Feature Papers in Medical Statistics and Data Science Section

Feature Papers in Medical Statistics and Data Science Section

Editor

Pentti Nieminen

MDPI

Basel • Beijing • Wuhan • Barcelona • Belgrade • Novi Sad • Cluj • Manchester

Editor
Pentti Nieminen
University of Oulu
Oulu
Finland

Editorial Office
MDPI
St. Alban-Anlage 66
4052 Basel, Switzerland

This is a reprint of articles from the Special Issue published online in the open access journal *BioMedInformatics* (ISSN 2673-7426) (available at: https://www.mdpi.com/journal/biomedinformatics/special_issues/Feature_Papers_in_Medical_Statistics_and_Data_Science_Section).

For citation purposes, cite each article independently as indicated on the article page online and as indicated below:

Lastname, A.A.; Lastname, B.B. Article Title. *Journal Name* **Year**, *Volume Number*, Page Range.

ISBN 978-3-7258-1043-7 (Hbk)
ISBN 978-3-7258-1044-4 (PDF)
doi.org/10.3390/books978-3-7258-1044-4

Cover image courtesy of Pentti Nieminen

Contents

About the Editor

Pentti Nieminen

Pentti Nieminen is a senior scientist at the University of Oulu. He completed his Ph.D. degree in 1996 and is employed as a professor in medical informatics and data analysis at the University of Oulu. He has worked for over 40 years as an academic teacher in knowledge management and data analysis. A lot of his teaching and research have been focused on the following fields: biostatistics, data analysis methods in health care and medicine, data informatics, statistics in scientific journals, statistical modelling, bibliometrics, information retrieval, and educational practices in teaching scientific research and communication. To date, he has published over 260 scientific articles. His current research projects include studies on statistical reporting and the quality of data presentation in medical articles, the meta-analysis of multivariable models, and e-professionalism among medical students. His goal is to improve the quality of published research papers and thus contribute to societal welfare and human well-being through his experience in data analysis. Outside of his professional interests, he enjoys orienteering, hiking, and traveling.

Preface

Medical data science, including the traditional science of statistics, contributes to the development and application of tools that are used for the design, analysis, and interpretation of empirical medical studies. The storage capacity of digital data and the technological advances achieved over recent decades have contributed to the proliferation of new analytical methods in medicine. The value of using these methods as a diagnostic and prognostic tool has steadily increased. Nevertheless, classical statistical approaches can often provide effective answers to important questions. The development of new data analysis methods for medical and related applications depends on the innovative use of biomedical technology, computer algorithms, statistical inference theory, a good understanding of clinical and epidemiological research questions, and an understanding of the importance of statistical software. The broader introduction and expansion of the new analysis tool for a medical audience might require this method to solve a data analysis problem where basic statistical methods have been neither useful nor applicable. The aim of this reprint is to emphasize the practical aspects of novel data analysis methods and to provide insights into the challenges in biostatistics, epidemiology, clinical medicine, and biomedicine. These contributions cover meta-analysis, the assessment of clinical outcomes, machine learning, medical diagnostics, and genomic factors. Each article is self-contained and may be read independently in line with the needs of the reader. The reprint comprises essential reading for postgraduate students as well as researchers from medicine and other scientific fields where statistical data analysis is central.

Pentti Nieminen
Editor

BioMedInformatics

Article

Comparing ANOVA and PowerShap Feature Selection Methods via Shapley Additive Explanations of Models of Mental Workload Built with the Theta and Alpha EEG Band Ratios

Bujar Raufi † and Luca Longo *,†

Artificial Intelligence and Cognitive Load Research Lab, Technological University Dublin, Grangegorman Lower, D07 H6K8 Dublin, Ireland; bujar.raufi@tudublin.ie
* Correspondence: luca.longo@tudublin.ie
† These authors contributed equally to this work.

Abstract: Background: Creating models to differentiate self-reported mental workload perceptions is challenging and requires machine learning to identify features from EEG signals. EEG band ratios quantify human activity, but limited research on mental workload assessment exists. This study evaluates the use of theta-to-alpha and alpha-to-theta EEG band ratio features to distinguish human self-reported perceptions of mental workload. **Methods**: In this study, EEG data from 48 participants were analyzed while engaged in resting and task-intensive activities. Multiple mental workload indices were developed using different EEG channel clusters and band ratios. ANOVA's F-score and PowerSHAP were used to extract the statistical features. At the same time, models were built and tested using techniques such as Logistic Regression, Gradient Boosting, and Random Forest. These models were then explained using Shapley Additive Explanations. **Results**: Based on the results, using PowerSHAP to select features led to improved model performance, exhibiting an accuracy exceeding 90% across three mental workload indexes. In contrast, statistical techniques for model building indicated poorer results across all mental workload indexes. Moreover, using Shapley values to evaluate feature contributions to the model output, it was noted that features rated low in importance by both ANOVA F-score and PowerSHAP measures played the most substantial role in determining the model output. **Conclusions**: Using models with Shapley values can reduce data complexity and improve the training of better discriminative models for perceived human mental workload. However, the outcomes can sometimes be unclear due to variations in the significance of features during the selection process and their actual impact on the model output.

Keywords: model explainability; mental workload; statistical feature selection; Shapley-based feature selection; alpha and theta EEG band ratios; machine learning

Citation: Raufi, B.; Longo, L. Comparing ANOVA and PowerShap Feature Selection Methods via Shapley Additive Explanations of Models of Mental Workload Built with the Theta and Alpha EEG Band Ratios. *BioMedInformatics* **2024**, *4*, 853–876. https://doi.org/10.3390/biomedinformatics4010048

Academic Editors: Pentti Nieminen and Carson K. Leung

Received: 28 January 2024
Revised: 6 March 2024
Accepted: 12 March 2024
Published: 19 March 2024

1. Introduction

In many practical machine learning tasks, including interpretability [1,2], data valuation [3], feature selection [4,5], ensemble pruning [6], federated learning [7] and universal explainability [8,9], measuring the achievement of a data attribute is a central issue. Although we heavily rely on machine learning models to perform various tasks, we rarely question the validity of the decisions made by the learning algorithms used to build them. This raises legitimate questions concerning the importance of a feature during the model learning process, the value of an individual data point in a dataset during learning, which models are more valuable during an ensemble learning procedure, which vote is more important, and why. While different methods exist to address these questions, the *transferable utility* cooperative game approach is a more general and holistic way to tackle them, with its most popular method being based on Shapley values [10]. Cooperative game theory aims to evaluate the value of coalitions that players can form. Shapley values effectively divide a cooperative game's overall value or payoff between its players. They assess a player's average marginal contribution to all potential coalitions they could be a part of and are calculated by averaging their marginal contributions across all possible coalition formations. Over the years, several enhancements have been made to Shapley values, such as enhancing efficiency, symmetry and fairness [11]. When considering machine learning and corporate game theory, each feature is treated as a player in a game, and the Shapley value of a feature represents its contribution to the model's overall prediction accuracy. To calculate Shapley values, one must consider all possible feature subsets and compute each feature's marginal contribution to the prediction accuracy. Although this process can be computationally intensive, recent algorithm and computing power advancements have made it viable for larger and more complex datasets.

Shapley values are widely used in machine learning to explain how individual features or variables contribute to a model's final prediction. Each feature is assigned a numerical value representing its impact on the output, resulting in a clear and understandable explanation of the model's behaviour. This information is invaluable for identifying critical features, improving model performance, and building trust and accountability in machine learning models [1,12,13]. Using Shapley values in machine learning offers a significant advantage as they support an unbiased way of interpreting the behaviour of various learnt models [14]. Additionally, Shapley values can be utilized to explain the predictions of black-box models, which are typically challenging to interpret using other methods [15]. Some examples of how Shapley values are applied in machine learning include:

1. **Feature selection:** Identifying the most significant features and eliminating any irrelevant or redundant ones is crucial for creating precise and efficient models, especially in datasets with numerous dimensions [5,16].
2. **Model comparison:** Comparing the performance of various models and pinpointing their strengths and weaknesses can aid in selecting the most suitable model for a particular task and identifying areas for enhancement [17].
3. **Bias detection:** Identify any potential features that may result in bias or discrimination in the model's predictions. It is imperative to take immediate action to address this bias and improve the model's fairness [9].
4. **Explainable AI:** It is important to clearly and unequivocally explain how the model behaves to establish trust and accountability in automated decision-making systems [1,8,18].

Calculating Shapley values for extensive datasets is computationally expensive, rendering its use in practical situations difficult. Studies have examined these difficulties and drawbacks in machine learning [19,20]. Moreover, understanding and interpreting Shapley values can be subjective and influenced by the selection of the model's starting point, potentially affecting the outcomes [1,21]. Algorithm design and computing power have recently made significant progress, broadening their applications and creating new research opportunities in this field. Shapley values can serve as a useful tool for evaluating intricate classification models. For instance, they can be applied to the models for distinguishing between the self-reported perceptions of mental workload via electroencephalographic activity. Research has shown that EEG band ratios, particularly those in the theta and alpha bands, are linked to various mental workload states [22,23]. Studies support the idea that these measures could be used as indicators of workload [24,25], and as a result, they could be incorporated into various machine-learned models to discriminate the self-reported perceptions of mental workload [26]. There have been numerous proposals for machine learning models aiming to distinguish the self-reported perceptions of mental workload [25–28]. However, mental workload research using EEG data in the area of model explainability with the use of Shapley values is currently limited.

This paper investigates the impact of Shapley-based feature selection methods in comparison to statistical feature selection methods on the capability of machine learning models to distinguish the self-reported perceptions of mental workload using alpha-to-theta and theta-to-alpha ratios extracted from EEG data. The formulated **research question** is: What is the difference in performance between these two methods? The innovative aspect of the paper resides in the fact that, by integrating explainability in feature selection methods, it is possible to unveil a potential new dimension for understanding the complex relationship between EEG band ratios and self-reported mental workload levels. This innovation would empower the machine learning models to make accurate predictions and provide invaluable insights into the specific EEG features that drive these predictions to human stakeholders. As a result, this might enhance the transparency and interpretability of these models, enabling researchers and clinicians to decipher the intricate neurological processes underpinning mental workload variations with a higher level of precision and clarity than existing research works. With the fusion of feature selection methods and model explainability with EEG band ratio data, it is possible to introduce a potential research path in comprehending cognitive states, paving the way for more targeted interventions, data-driven discoveries, and a deeper comprehension of mental workload dynamics. This paper is a step towards that direction.

The remainder of this paper is organised as follows: Section 2 provides the background concepts on alpha-to-theta and theta-to-alpha EEG band ratios as well as statistical and Shapley-based feature extraction on EEG data; Section 3 outlines the experiment design for feature extraction from EEG band-ratios using Shapley values and its comparison with the traditional statistical ANOVA method; Section 4 presents the result, while Section 5 critically discusses them. Eventually, Section 6 highlights the contribution to the body of knowledge and presents future directions of research.

2. Related Work

This section will thoroughly define Shapley values and examine their significant impact on machine learning. Furthermore, mental workload and its assessment methods will be precisely defined. Lastly, statistical and Shapley-based feature selection methods will be exhaustively explored.

2.1. Shapley Values in Machine Learning

To accurately define the Shapley values in collaborative game theory, it is crucial to have a thorough grasp of the fundamental formalisms and definitions involved. The definitions provided below are important in that regard [6,10].

Player sets and coalitions: Let us consider the machine learning features as being players in a cooperative game provided by a finite set: $\mathcal{F} = \{1, 2, 3, \ldots, n\}$. We denote a non-empty subset $\mathcal{N} \subseteq \mathcal{F}$ as a **coalition** and $\mathcal{F}$ as **grand coalition**.

Cooperative game: A cooperative game between features is represented by the pair $(\mathcal{F}, v)$. Here, $v : 2^{\mathcal{F}} \rightarrow \Re$ is a coalition function that assigns a real value to each feature coalition. It is worth noting that $v(\emptyset) = 0$ is also necessary to consider the function a collaborative game.

Feasible pay-off vector sets: In a cooperative game $(\mathcal{F}, v)$, the set of feasible payoff vectors is defined as $\mathcal{Z}(\mathcal{F}, v)$, which consists of all vectors $z \in \Re^{\mathcal{F}}$ that satisfy the condition $\sum_{i \in \mathcal{F}} z_i \leq v(\mathcal{F})$.

Solution concepts and vectors: When dealing with collaborative games, a solution concept Φ is a way of mapping a subset $\Phi(\mathcal{F}, v) \subseteq \mathcal{Z}((\mathcal{F}, v))$ to a specific game $(\mathcal{F}, v)$. In order for a solution vector $\phi(\mathcal{F}, v) \in \Re^{\mathcal{F}}$ to be considered a solution to the cooperative game $(\mathcal{F}, v)$, it must satisfy the solution concept Φ, meaning that $\phi(\mathcal{F}, v) \in \Phi(\mathcal{F}, v)$. A single-valued solution concept would exist if, for every $(\mathcal{F}, v)$, the set $\Phi(\mathcal{F}, v)$ only contains one element.

Feature set permutations: We can refer to the set of all permutations on a given set $\mathcal{F}$ as $\Pi(\mathcal{F})$. Within this set, there exists a specific subset of permutations represented by $\pi \in \Pi(\mathcal{F})$, where π_i denotes the position of feature i within the permutation π.

The predecessor set: of a feature $i \in \mathcal{F}$ in a permutation π is a coalition of the form: $\mathcal{P}_i^{\pi} = \{j \in \mathcal{F} | \pi_j < \pi_i\}$.

Assuming the given permutation of three features is $\pi = (3, 2, 1)$, the predecessor set for this permutation would be: $\mathcal{P}_1^{\pi} = (3, 2)$ for the first feature, $\mathcal{P}_2^{\pi} = (3)$ for the second feature, and $\mathcal{P}_3^{\pi} = \emptyset$ for the third feature.

Given these definitions, we can now define the Shapley values as:

$$\phi_i^s = \frac{1}{\Pi(\mathcal{F})} \sum_{\pi \in \Pi(\mathcal{F})} [v(\mathcal{P}_i^\pi \cup \{i\}) - v(\mathcal{P}_i^\pi)] \tag{1}$$

where the expression inside the sum represents the ith features marginal contribution within permutation π. According to the equation, the Shapley value for a feature is the average marginal contribution of that feature to the predecessor set's value, calculated across all possible permutations of the feature set.

2.2. The Concept of Mental Workload

Mental workload is crucial for studying human performance and is applied in various fields, such as medicine [29], education [30], web-design [31], and transportation [32], among others. The concept of mental workload is complex and has multiple levels, which can be difficult to define. It is often confused with cognitive effort [33], leading to ambiguities in its definition. This multifaceted complexity makes it challenging to understand the concept entirely. There are numerous interpretations of mental workload, as stated in the research by Hancock [34]. However, a recent comprehensive definition incorporating various perspectives is that *Mental Workload (MWL) reflects the level of engagement of a limited pool of resources during the cognitive processing of a primary task over time. This is influenced by both external stochastic environmental and situational factors, as well as the internal characteristics of the human operator, and it is necessary for managing static task demands through dedicated effort and attention* [35]. Based on the Multiple Resource Theory (MRT), this definition states that resources have a limited capacity and using multiple resources simultaneously can lead to reduced performance and increased mental workload. The theory suggests that resource selection and allocation depend on task demands, individual differences and context. To optimize the use of multiple resources, task design and training can minimize the mental workload and improve resource allocation and coordination, as outlined in Wickens' work on the subject.

Numerous techniques are utilized to measure mental workload [34]. One method uses *subjective measures*, which involves collecting feedback from individuals who have interacted with a task and system. This feedback is typically obtained through post-task surveys or questionnaires. Some common subjective measurement approaches are the NASA Task Load Index (NASATLX), the Workload profile (WP), and the Subjective Workload Assessment Technique (SWAT). Another method is *task performance measures*, which includes primary and secondary task measures. This method objectively measures an individual's performance related to a task. Examples of such measures include the time completion of a task, reaction time to secondary tasks, number of errors on the primary task and tracking and analyzing different actions performed by a user during a primary task. Lastly, *physiological measures* are based on analyzing the physiological responses of the human body. Examples of such measures include EEG (electroencephalogram), MEG (magnetoencephalogram), Brain Metabolism, Endogenous Eye blinks, Pupil diameter, heart rate measures, or electrodermal responses.

"EEG band ratios" refer to comparing power or amplitude between two frequency bands present in an electroencephalographic (EEG) signal. These ratios are widely utilized in neuroscience research to study brain activity during various states, including sleep, attention, alertness, emotion, and mental workload. In particular, the alpha and theta bands are frequently studied in the context of mental workload due to research indicating a correlation between these bands and increased mental workload. Specifically, an increase in the theta power band in the frontal brain region and a decrease in the alpha power in the parietal region is associated with increased mental workload [36]. Measuring mental workload through EEG band ratios and correlating objective brain activity (alpha-to-theta and theta-to-alpha) with the subjective self-reports of workload is difficult due to the disparity between the measures. It is crucial to investigate the convergence of measures between objective brain activity and the self-reported perception of mental workload [37]. Eventually, various analytical models of cognitive load have been built, with inductive and deductive techniques [35]. For example, Machine Learning has been used in conjunction with EEG data to inductively model cognitive load in a self-supervised way, without human intervention in selecting features [38]. Similarly, mental workload is represented and assessed via defeasible reasoning as a non-monotonic knowledge-representation technique that allows one to embed the deductive knowledge of a human reasoner together in a model [39,40]

2.3. Feature Selection with Statistical and Shapley-Based Methods

Various inductive data-driven techniques have been employed in mental workload modeling. However, one of the challenges is to create a group of independent features that can be mapped inductively to a target feature, which is typically a person's subjective perception of workload or a physiological measure of bodily activation. In Machine Learning, various methods are available to automatically select the most pertinent, descriptive and distinguishing features from a larger set of features for solving classification or regression tasks. These techniques are briefly described in the following sub-section.

2.3.1. Traditional Statistical Feature Selection Methods

Feature selection methods in statistics help pick out the most significant features from a large pool of available features. This process reduces the data's complexity while retaining as much important information as possible. A preferred approach is the *mutual information-based feature selection*, which assesses the dependence between the features and the target variable [41]. The mutual information score assesses the significance of features and chooses the most important K features. It is an effective and efficient method for both categorical and continuous variables. Another widely used method for selecting statistical features is the *chi-square test*. It determines the relationship between categorical variables and chooses the features that are most likely to be related to the target variable. This test calculates the chi-square statistic for each feature and sorts them based on their p-values. The features with lower p-values are more significant to the target variable. This method is effective in selecting features that are highly correlated with the target variable [42]. Another statistical method for feature selection is the ANOVA F-test. It is specifically used for choosing features with continuous variables and calculates the disparity between the means of the variables for the distinct categories of the target variable [43]. The ANOVA F-test evaluates features by their F-statistic or F-score. This ratio measures the difference in variance between groups and within groups. Features with a high F-statistic or F-score significantly impact the target variable when chosen. This method is effective for non-skewed data.

2.3.2. Shapley Values and Their Application as a Feature Selection Method

In the *Shapley-based feature selection* method, machine learning model input features are treated as players, while the model's performance is considered the payoff. The *Shapley values* quantify the contribution of each feature to the model's performance on a given set of data points [44]. The features can be ranked, selected, or removed based on these values. To define the Shapley values in machine learning, we consider the feature set $\mathcal{F} = \{1,\ldots,n\}$ and $\mathcal{S} \subseteq \mathcal{F}$. We also define the train and test feature vector sets as $X_{\mathcal{S}}^{train} = \{x_i^{train} | i \in \mathcal{S}\}$ and $X_{\mathcal{S}}^{test} = \{x_i^{test} | i \in \mathcal{S}\}$. We use $f_s(\cdot)$ to represent a machine learning model trained using $X_{\mathcal{S}}^{train}$ as input. The payoff is $v(\mathcal{S})) = g(y, \hat{y}_{\mathcal{S}})$, where $g(\cdot)$ is a goodness of fit function, y is the ground truth, and $y_{\mathcal{S}} = f_{\mathcal{S}}(X_{\mathcal{S}}^{test})$ is the predicted target. The Shapley values were widely used as a feature selection method across various contexts and applications [16,45]. It is important to note that both the ANOVA F-score and Shapley-based feature selection methods have been utilized to analyze EEG data. These selection methods have been applied and compared in various situations, such as the diagnosis of Parkinson's disease [46], recognizing emotions [47], detecting sleep apnea and depression [48,49], and diagnosing schizophrenia [50]. Although there is a considerable amount of research comparing the ANOVA F-score and Shapley-based feature selection methods in different problem scenarios, there is limited research on comparing these feature selection methods for measuring the mental workload physiologically using EEG band ratios. Considering the highly subjective nature of assessing mental workload conditions using machine learning, explaining the relevance of these features is of the utmost importance. In this regard, limited work is seen, for example, on brain state classification using EEG [51] or the cross-sectional classification of mental workload using eye tracking features [52].

3. Materials and Methods

To tackle the research question laid out in Section 1, a research hypothesis has been developed:

Hypothesis 1. *IF high-level EEG features are selected using the Shapley-value-based method. Then, the resulting machine learning model will demonstrate higher performance in discriminating the self-reported perceptions of mental workload compared to models that use statistical feature selection methods.*

This study follows the processing pipeline presented in [25], but with some modifications in the subsequent sections. The research hypotheses were tested through comparative empirical research, and more details can be found in Figure 1 and the following subsections.

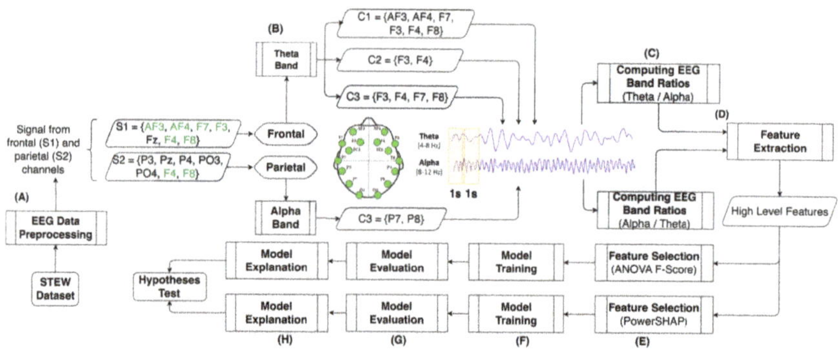

Figure 1. A step–by–step illustration for classifying self-reported mental workload perception using mental workload indexes created through the EEG analysis of the alpha and theta bands. (A) Signal denoising process. (B) Select electrodes from the frontal cortical areas for the theta band and the parietal cortical areas for the alpha band and group them to create electrode clusters. (C) Calculate the mental workload indexes using the alpha-to-theta and theta-to-alpha band ratios. (D) Extract high-level features from the mental workload indexes. (E) Use ANOVA F-Score and PowerSHAP to select the best features. (F) Train a machine learning model for classifying self-reported mental workload perception. (G) Evaluate the model. (H) Explain the model for hypothesis testing.

3.1. Dataset

The STEW (Simultaneous Task EEG Workload) dataset was selected for an experiment. This dataset consists of raw EEG data collected from 48 subjects through 14 channels [53]. Two experimental conditions were studied: the rest state and a multitasking cognitive processing speed test called SIMKAP. The Emotiv EPOC EEG headset was used to record the data, with a sampling frequency of 128 Hz. The recordings included 19,200 data samples across the 14 channels. After each task, the subjects rated their perceived mental workload on a scale of 1–9, which was used to determine whether there was an increase in cognitive load during the SIMKAP test compared to the rest state.

3.2. EEG Data Pre-Processing

Before analyzing the raw EEG data, removing noise through a denoising pipeline is important. This process is illustrated in point (A) of Figure 1 and follows Makoto's pre-processing pipeline [54]. The pipeline involves re-referencing channel data to average reference, high-pass filtering each channel at 1 Hz, and using Independent Component Analysis (ICA) for artefact removal. ICA separates the EEG signal sources into 14 independent components for each subject. To remove artefacts, 14 components are generated and it is checked whether the values are outside the "z-score±3" range [55], which are then considered artefacts and set to zero. The remaining "good" components are converted back to the original neural EEG signal using inverse ICA.

3.3. Computing EEG Band Ratios from the Theta and Alpha Bands as Indicators of Objective Mental Workload

The study utilized a baseline of frontal and parietal electrodes based on the 10–20 international system. These were cross-referenced with electrode availability from the Emotiv EPOC EEG headset. Due to the limited availability of electrodes, three frontal and one parietal cluster were created using specific combinations of electrodes and channel aggregation approaches. The channel clusters are depicted in Table 1 and marked as point (B) in Figure 1.

Table 1. Clusters and electrode combinations from the available electrodes in the frontal and parietal cortical regions.

Cluster Notation	Band	Electrodes
$c1-\theta$	Theta	AF3, AF4, F3, F4, F7, and F8
$c2-\theta$	Theta	F3 and F4
$c3-\theta$	Theta	F3, F4, F7, and F8
$c-\alpha$	Alpha	P7 and P8

The rationale for using the three selections from the theta band ($c1-\theta$, $c2-\theta$, and $c3-\theta$) was to use the symmetrical and iterative enlargement of the electrode numbers on the frontal brain region to provide better coverage. We utilized the average power spectral density (PSD) values from the alpha band in cluster $c-\alpha$, and the average PSD values from the theta band in clusters $c1-\theta$, $c2-\theta$, and $c3-\theta$ [23] to calculate the alpha-to-theta and theta-to-alpha ratios. We strategically selected different clusters from frontal and parietal electrodes, as depicted in Table 1 and point (C) in Figure 1, to acquire three alpha-to-theta and three theta-to-alpha ratios, resulting in six mental workload indexes. These indexes were then utilized for feature extraction, selection, and model training. Henceforth, we will refer to these indexes as our mental workload indexes given in Equation (2)

$$MWL_{indexes}\{at1, at2, at3, ta1, ta2, ta3\} \quad (2)$$

where: $at-1 = \frac{c-\alpha}{c1-\theta}$, $at-2 = \frac{c-\alpha}{c2-\theta}$, $at-3 = \frac{c-\alpha}{c3-\theta}$, $ta-1 = \frac{c1-\theta}{c-\alpha}$, $ta-2 = \frac{c2-\theta}{c-\alpha}$ and $ta-3 = \frac{c3-\theta}{c-\alpha}$

3.4. Feature Selection Using Statistical and Shapley-Based Methods

The rationale behind selecting statistical and Shapley-based feature selection methods for our study lies in their efficiency and easy interpretability. Table 2 outlines the comparison of feature selection methods outlined in our study against four other methods (Recursive Feature Elimination (RFE), Least Absolute Shrinkage, and Selection Operator (LASSO), Random Forest Feature Importance and Principal Component Analysis (PCA)) in terms of interpretability, assumptions, scalability, robustness, and performance.

Table 2. Comparison of statistical and Shapley-based feature selection methods compared to other methods.

Feature Selection Method	Method Type	Interpret-Ability	Assumptions	Scalability	Robustness	Performance
ANOVA F-Score	Statistical	Easy to interpret	Linearity assumed	Efficient	Susceptible to outliers and non-normal distributions	Effective in identifying significant differences between groups
PowerSHAP	Shapley-based	Variable interpretability	No assumptions	Computationally expensive	More robust to outliers and non-linear relationships	Can capture complex interactions and nonlinear relationships
RFE	Heuristic	Moderate	May overlook complex interactions	Model complexity dependent	Sensitive to noise	Performance based on underlying model
LASSO	Regularization	Moderate	Linearity assumed	Efficient	May shrink coefficients too fast during regularization	Effective on a sparse set of features
Random forest feature importance	Ensemble	Moderate	Assumes no interactions between features	Efficient	Handles outliers well	Captures nonlinear relationships
PCA	Dimensionality reduction	Challenging	Assumes linearity, orthogonality	Efficient	Loss of interpretability	Captures variance that is not specific to target

From the aforementioned table, the research strength assumptions of the study can be summarized around the following points:

- By applying the statistical (ANOVA F-score) and Shapley-based (PowerSHAP) methods, the research tends to demonstrate a comprehensive approach to feature selection, closely matching the type of data we explore (EEG) and model complexities that arise from it, thus providing a methodological diversity to the study.
- Whilst Shapley-based feature selection and model interpretability may vary, including ANOVA F-score ensures that at least one method in the study provides straightforward interpretability, which is expected to enhance the comprehensibility of the findings.
- The study also tends to benefit from the robustness to outliers and nonlinear relationships of Shapley-based feature selection methods, while still leveraging the efficiency and performance of ANOVA F-score in identifying significant feature differences.
- Comparing Shapley-based feature selection methods with other common feature selection techniques, the research aims to showcase a broad understanding of the importance of feature selection in Mental Workload Studies using EEG, offering insights into the strengths and limitations of various feature selection approaches in the context of model explainability.

3.4.1. Statistical Feature Selection Methods

It is important to extract high-level features from MWL indexes to discover unique properties that may not be detectable by solely considering the indexes. Time Series Feature Extraction Library (TSFEL) (https://tsfel.readthedocs.io/en/latest/index.html

accessed on 15 December 2023) is a tool that can extract high-level features from the MWL indexes described in Equation (2). TSFEL provides a variety of statistical properties that can be extracted from different types of data, including frequency and temporal data, and presented as point (D) in Figure 1. Initially, a large number of features are taken into consideration, and feature reduction is performed using statistical and Shapley-based feature selection methods, as explained in Section 2.3.1 and illustrated as point (E) in Figure 1. The "SelectKBest" feature selection algorithm is used for statistical feature selection, which ranks features based on the ANOVA F-score between a feature vector and a class label. Through an iterative process of supervised model performance evaluation [25], the optimal number of retained features is determined to be seven.

3.4.2. Shapley-Value-Based Feature Selection Methods

The Shapley-based feature selection method utilizes the "Powershap" algorithm [56]. Powershap is designed to identify features that have a greater impact on predictions than random features. The algorithm comprises the *Explain* and the *Core* Powershap components. In the *Explain* component, multiple models are created using different random features, and the average effect of all features is explained using Shapley values. In the *Core* Powershap component, the effects of the original features are statistically compared to the random feature, allowing for the selection of more informative features.

To evaluate the correlation and minimize multicollinearity, attention is given to the Pearson correlation between features selected with both the ANOVA F-score and PowerSHAP. Multicollinearity reduction is critical to maintaining the predictive power of each feature. Highly correlated features can negatively impact the model and not contribute to further training. Therefore, a correlation threshold of ± 0.5 is recommended for optimal model performance [57].

3.5. Model Training

The modeling and training process aims to develop classification models that can differentiate self-reported mental workload scores from independent features selected using statistical (SelectKBest with ANOVA-F score) and Shapley-based (Powershap) selection methods. This is illustrated under point (F) in Figure 1. Instead of task load conditions, mental workload self-assessment scores are selected as the target feature because they provide a more reliable indicator of user experience. Different task load conditions can result in varying levels of cognitive load, and mental workload can be influenced by factors such as prior knowledge, motivation, time of day, fatigue, and stress [34]. The target feature range is divided into two levels of mental workload, "suboptimal MWL" and "super optimal MWL", based on the parabolic relationship between mental workload and performance [30]. Scores ranging from 1 to 4 were grouped as "suboptimal MWL" while scores from 6 to 9 were categorized as "super optimal MWL". Scores of 5, indicating a neutral mental workload experience, were disregarded as they could potentially complicate the distinction between "suboptimal/super optimal". This approach simplified the model training into a binary classification problem. In this study, we utilized three techniques for learning classification models: Logistic Regression (L-R), Gradient Boosting (GB), and Random Forest (RF), which have been previously used in research involving longer EEG recordings [58]. Logistic regression and Gradient Boosting are error-based methods and are well suited for binary classification tasks, which is the focus of our study. On the other hand, Random Forest is an information-based ensemble learning technique that can identify important features by calculating their information gains during model training across multiple decision trees. We utilized separate training processes to train each classification model. These training processes involved selecting features using statistical methods like SelectKBest with ANOVA-F score and Shapley-based methods like PowerSHAP. Since our study used a small dataset of only 48 subjects, we employed a repeated Monte Carlo sampling for model training and validation, following this order:

1. For model training, a randomised 70% of subjects are chosen from both the "suboptimal MWL" and "super optimal MWL" categories, which are dependent features.
2. The remaining 30% of the data is reserved for model testing.
3. To capture the probability density of the target variable, the above splits are repeated 100 times to observe random training data.

To ensure the validity and robustness of the comparisons between different models and techniques a separated training, evaluation and explanation runs is performed for every Monte Carlo run. Figure 2 illustrates this process.

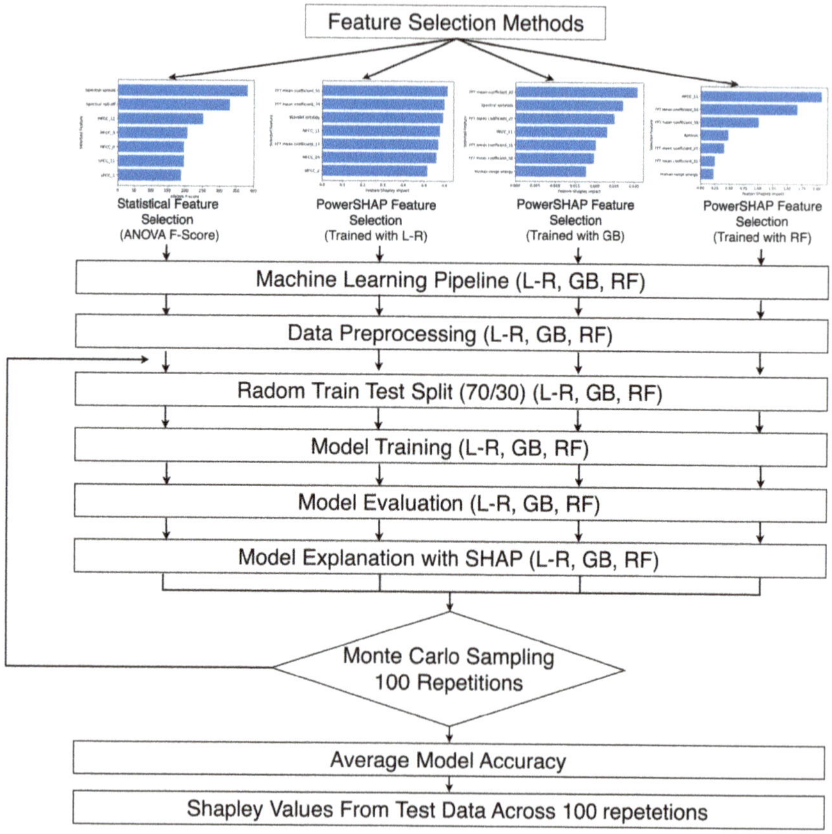

Figure 2. A step–by–step illustration of the model training procedure, evaluation and explanation for each feature selection method.

From the figure, it can bee seen that, for each feature selection methods, we put the selected features separately to the machine learning pipeline consisted of the steps such as: data preprocessing by scaling the data using the standard scaling method; a random 70/30 train test split across 100 iterations; model evaluation with accuracy, recall, precision and f1-score measurements and model explanation for each iteration during Monte Carlo sampling process. Finally, an averaging accuracy across 100 iterations represents the final model accuracy. The Shapley values across 100 repetitions are used to interpret the feature contributions to the model output for each of the machine learning techniques utilized (L-R, GB, and RF).

To overcome the issue of a small dataset, we implemented a synthetic data generation strategy using deep learning with GANs (Generative Adversarial Networks) [59]. We ensured the quality of the synthetic data was similar to that of the original training set by analyzing a synthetic quality score metric. This scoring metric assessed the Field Correlation Stability, Deep Structure Stability, and Field Distribution Stability [25] to provide an overall quality score. We used the same training process for the original and combined (original + synthetic) data with the same Monte Carlo sampling. To train the models, we randomly selected 70% of the subjects and used the remaining 30% for testing, with 100 iterations. During model training, we utilized Z-score normalization to minimize the mean and maximize the standard deviation. This approach allowed us to transform extreme values in the dataset into values that were no longer significant outliers, thus reducing their impact.

3.6. Model Explainability and Evaluation

The SHAP method is used to explain the model's output. This method attributes the importance of each feature to the model's predictions through Shapley values. SHAP calculates the contribution of each feature by considering all possible feature combinations and comparing the predictions with and without that feature. Considering their interactions allows for a more accurate attribution of importance to each feature. The SHAP values can be visualized through various SHAP plots, which depict the contribution of each feature to the model's predictions for a specific instance. Usually, these plots show features that either increase or decrease the target value. Overall, SHAP helps to interpret a machine learning model's output by explaining each feature's importance to the predictions. This can be useful in understanding the model's behavior and identifying areas for improvement. This research study uses evaluation metrics to measure how well-trained models perform when faced with new data. The metrics used include True Positives (*tp*), True Negatives (*tn*), False Positives (*fp*), and False Negatives (*fn*). These metrics calculate the model's accuracy, precision, recall, and f1-score. Using these metrics, the researchers can assess how well the models can distinguish the self-reported perceptions of mental workload. The best model minimizes either *fp* or *tn*, but this comes at a cost to the other metric. In this sense, the f1-score is also useful as it considers both precision and recall since it represents the harmonic mean between them. The evaluation of the model performance using these metrics was applied to the SelectKbest algorithm with the ANOVA-F score and Shapley-based feature selection methods using PowerSHAP with Logistic Regression (L-R), Gradient Boosting (GB), and Random Forest (RF).

4. Results

4.1. EEG Artifact Removal

For every one of the 48 subjects, both the "Rest" and "Simkap" task load conditions have their raw EEG signal undergo artefact removal separately. On average, between one and two ICA components are removed from the EEG data for both conditions according to the methodology outlined in [25,55]. These components are zeroed out, and the EEG multi-channel data are reconstructed through inverse ICA. Since most subjects had at least one bad component removed, it is reasonable to assume that some artefact was eliminated from the EEG signal, allowing for further computations of the alpha and theta bands [60].

4.2. Evaluation of Feature Selection

TSFEL extracted 210 (the complete list of features can be found in https://www.frontiersin.org/articles/10.3389/fninf.2022.861967/full#supplementary-material (accessed on 15 December 2023)) high-level features from the objective mental workload indexes across the frequency and temporal domains. ANOVA F-score and PowerSHAP impact values are calculated for each feature, and the ones with the highest values are kept for model training. To use the SelectKBest algorithm, an initial number of features is required, as mentioned in the design Section 3.4.1.

Therefore, we use an iterative approach to gradually include features during model training and evaluate the model's accuracy at each iteration. This process of optimal feature selection is performed on data from the original dataset, identifying seven optimal features as displayed in Figure 3 [25]. As a result, we retain the seven highest-ranked features with the highest ANOVA F-score values from SelectKbest and the seven highest feature impact from Shapley values retrieved from PowerSHAP with Logistic Regression (L-R), Gradient Boosting (GB), and Random Forest (RF) for the training process. Additionally, Pearson correlation among features shows a mild correlation between features as depicted in Figure 3, as grouped by task conditions ("Rest" and "Simkap").

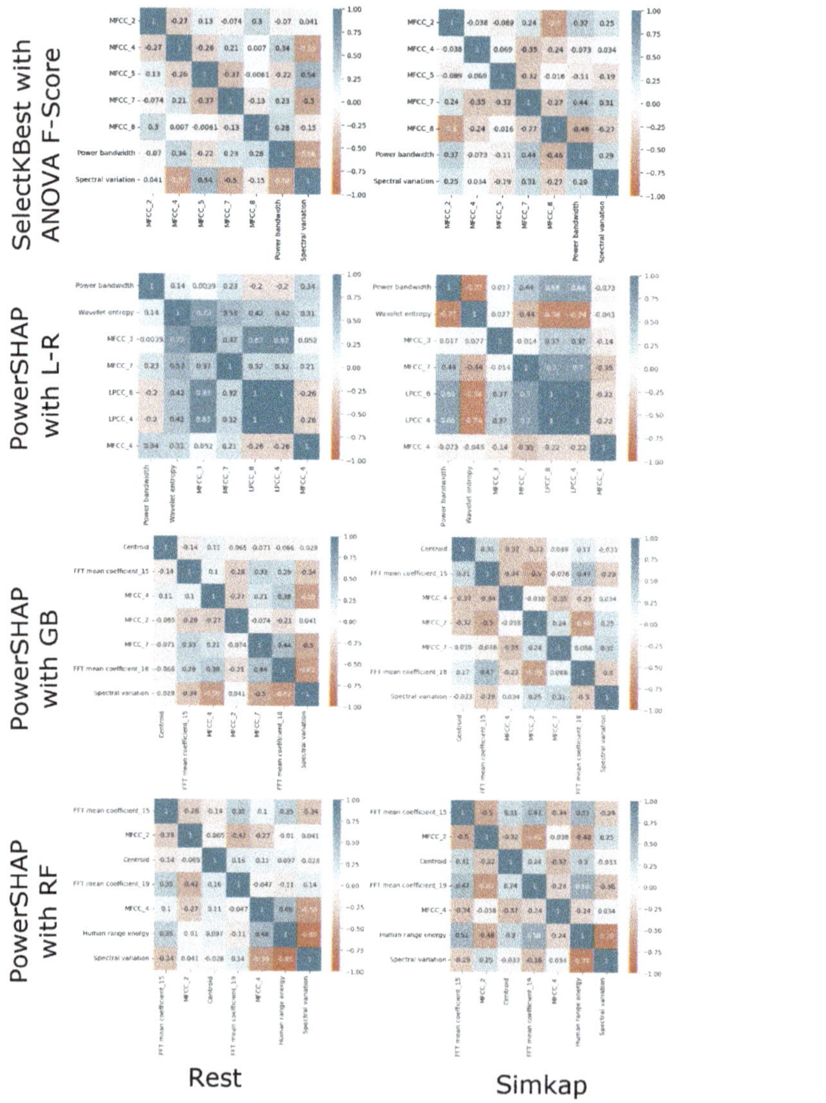

Figure 3. Pearson correlation of features selected with SelectKBest and PowerSHAP for the case of at-2 mental workload index.

4.3. Training Set Evaluation across Indexes

The "curse of dimensionality" issue arose due to the low number of training instances compared to the independent features. During the initial model evaluation with test data, the average accuracy was only 60%. The classifiers' learning curves indicated that the model was underfitting and could not generalize from test data. To overcome the bias caused by the small variance in data, synthetic data generation was used to train more accurate models. The study utilized the initial dataset of 48 subjects, with 150 data points (2.5 min of EEG activity divided into 150 segments of 1 s) for each of the indexes designed in Equation (2). Two synthetic datasets were generated, one for the "Rest" and "Simkap" task load conditions, respectively, to preserve the original dataset's characteristics. The findings indicated a synthetic quality score of more than 87% for all the chosen objectives and continuous mental workload indexes, demonstrating excellent quality and similarity to other research studies [61]. As a result, data were synthesized for an additional 180 subjects, generating 150 data points each for every mental workload index. Therefore, the final dataset includes both original and synthesized data, with 228 subjects and 150 data points for each mental workload index as defined in Equation (2). Figure 4 displays the quality scores for synthetic data for "Rest" and "Simkap" conditions, respectively.

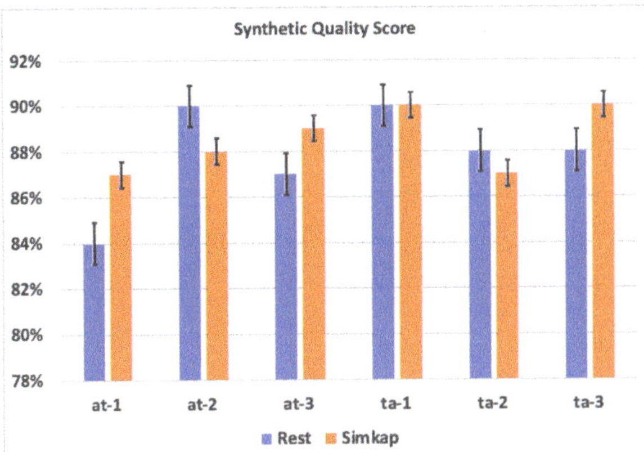

Figure 4. Quality scores of synthetic data for "rest" and "Simkap" task load conditions.

4.4. Model Explainability and Validation

Figure 5 showcases the classifiers' performance and the evaluation metrics for all mental workload objective indexes. The dashed red line depicts the threshold for below and above-average model performance, set at 90%.

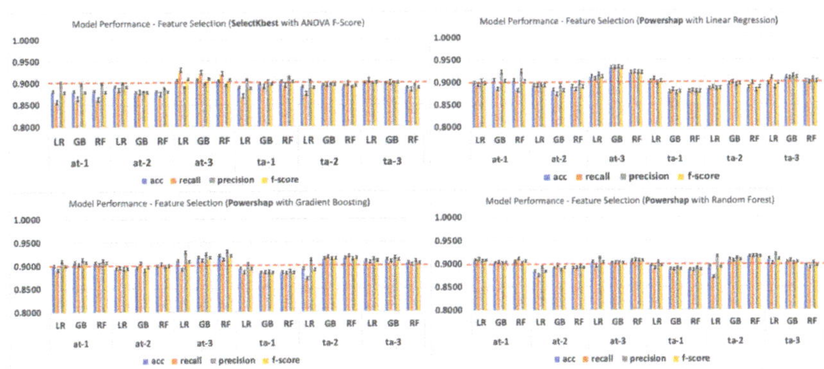

Figure 5. Model performance for features selected with ANOVA F-score and PowerSHAP methods.

Based on the figure data analysis, it is evident that the Shapley-based feature selection methods utilizing PowerSHAP with Logistic Regression (L-R) and Gradient Boosting (GB) demonstrated an exceptional performance for the mental workload index at-3. Furthermore, the PowerSHAP feature selection techniques utilized for theta-to-alpha ratio indexes ta-2 and ta-3 have shown an above-average performance of 90% when trained with Linear Regression and Gradient Boosting. However, the PowerSHAP features trained with Random Forest performance seems below the average threshold. On the other hand, the statistical feature selection method has shown a below-average performance of 90% across all mental workload objective indexes. To better analyze the results and see the model performance of the aforementioned ratios for both feature selection methods, Figure 6 outlines the density plots of the model training with Monte Carlo sampling provided in Section 3.5.

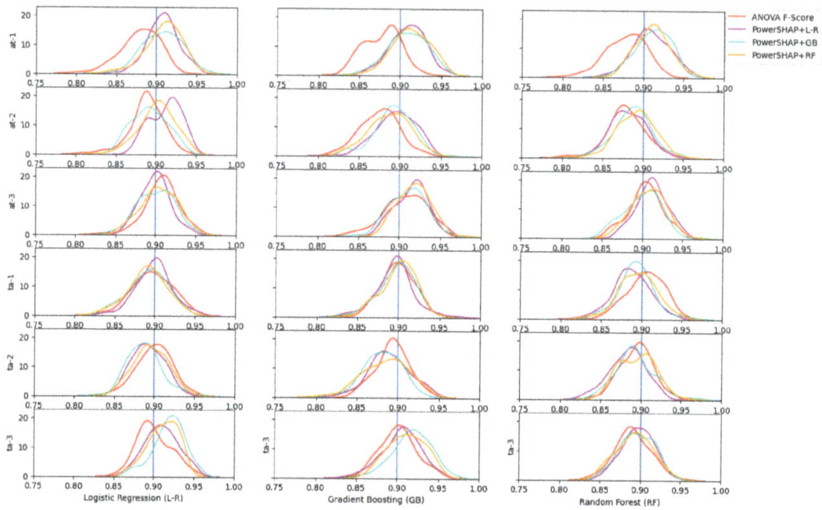

Figure 6. Density plots of model performance for features selected with ANOVA F-score and PowerSHAP methods. The comparison is made between ANOVA F-Score against PowerSHAP with L-R, GB, and RF, respectively.

Figure 6 shows a better performance of the PowerSHAP feature selection methods for the mental workload indexes at-3, ta-2, and ta-3. Furthermore, the mental workload index at-1 very clearly shows the best performance of the powerSHAP feature selection method compared to ANOVA F-score, even though the model's overall performance is below the mean threshold of 90%, as given in Figure 5. Table 3 showcases the two-tailed *t*-test results for model performance accuracy between ANOVA F-score and Shapley-based Powershap feature selection methods across all workload objective indexes.

We analyzed the effect size of the density plots using Cohen's d to determine the significance levels presented in Table 3. Cohen's d is a standardized measurement used to determine the difference between the means of two groups. It is utilized to compare a sample from PowerSHAP feature selection methods with the ANOVA feature selection method to validate the significance levels in Table 3. Cohen's d is an appropriate effect size alongside *t*-tests and ANOVA analyses. Table 3 shows medium and large effect sizes for the at-2, ta-2, and ta-3 mental workload indexes. Furthermore, very strong effect sizes are seen in at-1, even though the model performance for that index is under the threshold of 90%. To comprehensively analyze the models, we will thoroughly examine the significant feature selection methods outlined in Table 3. Furthermore, we will examine the top-performing indexes as per Figure 5, particularly at-3, ta-2, and ta-3. To better understand the crucial features and their characteristics, Table 4 provides a detailed overview of these features and their descriptions as they apply to our analysis.

Table 3. The two-tailed t-test performed against feature selection methods applied to accuracy evaluation metrics. The t-test is performed between ANOVA F-Score against PowerSHAP with L-R, GB and RF, respectively. Values for t-statistics, p-value, and Cohen's d (d) are given for every machine learning model across mental workload indexes. The (†) indicates the significant results within the threshold confidence value of $\alpha = 0.05$

Workload Index	Logistic Regression (L−R)			Gradient Boosting (GB)			Random Forest (RF)		
	t-Stat.	p-Value	(d)	t-Stat.	p-Value	(d)	t-Stat.	p-Value	(d)
	−9.20	5.01×10^{-17} †	1.309	−10.29	3.45×10^{-20} †	1.154	−9.63	2.88×10^{-18} †	1.26
at-1	−8.16	3.76×10^{-14} †	1.45	−9.52	5.85×10^{-18} †	1.34	−10.49	9.06×10^{-21} †	1.61
	−8.92	2.98×10^{-16} †	1.36	−11.40	1.72×10^{-23} †	1.48	−10.28	2.40×10^{-20} †	1.46
	−8.05	7.39×10^{-14} †	1.14	−5.90	1.50×10^{-8} †	0.15	−0.68	0.49	0.61
at-2	−1.08	0.27	0.83	−5.28	3.24×10^{-7} †	0.74	−2.47	0.01 †	0.50
	−4.33	2.36×10^{-5} †	0.09	−3.53	0.0004 †	0.35	−3.39	0.0008 †	0.48
	2.84	0.004 †	−0.40	−2.95	0.003 †	−0.32	−2.79	0.005 †	0.13
at-3	2.28	0.02 †	0.42	−0.95	0.34	0.13	1.12	0.26	0.52
	0.93	0.35	0.39	−3.68	0.0002 †	−0.15	−1.16	0.24	0.16
	−0.66	0.50	0.09	1.27	0.20	−0.23	5.66	5.24×10^{-8} †	−0.26
ta-1	1.66	0.09	−0.18	0.45	0.64	−0.06	3.98	9.60×10^{-5} †	0.05
	1.86	0.06	−0.80	−0.36	0.71	0.56	3.20	0.001 †	0.45
	2.90	0.004 †	−0.41	1.11	0.26	−0.58	3.78	0.0002 †	−0.22
ta-2	4.16	4.48×10^{-5} †	−0.15	4.10	5.86×10^{-5} †	−0.58	0.47	0.63	−0.33
	1.61	0.10 †	−0.53	2.35	0.01 †	−0.06	−0.29	0.76	0.04
	−3.02	0.002 †	0.42	−1.17	0.24	0.89	−2.29	0.02 †	0.52
ta-3	−6.29	1.96×10^{-9}	0.16	−5.25	3.83×10^{-7} †	0.74	−1.76	0.07	0.46
	−3.73	0.0002 †	0.32	−3.27	0.001 †	0.44	−0.77	0.44	0.10

Table 4. A list of important EEG features alongside their respective descriptions.

Feature Name	Feature Description
Histogram_8	Histogram 8 of the EEG signal (nine histogram features are extracted).
Histogram_9	Histogram 9 of the EEG signal (nine histogram features are extracted).
LPCC_3	Linear prediction cepstrum coefficients.
MFCC_2	The MEL cepstral coefficient 2 (ten MFCC coefficients are extracted).
MFCC_10	The MEL cepstral coefficient 10 (ten MFCC coefficients are extracted).
Wavelet absolute mean	Continuous wavelet transform absolute mean value of EEG signal.
Fundamental frequency	Fundamental frequency of the EEG signal.
Entropy	Entropy of the EEG signal using the Shannon Entropy method.

Figure 7 in the at-3 workload index clearly illustrates the importance of features as determined by feature selection methods. In addition, Figure 8 confidently presents the model explainability of feature importance through Shapley values in the form of beeswarm plots generated from the test set.

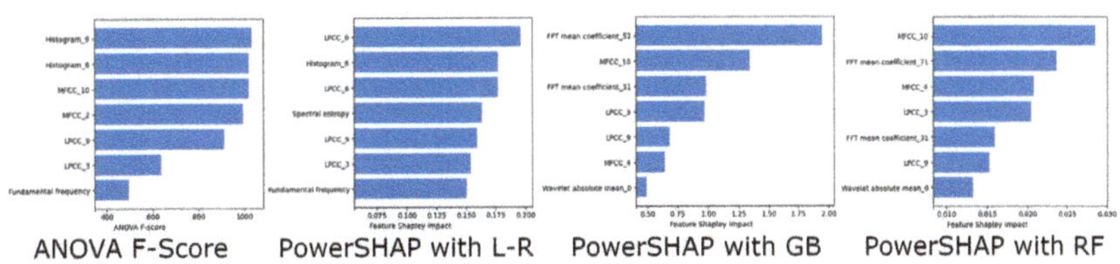

Figure 7. Feature importances selected from ANOVA F-score and PowerSHAP for the case of at-3.

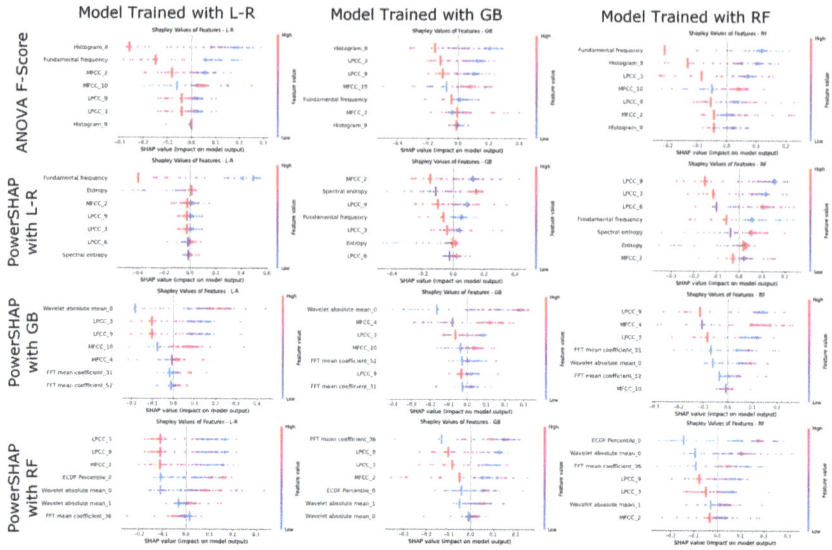

Figure 8. Shapley values on feature impact on model output selected with ANOVA F-score and PowerSHAP and trained with L-R, GB, and RF for the case of at-3.

Figures 7 and 8 revealed an interesting observation. During the feature selection process using ANOVA f-score, "Histogram_9" and "Histogram_8" had the highest f-score value, suggesting they were the most important features. However, upon examining the model's feature contributions using Shapley values, "Histogram_8", "Fundamental_frequency" and "LPCC_3" were the top four critical features. It is quite observable that "Histogram_9", which was the top ranking feature with ANOVA f-score selection method, when explained by SHAP, rank as the least contributing feature across all training methods (L-R, GB, and RF). When using PowerSHAP with L-R for feature selection, "spectral entropy" and "Entropy" features appear as the most important ones when selected using PowerSHAP with L-R. However, Shapley values retired with Shapley additive explanations showed "LPCC_9", "LPCC_3", "MFCC_9", and "Fundamental_frequency" that contributed the most to the model's output. When features are analyzed for the cases of feature selection methods using PowerSHAP with both Gradient Boosting (GB) and Random Forest (RF), we observe "FFT Mean Coefficient_52", "MFCC_10", "EDCF Percentile_0", and "Vawelet absolute mean_1" as the most important features. However, the model explainability provided with SHAP, brings the least important features from the feature selection method as the highest contributing ones. Features like "MFCC_4", "Wavelet absolute mean_0", and "LPCC_9" are the least ranked ones from the feature selection method; however, they appear as the most contributing ones appearing in the top two of most contributing features. Figure 9 shows the feature importance for the ta-2 workload index, and Figure 10 illustrates the model's explainability in terms of feature importance through the Shapley values generated from the test set in beeswarm plots.

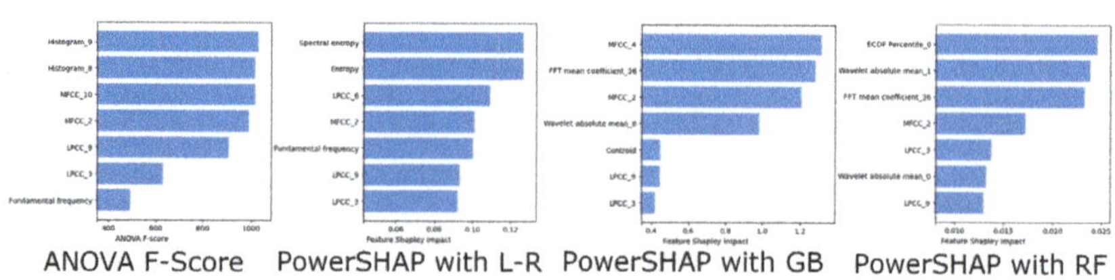

Figure 9. Feature importances selected from ANOVA F-score and PowerSHAP for the case of ta-2.

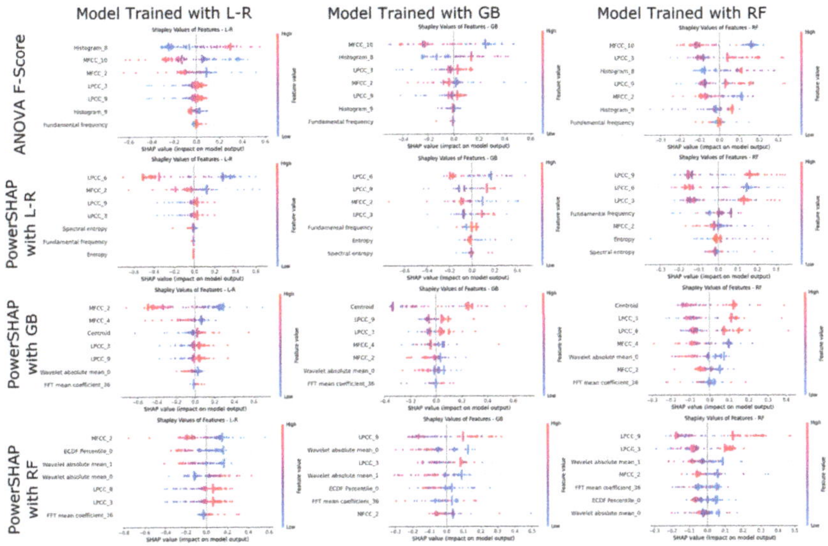

Figure 10. Shapley values on feature impact on model output selected with ANOVA F-score and PowerSHAP and trained with L-R, GB, and RF for the case of ta-2.

When analyzing the ta-2 mental workload index, we found that "Histogram_9" and "Histogram_8" were the most important features during ANOVA F-score feature selection. However, when explaining the contribution of features to the model output, "MFCC_10" and "LPCC_3" (Linear Prediction Cepstral Coefficients 3) also have the greatest impact along "Histogram_8". In the case of features selected with PowerSHAP+L-R and trained with L-R, GB, and RF, "MFCC_2", "LPCC_6", and "LPCC_9" (MEL Cepstral Coefficients 2 and Linear Prediction Cepstral Coefficients 6 and 9) are the most important features, despite being ranked relatively low in importance during feature selection. Another crucial observation is that highly ranked features during feature selection, like "Spectral Entropy" and "Entropy", are at the bottom of features that contribute to model output when explained with Shapley values. For features selected with PowerSHAP + GB and PowerSHAP + RF and trained with L-R, GB, and RF, the "LPCC_9" and "MFCC_2" features were found to be the most important for model explainability with test data. Even though "LPCC_3" and "LPCC_9" were ranked at the bottom in both cases, they were among the top three features contributing to the model output during model training and explainability with Shapley values. In reference to the ta-3 workload index, Figure 11 shows the feature importance as determined by feature selection methods.

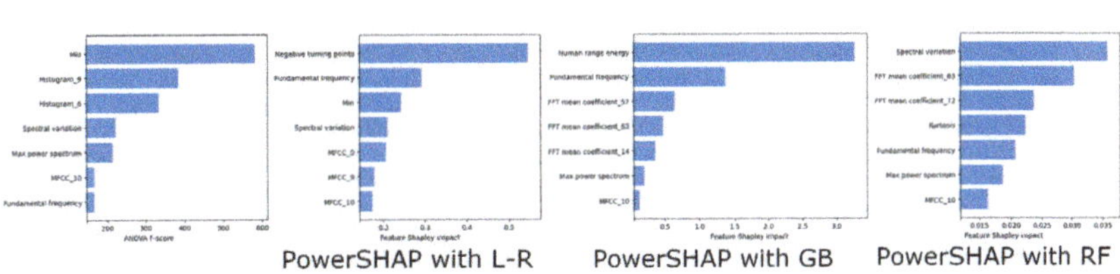

Figure 11. Feature importances selected from ANOVA F-score and PowerSHAP for the case of ta-3.

The Shapley values generated from the test set are presented as beeswarm plots in Figure 12, depicting the model explainability of feature importance.

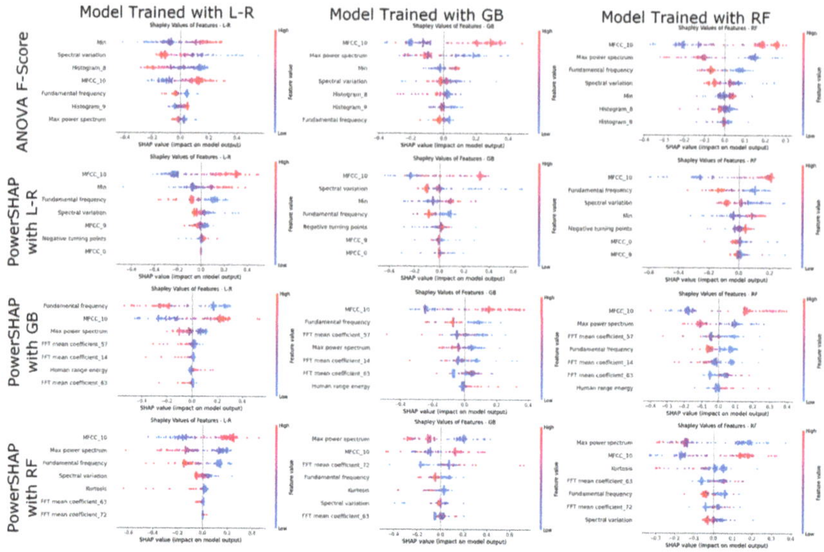

Figure 12. Shapley values on feature impact on model output selected with ANOVA F-score and PowerSHAP and trained with L-R, GB, and RF for the case of ta-3.

For the theta-to-alpha (ta-3) workload index, the feature MFCC_10 (MEL cepstral coefficients 10) is ranked at the bottom during feature selection using all statistical and Shapley-based feature selection methods. However, upon analyzing the Shapley value for their impact on the model output, it was found that this feature had the highest contribution across the board in all models explained with Shapley Additive Explanations.

5. Discussion

The findings presented in this paper suggest that using Shapley-value-based methods for model training leads to better performance than using statistical methods with an ANOVA F-score. This is particularly evident in the mental workload indexes at-3, ta-2, and ta-3. Additionally, the results from Table 3 demonstrate a statistically significant difference between ANOVA F-score and PowerSHAP methods, confirming the hypothesis outlined in Section 3 that high-level EEG features selected using the Shapley-based method have a greater impact on model performance for discriminating the self-reported perception of mental workload than statistical methods. When we analyze model explainability using SHAP, we notice an intriguing observation by comparing the features selected through both methods. When presented with testing data, the less important features tend to impact the model output significantly. Features such as "Wavelet absolute mean_0", "Wavelet absolute mean_1", and "Fundamental frequency", statistical histogram features like "Histogram_8" and "Linear" and MEL cepstral coefficients ("LPCC_3", "LPCC_6", "LPCC_9", and "MFCC_10") contribute the most to the model output in all trained and evaluated models. In Figure 13, we can compare the ranked features from feature selection methods (ANOVA F-score and PowerSHAP) and their respective contribution to the model output. The feature importance is normalized between the $[0 \ldots 1]$ range, where zero indicates a low impact of the feature on training, and one indicates a high impact.

Looking at Figure 13, we can observe a discrepancy between the features selected through the ANOVA F-score, namely "Histogram_8" and "MFCC_10", and those that contribute the most to the model output. Interestingly, the high-ranked features from ANOVA F-score appear to be the least important in model explainability and vice versa. This trend is also visible in the "linear and MEL cepstral coefficients" ("LPCC_3", "LPCC_9", and "MFCC_10") for both feature selection methods and their respective feature importance for model explainability.

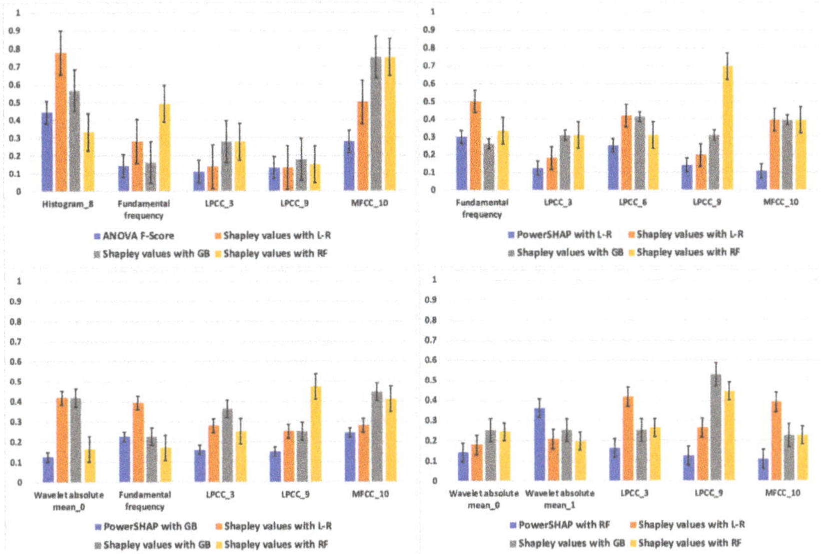

Figure 13. Comparison of feature importance across feature selection methods (ANOVA F-score and PowerSHAP with L-R, GB. and RF) and their Shapley value contribution on model input (L-R, GB, and RF).

The importance of Shapley values in model explainability is highlighted in the research. It is observed that people tend to trust the model explainability provided by Shapley values. This claim is based on the following points:

1. Methods based on Shapley values are not tied to any specific machine learning model and can be used with linear and nonlinear models, decision trees, and neural networks. These methods are effective, as they avoid common mistakes such as using a "one-size-fits-all" approach to interpretability, poor model generalization, over-reliance on complex models for explainability, and neglecting feature dependence [62]. On the other hand, statistical feature selection methods often require a particular model or make assumptions about data distribution.
2. When working with complex datasets, Shapley-based methods are crucial as they consider the interaction between features. On the other hand, statistical feature selection techniques like correlation-based feature selection only consider pairwise correlations between features and may overlook significant interactions.
3. Regarding ranking features, Shapley-based methods are more reliable because small changes do not easily influence them in the data or model. On the other hand, statistical feature selection methods may yield different results depending on the particular data sample or model being utilized.
4. Methods based on Shapley values are useful in clearly understanding each feature's importance. This is because it highlights the contribution of a feature to the prediction, making it easy to explain to domain experts. On the other hand, statistical feature selection methods may require an easily interpretable feature importance measure.

Even though Shapley-based feature selection methods are more effective than statistical methods, there are still some open research questions and inconclusive explanations regarding contradictory results. This is because the feature importance in the selection method may differ from the feature importance of the model output provided by SHAP.

Some researchers argue that using Shapley values for feature importance in machine learning models can lead to mathematical problems which may increase complexity and the need for causal reasoning. Moreover, Shapley values should be able to explain their results in a way that aligns with human-centric goals of explainability [63]. One particular study suggests that using model averaging directly for feature selection requires caution, as the average performance of a feature across all submodels may not reflect its specific performance in the optimal submodels. To ensure the selection of all features based on their optimal submodel contributions, it is best to select all features explicitly [44]. Furthermore, the authors demonstrate this claim with examples outlined through sets of axioms like efficiency, additivity, and balanced contributions. It is possible that the contradictions between feature selection methods and feature contributions, as seen in Figure 13, could be attributed to the direct averaging of features during Shapley Additive Explanations (SHAP) and the Monte Carlo simulation used during training. However, further research is necessary to confirm this hypothesis.

6. Conclusions

The paper outlined the need for a more comprehensive understanding of the performance and interpretability of different feature selection methods in machine learning models that discriminate self-reported perceptions of mental workload using EEG band ratios. This research issue is tackled through a comparative empirical study using a six-step process pipeline as outlined in Section 3. Logistic Regression (L-R), Gradient Boosting (GB), and Random Forest (RF) learning techniques were employed to train the models, with a focus on utilizing Shapley-based and ANOVA F-score feature selection methods. To ensure model explainability, we utilized Shapley Additive Explanations.

According to the analysis, it was discovered that feature selection methods that utilize Shapley values can improve model performance and partially explain how the model can distinguish between different mental workload perceptions using EEG data. These methods can identify the most crucial features and their corresponding impact on the model's predictions, thereby providing valuable insights into the factors contributing to successfully identifying mental workload perceptions through machine learning. In identifying the most impactful features contributing to model output, the study uncovered unexpected contradictions between the Shapley-based feature selection methods (PowerSHAP and ANOVA F-score) and the Shapley Additive Explanation (SHAP) method. It is important to note that possible explanations for these contradictions are hypothesized in Section 5, and further research will be necessary to validate these claims. Although the paper demonstrated that Shapley-based methods outperform traditional statistical approaches, it should be noted that Shapley-based feature selection methods can often lead to complex and inconclusive interpretations. This is due to the complex interplay between the perceived importance of features during the selection process and their actual significance in shaping the final output of the model. However, these conflicting outcomes provide valuable insights into the intricate dynamics of feature importance and model behavior. Therefore, it is essential to acknowledge these potential disparities when working with feature selection, as it can lead to a more comprehensive understanding of the model's inner workings and pave the way for refined methodologies that harness the true power of Shapley-based techniques.

It is important to note that this research has limitations in terms of the feature selection methods used to explain the models. This study focuses on statistical (ANOVA-F-score) and game theoretic (PowerSHAP) approaches. However, there are other selection methods based on explainable AI, such as wrapper-based selectors like Boruta, selection methods based on regression models or random forest, iterative dataset weighting, and targeted replacement values. The rationale behind using statistical and Shapley-based methods is that they have been proven to effectively select essential features and discard non-contributing ones, which not only maintains or improves classification accuracy, but also reduces the execution time in machine learning models, making the Shapley-based feature selection effective and efficient [64]. Additionally, Shapley values are relatively consistent across selected machine learning models, making the analysis of model explainability more straightforward. It is also essential to acknowledge that the explanations may vary depending on the model's outcome and application, as outlined in this study.

In future investigations, researchers can thoroughly examine the properties of these features to construct models that can precisely evaluate the model's accuracy. More research will elaborate on how the alpha-to-theta and theta-to-alpha ratio indexes can be employed to explain the model's efficiency regarding the following concerns. The first is a further confirmation of the findings of this study, aiming at replicating the experiment using additional publicly available datasets. The second is to enhance the explainability of models utilizing additional additive methods, such as LIME, DeepLIFT, and Layer-wise relevance estimation, in addition to the traditional Shapley value estimation.

Author Contributions: Conceptualization, B.R. and L.L.; methodology, B.R. and L.L.; software, B.R.; validation, B.R.; formal analysis, B.R. and L.L.; investigation, B.R.; resources, B.R.; data curation, B.R.; writing—original draft preparation, B.R.; writing—review and editing, B.R. and L.L.; visualization, B.R.; supervision, L.L.; project administration, B.R.; funding acquisition, L.L. All authors have read and agreed to the published version of the manuscript.

Funding: Supported by MCSA Post-doc CareerFIT fellowship, funded by Enterprise Ireland, TU Dublin School of Computer Science and the European Commission. Fellowship ref. number: MF2020 0144.

Institutional Review Board Statement: Not applicable.

Informed Consent Statement: Not applicable.

Data Availability Statement: Publicly available datasets were analyzed in this study. These data can be found here: [https://github.com/braufi/xai-2023-supplemental/tree/f6b3a9272a8dd63303634d858564ecb8ac2cf7f8 (accessed on 15 December 2023)].

Conflicts of Interest: The authors declare no conflicts of interest with this manuscript. The funders had no role in the study's design; in the collection, analyses, or interpretation of data; in the writing of the manuscript; or in the decision to publish the results.

References

1. Lundberg, S.M.; Lee, S.-I. A unified approach to interpreting model predictions. *Adv. Neural Inf. Process. Syst.* **2017**, *30*. 4765–4774.
2. Wang, J.; Jenna W.; Scott L. Shapley flow: A graph-based approach to interpreting model predictions. In Proceedings of the International Conference on Artificial Intelligence and Statistics, Virtual, 13–15 April 2021.
3. Sim, R. H. L.; Xu, X.; Low, B. K. H. Data valuation in machine learning: "ingredients", strategies, and open challenges. In Proceedings of the IJCAI, Vienna, Austria, 23–29 July 2022.
4. Zacharias, J.; von Zahn, M.; Chen, J.; Hinz, O. Designing a feature selection method based on explainable artificial intelligence. *Electron. Mark.* **2022**, *32*, 2159–2184. [CrossRef]
5. Cohen, S.; Dror, G.; Ruppin, E. Feature selection via coalitional game theory. *Neural Comput.* **2007**, *19*, 1939–1961. [CrossRef] [PubMed]
6. Rozemberczki, B.; Watson, L.; Bayer, P.; Yang, H.T.; Kiss, O.; Nilsson, S.; Sarkar, R. The shapley value in machine learning. *arXiv* **2022**, arXiv:2202.05594.
7. Wang, J.; Wiens, J.; Flow, S. L. S.: A Graph-based Approach to Interpreting Model Predictions. *arXiv* **2020**, arXiv:2010.14592.
8. Sundararajan, M.; Najmi, A. The many Shapley values for model explanation. In Proceedings of the International Conference on Machine Learning, Virtual , 13–18 July 2020; pp. 9269–9278.
9. Covert, I; Lee, S.I. Improving KernelSHAP: Practical Shapley value estimation using linear regression. In Proceedings of the International Conference on Artificial Intelligence and Statistics, Virtual, 13–15 April 2021.
10. Shapley, L. S. A Value for n-Person Games. In *Contributions to the Theory of Games (AM-28)*; Kuhn, H., Tucker, A., Eds.; Princeton University Press: Princeton, NJ, USA, 1953; Volume II, pp. 307–318. [CrossRef]
11. Chalkiadakis, G.; Elkind, E.; Wooldridge, M. Computational Aspects of Cooperative Game Theory. *Synth. Lect. Artif. Intell. Mach. Learn.* **2011**, *5*, 1–168.
12. Dondio, P.; Longo, L. Trust-based techniques for collective intelligence in social search systems. In *Next Generation Data Technologies for Collective Computational Intelligence*; Springer: Berlin/Heidelberg, Germany, 2011; pp. 113–135.
13. Shrikumar, A.; Greenside, P.; Kundaje, A. Learning important features through propagating activation differences. In Proceedings of the International conference on Machine Learning, Sydney, NSW, Australia, 6–11 August 2017; pp. 3145–3153.

14. Merrick, L.; Taly, A. The explanation game: Explaining machine learning models using shapley values. In Proceedings of the Machine Learning and Knowledge Extraction: 4th IFIP TC 5, TC 12, WG 8.4, WG 8.9, WG 12.9 International Cross-Domain Conference, CD-MAKE 2020, Dublin, Ireland, 25–28 August 2020; Proceedings 4; Springer International Publishing: Berlin/Heidelberg, Germany, 2020; pp. 17–38.
15. Louhichi, M.; Nesmaoui, R.; Mbarek, M.; Lazaar, M. Shapley Values for Explaining the Black Box Nature of Machine Learning Model Clustering. *Procedia Comput. Sci.* **2023**, *220*, 806–811. [CrossRef]
16. Tripathi, S.; Hemachandra, N.; Trivedi, P. Interpretable feature subset selection: A Shapley value based approach. In Proceedings of the 2020 IEEE International Conference on Big Data (Big Data), Atlanta, GA, USA, 10–13 December 2020; pp. 5463–5472.
17. Främling, K.; Westberg, M.; Jullum, M.; Madhikermi, M.; Malhi, A. Comparison of contextual importance and utility with lime and Shapley values. In Proceedings of the Explainable and Transparent AI and Multi-Agent Systems: Third International Workshop, EXTRAAMAS 2021, Virtual Event, 3–7 May 2021; pp. 39–54.
18. Longo, L.; Brcic, M.; Federico, C.; Jaesik, C.; Confalonieri, R.; Del Ser, J.; Guidotti, R.; Hayashi, Y.; Herrera, F.; Holzinger, A.; et al. Explainable Artificial Intelligence (XAI) 2.0: A manifesto of open challenges and interdisciplinary research directions. *Inf. Fusion* **2024**, *106*, 102301. [CrossRef]
19. Zhang, J.; Xia, H.; Sun, Q.; Liu, J.; Xiong, L.; Pei, J.; Ren, K. Dynamic Shapley Value Computation. In Proceedings of the 2023 IEEE 39th International Conference on Data Engineering (ICDE), Anaheim, CA, USA, 3–7 April 2023; pp. 639–652.
20. Jia, R.; Dao, D.; Wang, B.; Hubis, F.A.; Hynes, N.; Gürel, N.M.; Spanos, C.J. Towards efficient data valuation based on the shapley value. In Proceedings of the The 22nd International Conference on Artificial Intelligence and Statistics, Naha, Japan, 16–18 April 2019; pp. 1167–1176.
21. Ancona, M.; Ceolini, E.; Öztireli, C.; Gross, M. Towards better understanding of gradient-based attribution methods for deep neural networks. *arXiv* **2017**, arXiv:1711.06104.
22. Gevins, A.; Smith, M.E. Neurophysiological measures of cognitive workload during human–computer interaction. *Theor. Issues Ergon. Sci.* **2003**, *4*, 113–131. [CrossRef]
23. Borghini, G.; Astolfi, L.; Vecchiato, G.; Mattia, D.; Babiloni, F. Measuring neurophysiological signals in aircraft pilots and car drivers for the assessment of mental workload, fatigue and drowsiness. *Neurosci. Biobehav. Rev.* **2014**, *44*, 58–75. [CrossRef]
24. Fernandez Rojas, R.; Debie, E.; Fidock, J.; Barlow, M.; Kasmarik, K.; Anavatti, S.; Abbass, H. Electroencephalographic workload indicators during teleoperation of an unmanned aerial vehicle shepherding a swarm of unmanned ground vehicles in contested environments. *Front. Neurosci.* **2020** *14*, 40. [CrossRef]
25. Raufi, B.; Longo, L. An Evaluation of the EEG alpha-to-theta and theta-to-alpha band Ratios as Indexes of Mental Workload. *Front. Neuroinform.* **2022**, *16*, 44. [CrossRef] [PubMed]
26. Raufi, B. Hybrid models of performance using mental workload and usability features via supervised machine learning. In Proceedings of the Human Mental Workload: Models and Applications: Third International Symposium, H-WORKLOAD 2019, Rome, Italy, 14–15 November 2019; Springer International Publishing: Berlin/Heidelberg, Germany, 2019; pp. 136–155.
27. Mohanavelu, K.; Poonguzhali, S.; Janani, A.; Vinutha, S. Machine learning-based approach for identifying mental workload of pilots. *Biomed. Signal Process. Control* **2022**, *75*, 103623. [CrossRef]
28. Kakkos, I.; Dimitrakopoulos, G.N.; Sun, Y.; Yuan, J.; Matsopoulos, G.K.; Bezerianos, A.; Sun, Y. EEG fingerprints of task-independent mental workload discrimination. *IEEE J. Biomed. Health Inform.* **2021**, *25*, 3824–3833. [CrossRef]
29. Longo, L. Designing medical interactive systems via assessment of human mental workload. In Proceedings of the 2015 IEEE 28th International Symposium on Computer-Based Medical Systems, Sao Carlos, Brazil, 22–25 June 2015; pp. 364–365.
30. Longo, L.; Rajendran, M. A novel parabolic model of instructional efficiency grounded on ideal mental workload and performance. In Proceedings of the 5th International Symposium, H-WORKLOAD 2021, Virtual Event, 24–26 November 2021; pp. 11–36.
31. Longo, L. Formalising human mental workload as non-monotonic concept for adaptive and personalised web-design. In Proceedings of the International Conference on User Modeling, Adaptation, and Personalization, Montreal, QC, Canada, 16–20 July 2012
32. Jafari, M.J.; Zaeri, F.; Jafari, A.H.; Payandeh Najafabadi, A.T.; Al-Qaisi, S.; Hassanzadeh-Rangi, N. Assessment and monitoring of mental workload in subway train operations using physiological, subjective, and performance measures. *Hum. Factors Ergon. Manuf. Serv. Ind.* **2020**, *30*, 165–175. [CrossRef]
33. Longo, L.; Barrett, S. A computational analysis of cognitive effort. In Proceedings of the Asian Conference on Intelligent Information and Database Systems, Hue City, Vietnam, 24–26 March 2010
34. Hancock, G.M.; Longo, L.; Young, M.S.; Hancock, P.A. *Mental Workload. Handbook of Human Factors and Ergonomics*; Wiley Online Library: Hoboken, NJ, USA, 2021.
35. Longo, L.; Wickens, C.D.; Hancock, G.; Hancock, P.A. Human Mental Workload: A Survey and a Novel Inclusive Definition. *Front. Psychol.* **2022**, *13*, 883321. [CrossRef]
36. Käthner, I.; Wriessnegger, S.C.; Müller-Putz, G.R.; Kübler, A.; Halder, S. Effects of mental workload and fatigue on the P300, alpha and theta band power during operation of an ERP (P300) brain–computer interface. *J. Biol. Psychiatry* **2014**, *102*, 118–129. [CrossRef] [PubMed]

37. Muñoz-de-Escalona, E.; Cañas, J.J.; Leva, C.; Longo, L. Task demand transition peak point effects on mental workload measures divergence. In Proceedings of the Human Mental Workload: Models and Applications: 4th International Symposium, H-WORKLOAD 2020, Granada, Spain, 3–5 December 2020; Springer International Publishing: Berlin/Heidelberg, Germany, 2020; pp. 207–226.
38. Longo, L. Modeling Cognitive Load as a Self-Supervised Brain Rate with Electroencephalography and Deep Learning. *Brain Sci.* **2022**, *12*, 10, 1416. MDPI [CrossRef]
39. Rizzo, L. Middeldorf and Longo, Luca, Representing and inferring mental workload via defeasible reasoning: A comparison with the NASA Task Load Index and the Workload Profile. In Proceedings of the 1st Workshop on Advances in Argumentation in Artificial Intelligence AI3@AI*IA, Bari, Italy, 14–17 November 2017.
40. Rizzo L.; Luca, L. Inferential Models of Mental Workload with Defeasible Argumentation and Non-monotonic Fuzzy Reasoning: A Comparative Study. In Proceedings of the 2nd Workshop on Advances in Argumentation in Artificial Intelligence, Co-Located with XVII International Conference of the Italian Association for Artificial Intelligence, AI^3@AI*IA 2018, Trento, Italy, 20–23 November 2018; pp. 11–26.
41. Hoque, N.; Bhattacharyya, D.K.; Kalita, J.K. MIFS-ND: A mutual information-based feature selection method. *Expert Syst. Appl.* **2014**, *41*, 6371–6385. [CrossRef]
42. Zhai, Y.; Song, W.; Liu, X.; Liu, L.; Zhao, X. A chi-square statistics based feature selection method in text classification. In Proceedings of the 2018 IEEE 9th International Conference on Software Engineering and Service Science (ICSESS), Beijing, China, 23–25 November 2018; pp. 160–163.
43. Perangin-Angin, D.J.; Bachtiar, F.A. Classification of Stress in Office Work Activities Using Extreme Learning Machine Algorithm and One-Way ANOVA F-Test Feature Selection. In Proceedings of the 2021 4th International Seminar on Research of Information Technology and Intelligent Systems (ISRITI), Yogyakarta, Indonesia, 16–17 December 2021; pp. 503–508.
44. Fryer, D.; Strümke, I.; Nguyen, H. Shapley Values for Feature Selection The Good, the Bad, and the Axioms. *arXiv* **2021**, arXiv:2102.10936.
45. Williamson, B.; Feng, J. Efficient nonparametric statistical inference on population feature importance using Shapley values. In Proceedings of the International Conference on Machine Learning, Virtual, 13–18 July 2020; pp. 10282–10291.
46. Junaid, M.; Ali, S.; Eid, F.; El-Sappagh, S.; Abuhmed, T. Explainable machine learning models based on multimodal time-series data for the early detection of Parkinson's disease. *Comput. Methods Programs Biomed.* **2023** *234*, 107495. [CrossRef]
47. Msonda, J.R.; He, Z.; Lu, C. Feature Reconstruction Based Channel Selection for Emotion Recognition Using EEG. In Proceedings of the 2021 IEEE Signal Processing in Medicine and Biology Symposium, 2021 (SPMB), Philadelphia, PA, USA, 4 December 2021; pp. 1–7.
48. Moussa, M.M.; Alzaabi, Y.; Khandoker, A.H. Explainable computer-aided detection of obstructive sleep apnea and depression. *IEEE Access* **2022**, *10*, 110916–110933. [CrossRef]
49. Khosla, A.; Khandnor, P.; Chand, T. Automated diagnosis of depression from EEG signals using traditional and deep learning approaches: A comparative analysis. *Biocybern. Biomed. Eng.* **2022**, *42*, 108–142. [CrossRef]
50. Shanarova, N.; Pronina, M.; Lipkovich, M.; Ponomarev, V.; Müller, A.; Kropotov, J. Application of Machine Learning to Diagnostics of Schizophrenia Patients Based on Event-Related Potentials. *Diagnostics* **2023**, *13*, 509. [CrossRef] [PubMed]
51. Islam, R.; Andreev, A.V.; Shusharina, N.N.; Hramov, A.E. Explainable machine learning methods for classification of brain states during visual perception. *Mathematics* **2022**, *10*, 2819. [CrossRef]
52. Kaczorowska, M.; Plechawska-Wójcik, M.; Tokovarov, M. Interpretable machine learning models for three-way classification of cognitive workload levels for eye-tracking features. *Brain Sci.* **2021**, *11*, 210. [CrossRef]
53. Lim, W.L.; Sourina, O.; Wang, L.P. STEW: Simultaneous task EEG workload data set. *IEEE Trans. Neural Syst. Rehabil. Eng.* **2018**, *26*, 2106–2114. [CrossRef]
54. Mikayoshi, M. Makoto's Preprocessing Pipeline. 2018. Available online: https://sccn.ucsd.edu/wiki/Makotoś_preprocessing_pipeline (accessed on 4 April 2023).
55. Nolan, H.; Whelan, R.; Reilly, R.B. FASTER: Fully automated statistical thresholding for EEG artifact rejection. *J. Neurosci. Methods* **2010**, *192*, 152–162. [CrossRef]
56. Verhaeghe, J.; Van Der Donckt, J.; Ongenae, F.; Van Hoecke, S. Powershap: A power-full shapley feature selection method. In Proceedings of the Machine Learning and Knowledge Discovery in Databases: European Conference, ECML PKDD 2022, Grenoble, France, 19–23 September 2022; Springer International Publishing: Cham, Switzerland, 2022; pp. 71–87.
57. Lieberman, M.G.; Morris, J.D. The precise effect of multicollinearity on classification prediction. *Mult. Linear Regres. Viewpoints* **2014**, *40*, 5–10.
58. Mridha, K.; Kumar, D.; Shukla, M.; Jani, M. Temporal features and machine learning approaches to study brain activity with EEG and ECG. In Proceedings of the 2021 International Conference on Advance Computing and Innovative Technologies in Engineering (ICACITE), Greater Noida, India, 4–5 March 2021; pp. 409–414.
59. Goodfellow, I.; Pouget-Abadie, J.; Mirza, M.; Xu, B.; Warde-Farley, D.; Ozair, S.; Bengio, Y. Generative adversarial networks. *Commun. ACM* **2020**, *63*, 139–144. [CrossRef]
60. Frølich, L.; Dowding, I. Removal of muscular artifacts in EEG signals: A comparison of linear decomposition methods. *Brain Inform.* **2018**, *5*, 13–22. [CrossRef] [PubMed]

61. Hernandez-Matamoros, A.; Fujita, H.; Perez-Meana, H. A novel approach to create synthetic biomedical signals using BiRNN. *Inf. Sci.* **2020**, *541*, 218–241. [CrossRef]
62. Molnar, C.; König, G.; Herbinger, J.; Freiesleben, T.; Dandl, S.; Scholbeck, C. A.; Bischl, B. General pitfalls of model-agnostic interpretation methods for machine learning models. In Proceedings of the xxAI-Beyond Explainable AI: International Workshop, Held in Conjunction with ICML 2020, Vienna, Austria, 18 July 2020; Revised and Extended Papers; Springer International Publishing: Cham, Switzerland, 2022; pp. 39–68.
63. Kumar, I.E.; Venkatasubramanian, S.; Scheidegger, C.; Friedler, S. Problems with Shapley-value-based explanations as feature importance measures. In Proceedings of the International Conference on Machine Learning, Virtual, 21 November 2020; pp. 5491–5500.
64. Bolón-Canedo, V.; Sánchez-Maroño, N.; Alonso-Betanzos, A. Distributed feature selection: An application to microarray data classification. *Appl. Soft Comput.* **2015**, *30*, 136–150. [CrossRef]

BioMedInformatics

Article

The Effect of Data Missingness on Machine Learning Predictions of Uncontrolled Diabetes Using All of Us Data

Zain Jabbar [1,2] and Peter Washington [1,2,*]

1 Information and Computer Sciences Department, University of Hawai'i at Mānoa, 2500 Campus Road, Honolulu, HI 96822, USA; zjabbar@hawaii.edu
2 Hawai'i Digital Health Laboratory, 1680 East-West Road, Honolulu, HI 96822, USA
* Correspondence: pyw@hawaii.edu

Abstract: Electronic Health Records (EHR) provide a vast amount of patient data that are relevant to predicting clinical outcomes. The inherent presence of missing values poses challenges to building performant machine learning models. This paper aims to investigate the effect of various imputation methods on the National Institutes of Health's All of Us dataset, a dataset containing a high degree of data missingness. We apply several imputation techniques such as mean substitution, constant filling, and multiple imputation on the same dataset for the task of diabetes prediction. We find that imputing values causes heteroskedastic performance for machine learning models with increased data missingness. That is, the more missing values a patient has for their tests, the higher variance there is on a diabetes model AUROC, F1, precision, recall, and accuracy scores. This highlights a critical challenge in using EHR data for predictive modeling. This work highlights the need for future research to develop methodologies to mitigate the effects of missing data and heteroskedasticity in EHR-based predictive models.

Keywords: algorithmic fairness; electronic health records; data missingness; data imputation; diabetes

Citation: Jabbar, Z.; Washington, P. The Effect of Data Missingness on Machine Learning Predictions of Uncontrolled Diabetes Using All of Us Data. *BioMedInformatics* **2024**, *4*, 780–795. https://doi.org/10.3390/biomedinformatics4010043

Academic Editors: Carson K. Leung and Alexandre G. De Brevern

Received: 21 January 2024
Revised: 7 February 2024
Accepted: 26 February 2024
Published: 6 March 2024

1. Introduction

Diabetes is a health condition characterized by chronic hyperglycemia and resulting from issues with insulin secretion and action [1]. The onset of diabetes increases the risk for a number of health complications such as cardiovascular disease, kidney disease, retinopathy, and neuropathy [2,3]. The longer one has diabetes, the more complications are likely to occur [4]. Diabetes affects 464 million people in the world as of 2021, and it is predicted to increase to 638 million by 2045 [5]. Diabetes disproportionately affects minority populations [4,6].

Diabetes has also been studied using machine learning [7–9]. Oikonomou et al. [10] provide a comprehensive overview of how machine learning has been applied to precision diabetes care, particularly in cardiovascular risk prediction among diabetic patients. Their work underscores the significant potential of machine learning in transforming diabetes care by leveraging large datasets to identify risk factors and predict outcomes with high accuracy.

In recent years, the application of machine learning to electronic health records (EHR) has emerged as a promising tool for enhancing our understanding of diabetes and improving prediction models for its management. The integration of machine learning with EHR data offers a new frontier in diabetic research. Prior studies have shown that machine learning models can effectively predict the progression to pre-diabetes and type 2 diabetes using EHR data, emphasizing the role of established risk factors and identifying novel factors for further research [11]. Cahn et al. highlighted the use of machine learning models to improve the prediction of incident diabetes utilizing patient data from EHR, underscoring the potential for targeted interventions [12]. Additionally, leveraging large health records datasets has enabled significant progress in diabetes forecasting using machine learning, as demonstrated by research conducted using the health records of patients in Ontario, Canada [13]. This approach not only offers predictive insights, but also helps identify critical features contributing to diabetes onset.

Building upon this line of research, we study the prediction of diabetes using EHR data from the National Institutes of Health (NIH)'s All of Us (AoU) dataset. The program is a result of the Precision Medicine Initiative Cohort Program [14]. The cohort consists of over 1 million volunteers who contributed their biospecimen samples (such as blood and urine), physical measurements, and extensive surveys on health and lifestyle [15]. The overarching goal of All of Us is to advance precision medicine—a personalized approach to disease prevention and treatment that considers individual differences in lifestyle, environment, and biology. This approach is intended to overcome the limitations of a one-size-fits-all model in health care by factoring individual variation. The All of Us Research Program stands out for its commitment to diversity, striving to include participants from various racial and ethnic backgrounds, age groups, geographic regions, and health statuses to ensure the dataset reflects the broad diversity of the U.S. population [16]. By harnessing the power of big data and emphasizing inclusivity and participant engagement, the All of Us Research Program aspires to revolutionize our understanding of health and pave the way for more effective, personalized healthcare solutions.

We focus, in particular, on measuring the effect of data missingness on the prediction of health outcomes such as diabetes using All of Us data. We apply several data imputation techniques and measure their effect on various model performance metrics. This characterization of data missingness on large EHR datasets can inform future efforts that apply imputation strategies to such data.

2. Materials and Methods

2.1. Dataset

We used the National Institutes of Health (NIH) All of Us dataset. We selected 47 features from Abegaz et al.'s work [17]. We list them in Table 1 alongside the proportion of missing values per feature. For each measurement type, we created two features: one for the average reading and another for the number of times the feature is read.

Table 1. Model input features and missingness proportion for the total dataset for training and testing subsets.

	Total	Training	Testing
Age	0.000000	0.000000	0.000000
Median income	0.000000	0.000000	0.000000
Deprivation index	0.000000	0.000000	0.000000
Chloride	0.091448	0.091257	0.092210
Bicarbonate	0.653057	0.653368	0.651811
Alanine aminotransferase	0.144202	0.143750	0.146010
Albumin	0.138477	0.137825	0.141085
Alkaline phosphatase	0.140681	0.140218	0.142532
Anion gap	0.222889	0.222680	0.223723
Aspartate aminotransferase	0.145162	0.144927	0.146102
Basophils	0.155516	0.154991	0.157613
Bilirubin	0.159603	0.159277	0.160906
Height	0.006870	0.006940	0.006586
Weight	0.008790	0.008826	0.008649
Calcium	0.094230	0.093851	0.095750
Carbon dioxide	0.177928	0.177490	0.179681
HDL	0.331019	0.330497	0.333108
LDL	0.351579	0.350987	0.353944
Creatinine	0.083538	0.083301	0.084485
Eosinophil	0.151078	0.150606	0.152965
Erythrocytes	0.104615	0.104277	0.105968
Heart rate	0.008975	0.008941	0.009110

Table 1. *Cont.*

	Total	Training	Testing
Leukocyte	0.089564	0.089203	0.091010
Lymphocytes	0.144079	0.143765	0.145333
MCH	0.139400	0.139079	0.140685
MCHC	0.140034	0.139695	0.141393
MCV	0.169126	0.168842	0.170263
Monocytes	0.146879	0.146420	0.148718
Neutrophils	0.143371	0.142896	0.145271
Platelets	0.115707	0.115226	0.117633
Potassium	0.103088	0.102984	0.103506
Respiratory rate	0.310053	0.308913	0.314610
Sodium	0.092913	0.092681	0.093841
Triglyceride	0.339421	0.339068	0.340833
Urea nitrogen	0.112839	0.112733	0.113262
Vomiting	0.000000	0.000000	0.000000
Myocardial infarction	0.000000	0.000000	0.000000
Arthritis	0.000000	0.000000	0.000000
Polyuria	0.000000	0.000000	0.000000
Aspirin	0.098970	0.098952	0.099043
Beta blockers	0.098970	0.098952	0.099043
Steroids	0.098970	0.098952	0.099043
Acetaminophen	0.098970	0.098952	0.099043
Statin	0.098970	0.098952	0.099043
Opioids	0.098970	0.098952	0.099043
Nicotine	0.098970	0.098952	0.099043
Paraesthesia	0.098970	0.098952	0.099043

The total size of the dataset is 162,453, with 56,655 positive and 105,798 negative data points. The stratified train/test split is 80/20, yielding 129,962 training patients of whom 45,324 are positive and 84,638 are negative, and 32,491 test patients consisting of 11,331 positive and 21,160 negative patients.

2.2. Modeling

To increase uniformity for ease of comparison while maintaining a robust search for well-performing models, we employed Autosklearn2.0 [18,19]. This meta-model has a search space consisting of every model within Scikit-Learn and subsequently searches over hyperparameter space per model. The training is conducted on four CPUs, 26 GB of RAM, 3 h of training time, 6572 MB of memory per job, log loss as the objective function, and no limit to the number of models on disk.

We compare the following six imputation methods alongside an oversampling preprocessing step.

No Imputation: This method involves not performing any imputation on the dataset, leaving the missing values as they are. In this approach, the model chosen must inherently be capable of handling missing data. Techniques such as decision trees or certain ensemble methods can often process datasets with missing values directly. This method is based on the assumption that the model can interpret and manage the missingness in the data without any explicit intervention.

Automatic Imputation (via Autosklearn): This approach employs Autosklearn, an automated machine learning tool, to determine the best imputation method for the dataset. Autosklearn explores various imputation strategies as part of its preprocessing pipeline and selects the one that optimizes model performance. This method leverages the power of automated machine learning to identify the most effective imputation technique, which could range from simple strategies like mean or median substitution to more complex ones, based on the characteristics of the data.

Constant Fill: In this approach, missing values are filled with a constant value. This constant could be a number outside the normal range of values (such as −1) to differentiate imputed values from real ones. The advantage of this method is its simplicity and the clear demarcation it provides, which can be helpful in certain analytical contexts.

Mean Substitution: Mean substitution involves replacing missing values in a dataset with the mean value of the respective column. This method assumes that the missing values are randomly distributed and that the mean is a representative statistic for the missing data. It is a straightforward approach but may not always be suitable, particularly in cases where the data distribution is skewed or the mean is not a good representation of the central tendency.

Median Substitution: Similar to mean substitution, median substitution replaces missing values with the median of the respective column. This method is particularly useful in datasets where the distribution is skewed or there are outliers, as the median is less affected by extreme values than the mean. It is a robust approach that can provide a better central tendency estimate in certain types of data distributions.

Multiple Imputation with Bayesian Ridge: This is a more sophisticated approach where multiple imputation is performed using Bayesian Ridge regression. In this method, missing values are estimated based on observed data, with the Bayesian Ridge regression model used to predict the missing values. Specifically, one begins by denoting one column of the training input f and the other columns X_f. A Bayesian Ridge regression model is then fitted on (X_f, f). This is conducted for every feature and can be repeated so that in the next round, the previous rounds' predictions can be used to make better predictions of the missing value. In this paper, we use 15 imputation rounds. The number of imputation rounds, 15, is chosen arbitrarily. The higher the number, the more accurate the imputation should be. For a dataset as large as All of Us, we chose to keep it lower. This technique considers the uncertainty in the imputation process by creating several imputed datasets and combining the results, leading to more accurate and reliable imputation compared to single imputation methods.

Each of these imputation methods has its strengths and weaknesses and is suitable for different types of datasets and missing data patterns. The choice of imputation method can significantly impact the performance of the subsequent analysis or machine learning models.

Random oversampling is a technique used to address class imbalance in a dataset, particularly in situations where the dataset has a disproportionate number of instances in different classes. This imbalance can lead to biased or inaccurate model performance, as the model may tend to favor the majority class.

In random oversampling, the idea is to balance the dataset by increasing the size of the underrepresented class (minority class). This is accomplished by randomly duplicating instances from the minority class until the number of instances in both the minority and majority classes is approximately equal. This method creates additional samples from the minority class not by generating new samples but by resampling from the existing samples.

In total, there are 12 different models to test with the same underlying classifier.

2.3. Model Evaluation

Model performance is a catch-all term to describe the plethora of different metrics used to compare a model's predictions to the actual outcome. We can summarize the comparison of a classification model's predictions as compared to the number of actual classes in a confusion matrix.

We use the following abbreviations in the definitions of our performance metrics:

$$
\begin{aligned}
TP &= \text{True Positive} \\
FN &= \text{False Negative} \\
FP &= \text{False Positive} \\
TN &= \text{True Negative} \\
P &= \text{Positive} = TP + FN \\
N &= \text{Negative} = FP + TN
\end{aligned}
$$

We have the corresponding normalized quantities associated with the above counts:

$$
\begin{aligned}
TPR &= \text{True Positive Rate} = TP/P \\
FNR &= \text{False Negative Rate} = FN/P \\
FPR &= \text{False Positive Rate} = FP/N \\
TNR &= \text{True Negative Rate} = TN/N
\end{aligned}
$$

We may now define four of the five metrics:

$$
\begin{aligned}
\text{Balanced Accuracy} &= \frac{1}{2}\left(\frac{TP}{TP+FN} + \frac{TN}{TN+FP}\right) \\
\text{Precision} &= \frac{TP}{TP+FP} \\
\text{Recall} &= \frac{TP}{TP+FN} \\
\text{F1} &= \frac{2TP}{2TP+FP+FN}
\end{aligned}
$$

The final of the five metrics consists of the probability output of a model. Given an input, a model has a probability associated with the class and a threshold such that inputs with a probability larger than the threshold are predicted to be a member of the class. There are certain points on this curve that we know the values for.

If the threshold is set to 0, then the model predicts all inputs as positive. Thus, the true positive rate is 1 and the false positive rate is 1. If the threshold is set to 1, then the model predicts all inputs as negative. Thus, the true positive rate is 0 and the false positive rate is 0. This defines a curve in the space with coordinates (FPR, TPR) parameterized by the probability threshold with endpoints $(0,0)$ and $(1,1)$. This curve is called the Receiver Operating Characteristic (ROC) curve, and its integral is called the Area Under the ROC (AUROC).

2.4. Model Fairness Evaluation

Given the standard metrics above, we can consider some *fairness metrics* that are measured as discrepancies of some performance metric between members of a privileged group and the remaining groups. In this dataset, there are two primary sensitive attributes that fall into this regime: gender and race. In order to define these differences, we must introduce new notation. The exact notation will differ based on the source [20–23]. The quantities below will be numerically equivalent to those in the previous literature while remaining consistent with the notation used in this paper. Let μ_S denote the metric μ on the subset S within the data. For example, FPR_P will denote the False Positive Rate on the privileged group, whereas FPR_U will denote the False Positive Rate on the unprivileged group. We let y_i represent the test result for patient i and $\hat{y}_i$ represent the model's prediction for patient i. The final fairness metric shown below is described in detail by Speicher et al. [24].

$$\text{Average Odds Difference} = \frac{1}{2}[(\text{FPR}_U - \text{FPR}_P) + (\text{TPR}_P - \text{TPR}_U)]$$
$$\text{Average Odds Error} = \frac{1}{2}[|\text{FPR}_U - \text{FPR}_P| + |\text{TPR}_U - \text{TPR}_P|]$$
$$\text{Class Imbalance} = \frac{(P_U + N_U) - (P_P + N_P)}{P + N}$$
$$\text{Equal Opportunity Difference} = \text{TPR}_U - \text{TPR}_P$$
$$\text{Statistical Parity Difference} = (\text{TPR}_U + \text{FPR}_U) - (\text{TPR}_P + \text{FPR}_P)$$
$$\text{Between Group Generalized Entropy Error} = \frac{1}{2n}\sum_{i=1}^{n}\left[\left(\frac{\hat{y}_i - y_i + 1}{\frac{1}{n}(\sum_{i=1}^{n}\hat{y}_i - y_i + 1)}\right)^2 - 1\right]$$

2.5. *Measuring the Effect of Data Missingness*

We are interested in measuring the effect on the model's performance as the number of missing features varies. One expects that a higher number of missing features would lead to lower overall performance. Since the number of missing features is a large range, we can study the trend by fitting an ordinary least squares line between the performance versus the number of missing features. Our procedure is as follows:

1. Given a model fitted on the training data:
2. Select a subset of the testing data with a specified number of missing features.
3. Evaluate the model's performance on that subset.
4. Plot the performance versus the number of missing features.
5. Evaluate the F-test for the slope of the line and the Breuch–Pagan test for the heteroskedasticity of the residuals around the line.

3. Results

3.1. *Data Missingness*

We constructed a simple (but interpretable) linear regression model that predicts the number of missing features given race and gender. The coefficients are shown in Table 2. We observe that race and gender are predictors of missingness.

Table 2. Linear regression coefficients.

Sensitive Attribute	Coefficient
Female	−0.54
Male	0.39
Gender Other	0.14
Black	1.31
White	−1.34
Middle Eastern	0.48
Asian	−0.09
Race Other	−0.35

3.2. *Model Performance*

Figures 1 and 2 outline each imputation method's overall performance on the dataset when stratified by different sensitive attributes. For each imputation method, we measured the AUROC, balanced accuracy, F1, precision, and recall on the total population, each gender category, each racial category, and across the different missing feature bucketed groups. We then reran the analysis with an extra step of oversampling to balance the dataset for the number of people with diabetes.

Figures 3 and 4 compare the fairness metrics, average odds difference, average odds error, between-group generalized entropy error, class imbalance, equal opportunity difference, mean difference, and statistical parity difference. These are fairness metrics, which means that for a sensitive attribute, we denote one group to be privileged and one to be unprivileged. We evaluated the imputation methods on the model discrepancy across groups. Since there is no obvious privileged group for the missing feature sub-populations, we only compared gender (with *male* being the privileged group) and race (with *white* being the privileged group).

3.3. *Effect of Data Missingness*

We next seek to understand the effect of data missingness. In the previous section, the 0.2-quantile missing feature sub-populations had their AUROC, balanced accuracy, F1, precision, and recall tabulated. We may visualize how the models perform more easily by plotting the models performance as a grouped bar chart, both without (Figure 5) and with (Figure 6) oversampling.

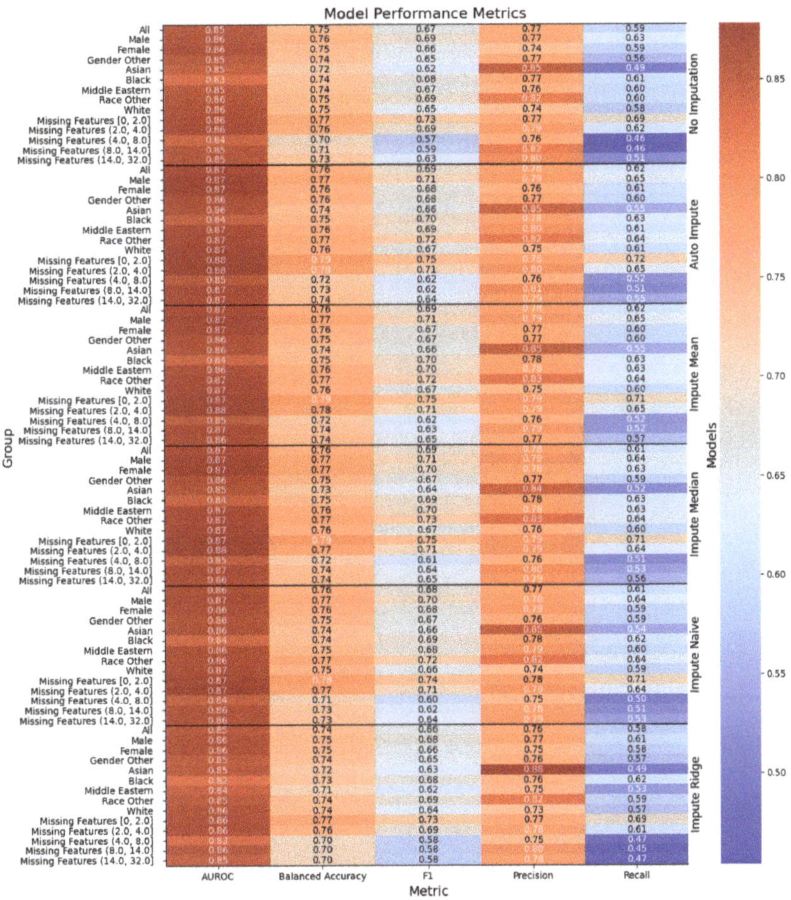

Figure 1. Performance of the models, with the columns denoting the specific metric, across the evaluated sub-population (left label) and the imputation method (right label). The color denotes the magnitude of the metric, warmer colors indicating higher performance. The text color is adjusted to be readable given the background color.

We plotted the line of best fit for each machine learning metric as a function of the number of missing features and across imputation strategies, both without oversampling (Figure 7, Table 3) and with oversampling (Figure 8, Table 4). We observed a statistically significant negative slope in all of the performance metrics and models except for the following imputation methods using balanced accuracy: impute mean, impute naive, impute median, impute ridge. Furthermore, any model apart from "No Imputation" and "Auto Impute" demonstrated statistically significant heteroskedasticity.

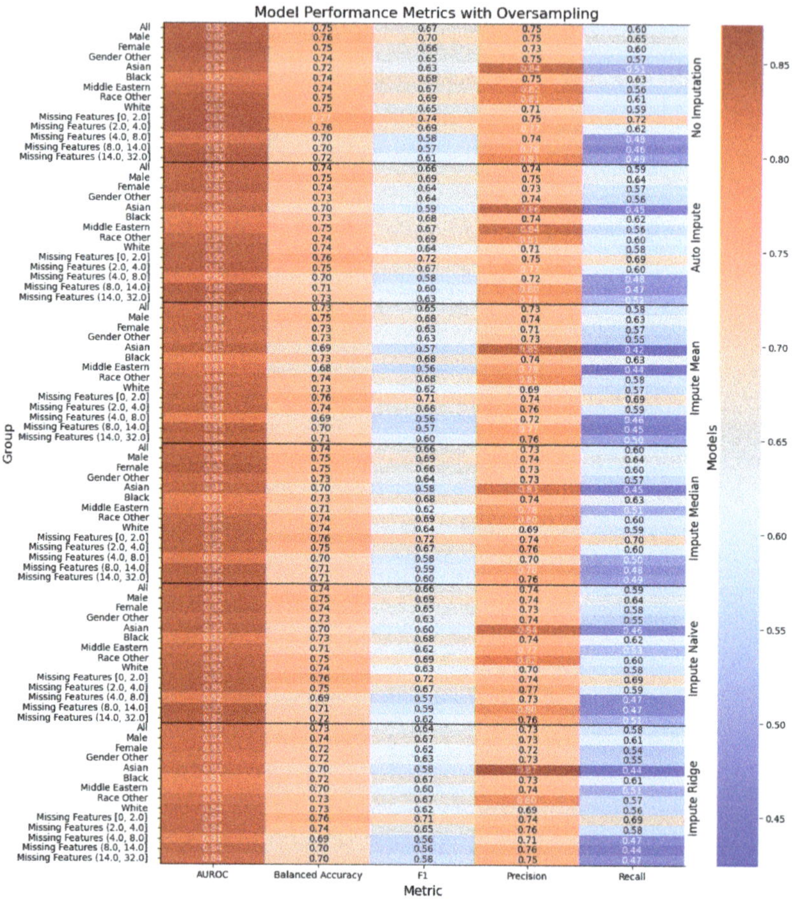

Figure 2. Performance of the models when oversampling, with the columns denoting the specific metric, across the evaluated sub-population (left label) and the imputation method (right label). The color denotes the magnitude of the metric, warmer colors indicating higher performance.

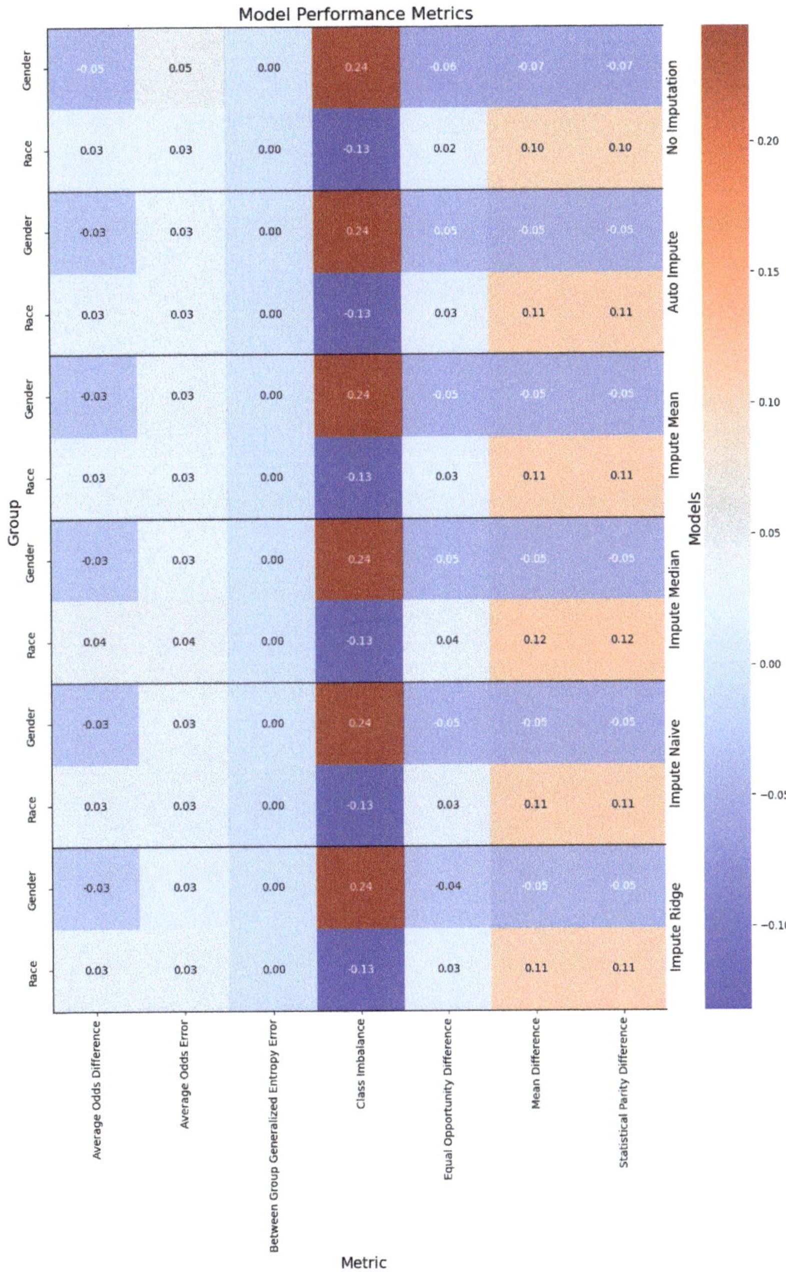

Figure 3. Performance of the models, with the columns denoting the specific metric, across the evaluated sub-population (left label) and the imputation method (right label).

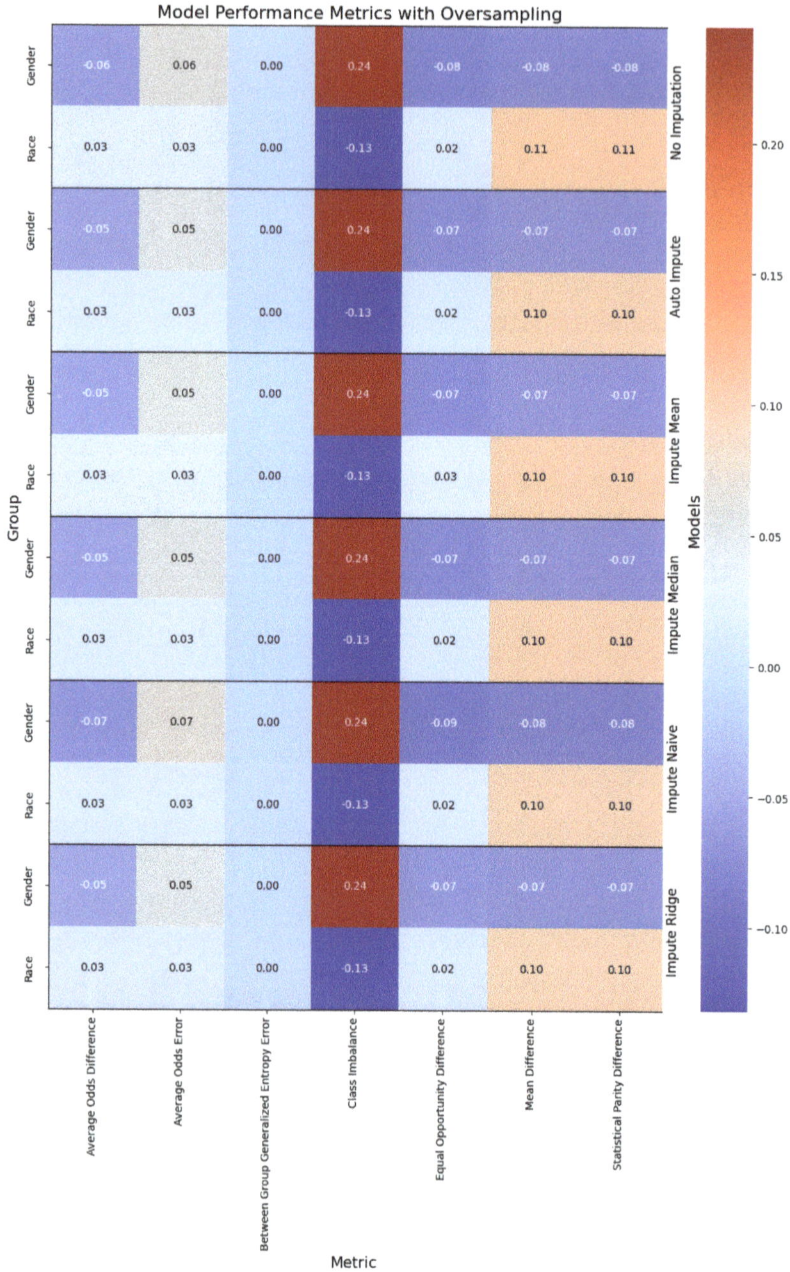

Figure 4. Performance of the models when oversampling, with the columns denoting the specific metric, across the evaluated sub-population (left label) and the imputation method (right label). The color denotes the magnitude of the metric, with warmer colors indicating better performance. The text color is adjusted to be readable given the background color.

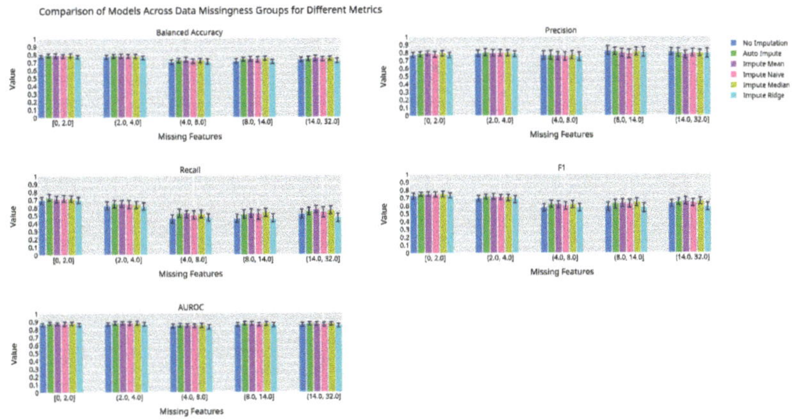

Figure 5. Machine learning performance exhibited by different imputation methods grouped by 0.2 quantiles.

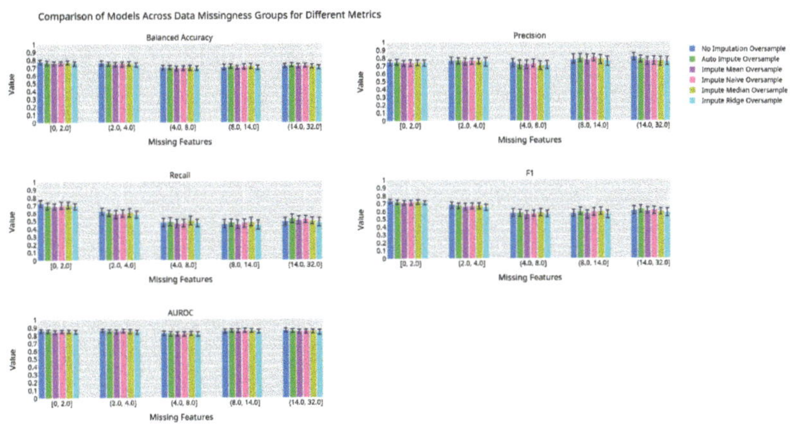

Figure 6. Machine learning performance exhibited by different imputation methods using an oversampling preprocessing step grouped by 0.2 quantiles.

Table 3. Tabular representation of Figure 7. We display the Y-intercept and slope of the lines of best fit for the estimator performance on a given metric. The F-Test p-value gives the probability of the null hypothesis that the line of best fit has a slope of zero. The Breusch–Pagan p-value, which gives the probability that the error of the line has constant variance, is also given.

Estimator	Metric	Y-Intercept	Slope	F-Test p-Value	Breusch–Pagan p-Value
No Imputation	Balanced Accuracy	0.938288	−0.014331	0.000000	0.372675
	Precision	1.038484	−0.015907	0.000000	0.683840
	Recall	0.688205	−0.010770	0.000000	0.380535
	F1	0.805173	−0.012496	0.000000	0.934875
	AUROC	0.938288	−0.014331	0.000000	0.372675
Auto Impute	Balanced Accuracy	0.962040	−0.014739	0.000000	0.352425
	Precision	1.023924	−0.015765	0.000000	0.681243
	Recall	0.742006	−0.011667	0.000000	0.657899
	F1	0.844082	−0.013165	0.000000	0.760720
	AUROC	0.962040	−0.014739	0.000000	0.352425

Table 3. *Cont.*

Estimator	Metric	Y-Intercept	Slope	F-Test *p*-Value	Breusch-Pagan *p*-Value
Impute Mean	Balanced Accuracy	0.744528	−0.000483	0.517161	0.000141
	Precision	0.887014	−0.006534	0.000078	0.000000
	Recall	0.680919	−0.005709	0.000068	0.001215
	F1	0.759957	−0.006277	0.000007	0.000021
	AUROC	0.825048	−0.004409	0.000089	0.000099
Impute Naive	Balanced Accuracy	0.736591	−0.000548	0.431844	0.000462
	Precision	0.867793	−0.006154	0.000095	0.000001
	Recall	0.649528	−0.005119	0.000186	0.005948
	F1	0.733024	−0.005788	0.000016	0.000159
	AUROC	0.812685	−0.004257	0.000106	0.000334
Impute Median	Balanced Accuracy	0.743865	−0.000620	0.384045	0.000024
	Precision	0.890143	−0.006735	0.000025	0.000000
	Recall	0.665581	−0.005631	0.000031	0.005150
	F1	0.752403	−0.006318	0.000002	0.000065
	AUROC	0.824385	−0.004546	0.000030	0.000131
Impute Ridge	Balanced Accuracy	0.695296	0.000247	0.724879	0.000051
	Precision	0.875240	−0.006566	0.000036	0.000002
	Recall	0.565600	−0.004039	0.002779	0.007240
	F1	0.671835	−0.005079	0.000164	0.000335
	AUROC	0.775816	−0.003679	0.000605	0.000196

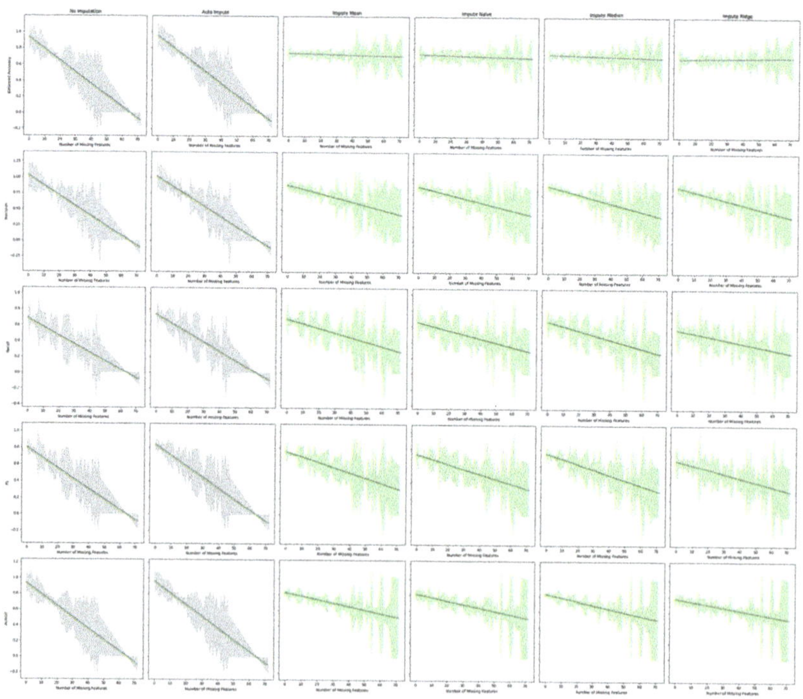

Figure 7. Best fit lines of machine learning metrics as a function of the number of missing features. The shading is the residual of the best fit line. The best fit line is colored green if we reject the null hypothesis that the line has a slope of zero. The shading is colored green if we reject the null hypothesis that the residuals have constant variance.

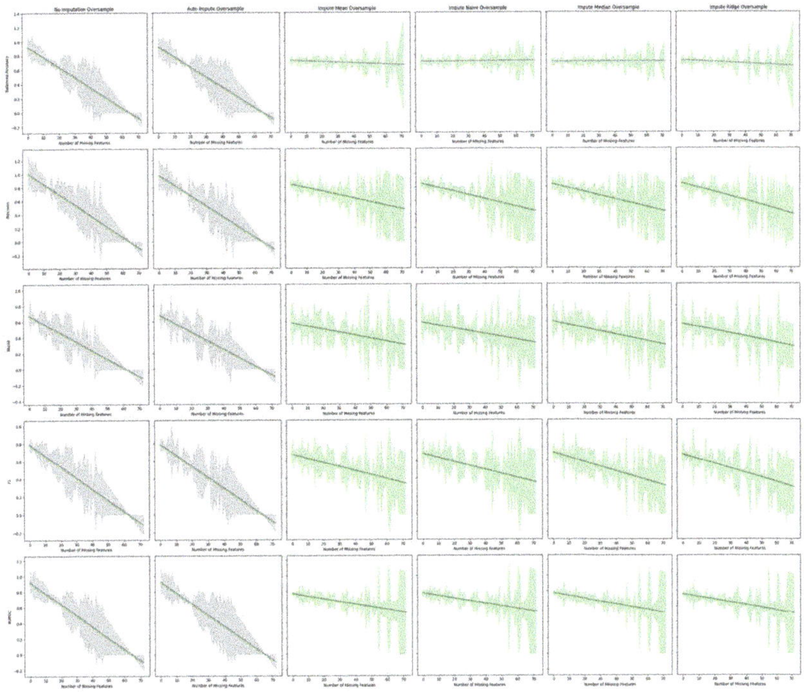

Figure 8. Best fit lines of machine learning metrics as a function of the number of missing features. The shading is the residual of the best fit line. All models contain an oversampling step. The best fit line is colored green if we reject the null hypothesis that the line has a slope of zero. The shading is colored green if we reject the null hypothesis that the residuals have constant variance.

Table 4. Tabular representation of Figure 8 displaying the Y-intercept and slope of the lines of best fit for the estimator performance with oversampling on a given metric. The F-Test p-value, which gives the probability of the null hypothesis that the line of best fit has a slope of zero, is given. The Breusch–Pagan p-value, which gives the probability that the error of the line has constant variance, is also given.

Estimator	Metric	Y-Intercept	Slope	F-Test p-Value	Breusch–Pagan p-Value
No Imputation	Balanced Accuracy	0.929096	−0.014328	0.000000	0.485545
	Precision	1.016151	−0.015712	0.000000	0.913311
	Recall	0.681390	−0.010974	0.000000	0.125074
	F1	0.793971	−0.012573	0.000000	0.761271
	AUROC	0.929096	−0.014328	0.000000	0.485545
Auto Impute	Balanced Accuracy	0.927235	−0.014183	0.000000	0.510401
	Precision	0.985620	−0.015222	0.000000	0.935550
	Recall	0.686184	−0.010758	0.000000	0.247551
	F1	0.793458	−0.012372	0.000000	0.783637
	AUROC	0.927235	−0.014183	0.000000	0.510401
Impute Mean	Balanced Accuracy	0.726784	−0.000887	0.257000	0.003557
	Precision	0.850450	−0.005228	0.000794	0.000000
	Recall	0.583068	−0.003841	0.003761	0.017359
	F1	0.676989	−0.004579	0.000297	0.000400
	AUROC	0.775188	−0.003411	0.001467	0.000415

Table 4. *Cont.*

Estimator	Metric	Y-Intercept	Slope	F-Test p-Value	Breusch–Pagan p-Value
Impute Naive	Balanced Accuracy	0.706228	0.000201	0.748666	0.000180
	Precision	0.856446	−0.005707	0.000332	0.000000
	Recall	0.588463	−0.003621	0.007300	0.003331
	F1	0.683514	−0.004533	0.000638	0.000028
	AUROC	0.780858	−0.003407	0.001658	0.000215
Impute Median	Balanced Accuracy	0.702667	0.000042	0.943492	0.000159
	Precision	0.846575	−0.005729	0.000216	0.000000
	Recall	0.597699	−0.004181	0.001187	0.017877
	F1	0.691866	−0.005232	0.000011	0.000528
	AUROC	0.778030	−0.003616	0.000513	0.000478
Impute Ridge	Balanced Accuracy	0.716799	−0.001077	0.172684	0.003920
	Precision	0.854813	−0.006436	0.000026	0.000025
	Recall	0.562891	−0.004000	0.002777	0.017178
	F1	0.666654	−0.005118	0.000037	0.000330
	AUROC	0.763755	−0.003537	0.000880	0.000269

4. Discussion

We observe that imputation methods homogenize the amount of information per patient. That is, without imputation, the models have a sharp performance loss, whereas imputation makes the slope less steep at the cost of increasing heteroskedasticity. We also note that every statistical test agrees between the oversampled and non-oversampled models. This trend underscores the sensitivity of predictive models to the method of handling missing data in electronic health records (EHR). The negative slope indicates that as the degree of imputation increases—implying more data are being estimated rather than observed—the accuracy, precision, and recall of the models tend to decrease. This phenomenon can be attributed to the fact that imputation, despite being a necessary process to address missing data, introduces a level of uncertainty or noise. This noise can distort the underlying patterns within the data, leading to less reliable predictions from the models.

We are not the first paper to study diabetes prediction using the All of Us dataset. A paper by Abegaz et al. studied the application of machine learning algorithms to predict diabetes in the All of Us dataset [17]. Their work presents the AUROC, recall, precision, and F1 scores stratified by gender of the random forest, XGBoost, logistic regression, and weighted ensemble models. Our work builds upon those foundations in three ways. First, we note that all of the models in Abegaz et al.'s work can be found in Scikit-Learn. Hence, we performed a deep search over all Scikit-learn models to find the best performing ones. Second, we presented our results for further substrata of the dataset. One of the most important features of AoU is the diversity of people within the dataset. We highlighted the five performance metrics on the total testing dataset on each gender, on each race, and on groups bucketed by the number of missing features. We also presented the models' performance on a number of fairness measurements when the sub-populations have a clear privileged group. Third, our largest deviation from the previous work was to show how the performance of a model changes as one changes the number of missing features.

The model performance in Figures 1 and 2 has been trained for only three hours (as opposed to the multiday- or multiweek-long training that some deep neural network solutions provide) and yields modest results. Our best performing model is the "Auto Impute" model. We may compare the performance of that model to Abegaz et al.'s work. "Auto Impute" has a higher AUROC, comparable precision, and worse recall and F1. We note, however, that these are not clinically ready. Further improvements need to be made in order to prefer this to a HbA1c test for diabetes testing. Since the multiple imputer only used 15 iterations, the algorithm likely did not stabilize and caused the performance to drop. We emphasize that the primary objective of our research was not to maximize the performance of machine learning models applied to AoU data, but instead to study the effects of data missingness and imputation strategies on model performance.

Our analysis also highlights the presence of statistically significant heteroskedastic variance in model performances across imputation methods. Heteroskedasticity, in this context, refers to the irregular variability in the performance of predictive models, dependent on the amount and pattern of missing data being imputed. This irregular variance poses a significant challenge in predictive modeling, as it implies that the error terms (or the differences between predicted and actual values) are not uniformly distributed. Models thus exhibit different levels of accuracy and reliability depending on the specific characteristics of the missing data in each patient record.

The presence of heteroskedastic variance can be particularly problematic in clinical settings. It implies that for some patients, especially those with more extensive or particular patterns of missing data, the predictions made by the models could be less reliable. This inconsistency could lead to disparities in clinical decision-making, potentially affecting the quality of care provided to certain patient groups. Since the "Auto Imputation" model has the largest Y-intercept and one of the most negative slopes, it might be most beneficial to use the "Auto Impute" method for patients with few missing values in a clinical setting. For patients with a lot of missing values, one may use another imputation method with a less steep slope or perform a cost–benefit analysis of ordering more tests to make the model more performant.

These findings highlight the critical need for developing more robust imputation techniques that can minimize the introduction of noise and ensure uniform model performance across varying degrees of missing data. It also underscores the importance of considering the nature and pattern of missing data when applying machine learning models in healthcare settings. Future research should focus on exploring advanced imputation methods, possibly incorporating domain knowledge or utilizing more sophisticated algorithms, to mitigate the effects of data missingness on predictive model performance. In conclusion, while imputation is a necessary step in dealing with incomplete datasets for some models, our study indicates that current methods have significant limitations.

Addressing these limitations is crucial for the development of reliable and consistent machine learning models for clinical predictions, ultimately enhancing the quality of patient care and health outcomes. Our analysis on data missingness revealed that individuals who are male and persons of color would be disproportionately affected by a loss in performance with respect to data missingness. This is due to the number of missing features being more highly correlated with males and non-white people.

Future work can be conducted to ensure the robustness of the findings. A number of unanswered questions remain, such as: (1) does heteroskedasticity depend on certain features included in the model over another? (2) Do these findings pertain to more modern and complex deep learning models? (3) What other forms of data augmentation can be performed to reduce heteroskedasticity? Another comparison of interest is exploring whether the testing dataset holds more missing values than the training dataset and how the performance differs compared to the case of having roughly similar missing values between training and testing. If the testing dataset does not require many labels, then hospitals could save time and money by not measuring every missing value.

Author Contributions: Conceptualization, Z.J. and P.W.; methodology, Z.J.; software, Z.J.; validation, Z.J. and P.W.; formal analysis, Z.J.; investigation, P.W.; resources, Z.J.; data curation, Z.J.; writing—original draft preparation, Z.J.; writing—review and editing, Z.J. and P.W.; visualization, Z.J.; supervision, P.W.; project administration, P.W. All authors have read and agreed to the published version of the manuscript.

Funding: This research received no external funding.

Institutional Review Board Statement: Not applicable.

Data Availability Statement: Restrictions apply to the availability of these data. Data were obtained from the National Institutes of Health's All of Us and are available at https://www.researchallofus.org/ (accessed on 12 January 2024) with the permission of National Institutes of Health's All of Us. Obtaining access to the data involves institutional agreement, verification of identity, and mandatory training.

Conflicts of Interest: The authors declare no conflicts of interest.

References

1. World Health Organization. *ICD-11: International Classification of Diseases 11th Revision: The Global Standard for Diagnostic Health Information*; World Health Organization: Geneva, Switzerland, 2019.
2. Cole, J.B.; Florez, J.C. Genetics of diabetes mellitus and diabetes complications. *Nat. Rev. Nephrol.* **2020**, *16*, 377–390. [CrossRef] [PubMed]
3. Association, A.D. Diagnosis and classification of diabetes mellitus. *Diabetes Care* **2010**, *33*, S62–S69. [CrossRef] [PubMed]
4. Group, T.S. Long-term complications in youth-onset type 2 diabetes. *N. Engl. J. Med.* **2021**, *385*, 416–426. [CrossRef] [PubMed]
5. Rooney, M.R.; Fang, M.; Ogurtsova, K.; Ozkan, B.; Echouffo-Tcheugui, J.B.; Boyko, E.J.; Magliano, D.J.; Selvin, E. Global prevalence of prediabetes. *Diabetes Care* **2023**, *46*, 1388–1394. [CrossRef] [PubMed]
6. Haw, J.S.; Shah, M.; Turbow, S.; Egeolu, M.; Umpierrez, G. Diabetes complications in racial and ethnic minority populations in the USA. *Curr. Diabetes Rep.* **2021**, *21*, 1–8. [CrossRef] [PubMed]
7. Khanam, J.J.; Foo, S.Y. A comparison of machine learning algorithms for diabetes prediction. *ICT Express* **2021**, *7*, 432–439. [CrossRef]
8. Hasan, M.K.; Alam, M.A.; Das, D.; Hossain, E.; Hasan, M. Diabetes prediction using ensembling of different machine learning classifiers. *IEEE Access* **2020**, *8*, 76516–76531. [CrossRef]
9. Krishnamoorthi, R.; Joshi, S.; Almarzouki, H.Z.; Shukla, P.K.; Rizwan, A.; Kalpana, C.; Tiwari, B. A novel diabetes healthcare disease prediction framework using machine learning techniques. *J. Healthc. Eng.* **2022**, *2022*, 1684017. [CrossRef] [PubMed]
10. Oikonomou, E.K.; Khera, R. Machine learning in precision diabetes care and cardiovascular risk prediction. *Cardiovasc. Diabetol.* **2023**, *22*, 259. [CrossRef] [PubMed]
11. Anderson, J.P.; Parikh, J.R.; Shenfeld, D.K.; Ivanov, V.; Marks, C.; Church, B.; Laramie, J.; Mardekian, J.; Piper, B.; Willke, R.; et al. Reverse Engineering and Evaluation of Prediction Models for Progression to Type 2 Diabetes. *J. Diabetes Sci. Technol.* **2016**, *10*, 6–18. [CrossRef] [PubMed]
12. Cahn, A.; Shoshan, A.; Sagiv, T.; Yesharim, R.; Goshen, R.; Shalev, V.; Raz, I. Prediction of progression from pre-diabetes to diabetes: Development and validation of a machine learning model. *Diabetes/Metabolism Res. Rev.* **2020**, *36*, e3252. [CrossRef] [PubMed]
13. Ravaut, M.; Sadeghi, H.; Leung, K.K.; Volkovs, M.; Rosella, L. Diabetes Mellitus Forecasting Using Population Health Data in Ontario, Canada. *arXiv* **2019**, arXiv:abs/1904.04137.
14. Hudson, K.; Lifton, R.; Patrick-Lake, B.; Burchard, E.G.; Coles, T.; Collins, R.; Conrad, A. *The Precision Medicine Initiative Cohort Program—Building a Research Foundation for 21st Century Medicine;* Precision Medicine Initiative (PMI) Working Group Report to the Advisory Committee to the Director, National Institutes of Health: Bethesda, MD, USA, 2015.
15. Sankar, P.L.; Parker, L.S. The Precision Medicine Initiative's All of Us Research Program: An agenda for research on its ethical, legal, and social issues. *Genet. Med.* **2017**, *19*, 743–750. [CrossRef] [PubMed]
16. Mapes, B.M.; Foster, C.S.; Kusnoor, S.V.; Epelbaum, M.I.; AuYoung, M.; Jenkins, G.; Lopez-Class, M.; Richardson-Heron, D.; Elmi, A.; Surkan, K.; et al. Diversity and inclusion for the All of Us research program: A scoping review. *PLoS ONE* **2020**, *15*, e0234962. [CrossRef] [PubMed]
17. Abegaz, T.M.; Ahmed, M.; Sherbeny, F.; Diaby, V.; Chi, H.; Ali, A.A. Application of Machine Learning Algorithms to Predict Uncontrolled Diabetes Using the All of Us Research Program Data. *Healthcare* **2023**, *11*, 1138. [CrossRef] [PubMed]
18. Feurer, M.; Eggensperger, K.; Falkner, S.; Lindauer, M.; Hutter, F. Auto-Sklearn 2.0: Hands-free AutoML via Meta-Learning. *arXiv* **2020**, arXiv:2007.04074 [cs.LG].
19. Feurer, M.; Klein, A.; Eggensperger, K.; Springenberg, J.; Blum, M.; Hutter, F. Efficient and Robust Automated Machine Learning. *Adv. Neural Inf. Process. Syst.* **2015**, *28*, 2962–2970.
20. Bellamy, R.K.E.; Dey, K.; Hind, M.; Hoffman, S.C.; Houde, S.; Kannan, K.; Lohia, P.; Martino, J.; Mehta, S.; Mojsilovic, A.; et al. AI Fairness 360: An Extensible Toolkit for Detecting, Understanding, and Mitigating Unwanted Algorithmic Bias. *arXiv* **2018**, arXiv:1810.01943.
21. Mehrabi, N.; Morstatter, F.; Saxena, N.; Lerman, K.; Galstyan, A. A survey on bias and fairness in machine learning. *ACM Comput. Surv. (CSUR)* **2021**, *54*, 1–35. [CrossRef]
22. Caton, S.; Haas, C. Fairness in machine learning: A survey. *ACM Comput. Surv.* **2020** . [CrossRef]
23. Barocas, S.; Hardt, M.; Narayanan, A. *Fairness and Machine Learning: Limitations and Opportunities;* MIT Press: Cambridge, MA, USA, 2023.
24. Speicher, T.; Heidari, H.; Grgic-Hlaca, N.; Gummadi, K.P.; Singla, A.; Weller, A.; Zafar, M.B. A unified approach to quantifying algorithmic unfairness: Measuring individual &group unfairness via inequality indices. In Proceedings of the 24th ACM SIGKDD International Conference on Knowledge Discovery & Data Mining, London, UK, 19–23 August 2018; pp. 2239–2248.

BioMedInformatics

MDPI

Article

Whole Slide Image Understanding in Pathology: What Is the Salient Scale of Analysis?

Eleanor Jenkinson and Ognjen Arandjelović *

School of Computer Science, University of St Andrews, St Andrews KY16 9AJ, UK; ej64@st-andrews.ac.uk
* Correspondence: oa7@st-andrews.ac.uk; Tel.: +44-(0)-1223-462824

Abstract: Background: In recent years, there has been increasing research in the applications of Artificial Intelligence in the medical industry. Digital pathology has seen great success in introducing the use of technology in the digitisation and analysis of pathology slides to ease the burden of work on pathologists. Digitised pathology slides, otherwise known as whole slide images, can be analysed by pathologists with the same methods used to analyse traditional glass slides. Methods: The digitisation of pathology slides has also led to the possibility of using these whole slide images to train machine learning models to detect tumours. Patch-based methods are common in the analysis of whole slide images as these images are too large to be processed using normal machine learning methods. However, there is little work exploring the effect that the size of the patches has on the analysis. A patch-based whole slide image analysis method was implemented and then used to evaluate and compare the accuracy of the analysis using patches of different sizes. In addition, two different patch sampling methods are used to test if the optimal patch size is the same for both methods, as well as a downsampling method where whole slide images of low resolution images are used to train an analysis model. Results: It was discovered that the most successful method uses a patch size of 256 × 256 pixels with the informed sampling method, using the location of tumour regions to sample a balanced dataset. Conclusion: Future work on batch-based analysis of whole slide images in pathology should take into account our findings when designing new models.

Keywords: WSI; patches; tumour; cancer; deep learning; Camelyon17

Citation: Jenkinson, E.; Arandjelović, O. Whole Slide Image Understanding in Pathology: What Is the Salient Scale of Analysis? *BioMedInformatics* **2024**, *4*, 489–518. https://doi.org/10.3390/biomedinformatics4010028

Academic Editors: Pentti Nieminen and Hans Binder

Received: 16 December 2023
Revised: 7 February 2024
Accepted: 9 February 2024
Published: 14 February 2024

1. Introduction

Digital pathology is a relatively new area of pathology wherein specimen slides are digitised for analysis, minimising the time needed for the diagnostic process of a patient. These digital tissue samples are called whole slide images (WSIs) and can be utilised similarly to glass pathology slides in the identification of disease. This technology has the potential to become routine in clinical pathology settings and has paved the way for the possibility of automated WSI classification using machine learning architectures.

The main concept behind the automated analysis of WSIs is to imitate the process that a pathologist ordinarily follows to complete analysis of a WSI. Often, the overarching goal of the analysis is to identify the presence of tumourous tissue in a WSI. As the nature of the analysis is to mimic the pathologists' cognitive process, deep learning methods are best suited to this task. In particular, deep learning methods have proven vastly superior to traditional machine learning models in extracting nuanced patterns from highly complex and high-dimensional data. For example, they have been widely used to learn from training images how to identify the presence and localize tumorous tissue in a WSI [1]. Unfortunately, due to the size of WSIs (often several gigapixels [2]), it is not possible to input the raw images into a network. Different methods have been researched to overcome this, namely downsampling of WSIs and patch extraction [3,4].

The focus of this work is on the patch-based method of WSI analysis. Patch-based methods involve splitting the WSIs into small patches and extracting a subset of these patches to input into a neural network [2,3]. Patch extraction can be performed using various sampling methods, two of which were implemented as part of this work. The patch-based method is the commonly preferred alternative to the downsampling method which retrieves lower resolution versions of the WSI that can be processed as entire images by a neural network [3,4].

Patch-based methods are common in the classification of WSIs. However, there is little research into the effect of patch size on the accuracy of the classification. A majority of the related work uses a relatively small patch size, typically around 256 × 256 pixels [5–7]. This is largely a choice borne out initially out of practical computational constraints and subsequently adopted for the sake of uniformity, ease of comparison with previous work, and tradition. No work has examined whether this choice is optimal and indeed any longer sensible, given the improvements in computational power—the use of small patches limits the amount of spatial information that is exploited which inevitably affects overall performance. Hence, the present work aims to implement a patch-based WSI analysis method in order to evaluate the effect of patch size on the automatic analysis of WSIs.

Four patch sizes were evaluated for the initial random sampling method (256, 384, 512, and 786), and three patch sizes were tested with the informed sampling method (256, 512, and 1024). Figure 1 shows the level of detail present in each of the patch sizes. Only the largest downsampling factor was used for the downsampling method.

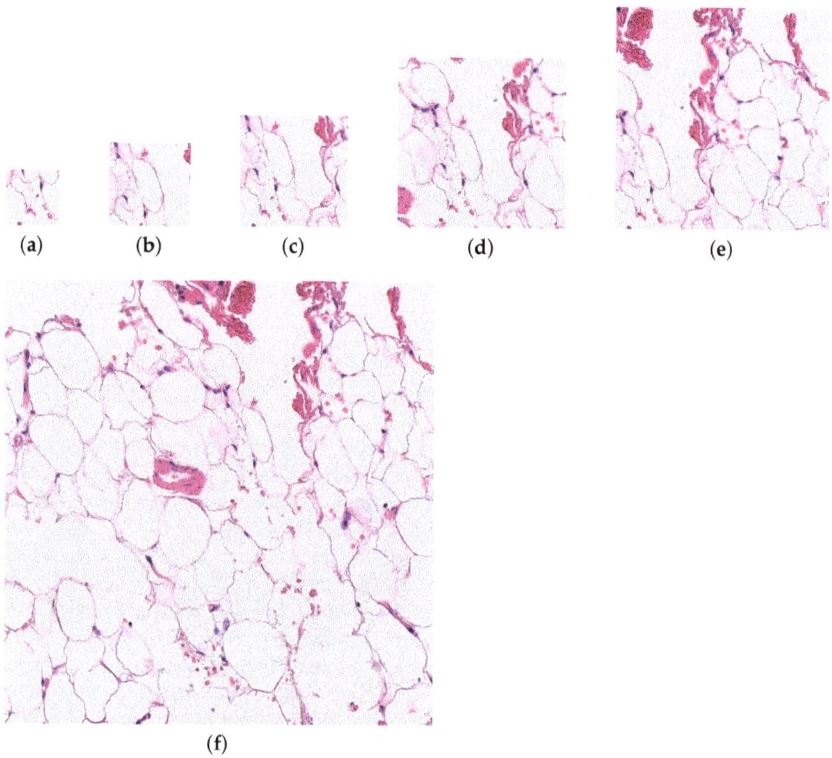

Figure 1. A patch from a whole slide image (test_016.tif) at each of the patch sizes evaluated for the paper. (**a**) Patch size = 256. (**b**) Patch size = 384. (**c**) Patch size = 512. (**d**) Patch size = 786. (**e**) Patch size = 1024. (**f**) Patch size = 2048.

2. Related Work

2.1. Introduction to Digital Pathology

Pathology is a field of medicine related to the diagnosis and staging of diseases, including cancer. Since the 1800s [8], pathologists have carried out this work by examining specimen on glass slides using a microscope. However, for the past few decades there has been increasing research in the digitisation of this process, resulting in the subfield of digital pathology. This began with the introduction of WSI scanners in the early 2000s [9]. These scanners produce WSIs, high-resolution images of glass pathology slides which contain billions of pixels and are around 2 gigabytes in size [10]. The use of WSIs as a replacement for the traditional glass slides means specimens can be displayed on large screens, viewed in locations outside the hospital and laboratory environment, and shared between pathologists and experts. These possibilities help to improve accuracy of diagnosis, allow for collaboration between medical personnel, and create a flexible work environment [9–11]. Another use of WSIs in digital pathology is for the automation of the analysis of WSIs, using deep learning. Applying this in a clinical setting would ease the workload of pathologists, reduce wait times, and standardise the analysis of pathology slides [5]. However, the nature of WSIs, the size, high morphological variance and artefacts present, prevent the use of conventional deep learning methods [5].

Research and advancements in digital pathology have positively impacted the healthcare industry; the ability to digitise pathology slides has eliminated the need for costly storage of glass slides, and allows for remote pathological analysis and faster diagnoses, without sacrificing any accuracy in the pathologists' results [12,13]. However, some of the concerns that occur in the analysis of pathology slides are not solved by the use of WSIs. The manual analysis of WSIs still remains to be a time-consuming process and there is no standardisation between pathologist's analyses or different pathologists' results. To solve this, research continues into the automation of WSI classification. By using machine learning algorithms to aid with the analysis, the time taken for this process can be reduced and there can be a level of standardisation between outcomes [5,12,14,15]. The computational analysis of WSIs also has the ability to account for more morphological information than a human can which leads to a better accuracy of diagnoses [4].

Future advances in digital pathology show a great deal of promise, but progress is slowed by various barriers, including ethical concerns and regulations [9]. In the near future, it is likely that this technology will be slowly introduced into the diagnostic process, aiding pathologists by analysing slides and prioritising those that the algorithm indicates contain disease [12,16,17]. The introduction of the Grand Challenges has fast-tracked research in this field, providing datasets and creating an environment for researchers to submit their work. Recent diagnostic models have shown a great deal of promise, performing better than pathologists, mimicking a time-pressured environment, in the diagnosis and staging of disease from imaging [18].

2.2. Analysis of Whole Slide Images

Deep learning algorithms have been successfully used for the classification of WSIs, producing results similar to that of pathologists. The automation of analysis of WSIs has many advantages over the traditional manual annotation of glass pathology slides. However, there are barriers to overcome in achieving a successful implementation for this process. In recent years, digital pathology research has focused on methods to overcome these issues, with the most significant being the large size of WSIs and a lack of annotated training data. The lack of data is due to the annotation process performed by pathologists being time-consuming and therefore yielding only a small amount of available training data.

Problems with Computational Analysis of Whole Slide Images

WSIs contain billions to trillions of pixels per image and, on average, range from 1 to 4 GB in size [9]. This makes the use of conventional deep learning algorithms computationally expensive and impractical [3–5,12,13,19]. There are two common methods for dealing with this issue: downsampling and patch extraction. Downsampling involves scaling down the WSI until it contains much fewer pixels and can be analysed by a conventional deep learning algorithm [4,12,20,21]. This method is not desirable as the process results in a significant loss of fine detail from the image, affecting the classification accuracy [6,15,19,22]. Patch extraction splits the WSI into many small patches that can be analysed individually by a deep learning algorithm and, using the patch-level classifications, produce a slide-level classification [4,12]. Patch-based methods usually involve assigning the relevant slide-level label to all patches in the training data. This can be misleading as some patches from tumour-containing slides will not contain any diseased tissue themselves, meaning the model is being given false information [12]. There is also a loss of spatial information using a patch-based method, the relationship between patches and the global information is lost. Therefore this method assumes that slide level analysis can be extrapolated from patch-level information [4]. Despite the loss of spatial information using patch-based methods, this method is preferable over downsampling as it retains more morphological information and detail from the WSI [4].

A major bottleneck in the use of deep learning for the analysis of WSIs is the insufficiency of training data. WSIs have multiple levels at which annotations can be performed; pixel-level, patch-level, slide-level, lesion-level, and patient-level. Ideally, the training data for an analysis model will contain patch-level annotations to produce results comparable to experts [5]. However, manual annotations must be carried out by pathologists which is an expensive and time-consuming process, particularly at the more detailed pixel- and patch-levels where the pathologist annotates the exact location of any disease [4,13,22,23]. This impedes the use of fully supervised models using patch-based labelling which has the advantage of predicting where disease is present in an image [16]. As an alternative, weakly supervised learning methods are being widely adopted in the analysis of WSIs [13]. These methods use only slide-level annotations, describing if there is any disease present in a WSI, but not where in the image the disease is [12], to train the model.

The above two problems are the most significant barriers to the computational analysis of WSIs. However, there are also many smaller issues that must be tackled to build a successful model. Depending on the laboratory, scanner, and a number of other factors, there can be a significant amount of stain variation between WSIs and various artefacts [7,10,15,24]. Pathologists adapt to ignore these variations and distractions. An AI model is not capable of doing this which can affect the results of the classification [5]. To counteract the stain variation, colour normalisation can be applied to the WSIs during pre-processing [7,24], and the use of, for example, image filters can eliminate artefacts [5]. The extraction of features for classification can be difficult as WSIs can contain a lot of heterogeneity and there is sometimes little noticeable difference between disease and normal tissue [15,25]. This makes it tricky for the model to learn disease patterns and is amplified by the previously mentioned issue of a lack of WSI annotations as the location of disease is not specified to the model [22]. There also tends to be significant class imbalance with a benign/normal tissue class containing many more samples compared to a malignant/disease tissue class. A reason for this is that all slides, malignant, benign, and other, usually contain some normal tissue, whereas slides which are labelled as benign contain no disease tissue [13]. This issue can be minimised by, prior to analysis, performing data augmentation which involves applying different geometric transformations to the images [19]. Other methods include hard negative mining, where false positives are added to the training data, and sampling patches using patch-level annotations rather than random sampling; although these rely on the availability of patch-level annotations [5].

2.3. Patch-Based Whole Slide Image Analysis

Much of the current research in digital pathology focuses on patch-based methods for the analysis of WSIs, however, the work varies on pre-processing techniques, including patch extraction, model architecture, and classification. These processes are outlined below.

The goal of these techniques is to optimise the accuracy of the model in predicting the presence of disease; this article will focus on the optimisation of patch size.

1. Pre-processing: Before the data is fed into a model, pre-processing must be applied first. For patch-based WSI analysis, there are four main steps for pre-processing:
    (a) Tissue segmentation detects unwanted areas of WSIs, such as any background or blurry areas. These areas are irrelevant in the analysis of the tissue and are usually large regions so take up a significant amount of computational power to process [10].
    (b) Colour normalisation alters the distribution of colour values in an image to standardise the range of colour used. In the case of WSIs, this ensures that only relevant colour differences appear between slides. This is essential in the pre-processing of WSIs as it minimises the stain variation between images which can lead to bias in the training data and affect the results [7,19].
    (c) Patch extraction involves taking square patches, often 256 × 256 pixels in size, from the WSI for patch-level analysis [5–7]. This step of pre-processing has many variables that can be optimised; patch size, magnification/resolution level, sampling method, and whether patches are tiled or overlapping. This is done due to the large size of WSIs and the limits of computational power to deal with images of this size.
    (d) Data augmentation is the transformation of training data to new training data. This prevents overfitting and can be used to deal with severe class imbalance.
2. Architecture: Commonly, convolutional neural networks (CNNs) are used for the analysis of WSIs. Due to the insufficiency of training data, these models are often weakly supervised. A form of weakly supervised learning that can be used is multiple-instance learning (MIL). This is suitable for data where a class label is assigned to many instances, for example a slide label assigned to patches of that slide [13]. Originally, this algorithm would apply max pooling to the instances, meaning that if disease is predicted to be in one patch, the whole slide is predicted to be in the disease class [13].
3. Classification: For the analysis of WSIs, there are two classifications, patch-level and slide-level classification [7]. Predictions for patches are aggregated to produce slide-level classifications. Heatmaps are often used to display the distribution of results for the patches in a slide which often correlates with a pathologist's annotation of the slide.

2.3.1. Techniques Used in Related Work

Wang et al. [26] use a CNN to make patch-level classifications which are then used to produce a probability heatmap to predict the slide-level classification. WSI background is removed to prevent unnecessary computation using a threshold segmentation method with Otsu's algorithm. The patches used for classification are extracted at 256 × 256 pixels at 40× magnification level.

Hou et al. [3] used a CNN for patch-level classification followed by a decision fusion model. 500 × 500 pixel patches extracted at 20× and 5× magnification levels were used to train the model. Any patches that included too much unnecessary tissue or blood were discarded. Three kinds of data augmentation were applied to the patches to prevent overfitting. This included rotation and reflection of part of each patch and colour augmentation to affect the Hematoxylin and Eosin (H&E) stain.

Cruz-Roa et al. [27] downsampled the WSIs by a factor of 16:1 and tiled them into 100 × 100 pixel patches using grid sampling, discarding any patches that were largely fatty tissue or background. These patches were then converted to YUV colour space and normalised and then input into a 3-layer CNN which outputs the log likelihoods of the patch being disease or not. The outputs were transformed to be interpreted as probabilities and used to form a probability map for each WSI.

Yue et al. [19] used the Reinhard normalisation to minimise stain variation on the WSIs. Each WSI is downsampled and normalised before patches of size 224 × 224 pixels are extracted. The data augmentation techniques, rotations, reflections, Gaussian blur, and all-channel multiplication, were applied to the data to prevent overfitting and to help with class imbalance.

Ruan et al. [28] first used a fixed-level threshold segmentation method to remove background from the WSIs. Patches were sampled using a novel adaptive sampling method at both the 20× and 40× magnification levels and were chosen to be 256 × 256 pixels. Sampling at alternative magnification levels was tested and a combination of sampling at 20× and 40× magnification was shown to give the best results.

Rodriguez et al. [7] performed a systematic review of AI used in the analysis of WSIs. All 26 studies included in the review used patch-based methods, with varied other pre-processing techniques. A majority used tissue segmentation to remove unwanted regions of the WSIs, and the most common technique used was a threshold. Colour normalisation was only used in six of the studies, with techniques of colour deconvolution and simple normalisation. Data augmentation was widely used with a variety of methods, including rotations, flipping, and colour augmentations. Most studies used deep learning models for patch-level classification, with many different methods used for slide-level classification, with some simply opting for the most common class and others using more complex deep learning models.

Mohammadi et al. [13] implemented an extended MIL method for multi-class classification. WSIs are downsampled and the tissue is segmented to eliminate unnecessary background in the image and converted to HSV colour space. Non-overlapping patches of size 256 × 256 pixels are taken from only the segmented tissue at magnification level 0.

Fell et al. [16] used a fully supervised CNN to predict the probability of each patch from a WSI containing disease. The outputs from the CNN were then aggregated to form a heatmap for the WSI to be used as input to a slide-level classification model. Colour normalisation and aggregation were not used in an attempt to increase variation within the data for generalisation. Background was removed from the thumbnail by applying greyscale and removing any values over a threshold. Patches were extracted at the highest resolution level, level 0, and multiple patch sizes were tested for optimisation, 256 × 256 pixels, 512 × 512 pixels, and 1024 × 1024 pixels. The largest patch size, 1024 × 1024 pixels, was chosen for this model.

2.3.2. Comparison of Patch Sizes

In the reviewed related work, patch sizes range from 100 × 100 pixels to 1024 × 1024 pixels. Bándi et al. [18] reviewed submissions for the Camelyon17 challenge, which used a range of patch sizes between 256 × 256 pixels to 1920 × 1920 pixels both at level 0, and found that the smallest patch size provided enough context and is sufficient for analysis. A smaller patch size is beneficial if it provides enough information to the model, as, if a patch is too large, it will encounter the same computational problems that a WSI does. Conversely, some believe, such as Komura et al. [6] and Khened et al. [23], a larger patch size will result in better accuracy as smaller patches do not include sufficient context [23]. Similarly, Fell et al. [16] consulted with pathologists who noted that, for manual annotation, the typical patch size of 256 × 256 pixels would be too small and so larger patches may imitate the manual annotation process more closely. However, Deng et al. [15] found that small patches did not provide sufficient context for analysis, but large patches are too computationally expensive. Due to the lack of consensus on patch size, more work is needed to definitively find the optimal patch size.

2.4. Relevant Concepts and Technology

To ensure the reproducibility of WSI analysis methods and standardise the details included in research papers, a checklist of important details was created by Fell et al. [10]. This is a useful guideline for the implementation of the work and the related section of this article. It is important to note not all points are relevant to the work, specifically lesion and patient classification. The checklist is as follows [10]:

1. The hardware and software platform the system was trained and tested on.
2. The source of the data and how it can be accessed.
3. How the data was split into train, validation, and testing sets.
4. How or if the slides were normalised.
5. How the background and any artefacts were removed from the slides.
6. How patches were extracted from the image and any data augmentation that was applied.
7. How the patches were labelled.
8. How the patch classifier was trained, including technique, architecture, and hyper-parameters.
9. How the slide classifier was trained, including pre-processing, technique, architecture, and hyper-parameters.
10. How lesion detection was performed.
11. How the patient classifier was trained, including, pre-processing, technique, architecture, and hyper-parameters.
12. All metrics that are relevant to all the tasks.

Wang et al. [26], the winners of the Camelyon16 challenge evaluated four different deep-learning architectures for the analysis of WSIs: GoogLeNet, AlexNet, VGG16, and FaceNet. The patch classification stage was tested using these models and the accuracy of the classification was measured. The model that produced the best result, and the one used by Wang et al. for the final results of the analysis, was GoogLeNet which is a CNN based on the model created by the winners of ImageNet in 2014.

3. Proposed Methodology

3.1. Camelyon16 Winning Paper

The winning paper of the Camelyon16 challenge [26] was the main inspiration for the structure of the system. The Camelyon16 challenge is the source of the dataset used for the paper, which consists of a training set of 160 "normal" WSIs and 111 "tumour" WSIs and a testing set of 129 WSIs.

The overarching methodology of the winning paper is image pre-processing, patch-level classification, post-processing production of tumour probability heatmaps, and slide-level classification [26]. The image pre-processing stage involved only tissue segmentation to remove irrelevant white background from the WSIs and patch extraction. No colour standardisation or data augmentation was mentioned in the paper. Millions of patches of size 256 × 256 pixels were randomly extracted from training WSIs and used to train the model for patch-level classification. The patch-level classification stage results in a model that can predict if a patch contains any tumours. This model was then applied, in the post-processing stage, to overlapping patches extracted from a testing WSI, to produce a tumour probability heatmap corresponding to the image. Finally, features were extracted from the heatmaps which were then input into the slide-level classification model, a random forest classifier, to give a probability value for the presence of tumour in the WSI.

3.2. GoogLeNet

During the patch-level classification stage, Wang et al. [26] tested four different deep learning networks by evaluating the accuracy of the patch classification. The GoogLeNet network produced the best accuracy out of the four, with 98.4%. As the work uses similar methods and the same dataset, the GoogLeNet network was chosen to be the patch-level classification model architecture. GoogLeNet is a pretrained 22-layer deep convolutional neural network with a minimum image input size of 224 × 224 pixels. The architecture of the network is shown in Figure 2.

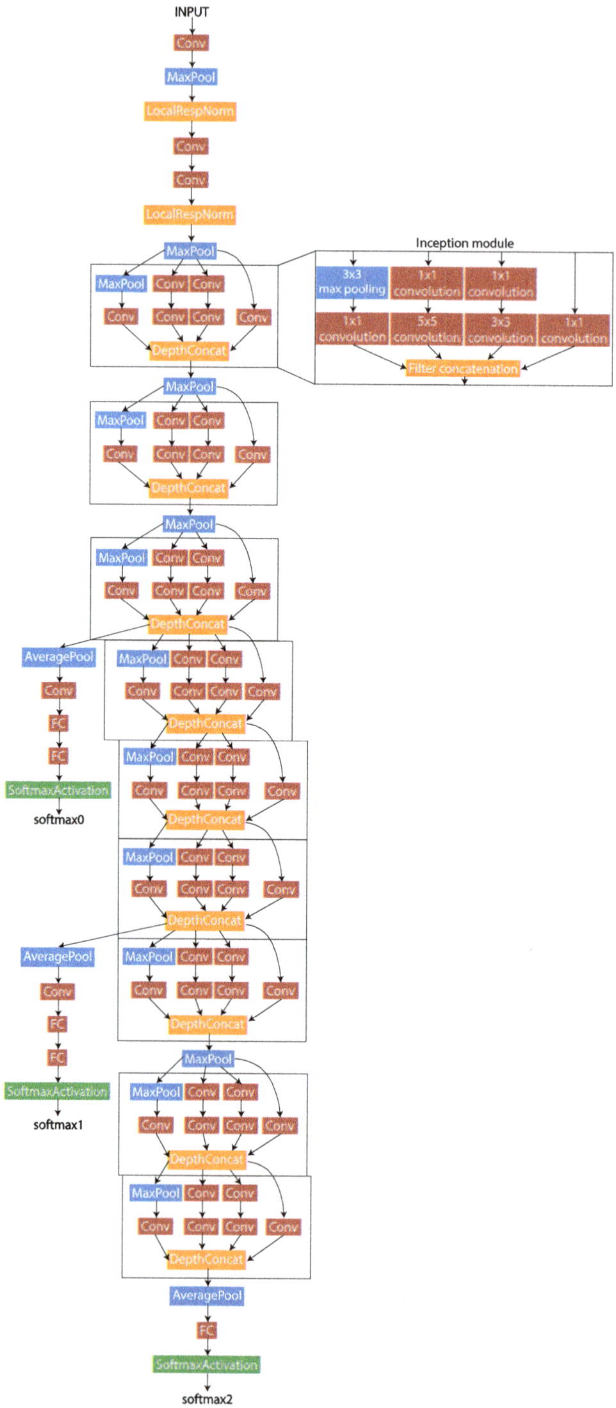

Figure 2. The structure of the GoogLeNet network.

3.3. System Structure

There are four distinguishable stages in the overall structure of the work: data pre-processing, patch-level classification, production of tumour probability heatmaps, and slide-level classification. These processes were all involved in producing the final artefact, an accurate patch-based WSI analysis method. However, due to the need to train the machine learning models, the structure of the system used to produce the final artefact differs from the structure of the final artefact itself. The differences between the systems can be seen in Figure 3.

Figure 3a shows the process of producing the final artefact. This system first applies pre-processing to the WSIs from the training dataset to retrieve many normal and tumour patches. These patches are then used to train the patch classification model. The WSIs from the testing dataset are then split into patches and, for each WSI, a heatmap is created to represent the probability of each patch being tumourous, predicted from the previously trained patch classification model. The slide-level classification is then trained using a training subset of the heatmaps from which features are extracted.

Figure 3b represents the final artefact. This allows an unseen WSI to be split into patches, which are then input directly to the post-processing step to produce a tumour probability heatmap corresponding to the WSI. This heatmap is then input to the slide classification model, extracting the features of the heatmap to predict the probability that the slide is tumourous.

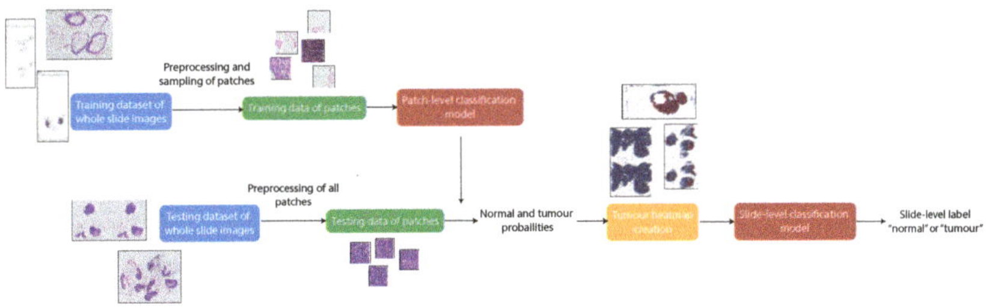

(a) The training structure

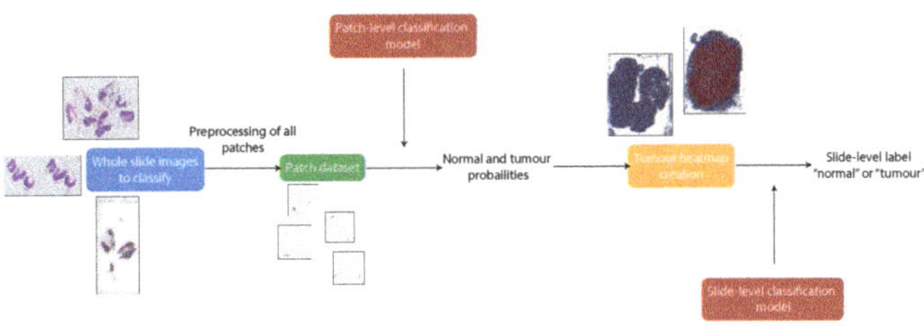

(b) The final structure

Figure 3. The structure that produces trained patch-level and slide-level classification models (**a**) and the structure that can be used to classify any unknown WSI using the trained models (**b**).

3.4. Camelyon16 Dataset

The dataset used for the work was the Grand Challenge Camelyon16 dataset of sentinel lymph node WSIs. This data is freely available to download from the Camelyon16 webpage [29].

The data is split into two folders, training and testing. The training folder contains the WSIs as .tif files and the lesion annotations as .xml files. There are 160 normal WSIs and 111 tumour WSIs for training, and the lesion annotations contain the coordinates of the tumours in each corresponding tumour WSI. The testing folder contains the WSIs as .tif files, the lesion annotations as .xml files, and a reference file. There are 129 WSIs to be used for testing, with the reference file containing the details for each file: the label i.e., normal or tumour, and the type of tumour. There is a lesion annotation file for each WSI in the test set that is labelled tumour. Figure 4 shows an example of a normal slide and a tumour slide.

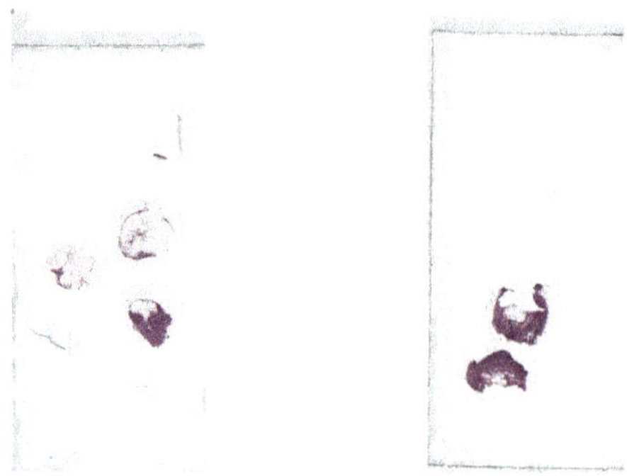

(a) (b)

Figure 4. An example of (**a**) a normal whole slide image (normal_005.tif), and (**b**) a tumour whole slide image (tumor_005.tif), both at the lowest resolution level.

The WSI is stored at multiple different resolution/magnification levels, shown by Figure 5. The images at different levels can be accessed separately to retrieve the WSI at the desired resolution. For this work, the WSIs are all retrieved at the highest resolution level, therefore containing the largest number of pixels possible. This is with the exception of the downsampling method where the aim is to use images of lower resolution.

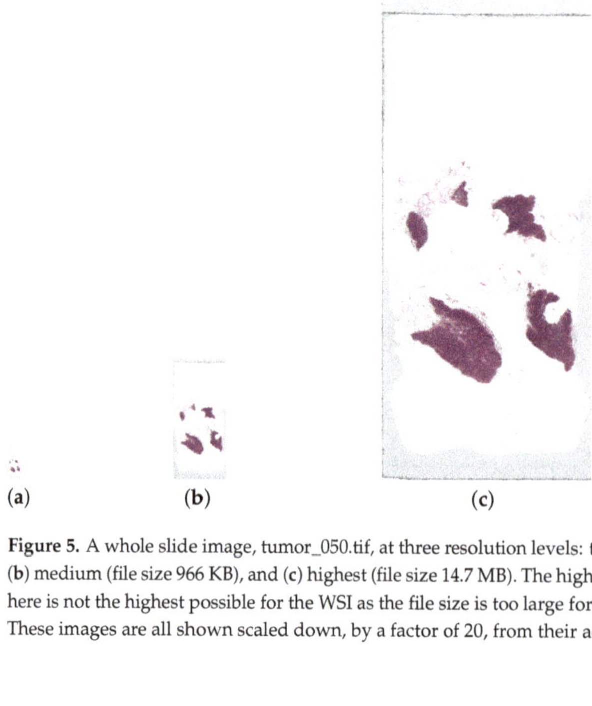

(a) (b) (c)

Figure 5. A whole slide image, tumor_050.tif, at three resolution levels: the (**a**) lowest (file size 75 KB), (**b**) medium (file size 966 KB), and (**c**) highest (file size 14.7 MB). The highest resolution level displayed here is not the highest possible for the WSI as the file size is too large for the highest resolution image. These images are all shown scaled down, by a factor of 20, from their actual size.

3.5. OpenSlide

The WSI .tif files contain multiple versions of the slide image, at different resolutions. These are stored in a pyramid-like structure which cannot be accessed unless using a specialised library [29]. The OpenSlide library is a C library that can read WSIs, the Python binding of the library also includes a Deep Zoom generator. For the work, this library was chosen as it has functions to read WSIs, get the dimensions of each level of the WSI, and fetch regions of the WSI at a specified level. The additional Deep Zoom generator also provides the ability to split the OpenSlide object into tiles of a given size which is ideal for the aim of this work.

3.6. Pre-Processing

There are four main pre-processing steps for WSI analysis: tissue segmentation, colour normalisation, patch extraction, and data augmentation. For this work, only two of these pre-processing steps, tissue segmentation and patch extraction, were implemented. The decision to not perform colour normalisation was influenced by the Camelyon16 winning paper [26], which used the same dataset as used for this work. As colour normalisation is usually performed to remove stain variation within the dataset, and Wang et al. [26] did not apply colour normalisation, it was decided not to perform any kind of colour normalisation. Data augmentation was not deemed necessary as it is possible to extract hundreds of thousands of patches from each image in the dataset. These patches can be used to form a large training dataset, therefore eliminating the risk of overfitting due to lack of training data.

The aim of the tissue segmentation stage is to remove any unnecessary areas from the WSIs. For this paper, this step is focused on removing the background of the images. As can be seen in Figure 6, a WSI can consist of majority background which is not useful for the classification model. Without this pre-processing step, many of the patches extracted from the image may be background and therefore the model would be largely trained on irrelevant data and predict non-background patches poorly. This would also lead to a great deal of unnecessary computational time and power spent training the model, as a larger number of patches per image, and therefore a larger training dataset, would be required to achieve accurate predictions.

Figure 6. An example of a whole slide image (normal_001.tif), at the lowest resolution level, to display the amount of white background typical in a whole slide image.

As the aim of the work is to implement a patch-based WSI analysis method, patch extraction is an essential pre-processing step. For this step, the entire WSIs are first split into patches. Most WSIs produce hundreds of thousands of patches per image, depending on the size which is specified when splitting up the WSI. The effect of using different patch sizes in this step will be investigated later in this report. The patches can also be overlapping by a specified number of pixels, which can provide some additional context to the patches to reduce the loss of spatial information.

The second part of patch extraction is to create a subset of patches from the entire set of patches, depending on the task. For the post-processing step using WSIs from test data, the entire patch dataset is used. However, to train the patch classification model, only a sample of patches from each WSI in the training dataset is used. There are multiple methods that can be used in patch extraction to choose a sample of patches from an image. In this paper, two of these methods, random sampling and informed sampling, are implemented and tested with the varied patch sizes.

For this work, there were two main pre-processing steps implemented: tissue segmentation (background removal) and patch extraction. The background removal pre-processing was implemented as part of the patch extraction pre-processing. The pre-processing stage results in the creation of a new dataset of patches and their labels, to be used as input to the patch-level classification model.

The pre-processing stage begins with the splitting of WSIs into all possible patches using a provided patch size. The total number of patches that this process results in varies as the WSIs have different dimensions. To retrieve a subset of patches for the training dataset, a sampling method must be used. The implementation of two sampling methods used for this work, random sampling and informed sampling, are described in Sections 3.6.2 and 3.6.3. A Patch class object is created for each of the patches in the subset which performs functions including label retrieval, background check, and transformations.

The label retrieval for a patch is dependent on the slide label. For the training data, the slide label is contained within the filename, either "normal" or "tumour". If a WSI has the "normal" slide label, all patches extracted from the WSI are labelled "normal" too. However, for slides labelled "tumour", the patch label must be inferred from the lesion annotations. The lesion annotations are contained in .xml files via the coordinates of the tumour regions in a slide. These coordinates were collated into tumour regions by creating polygon objects for each tumour and saving each in a list of tumours for the corresponding slide. Figure 7 shows an example of the polygons representing tumours in a WSI graphed. To check if a patch contains tumour, the centre of the patch was found and used to create a point object. The list of polygons representing tumours was then looped through, and each one checked if it contained the centre of the patch. If the patch was deemed to be within a tumour, it was labelled "tumour", if not it was labelled "normal".

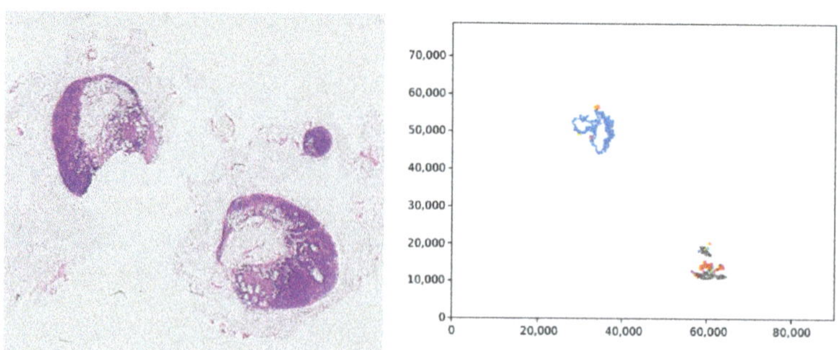

(a) (b)

Figure 7. (**a**) A whole slide image containing tumour (tumor_075.tif), with (**b**) the corresponding plot of the tumour regions from the lesion annotation file. Note that the whole slide image has been vertically flipped to match the orientation of the plot; the axis values are the pixel coordinates.

The "normal" and "tumour" labels for the patches were encoded using one hot encoding, with two values, the first representing the "normal" class and the second representing the "tumour" class. Therefore, a "normal" patch label contains a 1.0 in the first position and a 0.0 in the second position, and a "tumour" patch label has a 0.0 in the first position and a 1.0 in the second position.

3.6.1. Background Removal

The background removal step occurs when the patches are fetched in the sampling method. A background check was implemented by calculating the mean of the pixel values in the patch. If this mean is greater than a threshold, the patch is discarded and not added to the new training dataset. The threshold was determined with the aim of excluding as many background patches as possible without removing any tissue regions. This was achieved by comparison of example WSIs and corresponding images showing the pixels that would be discarded at the threshold. An image with all white pixels would have a mean pixel value of 256. However, to account for the slight off-white colour of the background of WSIs and general artefact, it was determined that any threshold above 240 would not remove significant background region. Therefore, a threshold of 240 was initially tested. However, this resulted in not all background region being removed, and in some cases none at all, so the threshold 230 was also tested and compared with 240. An example of this comparison is shown in Figures 8 and 9. Ultimately, a threshold of 230 was chosen for the background segmentation as this removed significantly more irrelevant patches for many WSIs, yet still kept all relevant information. This threshold is independent of patch size, its value being ultimately driven by image content, rather than size, and the staining protocol, that is the contrast between tissue and background, etc. An alternative approach would have been to employ some type of colour normalization prior to thresholding [24] which we decided not to do so as to avoid introducing a potential confound into our analysis though it should be noted that the most recent findings in this realm suggest that colour normalization becomes unnecessary if a sufficient feature extractor is used [30].

(a) (b) (c)

Figure 8. A comparison of a whole slide image (tumor_001.tif) and the detection of white background areas using different thresholds. The dark blue areas are the background and white are tissue. It is clear that a threshold of 240 is not strict enough for this image as no region in the image has been detected as background. From the WSI, it is possible to see that the background of this slide has a slight off-white colour, explaining why this has not been segmented correctly. (**a**) The original whole slide image. (**b**) Background region detected with threshold = 240. (**c**) Background region detected with threshold = 230.

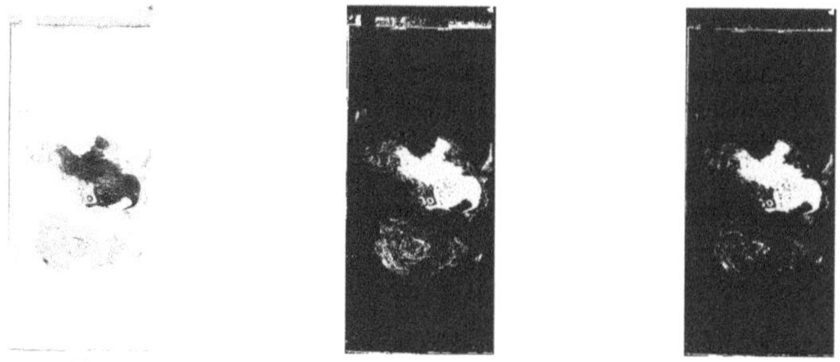

(a) (b) (c)

Figure 9. A comparison of a whole slide image (tumor_036.tif) and the detection of white background areas using different thresholds. The dark blue areas are the background and white are tissue. (**a**) The original whole slide image. (**b**) Background region detected with threshold = 240. (**c**) Background region detected with threshold = 230.

3.6.2. Random Sampling Method

The random sampling method involves choosing, at random, a given number of patches from all the possible patches for an image. This random selection is done without replacement to avoid duplicates in the training data. Random sampling is a simple sampling method, but it can result in a significantly large class imbalance. When randomly sampling from a normal slide, all patches will be "normal", either normal tissue or non-tissue regions. However, when sampling from a tumour slide, some patches will be tumour, but a large number are still "normal" patches. This means that the resulting dataset contains a much larger number of normal patches compared to tumour patches.

The random sampling method retrieves a subset of patches chosen at random. This was implemented by, for each WSI, iteratively fetching random patch addresses from the set of patches for the image and adding the corresponding patch to the training dataset. There is a defined maximum number of patches per image for the sampling method. The iterative process will continue until this maximum is reached or all patches have been fetched.

3.6.3. Informed Sampling Method

The informed sampling method counteracts the issue of class imbalance from the random sampling method. This method is more complex than random sampling as it uses the location of tumours in the slides. Normal slides are processed in the same way as in random sampling; a given number of patches are chosen randomly, all of which are "normal". However, for tumour slides, the patches are sampled based on the location of the tumours in the slides. A given number of tumour-labelled patches are extracted in addition to the usual "normal" patches which are still chosen from the tumour slides. By specifying a similar value for the number of both the tumour and normal patches, a more balanced dataset can be produced, ensuring a reasonable proportion of the training dataset is tumour.

The informed sampling method creates a more balanced dataset than the random sampling method. This method was implemented similarly to the random sampling, except, for tumour slides, the maximum number of patches is split into a maximum number for normal patches and a maximum number for tumour patches. The two maximum values for the tumour slides are chosen to be equal and the sum of them is equal to the maximum number of patches for the normal slides. The tumour patches are sampled from a list of patches in tumour regions fetched from the lesion annotation files. The resulting dataset remains slightly unbalanced, although to a much lesser degree. It is not possible to completely balance the dataset without using a small number of patches per image as there is significantly fewer tumour patches compared to normal patches.

3.7. Patch-Level Classification

The aim of the patch-level classification model is to predict the probability of a patch containing tumourous tissue. This model takes as input the pre-processed patches sampled from the training data. It outputs a probability value for both the normal class and the tumour class. The model is trained and optimised based only on the accuracy of the patch-level classification. The patch classification is the foundation of the remainder of the system, therefore it is essential that the model performs well.

As this stage focuses on performing patch-level classifications, rather than slide-level or lesion-level, the input patches are independent from their original WSIs. Therefore, the model learns only from the features and morphological information given by a patch individually. This also means there is no spatial information provided to the model which is the most significant drawback of patch-based analysis methods.

The patch-level classification stage focuses on the prediction of patch-level labels by training a neural network. This step was implemented using the GoogLeNet architecture described in Section 3.2 which was loaded from PyTorch in the PatchAnalysis script. As this network usually has 1000 output nodes, the number of classes for this problem, two, normal and tumour, was specified when loading the model.

The input data for the model originates from the pre-processing step. A custom dataset was created to take the directory of the patch files and create a dataset consisting of a list of the patch filenames and a list of the patch labels. The __getitem__ function of the dataset class then fetches the patch, as a tensor, from the file at the given index, alongside the label for the patch. To train and evaluate the model, the patch dataset was split into train and validation datasets using a stratified split based on the patch labels to ensure the tumour patches were evenly distributed between the datasets. The size of the validation dataset was specified to be 20% of the original dataset. All testing was performed using a separate test corpus provided as part of the challenge data set.

The version of WSI analysis performed in this work is a binary classification problem. However, as the GoogLeNet network has been used, which requires a minimum of two classes, the binary classification is implemented using one hot encoding with a class representing "normal" and a class representing "tumour". Therefore, despite this being a binary problem, the loss function, optimiser, and activation function were chosen based on the model architecture having two output nodes. Categorical cross entropy loss was chosen for the loss function as this is commonly used in classification problems with success; binary cross entropy loss was not possible to use given the one hot encoded outputs. The Adam optimiser was used due to its ability to adapt well to increase speed and accuracy of the predictions. The softmax activation function was used to convert the model outputs to probabilities. This was chosen over the sigmoid function as the classes are mutually exclusive and the probabilities output from the softmax function sum to one.

3.7.1. Testing

The patch classification model was tested using the validation set, the confusion matrix for which can be seen in Table 1, and by analysing the graphs for the loss, accuracy and recall of the predictions to ensure the model was learning properly. Figure 10 shows these graphs for the trained model with a patch size of 256; also see the summary in Table 2. From these, it is possible to see the model is predicting well overall and there is low loss. However, there is some overfitting, specifically for the tumour class as can be seen in Figure 10c, which was addressed during hyper-parameter testing.

Table 1. Confusion matrix for the patch classification model on the validation set.

		Actual	
		Positive	**Negative**
Predicted	**Positive**	201	0
	Negative	163	7798

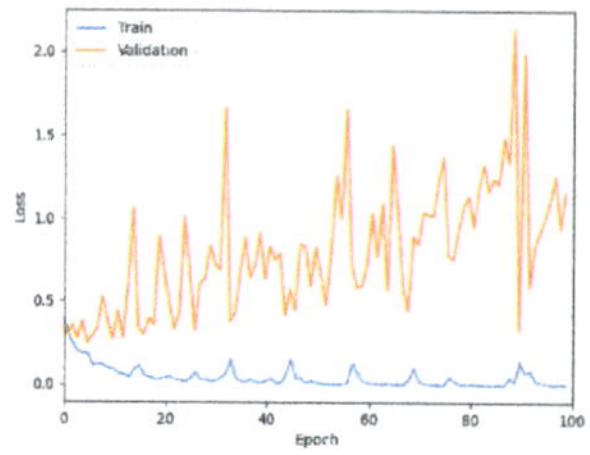

(**a**) Loss

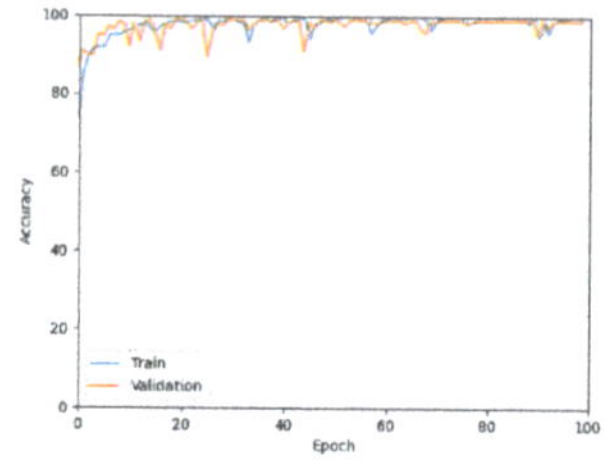

(**b**) Accuracy

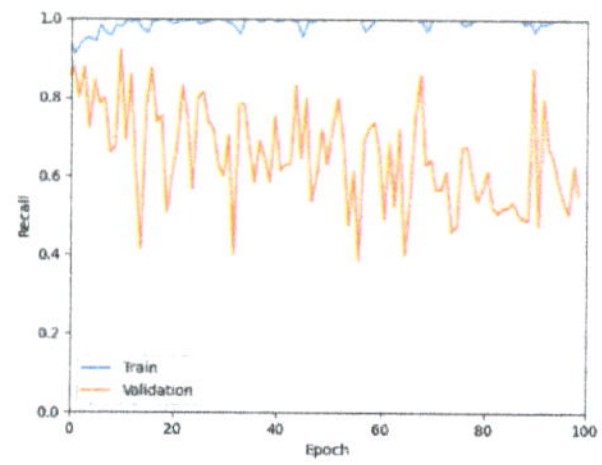

(**c**) Recall

Figure 10. The loss, accuracy, and recall graphs used for testing the patch classification model. Also see Table 2 for a numerical summary of the data.

Table 2. The loss, accuracy, and recall values used for testing the patch classification model. To account for stochastic fluctuations all values are reported for the exact epoch noted, followed by the average of the values corresponding to epochs in a window centred at the said epoch.

		Epoch			
		25	**50**	**75**	**100**
Train	Accuracy (%)	98.72/98.24	99.34/99.24	99.23/98.82	99.44/99.81
	Recall	0.99/0.99	1.0/0.99	1.0/0.99	1.0/1.0
	Loss	0.04/0.04	0.01/0.02	0.01/0.02	0.01/0.01
Validation	Accuracy (%)	90.03/94.94	99.03/98.72	99.03/98.72	98.83/98.93
	Recall	0.80/0.73	0.63/0.69	0.48/0.54	0.55/0.56
	Loss	0.67/0.67	0.83/0.67	1.37/1.13	0.95/1.12

3.7.2. Hyper-Parameter Tuning

The hyper-parameters that were tuned for this model were learning rate, class weights, patches extracted per image and number of epochs. These parameters were evaluated using the loss, accuracy, and recall measures for the model's predictions. All hyper-parameter tuning was performed on a patch dataset with 100 patches of size 256 × 256 per WSI, sampled using the random sampling method. Except where otherwise specified, the hyper-parameters were kept the same for all patch size and sampling method tests.

The learning rate was optimised by testing values on a log scale, from 10^{-1} to 10^{-5}, and comparing the loss, accuracy, and recall on the validation set. The results of these measurements are shown in Figure 11 (also see Table 3). From the accuracy graph, it is evident that the learning rate affects this metric very little, particularly by the end of the 100 epochs. Therefore, the final learning rate was chosen based on loss and recall measurements. From the loss, 10^{-1} appears to be the best choice, but also gives the lowest recall value. Consequently, a learning rate of 10^{-5} was chosen which also has low loss but gives a similar recall to other learning rates.

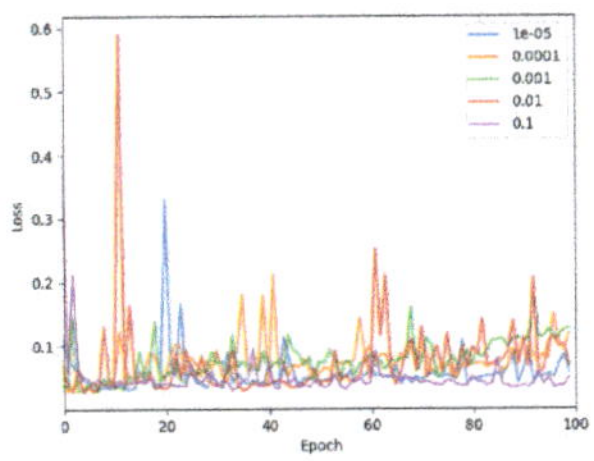

(**a**) Loss

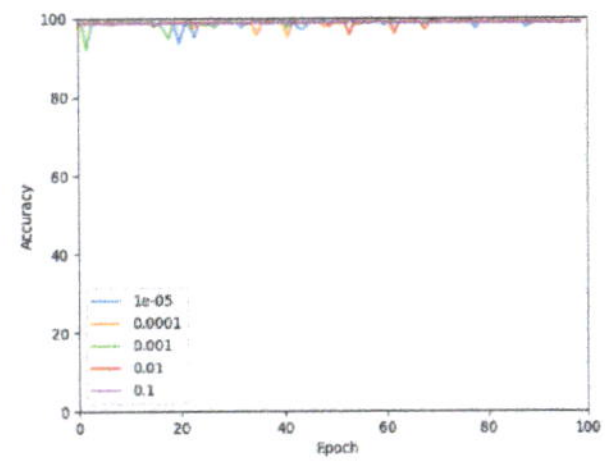

(**b**) Accuracy

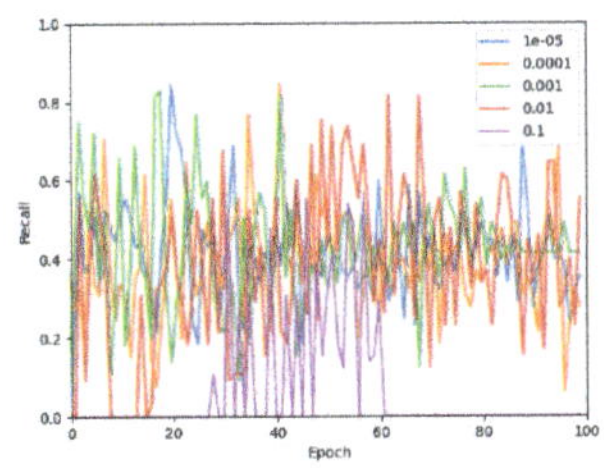

(**c**) Recall

Figure 11. The validation loss, accuracy, and recall graphs for a range of learning rates used to find the best hyper-parameter value. Also see Table 3 for a numerical summary of the data.

Table 3. The validation loss, accuracy, and recall values for a range of learning rates used to find the best hyper-parameter value. To account for stochastic fluctuations all values are reported for the exact epoch noted, followed by the average of the values corresponding to epochs in a window centred at the said epoch.

		Epoch			
Learning Rate		**25**	**50**	**75**	**100**
10^{-5}	Accuracy (%)	98.67/98.67	99.11/99.11	99.20/99.20	99.20/99.20
	Recall	0.18/0.30	0.47/0.41	0.37/0.43	0.33/0.31
	Loss	0.06/0.05	0.05/0.05	0.06/0.05	0.09/0.08
10^{-4}	Accuracy (%)	99.11/99.11	99.20/99.20	99.38/99.28	99.11/99.11
	Recall	0.31/0.35	0.49/0.47	0.43/0.41	0.32/0.28
	Loss	0.08/0.07	0.06/0.06	0.07/0.07	0.09/0.11
0.001	Accuracy (%)	98.32/98.67	99.56/99.56	99.38/99.38	99.38/99.38
	Recall	0.77/0.61	0.33/0.40	0.51/0.49	0.42/0.42
	Loss	0.07/0.06	0.08/0.07	0.07/0.07	0.13/0.13
0.01	Accuracy (%)	99.38/99.38	98.94/98.58	99.47/99.47	99.38/99.38
	Recall	0.52/0.39	0.43/0.64	0.23/0.43	0.23/0.40
	Loss	0.06/0.07	0.04/0.05	0.12/0.08	0.10/0.09
0.1	Accuracy (%)	99.03/99.03	99.20/99.20	99.03/99.03	99.03/99.03
	Recall	0.00/0.00	0.32/0.30	0.00/0.00	0.00/0.00
	Loss	0.07/0.05	0.04/0.04	0.05/0.04	0.04/0.04

From Figure 11, it is clear that the recall values are not ideal given that the aim of the work is to detect tumours. Therefore, class weights were added to the loss function in an attempt to improve the recall of the predictions. A comparison of class weights versus no class weights can be seen in Figure 12. It is obvious from these graphs that using class weights is much more optimal for this work.

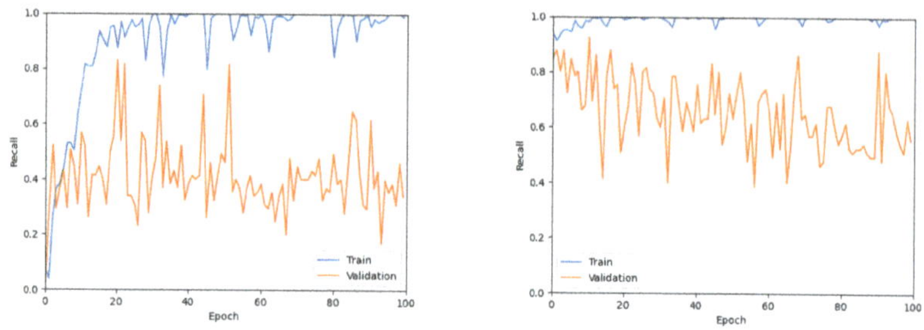

(**a**) Model without class weights (**b**) Model with class weights

Figure 12. The recall values for the model without using class weights for the loss function and with using weights.

Another hyper-parameter that was investigated is the number of patches sampled per image. The results of this investigation are shown in Figure 13 which shows the validation loss, accuracy, and recall for 10, 25, 50, 100, and 150 patches per image; a further summary can be found in Table 4. Many of the values are similar for the various numbers of patches. However, the largest number of patches per image gave the most stable values. Therefore, 150 patches were sampled from each image for the remainder of the work with the exception of the 1024 × 1024 patch size, which only had 50 samples from each image due to the large patch size.

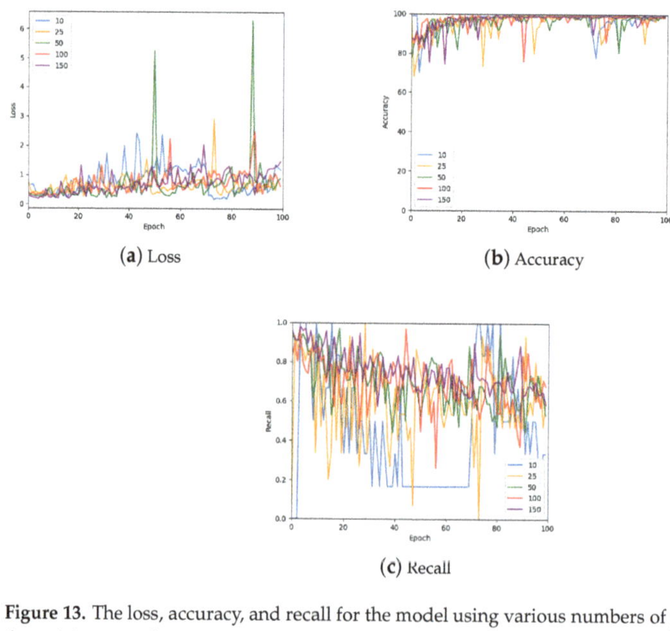

(**a**) Loss (**b**) Accuracy

(**c**) Recall

Figure 13. The loss, accuracy, and recall for the model using various numbers of patches per WSI in the training set. Also see Table 4 for a numerical summary of the data.

Table 4. The loss, accuracy, and recall for the model using various numbers of patches per WSI in the training set. To account for stochastic fluctuations all values are reported for the exact epoch noted, followed by the average of the values corresponding to epochs in a window centred at the said epoch.

		Epoch			
No. Patches		**25**	**50**	**75**	**100**
10	Accuracy (%)	98.23/98.32	99.03/99.03	94.06/94.62	99.03/99.03
	Recall	0.33/0.5	0.17/0.17	0.84/0.89	0.33/0.27
	Loss	0.76/0.48	1.26/1.38	0.22/0.22	1.27/1.28
25	Accuracy (%)	97.96/98.32	94.42/94.83	88.74/88.74	98.85/98.96
	Recall	0.51/0.51	0.73/0.73	0.81/0.85	0.47/0.60
	Loss	0.66/0.69	0.36/0.40	0.37/0.41	0.85/0.67
50	Accuracy (%)	92.11/95.83	99.03/98.97	98.85/99.14	98.67/98.75
	Recall	0.88/0.78	0.53/0.59	0.64/0.64	0.62/0.60
	Loss	0.32/0.39	5.26/2.22	0.70/0.72	0.84/0.80
100	Accuracy (%)	96.19/97.96	99.03/98.29	98.85/94.71	98.49/98.49
	Recall	0.77/0.64	0.45/0.64	0.62/0.70	0.71/0.64
	Loss	0.38/0.70	1.17/0.84	1.07/0.95	0.84/0.85
150	Accuracy (%)	98.67/94.42	99.03/99.16	98.85/99.14	99.56/99.26
	Recall	0.81/0.83	0.65/0.68	0.70/0.71	0.64/0.62
	Loss	0.57/0.63	0.92/0.98	0.89/0.88	1.37/1.39

As can be seen from previous hyper-parameter tuning, the maximum epoch value that was previously used is sufficient for training the model. The accuracy has plateaued and, based on recall graphs, the model is beginning to overfit for the tumour data. The trained model used for the production of heatmaps is selected individually for each classification using the loss, accuracy, and recall graphs to choose the best performing model.

The batch size used varied depending on the patch size as increasing the patch size led to issues with the CUDA memory so a decrease in batch size was required to run the patch classification.

3.8. Production of Tumour Probability Map

This stage of the system creates heatmaps that correspond to each WSI in the testing dataset. The testing data, one WSI at a time, undergoes patch extraction resulting in a set of all patches from a WSI. The trained patch-level classification model is applied to this set of patches and predicts, for each patch, the probability that the patch contains tumourous tissue. The tumour probabilities are then displayed in a heatmap. From the heatmaps, it is possible to see the correlation between areas of high tumour probability and the location of tumours in the corresponding WSI. Therefore, if a test WSI is classified as tumour, these heatmaps can be used to retrieve the location of tumours in the WSI for further analysis by a pathologist.

The production of the tumour probability heatmaps is a post-processing step which involves applying the trained model from the previous stage, rather than being a model itself. The heatmaps produced are split into training and testing data. The training heatmaps become the input for the second model of the system, and the testing data is used to test the accuracy of the model and the overall patch-based WSI analysis method.

The production of the tumour probability map from a WSI can be split into two parts, both of which are implemented in the CreateHeatmap script. The first part involves splitting the WSI into patches and the second part uses the trained patch-level classification model to get the predictions for the patches which form the heatmap.

The model is loaded from a file of the saved trained model produced by the previous step of the process. The WSI is then loaded and split into patches using the Deep Zoom generator. The columns and rows that formulate the addresses of the patches are iterated through and each patch address is added to a list, provided it is not part of the background of the slide. A custom dataset, AllPatchDataset, is then used to create a dataset with these patch addresses and the generator. The __getitem__ function in this dataset fetches the patch at the address given by the index and preprocesses it before returning the patch.

The heatmap data begins as an array of zeros with the dimensions of the number of columns and rows. This ensures that any background patches that are not in the dataset are automatically given a value of 0 for the heatmap. For each patch in the dataset, the probability predictions for the two classes are produced by the trained model. The probability values for the "normal" class are negated to give values between −1 and 0. The "tumour" class predictions are untouched. The highest absolute value between the predictions for each patch is added to the heatmap data in the position given by the column and row of the address of the patch.

Once the whole dataset has been predicted, the heatmap data is plotted using the seaborn package and the resulting heatmap is saved as an image into a directory of heatmaps. Every heatmap is plotted with the same minimum and maximum values to ensure the colour scale is equal for the next stage of feature extraction and training. A file containing a list of the probability values is also saved to aid in feature extraction in the next stage.

Each heatmap is saved with the label of the slide in the filename to be used for the slide classification. The label for each test WSI is contained within the reference.csv file from the dataset. This file is read using pandas and, for each WSI, the corresponding label is fetched from the dataset and added to the heatmap's filename.

Testing

This post-processing stage was tested by inspecting the resulting heatmaps. The heatmaps corresponding to both normal and tumour WSIs were compared to check that the heatmap creation was successful. Different colour maps and formats were also tested to identify the optimal parameters for the heatmaps. Figure 14 shows an alternative colour map that was tested prior to deciding to show normal probabilities in addition to tumour probabilities. This figure also shows a heatmap that only uses classification results rather than probabilities. Using the classification results did not provide the information required for the feature extraction that is required for slide classification.

(a) (b)

Figure 14. Two different heatmaps, both using a colourmap which was not used for the final work, with the left-hand heatmap displaying tumour probabilities and the right-hand heatmap showing classification predictions. (**a**) Heatmap using probabilities of tumour. (**b**) Heatmap using classification predictions.

The final style of heatmaps, including colour map, is shown in Figure 15. These heatmaps were created using the reversed "BuRd" colour map with the scale of probabilities being between -1 and 1. The regions that are saturations of blue are values between -1 and 0, normal tissue, and the regions that are saturations of red are between 0 and 1, tumour tissue.

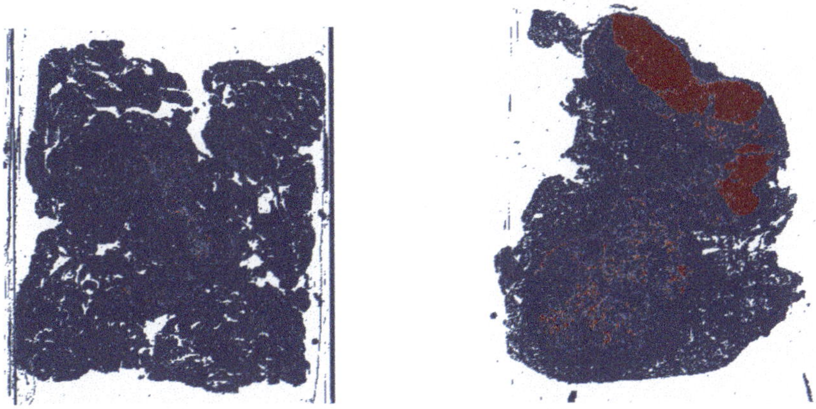

(**a**) Heatmap for a normal slide (**b**) Heatmap for tumour slide

Figure 15. Example of a heatmap for a normal whole slide image (test_037.tif) and for a tumour whole slide image (test_016.tif), where dark blue represents probability of 1 for normal tissue and dark red represents probability of 1 for tumour tissue.

3.9. Slide-Level Classification

The slide-level classification model is the final step in the classification of WSIs. This model is trained using features extracted from each of the tumour probability heatmaps, for example, the percentage of the slide that is tumour, the average probability values, and the frequency of high probability tumour areas. These features are input to the model alongside the labels for the corresponding WSIs.

The trained model is tested using extracted features from the heatmaps in the testing data. The metrics resulting from this testing are used to evaluate the accuracy of the entire WSI analysis. These measures will be used to evaluate and compare the various patch sizes and methods used in this work.

The slide-level classification task is the last in the analysis of WSIs. The aim of this classification is to predict the slide-level label for a WSI from the corresponding heatmap produced in the previous step. This is implemented with a random forest architecture, using the sci-kit learn package.

The dataset for the input of the model is the heatmap data. However, as this dataset consists of images of various sizes, the pre-processing step, feature extraction, must first be undertaken. Feature extraction is performed to collect features of the images and data, as numerical values, that can be input into the classifier. The feature extraction process is detailed in Section 3.9.1. This step is performed within a custom dataset class, HeatmapDataset. This class takes the path of the heatmap directory, extracts features from each of the images in the directory, and gets the label for the instance. The input data was split into training and test sets using a stratified split with a test set size of 0.2. A validation set was not necessary for this model as no hyper-parameter tuning was performed.

The output for this classification is the final classification result for the analysis of the WSI. The labels for the slides are one-hot encoded, in the same way as done for the patch-level classification model. Therefore, the output produced by the model, for each input, is either $[1.0, 0.0]$ for "normal" or $[0.0, 1.0]$ for "tumour".

3.9.1. Feature Extraction

Feature extraction is necessary for this model as the input images, the heatmaps, are of varying sizes. It is not possible to resize these images to make a dataset of images of the same dimensions as this would warp the information provided by the heatmap. A feature extraction process was implemented that extracts 22 statistical and mophological features from each heatmap image and corresponding probabilities. In choosing these features, inspiration was taken from both the Camelyon16 winning paper [26] and from Fu et al. who investigated tumour detection in whole slide images [31].

The first feature extracted is the percentage of tissue that is predicted to be tumour. This was implemented by getting the sum of positive probabilities, the tumour patches, and the sum of negative probabilities, the normal patches. The percentage of tumour patches over the entire tissue region, tumour and normal patches, was then calculated.

The next features are the number of tumour regions and the size of the largest tumour region in the heatmap. This is implemented by extracting a mask of the tumour regions. The number of tumour regions found in this mask is the first of these features. Then the largest continuous area of tumour patches is found and the size calculated in pixels. Figure 16 shows an example of the mask of the tumour regions in a WSI.

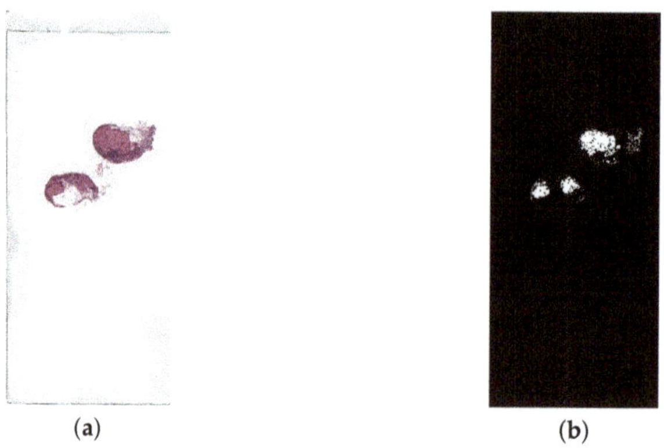

Figure 16. An example of a mask of the tumour regions in a whole slide image (test_040.tif). (**a**) The original whole slide image. (**b**) The mask of tumour regions.

The remaining extracted features are based on the statistics of the probabilities. The probability values are split into positive (tumour) probabilities and negative (normal) probabilities. The absolute value of each of the negative probabilities was taken for ease in calculations. From both of these sets of probabilities, nine values were calculated from the data. These values were the mean, median, mode, variance, standard deviation, minimum, maximum, range, and sum.

Other features were extracted to test for effectiveness, such as the class with the largest mean and the class with the largest number of patches. However, both of these values were largely the same for all slides, whether normal or tumour, and so were deemed not useful to the classifier.

3.9.2. Testing

This stage was tested using two methods. The feature extraction tasks were tested by printing out the features for various heatmap instances and analysing the values to ensure they appeared reasonable. The classifier was tested by analysing the accuracy, recall, and AUC measurements for the predictions to check that the predictions given were reasonable.

3.10. Testing the Effects of Patch Size

Using the final structure of the work, various patch sizes were tested. The entire process of patch dataset creation, patch classification, heatmap creation, and finally slide classification was performed for each patch size. The results of these tests are detailed in Section 4.1.

3.11. Downsampling Analysis Method

Downsampling is an alternative method used to counteract the problems faced when analysing WSIs. This can be used alone or in conjunction with patch extraction. As the original size of a WSI file is too large, downsampling reduces the resolution of the image, by a downsampling factor, therefore reducing the size of the image.

If the downsampling factor is large enough, the resulting downsampled image can be input directly into a model to predict the probability of tumour. This removes the need for splitting the image into patches and can be performed using only one model to predict the slide-level classification. Another option is using a combination of downsampling and patch extraction. An image can be moderately downsampled and then patch extraction can be performed on the downsampled image.

In general, patch-based methods are preferred over downsampling methods. When the resolution of a WSI is reduced, a significant amount of morphological information and fine detail can be lost. This can have a detrimental effect on the accuracy of the model and make the resulting model unusable in genuine clinical scenarios.

The downsampling-based WSI method involves inputting downsampled WSIs into a model for classification. This does not entail any patch extraction or related steps. The model used for this method was the GoogLeNet network, as used in the patch-level classification. As in the patch-level classification, the labels for the slides were one hot encoded to provide a two output node model as required by the GoogLeNet network.

This method was implemented by first creating a new dataset of the WSIs at the lowest resolution possible, from the training and testing WSIs. For the training of the model, the dataset of downsampled training WSIs was then split into training and validation sets using a stratified split with a validation set size of 0.2. For the testing and evaluation of the trained model, the set of downsampled testing WSIs was used.

Pre-processing for this method involved downsampling the images, resizing the images to 256×256, transforming to tensors, and normalisation. The downsampling occurs in the creation of the new dataset, prior to any analysis. When getting the items in the dataset with the dataloader, the remaining pre-processing steps are applied to the images. The resizing of the images is far from ideal as some are resized more significantly than others and so are not very comparable. However, this is necessary as the GoogLeNet network only accepts datasets of images of equal sizes. The transformation to tensor and normalisation is also required by the network.

The same loss function, optimiser, learning rate, and activation function as the patch classification model were used given the use of the same network and input image size. A few learning rates were tested but this appeared to have little effect on the accuracy of the model.

The final analysis of the WSIs was implemented by loading the best trained model and inputting the downsampled test WSIs. The predictions produced were evaluated using the accuracy and recall metrics.

Testing

This model was tested similarly to the patch-level classification model, using the loss, accuracy, and recall graphs. Figure 17 contains the corresponding three graphs (also see the summary in see Table 5) where it can be observed that the model is predicting the slide label well.

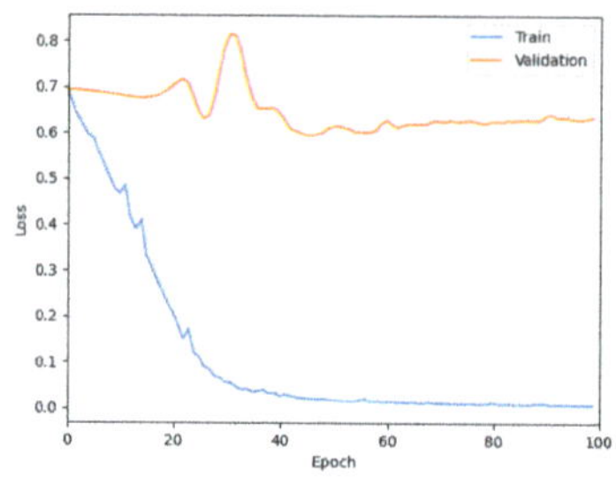

(**a**) Loss

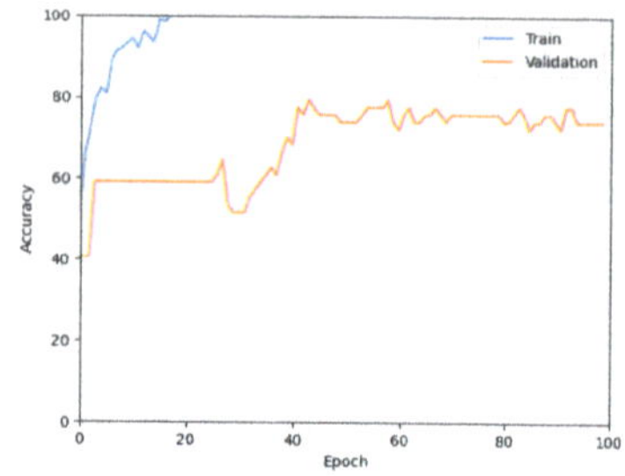

(**b**) Accuracy

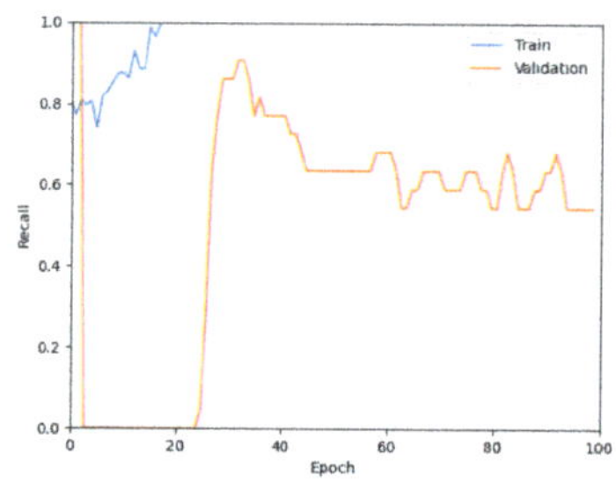

(**c**) Recall

Figure 17. The loss, accuracy, and recall graphs used for testing the downsampled slide classification model. Also see Table 5 for a numerical summary of the data.

Table 5. The loss, accuracy, and recall values used for testing the downsampled slide classification model. To account for stochastic fluctuations all values are reported for the exact epoch noted, followed by the average of the values corresponding to epochs in a window centred at the said epoch.

		Epoch			
		25	**50**	**75**	**100**
Train	Accuracy (%)	100.00/100.00	100.00/100.00	100.00/100.00	100.00/100.00
	Recall	1.0/1.0	1.0/1.0	1.0/1.0	1.0/1.0
	Loss	0.11/0.11	0.02/0.02	0.01/0.01	0.01/0.01
Validation	Accuracy (%)	59.35/60.00	74.26/74.26	76.04/76.04	74.26/74.26
	Recall	0.04/0.13	0.64/0.64	0.64/0.62	0.55/0.55
	Loss	0.65/0.65	0.62/0.62	0.63/0.63	0.63/0.63

3.12. Metrics

The metrics used for the evaluation of the models are dependent on the task. There were three sets of metrics used throughout the work, which consisted of some combination of the loss, accuracy, recall, and AUC measurements. The performance of the patch-level classification model was measured using loss, accuracy, and recall. The final slide-level classification for the patch-based method was evaluated with the accuracy, recall, and AUC metrics. For this model, AUC is included as this is the primary metric used to evaluate the model in the Camelyon16 winning paper [26]. In analysing the training, the downsampled slide classification model, loss, accuracy, and recall were used. The measures used for the slide classification model, using the downsampled method, were accuracy and recall.

The loss values used were calculated from the model's direct output, prior to softmax, using the cross entropy loss function. For the patch-level classification model, the loss function was given class weights due to the unbalanced nature of the datasets produced by random sampling. Cross entropy loss is used when a model's output is class probabilities. The calculated loss value will increase if the probabilities of the classes are getting further from the true values. The equation for calculating cross entropy loss is

$$H(x) = -(P(\text{"normal"}) * \log(Q(\text{"normal"}) + P(\text{"tumour"}) * \log(Q(\text{"tumour"}))$$

where $P(x)$ is the true probability of x and $Q(x)$ is the predicted probability of x.

The accuracy of the model is essentially the percentage of correctly predicted labels. In all instances, the predicted label is calculated by taking the class with largest probability for each patch/slide. The equation for calculating the accuracy is

$$\text{accuracy} = \text{number of correct predictions/size of dataset} * 100$$

Recall is a measure of the accuracy of only the positive class, the "tumour" class. A good recall is particularly important for the analysis of WSIs as the misclassification of a tumour slide could have dire consequences. The observation of recall values is also key for the randomly sampled datasets due to the significant class imbalance. The equation for calculating the recall is

$$\text{recall} = \text{number of correctly predicted "tumour"/number of "tumour" in the dataset}$$

The AUC measure is calculated for the slide-level classification to allow comparison between this model and related work as it is a commonly used metric in WSI analysis methods. AUC stands for area under the ROC (receiving operator characteristic) curve. This is calculated by taking the integral of the ROC curve.

For the patch-level classification, and both downsampling models, the accuracy and recall were calculated manually using these formulae. The slide-level classification used the scikit-learn metrics to get the accuracy, recall, and AUC.

4. Results and Evaluation

4.1. Results of the Effect of Patch Size

To investigate the effect of patch size, the patch-based WSI analysis method was performed using a variety of patch sizes with the final classification results recorded for evaluation. Although not formally evaluated, the patch-level classification accuracy was close to 100% for all patch sizes for both sampling methods. However, the informed sampling method gave higher recall values, 90–98%, for the patch sizes tested, compared to the corresponding patch sizes sampled using random sampling, 60–70%.

Different patch sizes for the random sampling method were tested first, the results of which can be found in Table 6. The typical patch size used in related work is 256 × 256 pixels, therefore, this was the first patch size tested. It was not possible to decrease the patch size by a significant amount from here, as the GoogLeNet network requires inputs of at least 224 × 224 pixels. While patches with smaller dimensions than this could be resized to input to the model, this could skew the patch size evaluation. Therefore, it was decided to double the patch size and observe the effects, testing the patch-based method using 512 × 512 patches. As can be seen in Table 6, this patch size caused a decrease in the accuracy of the model, with the tumour slide classification only correct 50% of the time. Figure 18 shows the heatmaps corresponding to the same test image for these two patch sizes. It is clear that a lot of detail in the heatmap is lost by increasing the patch size. Although the heatmap using 512 pixel size patches contains less uncertain predictions, where the colour of the patch is not at either of the extremes, dark blue for normal and dark red for tumour.

Table 6. Results for the random sampling method.

Patch Size (px)	Accuracy (%)	Recall	AUC
256	73	0.60	0.71
384	54	0.30	0.49
512	69	0.50	0.66
786	62	0.60	0.61

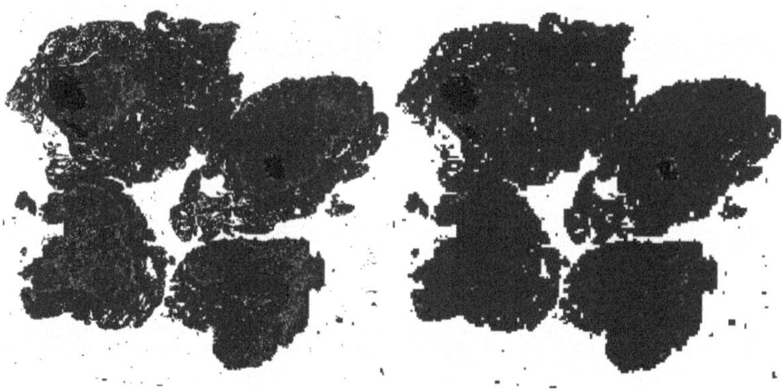

(**a**) Patch size = 256 (**b**) Patch size = 512

Figure 18. The heatmaps corresponding to a tumourous WSI (test_001.tif), using a patch size of 256 × 256 and 512 × 512.

As there was a decrease in the accuracy, the next patch size attempted was the mean of the previous two, 384 × 384. This was followed by testing 1.5 times the current largest patch size, giving a patch size of 786, to evaluate if the downward trend continued. Neither of these patch sizes yielded a model that proved to be as accurate as the first, 256 patch size, model. Testing with the 786 × 786 patch size shows that it continues the decrease that was observed between patch sizes 256 and 512 in two metrics, accuracy and AUC. However, the recall value for this model is higher than the 512 patch size and equal to the 256 patch size. Given the importance of the recall for this task, a patch size of 786 should be considered over patches of 512 × 512. Based on the results of the other patch sizes, the metrics for the 384 patch size test appear to be an anomaly given the significant decrease in all three measures. Extrapolating from the trend between the remaining three patch sizes, the random sampling method predicts best when used with a smaller patch size.

Given the trend observed for random sampling, increasing patch size leads to decrease in accuracy, the informed sampling method was evaluated next. This method was evaluated with two of the same patch sizes as the random sampling, 256 and 512, and one other, 1024. The smallest patch size, 256 was tested first as this proved to be the most successful for the random sampling method. Patches of size 512 × 512 were then tested to see if the same downward trend applies for this sampling method. This proved to be true, however, rather than try the same 1.5 times larger patch size as done in the random sampling method, it was decided to evaluate a more extreme patch size of 1024 × 1024. As can be seen in Table 7, a decrease in accuracy occurred between patch sizes 512 and 1024. However, the largest patch size gave the highest recall value, similarly to the random sampling method, where the largest patch size gave the equal highest recall value. Despite the significance of the recall for this task, the large decrease in overall accuracy between 256 patch size and 1024 patch size is too severe to ignore in favour of the higher recall.

Table 7. Results for the informed sampling method.

Patch Size (px)	Accuracy (%)	Recall	AUC
256	81	0.60	0.79
512	65	0.30	0.59
1024	58	0.70	0.60

4.2. Comparison of Methods

For both the random sampling method and informed sampling method, the smallest patch size tested, 256 × 256, produced the most accurate slide-level predictions. The informed sampling method proved to be superior to the random sampling method for this patch size giving an accuracy of 81% compared to 73%. However, the other patch size tested with both sampling methods, 512 × 512, achieved better results using the random sampling method, with a significant difference in the recall values, 0.5 for random sampling and 0.3 for informed sampling.

Here we also note that all of the achieved levels of accuracy could be further increased by the employment of techniques such as hard negative mining following the standard training protocol, as a means of reducing false positive errors. Had this been done the ultimate performance would have been higher, benefiting both from this feedback loop and the optimal patch size. However since our goal was not to employs all means available so as to engineer the highest performing systems based on the evaluated architectures but rather to assess the impact of patch size specifically, we made no such efforts.

The patch-based method and downsampling method can also be compared. The best patch method gave an accuracy of 81% and a recall of 0.60. The downsampling method gave significantly lower values, with accuracy at 64% and recall 0.49. This is the expected result, given the loss of fine detail that occurs in the downsampling of WSIs. However, given the lack of investigation into the best downsampling factor, this may not be a fair comparison. It is possible, by finding the optimal downsampling factor, the downsampling method could prove to be as accurate as the patch-based method.

4.3. Related Work

The Camelyon16 winning paper [26] was used throughout the work as guidance for the methodology of the system. This paper did not investigate the effect of patch size but was focused on the optimisation of the accuracy of the WSI analysis model for the Camelyon16 challenge. The research produced a model with an AUC score of 0.925 using patches of size 256 × 256. This is significantly higher than the one achieved by this work, 0.79 for the optimal method. However, the aim of this work was focused on the effect of patch size and used significantly fewer patches for training compared, with Wang et al. using millions of normal and tumour patches compared to around 40,000 used for this work.

The most significant related work is the paper by Fell et al. [16] who also did an investigation into patch size, using a similar methodology to this work and the Camelyon16 winning paper [26]. Three patch sizes were tested, 256, 512, and 1024. Fell et al. found that the largest patch size, 1024, provided the best model for analysis of the WSIs. This is in contrast to the findings of this paper, although not entirely when considering the recall rather than the accuracy. With a patch size of 1024 × 1024 pixels, an accuracy of 90% was achieved, compared to 81% for this work, and a recall of 97%, compared to 60%. The model implemented by Fell et al. was evidently very successful in the analysis of WSIs. However, it is difficult to compare as a dataset of 2909 WSIs was used compared to the dataset of 271 training WSIs and 129 testing WSIs that was used for this work.

4.4. Conclusions

The work successfully implemented a patch-based WSI analysis method and evaluated the effect of patch size, giving an optimal method using a patch size of 256 × 256 sampled using the informed sampling method. Both a random sampling method and an informed sampling method, using tumour region location, were implemented allowing for thorough investigation into the patch sizes using these different methods. Based on the classification results, the more accurate of the two sampling methods is dependent on the patch size. However, the optimal patch size/sampling method pair used the informed sampling method. A basic downsampling method was also tested, allowing for comparison of this with the patch-based method which was superior as expected from the literature. One of the significant achievements of the work is the production of the tumour probability heatmaps for use in identifying the location of tumours in a WSI. At small patch sizes, these heatmaps give fine detail of probable tumour regions that can be used by pathologists to aid their analysis and diagnosis of the specimens.

4.5. Future Work

Primarily, future work should continue the investigation into the effect of patch sizes to include larger patch sizes, and investigate more the informed sampling method. The tertiary objective to evaluate various downsampling factors for the downsampling method was not completed. This is another possible area for future work, however, due to the larger success of the patch-based method, this would be a low priority for further research. There is also a significant number of other factors that can be investigated in future work to try to optimise the accuracy of the patch-based WSI analysis method. Two factors that are already in use in related work are overlapping of patches and sampling patches at different magnification levels.

In the Camelyon16 winning paper [26], overlapping patches are used in the production of the tumour probability heatmaps, although it is not specified how many pixels the patches overlap by. This warrants further investigation, exploring the use of overlapping patches in the production of the tumour probability heatmaps, and the effect of different numbers of overlapping pixels. The DeepZoomGenerator used in this work has an overlap parameter which could be used for this work. This could also be extended to experiment with overlapping patches in the training of the patch-classification model.

Some work, reviewed in Section 2, e.g., Hou et al. [3] and Ruan et al. [28], chose to sample patches at differing magnification levels. Ruan et al. investigated different magnification levels as, when pathologists analyse slides, they alter the magnification level of the microscope throughout, and found sampling at a mixture of 20× and 40× magnification levels yielded the best results. However, more research could be done on different magnification level combinations alongside an optimal patch size. The same theory could also be applied to patch sizes, using a combination of patches sampled at different sizes. From the results of this work, with the largest patch size giving the best recall and the smallest the best accuracy, this could be beneficial to the accuracy of the classification and is therefore worth investigating.

Lastly, as noted in Section 4.1, the smallest patch size considered in our analysis was 256 × 256 pixels, which was a choice driven primarily by the constraint on input size of GoogLeNet. Considering that we found an overall benefit in the use of smaller patches, in future it is worth extending our work in this direction and any model constraints of the aforementioned kind circumvented by upscaling small input.

Author Contributions: Conceptualization, E.J. and O.A.; methodology, E.J. and O.A.; software, E.J.; investigation, E.J. and O.A.; resources, O.A.; data curation, E.J.; writing—original draft preparation, E.J. and O.A.; writing—review and editing, E.J. and O.A.; visualization, E.J.; supervision, O.A.; work administration, O.A. All authors have read and agreed to the published version of the manuscript.

Funding: This research received no external funding.

Institutional Review Board Statement: No ethics approval is applicable; only anonymized, publicly available data was used.

Informed Consent Statement: No informed consent is applicable; only anonymized, publicly available data was used.

Data Availability Statement: The data set used in the present article is already freely available online.

Conflicts of Interest: The authors declare no conflicts of interest.

References

1. Feng, R.; Liu, X.; Chen, J.; Chen, D.Z.; Gao, H.; Wu, J. A deep learning approach for colonoscopy pathology WSI analysis: accurate segmentation and classification. *IEEE J. Biomed. Health Inform.* **2020**, *25*, 3700–3708. [CrossRef]
2. Dimitriou, N.; Arandjelović, O. Magnifying networks for images with billions of pixels. *arXiv* **2021**, arXiv:2112.06121.
3. Hou, L.; Samaras, D.; Kurc, T.M.; Gao, Y.; Davis, J.E.; Saltz, J.H. Patch-based convolutional neural network for whole slide tissue image classification. In Proceedings of the IEEE Conference on Computer Vision and Pattern Recognition, Las Vegas, NV, USA, 26 June–1 July 2016; pp. 2424–2433.
4. Lomacenkova, A.; Arandjelović, O. Whole slide pathology image patch based deep classification: An investigation of the effects of the latent autoencoder representation and the loss function form. In Proceedings of the IEEE EMBS International Conference on Biomedical and Health Informatics, Athens, Greece, 27–30 July 2021; pp. 1–4.
5. Dimitriou, N.; Arandjelović, O.; Caie, P.D. Deep learning for whole slide image analysis: An overview. *Front. Med.* **2019**, *6*, 264. [CrossRef]
6. Komura, D.; Ishikawa, S. Machine learning methods for histopathological image analysis. *Comput. Struct. Biotechnol. J.* **2018**, *16*, 34–42. [CrossRef] [PubMed]
7. Rodriguez, J.P.M.; Rodriguez, R.; Silva, V.W.K.; Kitamura, F.C.; Corradi, G.C.A.; de Marchi, A.C.B.; Rieder, R. Artificial intelligence as a tool for diagnosis in digital pathology whole slide images: A systematic review. *J. Pathol. Inform.* **2022**, *13*, 100138. [CrossRef]
8. Jamaluddin, M.F.; Fauzi, M.F.A.; Abas, F.S. Tumor detection and whole slide classification of H&E lymph node images using convolutional neural network. In Proceedings of the IEEE International Conference on Signal and Image Processing Applications, Kuching, Malaysia, 12–14 September 2017; pp. 90–95.
9. Pantanowitz, L.; Sharma, A.; Carter, A.B.; Kurc, T.; Sussman, A.; Saltz, J. Twenty years of digital pathology: An overview of the road travelled, what is on the horizon, and the emergence of vendor-neutral archives. *J. Pathol. Inform.* **2018**, *9*, 40. [CrossRef] [PubMed]
10. Fell, C.; Mohammadi, M.; Morrison, D.; Arandjelović, O.; Caie, P.; Harris-Birtill, D. Reproducibility of deep learning in digital pathology whole slide image analysis. *PLoS Digit. Health* **2022**, *1*, 21. [CrossRef]
11. Bejnordi, B.E.; Veta, M.; Van Diest, P.J.; Van Ginneken, B.; Karssemeijer, N.; Litjens, G.; Van Der Laak, J.A.; Hermsen, M.; Manson, Q.F.; Balkenhol, M.; et al. Diagnostic assessment of deep learning algorithms for detection of lymph node metastases in women with breast cancer. *JAMA* **2017**, *318*, 2199–2210. [CrossRef]
12. Caie, P.D.; Dimitriou, N.; Arandjelović, O. Precision medicine in digital pathology via image analysis and machine learning. In *Artificial Intelligence and Deep Learning in Pathology*; Elsevier: Amsterdam, The Netherlands, 2021; pp. 149–173.
13. Mohammadi, M.; Cooper, J.; Arandjelović, O.; Fell, C.; Morrison, D.; Syed, S.; Konanahalli, P.; Bell, S.; Bryson, G.; Harrison, D.J.; et al. Weakly supervised learning and interpretability for endometrial whole slide image diagnosis. *Exp. Biol. Med.* **2022**, *247*, 2025–2037. [CrossRef] [PubMed]
14. Janowczyk, A.; Madabhushi, A. Deep learning for digital pathology image analysis: A comprehensive tutorial with selected use cases. *J. Pathol. Inform.* **2016**, *7*, 29. [CrossRef] [PubMed]
15. Deng, S.; Zhang, X.; Yan, W.; Chang, E.I.C.; Fan, Y.; Lai, M.; Xu, Y. Deep learning in digital pathology image analysis: A survey. *Front. Med.* **2020**, *14*, 470–487. [CrossRef]
16. Fell, C.; Mohammadi, M.; Morrison, D.; Arandjelović, O.; Syed, S.; Konanahalli, P.; Bell, S.; Bryson, G.; Harrison, D.J.; Harris-Birtill, D. Detection of malignancy in whole slide images of endometrial cancer biopsies using artificial intelligence. *PLoS ONE* **2023**, *18*, 28. [CrossRef]
17. Zhang, X.; Ba, W.; Zhao, X.; Wang, C.; Li, Q.; Zhang, Y.; Lu, S.; Wang, L.; Wang, S.; Song, Z.; et al. Clinical-grade endometrial cancer detection system via whole-slide images using deep learning. *Front. Oncol.* **2022**, *12*, 11. [CrossRef]
18. Bandi, P.; Geessink, O.; Manson, Q.; Van Dijk, M.; Balkenhol, M.; Hermsen, M.; Bejnordi, B.E.; Lee, B.; Paeng, K.; Zhong, A.; et al. From detection of individual metastases to classification of lymph node status at the patient level: The CAMELYON17 challenge. *IEEE Trans. Med. Imaging* **2019**, *38*, 550–560. [CrossRef]
19. Yue, X.; Dimitriou, N.; Arandjelović, O. Colorectal cancer outcome prediction from H&E whole slide images using machine learning and automatically inferred phenotype profiles. In Proceedings of the International Conference on Bioinformatics and Computational Biology, Honolulu, HI, USA, 18–20 March 2019; pp. 139–149.
20. Kumar, N.; Sharma, M.; Singh, V.P.; Madan, C.; Mehandia, S. An empirical study of handcrafted and dense feature extraction techniques for lung and colon cancer classification from histopathological images. *Biomed. Signal Process. Control* **2022**, *75*, 103596. [CrossRef]

21. Kumaraswamy, E.; Kumar, S.; Sharma, M. An Invasive Ductal Carcinomas Breast Cancer Grade Classification Using an Ensemble of Convolutional Neural Networks. *Diagnostics* **2023**, *13*, 1977. [CrossRef] [PubMed]
22. Wang, X.; Chen, H.; Gan, C.; Lin, H.; Dou, Q.; Huang, Q.; Cai, M.; Heng, P.A. Weakly supervised learning for whole slide lung cancer image classification. In Proceedings of the Medical Imaging with Deep Learning, Montreal, QC, Canada, 6–8 July 2018.
23. Khened, M.; Kori, A.; Rajkumar, H.; Krishnamurthi, G.; Srinivasan, B. A generalized deep learning framework for whole-slide image segmentation and analysis. *Sci. Rep.* **2021**, *11*, 14. [CrossRef] [PubMed]
24. Nazki, H.; Arandjelovic, O.; Um, I.H.; Harrison, D. MultiPathGAN: Structure preserving stain normalization using unsupervised multi-domain adversarial network with perception loss. In Proceedings of the 38th ACM/SIGAPP Symposium on Applied Computing, Tallinn, Estonia, 27–31 March 2023; pp. 1197–1204.
25. Kong, B.; Wang, X.; Li, Z.; Song, Q.; Zhang, S. Cancer metastasis detection via spatially structured deep network. In *Proceedings of the Information Processing in Medical Imaging: 25th International Conference*; Springer: Berlin/Heidelberg, Germany, 2017; pp. 236–248.
26. Wang, D.; Khosla, A.; Gargeya, R.; Irshad, H.; Beck, A.H. Deep learning for identifying metastatic breast cancer. *arXiv* **2016**, arXiv:1606.05718.
27. Cruz-Roa, A.; Gilmore, H.; Basavanhally, A.; Feldman, M.; Ganesan, S.; Shih, N.N.; Tomaszewski, J.; González, F.A.; Madabhushi, A. Accurate and reproducible invasive breast cancer detection in whole-slide images: A Deep Learning approach for quantifying tumor extent. *Sci. Rep.* **2017**, *7*, 14. [CrossRef]
28. Ruan, J.; Zhu, Z.; Wu, C.; Ye, G.; Zhou, J.; Yue, J. A fast and effective detection framework for whole-slide histopathology image analysis. *PLoS ONE* **2021**, *16*, 22. [CrossRef]
29. Ehteshami, B.; Geessink, O.; Hermsen, M.; Litjens, G.; van der Laak, J.; Manson, Q.; Veta, M.; Stathonikos, N. CAMELYON16—Grand Challenge. Available online: https://camelyon16.grand-challenge.org/ (accessed on 8 February 2024).
30. Wölflein, G.; Ferber, D.; Meneghetti, A.R.; El Nahhas, O.S.; Truhn, D.; Carrero, Z.I.; Harrison, D.J.; Arandjelović, O.; Kather, J.N. A Good Feature Extractor Is All You Need for Weakly Supervised Learning in Histopathology. *arXiv* **2023**, arXiv:2311.11772.
31. Fu, H.; Mi, W.; Pan, B.; Guo, Y.; Li, J.; Xu, R.; Zheng, J.; Zou, C.; Zhang, T.; Liang, Z.; et al. Automatic pancreatic ductal adenocarcinoma detection in whole slide images using deep convolutional neural networks. *Front. Oncol.* **2021**, *11*, 665929. [CrossRef] [PubMed]

BioMedInformatics

Article

Machine Learning Analysis of Genomic Factors Influencing Hyperbaric Oxygen Therapy in Parkinson's Disease

Eirini Banou, Aristidis G. Vrahatis, Marios G. Krokidis * and Panagiotis Vlamos

Bioinformatics and Human Electrophysiology Laboratory, Department of Informatics, Ionian University, 49100 Corfu, Greece; irene.banou@gmail.com (E.B.); aris.vrahatis@ionio.gr (A.G.V.); vlamos@ionio.gr (P.V.)
* Correspondence: mkrokidis@ionio.gr

Abstract: (1) Background: Parkinson's disease (PD) is a progressively worsening neurodegenerative disorder affecting movement, mental well-being, sleep, and pain. While no cure exists, treatments like hyperbaric oxygen therapy (HBOT) offer potential relief. However, the molecular biology perspective, especially when intertwined with machine learning dynamics, remains underexplored. (2) Methods: We employed machine learning techniques to analyze single-cell RNA-seq data from human PD cell samples. This approach aimed to identify pivotal genes associated with PD and understand their relationship with HBOT. (3) Results: Our analysis indicated genes such as MAP2, CAP2, and WSB1, among others, as being crucially linked with Parkinson's disease (PD) and showed their significant correlation with Hyperbaric oxygen therapy (HBOT) indicatively. This suggests that certain genomic factors might influence the efficacy of HBOT in PD treatment. (4) Conclusions: HBOT presents promising therapeutic potential for Parkinson's disease, with certain genomic factors playing a pivotal role in its efficacy. Our findings emphasize the need for further machine learning-driven research harnessing diverse omics data to better understand and treat PD.

Keywords: Parkinson's disease; hyperbaric oxygen therapy; machine learning; genomic factors; single-cell RNA-seq

Citation: Banou, E.; Vrahatis, A.G.; Krokidis, M.G.; Vlamos, P. Machine Learning Analysis of Genomic Factors Influencing Hyperbaric Oxygen Therapy in Parkinson's Disease. *BioMedInformatics* **2024**, *4*, 127–138. https://doi.org/10.3390/biomedinformatics4010009

Academic Editors: Pentti Nieminen and Alexandre G. De Brevern

Received: 31 August 2023
Revised: 1 October 2023
Accepted: 4 January 2024
Published: 9 January 2024

1. Introduction

The Parkinson's disease is characterized by a spectrum of symptoms that can differ in nature and intensity, making the prediction of treatment outcomes challenging [1]. Interestingly, the therapeutic potential of hyperbaric oxygen therapy (HBOT) for Parkinson's was sometimes identified in an unanticipated manner [2]. For example, a diabetic patient undergoing HBOT for a foot ulcer unexpectedly reported a marked alleviation in Parkinson's symptoms. Animal studies consistently indicate that HBOT exhibits anti-inflammatory properties [3], which could be beneficial in addressing the inflammatory conditions observed in the substantia nigra region of the brain in Parkinson's patients. Anecdotal evidence further suggests that some Parkinson's patients, even those with advanced stages of the disease, have shown significant improvements after HBOT sessions.

The realm of hyperbaric oxygen therapy (HBOT) in treating neurodegenerative diseases [4], particularly Parkinson's disease (PD), is burgeoning with potential. As we delve deeper into this field, a multitude of studies have emerged, shedding light on the transformative effects of HBOT on neuronal health, motor function, and overall quality of life for patients. For instance, recent research has illuminated the capacity of HBOT to target specific brain circuits, enhance neurotrophic factors, and even modulate epigenetic pathways, offering a beacon of hope for those grappling with the debilitating effects of PD.

For instance, research has demonstrated that HBOT can significantly increase the number of TH-positive neurons in MPTP-treated mice, enhancing the neurotrophic factor BDNF while reducing apoptotic signaling and attenuating inflammatory mediators in the midbrain [5]. This treatment also promotes mitochondrial biogenesis and improves locomotor activity and grip strength in these mice.

Further insights [6] highlighted the potential of HBOT in targeting specific brain circuits involved in "Kinesia Paradoxa", including the noradrenergic system, basal ganglia, and the cerebellum circuit. This study presented evidence supporting the "Norepinephrine Hypothesis", suggesting a role for HBOT in increasing norepinephrine levels, which could restore motor deficits in Parkinson's disease patients. When considering the combination of treatments, the research indicates that combining donepezil with HBOT and functional rehabilitation training can significantly enhance therapeutic effectiveness in Parkinson's disease dementia (PDD) patients. This combination not only improves cognitive function, self-care ability, and quality of life but also significantly reduces inflammatory markers like serum IL-1β and IL-6 [7].

In a broader context, the potential of HBOT as a therapeutic intervention for neurodegenerative diseases has been explored, with findings emphasizing its promising effects in conditions associated with neurodegeneration and functional impairments. A special focus has been given to the role of epigenetics in these effects [8]. Lastly, in a study focused on spinocerebellar ataxias (SCAs), HBOT was found to attenuate motor coordination and cognitive impairment in SCA17 mice, with effects persisting for about a month post-treatment. SCA17 is a rare subtype of SCAs (spinocerebellar ataxias), notable for its association with a myriad of neurological symptoms including motor coordination and cognitive impairments, often leading to a substantial reduction in the quality of life of affected individuals.

This neuroprotective effect of HBOT might be attributed to the promotion of BDNF production and the reduction of neuroinflammation [9].

Despite the promising strides made in this domain, the field is still in its infancy. The intricacies of HBOT's impact on the human brain, especially in the context of neurodegenerative diseases, remain vast and largely uncharted. While the preliminary results are indeed encouraging, they underscore the pressing need for more comprehensive, large-scale studies. Only through rigorous research, meticulous analysis, and collaborative efforts can we truly harness the full potential of HBOT and pave the way for groundbreaking therapeutic interventions in the future.

On the other hand, machine learning (ML) methodologies have been extensively applied to enhance the understanding and management of Parkinson's disease (PD). A comprehensive review of the literature reveals the utilization of ML models in conjunction with Internet of Things technologies, such as smart devices and various sensors, to optimize predictions and estimations regarding different aspects of PD [10]. These models are trained on data acquired via these technologies and address a myriad of PD-related problems, offering insights into the most effective algorithms and commonly addressed issues in PD management. Another study provides an extensive overview of the application of ML in categorizing PD, emphasizing the use of diverse data modalities and artificial intelligence techniques to facilitate informed and systematic clinical decision-making [11]. These studies collectively underscore the pivotal role of ML in advancing diagnostic processes and therapeutic interventions for PD, highlighting its potential in contributing to more nuanced and effective approaches in PD treatment and management.

The exploration of hyperbaric oxygen therapy (HBOT) in the context of Parkinson's disease (PD) has predominantly been rooted in traditional research methodologies [12]. Notably absent from this landscape is the integration of modern machine learning (ML) frameworks, which have the potential to revolutionize our understanding of the disease's intricacies [13]. While several studies have explored molecular biology to understand underlying mechanisms, many have not fully utilized advanced computational methods. Our endeavor represents a pioneering effort in this direction. By employing an ML approach, we aim to meticulously examine the behavior of key genes implicated in PD. This innovative methodology allows us to unravel the intricate relationships between these genes and the therapeutic effects of HBOT, offering a fresh perspective and potentially groundbreaking insights into the treatment of PD.

2. Materials and Methods

2.1. Dataset

In our study, we utilized single-cell RNA sequencing (scRNA-seq) data derived from the work of [14]. This dataset offers a comprehensive expression profiling of human induced pluripotent stem cell (iPSC)-derived midbrain dopaminergic neurons. These neurons were sourced from both Parkinson's disease patients and healthy controls. Novak and her team employed scRNA-seq to delve into the expression profiles of these neurons, aiming to uncover the underlying molecular networks associated with Parkinson's disease pathology. Their findings hint at a core molecular network linked to the disease, presenting a valuable resource for further exploration of this debilitating neurological disorder.

The scRNA-seq dataset under consideration comprises a total of 4495 cells, which are profiled for their expression across 18,098 genes. This extensive gene coverage ensures a comprehensive view of the transcriptional landscape of each individual cell, allowing for a detailed understanding of cellular heterogeneity and potential differences between the two conditions. The dataset is categorized into two distinct tags or conditions such as "Control" and "PD". The distribution of cells across these conditions is slightly imbalanced. The "Control" group consists of 2518 cells, which constitutes approximately 56% of the total cells. On the other hand, the "PD" group has 1977 cells, making up the remaining 44% of the dataset. This discrepancy in cell numbers between the two conditions should be taken into account during downstream analyses, especially when comparing gene expression patterns or inferring statistical significance. The presence of nearly 2000 cells in the "PD" group, despite being fewer than the "Control", still offers a substantial sample size for robust analysis. Given the depth of genes profiled, this dataset is poised to provide significant insights into the molecular differences and similarities between normal (Control) cells and those affected by Parkinson's Disease.

2.2. Hybrid Feature Selection Methodology

To ensure a comprehensive and robust feature selection, we devised a hybrid methodology that synergizes the strengths of both traditional differential gene expression (DEG) analysis and machine learning techniques. The DEG analysis offers a foundational understanding by pinpointing genes that exhibit significant expression differences, serving as an initial filter in the identification of potential key players. On the other hand, the variable importance (VI) from machine learning provides a data-driven perspective, highlighting genes that are most influential in predictive modeling. Building on these insights, we incorporated an ensemble voting scheme to establish a more robust gene ranking. This approach not only consolidates the insights from both methodologies but also prioritizes genes that are strongly associated with PD.

2.2.1. Differential Gene Expression Analysis

We initiated our feature selection process by applying the Wilcoxon test [15]. This non-parametric statistical test was used to identify genes that were differentially expressed between the PD and healthy cell samples. The Wilcoxon test, or Mann–Whitney U test, is a non-parametric method comparing the medians of two independent samples by ranking all observations and summing the ranks separately for each group to determine statistical significance. If R_1 and R_2 are the sum of ranks for the first and second groups, respectively, and n_1 and n_2 are the sizes of the two groups, the test statistic U is given by $U = n_1 n_2 + \frac{n_1(n_1+1)}{2} - R_1$. The Wilcoxon test is particularly useful when the data does not meet the assumptions of a t-test, such as when the data is not normally distributed. The outcome of the Wilcoxon test provided us with a ranked list of genes, organized based on their significance levels. We considered genes with a p-value of less than 0.05 as statistically significant. This threshold value of $p < 0.05$ is a conventional criterion in statistical hypothesis testing that helps in minimizing the Type I error, ensuring that the identified genes are truly differentially expressed and not due to random chance.

2.2.2. Machine Learning-Based Feature Selection Analysis

Regarding the machine learning-based feature selection, we used the XGBoost 2.0 Algorithm [16]. It is a gradient boosting framework, to further refine our feature selection. By training the model on our dataset, we extracted the variable importance scores for each gene. This allowed us to generate a second ranked list of genes, this time based on their importance in the predictive model. code. More specifically, XGBoost offers a robust mechanism to assess the importance of features in a predictive model through its variable importance (VI) metric. The VI in XGBoost is primarily derived from the number of times a feature is used to split the data across all trees, and the improvement it brings to the model, typically measured as the gain. Mathematically, if f_i represents a feature and $G(f_i)$ denotes the gain brought by f_i when used in splits, the importance $I(f_i)$ of the feature is proportional to the sum of gains over all splits where f_i is used: $I(f_i) \propto \sum G(f_i)$. This aggregated measure provides a ranking of features based on their contribution to the model's predictive power, allowing for the identification of the most influential predictors in the dataset. In our implementation of the XGBoost algorithm, we used a learning rate (eta) of 0.01, a max depth of 6, a subsample of 0.8, a colsample_bytree of 0.8, and built 1000 trees as the number of estimators.

2.2.3. Hybrid Ensemble Genes Ranking

To combine the insights from both the Wilcoxon test and the XGBoost algorithm, we utilized the Borda count, a consensus-based ensemble voting scheme [17]. By taking the two ranked gene lists from the previous steps, the Borda count method allowed us to derive a more robust and consolidated ranking. This combined ranking leverages the dynamics of both statistical testing and machine learning, ensuring a comprehensive selection of features that are both statistically significant and relevant for predictive modeling. The Borda count operates on the principle of assigning points to items (in this case, genes) based on their rank. For a given gene list of n genes, the top-ranked gene receives n points, the next receives $n-1$ points, and so on, with the last-ranked gene receiving 1 point.

Let us denote the ranking from the Wilcoxon test as R_W and from the XGBoost algorithm as R_X. For a particular gene g_i, its Borda count score $B(g_i)$ is computed as:

$$B(g_i) = n - R_W(g_i) + 1 + n - R_X(g_i) + 1,$$

where $R_W(g_i)$ and $R_X(g_i)$ represent the ranks of gene gigi in the Wilcoxon and XGBoost rankings, respectively. After computing the Borda count scores for all genes, we can then rank them based on these scores to derive a consolidated ranking. This ensemble approach ensures that genes which are both statistically significant (from the Wilcoxon test) and important for predictive modeling (from XGBoost) receive higher ranks, providing a more robust and comprehensive feature selection.

3. Results and Discussion

We ended up with a combined list of genes (Table S1) that are strongly related to PD and decided to explore closely at the top 100 genes since it's been demonstrated that in scRNA-seq, typically only a few dozen to a couple of hundred genes play a pivotal role in the dataset [18]. Also, focusing on the top 100 genes facilitated a more in-depth exploration of their biological functions, interactions, and roles in the context of the study, allowing for more meaningful interpretations and conclusions.

Also, by concentrating on the top genes, we're likely capturing the most important ones that have the biggest impact on PD. A key part of our study was to see how these genes are related to HBOT. This is important because if we know which genes are affected by this therapy, it could help doctors treat PD more effectively in the future.

Our study had three four parts. First, we examine the classification performance using the 100 key genes regarding differentiating healthy samples from Parkinson's disease samples. Furthermore, we looked at how HBOT affects each of the top 100 genes one by one. This helped us figure out which specific genes might be good targets for treatment. Next, we checked how our chosen genes fit into bigger groups of genes and how they might be linked to other diseases or treatments. This gave us a better idea of the bigger picture and how these genes work in the body. Lastly, we used a simple visual tool zooming out of the genes to show how our top genes are connected to each other along with the associated gene ontologies.

3.1. Classification Performance of Leading Genes

We investigated the role of specific genes in understanding the difference between healthy cells and those affected by Parkinson's disease. After we had our list of 100 genes, we used a tool called PyCaret to see how well we could separate or tell apart the healthy cells from the PD ones using only these genes (Figure 1). PyCaret offers a variety of classifiers for comparison in its classification module, such as logistic regression, K nearest neighbor (KNN), naive bayes, decision tree, random forest, gradient boosting machines, support vector machines (SVM), linear discriminant analysis (LDA), quadratic discriminant analysis (QDA), ridge classifier, extreme gradient boosting (XGBoost), light gradient boosting machine (LightGBM), catboost, adaboost, extra trees, stochastic gradient descent (SGD), and dummy classifier.

Model	Accuracy	AUC	Recall	Prec.	F1	Kappa	MCC	TT (Sec)
Logistic Regression	0.9959	0.9997	0.9964	0.9943	0.9953	0.9916	0.9917	34.7730
CatBoost Classifier	0.9956	1.0000	0.9964	0.9935	0.9950	0.9910	0.9910	98.5940
Extreme Gradient Boosting	0.9952	0.9998	0.9964	0.9928	0.9946	0.9903	0.9903	32.6920
Light Gradient Boosting Machine	0.9933	0.9998	0.9949	0.9900	0.9924	0.9865	0.9865	16.1080
Gradient Boosting Classifier	0.9914	0.9997	0.9906	0.9899	0.9902	0.9826	0.9826	27.2380
Ada Boost Classifier	0.9911	0.9996	0.9863	0.9935	0.9898	0.9819	0.9820	10.8870
SVM - Linear Kernel	0.9832	0.0000	0.9812	0.9807	0.9809	0.9658	0.9660	3.5550
Random Forest Classifier	0.9828	0.9991	0.9920	0.9699	0.9808	0.9653	0.9656	3.5500
Extra Trees Classifier	0.9746	0.9982	0.9863	0.9575	0.9716	0.9486	0.9491	4.5160
Decision Tree Classifier	0.9622	0.9616	0.9566	0.9575	0.9570	0.9232	0.9233	4.0940
Ridge Classifier	0.9431	0.0000	0.9097	0.9590	0.9336	0.8839	0.8849	4.6020
K Neighbors Classifier	0.9428	0.9818	0.9668	0.9097	0.9372	0.8848	0.8865	4.6390
Naive Bayes	0.8856	0.8979	1.0000	0.7953	0.8855	0.7744	0.7955	3.6570
Dummy Classifier	0.5601	0.5000	0.0000	0.0000	0.0000	0.0000	0.0000	2.5160
Quadratic Discriminant Analysis	0.4673	0.5117	0.8815	0.4471	0.5922	0.0214	0.0350	17.2700

Figure 1. Comprehensive classification performance of the top 100 genes. The figure displays the outcomes from 15 well-known classifiers, evaluated based on 7 performance measures alongside their execution time. This analysis underscores the efficacy of our selected genes in distinguishing between PD and healthy samples across diverse machine learning models.

The primary contribution of this task lies in its comprehensive examination of the performance of multiple classifiers in discerning between Parkinson's Disease and healthy cell states using the identified key genes. By leveraging a diverse set of classifiers, ranging from logistic regression to more complex models like CatBoost and Gradient Boosting Machines, we were able to gauge the robustness and reliability of these key genes as discriminative features. This approach not only underscores the significance of the selected genes but also provides a holistic view of their potential in different machine learning paradigms. The ability of these genes to consistently separate PD from healthy samples across various classifiers reinforces their importance in the realm of Parkinson's Disease research. This task, therefore, serves as a foundational step in understanding the potential of these genes as biomarkers and offers a blueprint for future studies aiming to harness the power of machine learning in biomedical research.

Our results were pretty clear. By using the top 100 genes we identified, the tool was able to clearly tell the difference between healthy and PD cells. This means that these genes are really important and can be key players in understanding Parkinson's Disease. In simple words, our study shows that with the right genes, we can easily spot the difference between a healthy cell and one that is affected by PD.

3.2. Gene-Based Analysis

The 100 genes derived from our analysis were individually examined to determine their established or potential links with Parkinson's disease and the impacts of HBOT. This targeted approach was designed to elucidate the molecular underpinnings that might be at play in the therapeutic response of Parkinson's patients to HBOT, providing a deeper understanding of the disease mechanism and potential intervention points. Furthermore, the distribution and the associations among the top 10 genes is illustrated in Figure 2 showing their potential in our framework.

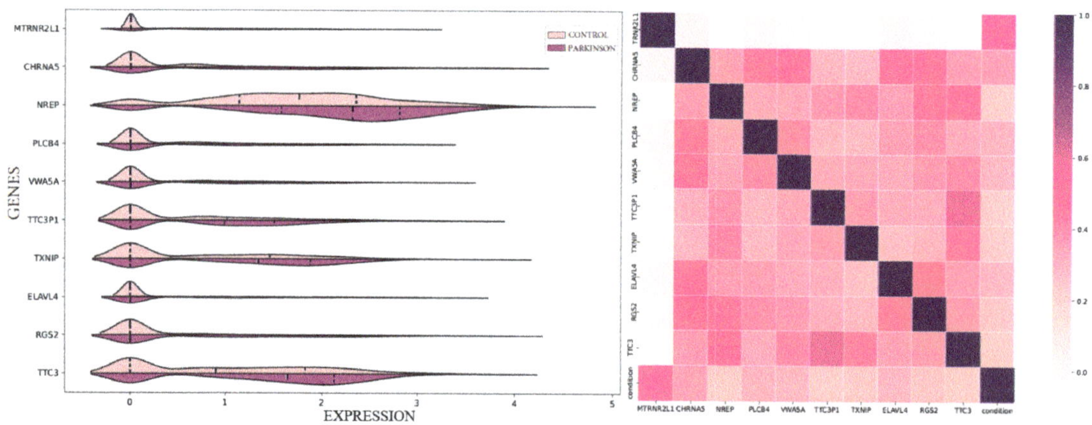

Figure 2. Comparative analysis of the 10 dominant genes. On the **left**, a violin plot illustrates the distribution of expression levels for each gene, highlighting their prominence in our framework. On the **right**, a heatmap showcases the correlation patterns among these genes, providing insights into their interrelated dynamics.

More specifically, TXNIP (Thioredoxin Interacting Protein) plays a pivotal role in the regulation of cellular redox balance [19]. By binding to thioredoxin, a primary antioxidant protein, TXNIP inhibits its antioxidant function, potentially leading to heightened oxidative stress within cells. This interaction becomes particularly relevant in the context of hyperbaric oxygen therapy (HBOT). Given that HBOT involves the administration of oxygen at elevated pressures, there's an inherent increase in the production of reactive oxygen species (ROS). As oxidative stress is a recognized factor in the pathogenesis of Parkinson's Disease, the modulation of this stress, potentially influenced by TXNIP, might be crucial in determining cellular responses to HBOT and its therapeutic implications for PD.

The ELAVL4 (ELAV Like RNA Binding Protein 4) gene, a member of the ELAVL family of RNA-binding proteins, is predominantly expressed in neurons [20]. Its primary function revolves around stabilizing mRNA, a process integral to neuronal differentiation and maintenance. In the realm of HBOT, where there's a proposed neuroprotective effect primarily through enhanced oxygen delivery to hypoxic tissues, ELAVL4's role in neuronal maintenance becomes significant. Neurons, when exposed to increased oxygen levels during HBOT, might leverage the stabilizing influence of ELAVL4, underscoring its potential importance. Furthermore, in neurodegenerative conditions like Parkinson's, where neuronal health is paramount, genes like ELAVL4 that bolster neuronal function could offer insights into disease progression and therapeutic responses.

Lastly, XBP1 (X-Box Binding Protein 1), a transcription factor, is activated as part of the unfolded protein response (UPR) [21]. The UPR is a cellular mechanism triggered by the accumulation of unfolded or misfolded proteins within the endoplasmic reticulum (ER). The relevance of XBP1 in HBOT stems from the therapy's potential to induce oxidative modifications to proteins, which can lead to their misfolding. As the UPR aims to restore cellular function in the face of such protein stress, XBP1 might be a key player in this restoration process. This becomes even more pertinent in Parkinson's Disease, where protein misfolding and aggregation are hallmark features. The potential activation of the UPR, and by extension the role of XBP1, could shed light on how Parkinsonian brain cells respond to both protein aggregation and treatments like HBOT.

3.3. Enrichment Analysis in Gene Ontologies, Disease and Pharmaceutical Terms

We conducted an enrichment analysis on the leading genes to ascertain if there was a notable overlap with predefined gene sets from established ontologies (Figure 3). We employed the EnrichR platform [22] to analyze our gene set in the context of GO cellular component processes, pathway maps, drug descriptors, and disease terms. EnrichR is a comprehensive web-based and mobile application that offers a range of gene-set libraries, a unique ranking method for enriched terms, and diverse visualization techniques for results presentation. The platform encompasses 35 gene-set libraries, accounting for a total of 31,026 gene-sets that span the entire human and mouse genome and proteome. Typically, each gene-set contains approximately 350 genes, leading to over six million interconnections between terms and genes. For the enrichment analysis, EnrichR utilizes the Fisher exact test, a standard method prevalent in many enrichment analysis tools. This test, based on a binomial distribution, evaluates the likelihood of a gene's association with a particular set, assuming independence.

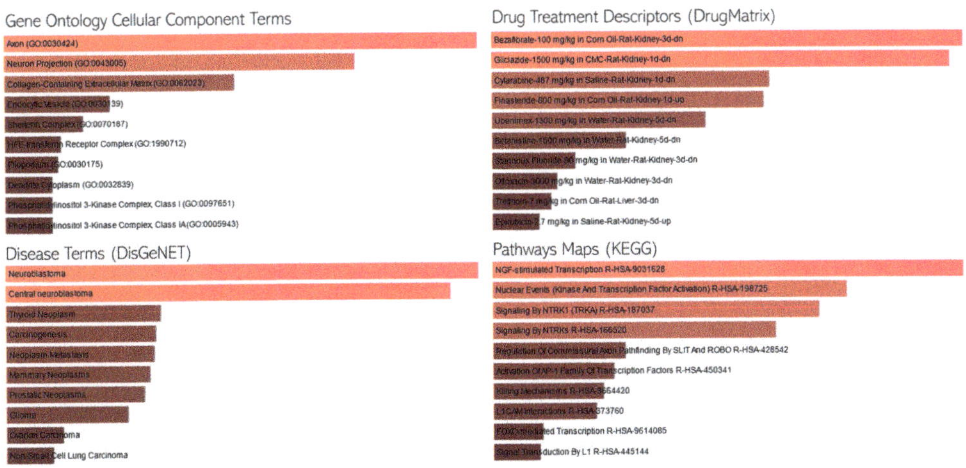

Figure 3. Enrichment Analysis of the Top 100 Genes. This figure presents the association of our selected genes with various gene ontology (GO) terms, disease annotations, and pharmaceutical implications. Longer bars indicate greater statistical significance, highlighting the genes' multifaceted roles and potential therapeutic significance in the broader biological and medical context.

Enrichment analysis in KEGG pathway terms reveals several intriguing pathways. Indicatively, the "NGF-stimulated Transcription R-HSA-9031628" pathway suggests a role in neurotrophic factor signaling, which is crucial for neuronal survival and has been implicated in Parkinson's disease [23]. Neurotrophic factors could potentially be modulated by HBOT, leading to neuroprotective effects. Additionally, the "Serotonin and Melatonin Biosynthesis R-HSA-209931" pathway is noteworthy, given that serotoninergic system dysfunction is often observed in Parkinson's disease, and HBOT might influence neurotransmitter levels or their biosynthetic pathways. Both pathways provide valuable insights into the potential mechanisms through which HBOT could exert therapeutic effects in Parkinson's disease.

Upon examining the GO cellular component terms, several cellular structures and complexes emerge as potentially relevant. Specifically, the term "Axon (GO:0030424)" is of particular interest, as axonal degeneration is a hallmark of Parkinson's disease, and any therapeutic intervention, including HBOT, that can influence axonal health could be beneficial. Similarly, "Neuron Projection (GO:0043005)" is another term that stands out, given that the integrity of neuronal projections is vital for proper neuronal communication, and its disruption is observed in Parkinson's disease [24]. HBOT's potential to modulate or protect these neuronal structures could provide a mechanistic insight into its therapeutic effects in the context of Parkinson's disease.

Regarding the drug terms, certain drugs emerge as potentially relevant in the context of Parkinson's disease and HBOT. Notably, epinephrine (adrenaline) plays a role in the autonomic nervous system and its dysregulation is observed in Parkinson's disease. The potential modulation of epinephrine levels or its pathways by HBOT could provide insights into its therapeutic effects. Several disease conditions stand out in the context of Parkinson's disease and HBOT. "Neuroblastoma" is particularly noteworthy, as it is a neural tumor that could provide insights into the neural mechanisms potentially influenced by HBOT. Additionally, "Glioma," another type of brain tumor, is of interest, given that any therapeutic intervention, including HBOT, that can influence neural health or growth mechanisms could be beneficial in understanding its broader implications for neurological conditions like Parkinson's disease.

These findings not only elucidate the potential biological processes influenced by the dominant genes separating PD from healthy states but also offer a preliminary understanding of how HBOT might interact with these processes. Further studies could dive deeper into these associations, paving the way for targeted therapeutic strategies in PD.

3.4. Graph-Based Analysis—Interconnectivity and Associations

In our graph-based analysis (Figure 4), we focused on understanding the relationships between genes and their associated gene ontologies, which describe their roles in molecular functions and broader biological processes. A key aspect of this was examining gene-gene interactions using protein-protein interaction (PPI) networks. These PPI networks provide a structured representation of how proteins, and by extension the genes that code for them, interact within a cell. By mapping our selected genes onto these networks, we gained insights into potential functional relationships that these genes might have with one another.

Alongside this, we aimed to determine how our genes fit within larger biological contexts. To do this, we conducted an enrichment analysis, which checks if certain biological categories or functions are more common among our selected genes than would be expected by chance [25]. It uses the standard hypergeometric distribution test, also known as the Fisher exact test, for this purpose, a widely accepted statistical method in gene enrichment analysis. By comparing our gene set to reference sets, this test helped us identify specific biological processes or molecular functions that our genes are likely involved in.

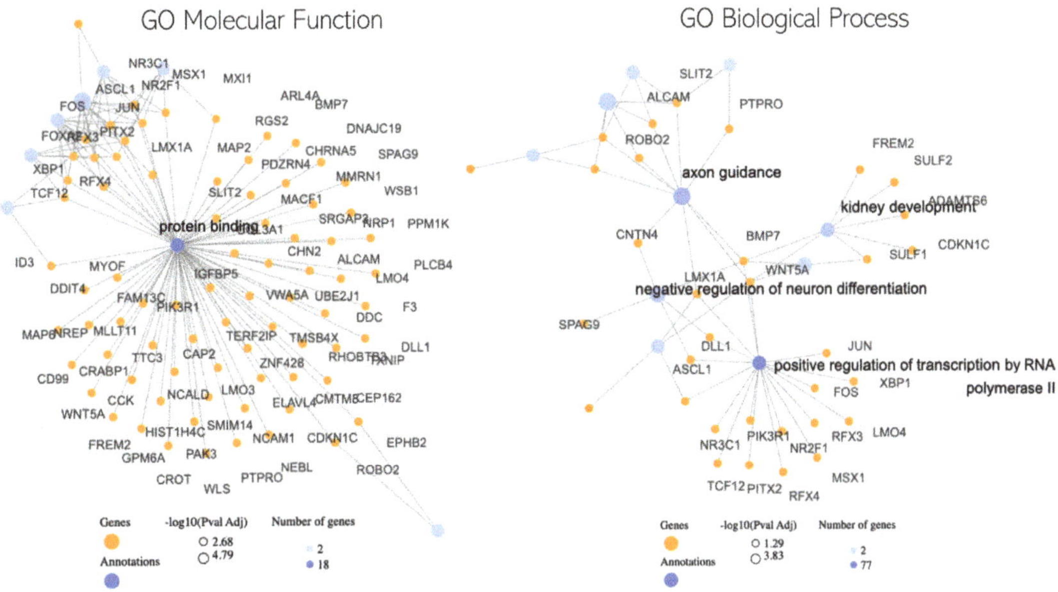

Figure 4. Interconnectivity Graph of the Top 100 Genes. This visualization depicts the Protein–protein Interaction (PPI) associations among our significant genes, emphasizing their interconnected roles. Additionally, key gene ontologies are highlighted as hubs, demonstrating their central role in bridging multiple significant genes and underscoring their biological importance.

In our exploration of the potential molecular interplay between hyperbaric oxygen therapy (HBOT) and Parkinson's disease (PD), the graph-based analysis has revealed several noteworthy findings. The central observation is the pronounced role of the "Protein Binding" term. Acting as a hub, this term suggests a nexus of interactions, with several genes like MAP2, CAP2, and WSB1 being pivotal [26–28]. The hub-like nature of "Protein Binding" implies that these genes might be central to many protein–protein interactions, potentially modulating a variety of cellular processes that could be influenced by HBOT in the context of PD [29].

Among these genes, for instance, MAP2 is known for its role in stabilizing microtubules [30], which are essential for maintaining cell structure and facilitating intracellular transport. Any modulation in its activity could impact neuronal health and function, making it a potential target of interest in PD and its response to HBOT. Furthermore, other gene ontology (GO) terms that stood out include "axon guidance" [31], "negative regulation of neuron differentiation" [32], and "positive regulation of transcription by RNA polymerase II" [33]. The presence of "axon guidance" is particularly intriguing, as it plays a crucial role in the proper formation of neural circuits. Disruptions in this process could contribute to neurodegenerative conditions like PD. The regulation of neuron differentiation and transcription further suggests that HBOT might influence the broader landscape of gene expression and neuronal development in PD.

In considering the translational potential of our findings, it is pivotal to acknowledge the prospective clinical implications. The identified genomic correlations with hyperbaric oxygen therapy (HBOT) in Parkinson's disease (PD) suggest avenues for the development of personalized and optimized treatment strategies, potentially enhancing therapeutic outcomes and patient quality of life. These genomic insights could inform the creation of targeted therapies and predictive models, allowing for individualized treatment plans based on specific genomic profiles. However, the realization of these clinical applications necessitates rigorous validation through clinical trials, collaborative integration into clinical workflows, adherence to ethical and regulatory standards, and comprehensive educational outreach to stakeholders about the benefits and limitations of such interventions.

Our study, while offering significant insights, is subject to several limitations. The single-cell RNA-seq data utilized may not fully capture the intricate cellular heterogeneity inherent to Parkinson's disease due to its inherent resolution and depth limitations, and the public datasets employed may harbor biases stemming from variations in sample collection, processing, and sequencing technologies across different studies. Additionally, the machine learning techniques applied in our analysis are susceptible to biases from the training data, model assumptions, and algorithmic constraints, potentially impacting the reliability of our identified gene correlations. Furthermore, the generalizability of our findings is constrained, necessitating validation in diverse and larger Parkinson's disease populations to confirm their universal applicability and clinical relevance.

4. Conclusions

Our comprehensive study, integrating both traditional and machine learning methodologies, has shed light on the intricate molecular landscape underpinning Parkinson's disease (PD) and its potential modulation by hyperbaric oxygen therapy (HBOT). By synergizing differential gene expression analysis with machine learning techniques, we've identified pivotal genes, such as MAP2, SLIT2, CAP2, DDC, WSB1, and MYOF, that play significant roles in PD and may be influenced by HBOT. The pronounced role of the "Protein Binding" term, acting as a hub in our analysis, underscores the importance of protein–protein interactions in understanding the therapeutic potential of HBOT in PD.

Furthermore, our exploration into gene ontologies and pathways, such as "axon guidance" and "negative regulation of neuron differentiation," has provided insights into the broader biological processes that might be at play. The enrichment analysis, leveraging the Fisher exact test, has highlighted potential biological pathways and drug interactions that could be pivotal in understanding the therapeutic mechanisms of HBOT in PD. In essence, our findings emphasize the intricate interplay of genes, pathways, and cellular processes in PD and how they might be modulated by HBOT. This research not only offers a deeper understanding of the molecular mechanisms of PD but also paves the way for future studies aiming to optimize therapeutic strategies for this debilitating neurodegenerative disorder.

Supplementary Materials: The following supporting information can be downloaded at: https://www.mdpi.com/article/10.3390/biomedinformatics4010009/s1, Table S1: List of genes that were found to be significant in the present approaches.

Author Contributions: Conceptualization, E.B. and P.V.; methodology, E.B. and A.G.V.; software, E.B.; validation, A.G.V. and M.G.K.; formal analysis, E.B. and A.G.V.; data curation, E.B. and A.G.V.; writing—original draft preparation, E.B. and A.G.V.; writing—review and editing, M.G.K. and P.V.; supervision, P.V.; funding acquisition, P.V. All authors have read and agreed to the published version of the manuscript.

Funding: This research is funded by the European Union and Greece (Partnership Agreement for the Development Framework 2014–2020) under the Regional Operational Programme Ionian Islands 2014–2020, project title: "Study of Clinical trial protocols with biomarkers that define the evolution of non-genetic neurodegenerative diseases- NEUROTRIAL", project number: 5016089.

Institutional Review Board Statement: Not applicable.

Informed Consent Statement: Not applicable.

Data Availability Statement: This study uses a public dataset available at Gene Expression Omnibus. The data presented in this study are available on request from the corresponding author.

Conflicts of Interest: The authors declare no conflicts of interest.

References

1. Bloem, B.R.; Okun, M.S.; Klein, C. Parkinso n's disease. *Lancet* **2021**, *397*, 2284–2303. [CrossRef] [PubMed]
2. Wilmshurst, P.; Bewley, S.; Murray, P. Hyperbaric oxygen therapy for the treatment of long COVID. *Clin. Med.* **2023**, *23*, 99–100. [CrossRef] [PubMed]
3. Taslipinar, M.Y.; Aydin, I.; Kaldirim, U.; Aydin, F.N.; Agilli, M.; Eyi, Y.E.; Cayci, T. Hyperbaric oxygen treatment and N-acetylcysteine ameliorate acetaminophen-induced liver injury in a rat model. *Hum. Exp. Toxicol.* **2013**, *32*, 1107–1116. [CrossRef] [PubMed]
4. Kidd, P.M. Multiple sclerosis, an autoimmune inflammatory disease: Prospects for its integrative management. *Altern. Med. Rev.* **2001**, *6*, 540–566. [PubMed]
5. Hsu, H.T.; Yang, Y.L.; Chang, W.H.; Fang, W.Y.; Huang, S.H.; Chou, S.H.; Lo, Y.C. Hyperbaric oxygen therapy improves Parkinson's disease by promoting mitochondrial biogenesis via the SIRT-1/PGC-1α pathway. *Biomolecules* **2022**, *12*, 661. [CrossRef]
6. Banou, E. Hyperbaric oxygen therapy effect on "Kinesia Paradoxa" brain circuits. GeNeDis 2020: Genetics and Neurodegenerative Diseases. *GeNeDis 2020: Genet. Neurodegener. Dis.* 2021; 1339, 139–146.
7. Fan, A.; Zhou, J. Effect of the combination of donepezil with hyperbaric oxygen therapy and functional rehabilitation training on parkinson's disease dementia and the neurological function system. *Int. J. Clin. Exp. Med.* **2020**, *13*, 5867–5875.
8. Mensah-Kane, P.; Sumien, N. The potential of hyperbaric oxygen as a therapy for neurodegenerative diseases. *GeroScience* **2023**, *45*, 747–756. [CrossRef]
9. Shi, Q.; Luo, Q.; Gong, Q.; Wang, G. Effects of rTMS Combined with Hyperbaric Oxygen-acupuncture-rehabilitation Therapy on Motor Function, Serum CRP and Plasma Dopamine in Patients with Parkinson's Disease. *Chin. Gen. Pract.* **2020**, *23*, 3460.
10. Giannakopoulou, K.M.; Roussaki, I.; Demestichas, K. Internet of things technologies and machine learning methods for Parkinson's disease diagnosis, monitoring and management: A systematic review. *Sensors* **2022**, *22*, 1799. [CrossRef]
11. Rana, A.; Dumka, A.; Singh, R.; Panda, M.K.; Priyadarshi, N.; Twala, B. Imperative role of machine learning algorithm for detection of Parkinson's disease: Review, challenges and recommendations. *Diagnostics* **2022**, *12*, 2003. [CrossRef]
12. Atzeni, F.; Masala, I.F.; Cirillo, M.; Boccassini, L.; Sorbara, S.; Alciati, A. Hyperbaric oxygen therapy in fibromyalgia and the diseases involving the central nervous system. *Clin. Exp. Rheumatol.* **2020**, *38*, 0094–0098.
13. Quazi, S. Artificial intelligence and machine learning in precision and genomic medicine. *Med. Oncol.* **2022**, *39*, 120. [CrossRef] [PubMed]
14. Novak, G.; Kyriakis, D.; Grzyb, K.; Bernini, M. Single-cell transcriptomics of human iPSC differentiation dynamics reveal a core molecular network of Parkinson's disease. *Commun. Biol.* **2022**, *5*, 49. [CrossRef] [PubMed]
15. Li, Y.; Ge, X.; Peng, F.; Li, W.; Li, J.J. Wilcoxon rank-sum test still outperforms dearseq after accounting for the normalization impact in semi-synthetic RNA-seq data simulation. *bioRxiv* **2022**, 2022-06. [CrossRef]
16. Chen, T.; He, T.; Benesty, M.; Khotilovich, V.; Tang, Y.; Cho, H.; Zhou, T. Xgboost: Extreme gradient boosting. *R Package Version 0.4-2* **2015**, *1*, 1–4.
17. Paplomatas, P.; Krokidis, M.G.; Vlamos, P.; Vrahatis, A.G. An ensemble feature selection approach for analysis and modeling of transcriptome data in alzheimer's disease. *Appl. Sci.* **2023**, *13*, 2353. [CrossRef]
18. Chatzilygeroudis, K.I.; Vrahatis, A.G.; Tasoulis, S.K.; Vrahatis, M.N. Feature Selection in single-cell RNA-seq data via a Genetic Algorithm. In Proceedings of the Learning and Intelligent Optimization: 15th International Conference, LION 15, Athens, Greece, 20–25 June 2021; Revised Selected Papers 15. Springer International Publishing: Berlin/Heidelberg, Germany, 2021; pp. 66–79.
19. Tezgin, D.; Giardina, C.; Perdrizet, G.A.; Hightower, L.E. The effect of hyperbaric oxygen on mitochondrial and glycolytic energy metabolism: The caloristasis concept. *Cell Stress Chaperones* **2020**, *25*, 667–677. [CrossRef]
20. Bowles, K.R.; Silva, M.C.; Whitney, K.; Bertucci, T.; Berlind, J.E.; Lai, J.D.; Temple, S. ELAVL4, splicing, and glutamatergic dysfunction precede neuron loss in MAPT mutation cerebral organoids. *Cell* **2021**, *184*, 4547–4563. [CrossRef]
21. Iwakoshi, N.N.; Lee, A.H.; Glimcher, L.H. The X-box binding protein-1 transcription factor is required for plasma cell differentiation and the unfolded protein response. *Immunol. Rev.* **2003**, *194*, 29–38. [CrossRef]
22. Chen, E.Y.; Tan, C.M.; Kou, Y.; Duan, Q.; Wang, Z.; Meirelles, G.V.; Ma'ayan, A. Enrichr: Interactive and collaborative HTML5 gene list enrichment analysis tool. *BMC Bioinform.* **2013**, *14*, 1–14. [CrossRef]
23. Zhou, L.; Too, H.P. Mitochondrial localized STAT3 is involved in NGF induced neurite outgrowth. *PLoS ONE* **2011**, *6*, e21680. [CrossRef] [PubMed]
24. Braak, H.; Braak, E. Pathoanatomy of Parkinson's disease. *J. Neurol.* **2000**, *247*, II3–II10. [CrossRef] [PubMed]
25. Garcia-Moreno, A.; López-Domínguez, R.; Villatoro-García, J.A.; Ramirez-Mena, A.; Aparicio-Puerta, E.; Hackenberg, M.; Pascual-Montano, A.; Carmona-Saez, P. Functional Enrichment Analysis of Regulatory Elements. *Biomedicines* **2022**, *10*, 590. [CrossRef] [PubMed]
26. D'Andrea, M.R.; Ilyin, S.; Plata-Salaman, C.R. Abnormal patterns of microtubule-associated protein-2 (MAP-2) immunolabeling in neuronal nuclei and Lewy bodies in Parkinson's disease substantia nigra brain tissues. *Neurosci. Lett.* **2001**, *306*, 137–140. [CrossRef] [PubMed]
27. Di Maio, A.; De Rosa, A.; Pelucchi, S.; Garofalo, M.; Marciano, B.; Nuzzo, T.; Usiello, A. Analysis of mRNA and protein levels of CAP2, DLG1 and ADAM10 genes in post-mortem brain of schizophrenia, Parkinson's and Alzheimer's disease patients. *Int. J. Mol. Sci.* **2022**, *23*, 1539. [CrossRef] [PubMed]

28. Nucifora Jr, F.C.; Nucifora, L.G.; Ng, C.H.; Arbez, N.; Guo, Y.; Roby, E.; Ross, C.A. Ubiqutination via K27 and K29 chains signals aggregation and neuronal protection of LRRK2 by WSB1. *Nat. Commun.* **2016**, *7*, 11792. [CrossRef] [PubMed]
29. Ruf, W.P.; Freischmidt, A.; Grozdanov, V.; Roth, V.; Brockmann, S.J.; Mollenhauer, B.; Danzer, K.M. Protein binding partners of dysregulated miRNAs in Parkinson's Disease Serum. *Cells* **2021**, *10*, 791. [CrossRef] [PubMed]
30. Dehmelt, L.; Halpain, S. The MAP2/Tau family of microtubule-associated proteins. *Genome Biol.* **2005**, *6*, 1–10.
31. Lesnick, T.G.; Papapetropoulos, S.; Mash, D.C.; Ffrench-Mullen, J.; Shehadeh, L.; De Andrade, M.; Maraganore, D.M. A genomic pathway approach to a complex disease: Axon guidance and Parkinson disease. *PLoS Genet.* **2007**, *3*, e98. [CrossRef]
32. Pirooznia, S.K.; Wang, H.; Panicker, N.; Kumar, M.; Neifert, S.; Dar, M.A.; Dawson, T.M. Deubiquitinase CYLD acts as a negative regulator of dopamine neuron survival in Parkinson's disease. *Sci. Adv.* **2022**, *8*, eabh1824. [CrossRef]
33. Majidinia, M.; Mihanfar, A.; Rahbarghazi, R.; Nourazarian, A.; Bagca, B.; Avci, Ç.B. The roles of non-coding RNAs in Parkinson's disease. *Mol. Biol. Rep.* **2016**, *43*, 1193–1204. [CrossRef] [PubMed]

BioMedInformatics

Article

Weighted Trajectory Analysis and Application to Clinical Outcome Assessment

Utkarsh Chauhan [1], Kaiqiong Zhao [2], John Walker [3] and John R. Mackey [3,*]

1 Faculty of Medicine and Dentistry, University of Alberta, Edmonton, AB T6G 2R7, Canada; uchauhan@ualberta.ca
2 Department of Mathematics and Statistics, York University, Toronto, ON M3J 1P3, Canada; kaiqiong@ualberta.ca
3 Division of Medical Oncology, Cross Cancer Institute, University of Alberta, 11560 University Ave NW, Edmonton, AB T6G 1Z2, Canada; john.walker2@albertahealthservices.ca
* Correspondence: jmackey@ualberta.ca

Abstract: The Kaplan–Meier (KM) estimator is widely used in medical research to estimate the survival function from lifetime data. KM estimation is a powerful tool to evaluate clinical trials due to simple computational requirements, its use of a logrank hypothesis test, and the ability to censor patients. However, KM estimation has several constraints and fails to generalize to ordinal variables of clinical interest, such as toxicity and ECOG performance. We devised weighted trajectory analysis (WTA) to combine the advantages of KM estimation with the ability to visualize and compare treatment groups for ordinal variables and fluctuating outcomes. To assess statistical significance, we developed a new hypothesis test analogous to the logrank test. We demonstrated the functionality of WTA through 1000-fold clinical trial simulations of unique stochastic models of chemotherapy toxicity and schizophrenia disease course. With increments in sample size and hazard ratio, we compared the performance of WTA to KM estimation and the generalized estimating equation (GEE). WTA generally required half the sample size to achieve comparable power to KM estimation; advantages over the GEE included its robust nonparametric approach and summary plot. We also applied WTA to real clinical data: the toxicity outcomes of melanoma patients receiving immunotherapy and the disease progression of patients with metastatic breast cancer receiving ramucirumab. The application of WTA demonstrated that using traditional methods such as KM estimation can lead to both type I and II errors by failing to model illness trajectory. This article outlines a novel method for clinical outcome assessment that extends the advantages of Kaplan–Meier estimates to ordinal outcome variables.

Keywords: weighted trajectory analysis; Kaplan–Meier estimator; clinical outcome assessment; logrank test; ordinal variables

Citation: Chauhan, U.; Zhao, K.; Walker, J.; Mackey, J.R. Weighted Trajectory Analysis and Application to Clinical Outcome Assessment. *BioMedInformatics* **2023**, 3, 829–852. https://doi.org/10.3390/biomedinformatics3040052

Academic Editors: Pentti Nieminen and Alexandre G. De Brevern

Received: 11 August 2023
Revised: 1 September 2023
Accepted: 25 September 2023
Published: 7 October 2023

1. Introduction

The Kaplan–Meier (KM) estimator [1], also referred to as the product-limit estimator, is widely used in medical research to estimate the survival function from lifetime data. KM estimation is a nonparametric approach for time-to-event data, which are often not normally distributed. To generate the KM estimates, the time-to-event and the status of each subject at the last observed timepoint are needed [2]. The event of interest may be death from any cause when we are determining overall survival and death due to a specific cause for cause-specific survival. KM estimates are frequently used in oncology and other medical disciplines. KM estimation is used to compare two or more treatment arms in clinical trials using the logrank test [3]. Patients that exit the trial without having experienced the event of interest at the last follow up are censored and omitted from further estimates.

The relatively simple computational requirements for KM estimation provide a powerful method to estimate time-to-event data. However, the advantages of KM estimation in clinical research cannot be extended to important ordinal outcomes, such as toxicity grade and Eastern Cooperative Oncology Group (ECOG) performance status [4]. Ordinal outcome variables are ubiquitous in medicine in the measurement of patient health status over time, but no statistical methods exist that combine censoring, graphical comparison of trajectories, and hypothesis testing for these variables. Often, ordinal clinical outcomes are collapsed to binary definitions to facilitate the use of KM estimation; this causes information loss, introduces an arbitrary cutpoint, and may lead to inaccurate conclusions. New methods are required to map the trajectory of ordinal outcomes and compare treatment arms in clinical trials.

The KM method has three conditions that limit its generalizability to other variables of interest in clinical research:

1. **Binary Condition**
   The event must be binary in nature or coded into binary form (0 for non-occurrence, 1 for occurrence). It is not possible to capture grades or stages of severity. For example, death is naturally binary (0 for alive, 1 for dead), but an outcome variable such as toxicity (measured in grades from zero to four) must be coded into binary form by setting a threshold for event occurrence, such as arbitrarily defining an event as any toxicity exceeding grade two;
2. **Descent Condition**
   Event occurrence always produces a drop in the KM curve (a consequence of plotting probability). It is not possible to track the trajectory of conditions that can both improve and worsen over time. For example, patients experiencing rising toxicity due to chemotherapy require additional interventions to tolerate therapy. The interventions may initially improve symptoms and reduce toxicity grade but fail to sustain benefits in subsequent treatment cycles. For a KM estimate following the above example, this complex trajectory would be simplified to an event occurrence the first time toxicity increases beyond grade two;
3. **Finality Condition**
   Once a patient experiences the event of interest, they are omitted from any subsequent analysis.

Weighted trajectory analysis (WTA) is a method that combines the simplicity and practicality of KM estimation with the ability to compare treatment groups for ordinal variables and bidirectional outcomes. Trajectories are presented using plots that track health status for treatment arms over time. WTA permits the censoring of patients that exit the study. To determine statistical significance, we developed a "weighted" logrank test.

In Section 2, we describe the methodology and theory of KM estimation and WTA, along with their respective hypothesis tests, and provide a computational approach to WTA that is robust with smaller datasets. We also outline GEE longitudinal analysis prior to its use as an additional comparator against WTA in subsequent simulation studies. In Sections 3 and 4, we describe unique simulation studies with chemotherapy toxicity grade and schizophrenia symptom stage as the variables of interest, respectively. In Section 5, we apply WTA to real clinical datasets: first, with the toxicity outcomes of melanoma patients receiving different immunotherapy protocols and, second, with tumor response outcomes of patients with metastatic breast cancer receiving an anti-angiogenic drug. Finally, we discuss the results and implications of both our simulations and real-world analyses in Section 6.

2. Methodology and Theory

2.1. Kaplan–Meier Estimator

The goal of the Kaplan–Meier (KM) estimator is to estimate a population survival curve from a sample with incomplete time-to-event observations [1]. "Survival" times need not relate to death but can refer to any event of interest, such as local recurrence or stroke. The event in this instance is a binary variable, meaning that samples have either experienced the event up to a given time point or not. The times to failure for each subject are thus characterized by two variables: (1) serial time and (2) outcome of event occurrence or censorship.

Suppose that $t_0 < t_1 < t_2 < \ldots < t_K$ are the K distinct failure times observed in the sample. We write n_j and d_j as the number of patients at risk and number of events at time t_j, respectively, where $j = 1, 2, \ldots, K$. Note that the patients who are lost to follow up or withdraw from the trial before experiencing the event of interest (i.e., censored samples) are taken out of the risk set at the subsequent time points.

The KM estimate at time t_j, $\widehat{S(t_j)}$, is calculated as the cumulative survival probability up to and including time t_j,

$$S(t_k) = \prod_{j=1}^{k} \left(1 - \frac{d_j}{n_j}\right), \quad (1)$$

where $S(t) = 1$ for $t < t_1$. The Kaplan–Meier curve is plotted as a stepwise function representing the change in survival probability over time.

To compare treatment arms, multiple survival functions are plotted together, enabling the comparison of differences in survival experience between groups. Treatment options can be compared using metrics such as median survival and hazard ratios. The logrank test is used to assess if the differences are statistically significant: this test and its modification for WTA are discussed in Sections 2.4 and 2.5, respectively.

2.2. Weighted Trajectory Analysis

Weighted trajectory analysis (WTA) is a modification of KM estimation that provides the following advantages:

- Assesses outcomes defined by various ordinal grades (or stages) of clinical severity;
- Permits continued analysis of participants following changes in the variable of interest;
- Demonstrates the ability of an intervention to both prevent the exacerbation of outcomes and improve recovery, as well as the time course of these effects.

Several properties of KM curves crucial for clinical trial evaluation are incorporated within WTA. The test is nonparametric and provides the ability to censor patients that withdraw or are lost to follow up. Outcomes for various treatment arms can be assessed using a summary plot that depicts all patients in serial time. The test for significance is a modification of the logrank test described by Peto et al., which is the standard method for comparing KM survival curves [3]. The logrank test is described in Section 2.4 and the weighted logrank test follows in Section 2.5. As the analytical form of the test is a conservative estimate that operates under the normal approximation, a more computationally intensive simulated approach is outlined in Section 2.6.

In WTA, an event is a change in grade or stage or, more generally, a severity score. The severity score must be ordinal but can have an arbitrary range of severity that depends on the variable of interest (for example, I–IV for heart failure class [5]). Unlike KM estimation, an event does not omit the patient from subsequent analysis. Both increases and decreases in variables of interest are captured as events. Participants can enter trajectory analysis at any starting stage, though inferences on trial results are most powerful if treatment arms are randomized to the same median starting stage.

Redefining the event allows clinical assessment of the overall trajectory of a group of patients, mapping both deterioration and improvement in health status over time. Graphically, the staircase representing survival in the Kaplan–Meier estimator always descends. The WTA staircase can both descend and rise over time to capture the dynamics of a patient's clinical status.

Variables of interest can include any ordinal outcome variables with a defined, finite range. Examples include ECOG performance [4] and Common Terminology Criteria for Adverse Events (CTCAE) toxicity scores [6], both with ordinal scoring that ranges from 0 to 5.

For this reason, a binary variable such as death (0, alive vs. 1, dead) is not an appropriate variable of interest. In this circumstance, the range of the ordinal variable is set to 1, and the modified significance test reduces to the standard logrank test. Conversely, ECOG performance is an appropriate variable of interest given that it is ordinal with a defined range and can both improve and worsen over time. In WTA, a higher score in the variable of interest generally represents poorer health status. Variables that follow the opposite trend can be adapted to WTA by simply reversing the polarity of the ordinal scale.

Censoring in WTA is similar to KM estimation. Patient loss to follow up and withdrawal requires censoring, but patients may experience several events prior to being censored. Censoring is represented on the plot using a Wye symbol (⅄). The number of patients remaining within the study is tabulated below the plot at evenly spaced time intervals for each treatment arm.

Table 1 directly compares KM estimation and WTA based on core features.

Table 1. Feature comparison between the Kaplan–Meier estimator and weighted trajectory analysis.

Feature	Kaplan–Meier Estimator	Weighted Trajectory Analysis
Event	Outcome with binary coding. A patient must begin at "0" and is removed from analysis following an event ("1")	An event is a change in clinical severity and does not remove a patient from further analysis. Must be discrete with a finite range that depends on the variable of interest
Variable of interest	Death, metastases, local recurrence, stroke, and more. Can include variables outside of medicine, such as postgraduate employment	Graded/staged outcomes: ECOG performance, toxicities, NYHA heart failure class, questionnaire scores, and more; also includes variables outside of medicine
Trajectory	Survival function always decreases	Bidirectional: severity function can decrease or increase
Censoring	Removes patients from subsequent analysis (for withdrawal, discharge, loss to follow up, etc.)	
Test for significance	Logrank test	Weighted logrank test
Y-axis	Survival probability	Weighted health status
X-axis	Time (discrete: days, weeks, months, etc.)	
Y-intercept	1.0	Between 0 and 1.0, inclusive

Weighted Trajectory Analysis, while retaining the serial time and censoring functionality of the Kaplan-Meier estimator, facilitates ordinal variables of interest and defines events as changes in severity that do not omit patients from subsequent analysis. In addition, the "weighted health status" is not a survival probability but rather a normalized aggregate score that dynamically falls with greater disease burden and increases with recovery.

2.3. Mathematical Overview of Weighted Trajectory Analysis

Weighted trajectory analysis plots the health status of treatment arms as a function of time. Time values must be discrete but can correspond to days, weeks, months, or any chosen interval. For each time value on the x-axis, there is a corresponding score on the y-axis: a weighted health status. The higher the weighted health status, the healthier the group is. This score is scaled by the initial size of the treatment arm to facilitate simple comparison of groups with unequal size.

Consider a group of n patients with toxicity grades ranging from grade zero (asymptomatic/mild toxicity) to grade five (death related to an adverse event). The weighted health status at time point j is denoted by U_j, where $j = 0, 1, \ldots, z$. For each treatment arm, U_j has a maximum value of 1 and a minimum value of 0. Suppose we begin a trial with all patients having no disease burden at grade zero: $U_j = U_0 = 1$. A trial with the highest possible morbidity requires all patients to experience grade five toxicity (death): at this point, U_j will drop to 0.

We let $g_{i,j}$ represent the severity score for the ith patient at time j, $i = 1, \ldots, n$. The severity score is identical to their ordinal score for the variable of interest. If the range of the ordinal variable of interest does not have 0 as one extreme end, all values must be shifted to set 0 as the starting score (the polarity may also be reversed so that 0 represents peak health status). All patients begin the trial at grade zero, which reflects $g_{i,0} = 0$. If a patient labeled with index 50 has a grade-three injury at the seventh time point, their severity score $g_{50,7} = 3$.

Scaling for the WTA curve is performed through normalizing to a minimum of 0 and a maximum of 1 by using the initial weight of the treatment arm. This weight, w_0, is the product of the starting patient count n_0 and the range of the ordinal variable of interest r:

$$w_0 = n_0 r. \tag{2}$$

Suppose the initial size of the group, n_0, is 100 patients. The range r for the ordinal variable (toxicity grade) is 5. Then, w_0 is 500. The value of the weight changes over time due to patient censoring reflected by a drop in n_j. The general equation for w_j is provided in Section 2.5 and is used in the weighted logrank test. However, for scaling and plotting U, only the initial weight of a given treatment arm, w_0, is required.

The initial value U_0 is a perfect score of 1.

$$U_0 = 1 \tag{3}$$

Subsequent values of U deviate based on observed event occurrences d_j. We define event occurrence as a change in the variable of interest for a given patient i at time j:

$$d_{i,j} = g_{i,j+1} - g_{i,j}. \tag{4}$$

Therefore, the observed event score for a group of n patients is defined as

$$d_j = \sum_{i=1}^{n} d_{i,j} = \sum_{i=1}^{n} (g_{i,j+1} - g_{i,j}), \tag{5}$$

with patients censored following time j not contributing to the sum. Events and resulting changes in treatment arm trajectory are always scaled by w_0. Using this event definition, U_j can be calculated iteratively from U_0:

$$U_{j+1} = U_j - \frac{d_j}{w_0}, j = 0, 1, 2 \ldots \tag{6}$$

Alternatively, U_j for any given time point can be computed as follows:

$$U_j = 1 - \frac{\sum_{j=0}^{j-1} d_j}{w_0}, j \epsilon \mathbb{Z}^+. \tag{7}$$

Values for d_j at a given time point can be negative, and these represent cases in which the treatment arm improved in overall health status. From Equations (6) and (7), it follows that a negative value of d_j produces an increase in the weighted health status U_j.

2.4. The Logrank Test

We present here the standard formula of the logrank test statistic.

- Let $t_1 < t_2 < \ldots < t_K$ be K distinct failure times observed in the data;
- n_j^A is the number of patients in group A at risk at t_j, where $j = 1, 2, \ldots, K$;
- n_j^B is the number of patients in group B at risk at t_j, where $j = 1, 2, \ldots, K$;

- $n_j = n_j^A + n_j^B$ is the total number of patients at risk at t_j, where $j = 1, 2, \ldots, K$;
- d_j^A is the number of patients who experienced the (binary) event in group A at t_j;
- d_j^B is the number of patients who experienced the (binary) event in group B at t_j;
- $d_j = d_j^A + d_j^B$ is the total number of patients who experienced the (binary) event at t_j;
- $S^A(t)$ and $S^B(t)$ are the survival functions for group A and B, respectively.

The information at t_j can be summarized in a 2 × 2 table.

	Observed to fail at t_j		At risk at t_j
Group A	d_j^A	$n_j^A - d_j^A$	n_j^A
Group B	d_j^B	$n_j^B - d_j^B$	n_j^B
	d_j	$n_j - d_j$	n_j

Under the null hypothesis $H_0 : S^A(t) = S^B(t), d_j^A$ follows a *hypergeometric distribution* conditional on the margins $(n_j^A, n_j^B, d_j, n_j - d_j)$. The expectation and variance of d_j^A take the form

$$e_j^A = E\left(d_j^A\right) = n_j^A \frac{d_j}{n_j} \tag{8}$$

$$V_j = Var\left(d_j^A\right) = \frac{n_j^A n_j^B (n_j - d_j)}{n_j^2 (n_j - 1)} d_j. \tag{9}$$

Define the observed aggregated number of failures in group A as

$$O^A = \sum_{j=1}^{K} d_j^A. \tag{10}$$

The expected aggregated number of failures in group A is thus

$$E\left(O^A\right) = E^A = \sum_{j=1}^{K} e_j^A. \tag{11}$$

The contributions from each t_j are independent and, thus, the variance of O^A is

$$Var\left(O^A\right) = V = \sum_{j=1}^{K} V_j. \tag{12}$$

Under the null hypothesis $H_0 : S^A(t) = S^B(t),$ the logrank test statistic shows

$$Z = \frac{O^A - E^A}{\sqrt{V}} = \frac{\sum_{j=1}^{K} (d_j^A - e_j^A)}{\sqrt{\sum_{j=1}^{K} V_j}} \sim N(0, 1). \tag{13}$$

This is an asymptotic result derived from the central limit theorem (CLT). Note that replacing O^A and E^A with O^B and E^B leads to the exact same p-value.

The extension to ordinal events in the following section is based on this Z test statistic.

2.5. The Weighted Logrank Test—Analytical Method

We define an event as a change in the severity score of a given condition. Let $g_{i,j}^A$ be the severity score for the ith individual in group A at time t_j, where $i = 1, 2, \ldots, n_j^A$ and $j = 1, 2, \ldots, K$. Define $d_{i,j}^A$ as the change in the severity score from time t_{j+1} to t_j.

$$d_{i,j}^A = g_{i,j+1}^A - g_{i,j}^A, j = 1, 2, K - 1. \tag{14}$$

Without loss of generality, we consider a severity score ranging from stage zero to stage four. As a result, $d_{i,j}^{A}$ has a total of nine possible values $(-4,-3,-2,-1,0,1,2,3,4)$ if the observation of this person is uncensored at t_{j+1}.

- Let L be the total number of possible values taken by the change variable $d_{i,j}^{A}$. When a severity score takes values from 0 to 4, $L = 9$;
- Let W be the ordered non-decreasing list of the L possible change values. When a severity score takes values from 0 to 4, $W = (-4,-3,-2,-1,0,1,2,3,4)$;
- Let w_l be the lth element of W;
- Let $d_j^{A,l}$ be the number of subjects in group A at t_j whose change values equal w_l:

$$d_j^{A,l} = \sum_{i=1}^{n_j^A} d_{i,j}^{A} I(d_{i,j}^{A} = w_l) \tag{15}$$

where $I\left(d_{i,j}^{A} = w_l\right) = 1$ when $d_{i,j}^{A} = w_l$ and 0 otherwise;

- Let $d_j^{B,l}$ be the number of subjects in group B at t_j whose change values equal w_l;
- $d_j^{(l)} = d_j^{A,l} + d_j^{B,l}$ is the total number of patients whose change values equal w_l at t_j.

The information at $t_j, j = 1,2,\ldots,K-1$ can be summarized in a 2×10 table:

Observed values of $d_{i,j}$ (w_l)	-4	-3	-2	-1	0	1	2	3	4		At risk at t_j
Group A	$d_j^{A,1}$	$d_j^{A,2}$	$d_j^{A,3}$	$d_j^{A,4}$	$d_j^{A,5}$	$d_j^{A,6}$	$d_j^{A,7}$	$d_j^{A,8}$	$d_j^{A,9}$	$n_j^A - \sum_{l=1}^{L} d_j^{A,l}$	n_j^A
Group B	$d_j^{B,1}$	$d_j^{B,2}$	$d_j^{B,3}$	$d_j^{B,4}$	$d_j^{B,5}$	$d_j^{B,6}$	$d_j^{B,7}$	$d_j^{B,8}$	$d_j^{B,9}$	$n_j^B - \sum_{l=1}^{L} d_j^{B,l}$	n_j^B
	$d_j^{(1)}$	$d_j^{(2)}$	$d_j^{(3)}$	$d_j^{(4)}$	$d_j^{(5)}$	$d_j^{(6)}$	$d_j^{(7)}$	$d_j^{(8)}$	$d_j^{(9)}$	$n_j - \sum_{l=1}^{L} d_j^{(l)}$	n_j

Under the null hypothesis $H_0 : S^A(t) = S^B(t)$, $\left(d_j^{A,1}, d_j^{A,2}, d_j^{A,3}, \ldots, d_j^{A,L}\right)$ follows a *multivariate hypergeometric distribution* conditional on the margins $\left(n_j^A, n_j^B, \left\{d_j^{(l)}\right\}_{l=1}^{L}, n_j - \sum_l d_j^{(l)}\right)$.

We can show that the mean and variance of $d_j^{A,l}$, where $l \in \{1,2,\ldots,L\}$, are

$$e_j^{A,l} \triangleq E\left(d_j^{A,l}\right) = n_j^A \frac{d_j^{(l)}}{n_j} \tag{16}$$

$$\sigma_{j,ll} \triangleq Var\left(d_j^{A,l}\right) = \frac{n_j^A n_j^B (n_j - d_j^{(l)})}{n_j^2 (n_j - 1)} d_j^{(l)}. \tag{17}$$

For distinct $l, q \in \{1,2,\ldots,L\}$, we can derive the covariance of $d_j^{A,l}$ and $d_j^{A,q}$

$$\sigma_{j,lq} \triangleq Cov\left(d_j^{A,l}, d_j^{A,q}\right) = -\frac{n_j^A n_j^B}{n_j^2 (n_j - 1)} d_j^{(l)} d_j^{(q)},\ l \neq q. \tag{18}$$

These moment results are derived from the definition of multivariate hypergeometric distribution. To account for the direction and the magnitude of the change variable, we define the *observed* weighted changes as

$$O_j^w = \sum_{l=1}^{L} w_l d_j^{A,l}. \quad (19)$$

When a severity score is defined as a range from 0 to 4, the weight w_l takes the values of $(-4, -3, -2, -1, 0, 1, 2, 3, 4)$ for $l = 1, 2, \ldots, 9.$. The expected value of O_j can be written as

$$E_j^w = \sum_{l=1}^{L} w_l e_j^{A,l}. \quad (20)$$

When the event is coded as a binary outcome, this weighted change O_j^w is reduced to the e_j^A defined above. Using the results in Equations (17) and (18), we can write the variance of the weighted score O_j^w as

$$V_j^w = Var\left(O_j^w\right) = \sum_{l=1}^{L} \sum_{q=1}^{L} w_l w_q \sigma_{j,lq}, \quad (21)$$

where $\sigma_{j,lq}$ is defined in Equation (18) when $l \neq q$ and in Equation (17) when $l = q$.

Similarly, we can aggregate the observed/expected weighted changes across all K time points and define a Z test statistic. The weighted logrank test statistic is defined as

$$Z = \frac{\sum_{j=1}^{K}\left(O_j^w - E_j^w\right)}{\sqrt{\sum_{j=1}^{K} V_j^w}}, \quad (22)$$

which follows the standard normal distribution $N(0,1)$, under the null hypothesis $H_0 : S^A(t) = S^B(t)$. Equivalently,

$$Z^2 = \frac{\left[\sum_{j=1}^{K}\left(O_j^w - E_j^w\right)\right]^2}{\sum_{j=1}^{K} V_j^w} \sim \chi_1^2; \quad (23)$$

i.e., the square of the Z test statistic follows a chi-square distribution with one degree of freedom.

The asymptotic result in Equation (22) is based on the assumption that the total number of distinct failure times recorded in the pooled samples (i.e., K) is sufficiently large. For smaller trials with shorter follow-up periods, this analytical method can provide conservative conclusions and result in type II errors below the designated significance level, as demonstrated in Section 3.3. To complement the analytical method, we also propose a bootstrap-based approach for calculating p-values, which, despite requiring greater computational effort, remains accurate and sensitive independent of trial sizes.

2.6. The Weighted Logrank Test—Computational Method

A completed trial can be analyzed either instantly with the analytical approach or through rigorous simulations in a more sensitive computational approach. Compared to the design phase, the advantage of a completed trial is the wealth of collected data. Multistate Markov modeling (MSM), available in the *msm* package in R, provides a powerful method to compute transition intensities of an inputted dataset through maximum likelihood estimation. The steps to analyze a complete trial are as follows:

1. Determine transition probabilities using *msm* to load into n-fold simulations blind to treatment assignment;
2. Generate a distribution of the null hypothesis using the test statistic (Equation (23));

3. Calculate a test statistic from the clinical data and then determine a p-value by comparison to the distribution of the null hypothesis.

Software with built-in tools to facilitate analytical and computational methods to streamline the use of WTA for investigators is in production.

2.7. GEE Longitudinal Analysis

The generalized estimating equation (GEE) (Liang and Zegar 1986) is a widely used regression-based tool for analyzing longitudinal data [7]. We compare the performance of our weighted trajectory approach to the GEE method. In the GEE method, we model the severity scores as outcomes and the treatment group as the covariate. We specify the autoregressive correlation structure to account for the dependence among the severity measures from the same patient. We use an identity mean-variance link function and leave the scale parameter unspecified. The significance test for the association between patients' severity score and treatment status is carried out using a Wald test statistic with the sandwich variance estimator.

A major advantage of the GEE over likelihood-based methods (e.g., multi-state models) is that the joint distribution of longitudinal outcomes does not have to be fully specified. Therefore, if the mean structure is accurately specified, the mean parameters (e.g., the treatment effect in our case) can be consistently estimated, regardless of whether or not the covariance structure is correctly characterized. Our weighted logrank test is more robust than the GEE because it is a nonparametric test and does not make any assumptions about the survival outcomes. In addition, a visual representation of the survival trajectory over time is naturally accompanied by our proposed test statistic, which tracks the number of changes in the severity score over time. On the other hand, the GEE enables simultaneous modeling of multiple covariates, while our approach focuses on comparison between two treatment groups. In the following simulation studies, we directly compared the performance of the GEE and WTA.

3. Simulation Study One—Toxicity

In our first clinical trial simulation study, we demonstrate the functionality of WTA and present its advantages over KM analysis. We establish the strength of our novel method through a rigorous power comparison between KM estimation, the GEE, and both analytical and simulated approaches to WTA.

The design was a phase III comparison of toxicity outcomes from chemotherapy between two treatment arms (control and treatment, 1:1 allocation). The variable of interest was CTCAE toxicity: grades range from one (mild/no toxicity) to five (death from toxicity) [6]. For example, the grades of oral mucositis are: (1) asymptomatic/mild, (2) moderate pain or ulcer that does not interfere with oral intake, (3) severe pain interfering with oral intake, (4) life threatening consequences indicating urgent intervention, and (5) death. For the purposes of WTA, the ordinal range of 1–5 was shifted to 0–4, with censoring thus taking place at grade four.

The simulation study was generated using Python 3.7 [8]. Study simulations are a stochastic process in which randomly generated numbers are programmed to mirror fluctuating toxicities experienced by groups of patients undergoing chemotherapy cycles with daily measurements of treatment toxicity. Each instance of the simulation requires a specified hazard ratio and sample size prior to the stochastic generation of toxicity. Table 2 provides a snapshot of the results for a single simulated clinical trial.

Table 2. A snapshot of the final results of a simulated chemotherapy toxicity-grade trial.

Patient ID	Treatment Arm	Duration	0	1	2	3	4	5	6	7	8	9	10
1	1	10	0	0	0	0	0	0	1	1	1	0	
2	1	10	0	0	0	0	0	1	1	1	1	1	
3	0	11	0	0	0	0	0	0	0	0	0	0	0
4	1	6	0	0	0	0	0	0					
5	0	13	0	0	0	0	0	0	0	0	0	1	1
6	1	9	0	0	0	0	0	0	0	0	0		
7	0	18	0	0	0	0	0	0	1	1	1	2	2
8	1	6	0	0	0	0	0	0					
9	1	29	0	0	0	0	0	0	0	0	0	1	0
10	0	4	0	0	0	0							

Treatment arms zero and one represent the control and treatment groups, respectively. Numbered columns indicate sequential days within the trial starting at day zero. Duration indicates the number of days the patient was hospitalized.

Each patient (represented by an ID number) has a risk of developing treatment toxicity over time. This risk is determined by their treatment group and the numbers of days they have spent in the study. The values within Table 2 were assigned as follows:

1. Treatment group: randomly assigned as zero or one with the constraint of having an equal number of patients allocated to each group;
2. Duration: the number of days a patient remains within the trial was programmed as a random value within a uniform distribution of 0 to 50 days;
3. Toxicity grade: computed for each patient on a daily basis for the extent of their assigned duration. To model the trajectory of toxicity grade over time, we made the following simplifying assumptions:
   (a) On any given day, patients can rise or fall by a single toxicity grade;
   (b) Transitions in toxicity grade are random, but a larger hazard ratio suggests a greater chance of exacerbation and lower chance of recovery;
   (c) A patient is censored once their pre-assigned duration within the trial has elapsed or they reach maximum toxicity, in this case representing death, whichever occurs first.

A hazard ratio for control:treatment was modeled for the control group to have a higher toxicity burden through time compared to the treatment group (the value was programmed as 1.0 or higher). For the control group, the probability of exacerbation was a base probability of 0.10 multiplied by the hazard ratio. If exacerbation did not occur and the current stage was above the minimum, the probability of recovery would be a base probability of 0.05 divided by the hazard ratio. Patients in the treatment group fluctuated based on base probabilities alone. Once a patient reached the maximum toxicity or their maximum assigned duration, they were censored.

3.1. *Kaplan–Meier Estimator: Toxicity Trial*

We performed Kaplan–Meier estimation using the Python 3.7 library "lifelines" [9]. This library was used to plot survival probabilities and conduct logrank tests. Results were validated by assessing the source code for accuracy and making a direct comparison to results from SPSS v26 (IBM Corp., Armonk, NY, USA) [10].

To permit comparison to KM estimation, all patients began the trial at stage zero, which represented grade-one toxicity. An "event" was considered exacerbation to the next stage. Following event occurrence, patients were removed from analysis. Censoring is represented by a Wye symbol (⅄).

A single toxicity comparison trial was conducted with the following parameters: 200 patients (1:1 treatment allocation at 100 patients/arm) and a 1.25:1 hazard ratio for control:treatment. Figure 1 depicts the corresponding Kaplan–Meier plot.

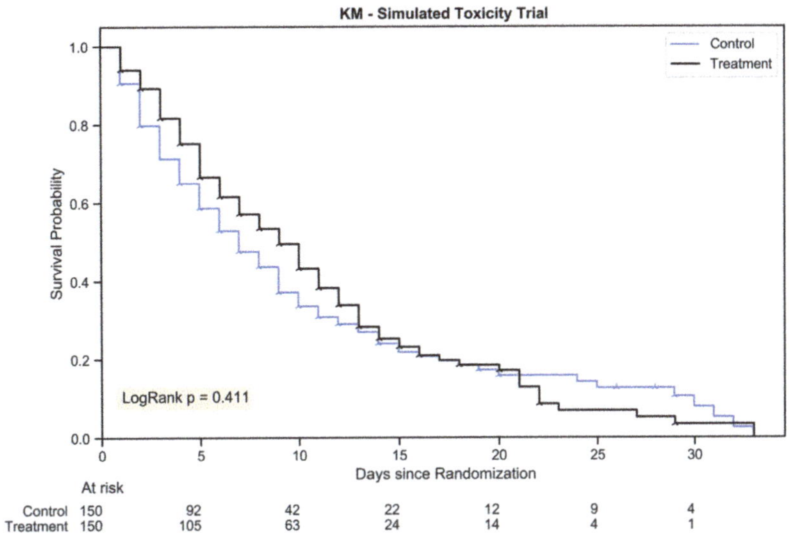

Figure 1. The Kaplan Meier estimator plot for a randomly generated chemotherapy toxicity trial of 300 patients with 1:1 allocation. An event was considered the onset of chemotherapy toxicity (beyond stage zero) and patients were censored once their assigned duration had been reached. The hazard ratio between treatment arms was 1.25:1.

The outcome for a logrank test conducted with this trial was $p = 0.411$; the result was not statistically significant. The Kaplan–Meier method was not sufficiently sensitive to distinguish between treatment arms for this simulated trial; high grades of toxicity may have differed between the groups, but standard time-to-event statistics failed to capture the complex trajectory of morbidity.

Next, we analyze and report an identical drug trial using weighted trajectory analysis.

3.2. Weighted Trajectory Analysis: Simulated Trial

The WTA was performed as described in Section 2.3 on an identical trial dataset of 200 patients. Censoring is represented by a Wye symbol (⅄) and occurred for each patient once they were no longer followed for toxicity grade. This took places under two conditions: either the assigned duration for the patient had been reached or the patient had suffered fatal toxicity. Figure 2 provides the plot of the WTA.

Note the change in x-axis range, the number of patients at risk, and the trajectory of health status: patients were followed for the full course of toxicity and both declines and improvements were mapped. As compared to the KM plot, the treatment arms in this trial were visually distinct across all time points, demonstrating a reduced disease burden for the treatment group, a difference sustained across time. By approximately day 30, a minor proportion of the original patients within the trial remained, and the delta between groups plateaued. Much like KM plot interpretation, the clinical significance of each trajectory dropped after a substantial fraction of patients had been censored.

Using the "weighted" logrank test, $p = 0.005$. WTA is a more powerful and more clinically relevant statistic for this dataset due to its ability to track toxicity severity across all grades. As KM estimation failed to reject the null hypothesis despite clinically meaningful group differences, a type II error occurred. The improved sensitivity of WTA prevented such an error from taking place.

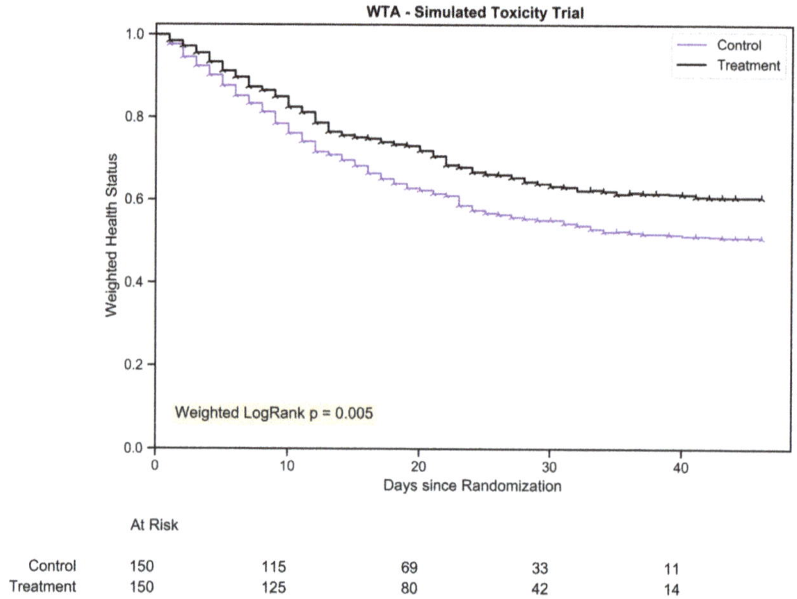

Figure 2. The weighted trajectory analysis plot for a randomly generated chemotherapy toxicity trial of 300 patients with 1:1 allocation. The weighted health status of both groups dropped due to increasing morbidity from chemotherapy toxicity following randomization. The hazard ratio between treatment arms was 1.25:1.

3.3. *Thousandfold Power Comparison—KM Estimation vs. WTA*

The trial analyzed in Sections 3.2 and 3.3 was a single instance of randomly generated data; the improved performance of WTA compared to KM estimation may have occurred by chance. To accurately compare the ability of the tests to distinguish between treatment arms, we ran 1000-fold analyses across increments in sample size from 20 to 300 and hazard ratio from 1.0 to 1.5. For each trial, a *p*-value was computed using both KM estimation and WTA. The fraction of tests that were significant (at $\alpha < 0.05$) represents the power of the test (correctly rejecting the null hypothesis that the two groups are the same).

Figure 3 demonstrates that WTA had a consistently higher power than KM estimation: it permitted comparable analyses with a smaller sample size. Given that trial data were randomly generated, the plots were not perfectly smooth but followed the expected logarithmic shape of power as a function of sample size.

For the simulated clinical trial at a 1.3 hazard ratio, WTA was able to reach 80% power at 180 patients while KM estimation required well over 300 patients. At a 1.4 hazard ratio, WTA required about 100 patients for 80% power while KM estimation required about 300. Across many hazard ratios, WTA required less than half the sample size to achieve a power equivalent to KM estimation. Note that the power of the KM method for these clinical trials at a 1.5 hazard ratio mirrored the power of WTA at a 1.3 hazard ratio.

In this simulated example, weighted trajectory analysis demonstrated greater sensitivity than Kaplan–Meier estimation to a dataset with ordinal severity scoring. With a greater likelihood of correctly rejecting the null hypothesis, the novel method reduced type II errors.

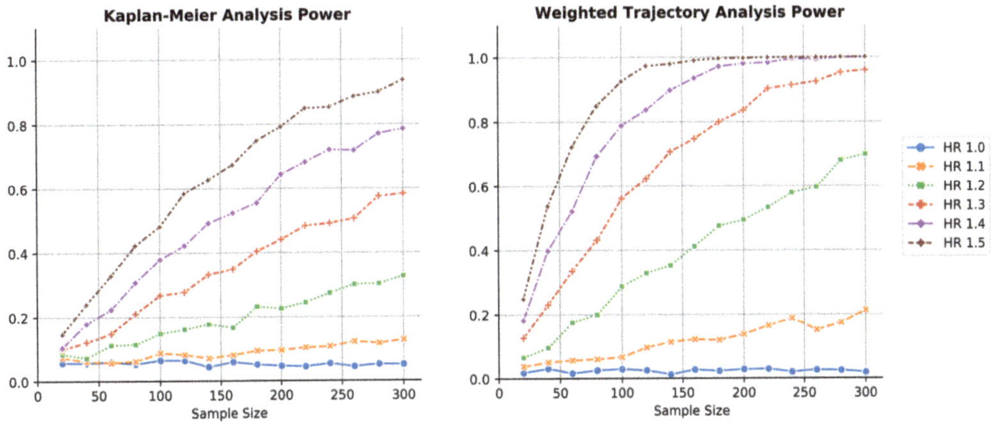

Figure 3. Thousandfold simulations of power as a function of sample size for both KM estimation and WTA across several hazard ratios. WTA demonstrated consistently higher power, reflecting a smaller sample size requirement during trial design. The type I error rate of WTA was approximately 0.025, indicating the method was conservative. The type I error approached 0.05 within the limit of larger trials with more distinct failure times.

3.4. Thousandfold Power Comparison—KM Estimation, WTA (Analytic and Computational), GEE

To demonstrate the differences between the analytical and computational approach with WTA (and reference these against standard approaches with KM estimation and the GEE), we ran 1000-fold analyses under 9 unique conditions at sample sizes of 100, 200, and 300 across hazard ratios of 1.0, 1.2, and 1.4. For each trial, a p-value was generated for all four of the KM estimation, WTA (analytical approach), WTA (simulated approach), and GEE longitudinal analysis using their respective hypothesis tests. The fraction of tests that were significant (at $\alpha < 0.05$) represented the power of the test (correctly rejecting the null hypothesis that the two groups were the same).

Figure 4 demonstrates that the analytical approach with WTA is less sensitive and less powerful than the computational approach. This is expected considering its computational effort and independence with regard to trial size. Importantly, the analytical approach provides conservative results: in this stochastic model, the type I error hovered at around half of the 0.05 standard met by KM estimation, the GEE, and the computational approach with WTA. In the second simulation study, the explanation for this discrepancy became evident; the analytical approach is based on a normal approximation that becomes more precise with a larger number of distinct failure times and longer follow up. As the second simulation study met these criteria, the simulated type I error correspondingly became closer to the 0.05 standard, the asymptotic limit.

GEE longitudinal analysis was found to be consistently weaker than both methods of WTA. This remained true in the second simulation study. The discrepancy was likely a trade-off related to the parametric nature of each test: WTA is nonparametric and does not require any assumptions about survival outcomes. The GEE is semi-parametric, which is less robust, but permits simultaneous modeling of multiple covariates as opposed to a sole comparison across treatment groups. As per this simulation study at a hazard ratio of 1.4, the analytical WTA met the 80% power standard for clinical trial design at 100 patients; the GEE required over 150 patients and KM estimation required 300. The most accurate method, the computational WTA, required fewer than 100 patients.

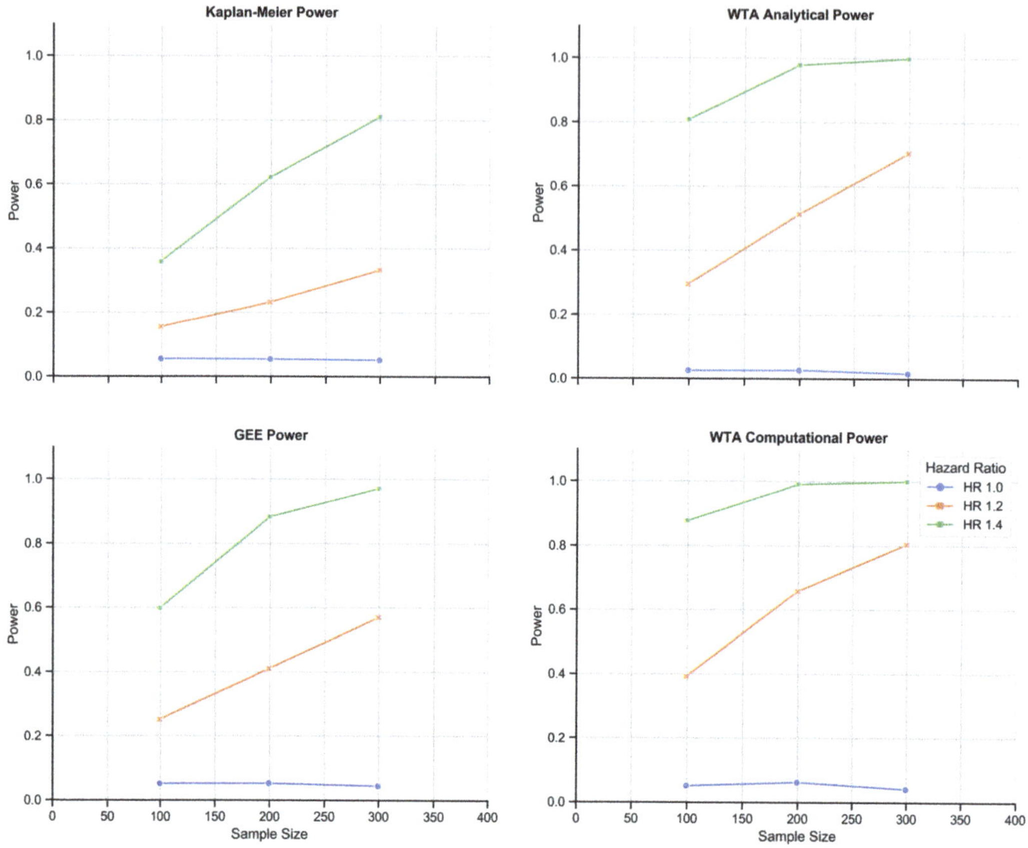

Figure 4. Chemotherapy toxicity simulation study: 1000-fold simulations of power as a function of sample size for KM estimation, the GEE, and WTA in both its analytical and computational forms. WTA outperformed KM estimation and the GEE with consistently higher power and, thus, a smaller sample size requirement. In addition, the computational approach with WTA outperformed the analytical approach in return for a more time- and resource-intensive methodology. The computational approach also met a standard type I error rate of 0.05 that was robust to changes in trial size.

4. Simulation Study Two—Schizophrenia

The first simulation study highlighted the functionality of WTA under restrictive and common trial conditions to permit analysis with KM estimation. However, some trials or datasets outside of medicine optimally analyzed using WTA may involve more extreme input parameters. Longer durations of patient participation and larger fluctuations within the data would also grant sensitivity to the analytical approach in Section 2.5. Accordingly, we developed a second simulation study to demonstrate the flexibility of WTA—in this case, solely in analytic form—and compared its power to the versatile GEE longitudinal analysis.

The design was a phase III comparison of antipsychotic efficacy in the management of schizophrenia. Compared to most chronic medical illnesses, psychiatric illness often demonstrates a more tumultuous course, with periods that may be completely asymptomatic interspersed with episodes of debilitating disease burden. Schizophrenia combines this generalization with a progressive disease course and often incomplete recovery following acute decompensations of the primary disorder or substance-induced episodes of psychosis.

As before, there were two treatment arms (control and treatment, 1:1 allocation). The variable of interest was symptom severity stage: stages ranged from zero (absence of symptoms) to six (life-threatening illness due to severe disease burden and neurocognitive decline). Patients entered the trial at stage two, which represented a symptom burden below the full threshold for a psychotic episode; in our scenario, these patients were recruited for the trial due to a positive symptom screen as opposed to emergency psychiatric admission typical of greater symptom severity. Measurement intervals represented months as opposed to days, which permitted larger transitions between stages in a single time interval, though loaded probabilities favor smaller transitions near extreme ends of the severity scale. Patients were enrolled into the trial for a randomized duration chosen from a uniform distribution between 36 and 84 months; they were censored when they reached the assigned duration or sooner if they reached stage six. The mechanics of the study otherwise mirrored simulation study one.

Thousandfold Power Comparison—WTA vs. GEE

Once again, we ran 1000-fold analyses under 9 unique conditions at sample sizes of 100, 200, and 300 across hazard ratios of 1.0, 1.2, and 1.4. For each trial, a p-value was generated for both WTA (analytical approach) and GEE longitudinal analysis using their respective hypothesis tests. The fraction of tests that were significant (at $\alpha < 0.05$) represented the power of the test (correctly rejecting the null hypothesis that the two groups were the same).

Figure 5 demonstrates that, under a vastly different stochastic model compared to the first simulation study, WTA once again outperformed the GEE. The type I error of WTA shifted to an average of 0.037, closer to 0.05 as the trial had increased follow up and failure times, which better satisfied the normal approximation underlying the method. This longer trial with more complex fluctuations in disease severity exhibited a higher power at identical hazard ratios and sample sizes compared to the previous study.

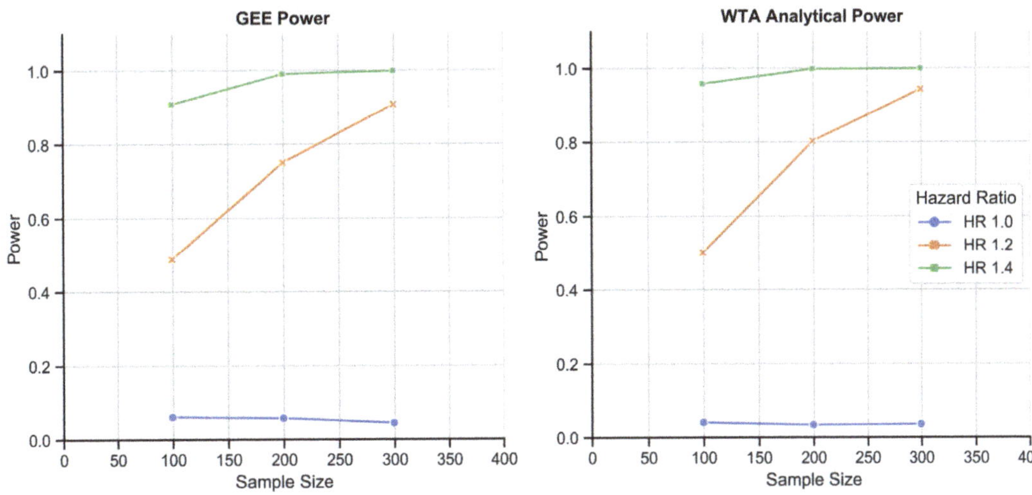

Figure 5. Schizophrenia disease course simulation study: 1000-fold simulations of power as a function of sample size for the GEE and WTA in its analytical form. WTA again outperformed the GEE and demonstrated a type I error rate of 0.037, closer to the 0.05 standard due to the larger size of each trial.

5. Illustrative Real-World Example

5.1. Immune Checkpoint Inhibitor Therapy for Melanoma

Immune checkpoint inhibitors (ICIs) have transformed the treatment landscape for melanoma [11]. Inhibitors targeting cytotoxic T lymphocyte antigen-4 (CTLA-4) and programmed death-1 (PD-1) produce a response in a large fraction of cancer patients. These responses are often durable and some are even curative. The use of anti-CTLA-4 and anti-PD-1 in combination has demonstrated the highest rate of durable responses among melanoma treatment protocols. In prescribing a treatment plan, the promising response rates must be balanced with concerns about toxicity outcomes. Toxic effects associated with ICIs are immune-related in nature, may impact any organ, and remain a major challenge in clinical care.

Published data comparing therapy protocols suggest that the use of combination CTLA-4/PD-1 therapy results in significantly higher immune-related toxicity when compared to monotherapy regimens [12]. These results may limit the use of combination therapy for patients with melanoma and remain a barrier to the development of new combinations.

However, when treatment outcomes are compared over a longer time horizon, the discrepancy in immune-related toxicities seen between patients treated with combination versus monotherapy disappears. Those patients treated with combination therapy do experience greater toxicity during active treatment but, because the large majority of toxicities are reversible, the health status of patients treated with combination therapy improves with time. Longitudinally, patients treated with combination immunotherapy receive fewer actual treatment infusions; however, the treatment response rate is higher and long-term survival comparable [13]. Put simply, the combination of CTLA-4- and PD-1-directed immunotherapy has greater efficacy despite a significantly shorter duration of therapy, and despite an initial increase in immune-related toxicities, the health status of patients who respond to therapy is excellent. The key limitation of existing statistical methods used to evaluate toxicity outcomes is the failure to capture improvement and accurately map changes through time.

The hypothesis that long-term health status is comparable between patients treated with combination versus monotherapy ICIs can be tested using weighted trajectory analysis. Rather than using percent incidence to inform treatment decisions (see Figure 6), WTA can enable clinicians to assess the time course of toxicity. The more detailed and sensitive mapping of toxicity outcomes can enable clinicians to more accurately translate patient data into standards for treatment.

In this example, retrospective toxicity data were used to compare monotherapy (anti-PD-1) with combination therapy (anti-PD-1 + anti-CTLA-4). Increases in alanine aminotransferase (ALT) levels indicate transient, immune-related hepatitis and were recorded for 195 melanoma patients on either protocol over 180 days. The increase in ALT from baseline was graded according to the National Cancer Institute Common Terminology Criteria for Adverse Events, version 5.0 [6]. The baseline ALT scores were assigned a toxicity of 0 by definition. This enabled comparison between KM estimation and WTA.

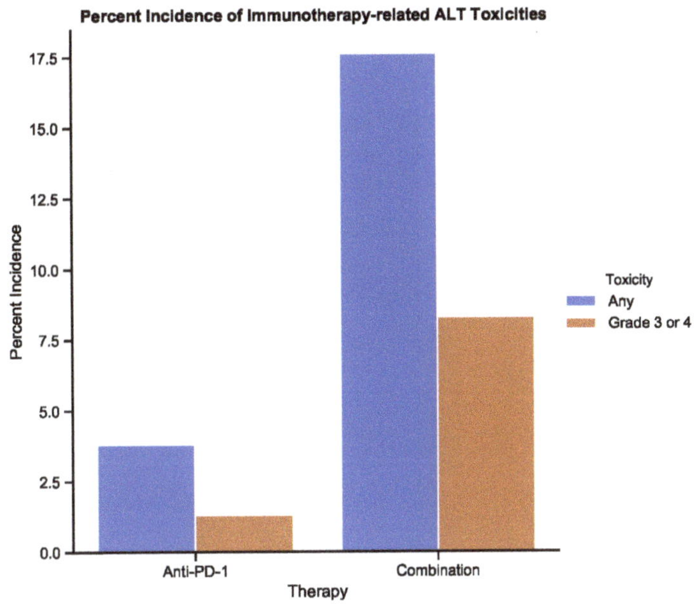

Figure 6. The incidence of treatment-related toxicities associated with an increase in alanine aminotransferase (ALT) for patients receiving anti-PD-1 therapy and combination therapy. Toxicities were graded using CTCAE v5.0 [6]. Data from Table 3 from the study by Larkin et al. (2015) [12].

5.1.1. Kaplan–Meier Estimator: Anti-PD-1 vs. Combination Therapy

To perform KM estimation, the occurrence of any nonzero toxicity score was considered an event. The KM estimation results in Figure 7 demonstrated that patients on combination therapy had a greater risk of experiencing nonzero toxicity over 100 days compared to the monotherapy group. This difference between groups was statistically significant with a p-value < 0.001.

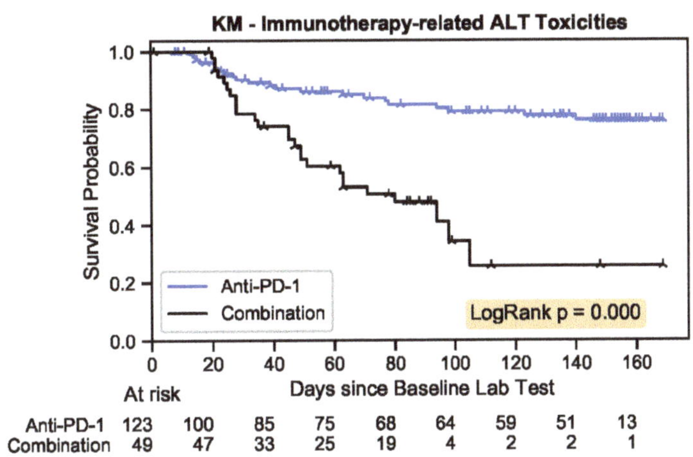

Figure 7. The Kaplan–Meier estimator plot for immunotherapy-related toxicities associated with an increase in ALT. An event was considered the onset of a nonzero toxicity grade.

5.1.2. Weighted Trajectory Analysis: Anti-PD-1 vs. Combination Therapy

The WTA results are depicted in Figure 8. The anti-PD-1 group had a steady accumulation of toxicity-related events, while the combination group featured a faster decline that plateaued at approximately 60 days. However, the trajectory of the combination group recovered, and by 160 days, the two trajectories nearly converged. As immune-related toxicities are often reversible, the ability to model both exacerbation and recovery provides a more accurate picture of clinical outcomes.

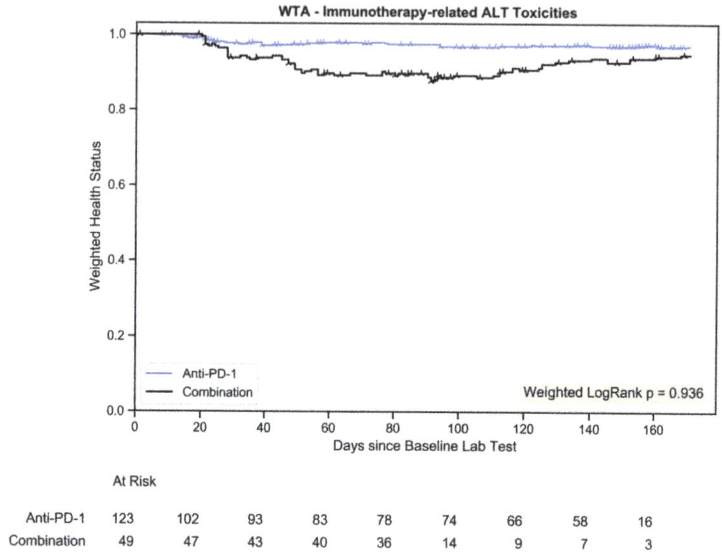

Figure 8. Weighted trajectory analysis plot for immunotherapy-related toxicities associated with an increase in ALT. The weighted health status of the combination group initially diverged from the anti-PD-1 group but subsequent recovery led to similar longitudinal outcomes.

The weighted logrank test had a *p*-value of 0.936, which was not statistically significant. The ability of recovery events to be captured within the weighted logrank hypothesis test demonstrates that differences in toxicity outcomes between these groups are misrepresented by prevalence data and the use of time-to-event curves, like in Kaplan–Meier estimation. The absence of significant differences in more robust analysis suggests incidence data provide an incomplete picture of toxicity outcomes, leading to a false rejection of the null hypothesis. In the simulated example examining the development of toxicity to chemotherapy, WTA avoided a type II error. In this real-world example, the use of WTA avoided a type I error.

5.2. Rose/Trio-012 Trial

Treatment using agents that disrupt tumor angiogenesis (the process of generating new blood vessels) have shown clinical benefits with colorectal cancer, renal cell carcinoma, and several gynecological cancers. The ROSE/TRIO-012 trial sought to evaluate ramucirumab, an anti-angiogenic drug, for the treatment of metastatic breast cancer [14]. Investigators compared ramucirumab to a placebo when added to standard docetaxel chemotherapy.

Many phase III trials within oncology are evaluated using Kaplan–Meier estimates and additional metrics based on the Response Evaluation Criteria in Solid Tumors (RECIST) [15]. In ROSE/TRIO-012, KM estimation was performed to determine progression-free survival, in which disease progression and death were considered events, and overall survival, where death alone was an event. The RECIST framework (Table 3) was used to determine overall response metrics. These metrics reflected patients whose cancer improved through the course of the trial (objective response rate (ORR)) and patients who did not experience progressive disease or death (disease control rate (DCR)).

The ORR and DCR are defined as follows:

$$ORR = CR + PR \tag{24}$$

$$DCR = CR + PR + SD \tag{25}$$

Table 3. RECIST 1.1 criteria definitions.

Treatment Outcome	Definition
Complete response (CR)	Disappearance of all target lesions. Any pathological lymph nodes (whether target or non-target) must show reduction in short axis to <10 mm
Partial response (PR)	At least a 30% decrease in the sum of diameters of target lesions, taking as reference the baseline sum diameters
Progressive disease (PD)	At least a 20% increase in the sum of diameters of target lesions, taking as reference the smallest sum in the study (this includes the baseline sum that is the smallest in the study). In addition to the relative increase of 20%, the sum must also demonstrate an absolute increase of at least 5 mm (note: the appearance of one or more new lesions is also considered progression)
Stable disease (SD)	Neither sufficient shrinkage to qualify as PR nor sufficient increase to qualify as PD, taking as reference the smallest sum of diameters in the study

Response Evaluation Criteria in Solid Tumours (RECIST) version 1.1 offers a standardized definition for endpoints in clinical trials that evaluate changes in tumour burden secondary to cancer therapeutics [15].

Together, the several endpoints provide a detailed picture of patient outcomes following randomization. However, the individual metrics take time to interpret and can sometimes provide conflicting signals regarding trial success. ROSE/TRIO-012 provides an example: although investigator-assessed PFS ($p = 0.077$) was insignificant at $p < 0.05$, endpoints, including ORR and DCR, were significantly higher in the ramucirumab group. The final verdict on the trial was that it failed to meaningfully improve important clinical outcomes—a decision based solely on the absence of significance in investigator-assessed PFS, the trial's primary endpoint. Had trial success been defined as a composite of several endpoints, the investigators may have concluded that ramucirumab conferred a significant benefit to the patients within the study. Currently, ramucirumab is not approved for use in the treatment of metastatic breast cancer.

The ability to combine the RECIST framework with mortality in a single plot would allow oncologists to rapidly interpret the totality of results of a clinical trial. A judgment on trial success can remain tied to the significance of a primary objective, but this objective should capture a wide array of important patient outcomes. In this example, ROSE/TRIO-012 trial results from Mackey et al.'s 2014 paper [14] were compared to weighted trajectory analysis with the original data.

5.2.1. Kaplan–Meier: Ramucirumab vs. Placebo + Docetaxel

Figure 2A,C from Mackey et al.'s 2014 paper are depicted in Figure 9. Respectively, they represent progression-free survival (the primary endpoint) and overall survival, both using standard Kaplan–Meier techniques. Upon inspection, progression-free survival appears slightly higher within the ramucirumab group. The logrank p-value of 0.077 did not indicate statistical significance. As PFS was the primary endpoint, the intervention was deemed unsuccessful. Overall survival outcomes were no different between groups ($p = 0.915$).

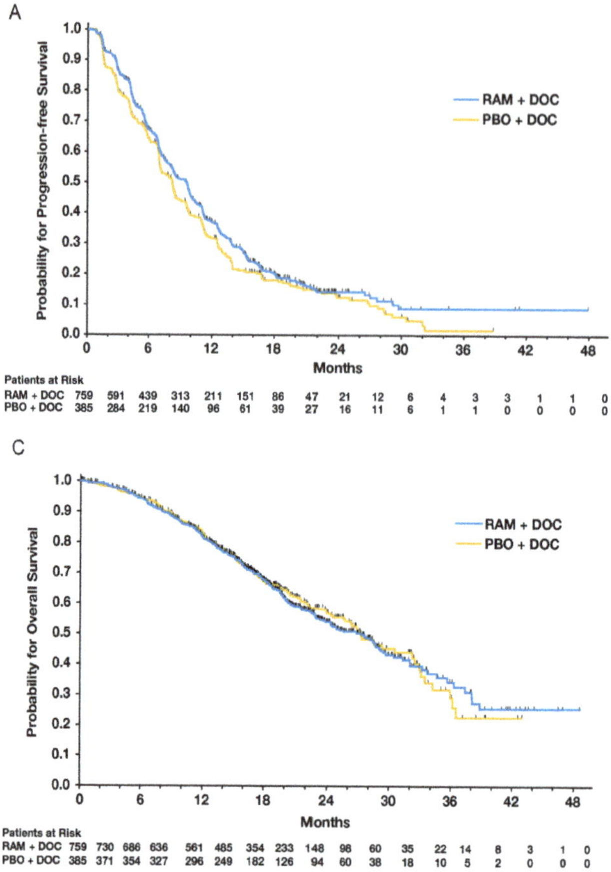

Figure 9. Figure 2A,C from Mackey et al.'s 2014 paper comparing ramucirumab to a placebo added to standard docetaxel chemotherapy [14]. The figures provide patient outcomes using KM estimates of progression-free survival (PFS) and overall survival (OS), respectively.

5.2.2. RECIST Endpoints: Ramucirumab vs. Placebo + Docetaxel

Conflicting signals about the efficacy of ramucirumab arise when analyzing secondary endpoints. ORR and DCR were significantly higher in the ramucirumab arm (44.7% vs. 37.9%, $p = 0.027$; 86.4% vs. 81.3%, $p = 0.022$).

ORR and DCR provide no time-to-event information. The goal of combining RECIST metrics with KM estimation is to generate a complete picture of patient outcomes. However, by omitting information on time and severity, respectively, the distinct methods may disagree on intervention efficacy. The whole is less than the sum of its parts.

The existing solution to this apparent conflict was a decision made by the investigators prior to the study to select a single metric as the primary objective to determine success. This both focuses and simplifies any conversation about study outcomes. Had this primary objective been ORR, the conclusion of the study would have supported the use of ramucirumab for these patients.

5.2.3. Weighted Trajectory Analysis: Ramucirumab vs. Placebo in Addition to Docetaxel

We used weighted trajectory analysis to combine the RECIST framework with mortality to depict comprehensive time-to-event outcomes. To perform the method, we employed the ordinal severity scoring framework in Table 4.

Table 4. RECIST 1.1 mapped to ordinal severity scores.

Outcome	Score
Complete response (CR)	0
Partial response (PR)	1
Stable disease (SD)	2
Progressive disease (PD)	3
Death	4

Response Evaluation Criteria in Solid Tumours (RECIST) version 1.1 [15] adapted to Weighted Trajectory Analysis using ordinal severity scores. By convention, a score of zero is assigned to the lowest illness burden (complete response) and the maximum score to the highest illness burden (death).

The starting point of each patient at the time of randomization was stable disease (SD), a score of 2. At the ends of the ordinal scale were complete response (CR, the best outcome) and death (the worst outcome). Patients were censored upon withdrawal or loss to follow up or directly following death.

Using the original ROSE/TRIO-012 dataset and the ordinal framework above, we generated Figure 10. Censoring is indicated using vertical tick marks.

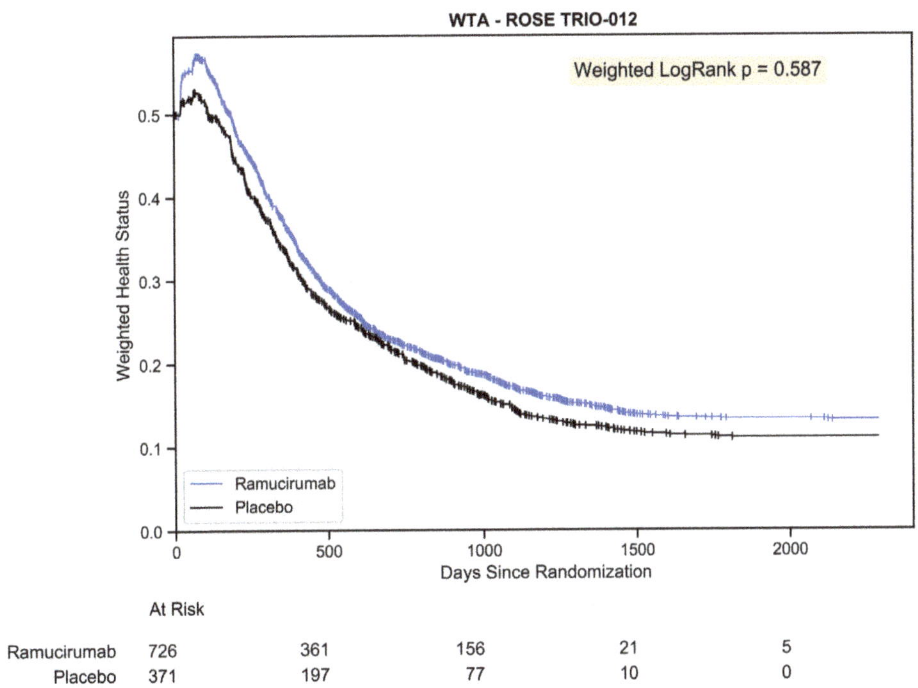

Figure 10. Weighted trajectory analysis of the original ROSE/TRIO-012 dataset using an ordinal scale that merges RECIST criteria with mortality. The trajectory of patient outcomes demonstrates that partial and complete response initially outweighed progressive disease and mortality for the first few chemotherapy cycles. Following this peak, patient prognosis was generally poor, as both treatment arms experienced growing disease burden and death.

This plot provides a comprehensive view of all patient outcomes for the full study duration. A few months into the trial, we see the peak in weighted health status for both groups. This occurred at 68 days for the placebo group and 76 days for the ramucirumab group. At this phase, some patients had experienced partial or complete response. Following this peak was a gradual descent that represented progressively increasing morbidity and death across both groups. The trajectories were strikingly similar, with the ramucirumab group experiencing slightly better outcomes throughout the study. The difference was not statistically significant ($p = 0.587$). This corroborates the current regulatory standard that ramucirumab should not be approved for the treatment of metastatic breast cancer.

With the WTA plot alone, investigators can easily interpret the time course of disease response. Patients likely to respond or recover generally do so following the first two chemotherapy cycles. After three months, the prognosis is poor: both treatment arms are characterized by progressive disease and death.

6. Discussion

WTA was created to (a) evaluate phase III clinical trials that assess outcomes defined by various ordinal grades (or stages) of severity; (b) permit continued analysis of participants following changes in the variable of interest; and (c) demonstrate the ability of an intervention to both prevent the exacerbation of outcomes and improve recovery and the time course of these effects. Its development was inspired by a pressure injury study—a disease process characterized by several stages of severity—for which Kaplan–Meier estimates would fail to capture the complete trajectory. Despite its limitations, KM estimation provides crucial advantages, such as patient censoring, rapid interpretation of survival plots, and a simple hypothesis test. To this end, we sought to create a statistical method that built on the foundations of Kaplan–Meier analysis but would overcome the inherent limitations of the technique.

We built the WTA toolkit based on expansion and extension of the Kaplan–Meier methodology. We adapted KM estimation to support analysis of ordinal variables by redefining events as changes in disease scores rather than assigning "1" and omitting the patient from further analysis. We adapted KM estimation to permit fluctuating outcomes (worsening and improvement of the ordinal outcome) by plotting a novel weighted health status as opposed to probability. We retained the ability to censor patients at the time of non-informative status. These changes warranted a novel significance test, for which we developed a modification of Peto et al.'s logrank test [3] This analytical approach is rather conservative in its type I error rates for smaller trials, but the rate approaches 0.05 within the limit of massive trials with many distinct failure times. Thus, we developed a computational approach that is more resource-intensive but remains precise and accurate independent of trial size.

In order to explore and demonstrate the utility of WTA, we applied WTA to two randomized clinical trial simulation studies. The first clinical setting was chemotherapy toxicity, a trial in which the variable of interest ranged from one to five (shifted to zero to four), stage transitions were singular and started at zero, and up to 50 discrete time points were measured for each patient. The second setting was schizophrenia disease course, a more complex trial in which the variable of interested ranged from zero to six, stage transitions were often multiple and started at two, and up to 84 discrete time points were measured for each patient. We performed sensitivity and power comparisons across both sample size and hazard ratio. Through 1000-fold validation, WTA showed greater sensitivity and power, often requiring fewer than half the patients for comparable power to KM estimation. WTA also showed increased power compared to the GEE, likely secondary to its more robust nonparametric methodology compared to the semi-parametric GEE, at the cost of the GEE's ability to model covariate effects. This demonstrates that designing a phase III clinical trial using our novel method as the primary endpoint can substantially lower cost, duration, and the risk of type II errors.

We also applied WTA to real-world clinical trial data. The first application was the assessment of time-dependent toxicity grades in melanoma patients receiving one of two immunotherapy treatment regimens. Although toxicities are generally reported in oncology trials as the worst grade experienced by each individual patient, this fails to capture those toxicities that resolve with treatment modification or targeted intervention. As such, the published literature suggests the prohibitive toxicity of the most effective therapy, while practitioners' experience is that high-grade toxicities are often transient and treatable.

The WTA we conducted confirmed that treatment-related toxicities of combination therapy resolved to rates close to that seen with less effective monotherapy regimens. The second application was the re-evaluation of a published phase III registration trial of an anti-angiogenic drug for the treatment of metastatic breast cancer. Although this study failed to demonstrate statistically significant improvement in the pre-defined primary endpoint, a number of secondary endpoints suggested the possibility of meaningful clinical benefit from the antiangiogenic therapy. By using an ordinal scale to describe the spectrum of clinical outcomes after therapy, spanning complete disease response, partial response, disease stability, disease progression, and death, WTA demonstrated that, although patients derived a modest benefit from antiangiogenic therapy when compared to control therapy, the difference was neither clinically nor statistically significant. The resulting graph captured the full clinical course of patients in a single figure. This result underscores that WTA did not inappropriately provide an overly sensitive analytic tool and justifies the regulatory stance that the intervention did not warrant approval for the market. Overall, the novel method affords greater specificity and reduces the likelihood of type I errors.

In aggregate, we feel the strengths of the weighted trajectory analysis statistic are its ability to capture detailed trajectory outcomes in a simple summary plot, its greater power, and its ability to map exacerbation and improvement. These strengths are built upon key advantages that make KM estimation a favored tool for clinical trial evaluation: namely, the ability to censor patients and compare treatment arms using a simple hypothesis test. WTA-dependent trial design can substantially reduce sample size requirements, increasing the practicality and lowering the cost of phase III clinical trials. However, we acknowledge several limitations of this method. WTA does not facilitate Cox regression analysis or generate the equivalent of a hazard ratio. WTA is a new technique and does not yet have a clinical or regulatory track record. WTA relies on the assumption of non-informative censoring, and investigation into alternative approaches to censoring, such as inverse-probability-of-censoring weighting (IPCW), remains important future work [16]. Lastly, WTA requires an assumption that the change between adjacent ordinal severities is equally important independent of the levels transitioned by applying a direct numerical weight. This conversion is not always medically appropriate: taking the example of pressure injuries, a transition from stage zero to one may necessitate a topical ointment, whereas a transition from stage three to four may warrant surgical repair. Thus, the method relies on a simplifying assumption and future research will be conducted to evaluate nonlinear scoring systems. For multi-stage systems, this method remains more precise than collapsing scores to binary systems in order to use KM estimation. Alternative statistical methods, such as multi-state modeling, are recommended to elicit the transition intensities of each unique level as necessary. To encourage the evaluation and improvement of WTA, software is in development to permit biostatisticians to further test and apply WTA and potentially expand its utility.

In summary, we report the development and validation of a flexible new analytic tool for analysis of clinical datasets that permits high-sensitivity assessment of ordinal time-dependent outcomes. We see multiple clinical applications and have successfully applied the new tool in the analysis of both simulated and real-world studies with complex illness trajectories. Future directions with weighted trajectory analysis include the addition of confidence intervals to group trajectories, the addition of nonlinear weights to mirror disease burden, exploration of alternative censoring assumptions, and a regression method analogous to the Cox model.

Author Contributions: Conceptualization, U.C. and J.R.M.; methodology, U.C. and K.Z.; software, U.C.; validation, U.C. and K.Z.; formal analysis, U.C.; investigation, U.C.; resources, J.W. and J.R.M.; data curation, U.C.; writing—original draft preparation, U.C.; writing—review and editing, K.Z., J.W. and J.R.M.; visualization, U.C.; supervision, J.R.M. All authors have read and agreed to the published version of the manuscript.

Funding: This research received no external funding.

Data Availability Statement: The data that support the findings of this research are available on request from the corresponding author. The data are not publicly available due to privacy or ethical restrictions.

Acknowledgments: The authors thank Britsol Myers Squibb for access to their melanoma clinical trial dataset and the TRIO-012/ROSE study team, along with the TRIO Science Committee, for access to their database.

Conflicts of Interest: The authors declare no conflict of interest.

References

1. Kaplan, E.L.; Meier, P. Nonparametric Estimation from Incomplete Observations. *J. Am. Stat. Assoc.* **1958**, *5*, 457–481. [CrossRef]
2. Peto, R.; Pike, M.; Armitage, P.; Breslow, N.E.; Cox, D.R.; Howard, S.V.; Mantel, N.; McPherson, K.; Peto, J.; Smith, P.G. Design and analysis of randomized clinical trials requiring prolonged observation of each patient. I. Introduction and design. *Br. J. Cancer* **1976**, *34*, 585–612. [CrossRef] [PubMed]
3. Peto, R.; Pike, M.; Armitage, P.; Breslow, N.E.; Cox, D.R.; Howard, S.V.; Mantel, N.; McPherson, K.; Peto, J.; Smith, P.G. Design and analysis of randomized clinical trials requiring prolonged observation of each patient. II. Analysis and examples. *Br. J. Cancer* **1977**, *35*, 1–39. [CrossRef] [PubMed]
4. Oken, M.M.; Creech, R.H.; Tormey, D.C.; Horton, J.; Davis, T.E.; McFadden, E.T.; Carbone, P.P. Toxicity and response criteria of the Eastern Cooperative Oncology Group. *Am. J. Clin. Oncol.* **1982**, *5*, 649–655. [CrossRef] [PubMed]
5. American Heart Association. Classes of Heart Failure. Published 2 June 2022. Available online: https://www.heart.org/en/health-topics/heart-failure/what-is-heart-failure/classes-of-heart-failure (accessed on 29 September 2022).
6. U.S. Department of Health and Human Services. Common Terminology Criteria for Adverse Events (CTCAE) Version 5.0. Published 27 Nov 2017. Available online: https://ctep.cancer.gov/protocoldevelopment/electronic_applications/docs/ctcae_v5_quick_reference_5x7.pdf (accessed on 23 March 2020).
7. Liang, K.; Zeger, S.L. Longitudinal data analysis using generalized linear models. *Biometrika* **1986**, *73*, 13–22. [CrossRef]
8. Python Software Foundation. Python Language Reference, Version 3.7. Available online: http://www.python.org (accessed on 16 March 2020).
9. Davidson-Pilon, C. Lifelines: Survival analysis in Python. *J. Open Source Softw.* **2019**, *4*, 1317. [CrossRef]
10. IBM Corp. *IBM SPSS Statistics for Windows*; Version 26.0; IBM Corp.: Armonk, NY, USA, 2017.
11. Wang, D.Y.; Salem, J.E.; Cohen, J.V.; Chandra, S.; Menzer, C.; Ye, F.; Zhao, S.; Das, S.; Beckermann, K.E.; Ha, L.; et al. Fatal toxic effects associated with immune checkpoint inhibitors: A systematic review and meta-analysis. *JAMA Oncol.* **2018**, *4*, 1721–1728. [CrossRef] [PubMed]
12. Larkin, J.; Chiarion-Sileni, V.; Gonzalez, R.; Grob, J.J.; Cowey, C.L.; Lao, C.D.; Schadendorf, D.; Dummer, R.; Smylie, M.; Rutkowski, P.; et al. Combined nivolumab and ipilimumab or monotherapy in untreated melanoma. *N. Engl. J. Med.* **2015**, *373*, 23–34. [CrossRef] [PubMed]
13. Larkin, J.; Chiarion-Sileni, V.; Gonzalez, R.; Grob, J.J.; Rutkowski, P.; Lao, C.D.; Cowey, L.; Schadendorf, D.; Wagstaff, J.; Dummer, R.; et al. Five-year survival with combined nivolumab and ipilimumab in advanced melanoma. *N. Engl. J. Med.* **2019**, *381*, 1535–1546. [CrossRef] [PubMed]
14. Mackey, J.R.; Ramos-Vazquez, M.; Lipatov, O.; McCarthy, N.; Krasnozhon, D.; Semiglazov, V.; Manikhas, A.; Gelmon, K.; Konecny, G.; Webster, M.; et al. Primary results of ROSE/TRIO-12, a randomized placebo-controlled phase III trial evaluating the addition of ramucirumab to first-line docetaxel chemotherapy in metastatic breast cancer. *J. Clin. Oncol.* **2015**, *33*, 141–148. [CrossRef]
15. Schwartz, L.H.; Litière, S.; De Vries, E.; Ford, R.; Gwyther, S.; Mandrekar, S.; Shankar, L.; Bogaerts, J.; Chen, A.; Dancey, J.; et al. RECIST 1.1-Update and clarification: From the RECIST committee. *Eur. J. Cancer* **2016**, *62*, 132–137. [CrossRef] [PubMed]
16. Robins, J.M.; Rotnitzky, A.; Zhao, L.P. Analysis of Semiparametric Regression Models for Repeated Outcomes in the Presence of Missing Data. *J. Am. Stat. Assoc.* **1995**, 90, 106–121. [CrossRef]

BioMedInformatics

MDPI

Article

Evaluation of Transmembrane Protein Structural Models Using HPMScore

Stéphane Téletchéa [1,†], Jérémy Esque [2,†], Aurélie Urbain [3], Catherine Etchebest [4] and Alexandre G. de Brevern [4,5,*]

1 Nantes Université, CNRS, U2SB, UMR 6286, F-44000 Nantes, France
2 Toulouse Biotechnology Institute, Université de Toulouse, CNRS, INRAE, INSA, 31077 Toulouse, France
3 Institut Jean-Pierre Bourgin, INRAE, AgroParisTech, Université Paris-Saclay, F-78000 Versailles, France
4 Université Paris Cité and Université de la Réunion and Université des Antilles, INSERM, BIGR, DSIMB, F-75014 Paris, France
5 Université Paris Cité and Université de la Réunion and Université des Antilles, INSERM, BIGR, DSIMB, F-97715 Saint Denis, France
* Correspondence: alexandre.debrevern@univ-paris-diderot.fr; Tel.: +33-1-4449-3000
† These authors contributed equally to this work.

Abstract: Transmembrane proteins (TMPs) are a class of essential proteins for biological and therapeutic purposes. Despite an increasing number of structures, the gap with the number of available sequences remains impressive. The choice of a dedicated function to select the most probable/relevant model among hundreds is a specific problem of TMPs. Indeed, the majority of approaches are mostly focused on globular proteins. We developed an alternative methodology to evaluate the quality of TMP structural models. HPMScore took into account sequence and local structural information using the unsupervised learning approach called hybrid protein model. The methodology was extensively evaluated on very different TMP all-α proteins. Structural models with different qualities were generated, from good to bad quality. HPMScore performed better than DOPE in recognizing good comparative models over more degenerated models, with a Top 1 of 46.9% against DOPE 40.1%, both giving the same result in 13.0%. When the alignments used are higher than 35%, HPM is the best for 52%, against 36% for DOPE (12% for both). These encouraging results need further improvement particularly when the sequence identity falls below 35%. An area of enhancement would be to train on a larger training set. A dedicated web server has been implemented and provided to the scientific community. It can be used with structural models generated from comparative modeling to deep learning approaches.

Keywords: structural models; protein structures; membrane bilayer; DOPE; Modeller; AlphaFold2

Citation: Téletchéa, S.; Esque, J.; Urbain, A.; Etchebest, C.; de Brevern, A.G. Evaluation of Transmembrane Protein Structural Models Using HPMScore. *BioMedInformatics* **2023**, *3*, 306–326. https://doi.org/10.3390/biomedinformatics3020021

Academic Editor: Pentti Nieminen

Received: 3 March 2023
Revised: 25 March 2023
Accepted: 3 April 2023
Published: 6 April 2023

1. Introduction

Protein structure knowledge allows the atomistic understanding of biological mechanisms. Nonetheless, most of the available protein structures in the Protein DataBank (PDB) [1] are globular. Indeed, despite their great functional importance, e.g., 20% of all human proteins [2], transmembrane proteins (TMPs) represent less than 0.7% of the PDB (at 8 December 2020). They are implicated in a large series of pathologies [3] and are targeted by more than 60% of current drug [4]. Thus, methods to propose efficient structural models of TMPs are of high importance [5,6].

Although the number of templates was limited, comparative modeling methods have been applied to TMPs de novo, and now, deep learning protein structure predictions are used with the most recent developments [7,8]. Whatever the approach, the major challenge is to detect the structural model with the closest conformation to the native structure, which is accomplished by the so-called model quality assessment programs (MQAPs). By definition, free energy potentials would theoretically allow this selection. Physics-based potentials taken from molecular mechanics [9,10] might be considered. It was actually proposed by Feig's group [11], which calculated the energy of models as a sum of the force field conformational energy of the membrane protein plus the interaction energy of the protein with an implicit model of membrane environment. A web server (not available at the present time) was developed to calculate what is designated as memscore. As stated by the authors, the strategy was rather good for decoy close to the native state but further improvements are required for models further from the native state. Thus, even by accounting the membrane environment, force-field-based scoring functions are not the most efficient ones in practice because most of them are not calibrated on free energies.

The statistical potentials derived from experimentally determined protein structures remain the most efficient ones. MQAPs can be divided into different approaches; the most important ones take into account the local 3D environment of the protein structures. Briefly speaking, the scoring is based on the counting of the observed contacts and compared to a reference. However, although based on the same spirit and the same datasets, the formalism of the scoring function itself may be very different (see [12]). In this field, the most widely used was discrete optimized protein energy, or DOPE [13], which was implemented in the Modeller software [14,15]. It is mainly based on the distance between atoms in the analyzed models compared to the ones observed in the dataset of reference. Prosa [16] and its latest incarnation Prosa-web [17] are based on a classical potential of mean force; the output provided by Prosa-web was interesting as it compared the quality of the structural models in regard to a large dataset of X-ray and NMR structures. Verify3D proposed a slightly different view by considering the compatibility of the model (3D) with its sequence (1D) by looking at the environment (secondary structure, hydrophobicity, etc.) as seen in known structures [18,19]. Since this first generation, different improvements have been introduced; they consisted of adding different parameters, such as the residue distance, solvent accessibility and secondary structure content [20–23]. The weighting of these parameters was optimized with artificial neural networks, support vector machines or machine learning approaches [24–27]. Consequently, they were in general more dependent on the training procedure and on the training set than classical approaches.

TMPs structural models have often been assessed using this approach. However, these MQAPs were often optimized on water-soluble proteins that bathe in a homogenous environment. In the case of TMPs, the situation is more complex because they are in contact with two very distinct environments; a water environment for the soluble part of the protein and the lipid environment for the membrane embedded region, and even a third one corresponding to the membrane interface. This also corresponds to a striking difference in the amino acid distribution of TMPs [28]. Thus, to make sure these specificities were taken into account, the IQ method was proposed. It is based on the analysis of four types of inter-residue interactions within the transmembrane domains [29]. The ProQM approach used support vector machines trained on contacts, solvent-accessible surface, secondary structure, topology of TM region, Z-coordinate, and evolutionary information [30,31]. It was sensitive to the side-chain positioning.

MEMEMBED is a dedicated statistical potential that considers the membrane depth of residues [32]. More recently, MAIDEN proposed an interesting and innovative development, computing the interatomic distance between all 20 standard residue types, focusing on intramembrane residues [33,34]. QMEANBrane is a more simple approach also using the delineation of a theoretical membrane region to focus on the transmembrane region [35]. It was only tested on a GPCR, while MAIDEN was tested on the most diverse set of protein folds.

In the RosettaMembrane/RosettaMP approach [36–38], a specific function for TMP has been established in a Rosetta way, namely the force field is a linear combination of a Lennard–Jones potential to model the VDW interactions, a backbone torsional term, a knowledge-based pair interaction term for the electrostatic interactions, reference energies to normalize the overall amino acid composition, an implicit atomic solvation term, and an orientation-dependent hydrogen bonding term [39]. This development is highly dependent on the specific generation of the models by Rosetta. All these scoring functions can only compare a set of equivalent structural models, but not different sequences. AlphaFold2 has its own quality schema evaluation, called pLDDT, for "predicted local distance difference test", which is a per-residue confidence metric [40]. pLDDT is not a score for comparing models but rather a local confidence measure of regions of the structural models [40]; it appears worse for qualifying regions in membrane protein compared to those in globular proteins [8,41–44].

In a previous study [45], we learnt and analyzed the sequence–structure relationship of TMPs with an unsupervised learning approach, called the hybrid protein model (HPM) [46,47]. HPM was also shown to be efficient in analyzing globular proteins, e.g., building of overlapping local structural prototypes [48–50] or the prediction [51–53] of flexibility. HPM was used to analyze protein fragments present in a non-redundant databank of all-α transmembrane proteins. The method has many advantages, which are: (i) A simultaneous learning of sequence (polarity, volume, and hydrophobicity) and structures (φ and ψ dihedral angles) properties, e.g., distribution of amino acids associated with different local conformations; (ii) Unsupervised learning due to the given descriptors (sequence and structure), i.e., without any a priori; and (iii) The learning of the overlapping of protein fragments, taking into account the sequentiality (or continuity) essential in proteins, i.e., without any constraints. After a fine-tuning of learning parameters, the sequence–structure relationship was analyzed in light of a structural alphabet, called protein blocks [54,55], underlining two helical regions with very different hydrophobic patterns, identifying groups with properties specific to extremities of helices, or to loops, or to helices. Moreover, some groups showed preferential localizations for the periphery of the membrane or inside the membrane. This can be used for annotation as channel/non-channel, but also for the assessment of the quality of structures and structural models.

In this study, we have generated a large set of structural models ranging from very good to poor models for a various number of folds. The models were evaluated using classical root mean square deviation (rmsd) and GDT_TS. The latter is the most classical reference metric for comparing diverse structural models [56]. Its interest is to limit the influence of poorly modeled substructures for the protein considered. We also used the famous DOPE scores [13], as using them is one of the most classical approaches to selecting protein structural models though comparative/homology modeling.

In some aspects, the HPM approach can be related to the Verify3D methodology, which encompasses sequence, structure, and environment properties to evaluate the compatibility of a given sequence with a given 3D structure. The Verify3D approach was never dedicated to TMPs. HPM does not need, as is true of other approaches, to localize helical regions and take into account the connecting loops. We then compared the discrimination of the quality of the models using HPMScore values compared to DOPE scores, and we propose a dedicated webserver HPMScore (https://www.dsimb.inserm.fr/dsimb_tools/hpmscore/index.php, accessed on 1 March 2023).

2. Materials and Methods

2.1. Protein Structure Dataset

The membrane protein dataset was derived from the HOMEP dataset [57]. This set of proteins is composed of 76 membrane proteins, separated in 23 categories, depending on their biological function (https://zenodo.org/record/2646540#.Y7b99C3pNTY, accessed on 1 March 2023). This dataset was completed by 13 GPCR structures. The entire dataset is composed of 89 proteins. The protein structures composed of all-α transmembrane domain were taken from the PDB [1]. For analysis purposes, the number of TM domains and their boundaries over the whole protein sequence were predicted using the PPM web server or directly imported from the orientation of protein in a membrane (OPM) database [58,59]. We defined three main categories of protein structures according to the transmembrane content: large (more than 40% of amino acids associated with the transmembrane domain), medium (40%< and >15%), and few (>15%). Please notice that HOMEP was later expanded in EncoMPASS [60].

2.2. Generation of Alternative Structural Models

We have generated a large set of structural models ranging from good quality to bad, i.e., to mimic what often happens in daily research. For a given protein, the original sequence from the PDB was extracted and duplicated to create an ideal alignment where the template and the target sequence are initially identical. The alignment was further processed to reproduce point mutations or gap insertions using two strategies. First, we created a similar sequence by randomly picking an amino acid position and exchanging it with another position. This procedure kept the amino acid composition, but varied the sequence identity with the template sequence. The procedure was repeated until a target percentage of identity was obtained or a maximum number of iterations was reached. This iteration number was set arbitrarily at twice the length of the amino acid sequence to save time. The second strategy consisted of perturbing the alignment by random gap modifications, up to 5 random gaps of length between 1 and 8, either on the parent sequence or on its children. Once the alignment was produced, its overall percentage of identity was calculated using BioPerl [61]. The structural models for each alignment were created using Modeller v9.18 [14,15] (the entire process of generation and evaluation of structural models is presented in Figure A1).

2.3. Assessment Scores

DOPE scores [13] are directly provided by Modeller [14,15]. HPM scores [45] are determined as follows: (i) The protein structures are cut into fragments of length L ($L = 13$, as obtained in [45] and recommended from previous studies [46,47,54], see next paragraph); (ii) Each fragment is translated in terms of polarity, volume, and hydrophobicity for their sequence and in the cosine and sine functions of their dihedral angles for their structure; (iii) The fragment and its local environment are then compared to each position of the optimal HPM matrix (determined in [45]); (iv) The maximal score provides the best matching between this position and the HPM matrix that reflects our current knowledge of TMP sequence–structure relationship. The HPMScore value is the sum of all these maximum scores. For further analyses, local DOPE and local HPMScore values were also investigated per domain, i.e., transmembrane region or not, using the segments defined as membranous in OPM [58,59].

From a practical point of view, HPM depends on its total length and the length of the fragments presented. These two parameters were tested in [45] to end with a total length of 100 and fragments of $L = 13$ positions. With several simulations, these two choices made it possible to have a sufficient occurrence number at each position, and also two distinct types of helices. Then, with these parameters, 100 independent simulations were carried out with a high learning rate similar to the self-organizing maps (SOM) type [62,63]; this high value limits the importance of initializing. The most central HPM (with a minimum distance from all the others) was then taken up as a new initial HPM for a new training. Here, the learning coefficient was quite limited to fix the optimal HPM. These two stages have a strong analogy with the two main phases of learning the SOMS, i.e., diffusion then specialization.

2.4. Data Analyses

The 3D structure representation is generated using the PyMOL software (http://www.pymol.org, accessed on 1 March 2023) [64]. The protein superimposition was carried out using the iPBA software [65] based on the protein block description [54]. RMSD was computed using profit [66], through the iPBA software. In the following step, the computation of the GDT_TS and PBscore alignment was performed [65]. TMalign was also used for comparison [67]. The GDT_TS value is a reference metric for comparing diverse structural models [56]. It weights close to large local RMSD variations to limit the influence of poorly modeled substructures for the protein considered. An ideal GDT_TS value is 100 for a "perfect" match between the model and the experimental structure; the worst value is 0. For each experiment, the best model is defined by the highest GDT_TS in regard to the true

3D structure. It is named "G-model" in the following. Most of the analyses were carried out using the Python language and R software [68]. We have made available a companion website that contains a large number of analyses (https://clipperton.ufip.univ-nantes.fr/hpmeval/, accessed on 1 March 2023). The analyses can be viewed at the level of the whole dataset, but also by a single protein and by protein type. Various data analyses have been performed. The most classic is the calculation of the Top 1, Top 5, and Top 10. The metric is simple and corresponds to the number of times that for the same simulation, the HPM or DOPE method allow you to select the best model. For Top 1, it is a direct comparison, while for Top 5 and Top 10, it is the best as selected by DOPE and/or HPM within their best 5 and 10 scores. The only specificity of these results is that sometimes DOPE and HPM can select the same result (hence, the category HPM and DOPE).

2.5. Scripting and Web Server of HPMScore

The original code of HPMScore was developed with the use of a local PDB reader coded in C language that generated a flat file with all the information (sequence in terms of polarity, volume, and hydrophobicity, and structure in terms of φ and ψ dihedral angles). The latter is used by the HPM program (also coded in C language) that performs the evaluation. A dedicated web server that encompasses all these properties is made available to the scientific community. It provides a simple interface with a nice visualization (https://www.dsimb.inserm.fr/dsimb_tools/hpmscore/index.php, accessed on 1 March 2023).

3. Results

3.1. Generation of a Set of Structural Models for Sequences with Various Sequence Identities with Templates

The assessment of protein model quality is essential to guide computational biologists to select the best structure for further evaluation and analysis. The main idea was to simulate a large sampling of structural models derived from TMP resolved structures, ranging from sequences close to the sequence of a known structure to sequences far from any structural template sequences leading to very poor models, as it may occur. To mimic the drift of protein sequences through evolution, the initial protein sequence of each protein model was subjected to permutations or mutations to reach a given percentage of identity.

For example, a 100amino-acid-length protein sequence will attain 99% of sequence identity if one mutation is virtually performed, or 98% with a permutation since two positions are exchanged between different amino acids. This degenerated sequence and the original protein structure is then used as inputs for Modeller [14] for producing 3D models of the "drifted" protein. We will detail below how the models are assessed using our original method, HPMScore [45] and DOPE [13].

From the dataset of 89 proteins, a total of 29,571 alignments were generated, which correspond to an average value of 332 degenerated alignments per protein. This value depends on the protein length. The distribution of scrambled sequences ranked by sequence identity is shown in Figure 1. The average sequence identity is 38.9% (for a median of 32.55%) and reaches a peak for the 10–15% interval with more than 3500 alignments available. As the generation of sequences with very low identity percentages (<10%) can be time-consuming, we limited the number of sequence generation, which resulted in a drop in this category. This distribution, which looks roughly as an extreme value distribution, shows that it is easier to generate sequences with low sequence identity than with high sequence identity. It also underlines the interest of categorizing 3 main classes of alignments: good for a sequence identities higher than 75% (3682 sequences), bad for sequence identities less than 35% (15,786 sequences), and medium for the sequences between them (10,102 sequences). For each alignment, 25 models were built using Modeller [49].

Thus, a particularly large number of structural models of very different quality have been proposed, allowing a broad view of all the different types of protein folding of TMPs. This approach allows the evaluation of HPMScore and its comparison with DOPE.

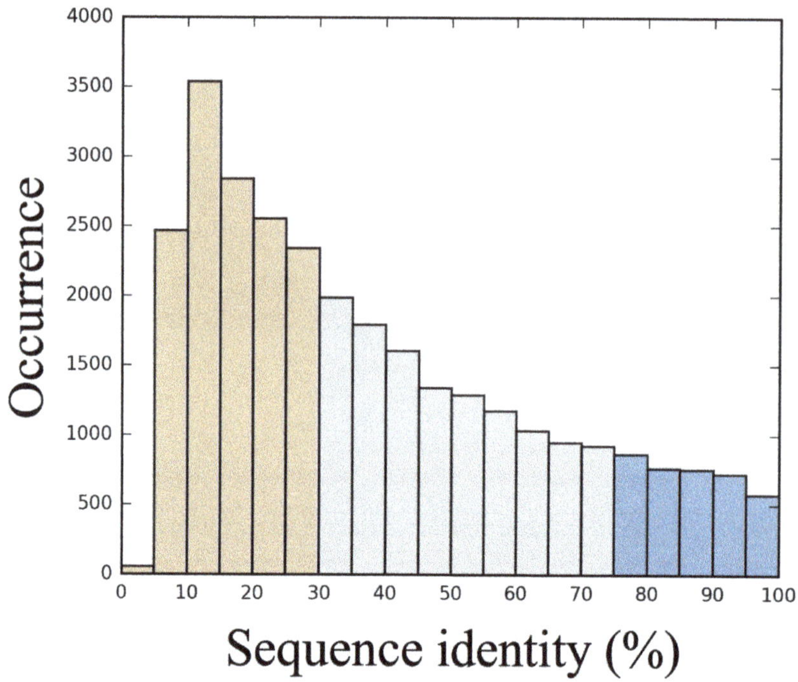

Figure 1. Distribution of sequence alignments. This histogram provides the distribution of sequence alignments percentage identity (%) between the true sequence and the simulated ones. A simulated sequence is classified as a good sequence if the sequence shares 75% or more sequence identity with the reference (in blue), as medium for a sequence identity above 30% and below 75% (grey), and as bad in other cases (<30%, in tan).

3.2. HPM Selects Better Models Than DOPE

To determine which model is the closest to the experimental structure, GDT_TS values [56] were computed for all models proposed from the degenerated sequences. In ideal situations, we should observe a correlation between the scoring functions and the GDT_TS values. Consequently, we addressed two questions: (i) What is the capacity of each scoring function to rank the model with the highest GDT_TS score first? and (ii) What is the quality of the best model (Rank 1) defined by each scoring function? For the first question, we found that both DOPE and HPM can identify the absolute G-model (the one with the highest GDT_TS) with a very limited prediction rate of 7.4% for HPM and 3.7% for DOPE. Although the capacity of each scoring function to identify the absolute G-model is limited, HPM appears slightly more efficient than DOPE.

This result still stands when addressing the second question, i.e., the quality of the model ranked best by each method. Indeed, the first model ranked by HPM has a lower GDT_TS score in 46.9% of cases compared to 40.1% for DOPE, and both select the same in 13.0% of the cases (see Table 1(A)). If the first 5 HPM or DOPE best scores are considered, HPM still outperforms DOPE (48.4% vs. 44.0%), and this situation stands true even if the first 10 models are considered (48.4% vs. 45.5%). This average lower sensitivity of DOPE may be attributed to a more important weight of loop regions in the scoring function. In contrast, when only transmembrane segments are taken into account (see Table 1(B)), DOPE slightly outperforms HPM (47.2% vs. 45.6%) only if the best model is considered. Indeed, when more models are considered (Top 5 or 10 models selected by each method), the differences between the two scoring functions are small but systematically in favor of HPM (46.8% vs. 46.4%, and 47.0% vs. 46.3%, respectively).

Table 1. Relative performance of HPM vs. DOPE. The percentages of best models, i.e., best GDT_TS found by HPM, DOPE or both within TOP 1, TOP 5 and TOP 10 results, are provided. (A) For the complete structure. (B) Only on transmembrane segments.

(A)			
Scoring Method/Models Considered for Ranking	**TOP 1**	**TOP 5**	**TOP 10**
DOPE	40.1%	44.0%	45.5%
HPM	46.9%	48.4%	48.4%
HPM and DOPE	13.0%	7.6%	6.1%
(B)			
Scoring Method/Models Considered for Ranking	**TOP 1**	**TOP 5**	**TOP 10**
DOPE	47.4%	46.4%	46.3%
HPM	45.6%	46.8%	47.0%
HPM and DOPE	7.0%	6.8%	6.7%

In a second step, we examined the influence of the sequence identity on the capacity of identifying the best model and the quality of the ranked models for each method (see Table 2). For models produced with medium sequence identity (35–75% of sequence identity), or with high sequence identity, i.e., good sequence alignment (75–100%), the quality of the best ranked model by HPM largely outperforms the quality of the best ranked model by DOPE, with about 52% for models in both medium and good categories detected by HPMScore, 36% detected using DOPE, and 12% where both models find the same model. For sequences below 35% of sequence identity, considered as poor alignments, DOPE (43.8%) performs slightly better than HPM (42.6%), and both methods find the best model in 13.6% of alignments.

Table 2. Relative performance of HPM vs. DOPE. The percentages of best models, i.e., the best GDT_TS, found by HPM, DOPE or both when the sequence percentage id of the reference model is taken into account, are provided.

Scoring Method/% Sequence Identity Range	**Poor Alignments (0–35%)**	**Average Alignments (35–75%)**	**Good Alignments (75–100%)**
Sequence count	15,786	10,102	3682
DOPE	43.8%	35.5%	36.8%
HPM	42.6%	51.8%	52.6%
HPM and DOPE	13.6%	12.7%	10.6%

In summary, for target sequences with a sequence identity compatible with comparative modeling (>35%), HPM is on average more effective than DOPE. When the sequence identity decreases, the differences between the two scoring schemas are much lower, and slightly in favor of the DOPE scoring function. Please note that for poor alignment quality, it is difficult to be sure that the aliasing is properly preserved. It is certain that a significant number of cases are not correct TMPs.

Figure 2 illustrates an example of the putative metal-chelate type ABC transporter (PDB ID 2NQ2) and the relationship between the generated alignments, the HPMScore value of the corresponding structural models, and the structural approximation (evaluated here by the GDT_TS). The protein is a homodimer, each monomer being composed of a large transmembrane domain containing eight TM helices and an intracellular domain composed of α-helices mainly and a few β-sheets (Figure 2a). Only Chain A has been evaluated, since Chain B is similar. Figure 2b shows the dependence of the HPM score with the percentage of identity of the target sequences with the template sequences. Since the HPM score is equivalent to a distance, the lower the HPMScore value, the better it is. Figure 2b clearly illustrates the nice correlation between the HPMScore and the sequence identity. Figure 2c shows that the quality of the models (evaluated with the GDT_TS score) is obtained after a strong randomization of the sequence alignment. This figure points out that even with a low sequence identity, the GDT_TS score can be very high, which means that it is possible to keep a native fold. It is clear, however, that the better the alignment, the lower the standard deviation of the category (good, medium, and bad). Figure 2d highlights the correlation between scores from HPMScore and GDT_TS scores. It is clear that for the lowest HPMScore values (associated with good quality alignments), the structural approximation is the best. Moreover, the HPMScore is able to distinguish the best ones from the worst.

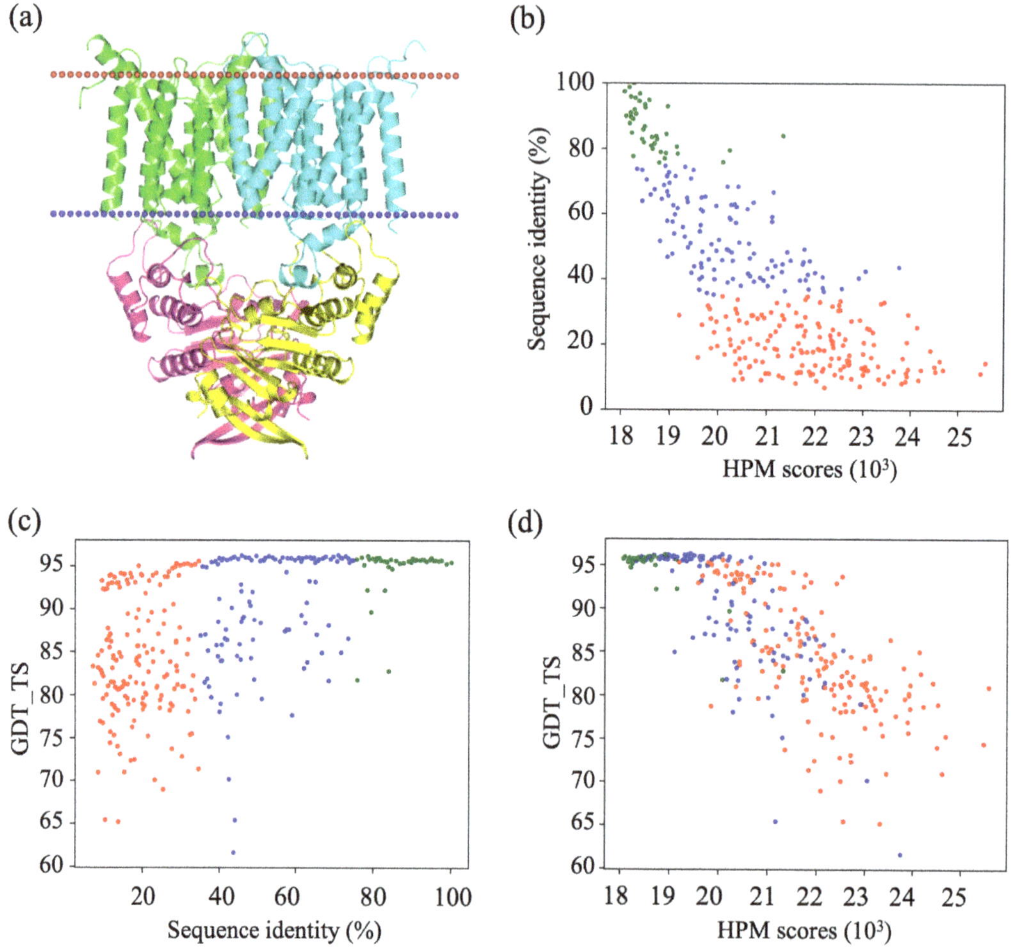

Figure 2. Example of putative metal-chelate type ABC transporter (PDB ID 2NQ2). (**a**) Three-dimensional visualization, (**b**) sequence identity of the alignments (%) vs. HPM scores (103), (**c**) GDT_TS vs. sequence identity of the alignments (%), and (**d**) GDT vs. HPM scores (103). (**b–d**) good alignment (green), intermediate alignment (blue) and bad alignment (red).

Hence, the example in Figure 2 shows the complexity of proposing structural models of different quality, but also how essential it is. TMPs are more often difficult cases than simple ones. The analysis of Top 1 to Top 10 shows that the HPMScore allows on average a better selection of models. The analysis of the alignments compatible with the comparative modeling (average and good quality) shows that the HPMScore gives a better selection in

52% of the cases, 12% are common with DOPE, and DOPE performed better in 36% of the cases. The difference is clear.

3.3. Assessment of Protein Model Quality

After evaluating how HPM correlates with a robust global measure, such as the GDT_TS, we go further in the evaluation of the quality of the models ranked by HPM and DOPE, respectively. An example of the models obtained for medium sequence identity to the reference protein (38%) is presented in Figure 3. The best model according to HPM is more compact and possesses slightly more secondary structures than the model with the best DOPE score. A closer inspection reveals a more consistent architecture of the seven transmembrane segments, a better orientation of the third intracytoplasmic loop characteristic of GPCR proteins, and the conservation of the extracellular loop involved as a lid for the ligand binding pocket. Overall, both models are of poor quality and would not be considered as sufficient for further use as support models, but the HPM-selected models are better candidates for further modeling studies.

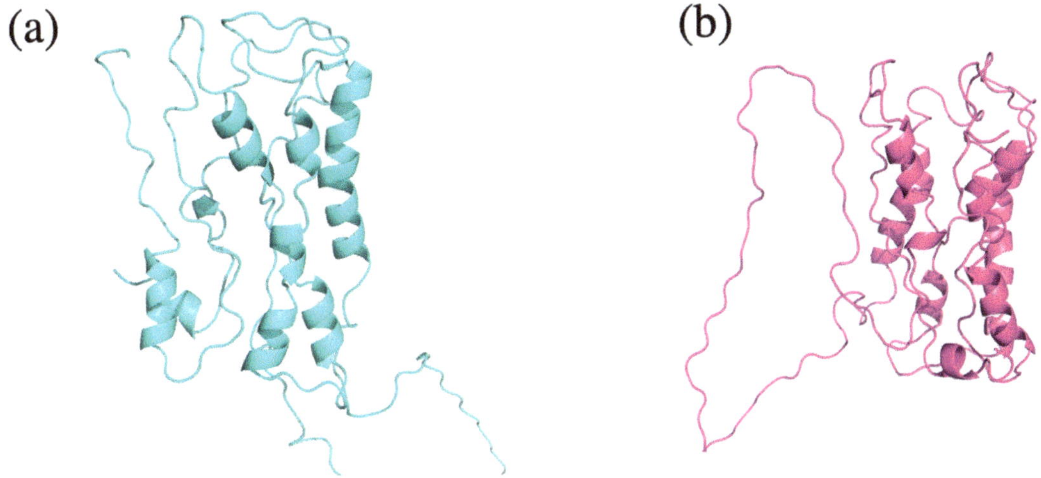

Figure 3. Comparison of models identified using HPM or DOPE. Cartoon representation of the models selected by HPM ((**a**), in cyan) or DOPE ((**b**), in pink) for a degenerated sequence of 38.8% sequence identity with the human M2 muscarinic acetylcholine receptor (PDB ID 3UON). The HPM-selected model is more compact than the DOPE-selected model.

All analyses for all proteins have been made available on the companion site (https://clipperton.ufip.univ-nantes.fr/hpmeval/, accessed on 1 March 2023). The analyses can be viewed at the level of the whole dataset, but also by single protein and by protein type.

3.4. Web Server Usage and Example

The web server can be accessed at the following url: https://www.dsimb.inserm.fr/dsimb_tools/hpmscore/index.php, accessed on 1 March 2023). The main page gives a small introduction and a direct access to the section for uploading the structural models (see Figure 4). Two options are possible that consist of: (i) Analyzing models one by one (see Figure 4B); or (ii) A set of models uploaded from an archive (see Figure 4A). Please note that structural models must be provided in a classical PDB format, as generated by Modeller [14], Robetta [69], RoseTTAfold [70], AlphaFold2 [40], I-Tasser and other classical approaches.

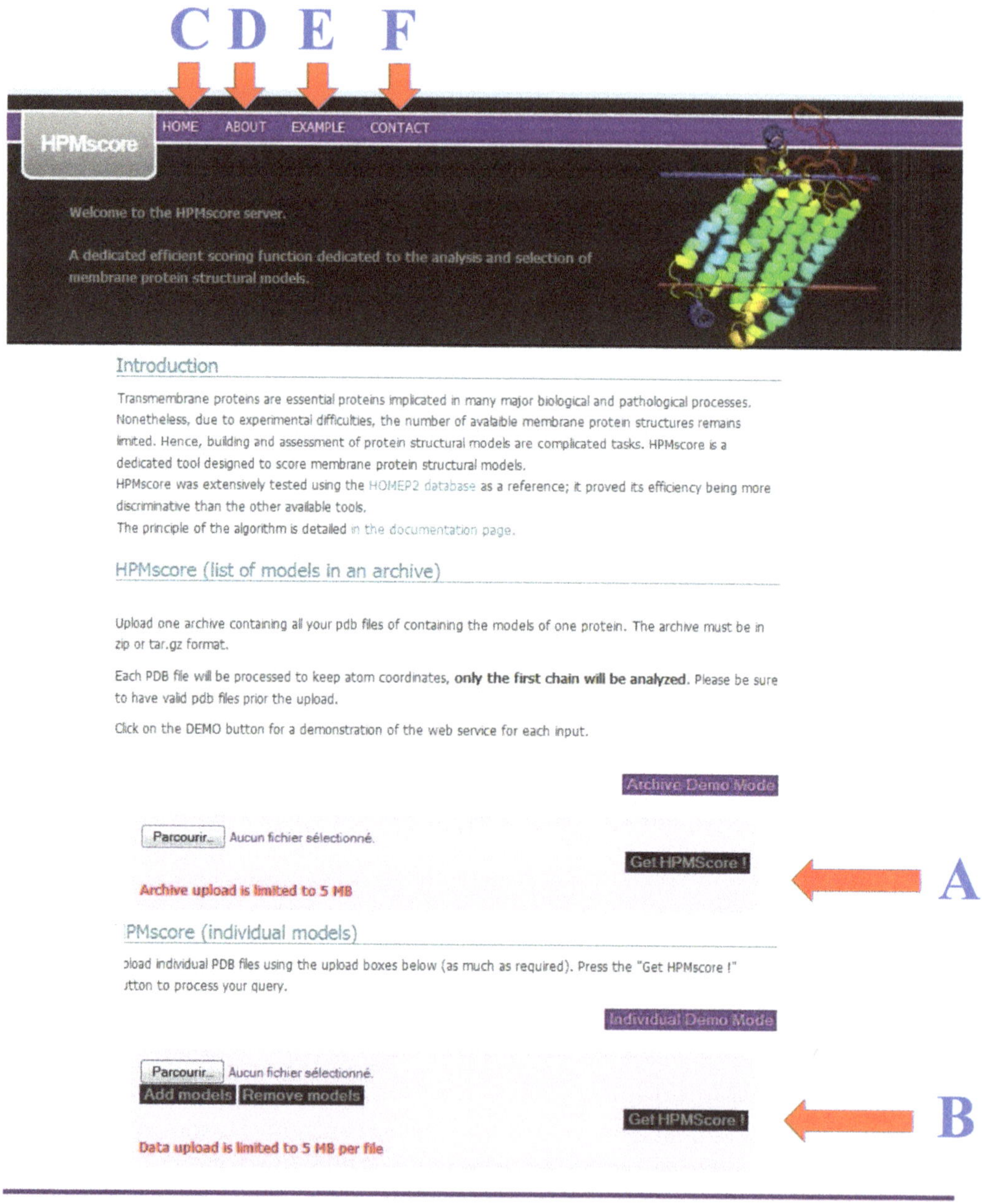

Figure 4. HPMScore homepage. Two options are provided to upload the structural models: (**A**) all files being in an unique archive or (**B**) added one by one. Links to the different pages are shown on the top of the page (**C**) this page, (**D**) a description of the methodology, (**E**) a dedicated example and (**F**) the contact page.

At the top, links to access other pages are found on all pages. The first page is the Home page (see Figure 4C), followed by a page of explanation of the HPM methodology (see Figure 4D), a concrete example of usage and analysis (see Figure 4E), and finally, the last page contains the contacts of the people involved in this research (see Figure 4F).

When the files have been loaded, the program launches an intermediate note page stating 'Please wait while HPMScore is computed'. Each job is associated with a temporary directory, which will be kept for two months.

The results page (see Figure 5) is divided into six main parts. The example proposed here can be found on the website, and corresponds to a putative Halorhodopsin with no known structure and less than 40% sequence identity to related ones, i.e., a classical case of structural modeling.

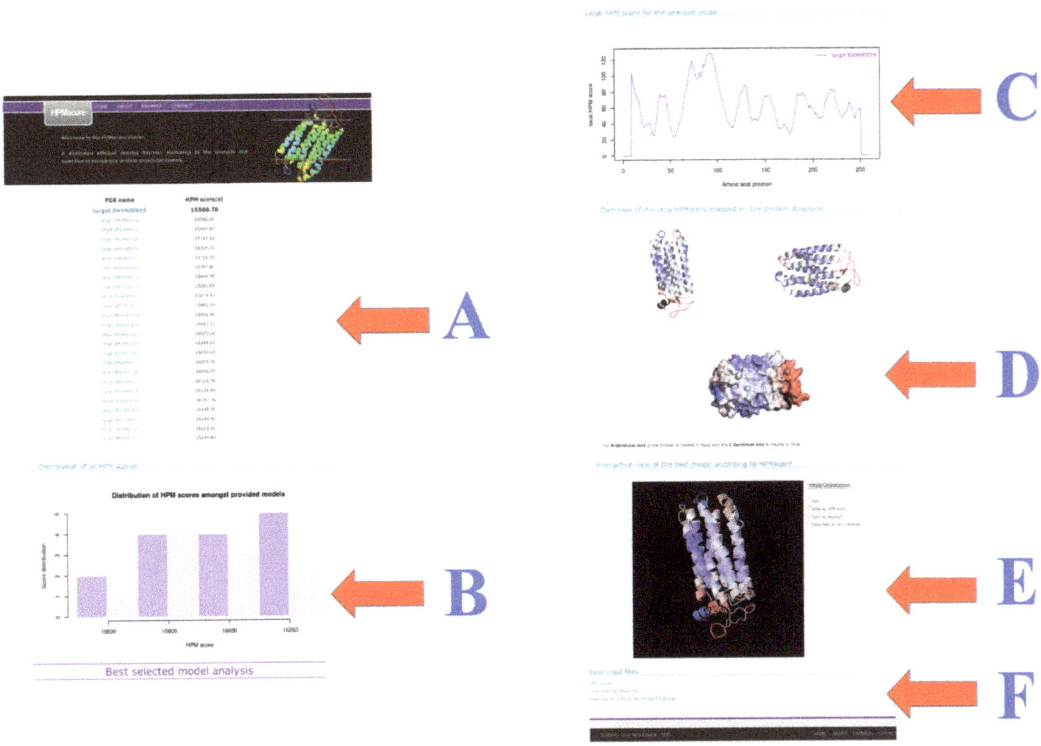

Figure 5. HPMScore results. The page results have been split in two columns. (**A**) The list of the different models ranging from best (smallest HPM score) to worst is provided; (**B**) A histogram of these HPM scores is provided; (**C**) A local plot of HPM score is shown for the best model (it can be found in the archive files for the other models); (**D**) Two orientations of the best structural models colored with the local HPM score are provided with an extra one within the protein surface; (**E**) An interactive visualization; and (**F**) Links to the different files and archive. The example shown here is provided on the website and corresponds to a Halorhodopsin far away from other related sequences and structures.

The first section lists the structural models by HPM score in descending order (the best being the first, see Figure 5A). Then, a histogram shows the distribution of the HPM scores of the different models (see Figure 5B). This information allows the user to carry out analyses, for example, to compare the best and the worst model, or other ranking questions. HPM, like DOPE score or Verify3D and PROSA, computes a local score, it uses an overlapping sequence window of 13 residues. The third section provides this information for the first model with a plot (see Figure 5C). It could allow comparing alternative proposed conformations. The fourth part shows the 3D model in two orientations (and an extra one with the surface) thanks to the software PyMOL. The structural model is colored according to the quality considered by the HPM score (see Figure 5D). The user can directly interact with the structural model (see Figure 5E). An essential point is the availability of an archive summarizing all this information (see Figure 5F), which can be downloaded locally. It contains all the information detailed here, but also provided for every model not shown on the website. Structural models are provided with an HPM score. It is possible to observe them with visualization software, such as the PyMOL software. All of this information makes it easy to choose the model that seems the most relevant, knowing the difficulty of this type of question for transmembrane proteins.

Thus, the HPMScore webserver allows the specialist and the neophyte (it has been particularly used in several training sessions) to evaluate models in a simple way. It then allows visualizing the areas considered as the most successful. The specialist can also use it to go further in comparative modeling by combining multiple models according to their local HPMScore values.

3.5. Use with Structural Models Coming from Different Approaches

We have assessed the interest of our approach based on comparative modeling, while new approaches of interest exist (see Figure 6). We have so built a 3D structural model of the putative Halorhodopsin used in Figure 5 with the threading approach Phyre [71] and deep learning approaches RoseTTAfold [70], ESMFold [72], and AlphaFold2 [40]. Other approaches were tested but they cannot provide complete models.

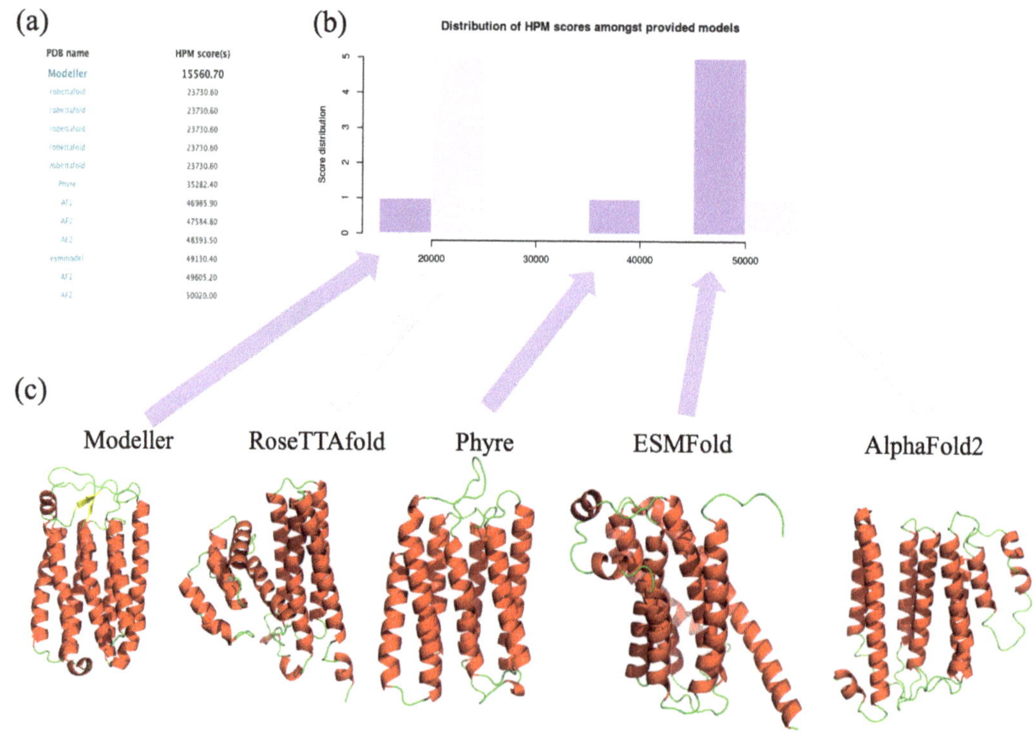

Figure 6. Comparison of different structural models coming from different methodologies for a Halorhodopsin. (**a**) The list of the different methodologies is provided, (**b**) the corresponding HPM score histogram with (**c**) the visualization of different structural models from Modeller, RoseTTAfold, Phyre, ESMFold, and AlphaFold2. Please notice that PDB files of RoseTTAfold have been saved in proper PDB format with PyMOL.

We have only added the best Modeller results. This works well and shows the diversity and difficulty of proposing TMP structural models. HPMScore values are distant, so the lower the better. Hence, AlphaFold2 [40] is very far away (and close to ESMFold) with the highest HPMScore values. Phyre is the intermediate when our supervised Modeller is the one associated with the lowest (best) HPMScore value. Interestingly, RoseTTAfold is not too far away but has a wrong local topology. This last example clearly underlines the interest of HPMScore, which is a specific development for protein of high pharmaceutical interest. Structure models were evaluated on a large scale with a very large set of model quality showing its stability. The HPM scoring function, performing on average better than DOPE, is the reference scoring function in the Modeller suite [14] (that can be used to rank models made from other approaches).

This example highlights the importance of having an external and simple tool to test results from different tools, even in this period of Deep Learning with AlphaFold2 and related methods.

4. Discussion

The modeling of TMPs has existed for a long time, even when the number of structures was very limited [7,73]. To analyze the properties of TMPs, the first step has long been the prediction of the transmembrane segments. PHDtm was the first method linking artificial neural networks (ANNs) and evolutionary data [74,75]. PsiPred [76,77] is a widely used platform for secondary structure prediction, which uses position-specific scoring matrices (PSSMs) with ANN [78]. Although this approach is hardly specific to TMPs, it has shown good results. Initially, the addition of hydrophobicity scales to the prediction of secondary structures gave better results [79,80]. An impressive number of methods were proposed, such as MEMSAT [81,82], HTP [83], DAS [83], SOSUI [84], HMMTOP [85,86], TMHMM 1.0 [87], PRED-TMR [88], OCTOPUS [89], TOPCONS [90,91], MINNOU [92], SVMtm [93], TUPS [94], Localizome [95], MemBrain [96], AllesTM [97], TMPSS [98], and TMbed [99]. The most recent approaches also take into account other features, such as the regions of the protein that actually face the membrane, the cytosolic or extracellular sides, and the motifs responsible for the interactions [97,100–102].

These approaches do not provide 3D structural models but they provide interesting behaviors. The first and most common proposition of TMP structural models is homology modeling with Modeller [14] and SwissModel [103]. Based on sequence alignment with a structural template, it remains essential in the TMP area. Some methods have been developed specifically for TMP. For instance, MEMOIR (membrane protein modeling pipeline) [104], and MEDELLER [105], which proposed only high-quality regions and did not complete others. Threading was used in TMFoldWeb [106], a web implementation of TMFoldRec [107]. Rosetta had interestingly incorporated a specific membrane-specific version of the original Rosetta energy function, which considers the membrane environment as an additional variable next to amino acid identity, inter-residue distances, and density [108]. It was included in RosettaMP [98]. In fact, all structural modeling methods, e.g., Phyre [71], Modeller [14], SwissModel [103], RoseTTAfold [70], ESMFold [72], and AlphaFold2 [40] can be used for TMPs (see Section 3.5).

However, a quasi-systematic bias is the use of score functions related to globular proteins and not to transmembrane proteins, such as DOPE. Independent tools, such as Verify3D [18] or Prosa II [16,17], are based on data that mainly emphasize globular proteins largely over-represented in PDB globular proteins compared to TMPs.

It is worth noting some studies of interest. Postic and collaborators have, thus, set up an empirical energy function for the structural assessment of protein transmembrane domains [33]. This statistical potential quantifies the interatomic distance between residues located in the lipid bilayer. Following a leave-one-out cross-validation procedure, they show that their method outperforms statistical potentials in discriminating correct from incorrect membrane protein models. The approach must be locally installed. Studer and coworkers proposed an equivalent method named QMEANBrane [35] derived from the original QMEAN scoring function [20,109]. It is integrated in the SwissModel environment but cannot be used with external models [103]. More recently, AlphaFold2 had proposed its pLDDT scores [40] associated with the quality of the proposed structural models. However, it cannot be used with results from other approaches. It seems so interesting to see if the HPMScore could be interesting for the scientific community.

Our work can easily raise three questions: (i) Which proteins can be used? (ii) Which structural models can be generated? and (iii) How can the results be assessed?.

Transmembrane proteins are difficult to obtain experimentally. In 2000, only one structure was in the protein data bank. Thanks to new methodologies, their number had greatly increased. Now, 1561 unique PTM structures can be found, for all-α and all-β TMPs, as stated by mpstruct [110,111] (https://blanco.biomol.uci.edu/mpstruc/#news, accessed on 17 January 2023). However, the number of different folds had not really increased, and redundancies exist. We have kept the HOMEP dataset as we know it very well and represent correctly the different known TMP folds.

From this dataset, we need to generate a series of structural models. Different approaches have been proposed to generate decoys that deviated from the real structure. As no dataset was available, we generated our own. To do this, we decided to make point mutations, insertions, and deletions to move further and further away from the real structure. Of course, this does not represent a directed (or rather degenerated) evolution [112], but it does allow for an important sampling of conformational space. The conservation of the membrane part plays on a weaker amino acid alphabet [113] than the one we used. Figure 2c shows how complex this is. Even with a 25% alignment, it is possible to have GDT_TS ranging from 10 to 90.

Finally, we have analyzed the results with RMSD [114], PBscore [65], and GDT_TS [56]. They all provide the same trends. Top 1, Top 5 and Top 10 underline the interest of the HPMScore to select the best models. As discussed before, we are in the idea of comparative modeling, i.e., for sequence alignment higher than 35%; the HPMScore gives a better selection in 52% of the cases, 12% are common with DOPE, and DOPE is associated with it in 36% of the cases. Figure 7 shows a visualization of the quality of the prediction by a slice of 5% of sequence identity. A regression is performed for the HPM results of DOPE and cases where both give the same result. The direction of the lines highlights the superiority of HPM. This evaluation unequivocally demonstrates the value of the approach. A Welsh test on the question of whether HPM is better than a DOPE score alone (data in Figure 7) gave a significant positive answer (0.01). A rather complex point to apprehend is the variability of the results simply by protein. The generation of unsupervised alternative alignments gives very different results depending on the topology of the protein, its amino acid composition or the impacts of insertions–deletions.

Lastly, we should remember that the HPMScore is built on the HPM matrix, fully described in [45]. The HPM strategy is based on a learning process combining sequence and structural properties, which depends on a few parameters.

In the present work, we kept the optimal HPM matrix finely tuned after an extensive grid search of the parameters and trained on 52 PDB files. Despite its small size, this dataset contains most of the representative folds of α-helical TM protein. Given the good results with the present version of the HPM matrix, we may reasonably expect improvement with new training on a larger dataset that includes 3D structures solved since. This will be the subject of a forthcoming study. For convenience, we have made available an additional website (https://clipperton.ufip.univ-nantes.fr/hpmeval/, accessed on 1 March 2023) with a large number of analyses, which highlights this complexity.

The HPMScore web server allows a simple and efficient use; we used it regularly (and also for courses). The example presented with results from very different predictive tools clearly demonstrates the usability of the methodology.

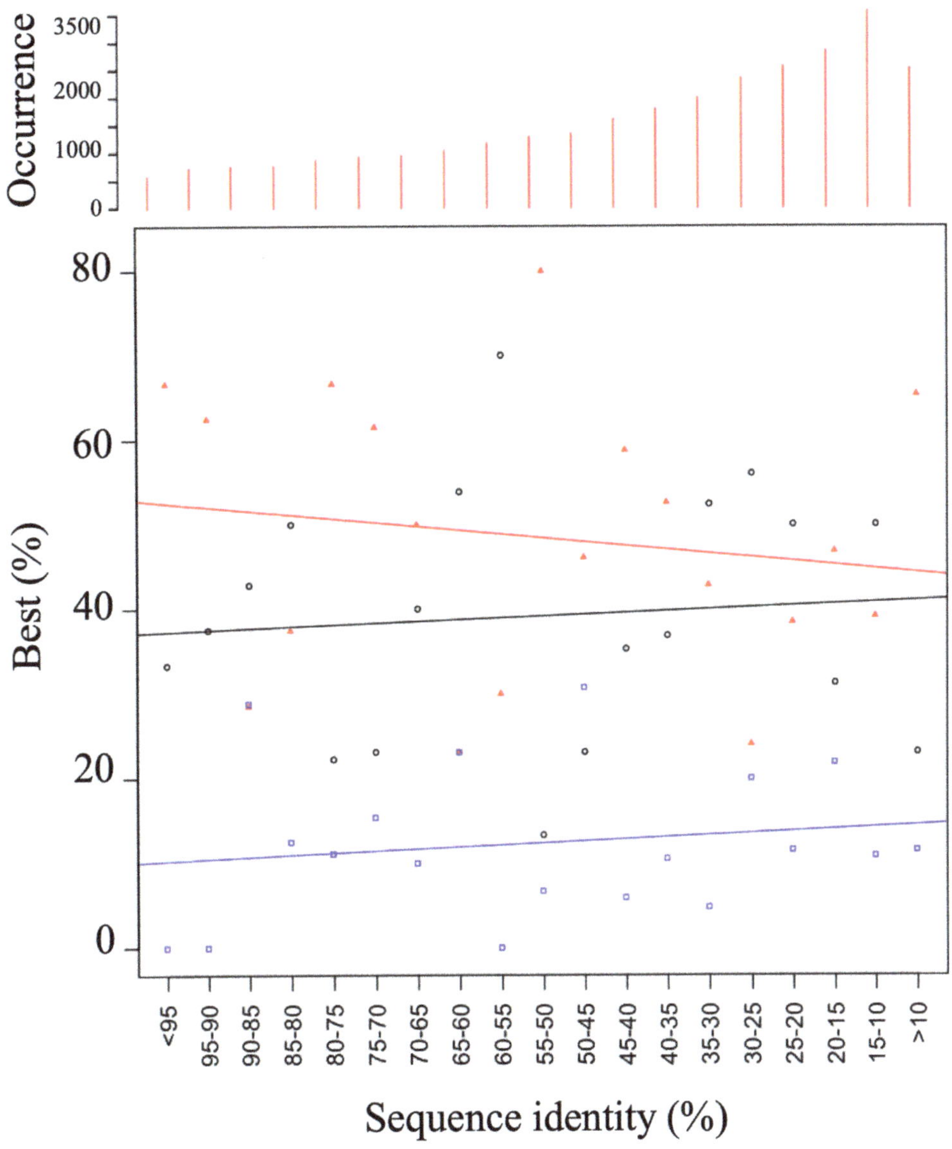

Figure 7. Evaluation summary. Per bins of 5% of sequence identity has shown the best results with HPMScore (red), DOPE (black) or both (blue). On the upper part, the number of evaluated models is given.

5. Conclusions

When one wants to produce a model and evaluate its quality, it is important to understand how the scoring procedure will indicate the overall quality of the model. Most of the proposed structural models have been created using comparative modeling [7], while AlphaFold2 can provide an interesting alternative [41,115,116]. In our study, we first simulated the evolutionary drift in protein sequence between homologous proteins by creating degenerated sequences using amino acids mutations or permutations. For each resulting sequence, we modeled the putative target protein from the template protein where the 3D structure was available. We then assessed the performance of our new method against the reference DOPE function, reportedly very effective for membrane proteins. Our new scoring function is based on the hybrid protein model approach, trained on a set of representative membrane proteins. It is widely accepted that membrane proteins are difficult to model since the amino acids forming the transmembrane segments are densely packed due to the hydrophobic environment and the lipid compaction surrounding the protein, whilst the extra- and intra-cellular amino acids are exposed to a more hydrophilic medium.

This study is interesting as the HPMScore is a non-classical approach, and was tested with the greatest number of different TMPs and the largest number of generated models. Moreover, Top 1 was used, but also Top 5 and Top 10; sequence identity rate influence was evaluated and even the analysis of the transmembrane region was assessed. It is, therefore, a systematic large-scale study.

A server is up for model validation. It can take as input a single model or a large number of models coming from various prediction methods. Interestingly, it can be used to select models and to analyze them at residue level (and so potentially combine different structural models).

Author Contributions: Conceptualization, A.G.d.B.; methodology, S.T., J.E., A.U. and A.G.d.B.; HPM coding, A.U.; formal analysis, S.T., J.E., A.U. and A.G.d.B.; resources, S.T., J.E., A.U. and A.G.d.B.; data curation, A.U. and A.G.d.B.; webserver developments, S.T. and J.E.; writing—original draft preparation, A.U. and A.G.d.B.; writing—review and editing, S.T., J.E., A.U., C.E. and A.G.d.B.; visualization, C.E., S.T., J.E. and A.G.d.B.; supervision, A.G.d.B.; project administration, C.E. and A.G.d.B.; funding acquisition, A.G.d.B. All authors have read and agreed to the published version of the manuscript.

Funding: This work was supported by grants from the Ministry of Research (France), Université Paris Cité (formerly University Paris Diderot, Sorbonne, Paris Cité, France and formerly Université de Paris), Université de la Réunion, National Institute for Blood Transfusion (INTS, France), National Institute for Health and Medical Research (INSERM, France), IdEx ANR-18-IDEX-0001 and labex GR-Ex. The labex GR-Ex, reference ANR-11-LABX-0051 is funded by the program "Investissements d'avenir" of the French National Research Agency, reference ANR-11-IDEX-0005-02. A.G.d.B. acknowledges the French National Research Agency with grant ANR-19-CE17-0021 (BASIN). Calculations were also performed on an SGI cluster granted by Conseil Régional Ile de France and INTS (SESAME Grant).

Institutional Review Board Statement: Not applicable.

Informed Consent Statement: Not applicable.

Data Availability Statement: Not applicable.

Acknowledgments: We would like to thank the anonymous reviewers who helped to improve the manuscript, Jean-Christophe Gelly for the fruitful discussions, and Sylvain Léonard for the technical support.

Conflicts of Interest: The authors declare no conflict of interest. The funders had no role in the design of the study; in the collection, analyses, or interpretation of data; in the writing of the manuscript, or in the decision to publish the results.

Appendix A

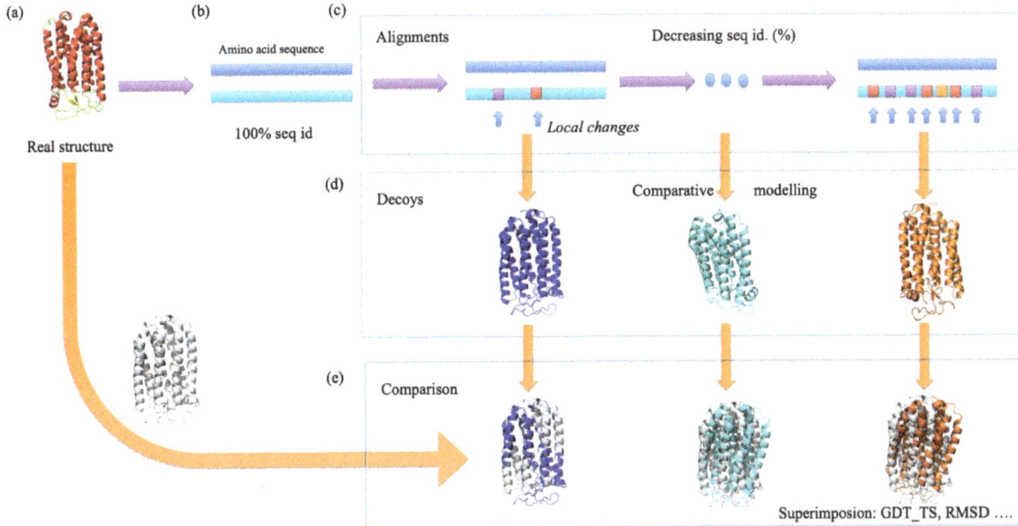

Figure A1. Study principle. (**a**) From a real structure taken from the protein data bank, (**b**) its sequence is extracted, an original alignment at 100% is performed, (**c**) then different changes are made to create alignments with decreasing sequence identity, (**d**) each alignment is used to generate structural models, (**e**) these models are superimpose with the true structural allowing to compute GDT_TS and RMSD.

References

1. Berman, H.M.; Westbrook, J.; Feng, Z.; Gilliland, G.; Bhat, T.N.; Weissig, H.; Shindyalov, I.N.; Bourne, P.E. The protein data bank. *Nucleic Acids Res.* **2000**, *28*, 235–242. [CrossRef] [PubMed]
2. Dobson, L.; Reményi, I.; Tusnády, G.E. The human transmembrane proteome. *Biol. Direct* **2015**, *10*, 31. [CrossRef] [PubMed]
3. Zaucha, J.; Heinzinger, M.; Kulandaisamy, A.; Kataka, E.; Salvádor, Ó.L.; Popov, P.; Rost, B.; Gromiha, M.M.; Zhorov, B.S.; Frishman, D. Mutations in transmembrane proteins: Diseases, evolutionary insights, prediction and comparison with globular proteins. *Brief. Bioinform.* **2020**, *22*, bbaa132. [CrossRef] [PubMed]
4. Gong, J.; Chen, Y.; Pu, F.; Sun, P.; He, F.; Zhang, L.; Li, Y.; Ma, Z.; Wang, H. Understanding membrane protein drug targets in computational perspective. *Curr. Drug Targets* **2019**, *20*, 551–564. [CrossRef] [PubMed]
5. Varga, J.; Dobson, L.; Reményi, I.; Tusnády, G.E. Tstmp: Target selection for structural genomics of human transmembrane proteins. *Nucleic Acids Res.* **2017**, *45*, D325–D330. [CrossRef]
6. Latek, D.; Trzaskowski, B.; Niewieczerza, S.; Miszta, P.; Mynarczyk, K.; Dębiński, A.; Puławski, W.; Yuan, S.; Sztyler, A.; Orze, U.; et al. Modeling of membrane proteins. In *Computational Methods to Study the Structure and Dynamics of Biomolecules and Biomolecular Processes*; Liwo, A., Ed.; Springer: Berlin/Heidelberg, Germany, 2018; pp. 371–451.
7. Almeida, J.G.; Preto, A.J.; Koukos, P.I.; Bonvin, A.; Moreira, I.S. Membrane proteins structures: A review on computational modeling tools. *Biochim. Biophys. Acta. Biomembr.* **2017**, *1859*, 2021–2039. [CrossRef] [PubMed]
8. Dobson, L.; Szekeres, L.I.; Gerdán, C.; Langó, T.; Zeke, A.; Tusnády, G.E. Tmalphafold database: Membrane localization and evaluation of alphafold2 predicted alpha-helical transmembrane protein structures. *Nucleic Acids Res.* **2022**, *51*, D517–D522. [CrossRef]
9. Lazaridis, T.; Karplus, M. Discrimination of the native from misfolded protein models with an energy function including implicit solvation. *J. Mol. Biol.* **1999**, *288*, 477–487. [CrossRef]
10. Felts, A.K.; Gallicchio, E.; Wallqvist, A.; Levy, R.M. Distinguishing native conformations of proteins from decoys with an effective free energy estimator based on the opls all-atom force field and the surface generalized born solvent model. *Proteins* **2002**, *48*, 404–422. [CrossRef] [PubMed]
11. Dutagaci, B.; Wittayanarakul, K.; Mori, T.; Feig, M.A.-O. Discrimination of native-like states of membrane proteins with implicit membrane-based scoring functions. *J. Chem. Comput.* **2017**, *13*, 3049–3059. [CrossRef]
12. Postic, G.; Janel, N.; Tufféry, P.; Moroy, G. An information gain-based approach for evaluating protein structure models. *Comput. Struct. Biotechnol. J.* **2020**, *18*, 2228–2236. [CrossRef]

13. Shen, M.Y.; Sali, A. Statistical potential for assessment and prediction of protein structures. *Protein Sci.* **2006**, *15*, 2507–2524. [CrossRef]
14. Sali, A.; Blundell, T.L. Comparative protein modelling by satisfaction of spatial restraints. *J. Mol. Biol.* **1993**, *234*, 779–815. [CrossRef] [PubMed]
15. Webb, B.; Sali, A. Protein structure modeling with modeller. *Methods Mol. Biol.* **2021**, *2199*, 239–255. [PubMed]
16. Sippl, M.J. Recognition of errors in three-dimensional structures of proteins. *Proteins* **1993**, *17*, 355–362. [CrossRef] [PubMed]
17. Wiederstein, M.; Sippl, M.J. Prosa-web: Interactive web service for the recognition of errors in three-dimensional structures of proteins. *Nucleic Acids Res.* **2007**, *35*, W407–W410. [CrossRef]
18. Eisenberg, D.; Lüthy, R.; Bowie, J.U. Verify3d: Assessment of protein models with three-dimensional profiles. *Methods Enzymol.* **1997**, *277*, 396–404. [CrossRef]
19. Lüthy, R.; Bowie, J.U.; Eisenberg, D. Assessment of protein models with three-dimensional profiles. *Nature* **1992**, *356*, 83–85. [CrossRef]
20. Benkert, P.; Biasini, M.; Schwede, T. Toward the estimation of the absolute quality of individual protein structure models. *Bioinformatics* **2011**, *27*, 343–350. [CrossRef]
21. Kortemme, T.; Morozov, A.V.; Baker, D. An orientation-dependent hydrogen bonding potential improves prediction of specificity and structure for proteins and protein-protein complexes. *J. Mol. Biol.* **2003**, *326*, 1239–1259. [CrossRef]
22. Shin, W.H.; Kang, X.; Zhang, J.; Kihara, D. Prediction of local quality of protein structure models considering spatial neighbors in graphical models. *Sci. Rep.* **2017**, *7*, 40629. [CrossRef] [PubMed]
23. Tosatto, S.C. The victor/frst function for model quality estimation. *J. Comput. Biol. A J. Comput. Mol. Cell Biol.* **2005**, *12*, 1316–1327. [CrossRef]
24. Conover, M.; Staples, M.; Si, D.; Sun, M.; Cao, R. Angularqa: Protein model quality assessment with lstm networks. *Comput. Math. Biophys* **2019**, *7*, 1–9. [CrossRef]
25. Uziela, K.; Shu, N.; Wallner, B.; Elofsson, A. Proq3: Improved model quality assessments using rosetta energy terms. *Sci. Rep.* **2016**, *6*, 33509. [CrossRef] [PubMed]
26. Cao, R.; Bhattacharya, D.; Hou, J.; Cheng, J. Deepqa: Improving the estimation of single protein model quality with deep belief networks. *BMC Bioinform.* **2016**, *17*, 495. [CrossRef]
27. Studer, G.; Rempfer, C.; Waterhouse, A.M.; Gumienny, R.; Haas, J.; Schwede, T. Qmeandisco-distance constraints applied on model quality estimation. *Bioinformatics* **2020**, *36*, 1765–1771. [CrossRef] [PubMed]
28. Gao, C.; Stern, H.A. Scoring function accuracy for membrane protein structure prediction. *Proteins* **2007**, *68*, 67–75. [CrossRef]
29. Heim, A.J.; Li, Z. Developing a high-quality scoring function for membrane protein structures based on specific inter-residue interactions. *J. Comput.-Aided Mol. Des.* **2012**, *26*, 301–309. [CrossRef]
30. Ray, A.; Lindahl, E.; Wallner, B. Model quality assessment for membrane proteins. *Bioinformatics* **2010**, *26*, 3067–3074. [CrossRef]
31. Wallner, B. Proqm-resample: Improved model quality assessment for membrane proteins by limited conformational sampling. *Bioinformatics* **2014**, *30*, 2221–2223. [CrossRef]
32. Nugent, T.; Jones, D.T. Membrane protein orientation and refinement using a knowledge-based statistical potential. *BMC Bioinform.* **2013**, *14*, 276. [CrossRef]
33. Postic, G.; Ghouzam, Y.; Gelly, J.C. An empirical energy function for structural assessment of protein transmembrane domains. *Biochimie* **2015**, *115*, 155–161. [CrossRef] [PubMed]
34. Postic, G.; Ghouzam, Y.; Guiraud, V.; Gelly, J.C. Membrane positioning for high- and low-resolution protein structures through a binary classification approach. *Protein Eng. Des. Sel. PEDS* **2016**, *29*, 87–91. [CrossRef] [PubMed]
35. Studer, G.; Biasini, M.; Schwede, T. Assessing the local structural quality of transmembrane protein models using statistical potentials (*qmeanbrane*). *Bioinformatics* **2014**, *30*, i505–i511. [CrossRef]
36. Barth, P.; Schonbrun, J.; Baker, D. Toward high-resolution prediction and design of transmembrane helical protein structures. *Proc. Natl. Acad. Sci. USA* **2007**, *104*, 15682–15687. [CrossRef] [PubMed]
37. Alford, R.F.; Koehler Leman, J.; Weitzner, B.D.; Duran, A.M.; Tilley, D.C.; Elazar, A.; Gray, J.J. An integrated framework advancing membrane protein modeling and design. *PLoS Comput. Biol.* **2015**, *11*, e1004398. [CrossRef]
38. Duran, A.M.; Meiler, J. Computational design of membrane proteins using rosettamembrane. *Protein Sci.* **2018**, *27*, 341–355. [CrossRef]
39. Yarov-Yarovoy, V.; Schonbrun, J.; Baker, D. Multipass membrane protein structure prediction using rosetta. *Proteins* **2006**, *62*, 1010–1025. [CrossRef]
40. Jumper, J.; Evans, R.; Pritzel, A.; Green, T.; Figurnov, M.; Ronneberger, O.; Tunyasuvunakool, K.; Bates, R.; Žídek, A.; Potapenko, A.; et al. Highly accurate protein structure prediction with alphafold. *Nature* **2021**, *596*, 583–589. [CrossRef]
41. Hegedűs, T.; Geisler, M.; Lukács, G.L.; Farkas, B. Ins and outs of alphafold2 transmembrane protein structure predictions. *Cell. Mol. Life Sci. CMLS* **2022**, *79*, 73. [CrossRef]
42. Tunyasuvunakool, K.A.-O.; Adler, J.A.-O.; Wu, Z.; Green, T.A.-O.; Zielinski, M.; Žídek, A.; Bridgland, A.; Cowie, A.; Meyer, C.; Laydon, A.; et al. Highly accurate protein structure prediction for the human proteome. *Nature* **2021**, *596*, 590–596. [CrossRef] [PubMed]
43. De Brevern, A.G. An agnostic analysis of the human alphafold2 proteome using local protein conformations. *Biochimie* **2023**, *207*, 11–19. [CrossRef] [PubMed]

44. Akdel, M.; Pires, D.E.V.; Pardo, E.P.; Jänes, J.; Zalevsky, A.O.; Mészáros, B.; Bryant, P.; Good, L.L.; Laskowski, R.A.; Pozzati, G.; et al. A structural biology community assessment of alphafold2 applications. *Nat. Struct. Mol. Biol.* **2022**, *29*, 1056–1067. [CrossRef] [PubMed]
45. Esque, J.; Urbain, A.; Etchebest, C.; de Brevern, A.G. Sequence-structure relationship study in all-alpha transmembrane proteins using an unsupervised learning approach. *Amino Acids* **2015**, *47*, 2303–2322. [CrossRef]
46. De Brevern, A.G.; Hazout, S. Hybrid protein model (hpm): A method to compact protein 3d-structure information and physicochemical properties. *IEEE-Comp. Soc. (SPIRE 2000)* **2000**, *S1*, 49–54.
47. De Brevern, A.G.; Hazout, S. 'Hybrid protein model' for optimally defining 3d protein structure fragments. *Bioinformatics* **2003**, *19*, 345–353. [CrossRef]
48. Benros, C.; de Brevern, A.G.; Etchebest, C.; Hazout, S. Assessing a novel approach for predicting local 3d protein structures from sequence. *Proteins: Struct. Funct. Bioinform.* **2005**, *62*, 865–880. [CrossRef]
49. Benros, C.; de Brevern, A.G.; Hazout, S. Analyzing the sequence–structure relationship of a library of local structural prototypes. *J. Theor. Biol.* **2009**, *256*, 215–226. [CrossRef]
50. Bornot, A.; Etchebest, C.; de Brevern, A.G. A new prediction strategy for long local protein structures using an original description. *Proteins* **2009**, *76*, 570–587. [CrossRef]
51. Bornot, A.; Etchebest, C.; de Brevern, A.G. Predicting protein flexibility through the prediction of local structures. *Proteins* **2011**, *79*, 839–852. [CrossRef]
52. Narwani, T.J.; Etchebest, C.; Craveur, P.; Léonard, S.; Rebehmed, J.; Srinivasan, N.; Bornot, A.; Gelly, J.C.; de Brevern, A.G. In silico prediction of protein flexibility with local structure approach. *Biochimie* **2019**, *165*, 150–155. [CrossRef]
53. De Brevern, A.G.; Bornot, A.; Craveur, P.; Etchebest, C.; Gelly, J.C. Predyflexy: Flexibility and local structure prediction from sequence. *Nucleic Acids Res.* **2012**, *40*, W317–W322. [CrossRef]
54. De Brevern, A.G.; Etchebest, C.; Hazout, S. Bayesian probabilistic approach for predicting backbone structures in terms of protein blocks. *Proteins* **2000**, *41*, 271–287. [CrossRef]
55. Joseph, A.P.; Agarwal, G.; Mahajan, S.; Gelly, J.C.; Swapna, L.S.; Offmann, B.; Cadet, F.; Bornot, A.; Tyagi, M.; Valadie, H.; et al. A short survey on protein blocks. *Biophys. Rev.* **2011**, *2*, 137–147. [CrossRef] [PubMed]
56. Zemla, A.; Venclovas, C.; Fidelis, K.; Rost, B. A modified definition of sov, a segment-based measure for protein secondary structure prediction assessment. *Proteins* **1999**, *34*, 220–223. [CrossRef]
57. Stamm, M.; Forrest, L.R. Structure alignment of membrane proteins: Accuracy of available tools and a consensus strategy. *Proteins* **2015**, *83*, 1720–1732. [CrossRef]
58. Lomize, M.A.; Lomize, A.L.; Pogozheva, I.D.; Mosberg, H.I. Opm: Orientations of proteins in membranes database. *Bioinformatics* **2006**, *22*, 623–625. [CrossRef]
59. Lomize, M.A.; Pogozheva, I.D.; Joo, H.; Mosberg, H.I.; Lomize, A.L. Opm database and ppm web server: Resources for positioning of proteins in membranes. *Nucleic Acids Res.* **2012**, *40*, D370–D376. [CrossRef] [PubMed]
60. Sarti, E.; Aleksandrova, A.A.; Ganta, S.K.; Yavatkar, A.S.; Forrest, L.R. Encompass: An online database for analyzing structure and symmetry in membrane proteins. *Nucleic Acids Res.* **2019**, *8*, D315–D325. [CrossRef]
61. BioPerl. 2020. Available online: https://github.com/bioperl/bioperl-live (accessed on 1 March 2023).
62. Kohonen, T. Self-organized formation of topologically correct feature maps. *Biol. Cybern* **1982**, *43*, 59–69. [CrossRef]
63. Kohonen, T. *Self-Organizing Maps*, 3rd ed.; Springer: Berlin/Heidelberg, Germany, 2001; p. 501.
64. Delano, W.L. The Pymol Molecular Graphics System. 2002. Available online: http://www.pymol.org (accessed on 1 March 2023).
65. Joseph, A.P.; Srinivasan, N.; de Brevern, A.G. Improvement of protein structure comparison using a structural alphabet. *Biochimie* **2011**, *93*, 1434–1445. [CrossRef] [PubMed]
66. Martin, A.; Porter, C. ProFit Software. Available online: http://www.bioinf.org.uk/software/profit/ (accessed on 1 March 2023).
67. Zhang, Y.; Skolnick, J. Tm-align: A protein structure alignment algorithm based on the tm-score. *Nucleic Acids Res.* **2005**, *33*, 2302–2309. [CrossRef] [PubMed]
68. R Core Team. *R: A Language and Environment for Statistical Computing*; R Foundation for Statistical Computing: Vienna, Austria, 2020.
69. Kim, D.E.; Chivian, D.; Baker, D. Protein structure prediction and analysis using the robetta server. *Nucleic Acids Res.* **2004**, *32*, W526–W531. [CrossRef] [PubMed]
70. Baek, M.; DiMaio, F.; Anishchenko, I.; Dauparas, J.; Ovchinnikov, S.; Lee, G.R.; Wang, J.; Cong, Q.; Kinch, L.N.; Schaeffer, R.D.; et al. Accurate prediction of protein structures and interactions using a three-track neural network. *Science* **2021**, *373*, 871–876. [CrossRef]
71. Kelley, L.A.; Sternberg, M.J. Protein structure prediction on the web: A case study using the phyre server. *Nat. Protoc.* **2009**, *4*, 363–371. [CrossRef]
72. Lin, Z.; Akin, H.; Rao, R.; Hie, B.; Zhu, Z.; Lu, W.; Smetanin, N.; Verkuil, R.; Kabeli, O.; Shmueli, Y.; et al. Evolutionary-scale prediction of atomic level protein structure with a language model. *bioRxiv* **2022**. [CrossRef]
73. Koehler Leman, J.; Ulmschneider, M.B.; Gray, J.J. Computational modeling of membrane proteins. *Proteins* **2015**, *83*, 1–24. [CrossRef]
74. Rost, B.; Casadio, R.; Fariselli, P.; Sander, C. Transmembrane helices predicted at 95% accuracy. *Protein Sci.* **1995**, *4*, 521–533. [CrossRef]
75. Bernhofer, M.; Dallago, C.; Karl, T.; Satagopam, V.; Heinzinger, M.; Littmann, M.; Olenyi, T.; Qiu, J.; Schütze, K.; Yachdav, G.; et al. Predictprotein-predicting protein structure and function for 29 years. *Nucleic Acids Res.* **2021**, *49*, W535–W540. [CrossRef]

76. Buchan, D.W.A.; Jones, D.T. The psipred protein analysis workbench: 20 years on. *Nucleic Acids Res.* **2019**, *47*, W402–W407. [CrossRef]
77. McGuffin, L.J.; Bryson, K.; Jones, D.T. The psipred protein structure prediction server. *Bioinformatics* **2000**, *16*, 404–405. [CrossRef]
78. Jones, D.T. Protein secondary structure prediction based on position-specific scoring matrices. *J. Mol. Biol.* **1999**, *292*, 195–202. [CrossRef]
79. Cid, H.; Bunster, M.; Arriagada, E.; Campos, M. Prediction of secondary structure of proteins by means of hydrophobicity profiles. *FEBS Lett.* **1982**, *150*, 247–254. [CrossRef]
80. Hessa, T.; Kim, H.; Bihlmaier, K.; Lundin, C.; Boekel, J.; Andersson, H.; Nilsson, I.; White, S.H.; von Heijne, G. Recognition of transmembrane helices by the endoplasmic reticulum translocon. *Nature* **2005**, *433*, 377–381. [CrossRef]
81. Jones, D.T.; Taylor, W.R.; Thornton, J.M. A model recognition approach to the prediction of all-helical membrane protein structure and topology. *Biochemistry* **1994**, *33*, 3038–3049. [CrossRef]
82. Jones, D.T. Improving the accuracy of transmembrane protein topology prediction using evolutionary information. *Bioinformatics* **2007**, *23*, 538–544. [CrossRef]
83. Fariselli, P.; Casadio, R. Htp: A neural network-based method for predicting the topology of helical transmembrane domains in proteins. *Comput. Appl. Biosci. CABIOS* **1996**, *12*, 41–48. [CrossRef]
84. Hirokawa, T.; Boon-Chieng, S.; Mitaku, S. Sosui: Classification and secondary structure prediction system for membrane proteins. *Bioinformatics* **1998**, *14*, 378–379. [CrossRef]
85. Tusnády, G.E.; Simon, I. Principles governing amino acid composition of integral membrane proteins: Application to topology prediction. *J. Mol. Biol.* **1998**, *283*, 489–506. [CrossRef]
86. Dosztányi, Z.; Magyar, C.; Tusnády, G.E.; Cserzo, M.; Fiser, A.; Simon, I. Servers for sequence-structure relationship analysis and prediction. *Nucleic Acids Res.* **2003**, *31*, 3359–3363. [CrossRef]
87. Sonnhammer, E.L.; von Heijne, G.; Krogh, A. A hidden markov model for predicting transmembrane helices in protein sequences. *Proc. Int. Conf. Intell. Syst. Mol. Biol.* **1998**, *6*, 175–182.
88. Pasquier, C.; Promponas, V.J.; Palaios, G.A.; Hamodrakas, J.S.; Hamodrakas, S.J. A novel method for predicting transmembrane segments in proteins based on a statistical analysis of the swissprot database: The pred-tmr algorithm. *Protein Eng.* **1999**, *12*, 381–385. [CrossRef]
89. Viklund, H.; Elofsson, A. Octopus: Improving topology prediction by two-track ann-based preference scores and an extended topological grammar. *Bioinformatics* **2008**, *24*, 1662–1668. [CrossRef]
90. Bernsel, A.; Viklund, H.; Hennerdal, A.; Elofsson, A. Topcons: Consensus prediction of membrane protein topology. *Nucleic Acids Res.* **2009**, *37*, W465–W468. [CrossRef]
91. Tsirigos, K.D.; Peters, C.; Shu, N.; Käll, L.; Elofsson, A. The topcons web server for consensus prediction of membrane protein topology and signal peptides. *Nucleic Acids Res.* **2015**, *43*, W401–W407. [CrossRef]
92. Cao, B.; Porollo, A.; Adamczak, R.; Jarrell, M.; Meller, J. Enhanced recognition of protein transmembrane domains with prediction-based structural profiles. *Bioinformatics* **2006**, *22*, 303–309. [CrossRef]
93. Yuan, Z.; Mattick, J.S.; Teasdale, R.D. Svmtm: Support vector machines to predict transmembrane segments. *J. Comput. Chem.* **2004**, *25*, 632–636. [CrossRef]
94. Zhou, H.; Zhang, C.; Liu, S.; Zhou, Y. Web-based toolkits for topology prediction of transmembrane helical proteins, fold recognition, structure and binding scoring, folding-kinetics analysis and comparative analysis of domain combinations. *Nucleic Acids Res.* **2005**, *33*, W193–W197. [CrossRef]
95. Lee, S.; Lee, B.; Jang, I.; Kim, S.; Bhak, J. Localizome: A server for identifying transmembrane topologies and tm helices of eukaryotic proteins utilizing domain information. *Nucleic Acids Res.* **2006**, *34*, W99–W103. [CrossRef]
96. Yin, X.; Yang, J.; Xiao, F.; Yang, Y.; Shen, H.B. Membrain: An easy-to-use online webserver for transmembrane protein structure prediction. *Nano-Micro Lett.* **2018**, *10*, 2. [CrossRef]
97. Hönigschmid, P.; Breimann, S.; Weigl, M.; Frishman, D. Allestm: Predicting multiple structural features of transmembrane proteins. *BMC Bioinform.* **2020**, *21*, 242. [CrossRef] [PubMed]
98. Koehler Leman, J.; Mueller, B.K.; Gray, J.J. Expanding the toolkit for membrane protein modeling in rosetta. *Bioinformatics* **2017**, *33*, 754–756. [CrossRef] [PubMed]
99. Bernhofer, M.; Rost, B. Tmbed: Transmembrane proteins predicted through language model embeddings. *BMC Bioinform.* **2022**, *23*, 326. [CrossRef]
100. Von Heijne, G. Membrane-protein topology. *Nat. Rev. Mol. Cell Biol.* **2006**, *7*, 909–918. [CrossRef] [PubMed]
101. Li, B.; Mendenhall, J.; Capra, J.A.; Meiler, J. A multitask deep-learning method for predicting membrane associations and secondary structures of proteins. *J. Proteome Res.* **2021**, *20*, 4089–4100. [CrossRef]
102. Qu, J.; Yin, S.S.; Wang, H. Prediction of metal ion binding sites of transmembrane proteins. *Comput. Math. Methods Med.* **2021**, *2021*, 2327832. [CrossRef] [PubMed]
103. Waterhouse, A.; Bertoni, M.; Bienert, S.; Studer, G.; Tauriello, G.; Gumienny, R.; Heer, F.T.; de Beer, T.A.P.; Rempfer, C.; Bordoli, L.; et al. Swiss-model: Homology modelling of protein structures and complexes. *Nucleic Acids Res.* **2018**, *46*, W296–W303. [CrossRef]
104. Ebejer, J.-P.; Hill, J.R.; Kelm, S.; Shi, J.; Deane, C.M. Memoir: Template-based structure prediction for membrane proteins. *Nucleic Acids Res.* **2013**, *41*, W379–W383. [CrossRef]

105. Kelm, S.; Shi, J.; Deane, C.M. Medeller: Homology-based coordinate generation for membrane proteins. *Bioinformatics* **2010**, *26*, 2833–2840. [CrossRef]
106. Kozma, D.; Tusnády, G.E. Tmfoldweb: A web server for predicting transmembrane protein fold class. *Biol. Direct.* **2017**, *10*, 54. [CrossRef]
107. Kozma, D.; Tusnády, G.E. Tmfoldrec: A statistical potential-based transmembrane protein fold recognition tool. *BMC Bioinform.* **2015**, *16*, 201. [CrossRef]
108. Yarov-Yarovoy, V.; Baker, D.; Catterall, W.A. Voltage sensor conformations in the open and closed states in ROSETTA structural models of K(+) channels. *Proc. Natl. Acad. Sci. USA* **2006**, *103*, 7292–7297. [CrossRef]
109. Benkert, P.; Künzli, M.; Schwede, T. Qmean server for protein model quality estimation. *Nucleic Acids Res.* **2009**, *37*, W510–W514. [CrossRef]
110. Snider, C.; Jayasinghe, S.; Fau-Hristova, K.; Hristova, K.; Fau-White, S.H.; White, S.H. Mpex: A tool for exploring membrane proteins. *Protein Sci.* **2009**, *18*, 2624–2628. [CrossRef] [PubMed]
111. Jayasinghe, S.; Hristova, K.; Fau-White, S.H.; White, S.H. Mptopo: A database of membrane protein topology. *Protein Sci.* **2001**, *10*, 455–458. [CrossRef] [PubMed]
112. Mokrab, Y.; Stevens, T.J.; Mizuguchi, K. A structural dissection of amino acid substitutions in helical transmembrane proteins. *Proteins* **2010**, *78*, 2895–2907. [CrossRef] [PubMed]
113. Olivella, M.; Gonzalez, A.; Pardo, L.; Deupi, X. Relation between sequence and structure in membrane proteins. *Bioinformatics* **2013**, *29*, 1589–1592. [CrossRef]
114. Kabsch, W. A discussion of the solution for the best rotation to relate two sets of vectors. *Acta Crystallogr. Sect. A* **1978**, *34*, 827–828. [CrossRef]
115. Del Alamo, D.; Govaerts, C.; McHaourab, H.S. Alphafold2 predicts the inward-facing conformation of the multidrug transporter lmrp. *Proteins* **2021**, *89*, 1226–1228. [CrossRef]
116. Xiao, Q.; Xu, M.; Wang, W.; Wu, T.; Zhang, W.; Qin, W.; Sun, B. Utilization of alphafold2 to predict mfs protein conformations after selective mutation. *Int. J. Mol. Sci.* **2022**, *23*, 7235. [CrossRef]

BioMedInformatics

MDPI

Article

Enhancing Explainable Machine Learning by Reconsidering Initially Unselected Items in Feature Selection for Classification

Jörn Lötsch [1,2,*] and Alfred Ultsch [3]

[1] Institute of Clinical Pharmacology, Goethe-University, Theodor-Stern-Kai 7, 60590 Frankfurt Am Main, Germany
[2] Fraunhofer Institute for Translational Medicine and Pharmacology ITMP, Theodor-Stern-Kai 7, 60596 Frankfurt Am Main, Germany
[3] DataBionics Research Group, University of Marburg, Hans-Meerwein-Straße 22, 35032 Marburg, Germany
* Correspondence: j.loetsch@em.uni-frankfurt.de

Abstract: Feature selection is a common step in data preprocessing that precedes machine learning to reduce data space and the computational cost of processing or obtaining the data. Filtering out uninformative variables is also important for knowledge discovery. By reducing the data space to only those components that are informative to the class structure, feature selection can simplify models so that they can be more easily interpreted by researchers in the field, reminiscent of explainable artificial intelligence. Knowledge discovery in complex data thus benefits from feature selection that aims to understand feature sets in the thematic context from which the data set originates. However, a single variable selected from a very small number of variables that are technically sufficient for AI training may make little immediate thematic sense, whereas the additional consideration of a variable discarded during feature selection could make scientific discovery very explicit. In this report, we propose an approach to explainable feature selection (XFS) based on a systematic reconsideration of unselected features. The difference between the respective classifications when training the algorithms with the selected features or with the unselected features provides a valid estimate of whether the relevant features in a data set have been selected and uninformative or trivial information was filtered out. It is shown that revisiting originally unselected variables in multivariate data sets allows for the detection of pathologies and errors in the feature selection that occasionally resulted in the failure to identify the most appropriate variables.

Keywords: data science; machine-learning; digital medicine; artificial intelligence

Citation: Lötsch, J.; Ultsch, A. Enhancing Explainable Machine Learning by Reconsidering Initially Unselected Items in Feature Selection for Classification. *Biomedinformatics* **2022**, 2, 701–714. https://doi.org/10.3390/biomedinformatics2040047

Academic Editors: Pentti Nieminen and José Manuel Ferreira Machado

Received: 4 November 2022
Accepted: 5 December 2022
Published: 12 December 2022

1. Introduction

Feature selection (for an overview, see e.g., [1]), is a frequent step of data preprocessing preceding machine-learning to reduce the data space and the computational load to process it, or the costs to acquire relevant data. Feature selection thus filters the information contained in a data set and removes uninformative variables, considering that machine learning algorithms need examples of the relevant structures in an empirical data set. Filtering out uninformative variables is also relevant to knowledge discovery. By reducing the data space to its components informative for the class structure, feature selection can simplify models to make them easier to interpret by field researchers, addressing explainable artificial intelligence (XAI) [2].

Too much information represented in many variables can prevent field experts from grasping the main mechanistic processes underlying a class structure in a data set. This is consistent with an observation more than half a century old that human intelligibility is limited, with a proposed optimum of 7 ± 2 [3]. On the other hand, too few features resulting from rigorous selection may be sufficient for successful classification by the AI, but insufficient for field experts to understand the key processes underlying the structure in the data. For example, of two highly correlated variables, one may be technically better for the AI to function and is therefore selected, but the other would make sense in the context of the actual research topic. Few selected variables may be functioning for an algorithm. However, they may provide a fragmented picture of the underlying process. The additional consideration of variables that were discarded during feature selection could make the scientific result very clear.

Knowledge discovery in complex data thus appears to potentially benefit from feature selection aimed at understandable feature sets in the topical research context from which the data set originates. Knowledge discovery via feature selection for classifiers is based on the idea that if an algorithm can be trained to assign a case to the correct class, the data contains a structure relevant to the class structure, and the variables that the algorithm needs to successfully perform its task are the class-relevant variables or features in the actual data set. However, the interpretation of a feature set in a specific research context may vary depending on whether it can be stated that only the selected features, but not the unselected features, provide a the information necessary for correct class assignment. This would allow the variables not selected to be discarded as uninteresting, and the result of the analysis will be that the process studied is characterized by the variables selected, which may represent scientific progress. For example, if the variables contained genetic information, then the selected features will give a clear indication of the genetic background of the biological process under study. A rigorous feature selection process that provides the minimum amount of information required by an AI for classification might have discarded variables that also provide class-relevant information, only to a lesser extent than the selected variables. In this case, the interpretation of the feature set in the topical context may differ from the one above, i.e., it cannot be claimed that the background mechanisms of the process of interest has been comprehensively captured when interpreting the selected features.

Thus, while usually the interest in the variables omitted during feature selection vanishes, they may still contain relevant information for the topical interpretation unless proven otherwise. Specific attempts on this topic are so far limited, such as highlighting that extracting a subset of the most important features could help researchers understand the biological processes underlying the disease [4]. Therefore, this report shows that classification performance obtained with the unselected features can be used to improve the interpretation of feature sets. The evaluation of classification performance with both the selected and unselected features provides an indication of whether informative features have been left aside. This information can critically affect the interpretation of a feature set if the selection process was conducted with the goal of knowledge discovery. Therefore, this report proposes an explainable feature selection (XFS) approach based on a systematic reconsideration of the unselected features.

2. Methods

2.1. Algorithm

Three criteria are proposed that a set of features should satisfy in order to both capture the background mechanisms of the process in terms of the explainable feature selection (XFS) and to have identified the most appropriate variables for the class assignment.

1. Classification performance of algorithms trained with the selected features should be satisfactory, which is routinely checked. Ideally, it should not drop significantly from the performance obtained with all features. The classification performance must be at least better than chance, including the lower bound of the 95% confidence interval of classification performance measures, which should be higher than the level of guessing of the class assignment.
2. Classification performance with the selected features should be better than classification performance when the training is conducted with the unselected features. This is not routinely checked. The difference between the respective classifications when training the algorithms with the selected features and when training the algorithm

with the unselected features should be positive, e.g., with a lower bound of the 95% confidence interval > 0.

3. If the difference in point 2 above is not satisfactorily greater than zero, but the classifier trained with the full set of features has satisfactory accuracy, then the unselected features should be reconsidered. If variables are omitted that are very strongly correlated with selected features, an assessment should be triggered of whether correlated variables might add relevant information that improves the (domain expert's) interpretation of the feature set. In a new feature selection pass, the features already selected from the first pass are omitted. The final feature set is then the union of the two feature sets, provided that the second pass did not fail criterion 1.

2.2. *Evaluations*

2.2.1. Quantification of Feature Importance

Several different methods of feature selection have been proposed. Overviews on feature selection methods are available in the literature, e.g., [1,5]. Feature selection methods [1] are typically presented in three classes: filter, wrapper and embedded methods. Filter methods suppress the least interesting variables, where interestingness is typically measured as a correlation to the variable to predict [6]. In wrapper methods, subsets of variables are evaluated for an overview, see for example [7]. Ensemble methods try to combine wrapper and filter methods [8]. Implementations include "brute force" approaches limited only by computational power, and various unsupervised and supervised methods. Supervised methods aim at identifying the variable importance via classification performance. Among supervised methods, both univariate and multivariate methods are available in which informative features can be obtained by, for example, recursive feature elimination or sequential feature selection. Particular implementations include the regression-based least absolute shrinkage and selection operators (LASSO [9]), or make use of usually well-performing machine learning methods such as random forests [10,11] and combine them with statistical tests as in the "Boruta" method [12].

Among popular multivariate supervised methods figures selecting features based on the variable importance in random forests classifiers. This can be obtained via permutation weighting [11] from out-of-bag (OOB) cases as the decrease in classification accuracy when the respective feature is omitted from the class assignment, as implemented in the R package "randomForest" (https://cran.r-project.org/package=randomForest (accessed on 3 September 2022) [13]), and callable via "importance=TRUE" in the random forest model constructor and "type=1" in the "importance()" read out function. Of note, the default method of the mentioned R libary, which measures how effective the feature is at reducing theuncertainty when constructing decision trees based on the mean reduction in impurity (or "Gini importance"), was not used because its use has been discouraged, as it has been demonstrated to occasionally produce biased results with inflated importance of numerical features not predictive for unseen data [14,15].

2.2.2. Computation of the Set Size of the Selected Features

Most feature selection methods, including the OOB permutation importance used in the present analyses, do not immediately provide a decision of how many "best" features to select but just a measure of the importance of each feature. Therefore, the size k of the final feature set is often determined arbitrarily.

Typically, feature importance has a highly skewed distribution, i.e., a few variables have high importance, but many have a low importance. This kind of distribution can be addressed with the computed ABC analysis (cABC) [16]. This is an item categorization method that aims to identify the most relevant items by dividing a set of non-negative numeric elements into subsets named "A", "B" and "C", such that subset "A" contains the "important few" items while subset "C" contains the "trivial many" items [17]. The algorithmic computation of the set sizes from the data has been described in detail previously [16]. Combining random forests with cABC analysis for feature selection has recently been proposed [18].

2.3. Experimental Setup

Programming was performed in the R language [19] using the R software package [20], version 4.2.1 for Linux, available free of charge from the Comprehensive R Archive Network (CRAN) at https://CRAN.R-project.org/ (accessed on 3 September 2022). Experiments were performed on 1 – 64 cores/threads on an AMD Ryzen Threadripper 3970X (Advanced Micro Devices, Inc., Santa Clara, CA, USA) computer with 256 GB random access memory (RAM) running Ubuntu Linux 22.04.1 LTS (Canonical, London, UK)). The main R packages used for the experiments were "randomForest" (https://cran.r-project.org/package=randomForest (accessed on 3 September 2022) [13]), "caret" (https://cran.r-project.org/package=caret (accessed on 3 September 2022) [21] and our package "ABCanalysis" (https://cran.r-project.org/package=ABCanalysis, (accessed on 3 September 2022) [16]). The computational requirements could be met by parallel processing using the "parallel" library included in the R base environment.

Twenty percent of the original data was separated as a validation data set, which was not further touched during feature selection. To obtain a representative subsample, our R package "opdisDownsampling" (https://cran.r-project.org/package=opdisDownsampling (accessed on 3 September 2022)) was used for this task. The package selects from 10,000–100,000 random samples the one in which the distributions of the variables are most similar to those of the original data. The details of this sampling procedure have been described previously [22].

Random forests were tuned with respect to hyperparameters, as reported previously [23], in order to ensure that the performance of the classifier during feature selection and classification was optimized for the actual data sets. Specifically, tuning was performed via a grid search and using a 100-fold cross-validation precluding each feature selection run. For example, tuning the hyperparameters indicated that for the iris data set (see next chapter) the classifier should be run with $n_{tree} = 1100$ trees, $\sqrt{n_{variables}} = 2$ features per tree and nodesize = 4. For the wine properties data set (see next chapter), the respective hyperparameter settings were $n_{tree} = 100$, $n_{variables} = 1$, nodesize = 1.

All feature selection experiments were performed in a 1,000 cross-validation scenario. In each run, from the 80% of the full data sets available for this task after having separated the 20% validation sample (see above), 2/3 were randomly drawn as training data subset using Monte Carlo resampling [24] implemented in the R library "sampling" (https://cran.r-project.org/package=sampling (accessed on 3 September 2022) [25]). The permutation variable importance was calculated directly using the OOB samples created during training with these 2/3 randomly drawn cases.

After feature selection, classification performance was evaluated after training random forests with 2/3 randomly drawn cases from the 80% of the data using only the selected or unselected features, and classification performance was tested with random samples of 80% of the 20% validation sample that were not touched during feature selection or classifier training. Classification performance was measured using balanced accuracy [26] implemented in the R library "caret".

2.4. Data Sets

2.4.1. Iris Flower Data Example

The iris flower data set set [27,28] contains measurements of the four variables, sepal length and width or petal length and width in centimeters, for 50 flowers of each of the three species, Iris setosa, versicolor, and virginica, providing a 150 × 4 data matrix. The data set was expanded by repeating variables to obtain very strongly correlated variables, or by adding variables as their permuted versions to obtain nonsense variables or by adding trivial information using the class information as the variable. Previous analyses indicated that petal dimensions were the most informative for species separation [29].

2.4.2. Wine Quality Data Set

A second data set was a wine data set from https://www.kaggle.com/datasets/shelvigarg/wine-quality-dataset (accessed 2 November 2022). It contains physicochemical properties of a collection of white and red wines and consists of 4898 samples of white wine and 1599 samples of red wine. Eleven variables on chemical properties are solid acidity, volatile acidity, citric acidity, residual sugar, chlorides, free sulfur dioxide, total sulfur dioxide, density, pH, sulfates, and alcohol. A 12th variable, quality, contains the median of at least three ratings from wine experts who ranked the wine quality of each sample between 0 (very poor) and 10 (very good). The wine data set was used for method development in feature selection for regression problems [30,31]. This provided the relevant features to be identified in the present analysis. Fuzzy techniques were used to identify the variables that had the greatest causal relationship with wine quality: Alcohol, fixed acidity, free sulfur dioxide, residual sugar and volatile acidity, while citric acid and sulfates were also variables that show a causal relationship with wine quality, but not in the same strength as the previous ones [31]. For the present experiments, the regression problem with the normally distributed wine quality variable was transferred into a classification problem via a median split into "low" and "high" quality wines.

3. Results

3.1. Iris Flower Data Set

Several modifications of the iris data set were assessed, including (i) the omission of very strongly correlated variables, (ii) the addition of more variables that are perfectly correlated with the existing variables, (iii) the addition of nonsense variables, (iv) the addition of perfect class discriminators, i.e., of the class membership as a variable. Experiments using these modifications allowed for four main conclusions, which are highlighted under the following subheadings.

3.1.1. Default Feature Selection Often Suffices and Removing Strongly Correlated Variables Is Not Necessary

In the iris data set, feature selection identified the two petal dimensions as the most informative for the training of a random forests classifier (Figure 1A(a–c)). Training with these two variables allowed the algorithm to classify the validation data set better than training with the unselected features, i.e., sepal dimensions, as indicated by the 95% confidence interval of the differences in the balanced accuracy located to the right of the zero difference. The median classification performance was even slightly better than when all variables were used for training. Reconsidering the unselected variables in a second round of feature selection added the sepal length to the set of selected features. However, the positive difference in classification performance between selected and unselected features had already indicated that this was unnecessary, and indeed the now larger feature set did not provide a better basis for training the classifier than the two variables selected first.

The petal dimensions were correlated very strongly [32] at a rank correlation [33] coefficient of $\rho > 0.9$. Petal width was selected as their prototype. In the feature selection among the remaining three variables (Figure 1), it was selected in the first round, while sepal length was added in a second round. However, both sets provided a poorer basis for random forest training than the sets obtained from the full data set without the removal of very strongly correlated variables (see above). The balanced accuracy of the class assignment was not better than with the full data set. When the four variables of the iris data set were added again to the data set (Figure 1 feature selection among the now eight variables remained unaffected and consistent by first referring to the petal dimensions and adding the sepal length in a second round.

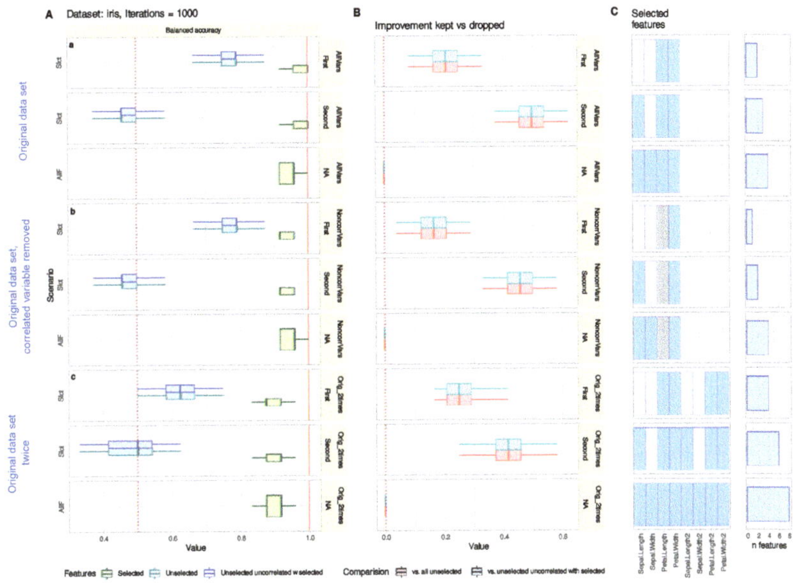

Figure 1. Feature selection and classification performance evaluation with different feature sets in the iris data set [28]. The graph is divided into subgraphs a–c from top to bottom. Experiments were performed (**a**) with the original data, (**b**) with the iris data set omitting one highly correlated variable, and (**c**) with the data set adding all variables twice. Each subgraph is organized in three further subgraphs, showing from top to bottom (i) the results when using the features selected in the default feature selection, (ii) the features added when performing a second feature selection on the unselected features from the first selection, and (iii) when training the algorithm with the full feature set. The boxes show the 25th, 50th (blue vertical line), and 75th percentiles of balanced accuracies obtained in 1000 repeated runs with a random selection of 67% from the training data set and 80% from a validation data set separated from the data set before feature selection. Whiskers span the 95% confidence interval from the 2.5th to the 97.5th percentiles. (**A**): Balanced accuracy obtained with a random forests classifier trained with (i) the selected features, (ii) the unselected features, and (iii) the unselected features that were not highly correlated with the selected features, with the correlation threshold set at a very strong correlation of $\rho > 0.9$. (**B**): Difference in balanced accuracy when algorithms were trained with the selected versus unselected features. (**C**): Selected features (blue) and unselected features (white). Features excluded from the experiments due to very strong correlation are shown in gray.

3.1.2. Reconsidering Unselected Features Captures Information When Bad or Trivial Features Were Initially Selected

If the data set contained a variable that is the class membership information, either by mistake or by accidental coincidence, the feature selection will identify that the variable is sufficient to train a perfect classifier (Figure 2) However, there are reasons that renamed class information, or variables identical to class information by any reason, can be a banality in the specific research domain from which the data set originates, and reconsidering the unselected features leads to petal dimension selection as described above, which allows the selected features to be interpreted in the current research field context.

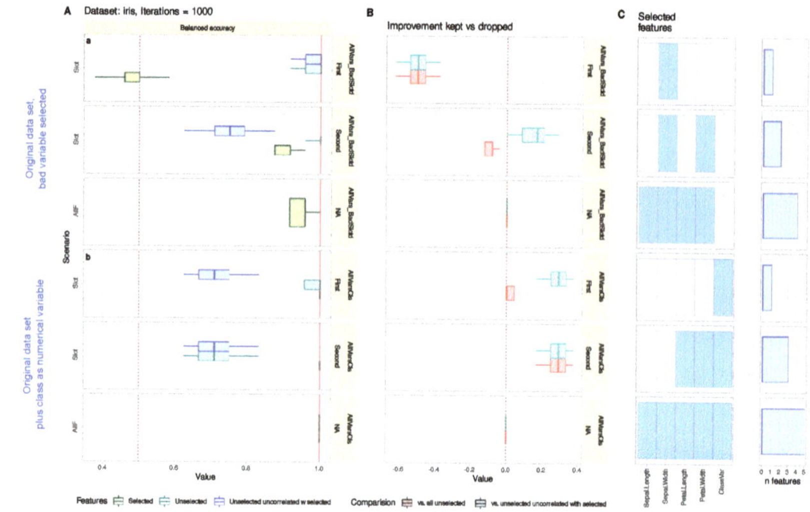

Figure 2. Feature selection and classification performance evaluation with different feature sets in the iris data set [28]. The graph is divided into subgraphs a–b from top to bottom. Experiments were performed (**a**) with the original data but sepal length was defined to be selected in a first run of feature selection, (**b**) with the iris data set where the class information was added as a numerical variable. Each subgraph is organized in three further subgraphs, showing from top to bottom (i) the results when using the features selected in the default feature selection, (ii) the features added when performing a second feature selection on the unselected features from the first selection, and (iii) when training the algorithm with the full feature set. The boxes show the 25th, 50th (blue vertical line), and 75th percentiles of balanced accuracies obtained in 1000 repeated runs with a random selection of 67% from the training data set and 80% from a validation data set separated from the data set before feature selection. Whiskers span the 95% confidence interval from the 2.5th to the 97.5th percentiles. (**A**): Balanced accuracy obtained with a random forests classifier trained with (i) the selected features, (ii) the unselected features, and (iii) the unselected features that were not highly correlated with the selected features, with the correlation threshold set at a very strong correlation of $\rho > 0.9$. (**B**): Difference in balanced accuracy when algorithms were trained with the selected versus unselected features. (**C**): Selected features (blue) and unselected features (white).

3.1.3. Reconsidering Unselected Features Does Not Tend to Add Uninformative Variables

When permuted versions of the four variables were added to the data set (Figure 3), none of them were selected in either the first or second round of feature selection. In the extreme case, when all variables were permuted (Figure 3 the unsuitability of the then seemingly random selection could be observed immediately from the poor performance of the trained classifiers, with confidence intervals of balanced accuracy 50%. In this case, the difference around zero between the performance of classifiers trained with selected and unselected features clearly indicated that no relevant information had been overlooked in the feature selection.

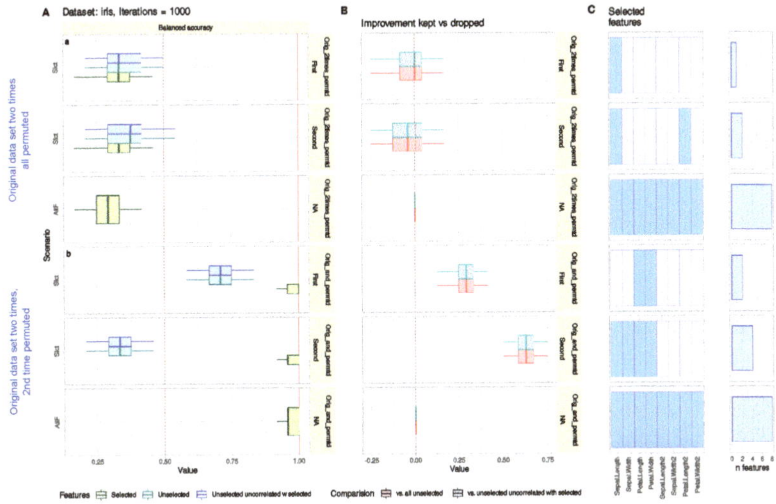

Figure 3. Feature selection and classification performance evaluation with different feature sets in the iris data set [28]. The graph is divided into subgraphs a - b from top to bottom. Experiments were performed (**a**) with doubling each variable and randomly permuting all variables, (**b**) doubling the data set and randomly permuting the second version of each variable while leaving the first versions in their original stage. Each subgraph is organized in three further subgraphs, showing from top to bottom (i) the results when using the features selected in the default feature selection, (ii) the features added when performing a second feature selection on the unselected features from the first selection, and (iii) when training the algorithm with the full feature set. The boxes show the 25th, 50th (blue vertical line), and 75th percentiles of balanced accuracies obtained in 1000 repeated runs with a random selection of 67% from the training data set and 80% from a validation data set separated from the data set before feature selection. Whiskers span the 95% confidence interval from the 2.5th to the 97.5th percentiles. (**A**): Balanced accuracy obtained with a random forests classifier trained with (i) the selected features, (ii) the unselected features, and (iii) the unselected features that were not highly correlated with the selected features, with the correlation threshold set at a very strong correlation of $\rho > 0.9$. (**B**): Difference in balanced accuracy when algorithms were trained with the selected versus unselected features. (**C**): Selected features (blue) and unselected features (white).

3.1.4. Reconsidering Unselected Features Indicates Relevant Information That May Have Been Missed in The Knowledge Discovery Process

Assembling the data set from similarly informative variables by just repeating the petal width 12 times led to an arbitrary selection of some of the same features (Figure 4), since all features are similarly informative and there is no better feature pick. The classification accuracy was satisfactory because feature selection came at no cost, allowing similar accuracy as when training was conducted with all features. However, training the classifier with the selected features was no better than with the unselected features, and the difference between the balanced accuracies was zero. This clearly indicated an error in feature selection and a need to re-examine the feature set, since it cannot be assumed that the best features were selected from the set of variables. While this may be irrelevant for training classifiers, it is likely relevant for knowledge discovery. Examination of the data set, as indicated by the zero-difference signal, would likely prevent biased interpretation of the selected features that would have gone unnoticed without assessing the classification performance with unselected features.

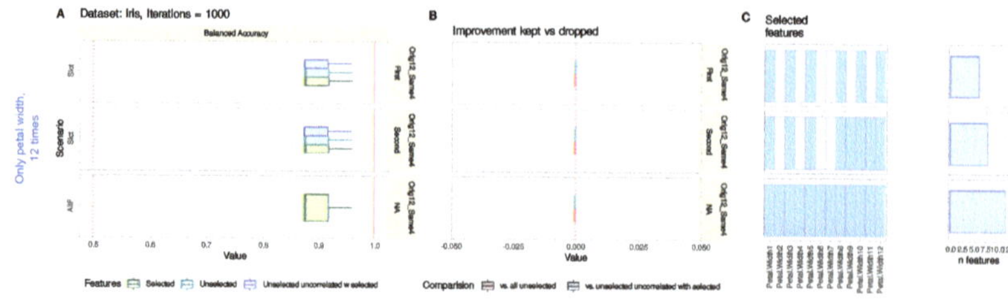

Figure 4. Feature selection and classification performance evaluation with different feature sets in the iris data set [28]. Experiments were performed only on petal width, added 12 times to the data set. The graph is organized in three subgraphs, showing from top to bottom (i) the results when using the features selected in the default feature selection, (ii) the features added when performing a second feature selection on the unselected features from the first selection, and (iii) when training the algorithm with the full feature set. The boxes show the 25th, 50th (blue vertical line), and 75th percentiles of balanced accuracies obtained in 1000 repeated runs with a random selection of 67% from the training data set and 80% from a validation data set separated from the data set before feature selection. Whiskers span the 95% confidence interval from the 2.5th to the 97.5th percentiles. (**A**): Balanced accuracy obtained with a random forests classifier trained with (i) the selected features, (ii) the unselected features, and (iii) the unselected features that were not highly correlated with the selected features, with the correlation threshold set at a very strong correlation of $\rho > 0.9$. (**B**): Difference in balanced accuracy when algorithms were trained with the selected versus unselected features. (**C**): Selected features (blue) and unselected features (white).

3.2. Wine Quality Data Set

Comparison Of Classification Performance with Selected and Unselected Features Can Reveal Feature Selection Problems

When not re-tuning the hyperparameters for the actual data set, feature selection using random forest permutation importance identified alcohol, free sulfur dioxide, and volatile acidity as the best variables for training the algorithm to discriminate between low- and high-quality wines (Figure 5). All of them were included in the result of the fuzzy logic techniques-based identification of relevant predictors of wine quality [31]. Moreover, these are also the variables that were found to be important predictors of wine quality for both wine types in a regression analysis, where red and white wines were evaluated separately [30]. This could have been accepted as a satisfactory result.

However, evaluation of the classification performance obtained when the unselected features were used for training demonstrated that a negative difference (Figure 5A(b)), i.e., it was not better than with the full feature set and, importantly, also not better than with the unselected features. This was indicated by the inclusion of the value zero in the 95% confidence intervals of the differences between the classification performance measures obtained with the selected features versus the full feature set or the non-selected features (Figure 5A(a,b)). The median difference in balanced class assignment accuracy was even smaller than for the unselected characteristics, although it was not significant because the 95% bootstrap confidence interval included the difference of zero.

Following the re-tuning of the random forests for the wine quality data set (see Section 2), the feature selection in the first round already resulted in a larger feature set that was closer to those identified in [30,31] and provided better classification results than the unselected features. This was further improved in the second round when the selected features. The resulting combined feature set thus met both the criterion of achieving classification performance as high as with all features and of selecting those features known from independent evaluations to be relevant to the target.

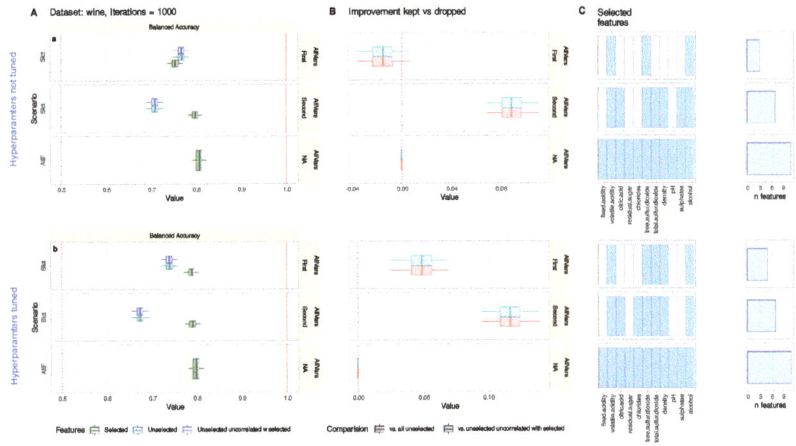

Figure 5. Feature selection and classification performance evaluation with different feature sets in the wine quality data set from https://www.kaggle.com/datasets/shelvigarg/wine-quality-dataset (accessed 2 November 2022). The graph is divided into subgraphs a–b from top to bottom. Experiments were performed (**a**) with non-tuned (**a**) and tuned (**b**) hyperparameters. The two subgraphs show from top to bottom (i) the results when using the features selected in the default feature selection, (ii) the features added when performing a second feature selection on the unselected features from the first selection, and (iii) when training the algorithm with the full feature set. The boxes show the 25th, 50th (blue vertical line), and 75th percentiles of balanced accuracies obtained in 1,000 repeated runs with a random selection of 67% from the training data set and 80% from a validation data set separated from the data set before feature selection. Whiskers span the 95% confidence interval from the 2.5th to the 97.5th percentiles. (**A**): Balanced accuracy obtained with a random forests classifier trained with (i) the selected features, (ii) the unselected features, and (iii) the unselected features that were not highly correlated with the selected features, with the correlation threshold set at a very strong correlation of $\rho > 0.9$. (**B**): Difference in balanced accuracy when algorithms were trained with the selected versus unselected features. (**C**): Selected features (blue) and unselected features (white).

4. Discussion

This report addresses a typical problem in the analysis of multivariate biomedical data, usually consisting of a set of individuals (cases) belonging to a particular diagnosis (class) and for which multiple measurements have been made (multivariate data). The first question that arises is whether there is any structure in these measurements that is relevant to the class structure and can be used to diagnose (classify) the subjects. To answer this question, a powerful machine-learned classifier can be trained on a subset of the data. If this classifier is able to classify the cases not used in learning (OOB data) such that this classification is close to the true class membership (e.g., a medical diagnosis), this indicates that there is structure in the multivariate data that supports the class structure. This structure could be used to assign future cases to the correct class, e.g., to make an (almost) accurate medical diagnosis for a person about whom the same type of information is available as that on which the algorithm was trained.

However, there are several pitfalls in this context. For example, the diagnosis may be accidentally coded in one or more variables. A typical example is the inclusion of a patient number in the data that contains a numeric code that already indicates the diagnosis. Then, the algorithm is trained on trivial information and is rather useless on future data. Other pitfalls include the problem of correlations and dealing with strongly correlated data. Filtering out correlated variables before machine learning fixes technical sensitivities of algorithms to avoid redundant information. However, this is not necessarily ideal for knowledge discovery. It also requires setting an arbitrary threshold above which the variables are considered highly correlated. A prototypical variable formally selected as the most strongly correlated feature of a group of features may be topically uninformative. On the other hand, selecting a topically meaningful prototype variable may disrupt the data-driven approach to information extraction because it introduces prior assumptions. Intermediate or latent variables computed from the original ones, such as projections onto principal component planes, may be difficult to interpret.

The basic idea presented here is to use the classifier not only for the selected features but also for the unselected features. If the performance of the classifier used is the same for both sets of features, there is no gain in information if only the selected features are used. Moreover, the selected features cannot be claimed to capture the nature of the mechanisms underlying the class structure of the data set. The selected features qualify for valid topical interpretation, if the performance of the classifier is better for the selected features. This is the case if the difference between the performance measures obtained when the algorithm was trained with either the selected features or the unselected features is positive and its 95% confidence interval in cross-validation runs does not include the difference of zero. In such a case, the feature selection can also be considered successful for knowledge discovery or explainable AI. The selected features qualify for valid topical interpretation.

Thus, this report emphasizes that there can be two different goals for feature selection (Figure 6). First, the technical goal of looking for the smallest number of features with which an algorithm can be trained to classify the data with sufficient accuracy ("technical feature selection" (TFS)). Second, the goal of knowledge discovery or XAI, where the features required for successful AI training are also interpreted in the topical context of the research data. In this scenario, the set of features must allow the, e.g., medical, field expert to understand how a machine system for class assignment, e.g., diagnosis, proceeds in order to arrive at a sufficiently accurate diagnosis. ("explainable feature selection" (XFS)). This might require more features than are technically necessary for a successful classification to enable a logical chain of reasoning that explains the class assignment within the particular research area. Thus, there can be different solutions for feature selection depending on the topical context and final aim of the analysis. The proposed approach facilitates explainable AI [2] because experts in the field will better understand an AI's decision if the key features on which the decision is based make sense to them in the context of their expertise, rather than simply accepting that the "black box" algorithm can use the information to make a diagnosis, to remain in the medical example.

Moreover, as demonstrated with the wine quality data set, the proposed method implicitly provides a signal for pathologies in feature selection that might escape attention without the reexamination of the unselected features. In machine learning reports, usually only the performance of the classifiers trained with the selected features is compared to the performance obtained when all variables were used for training. Given that feature selection methods can produce biased results [14,15], the proposed method provides a signal to identify missing informative variables and ensure that the most appropriate features were indeed selected for classifier training. To ensure that the best features were selected, the classifier performance when the unselected features were used for training should also be reported. There are valid reasons why performances may not be different, e.g., strongly correlated variables across selected and unselected features. However, this can be easily identified and interpreted to provide a complete picture of the information contained in the selected features compared to all variables. Moreover, the present example with the wine quality data set reemphasizes that random forests benefit from hyperparameter tuning, despite the suggestions to the contrary cited above and consistent with a recent case, published separately [23].

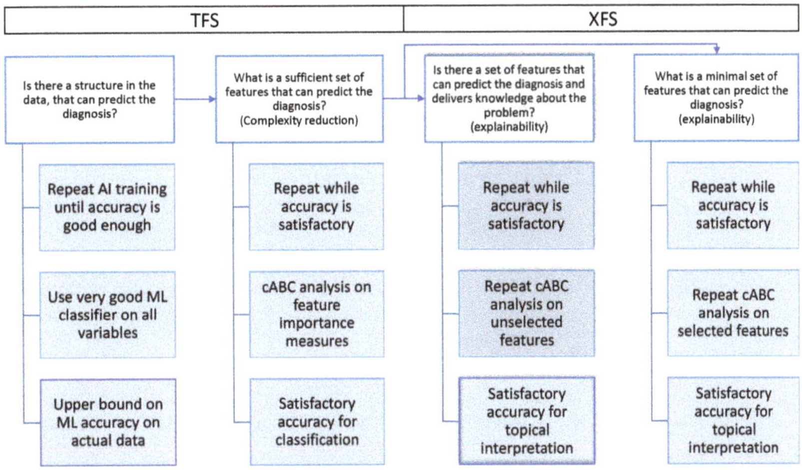

Figure 6. Flowchart showing the proposed feature selection workflow, with a distinction of the final goal into (i) "technical feature selection" (TFS), where the goal can be defined as training a powerful classifier, and (ii) "explainable feature selection" (XFS), where the goal can be defined that the selected features should be interpretable by a domain expert. Based on the evaluation of whether the entire input data space has a structure that matches the class structure of the output data space, for TFS the selected features are sufficient if the classifier computes the classification with the same accuracy as with all features in the data set. However, relevant information that makes the feature sets interpretable by the expert in the field may be lost in the process. For XFS, the selected features should therefore be interpretable by an expert in the field, i.e., they should contain relevant variables that provide information about the processes underlying the class structure. This can be facilitated by including the initially unselected features in the interpretation, as proposed in this report, or alternatively by reducing the data set to a bare informative minimum.

Limitations of the present assessments include the limited choice of machine-learning methods. While the proposed method should be generally suitable for the machine learning-based feature selection, here it was tested only with the OOB permutation feature importance of random forests. In addition, only one measure of classification performance was used, namely balanced accuracy. In the present experiments, the area under the receiver operating characteristic [34] was calculated in parallel, but it did not provide any additional insight, but merely repeated the observations based on the balanced accuracy, and therefore, for brevity, it is not included in the report. It is advisable to test the utility of further classification performance measures in the present XFS context separately when needed.

It should be noted that the present evaluations did not aim at benchmarking feature selection procedures for classification problems, but mainly at the importance of re-testing unselected features before declaring a machine learning-based analysis of a data set complete. In a review of feature selection methods for bioinformatics, especially for disease risk prediction [4], a classification was proposed according to which the approach proposed in the present report, especially to consider the unselected features, would belong to the class of feature selection algorithms that are independent of the details of the particular classifier algorithm. The other methods, on the other hand, depend on the details of the classifier algorithm. In particular, the approach presented here does not depend on the details of a particular feature selection algorithm or on a particular method for computing feature importance. In [35], different methods for evaluating the performance of different algorithms are compared with the result that none of them has a clear advantage. Moreover, the present experiments were conducted with classification problems. The re-evaluation of unselected features in regression problems has not been explicitly addressed. This would require the specification of modified signals, since balanced accuracy addresses classification, while an analogous measure must be found for regression before extending the currently proposed method to regression problems.

5. Conclusions

This work is particularly concerned with the features that are discarded by feature selection algorithms. When a classification task is attempted with such features omitted, there are two possible outcomes: The task fails or the task is possible even with the features not considered. If the task fails with the features not considered, then the conclusion is valid that the feature selection has chosen the best features for the task. If the classification is still possible, then either other features can be selected or the feature selection algorithm is not working correctly. If the algorithm is working correctly, then feature set can be extended to features that well describe the data generation process from an expert's point of view. Thus, the present proposal makes a distinction between whether the feature set can be described as containing relevant information for class assignment or whether as containing the only relevant information for class assignment. The former allows the unselected features to be included in the mechanistic interpretation, while the latter excludes them, i.e., adds a logical "NOT" to the argument in the sense of "these features are relevant, but not those". Thus, we propose, in line with [4], that extracting a subset of the most relevant features (through feature selection) could help researchers to understand the biological process(es) that underlie the disease.

Reconsideration of originally unselected items in multivariate data sets is proposed as a method to enhance the topical interpretation of variables emerging from feature selection aimed at knowledge discovery or explainable machine learning. This can be useful to filter out uninformative or trivial information or to add relevant topical information from variables originally overlooked in the feature selection. In addition, it can help to detect pathologies and errors in the feature selection that occasionally fail to identify the most appropriate variables. The method is generic to feature selection methods based on the supervised machine learning-based and can be implemented in the feature selection workflows.

Author Contributions: J.L.—Conceptualization and implementation of the algorithm, programming, data analysis, interpretation of the results, writing of the manuscript, creation of the figures, revision of the manuscript. A.U.—Critical revision of the manuscript for important intellectual content, conceptionalization of Figure 6, interpretation of the results, revision of the manuscript. All authors have read and agreed to the published version of the manuscript.

Funding: J.L. was supported by the Deutsche Forschungsgemeinschaft (DFG LO 612/16-1).

Institutional Review Board Statement: Not applicable.

Informed Consent Statement: Not applicable.

Data Availability Statement: Data have been taken from publicly available sources.

Conflicts of Interest: The authors declare no conflict of interest.

References

1. Guyon, I. An introduction to variable and feature selection. *J. Mach. Learn. Res.* **2003**, *3*, 1157–1182.
2. Lotsch, J.; Kringel, D.; Ultsch, A. Explainable Artificial Intelligence (XAI) in Biomedicine: Making AI Decisions Trustworthy for Physicians and Patients. *BioMedInformatics* **2022**, *2*, 1. [CrossRef]
3. Miller, G.A. The magical number seven plus or minus two: Some limits on our capacity for processing information. *Psychol. Rev.* **1956**, *63*, 81–97. [CrossRef] [PubMed]
4. Pudjihartono, N.; Fadason, T.; Kempa-Liehr, A.W.; O'Sullivan, J.M. A Review of Feature Selection Methods for Machine Learning-Based Disease Risk Prediction. *Front. Bioinform.* **2022**, *2*, 927312. [CrossRef]
5. Saeys, Y.; Inza, I.; Larranaga, P. A review of feature selection techniques in bioinformatics. *Bioinformatics* **2007**, *23*, 2507–2517. [CrossRef]
6. Yu, L.; Liu, H. Feature Selection for High-Dimensional Data: A Fast Correlation-Based Filter Solution. In Proceedings of the Twentieth International Conference on Machine Learning (ICML-2003), Washington, DC, USA, 21–24 August 2003.

7. Aboudi, N.E.; Benhlima, L. Review on wrapper feature selection approaches. In Proceedings of the 2016 International Conference on Engineering & MIS (ICEMIS), Agadir, Morocco, 22–24 September 2016; pp. 1–5.
8. Chen, C.W.; Tsai, Y.H.; Chang, F.R.; Lin, W.C. Ensemble feature selection in medical datasets: Combining filter, wrapper, and embedded feature selection results. *Expert Syst.* **2020**, *37*, e12553. [CrossRef]
9. Santosa, F.; Symes, W.W. Linear Inversion of Band-Limited Reflection Seismograms. *Siam J. Sci. Stat. Comput.* **1986**, *7*, 1307–1330. [CrossRef]
10. Ho, T.K. Random Decision Forests. In Proceedings of the 3rd International Conference on Document Analysis and Recognition, Montreal, QC, Canada, 14–16 August 1995. [CrossRef]
11. Breiman, L. Random Forests. *Mach. Learn.* **2001**, *45*, 5–32. [CrossRef]
12. Kursa, M.B.; Rudnicki, W.R. Feature Selection with the Boruta Package. *J. Stat. Softw.* **2010**, *36*, 1–13. [CrossRef]
13. Liaw, A.; Wiener, M. Classification and Regression by randomForest. *R N.* **2002**, *2*, 18–22.
14. Parr, T.; Turgutlu, K.; Csiszar, C.; Howard, J. Beware Default Random Forest Importances 2018. Available online: https://explained.ai/rf-importance (accessed on 3 September 2022).
15. Strobl, C.; Boulesteix, A.L.; Zeileis, A.; Hothorn, T. Bias in random forest variable importance measures: Illustrations, sources and a solution. *BMC Bioinform.* **2007**, *8*, 25. [CrossRef]
16. Ultsch, A.; Lotsch, J. Computed ABC Analysis for Rational Selection of Most Informative Variables in Multivariate Data. *PLoS ONE* **2015**, *10*, e0129767. [CrossRef]
17. Juran, J.M. The non-Pareto principle; Mea culpa. *Qual. Prog.* **1975**, *8*, 8–9.
18. Lotsch, J.; Ultsch, A. *Random Forests Followed by Computed ABC Analysis as a Feature Selection Method for Machine Learning in Biomedical Data*; Advanced Studies in Classification and Data Science; Springer: Singapore, 2020; pp. 57–69.
19. Ihaka, R.; Gentleman, R. R: A Language for Data Analysis and Graphics. *J. Comput. Graph. Stat.* **1996**, *5*, 299–314. [CrossRef]
20. R Core Team. R: A Language and Environment for Statistical Computing. Available online: https://www.R-project.org/ (accessed on 3 September 2022).
21. Kuhn, M. Caret: Classification and Regression Training. 2018. Available online: https://cran.r-project.org/package=caret (accessed on 3 September 2022).
22. Lötsch, J.; Malkusch, S.; Ultsch, A. Optimal distribution-preserving downsampling of large biomedical data sets (opdisDownsampling). *PLoS ONE* **2021**, *16*, e0255838. [CrossRef]
23. Lötsch, J.; Mayer, B. A Biomedical Case Study Showing That Tuning Random Forests Can Fundamentally Change the Interpretation of Supervised Data Structure Exploration Aimed at Knowledge Discovery. *BioMedInformatics* **2022**, *2*, 544–552. [CrossRef]
24. Good, P.I. *Resampling Methods: A Practical Guide to Data Analysis*; Birkhauser: Boston, MA, USA, 2006.
25. Tille, Y.; Matei, A. Sampling: Survey Sampling. 2016. Available online: https://cran.r-project.org/package=sampling (accessed on 3 September 2022).
26. Brodersen, K.H.; Ong, C.S.; Stephan, K.E.; Buhmann, J.M. The Balanced Accuracy and Its Posterior Distribution. In Proceedings of the 2010 20th International Conference on Pattern Recognition (ICPR), Istanbul, Turkey, 23–26 August 2010; pp. 3121–3124. [CrossRef]
27. Anderson, E. The irises of the Gaspe peninsula. *Bull. Am. Iris Soc.* **1935**, *59*, 2–5.
28. Fisher, R.A. The use of multiple measurements in taxonomic problems. *Ann. Eugen.* **1936**, *7*, 179–188. [CrossRef]
29. Bannerman-Thompson, H.; Bhaskara Rao, M.; Kasala, S. Chapter 5-Bagging, Boosting, and Random Forests Using R. In *Handbook of Statistics*; Rao, C.R., Govindaraju, V., Eds.; Elsevier: Amsterdam, The Netherlands, 2013; Volume 31, pp. 101–149. [CrossRef]
30. Gupta, Y.K. Selection of important features and predicting wine quality using machine learning techniques. *Procedia Comput. Sci.* **2018**, *125*, 305–312. [CrossRef]
31. Nebot, A.; Mugica, F.; Escobet, A. Modeling Wine Preferences from Physicochemical Properties using Fuzzy Techniques. In Proceedings of the 5th International Conference on Simulation and Modeling Methodologies, Technologies and Applications—SIMULTECH, Colmar, France, 21–23 July 2015. [CrossRef]
32. Schober, P.; Boer, C.; Schwarte, L.A. Correlation Coefficients: Appropriate Use and Interpretation. *Anesth. Analg.* **2018**, *126*, 1763–1768. [CrossRef]
33. Spearman, C. The proof and measurement of association between two things. *Am. J. Psychol.* **1904**, *15*, 72–101. [CrossRef]
34. Peterson, W.; Birdsall, T.; Fox, W. The theory of signal detectability. *Trans. Ire Prof. Group Inf. Theory.* **1954**, *4*, 171–212. [CrossRef]
35. Khaire, U.M.; Dhanalakshmi, R. Stability of feature selection algorithm: A review. *J. King Saud Univ.-Comput. Inf. Sci.* **2022**, *34*, 1060–1073. [CrossRef]

BioMedInformatics

MDPI

Article

Analysis of Differentially Expressed Genes, MMP3 and TESC, and Their Potential Value in Molecular Pathways in Colon Adenocarcinoma: A Bioinformatics Approach

Constantin Busuioc [1,†], Andreea Nutu [1,†], Cornelia Braicu [1,*], Oana Zanoaga [1], Monica Trif [2] and Ioana Berindan-Neagoe [1]

1 Research Center for Functional Genomics, Biomedicine and Translational Medicine, Iuliu Haţieganu University of Medicine and Pharmacy, 23 Marinescu Street, 40015 Cluj-Napoca, Romania
2 Centre for Innovative Process Engineering (CENTIV) GmbH, 28857 Bremen Stuhr, Germany
* Correspondence: braicucornelia@yahoo.com
† These authors contributed equally to this work.

Abstract: Despite the great progress in its early diagnosis and treatment, colon adenocarcinoma (COAD) is still poses important issues to clinical management. Therefore, the identification of novel biomarkers or therapeutic targets for this disease is important. Using UALCAN, the top 25 upregulated and downregulated genes in COAD were identified. Then, a Kaplan–Meier plotter was employed for these genes for survival analysis, revealing the correlation with overall survival rate only for MMP3 (Matrix Metallopeptidase 3) and TESC (Tescalcin). Despite this, the mRNA expression levels were not correlated with the tumor stages or nodal metastatic status. MMP3 and TESC are relevant targets in COAD that should be additionally validated as biomarkers for early diagnosis and prevention. Ingenuity Pathway Analysis revealed the top relevant network linked to Post-Translational Modification, Protein Degradation, and Protein Synthesis, where MMP3 was at the core of the network. Another important network was related to cell cycle regulation, TESC being a component of this. We should also not underestimate the complex regulatory mechanisms mediated by the interplay of the multiple other regulatory molecules, emphasizing the interconnection with molecules related to invasion and migration involved in COAD, that might serve as the basis for the development of new biomarkers and therapeutic targets.

Keywords: colon adenocarcinoma; bioinformatic analysis; MMP3 and TESC

Citation: Busuioc, C.; Nutu, A.; Braicu, C.; Zanoaga, O.; Trif, M.; Berindan-Neagoe, I. Analysis of Differentially Expressed Genes, MMP3 and TESC, and Their Potential Value in Molecular Pathways in Colon Adenocarcinoma: A Bioinformatics Approach. *Biomedinformatics* **2022**, *2*, 474–491. https://doi.org/10.3390/biomedinformatics2030030

Academic Editor: Pentti Nieminen

Received: 1 August 2022
Accepted: 30 August 2022
Published: 3 September 2022

1. Introduction

Although great improvements have been made in the management of colon cancer, it still represents an unmet clinical need, especially in the late stages of the disease, where the limited response to therapy and an important alteration in quality of life threaten patients' outcomes. Colon adenocarcinoma (COAD) is a common malignant tumor of the digestive tract, with an incidence of 37.7% with 114,515 new cases and a 13.4% mortality rate with 576,858 deaths reported by Globocan in 2021 [1,2]. In most cases, this cancer is asymptomatic until late stages, with widely available screening programs only in developed countries. Meanwhile, a reduced reported screening rate in low and middle-income countries is reflected by increasing mortality for these patients [3].

Treatments in advanced stages, which are often accompanied by metastasis or locally advanced disease, face limitations in regards to systemic chemotherapy and radiotherapy due to high toxicity, while surgical removal is a viable option mostly for earlier stages [1]. With such a high number of deaths annually, it is vital to search among the many altered molecules from cancer tissue, some of them with yet unknown roles, to identify more effective molecular actors and to investigate their potential role in colon cancer, thus possibly improving patient survival [4].

Multiple molecular alterations occur during COAD development and progression, impacting the patient's prognosis [5–7]. Their identification and study will improve disease management [8–11]. In the last few years, several molecular signatures have been validated as being correlated with prognostic and prediction significance [5,8,12,13].

Bioinformatic analysis of omics data has been widely used to explore the pathogenesis of human diseases [14]. The Cancer Genome Atlas (TCGA) is a comprehensive database where the molecular profiles and clinical parameters of 34 different tumor types on multiple levels (level of expression for coding and non-coding genes, mutational status, methylation patterns, or proteomic/metabolomic profile) are included [15]. The use of datasets from TCGA expands the opportunities for data mining and can provide a deeper understanding of cancer biology and tumor-specific vulnerabilities [16]. Previous studies concerning COAD gene expression profiling identified genes with an altered expression level [16–18]. These findings allow for the discovery of potential new molecules that may lead to a significantly more accurate diagnosis if found in the early stages, better patient stratification, and the development of new targeted therapies [19].

The more in-depth the studies are extended, the more the extracted information can define new potential molecules that can help the improvement of colon adenocarcinoma management. To identify potentially powerful "actors" in COAD progression, we chose to investigate the pathways and interaction networks associated with the most altered identified genes in COAD (top 25 upregulated coding genes and top 25 down-regulated coding genes, based on the UALCAN database (http://ualcan.path.uab.edu, 12 August 2022) using Ingenuity Pathway Analysis from Qiagen (IPA). The UALCAN portal has been widely used since its release in 2017 and has received immense praise and popularity. IPA is used to identify the interactions among the altered genes and integrate and identify the most relevant pathways associated with COAD.

This study aimed to identify the potential candidate *genes* in COAD and to further uncover their roles in this pathology. Among the top 25 up and 25 down-regulated genes, we explored two specific genes involved in several mechanisms from early stage to late stage colon adenocarcinomas, specifically the MMP3 and TESC genes, the only two genes among these top up and down-regulated genes that were correlated with overall survival rates (according to STARBASE).

The TESC (tescalcin) gene codifies for a protein with an intracytoplasmic localization that is expressed in several cancer types. It was recently proposed as a target for colon cancer therapy. MMP3 is known to be located intracellularly and is involved in the degradation of collagen, possessing the molecular functions of a hydrolase, metalloprotease, and protease. It is also involved in the epithelial to mesenchymal transition. In our study, the genes' level of expression was correlated with the overall survival rate. Both genes are still not often studied in this cancer type; therefore, due to their statistical power in overall survival, we investigated the bioinformatics data related to them. For validation, we used another cohort of patients found in the COLONOMICs project [20]. In addition, these data should be further validated in additional patient cohorts on biological samples from both tumor tissue and plasma. This part was not the purpose of our study at this time.

2. Materials and Methods

2.1. Study Design

A flow chart of the study design with datasets and analysis for COAD is shown in Figure 1.

2.2. Data Mining of TCGA Data Set in COAD

The bioinformatics portal UALCAN (http://ualcan.path.uab.edu, accessed on 8 June 2022) used TCGA level 3 RNA-sequencing and clinical data from COAD. This database was used to access the altered gene expression pattern [21]. The COAD cohort is represented by 286 primary COAD tumors and 41 adjacent normal tissue to some of the samples, comparing cancer tissue samples with normal tissue samples. UALCAN lists genes that show high differential expression among normal and tumor samples in the form of an interactive heatmap. The database delivers a graphical representation of the expression profile as a heatmap with the top 25 altered genes or as a box plot for individual genes; the expression level of the searched gene is normalized as transcript per million reads, and the p-value < 0.01 is considered to be significant. In UALCAN, the difference among the groups is performed using a t-test using a PERL script with the Comprehensive Perl Archive Network (CPAN) module "Statistics: t-test" [21].

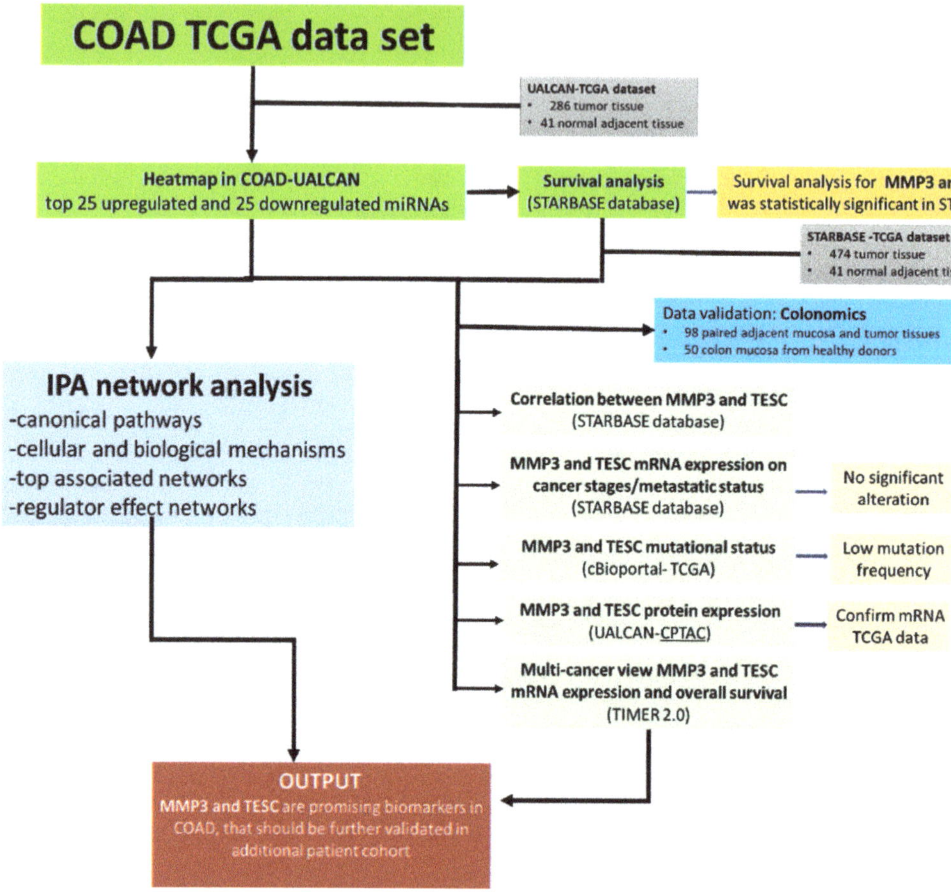

Figure 1. Flow diagram of the study design. Initial data sets from TCGA colon adenocarcinoma patients were analyzed using the UALCAN portal (comprising data from 286 tumor samples and 41 adjacent tissue), then survival analyses were performed for the top 25 upregulated and down-regulated genes using the STARBASE-TCGA data set (474 tumor samples and 41 adjacent tissue). The selected genes MMP3 and TESC (based on survival analysis-STARBASE) were validated on the Colonomics database, which contains a different set of patients than TCGA. Our data from two different patient cohorts showed that both genes can be found in all stages of colon adenocarcinoma patients, that their association with overall survival is significant, and that their protein profiling confirms the mRNA level of expression in UALCAN-CPTAC. These initial data suggest that they could be indicators of colon adenocarcinoma and, due to their link with overall survival, can become therapeutic targets. Further validation on patients' needs to be performed for data consistency.

2.3. Inclusion and Exclusion Criteria

To perform the bioinformatics analysis, we selected only patients with colon adenocarcinoma. A total of 286 patients with COAD were found in the UALCAN database, with 41 matched pairs of normal adjacent tissue according to the following table. We collected data from all 286 patients, who were of both sexes, with tumors at all stages, including lymph node involvement data. The exclusion criteria were patients with rectal cancer. Data of the patients included in our bioinformatics analysis are summarized in Table 1.

Table 1. UALCAN patient's characteristics.

Demographics		COAD Tumor (n = 286) Normal (n = 41)
Age—Range (years)		31–90
Gender	F	127
	M	156
	Unknown	3
Histological subtype	Adenocarcinoma	243
	Mucinous adenocarcinoma	37
	Unknown	3
Tumor stage	I	45
	II	110
	III	80
	IV	39
	Unknown	2
Nodal metastasis status	N0	166
	N1	70
	N2	47
	Unknown	3

For the evaluation of the significance of differences in expression levels between normal and primary tumors, or tumor subgroups based on clinicopathological features, Welch's t-test estimations were used (* $p \leq 0.05$, ** $p \leq 0.01$, *** $p \leq 0.001$, **** $p \leq 0.0001$) [22].

The UALCAN database was used for the identification of the top 25 upregulated and top 25 downregulated genes. Additionally, UALCAN was used for the graphical representation of protein expression levels for the same transcripts. Data from The Cancer Omics Atlas (TCOA) repository database provides information about gene expression, somatic mutations, miRNA expression, and protein expression data based on an individual molecule or a specific cancer type [23]. We used it for the downloaded top 25 upregulated and top 25 down-regulated genes in COAD for analysis and mechanistic insights.

2.4. Survival Analysis STARBASE Database

The StarBase database (https://starbase.sysu.edu.cn/panGeneCoExp.php#, accessed on 14 June 2022) is a portal that can facilitate tumor subgroups' gene expression and survival analyses, providing easy access to publicly available cancer transcriptome data contained by TCGA [24]. We evaluated the COAD patients' survival related to the top 25 upregulated and top 25 downregulated genes. The genes' names were keyed into the STARBASE database, and Kaplan–Meier survival plots, hazard ratio (HR), 95% confidence interval (CI), and log-rank p values were displayed directly on the web page; a log-rank $p < 0.05$ was considered statistically significant.

2.5. Pearson Correlation Analysis for Gene Expression Data

Data from survival analysis revealed the MMP3 and TESC coding genes that were further used for correlation analysis in COAD, using the STARBASE database [24,25]. A Pearson correlation coefficient $r > 0.40$, which was set as a cutoff, and a p-value ≤ 0.05 were considered statistically significant (https://starbase.sysu.edu.cn/panGeneCoExp.php, accessed on 12 June 2022).

2.6. Genetic Alterations Using cBioPortal

The frequency of gene alterations (amplification, deep deletion, and missense mutations) in cancer can be assessed by using cBioPortal (http://www.cbioportal.org, accessed on 2 August 2022). cBioportal is an interactive open-source platform that provides large-scale cancer genomics datasets [26].

2.7. MMP3 with TESC in COAD Protein Expression Levels

UALCAN also provides a protein expression analysis option for COAD, based on data available from the Clinical Proteomic Tumor Analysis Consortium (CPTAC, http://ualcan.path.uab.edu/analysis-prot.html accessed on 10 June 2022) [27].

2.8. Validation of MMP3 and TESC Expression Level with the Colonomics Database

Colonomics is a web resource for analyzing biomarkers of diagnosis and prognosis in colorectal cancer (https://www.colonomics.org/expression-browser/, accessed on 9 August 2022). It can be used to generate plots of the gene expression profiles based on a patient cohort of 98 paired adjacent mucosa and tumor tissues from colorectal cancer patients and 50 colon mucosa from healthy donors; the patient's characteristics have been described previously by Sanz-Pamplona et al., 2014 [18]; p-value < 0.01 is considered to be significant.

2.9. Pathway Analysis in COAD

Functional annotation was performed using Ingenuity Pathway Analysis (IPA, https://digitalinsights.qiagen.com/products-overview/discovery-insights-portfolio/analysis-and-visualization/qiagen-ipa/, accessed on 2 August 2022) applying predefined pathways and functional categories of the Ingenuity Knowledge Base [28]. The "Core Analysis' function included in IPA was used to interpret the top 25 upregulated and top 25 downregulated genes in COAD, downloaded from TCOA. After the analysis, the generated networks were arranged by a score in order of significance using the Ingenuity Knowledge Base. The significance of the bio functions and the canonical pathways were judged based on the Fisher Exact test p-value; being grouped into Disease and Disorders; Molecular and Cellular Functions; and Physiological System Development and Function. Additionally, the implication in canonical pathways was considered and ranked by the ratio value (number of molecules in a particular pathway that has the cut criteria, divided by the total number of molecules of the pathway). IPA generates networks for the altered signature in COAD that are correlated with previously identified associations between genes or proteins but independently of established canonical pathways. Moreover, these networks are linked to functions based on the molecules involved.

2.10. Multi-Cancer View of MMP3 and TESC in Cancer

Additional multi-cancer view graphical representations for MMP3 and TESC of the expression levels were downloaded from TIMER2.0 (http://timer.cistrome.org, accessed on 1 June 2022) [29,30].

3. Results

3.1. Altered Gene Expression Pattern in COAD Based on TCGA Dataset

A total number of 628 altered genes with an altered expression level (363 overexpressed and 265 downregulated genes), using as a cut-off value a fold change of ± 2 and a p-value ≤ 0.05 (TCGA patient cohort linked to the TCOA online tool) was found [5]. Gene expression analysis using TCGA data portal analysis with the UALCAN database for COAD permits emphasis on the top 25 upregulated and top 25 downregulated genes, displayed as a heatmap in Figure 2 and Table S1. The Log2(fold change) and p-value are based on the analysis done using TCOA online tool.

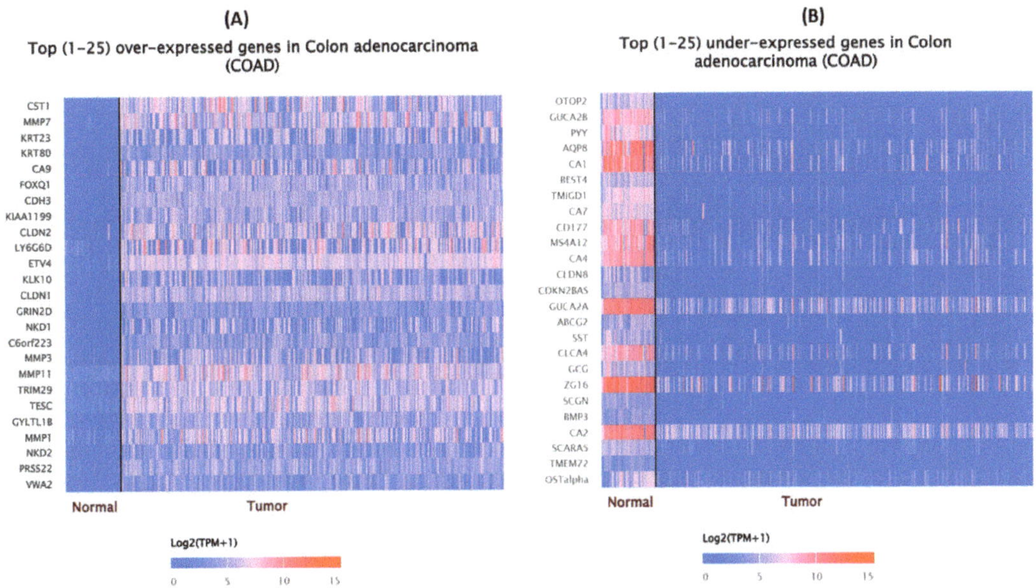

Figure 2. Heatmap showing patterns of most altered genes in COAD. (**A**) Heatmap graphical representation of the top 25 overexpressed genes, (**B**) top 25 under expressed genes in COAD versus adjacent normal tissue, data available from the TCGA dataset, generated by web-portal UALCAN. The expression level of genes in COAD is represented as a log2(TPM+ 1) scale.

3.2. Significance of the MMP3 and TESC in COAD

Among the top 25 upregulated and top 25 downregulated genes in COAD, two genes (MMP3 and TESC) were correlated with overall survival (OS) in COAD. Both genes are upregulated in COAD. The prognostic values of MMP3 and TESC mRNA in COAD evaluated by STARBASE online databases are displayed in Figure 3; we found that the expression of MMP3 and low expression of TESC suggest an unfavorable prognosis for patients with COAD.

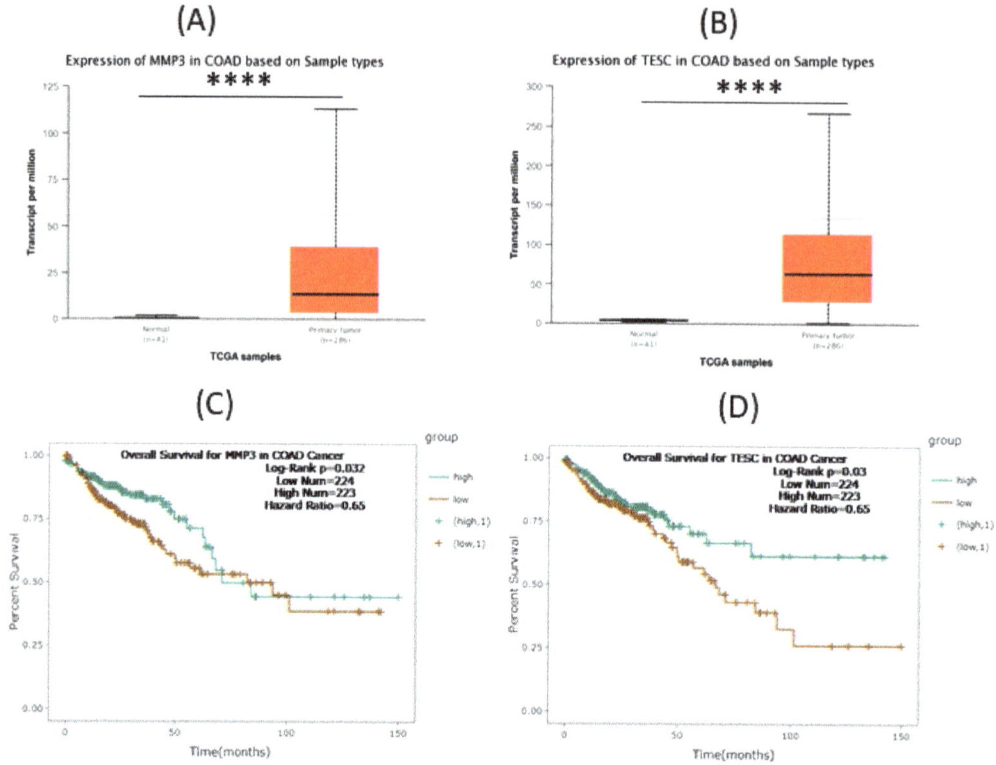

Figure 3. Expression levels and prognostic value of MMP3 and TESC in COAD. (**A**) the expression level for MMP3, graphical representation using UALCAN based on COAD TGCA data set; statistical significance was evaluated using Welch's *t*-test (UALCAN interface), **** $p \leq 0.0001$. (**B**) expression level for TESC, graphical representation using UALCAN based on the COAD TGCA data set; statistical significance was evaluated using Welch's *t*-test (UALCAN interface), **** $p \leq 0.0001$. (**C**) High expression of MMP3 indicates a better OS in COAD, using Kaplan-Meier Plotter database); (**D**) High expression of TESC indicates a better OS. Graphical representation of Kaplan-Meier Plotter was done using the STARBASE database). This can be explained by a lower number of patients with lymph node-positive/metastasis in the entire cohort.

No direct correlation between TESC and MMP3 (r = 0.004 and a p value = 0.925) has been revealed, as can be observed in Figure 4.

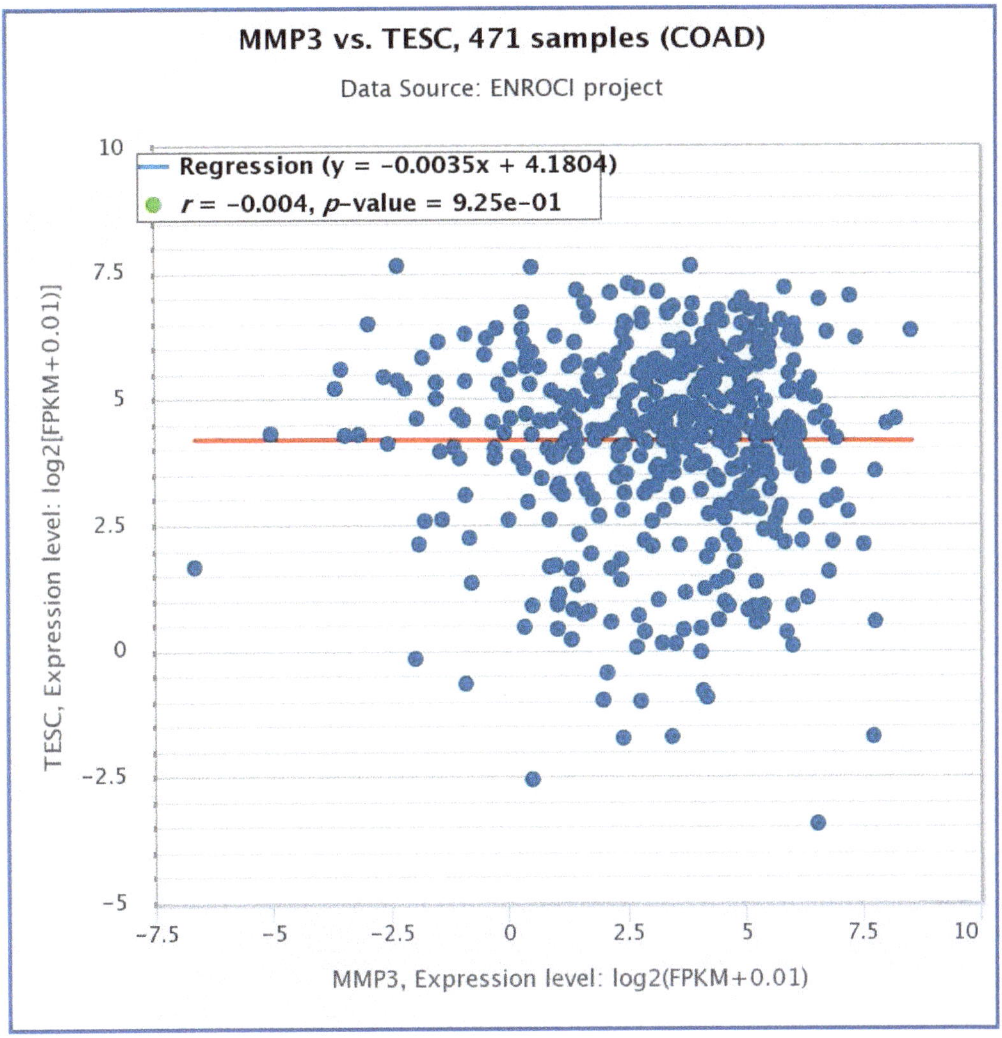

Figure 4. Pearson correlation between MMP3 and TESC expression in COAD samples ($n = 471$) using the STARBASE database.

3.3. MMP3 and TESC mRNA Expression and Cancer Stages and Lymph Node-Positive/Metastatic Status in COAD

The mRNA expression levels of MMP3 and TESC in tumor tissue were much higher compared to normal tissues. The relationship between the mRNA expression levels of MMP3 and TESC and the tumor stage of COAD patients was analyzed based on the UALCAN database (Figure 5). As shown in Figure 6, the mRNA expressions of MMP3 and TESC are statistically significant across all tumor stages and lymph node status of COAD.

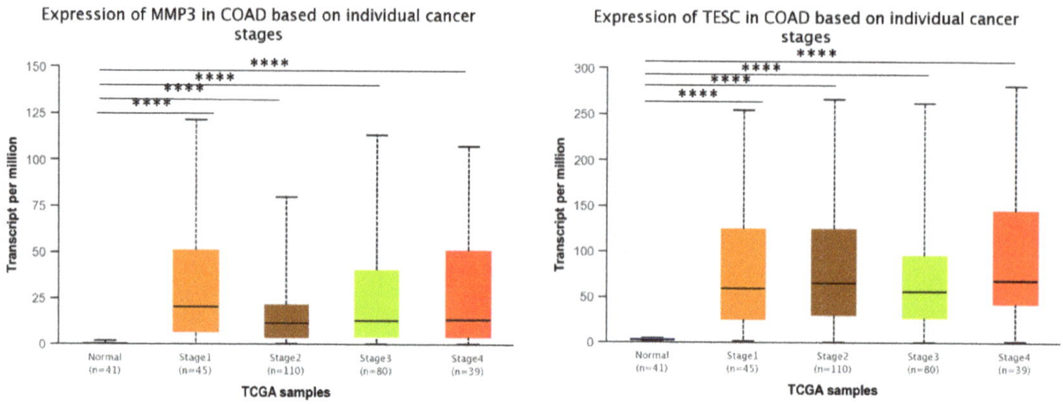

Figure 5. The relationship between MMP3 and TESC mRNA expression and cancer stages (UALCAN). Cancer stages include COAD from stage 1 to stage 4. Statistical significance was evaluated using Welch's t-test (UALCAN interface), **** $p \leq 0.0001$.

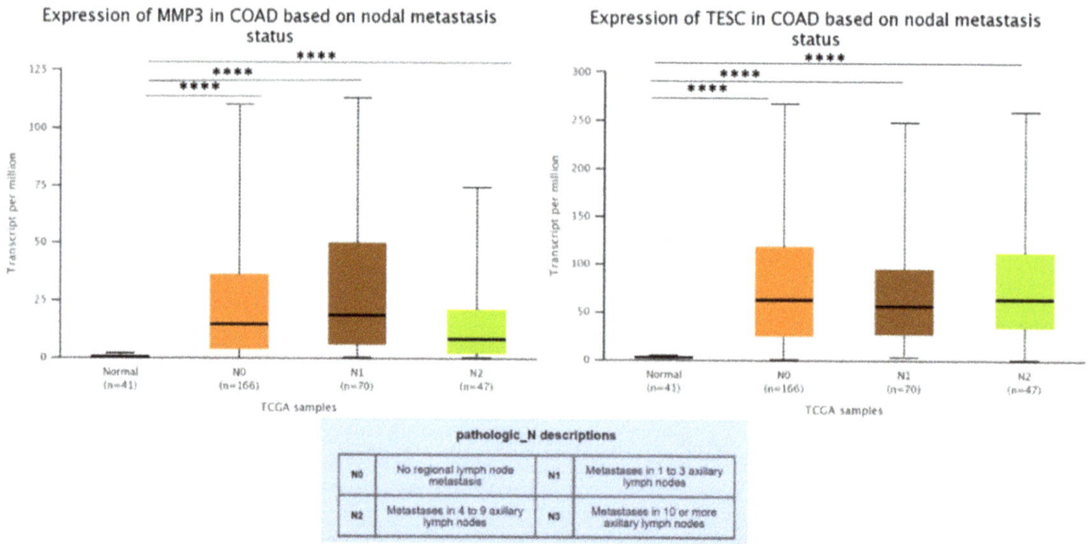

Figure 6. The relationship between MMP3 and TESC mRNA expression and status (UALCAN) in COAD. Statistical significance was evaluated using Welch's t-test (UALCAN interface), **** $p \leq 0.0001$.

3.4. MMP3 and TESC Mutational Signature in COAD Evaluated Using cBioPortal

The application of cBioPortal was for the evaluated mutational signature to show the mutational frequency of the selected genes (MMP3, TESC compared with TP53, which was identified to be highly mutated in COAD [5]) in the COAD TCGA cohort. The data is presented in Figure 7.

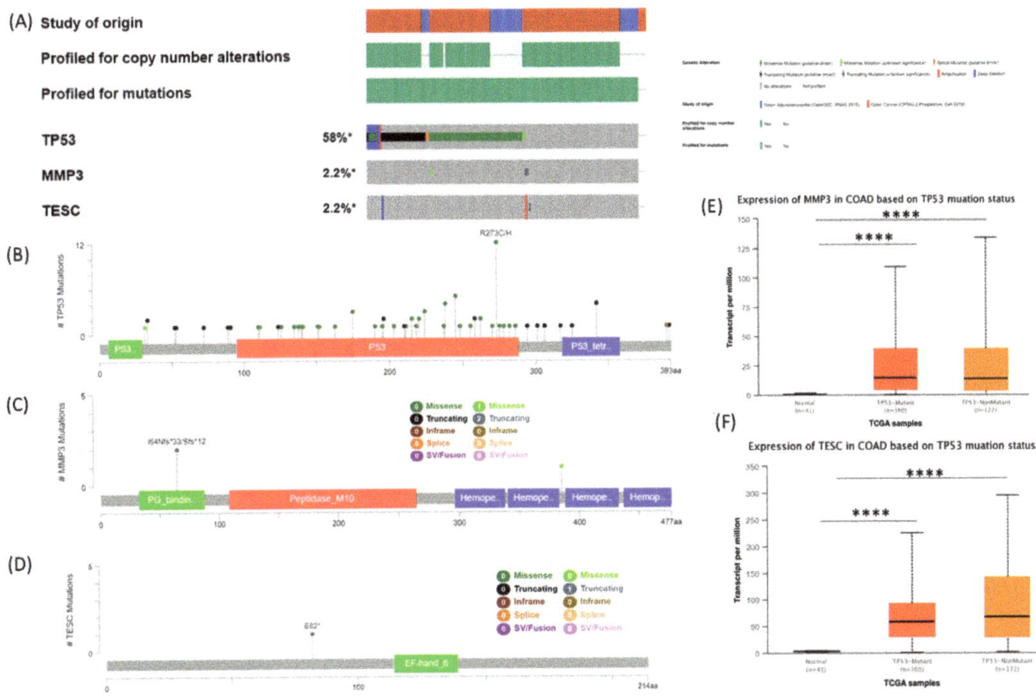

Figure 7. Analysis of genomic alterations in the identified hub genes and their correlations with survival prognosis in COAD using cBioPortal. (**A**) In the genomic alterations representation of the hub genes in the selected TCGA dataset of COAD, each column represents a patient. Localization and frequency of all mutations for (**B**) TP53, (**C**) MMP3, (**D**) TESC, (**E**) MMP3 expression level in COAD based on TP53 mutation status; statistical significance was evaluated using Welch's *t*-test (UALCAN interface), **** $p \leq 0.0001$, (**F**) TESC expression level in COAD based on TP53 mutation status; statistical significance was evaluated using Welch's *t*-test (UALCAN interface), **** $p \leq 0.0001$.

3.5. Validation of MMP3 and TESC with the Colonomics Patient Cohort

As represented in Figure 8, expression levels of two genes, *MMP3* and *TESC*, were validated in an additional transcriptomic dataset, consisting of 98 paired adjacent mucosa and tumor tissues from colorectal cancer patients and 50 colon mucosa from healthy donors. Compared with normal mucosa or normal adjacent tissue, expression levels of MMP3 and TESC were significantly increased in colon cancer.

3.6. MMP3 and TESC Protein Expression Levels

Additional analysis was performed to validate the mRNA expression levels for MMP3 and TESC at the protein level (Figure 9), revealing an overexpression at the protein level. The data is in agreement with those from the mRNA level.

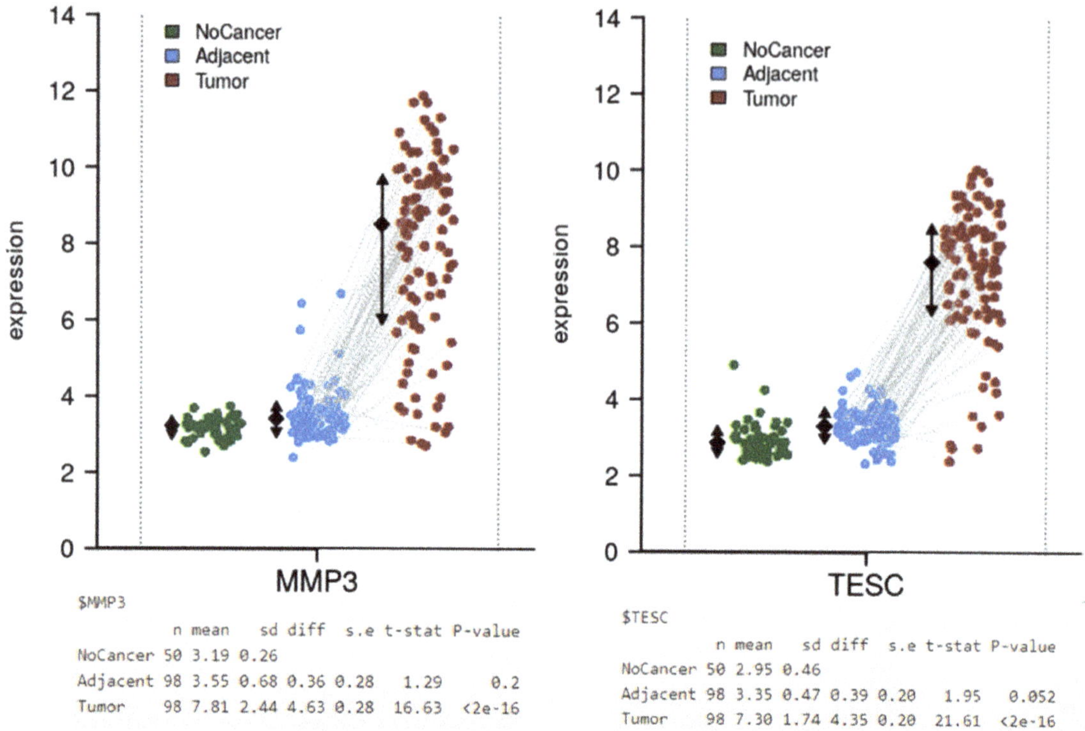

Figure 8. Validation of the MMP3 and TESC with the Colonomics patient cohort, $p < 0.05$ was considered statistically significant.

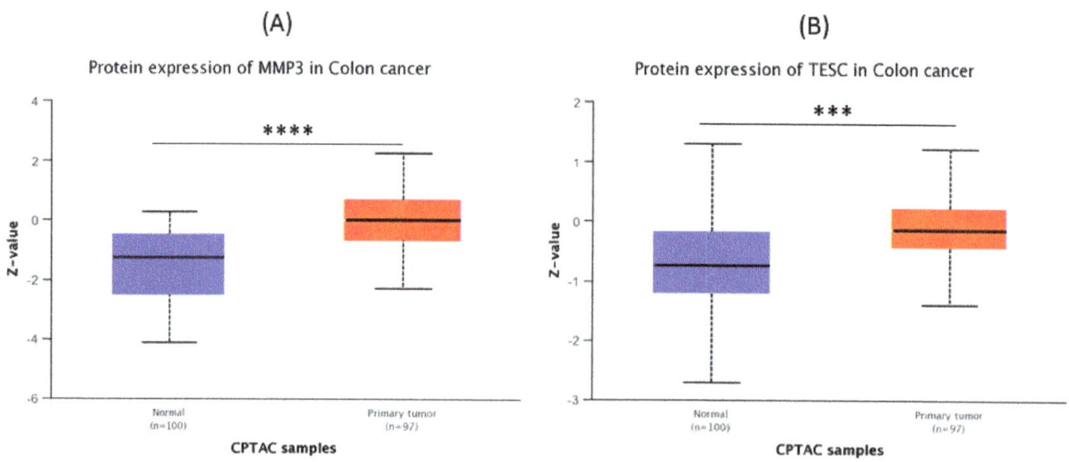

Figure 9. MMP3 and TESC protein expression in COAD samples (comprising data from 100 normal adjacent tissue and 97 primary COAD tumors) using the CPTAC-UALCAN platform. Statistical significance was evaluated using Welch's t-test (UALCAN interface), *** $p < 0.001$ and **** $p < 0.0001$.

3.7. *IPA Network Analysis*

The main canonical pathways generated using IPA based on the top 25 upregulated and downregulated genes in COAD are related to Granulocyte Adhesion and Diapedesis, Leukocyte Extravasation Signaling, Agranulocyte Adhesion, and Diapedesis or Inhibition of Matrix Metalloproteases (Figure 10A). Using the same data set for analysis, the top associated networks were generated, as displayed in Table 2. The network N1 (related to Post-Translational Modification, Protein Degradation, and Protein Synthesis) is displayed in Figure 10B, revealing the MMPs as a core element of this network. Additional graphical representation of the N4 network (related to Cell Cycle, Cancer, and Neurological Disease), revealing TESC's direct relationship with HIT and HRAS, as displayed in Figure 10B. Additional valuable data related to the prognostic value and main target molecules for the altered genes are displayed in Table 2. Additional IPA regulator networks are presented in Figure 11, and the Top Molecular and Cellular Functions generated using IPA are displayed in Table S2.

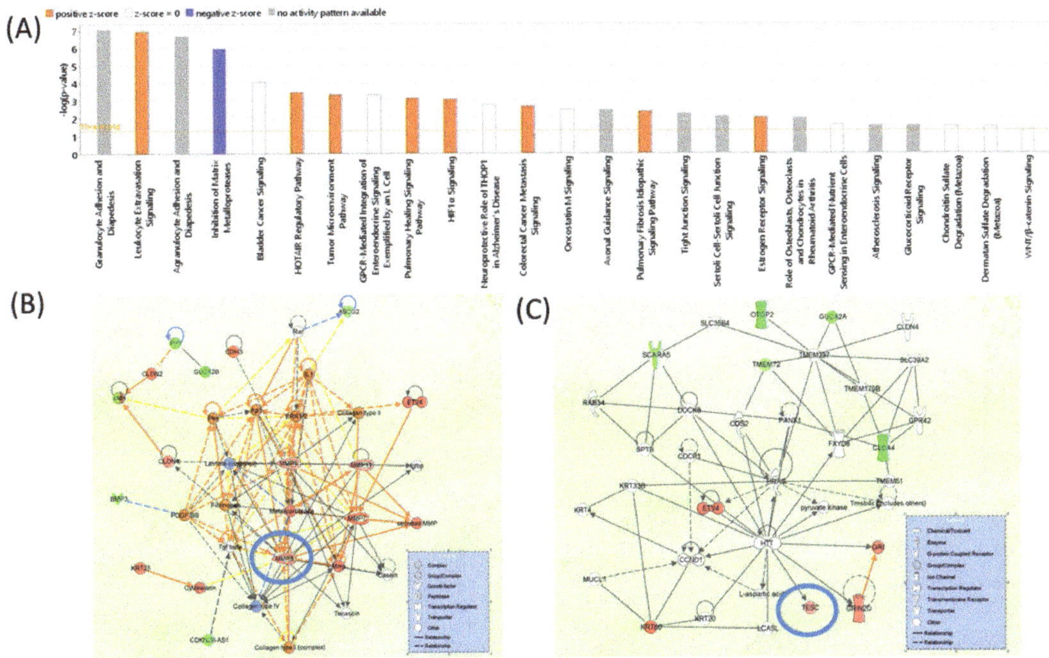

Figure 10. Mechanistic insights in COAD were generated based on the top 25 upregulated and downregulated genes generated using IPA. (**A**) Canonical pathways identified by IPA (**B**) Top-ranked enriched network, related to Post-Translational Modification, Protein Degradation, Protein Synthesis. (**C**) Network related to Cell Cycle, Cancer, and Neurological Disease. Red: significantly increased expression level; green: significantly decreased expression level. The regulators are colored by their predicted activation state: activated (orange) or inhibited (blue). Darker colors indicate higher absolute Z-scores. MMP3 and TESC are highlighted with blue circles.

Table 2. Top associated networks were generated using IPA, based on the altered signature on COAD.

ID	Associated Network	Score
N1	Post-Translational Modification, Protein Degradation, Protein Synthesis	32
N2	Developmental Disorder, Ophthalmic Disease, Organismal Injury and Abnormalities	29
N3	Hereditary Disorder, Ophthalmic Disease, Organismal Injury and Abnormalities	29
N4	Cell Cycle, Cancer, Neurological Disease	18

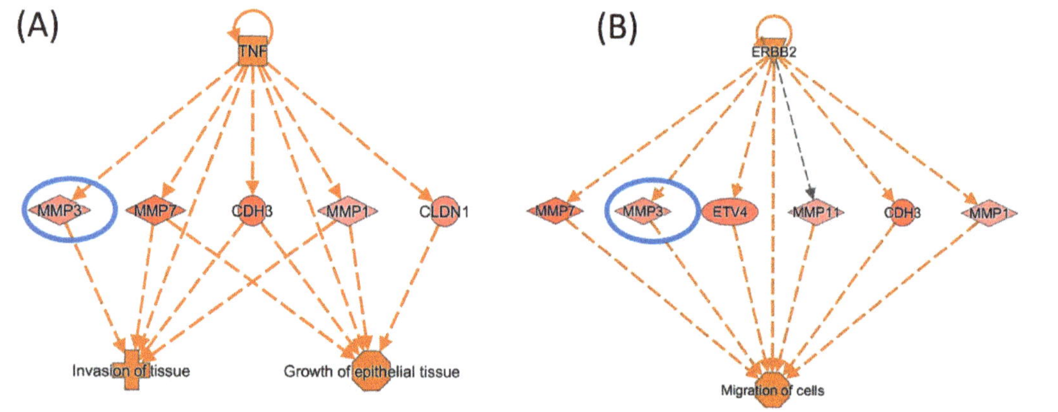

Figure 11. IPA regulator effect networks analysis of the top 25 upregulated and top 25 downregulated genes in COAD. Upstream regulators are located at the top of the network, target genes are in the middle of the network (orange color), and predicted disease or function in the bottom of the network. (**A**) TNF target molecule, network related to invasion of tissue and growth of epithelial tissue; (**B**) ERBB2 target molecule, related to the migration of cells. The data are generated using the Regulator Effects module in IPA. The MMP3 gene is highlighted with a blue circle.

4. Discussion

The initiation and progression of COAD involve important alterations at the transcriptomic level [18,31]. The TCGA cohort is an open-access database, comprising 34 types of cancer tissue and normal tissue. In our study, we extracted the top 25 upregulated and top 25 downregulated coding genes in COAD to assess their prediction of the overall survival rate. For further analysis, we selected two key genes involved in epithelial to mesenchymal transition and angiogenesis (MMP3) and a potential oncotarget (TESC), for which the previous data found in the literature correlated with our findings. Both genes, MMP3 and TESC, were correlated with overall survival rate according to the Starbase online tool. We compared the level of expression of these two genes with other cancers where they appear with a dysregulated expression compared to normal epithelial cells of the colon. A pan-cancer view of the expression levels for MMP3 and TESC downloaded from UALCAN displays interesting aspects related to these genes in solid cancer (Figure 12). MMP3 was found to have a prognostic role in pancreatic cancer and cervical cancer, while

TESC showed no prognostic role in investigated cancers. TESC was also proposed as an oncotarget. Furthermore, TESC was investigated in a patient's cohort by Kang et al., revealing that the cases with overexpression of TESC are related to reduced survival compared to the cases displaying high expression value; this study proposes TESC as a potential diagnostic marker in colorectal cancer, due to a high difference in the expression level between normal tissue and tumor tissue. The authors show inhibition of TESC decreases cell survival in vitro conditions [32].

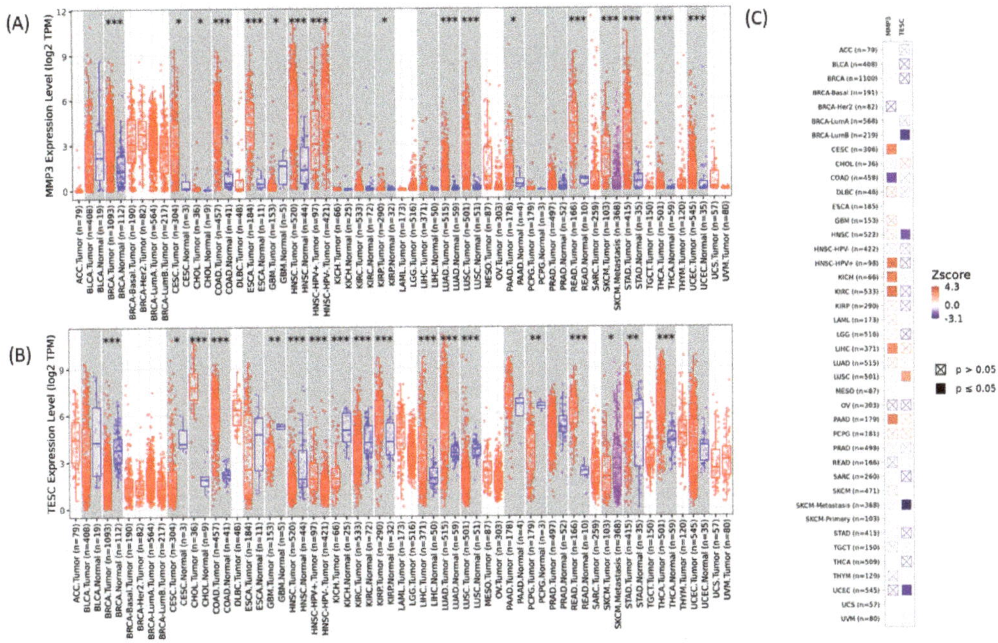

Figure 12. Multi-cancer view of the expression levels and survival analysis for MMP3 and TESC downloaded from TIMER2.0. (**A**) Multi-cancer view of the expression levels of MMP3. (**B**) Multi-cancer view of the expression levels for TESC. (**C**) Multi-cancer view of the correlation between overall survival with MMP3 and TESC (* $p \leq 0.05$, ** $p \leq 0.01$, *** $p \leq 0.001$).

The matrix metalloproteinases (MMPs) family consists of at least 24 calcium-dependent, zinc-containing endopeptidases. The pattern of these proteins in cancer is dependent on the MMP variant and the type of cancer [33,34]. MMPs belong to a large group of proteases capable of breaking all components of the extracellular matrix, being involved in all steps of tumorigenesis, cancer invasion, and metastasis [35–42]. MMP3, along with CXCL1, is considered an important stromal protein marker of the dysplasia–carcinoma transition in sporadic colorectal cancer [43]. Moreover, MMP3 is one of the colorectal cancer biomarkers related to the inflammatory microenvironment [44].

In several cancer types, MMP3 is considered a biomarker alone or in combination with other molecules [14,19,37,38,41,42,45–48]. Tumor cells typically express a high level of different MMPs [33,37,38]. As previously shown, MMP1, -3, -7, -9, -10, -11, -12, and -14 are upregulated in COAD samples [38,39]. Expression levels of MMP-1, -2, -7, -9, and -13 were observed to be related to worse outcomes; meanwhile, in the case of MMP-12, expression was observed to have a protective role [37].

MMP3, coding stromelysin-1, is upregulated in colon cancers [33] and its expression level affects the survival of patients with colon adenocarcinoma [14], also confirmed by the TCGA data presented in Figure 2. MMP3 has an important role in COAD tumor growth and metastasis [33]. Another study revealed that C/EBPβ upregulation was correlated with MMP3 expression and it is associated with metastatic status in colorectal cancer [49]. IPA data has revealed MMP3 to be involved in cellular movement along with other altered genes in COAD.

The prognostic value of MMP3 shows a divergence between different databases. This is possible because the cellular source of a specific MMP might have an impact on the biological outcome related to its expression [19,50].

TESC (Tescalcin) regulates the activities of the Na^+/H^+ exchanger and is related to the activation of the extracellular signal-regulated kinase (ERK) cascade to the expression of transcription factors that control cell growth and differentiation [51]. TESC is altered in several cancers [51]; TESC expression promotes the invasive and metastatic effects of colorectal cancer [52]. TESC was observed to be overexpressed in tumor tissue, as it was shown based on TCGA data, but also in serum from colorectal cancer patients, underlining its oncogenic role in this pathology [52], with prognostic significance in several other cancer types such as hepatocellular carcinoma [53] and gastric cancer [54]. TESC is overexpressed in colorectal cancer (CRC), but not in normal mucosa and premalignant dysplastic lesions, the high expression levels being related to an increased cell proliferation rate, invasiveness, and metastatic features [32,52,55]. TESC is presented as a potential oncotarget in colon adenocarcinoma, as revealed in data found by Kand et al., who indicated that depletion of TESC in this cancer type results in decreased tumor growth [32].

The genomic landscapes result from a combination of multiple overlapping mutational processes, making their deconvolution from genomic data a difficult challenge [56]. According to the analysis using cBioportal, based on TCGA data (Figure 7), we can observe that MMP3 and TESC have a low mutation rate, versus TP53, which has a higher mutation rate in COAD, as we observed in a previous study [5]. Additionally, in colorectal cancers, the presence of specific MMP3 polymorphisms was observed [57].

Alteration of genes involved in post-translational modification, protein degradation, and protein synthesis can lead to important structural alterations in existing proteins that participate in multiple biological processes [58]. Additionally, studies related to these alterations will have an important role in the immune recognition of tumor therapy [58].

The limitation of the present study is related to the type of analysis based on conclusions drawn from bioinformatics and analysis of previous experimental results. Even so, data generated by bioinformatics tools have an important advantage for cancer with a high number of cases, as all platforms collect a higher number of samples associated with clinical data and pathological data. In addition, analytical methods such as IPA applied in the present study revealed an important role in Post-Translational Modification, Protein Degradation, and Protein Synthesis in COAD, where an important element of this network is MMP3, a gene correlated with overall survival. Another important network was related to the cell cycle, with the TESC gene being a key component of this network. Our studies provide the clue that bioinformatics strategies could identify key genes associated with the pathogenesis of COAD, which can be exploited as biomarker candidates or therapeutic targets. However, these data alone do not provide sufficient insights into patient prognosis or treatment. Therefore, other molecular data should be considered in combination with our candidate genes for further understanding of COAD and to improve patient care.

5. Conclusions

An analysis of the top 25 upregulated and downregulated genes that were screened for the prediction of the overall survival rate in COAD was performed. Thus, we were able to identify two key genes (MMP3 and TESC) that may be associated with the prognosis of patients with COAD. Additional validation of the expression levels for MMP3 and TESC on the colonomics data set was subsequently performed. Additional validation studies in the large patient cohort will decipher the role of the two genes and will bring novel insights regarding stage correlation with expression level and hallmarks of cancer where these genes could serve as potential biomarkers and oncotargets. At the time when this study was performed, limited information about both genes was provided by studies done on patients with colon adenocarcinoma, leaving a lot of space for validation or discoveries about their potential value in different cancers.

IPA network analysis revealed further insights into the MMP3 and TESC profiles and provides a basis to investigate the regulatory mechanisms involved in COAD research, particularly in the context of the tumor microenvironment.

Supplementary Materials: The following supporting information can be downloaded at: https://www.mdpi.com/article/10.3390/biomedinformatics2030030/s1, Table S1: Top 25 upregulated and top 25 downregulated genes in COAD; Table S2. Main biomarkers application and target drugs, downloaded from IPA.

Author Contributions: Conceptualization, investigation, and writing—original draft preparation C.B. (Constantin Busuioc), A.N. and C.B. (Cornelia Braicu); O.Z., M.T. and I.B.-N., writing—review and editing. All authors have read and agreed to the published version of the manuscript.

Funding: Our work was part of the following projects: H2020-MSCA-RISE-2019- Grant Agreement no.: 872391—"DevelOpmeNt of Cancer RNA TherapEutic"—cONCReTE and H2020-MSCA-RISE-2018 No. 824036/2019'Excellence in research and development of non-coding RNA DIAGnostics in Oncology' (RNADIAGON).

Institutional Review Board Statement: Not applicable.

Informed Consent Statement: Not applicable.

Data Availability Statement: Not applicable.

Conflicts of Interest: The authors declare no conflict of interest.

References

1. Yue, F.R.; Wei, Z.B.; Yan, R.Z.; Guo, Q.H.; Liu, B.; Zhang, J.H.; Li, Z. SMYD3 promotes colon adenocarcinoma (COAD) progression by mediating cell proliferation and apoptosis. *Exp. Ther. Med.* **2020**, *20*, 11. [CrossRef] [PubMed]
2. Sung, H.; Ferlay, J.; Siegel, R.L.; Laversanne, M.; Soerjomataram, I.; Jemal, A.; Bray, F. Global Cancer Statistics 2020: GLOBOCAN Estimates of Incidence and Mortality Worldwide for 36 Cancers in 185 Countries. *CA Cancer J. Clin.* **2021**, *71*, 209–249. [CrossRef] [PubMed]
3. Schliemann, D.; Ramanathan, K.; Matovu, N.; O'Neill, C.; Kee, F.; Su, T.T.; Donnelly, M. The implementation of colorectal cancer screening interventions in low-and middle-income countries: A scoping review. *BMC Cancer* **2021**, *21*, 1125. [CrossRef]
4. Gurzu, S.; Silveanu, C.; Fetyko, A.; Butiurca, V.; Kovacs, Z.; Jung, I. Systematic review of the old and new concepts in the epithelial-mesenchymal transition of colorectal cancer. *World J. Gastroenterol.* **2016**, *22*, 6764–6775. [CrossRef]
5. Busuioc, C.; Ciocan-Cartita, C.A.; Braicu, C.; Zanoaga, O.; Raduly, L.; Trif, M.; Muresan, M.S.; Ionescu, C.; Stefan, C.; Crivii, C.; et al. Epithelial-Mesenchymal Transition Gene Signature Related to Prognostic in Colon Adenocarcinoma. *J. Pers. Med.* **2021**, *11*, 476. [CrossRef]
6. Nguyen, H.T.; Duong, H.Q. The molecular characteristics of colorectal cancer: Implications for diagnosis and therapy. *Oncol. Lett.* **2018**, *16*, 9–18. [CrossRef]
7. Gurzu, S.; Banias, L.; Kovacs, Z.; Jung, I. Epithelial-mesenchymal transition of tumor budding in colorectal cancer: The mystery of CD44-positive stromal cells. *Hum. Pathol.* **2018**, *71*, 168–169. [CrossRef]
8. Cojocneanu, R.; Braicu, C.; Raduly, L.; Jurj, A.; Zanoaga, O.; Magdo, L.; Irimie, A.; Muresan, M.S.; Ionescu, C.; Grigorescu, M.; et al. Plasma and Tissue Specific miRNA Expression Pattern and Functional Analysis Associated to Colorectal Cancer Patients. *Cancers* **2020**, *12*, 843. [CrossRef]
9. Ionescu, C.; Braicu, C.; Chiorean, R.; Cojocneanu Petric, R.; Neagoe, E.; Pop, L.; Chira, S.; Berindan-Neagoe, I. TIMP-1 expression in human colorectal cancer is associated with SMAD3 gene expression levels: A pilot study. *J. Gastrointestin. Liver Dis.* **2014**, *23*, 413–418. [CrossRef]
10. Tomuleasa, C.; Braicu, C.; Irimie, A.; Craciun, L.; Berindan-Neagoe, I. Nanopharmacology in translational hematology and oncology. *Int. J. Nanomed.* **2014**, *9*, 3465–3479. [CrossRef]
11. Jurj, A.; Zanoaga, O.; Braicu, C.; Lazar, V.; Tomuleasa, C.; Irimie, A.; Berindan-Neagoe, I. A Comprehensive Picture of Extracellular Vesicles and Their Contents. Molecular Transfer to Cancer Cells. *Cancers* **2020**, *12*, 298. [CrossRef]
12. Alajez, N.M. Large-Scale Analysis of Gene Expression Data Reveals a Novel Gene Expression Signature Associated with Colorectal Cancer Distant Recurrence. *PLoS ONE* **2016**, *11*, e0167455. [CrossRef]
13. Bochis, O.V.; Irimie, A.; Pichler, M.; Berindan-Neagoe, I. The role of Skp2 and its substrate CDKN1B (p27) in colorectal cancer. *J. Gastrointestin. Liver Dis.* **2015**, *24*, 225–234. [CrossRef]

14. Zeng, C.; Chen, Y. HTR1D, TIMP1, SERPINE1, MMP3 and CNR2 affect the survival of patients with colon adenocarcinoma. *Oncol. Lett.* **2019**, *18*, 2448–2454. [CrossRef]
15. Weinstein, J.N.; Collisson, E.A.; Mills, G.B.; Shaw, K.R.; Ozenberger, B.A.; Ellrott, K.; Shmulevich, I.; Sander, C.; Stuart, J.M. The Cancer Genome Atlas Pan-Cancer analysis project. *Nat. Genet.* **2013**, *45*, 1113–1120. [CrossRef]
16. Wang, Y.; Gao, X.; Ru, X.; Sun, P.; Wang, J. Identification of gene signatures for COAD using feature selection and Bayesian network approaches. *Sci. Rep.* **2022**, *12*, 8761. [CrossRef]
17. Lin, J.; Cao, Z.; Yu, D.; Cai, W. Identification of Transcription Factor-Related Gene Signature and Risk Score Model for Colon Adenocarcinoma. *Front. Genet.* **2021**, *12*, 709133. [CrossRef]
18. Sanz-Pamplona, R.; Berenguer, A.; Cordero, D.; Mollevi, D.G.; Crous-Bou, M.; Sole, X.; Paré-Brunet, L.; Guino, E.; Salazar, R.; Santos, C.; et al. Aberrant gene expression in mucosa adjacent to tumor reveals a molecular crosstalk in colon cancer. *Mol. Cancer* **2014**, *13*, 46. [CrossRef]
19. Buttacavoli, M.; Di Cara, G.; Roz, E.; Pucci-Minafra, I.; Feo, S.; Cancemi, P. Integrated Multi-Omics Investigations of Metalloproteinases in Colon Cancer: Focus on MMP2 and MMP9. *Int. J. Mol. Sci.* **2021**, *22*, 12389. [CrossRef]
20. Available online: https://www.colonomics.org (accessed on 28 August 2022).
21. Chandrashekar, D.S.; Bashel, B.; Balasubramanya, S.A.H.; Creighton, C.J.; Ponce-Rodriguez, I.; Chakravarthi, B.; Varambally, S. UALCAN: A Portal for Facilitating Tumor Subgroup Gene Expression and Survival Analyses. *Neoplasia* **2017**, *19*, 649–658. [CrossRef]
22. Chandrashekar, D.S.; Karthikeyan, S.K.; Korla, P.K.; Patel, H.; Shovon, A.R.; Athar, M.; Netto, G.J.; Qin, Z.S.; Kumar, S.; Manne, U.; et al. UALCAN: An update to the integrated cancer data analysis platform. *Neoplasia* **2022**, *25*, 18–27. [CrossRef]
23. Sun, Q.; Li, M.; Wang, X. The Cancer Omics Atlas: An integrative resource for cancer omics annotations. *BMC Med. Genom.* **2018**, *11*, 63. [CrossRef]
24. Li, J.-H.; Liu, S.; Zhou, H.; Qu, L.-H.; Yang, J.-H. starBase v2.0: Decoding miRNA-ceRNA, miRNA-ncRNA and protein–RNA interaction networks from large-scale CLIP-Seq data. *Nucleic Acids Res.* **2014**, *42*, D92–D97. [CrossRef] [PubMed]
25. Zhou, K.R.; Liu, S.; Cai, L.; Bin, L. ENCORI: The Encyclopedia of RNA Interactomes. Available online: http://starbase.sysu.edu.cn/index.php (accessed on 20 August 2022).
26. Cerami, E.; Gao, J.; Dogrusoz, U.; Gross, B.E.; Sumer, S.O.; Aksoy, B.A.; Jacobsen, A.; Byrne, C.J.; Heuer, M.L.; Larsson, E.; et al. The cBio cancer genomics portal: An open platform for exploring multidimensional cancer genomics data. *Cancer Discov.* **2012**, *2*, 401–404. [CrossRef]
27. Chen, F.; Chandrashekar, D.S.; Varambally, S.; Creighton, C.J. Pan-cancer molecular subtypes revealed by mass-spectrometry-based proteomic characterization of more than 500 human cancers. *Nature Commun.* **2019**, *10*, 5679. [CrossRef] [PubMed]
28. Krämer, A.; Green, J.; Pollard, J., Jr.; Tugendreich, S. Causal analysis approaches in Ingenuity Pathway Analysis. *Bioinformatics* **2014**, *30*, 523–530. [CrossRef]
29. Li, B.; Severson, E.; Pignon, J.C.; Zhao, H.; Li, T.; Novak, J.; Jiang, P.; Shen, H.; Aster, J.C.; Rodig, S.; et al. Comprehensive analyses of tumor immunity: Implications for cancer immunotherapy. *Genome Biol.* **2016**, *17*, 174. [CrossRef]
30. Li, T.; Fu, J.; Zeng, Z.; Cohen, D.; Li, J.; Chen, Q.; Li, B.; Liu, X.S. TIMER2.0 for analysis of tumor-infiltrating immune cells. *Nucleic Acids Res.* **2020**, *48*, W509–W514. [CrossRef]
31. Sharma, A.; Yadav, D.; Rao, P.; Sinha, S.; Goswami, D.; Rawal, R.M.; Shrivastava, N. Identification of potential therapeutic targets associated with diagnosis and prognosis of colorectal cancer patients based on integrated bioinformatics analysis. *Comput. Biol. Med.* **2022**, *146*, 105688. [CrossRef]
32. Kang, Y.H.; Han, S.R.; Kim, J.T.; Lee, S.J.; Yeom, Y.I.; Min, J.K.; Lee, C.H.; Kim, J.W.; Yoon, S.R.; Yoon, D.Y.; et al. The EF-hand calcium-binding protein tescalcin is a potential oncotarget in colorectal cancer. *Oncotarget* **2014**, *5*, 2149–2160. [CrossRef]
33. Liang, M.; Wang, J.; Wu, C.; Wu, M.; Hu, J.; Dai, J.; Ruan, H.; Xiong, S.; Dong, C. Targeting matrix metalloproteinase MMP3 greatly enhances oncolytic virus mediated tumor therapy. *Transl. Oncol.* **2021**, *14*, 101221. [CrossRef] [PubMed]
34. Curran, S.; Murray, G.I. Matrix metalloproteinases: Molecular aspects of their roles in tumour invasion and metastasis. *Eur. J. Cancer* **2000**, *36*, 1621–1630. [CrossRef]
35. Zinzindohoué, F.; Lecomte, T.; Ferraz, J.M.; Houllier, A.M.; Cugnenc, P.H.; Berger, A.; Blons, H.; Laurent-Puig, P. Prognostic significance of MMP-1 and MMP-3 functional promoter polymorphisms in colorectal cancer. *Clin. Cancer Res.* **2005**, *11*, 594–599. [CrossRef]
36. Chen, H.; Ye, Y.; Yang, Y.; Zhong, M.; Gu, L.; Han, Z.; Qiu, J.; Liu, Z.; Qiu, X.; Zhuang, G. TIPE-mediated up-regulation of MMP-9 promotes colorectal cancer invasion and metastasis through MKK-3/p38/NF-κB pro-oncogenic signaling pathway. *Signal Transduct. Target. Ther.* **2020**, *5*, 163. [CrossRef]
37. Pezeshkian, Z.; Nobili, S.; Peyravian, N.; Shojaee, B.; Nazari, H.; Soleimani, H.; Asadzadeh-Aghdaei, H.; Ashrafian Bonab, M.; Nazemalhosseini-Mojarad, E.; Mini, E. Insights into the Role of Matrix Metalloproteinases in Precancerous Conditions and in Colorectal Cancer. *Cancers* **2021**, *13*, 6226. [CrossRef] [PubMed]
38. Yu, J.; He, Z.; He, X.; Luo, Z.; Lian, L.; Wu, B.; Lan, P.; Chen, H. Comprehensive Analysis of the Expression and Prognosis for MMPs in Human Colorectal Cancer. *Front. Oncol.* **2021**, *11*. [CrossRef]
39. Baker, E.A.; Bergin, F.G.; Leaper, D.J. Matrix metalloproteinases, their tissue inhibitors and colorectal cancer staging. *Br. J. Surg.* **2000**, *87*, 1215–1221. [CrossRef]

40. Coussens, L.M.; Fingleton, B.; Matrisian, L.M. Matrix metalloproteinase inhibitors and cancer: Trials and tribulations. *Science* **2002**, *295*, 2387–2392. [CrossRef]
41. Honda, T.; Yamamoto, I.; Inagawa, H. Angiogenesis-, Metastasis- and Signaling Pathway-related Factor Dynamics in Human Colon Cancer Cells Following Interaction with Monocytes. *Anticancer Res.* **2013**, *33*, 2895–2900.
42. Gobin, E.; Bagwell, K.; Wagner, J.; Mysona, D.; Sandirasegarane, S.; Smith, N.; Bai, S.; Sharma, A.; Schleifer, R.; She, J.-X. A pan-cancer perspective of matrix metalloproteases (MMP) gene expression profile and their diagnostic/prognostic potential. *BMC Cancer* **2019**, *19*, 581. [CrossRef]
43. Sipos, F.; Germann, T.M.; Wichmann, B.; Galamb, O.; Spisák, S.; Krenács, T.; Tulassay, Z.; Molnár, B.; Műzes, G. MMP3 and CXCL1 are potent stromal protein markers of dysplasia-carcinoma transition in sporadic colorectal cancer. *Eur. J. Cancer Prev.* **2014**, *23*, 336–343. [CrossRef] [PubMed]
44. Calu, V.; Ionescu, A.; Stanca, L.; Geicu, O.I.; Iordache, F.; Pisoschi, A.M.; Serban, A.I.; Bilteanu, L. Key biomarkers within the colorectal cancer related inflammatory microenvironment. *Sci. Rep.* **2021**, *11*, 7940. [CrossRef] [PubMed]
45. Wen, Y.; Zhang, X.; Li, X.; Tian, L.; Shen, S.; Ma, J.; Ai, F. Histone deacetylase (HDAC) 11 inhibits matrix metalloproteinase (MMP) 3 expression to suppress colorectal cancer metastasis. *J. Cancer* **2022**, *13*, 1923–1932. [CrossRef]
46. Mehner, C.; Miller, E.; Khauv, D.; Nassar, A.; Oberg, A.L.; Bamlet, W.R.; Zhang, L.; Waldmann, J.; Radisky, E.S.; Crawford, H.C.; et al. Tumor cell-derived MMP3 orchestrates Rac1b and tissue alterations that promote pancreatic adenocarcinoma. *Mol. Cancer Res.* **2014**, *12*, 1430–1439. [CrossRef] [PubMed]
47. El-Sharkawi, F.; El Sabah, M.; Hassan, Z.; Khaled, H. The biochemical value of urinary metalloproteinases 3 and 9 in diagnosis and prognosis of bladder cancer in Egypt. *J. Biomed. Sci.* **2014**, *21*, 72. [CrossRef]
48. Ligi, D.; Mannello, F. Do matrix metalloproteinases represent reliable circulating biomarkers in colorectal cancer? *Br. J. Cancer* **2016**, *115*, 633–634. [CrossRef]
49. Ji, Y.; Li, J.; Li, P.; Wang, L.; Yang, H.; Jiang, G. C/EBPβ Promotion of MMP3-Dependent Tumor Cell Invasion and Association with Metastasis in Colorectal Cancer. *Genet. Test Mol. Biomark.* **2018**, *22*, 5–10. [CrossRef]
50. Piskór, B.M.; Przylipiak, A.; Dąbrowska, E.; Niczyporuk, M.; Ławicki, S. Matrilysins and Stromelysins in Pathogenesis and Diagnostics of Cancers. *Cancer Manag. Res.* **2020**, *12*, 10949–10964. [CrossRef]
51. Kolobynina, K.G.; Solovyova, V.V.; Levay, K.; Rizvanov, A.A.; Slepak, V.Z. Emerging roles of the single EF-hand Ca2+ sensor tescalcin in the regulation of gene expression, cell growth and differentiation. *J. Cell Sci.* **2016**, *129*, 3533–3540. [CrossRef]
52. Kang, J.; Kang, Y.H.; Oh, B.M.; Uhm, T.G.; Park, S.Y.; Kim, T.W.; Han, S.R.; Lee, S.J.; Lee, Y.; Lee, H.G. Tescalcin expression contributes to invasive and metastatic activity in colorectal cancer. *Tumour. Biol.* **2016**, *37*, 13843–13853. [CrossRef]
53. Zhou, Z.-G.; Chen, J.-B.; Zhang, R.-X.; Ye, L.; Wang, J.-C.; Pan, Y.-X.; Wang, X.-H.; Li, W.-X.; Zhang, Y.-J.; Xu, L.; et al. Tescalcin is an unfavorable prognosis factor that regulats cell proliferation and survival in hepatocellular carcinoma patients. *Cancer Commun.* **2020**, *40*, 355–369. [CrossRef] [PubMed]
54. Kim, T.W.; Han, S.R.; Kim, J.T.; Yoo, S.M.; Lee, M.S.; Lee, S.H.; Kang, Y.H.; Lee, H.G. Differential expression of tescalcin by modification of promoter methylation controls cell survival in gastric cancer cells. *Oncol. Rep.* **2019**, *41*, 3464–3474. [CrossRef] [PubMed]
55. Lee, J.H.; Choi, S.I.; Kim, R.K.; Cho, E.W.; Kim, I.G. Tescalcin/c-Src/IGF1Rβ-mediated STAT3 activation enhances cancer stemness and radioresistant properties through ALDH1. *Sci. Rep.* **2018**, *8*, 10711. [CrossRef]
56. Karolak, A.; Levatić, J.; Supek, F. A framework for mutational signature analysis based on DNA shape parameters. *PLoS ONE* **2022**, *17*, e0262495. [CrossRef] [PubMed]
57. Biondi, M.L.; Turri, O.; Leviti, S.; Seminati, R.; Cecchini, F.; Bernini, M.; Ghilardi, G.; Guagnellini, E. MMP1 and MMP3 Polymorphisms in Promoter Regions and Cancer. *Clin. Chem.* **2000**, *46*, 2023–2024. [CrossRef] [PubMed]
58. Li, W.; Li, F.; Zhang, X.; Lin, H.-K.; Xu, C. Insights into the post-translational modification and its emerging role in shaping the tumor microenvironment. *Signal Transduct. Target. Ther.* **2021**, *6*, 422. [CrossRef]

BioMedInformatics

MDPI

Article

A Preliminary Evaluation of "GenDAI", an AI-Assisted Laboratory Diagnostics Solution for Genomic Applications †

Thomas Krause [1,*], Elena Jolkver [1], Sebastian Bruchhaus [1], Paul Mc Kevitt [2], Michael Kramer [3] and Matthias Hemmje [2]

1 Faculty of Mathematics and Computer Science, University of Hagen, 58097 Hagen, Germany; elena.jolkver@studium.fernuni-hagen.de (E.J.); sebastian.bruchhaus@fernuni-hagen.de (S.B.)
2 Research Institute for Telecommunication and Cooperation (FTK), 44149 Dortmund, Germany; pmckevitt@ftk.de (P.M.K.); mhemmje@ftk.de (M.H.)
3 ImmBioMed Business Consultants GmbH & Co. KG, 64319 Pfungstadt, Germany; m.kramer@immbiomed.de
* Correspondence: thomas.krause@fernuni-hagen.de

† This paper is an extended version of our paper published in the 2021 IEEE International Conference on Bioinformatics and Biomedicine (BIBM 2021), Machine Learning and Artificial Intelligence in Bioinformatics and Medical Informatics (MABM 2021) Workshop, 9–12 December 2021.

Abstract: Genomic data enable the development of new biomarkers in diagnostic laboratories. Examples include data from gene expression analyses or metagenomics. Artificial intelligence can help to analyze these data. However, diagnostic laboratories face various technical and regulatory challenges to harness these data. Existing software for genomic data is usually designed for research and does not meet the requirements for use as a diagnostic tool. To address these challenges, we recently proposed a conceptual architecture called "GenDAI". An initial evaluation of "GenDAI" was conducted in collaboration with a small laboratory in the form of a preliminary study. The results of this pre-study highlight the requirement for and feasibility of the approach. The pre-study also yields detailed technical and regulatory requirements, use cases from laboratory practice, and a prototype called "PlateFlow" for exploring user interface concepts.

Keywords: laboratory diagnostics; requirements engineering; genomics; gene expression; metagenomics; medical diagnostics

Citation: Krause, T.; Jolkver, E.; Bruchhaus, S.; Mc Kevitt, P.; Kramer, M.; Hemmje, M. A Preliminary Evaluation of "GenDAI", an AI-Assisted Laboratory Diagnostics Solution for Genomic Applications. *Biomedinformatics* **2022**, *2*, 332–344. https://doi.org/10.3390/biomedinformatics2020021

Academic Editor: Pentti Nieminen

Received: 17 May 2022
Accepted: 8 June 2022
Published: 10 June 2022

1. Introduction

The field of biology that focuses on the genetic material of organisms is known as genomics. The goal of genomics is to understand the function, mechanisms, and regulation of genes and other genomic elements. This includes, for example, understanding the complex relationship between the genome, the expression of individual genes, environmental factors, and the resulting physiological and pathophysiological states of a cell or organism as a whole.

Once these relationships are discovered, they can be used in laboratory diagnostics to identify pathophysiological conditions and potentially improve patient care. Two examples are gene expression analysis and metagenomic analysis. The former is used to measure the activity of certain genes, while the latter is used to analyze the genomes of a patient's microbiota (e.g., the gut microbiota). Medical laboratories must constantly evolve and adapt to bring new insights into clinical practice. This includes generating, transforming, combining, and evaluating data to deliver individualized diagnostic results.

Genomic applications often generate large quantities of data [1], which presents processing and analysis challenges. For example, human genome sequencing regularly generates hundreds of gigabytes of raw data for a single sample. It is foreseeable that the total quantity of data will continue to increase as new technologies are developed and existing technologies are used more extensively. The type of data generated in these genomic applications is also quite heterogeneous and they sometimes need to be combined with other available data in the context of personalized medicine. This combination of volume (of data), velocity (of increase in data), and variety, identifies genomic applications as a Big Data problem [2]. Big Data application requirements often exceed the limits of individual machines and thus depend on architectures that are scalable across machine boundaries.

Artificial intelligence (AI) can identify patterns in such large data sets. In particular, "deep learning" [3] has proven to be a powerful technique for detecting even complex relationships in data. It has found application in a number of complex problems, such as phenotype prediction and regulatory genomics [4]. Due to its increased computational power, this technique can process large quantities of data. At the same time, deep learning often requires less data preprocessing than other approaches. For AI to support data analysis, several other challenges must be addressed, such as model selection, feature engineering, model explainability, and reproducibility, which are exacerbated by high dimensionality and a relatively small number of samples, often referred to as the "curse of dimensionality" [5]. In laboratory diagnostics, too, the number of samples available for AI methods is usually limited, since obtaining a larger number of samples is often complex and expensive. AI is also applied beyond analysis [5,6]. Examples include its use for dimensionality reduction in the visualization of high-dimensional data or clustering of similar sequences [7].

Regardless of the application area, the explainability of AI models is a further challenge. Powerful methods such as deep learning often represent a "black box", where it is unclear according to the criteria through which the model arrives at a certain decision. This is not only a purely technical challenge, but also a regulatory challenge in which legislators and regulators must create clear criteria according to which the use of AI in laboratory diagnostics is permitted. Initial proposals in this regard were published, for example, in 2020 by the Joint Research Center (JRC) of the European Commission [8]. In this report, transparency, reliability, and data protection are named as core criteria against which AI models must be measured.

In the context of laboratory diagnostics, genomic applications and AI face additional regulatory and technical challenges. Applicable standards and regulations such as ISO standards (including ISO 13485 [9], ISO 15189 [10], and IEC 62304 [11]) and the European Union's In Vitro Diagnostics Regulation (IVDR) [12] require that instruments used in diagnostics, as well as software, be certified and meet numerous criteria.

"Health institutions", defined in the IVDR as "... an organization the primary purpose of which is the care or treatment of patients or the promotion of public health" [12], have the privilege of using so-called "Laboratory-Developed Tests (LDTs)" [13]. For these tests, the laboratory takes full responsibility for validation and IVDR compliance. These tests may require the application of laboratory-developed software to convert raw data into reportable results. Taking responsibility for conformity with IVDR requirements means that the health institution has to establish and document that the LDT complies with the essential safety and performance requirements as specified in Annex I of the IVDR. Moreover, the institution has to establish and operate a Quality Management System (QMS) [10], including a Risk Management System (RMS) [13], Post-Market Surveillance (PMS), and Post-Marketing Performance Follow-Up (PMPF) for the respective LDTs. PMS and PMPF are intended to make sure that new scientific findings or technical developments are recognized, taken into account, and—when appropriate—implemented even after the tests have been introduced. This is to ensure that the performance of diagnostic tests always reflects the current state of the art. For software used in conjunction with LDTs, the same requirements apply as this software was not approved by the manufacturer for diagnostic purposes. It may thus be termed "RUO software" (Research Use Only).

However, because RUO applications have not been optimized for laboratory diagnostics, they may be difficult to integrate into the laboratory workflow, reducing efficiency and thus increasing costs. An example of this is software that is based on the concept of projects or individual experiments rather than automating repetitive tasks. Another example is data transfer between the RUO software and other parts of the solution, such as the compliance systems mentioned earlier.

Whether the required software is being developed from scratch or existing software is being repurposed for the task, careful analysis of the requirements for such software must be undertaken to ensure that a solution complies with all applicable regulations, supports laboratory use cases, integrates with other relevant systems, and does all this in an efficient manner, automating processes where possible to reduce the possibility of errors and overall costs. Due to these numerous aspects, involving different areas such as biology, informatics, and regulations, requirements engineering for laboratory diagnostic software is challenging.

In summary, challenges arise from the constant advancement of science and technology, the quantity and type of data, the use of machine learning to process these data, regulations governing the laboratory process, and the identification and analysis of requirements for laboratory diagnostic software. Combining genomic applications with AI and applying them in the context of laboratory diagnostics has potential for improved diagnostics, but only if the above challenges can be overcome (Figure 1).

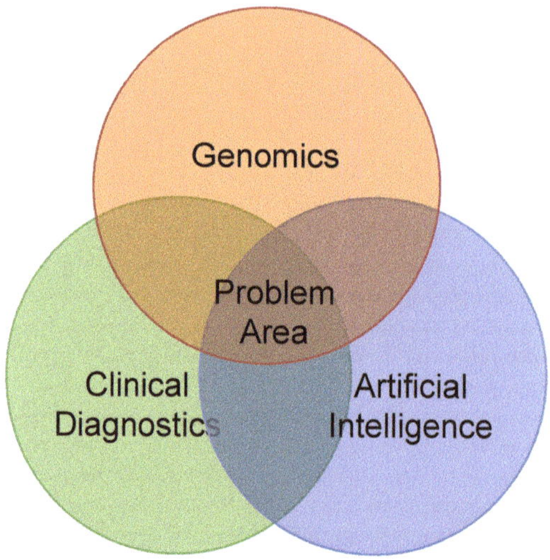

Figure 1. Problem area adressed in this paper, © 2021 IEEE. Reprinted, with permission, from Krause et al. [14].

Towards this goal, we recently introduced [14] a conceptual model called "GenDAI" (GENomic applications for laboratory Diagnostics supported by Artificial Intelligence). This extended paper discusses the rationale behind GenDAI in more detail and provides an initial evaluation of the model with the help of a recently conducted pre-study. The remainder of the paper discusses existing conceptual models that were developed before "GenDAI". "GenDAI" is then introduced as a new conceptual model that was developed to comprehensively cover the outlined challenges and the use cases in laboratory diagnostics. Finally, we discuss the pre-study, exploring detailed regulatory and technical requirements for the future implementation of our conceptual model and providing a preliminary evaluation of the concept and ideas behind "GenDAI".

2. State of the Art

Bioinformatics software solutions exist to support the analysis of instrument data generated by genomic applications. These solutions can be broadly classified into (i) generic bioinformatics data processing solutions and (ii) application-specific solutions. Generic solutions are developed to support all types of bioinformatics problems and are typically characterized by a flexible workflow approach, where individual tasks are connected as needed to achieve the intended goal. The flexible workflow concepts can better adapt to the constant progress in science and technology, as individual components can be replaced without altering other components of the system. Their disadvantage is that they are more difficult to set up and use than application-specific standard solutions since the latter can optimize the user experience for specific, relevant use cases.

An example of a generic workflow-based solution is the Galaxy project [15], which has several thousand tools that can be used as tasks in a workflow. It provides a multi-user web interface and is scalable to many concurrent compute nodes. It is available on free public servers, but can also be installed locally. With public servers, there are limitations on the available tools and the maximum amount of resources that can be consumed. Application-specific solutions are inherently less flexible. In the case of metagenomics, these include, for example, MG-RAST [16], MGnify (formerly EBI Metagenomics) [17], and QIIME 2 [18]. A popular and feature-rich solution for gene expression analysis is qBase+ [19,20].

The solutions in both categories have in common that they do not use AI to improve user interaction, e.g., by suggesting appropriate analysis methods or visualizations. Although, in some cases, machine learning algorithms are used in certain analysis steps of these products, this is also rarely enacted [5]. To overcome these and other problems, a conceptual architecture for the specific use case of rumen microbiome analysis was introduced in [6] (Figure 2). It was designed from the beginning to enable the use of AI in all relevant domains. It has a distributed architecture with a workflow engine and task scheduler at its core. To incorporate AI into all aspects of the solution, it was built on the AI2VIS4BigData reference model [21]. Recently, it has also been extended for the use case of human metagenome analysis [5]. As the name implies, AI2VIS4BigData also targets the challenges associated with Big Data processing. While some of the previously mentioned tools, particularly in the context of metagenomics, support the analysis of large data sets through parallel processing and streaming mechanisms, they do not fully address the challenge, as the actual analysis is only one of several steps in a Big Data process.

Another challenge with biomedical software solutions is the difficulty of using most products in laboratory diagnostics due to strict regulatory requirements. Although this use case is explicitly mentioned in the AI2VIS4BigData conceptual architecture for metagenomics, the assessment is very preliminary and does not take into account the applicable standards, such as the ISO standards mentioned above [9–11], and the recent regulation introduced by the IVDR in the European Union [12]. For the use case of gene expression analysis (Figure 3), a model was presented in [22] that is more focused on these regulatory issues and the specific needs of laboratory diagnostics. It is based on the CRISP4BigData reference model [23] (Figure 4). Unfortunately, it was not specifically designed for use with AI and is also limited to the use case of gene expression analysis. To our knowledge, there is no conceptual model that could serve as a template to support large-scale (in terms of Big Data), AI-driven genomic applications specifically tailored to high-throughput laboratory diagnostics.

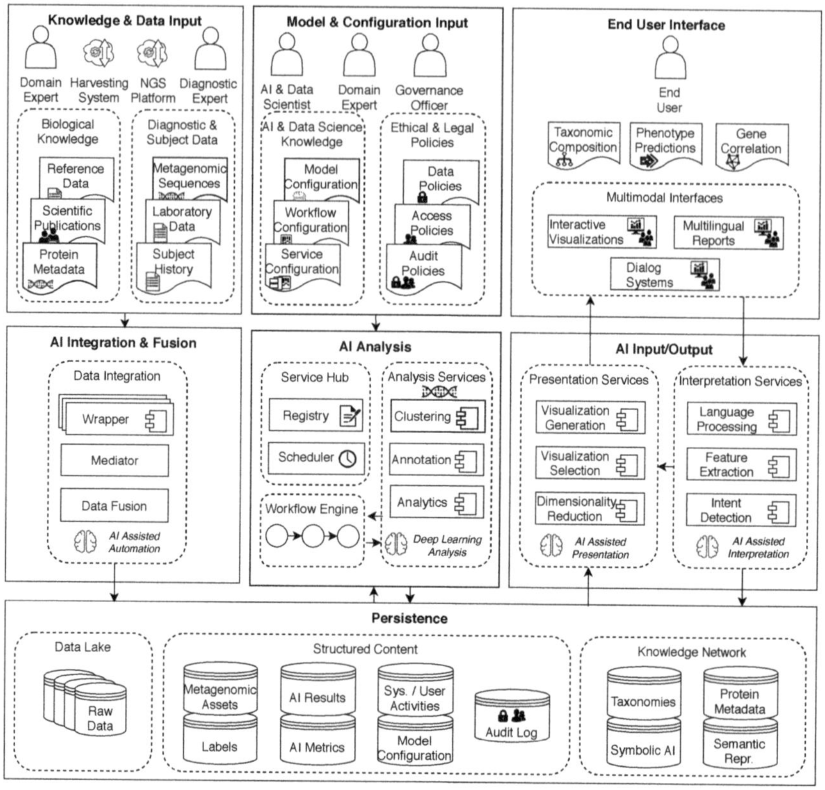

Figure 2. A conceptual architecture for AI and Big Data supporting metagenomics research [6].

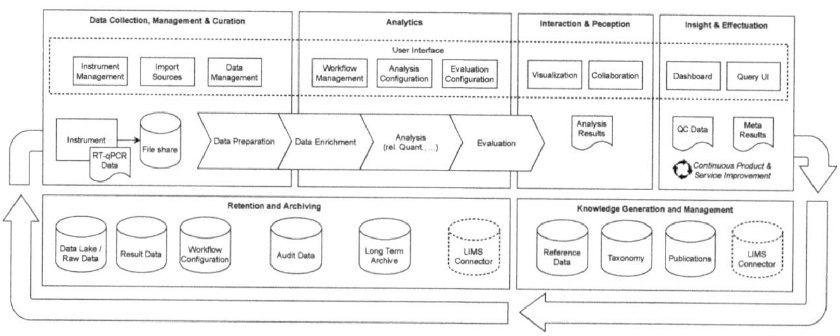

Figure 3. CRISP4BigData-based architecture of gene expression analysis platform [22].

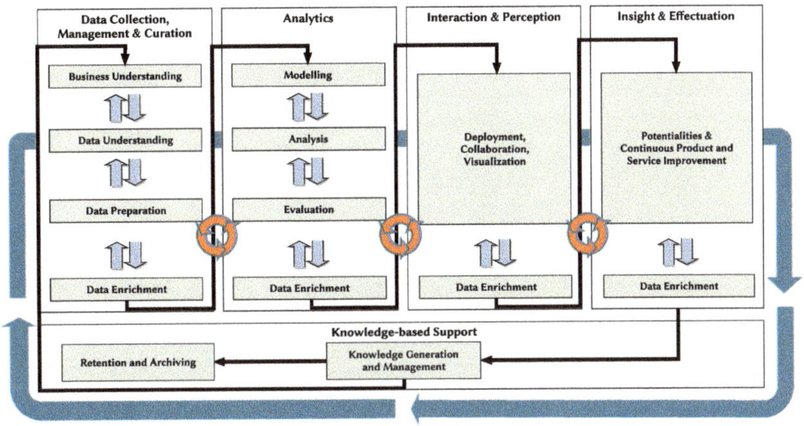

Figure 4. CRISP4BigData reference model [23].

3. Conceptual Model

We propose GenDAI (Figure 5) as a new model that combines the AI-driven nature of the AI2VIS4BigData conceptual architecture for metagenomics with the CRISP4BigData-based model for gene expression diagnostics. GenDAI incorporates elements from both of these earlier models.

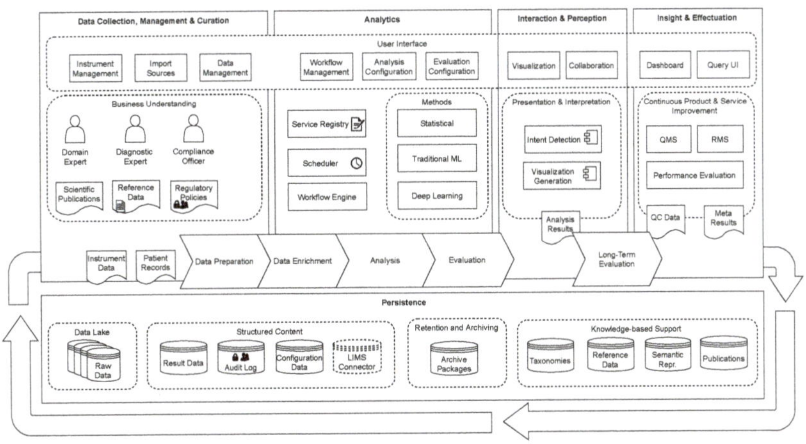

Figure 5. GenDAI conceptual model, © 2021 IEEE. Reprinted, with permission [14].

The general structure of the model is based on the CRISP4BigData reference model, with different phases for "data collection, management, and curation", "analytics", "interaction and perception", and "insight and effectuation". It also follows a three-layer design, with the user interface at the top and a persistence layer at the bottom. In the middle of Figure 5, the data flow through the system is shown as a series of generic processing steps. These steps are mapped by CRISP4BigData and are more granular than their phases.

Unlike the model based on AI2VIS4BigData, there is no explicit, conceptual "AI layer". Instead, the AI components are integrated into their respective phases, simplifying the model in this respect. This change also helps to emphasize the data flow between phases. Even if the specific use of AI is ultimately subject to the respective implementation, the goal of GenDAI is to define interfaces at which AI can be used by clearly naming the individual components and their interaction. Technically, the fundamentally modular approach of

GenDAI supports the flexible replacement of individual components by components with AI support as soon as they have been clinically evaluated and accepted.

Explicit references to specific genomic applications such as metagenomics or gene expression analysis have been removed from the model or generalized so that the model can be used for other applications. The importance of regulatory requirements was enhanced in respect to both models by including (i) the compliance officer as an explicit actor, (ii) regulatory policies as a possible data artifact, and (iii) "long-term evaluation", as an explicit requirement for use in laboratory diagnostics. When analysis is performed using an LDT, part of this long-term evaluation is tracking the LDT within a Quality Management System (QMS), Risk Management System (RMS), and continuous performance evaluation during the entire life cycle of the test. These have been explicitly added as part of the "continuous product and service improvement" topic within the "insight and effectuation" phase.

Looking at the different phases in detail, the first phase, "data collection, management, and curation", concerns all aspects related to data input. In addition to instrument or patient data for analysis, this also includes additional data such as reference data, scientific publications, or applicable policies. These data have been linked to relevant actors and they are considered together as part of the "business understanding" step of CRISP4BigData. This phase also includes the "data preparation" and "data enrichment" steps of CRISP4BigData. However, as a slight deviation from the reference model, the "data enrichment" step has also been pulled into the "analytics" phase, as we believe that with the increasing use of AI and deep learning, data enrichment is often closely related to and dependent on analytics itself. The user interface for this first phase will provide ways to manage import sources, instruments, and (imported) data.

The "analytics" phase includes components required for the actual data analysis, as well as components that manage, organize, and schedule these analytic processes. Examples included in Figure 5 are a workflow engine to orchestrate tasks and data flow, a scheduler to distribute work among compute nodes, and a service registry to manage the list of available tasks and methods. These analysis methods were grouped into three different categories. In addition to statistical methods or classical machine learning approaches, deep learning is included as a separate category to highlight its potential for improved diagnostics. Following the "analysis" step, another important step in the phase is "evaluation". For laboratory diagnostics, it is crucial that the results are checked for plausibility and interpreted. Here, we see potential for future applications of AI to help with both of these challenges.

The third phase, "interaction and perception", concerns the creation of result visualizations. These can be automatically generated reports sent from the lab to the responsible physician, but also visualizations created on demand. For the latter, AI can help to select appropriate visualizations and create them. "Insight and effectuation" in the context of laboratory diagnostics is a phase that focuses on long-term results and meta-analyses rather than single results. Examples include performance evaluation of diagnostic tests performed, as well as risk management systems and quality management systems, which in many cases are required by regulation.

"Persistence" can be considered as both a layer and a phase, because the data are retained and archived after the analysis is complete. However, here, we will consider it a layer because it interacts with all other phases to store intermediate results and can also serve as a data source for initial data import. It should be noted that CRISP4BigData includes a phase called "knowledge-based support", which includes "retention and archiving" as a step, in addition to "knowledge generation and management". We believe that "persistence" is a better term for the heterogeneous types of data managed by the system. However, we retain both steps in the form of data categories in the model. Within the persistence layer are several logical data stores for different data types. The data lake stores, e.g., raw, unprocessed data originating from an instrument. Structured data, on the other hand, may contain, e.g., (interim) results, audit data, or configuration data. A connector for a Laboratory Information Management System (LIMS) is also included, which serves as an interface to an existing system into which the solution is to be integrated. As a final category, "knowledge-based support" contains knowledge-based data that are independent of individual results. This includes entities such as reference data or taxonomies. They can also be used by AI methods to extract relevant, context-specific information.

In summary, the three core ideas that make up GenDAI are "artificial intelligence" to support end-users in all steps and aspects of the application, "laboratory diagnostics" as a core target market with distinct challenges, and a focus on "genomics" with all its applications.

4. Evaluation and Requirement Engineering

As an initial evaluation of the conceptual model as a valid basis for future implementations, a pre-study was conducted. The pre-study determined the detailed technical and legal requirements of the planned solution. For this, we partnered with a small medical laboratory of ImmBioMed GmbH & Co. KG in Heidelberg, Germany, which provided insights into detailed use cases and processes. The laboratory was selected because it offers various tests for genomic parameters, and the company ImmBioMed also offers consulting services for other laboratories and thus has great experience in the field of laboratory processes. However, as this is only a single laboratory, this evaluation can necessarily only be preliminary. As a practical application for evaluation, we used gene expression analysis of cytokine-dependent genes, which can be an important diagnostic indicator for inflammatory or antiviral defense reactions [24].

Requirements were gathered using a structured approach based on the research framework of Nunamaker et al. [25]. Methods utilized in the approach included a literature review, transcribed interviews, on-site visits, use case modeling, market analysis, and cognitive walkthroughs. A particular focus of the pre-study was the execution of already developed tests as opposed to the development of new tests. In this area, the use cases mapped in Figure 6 were examined in more detail. These use cases can be assigned to the four user stereotypes, "Lab Biologist", "Data Analyst", "Clinical Pathologist", and "QM and Compliance Officer". The evaluation was conducted by matching the identified challenges in the current process and requirements for future solutions with the "GenDAI" model, to determine if and how the model addresses this challenge or requirement. Hence, it is a qualitative approach. Quantification, e.g., in the form of a target benchmark, did not seem appropriate at this time due to the complexity of the various requirements and the early stage of the evaluation. A prototype called "PlateFlow" was used to evaluate user interface concepts with a cognitive walkthrough.

The preliminary study revealed that there are several points in the current laboratory workflow where processes could be more automated. For example, data have to be transferred manually between different systems several times. Due to different data formats and lack of import/export interfaces, this transfer is sometimes conducted by manual entry. Such manual transfer requires special attention and measures, such as a 4-eyes principle to avoid or detect incorrect entries. These, and similar manual steps, cost time and increase throughput times. This confirms the need for GenDAI's holistic approach, where the entire process is mapped and integrated. Table 1 shows an overview of the use cases and an assessment of the automation potential (low/medium/high) in the laboratory studied.

Table 1. Estimated potential for automatization of use cases.

Use Case	Potential			Limitations
	Low	Med.	High	
U1. Prepare Test		x		
U1.1. Program Cycler		x		Cycler Capabilities
U2. Execute Test		x	x	
U2.1. Document Test Protocol		x		User Input
U2.2. Quality Control			x	
U2.3. Store Results			x	

Table 1. *Cont.*

Use Case	Potential Low	Potential Med.	Potential High	Limitations
U3. Retrieve Results			x	
U3.1. Quality Control			x	
U4. Determine Gene Expression Level			x	
U4.1. Calculate (Δ)ΔCq			x	
U4.2. Apply Formulas			x	
U4.3. Store Analysis Results			x	
U5. Prepare Findings Report		x	x	
U5.1. Summarize Results			x	
U5.2. Summarize interpretation		x		Plausibility Checks
U6. Run Metaanalysis		x		
U6.1. Inter-Run QC		x		Not Formalized
U7. Create Findings Report	x		x	
U7.1. Verify Report	x			Legal Responsibility
U7.2. Submit Report			x	

Figure 6. Use cases analyzed in laboratory.

The interviews also confirmed the notion that laboratories are in an ongoing process of improving existing tests and developing new tests. In addition, there are evolving requirements from the regulatory area. These changes can also have an impact on the IT-supported processes, which is why the software and systems used need to be flexible or adaptable enough to meet changing requirements. In GenDAI, this need is underscored by the use of individual interchangeable and extensible components and by a flexible overarching workflow.

The market analysis revealed that most of the tools were outdated or did not offer all the analysis and processing functions needed. Moreover, none of the tools examined were specifically designed to meet the needs of medical laboratories. For example, the tools did not meet the necessary regulatory requirements, did not cover the complete workflow, and their user interface was also designed more for scientific research or the development of new tests, rather than the efficient processing of tests already developed. This also confirms the need for a new solution specifically designed for laboratory processes. Table 2 shows an overview of the different software tools for gene expression analysis that were evaluated, including their basic functionalities and last update date. Table 2 is a summary of the results given in Krause et al. [26], which were, in turn, based on the results of Pabinger et al. [27]. A "+" symbolizes the presence of a feature, a "+" the absence. Features whose existence could not be reliably determined have been marked as "nd" (not determined).

Table 2. qPCR software evaluation. Summarized from Krause et al. [26], Pabinger et al. [27].

Tool	**PCR Efficiency Estimation**	**Melt Curve Analysis**	**Reference Gene Selection**	**Cq Calculation**	**Error Propagation**	**Normalization**	**Absolute Quantifcation**	**Relative Quantification**	**Outlier Detection**	**NA Handling**	**Statistics**	**Graphs**	**MIQE Compliant**	**Last Update**
CAmpER	+	nd	nd	+	–	–	–	+	nd	–	–	+	–	2009
Cy0 Method	–	–	–	+	–	–	–	–	–	–	–	–	+	2010
DART-PCR	–	–	–	+	–	+	–	+	+	–	–	+	–	2002
Deconvolution	–	–	–	–	–	–	+	–	–	–	–	–	+	2010
ExpressionSuite Software	–	+	–	+	–	+	–	+	+	–	+	+	+	2019
Factor-qPCR	–	–	–	–	–	+	–	–	–	–	–	–	+	2020
GenEx	+	–	+	–	–	+	+	+	+	+	+	+	+	2019
geNorm	–	–	+	–	–	–	–	–	–	–	–	–	–	2018
LinRegPCR	+	–	–	+	–	–	+	–	+	–	–	+	+	2021
LRE Analysis	–	–	–	–	–	–	+	–	–	–	–	–	+	2012
LRE Analyzer	–	–	–	–	–	–	+	–	–	–	–	+	+	2014
MAKERGAUL	–	–	–	+	–	–	+	–	–	–	–	–	+	2013
PCR-Miner	+	–	–	+	–	–	–	–	–	–	–	–	+	2011
PIPE-T	–	–	–	–	–	+	+	+	+	+	+	+	–	2019
pyQPCR	+	–	–	–	+	+	–	+	–	+	–	+	+	2012
Q-Gene	+	–	–	–	–	+	–	+	–	–	–	+	–	2002
qBase	+	–	+	–	+	+	–	+	+	–	+	+	+	2007
qbase+	+	–	+	–	+	+	+	+	+	–	+	+	+	2017
qCalculator	+	–	–	–	–	+	–	+	–	+	–	+	–	2004
QPCR	+	–	–	+	+	+	–	+	–	+	+	+	+	2013
qPCR-DAMS	–	–	–	–	–	+	+	+	–	+	–	–	+	2006
RealTime StatMiner	–	–	+	–	+	+	–	+	+	+	+	+	+	2014
REST	–	–	–	–	+	+	–	+	–	–	+	+	+	2009
SARS	–	nd	nd	–	–	+	–	+	nd	–	+	–	+	2011
SoFAR	+	+	–	+	–	–	–	–	–	–	–	+	–	2003

In order to validate possible operating concepts for a solution, the PlateFlow proof-of-concept prototype was developed as part of the pre-study, which allows relevant analyses to be performed from the raw data and the results to be summarized in a report. Figure 7 shows one of the screens of PlateFlow. PlateFlow was evaluated through a cognitive walk-through, which resulted in positive feedback regarding the scope of functions. In addition, the need to further evaluate usability in future development was highlighted.

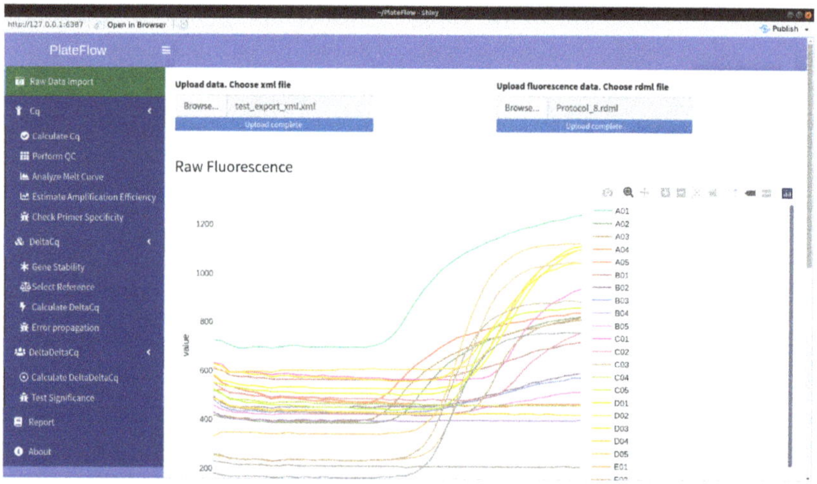

Figure 7. "PlateFlow" prototype user interface.

5. Conclusions and Future Work

The use of AI-assisted genomic applications has the potential to improve laboratory diagnostics. However, regulatory and other challenges currently hinder greater innovation in this area. There is a need for a software platform for genomic applications in laboratory diagnostics that leverages AI whilst providing the necessary foundation for regulatory compliance.

Here, we have presented GenDAI as one possible solution. It combines the knowledge of previous architectural models developed for specific genomic applications in different focus areas. Unlike these previous models, GenDAI is independent of specific genomic applications. Unlike the AI2VIS4BigData-based model, it considers the specific requirements of laboratory diagnostics to a much greater extent. Unlike the CRISP4BigData-based model, the integration of AI is also an essential feature of the model. GenDAI thus represents an improvement over both models.

A pre-study in cooperation with a small laboratory enabled a first practical evaluation of the concepts. Part of the preliminary study included the creation of use cases, evaluation of existing software components, requirement engineering, and development of the PlateFlow prototype. The remaining challenges include further practical validation of the model for additional use cases and in other laboratories, a technical architecture, implementation of missing components, and, ultimately, certification of the solution for clinical diagnostics.

Author Contributions: Conceptualization, T.K. and M.H.; investigation, T.K. and E.J.; writing—original draft preparation, T.K. and E.J.; writing—review and editing, S.B., P.M.K., M.K. and M.H.; visualization, T.K. and E.J.; supervision, M.K. and M.H.; project administration, T.K. All authors have read and agreed to the published version of the manuscript.

Funding: This research received no external funding.

Institutional Review Board Statement: Not applicable.

Informed Consent Statement: Not applicable.

Data Availability Statement: Not applicable.

Conflicts of Interest: The authors declare no conflict of interest.

References

1. Stephens, Z.D.; Lee, S.Y.; Faghri, F.; Campbell, R.H.; Zhai, C.; Efron, M.J.; Iyer, R.; Schatz, M.C.; Sinha, S.; Robinson, G.E. Big Data: Astronomical or Genomical? *PLoS Biol.* **2015**, *13*, e1002195,
2. Abawajy, J. Comprehensive analysis of big data variety landscape. *Int. J. Parallel Emergent Distrib. Syst.* **2015**, *30*, 5–14. [CrossRef]
3. LeCun, Y.; Bengio, Y.; Hinton, G. Deep learning. *Nature* **2015**, *521*, 436–444. [CrossRef] [PubMed]
4. Zou, J.; Huss, M.; Abid, A.; Mohammadi, P.; Torkamani, A.; Telenti, A. A primer on deep learning in genomics. *Nat. Genet.* **2019**, *51*, 12–18.
5. Krause, T.; Wassan, J.T.; Mc Kevitt, P.; Wang, H.; Zheng, H.; Hemmje, M.L. Analyzing Large Microbiome Datasets Using Machine Learning and Big Data. *BioMedInformatics* **2021**, *1*, 138–165. [CrossRef]
6. Reis, T.; Krause, T.; Bornschlegl, M.X.; Hemmje, M.L. A Conceptual Architecture for AI-based Big Data Analysis and Visualization Supporting Metagenomics Research. In Proceedings of the Collaborative European Research Conference (CERC 2020), Belfast, UK, 10–11 September 2020; Afli, H., Bleimann, U., Burkhardt, D., Loew, R., Regier, S., Stengel, I., Wang, H., Zheng, H., Eds.; CEUR Workshop Proceedings; CERC: New Delhi, India, 2020; pp. 264–272.
7. Soueidan, H.; Nikolski, M. Machine learning for metagenomics: Methods and tools. *arXiv* **2015**, arXiv:1510.06621.
8. Hamon, R.; Junklewitz, H.; Sanchez, I. *Robustness and Explainability of Artificial Intelligence*; EUR, Publications Office of the European Union: Luxembourg, 2020; Volume 30040.
9. *Standard ISO 13485:2016*; Medical Devices—Quality Management Systems—Requirements for Regulatory Purposes. ISO International Organization for Standardization: Geneva, Switzerland, 2016.
10. *Standard ISO 15189:2012*; Medical Laboratories—Requirements for Quality and Competence. ISO International Organization for Standardization: Geneva, Switzerland, 2012.
11. *Standard IEC 62304:2006*; Medical Device Software—Software Life Cycle Processes. IEC International Electrotechnical Commission: Geneva, Switzerland, 2006.
12. The European Parliament; The Council of the European Union. *In Vitro Diagnostic Regulation*; European Commission: Brussels, Belgium, 2017.
13. Spitzenberger, F.; Patel, J.; Gebuhr, I.; Kruttwig, K.; Safi, A.; Meisel, C. Laboratory-Developed Tests: Design of a Regulatory Strategy in Compliance with the International State-of-the-Art and the Regulation (EU) 2017/746 (EU IVDR In Vitro Diagnostic Medical Device Regulation). *Ther. Innov. Regul. Sci.* **2021**, 56, 47–64.
14. Krause, T.; Jolkver, E.; Bruchhaus, S.; Kramer, M.; Hemmje, M.L. GenDAI—AI-Assisted Laboratory Diagnostics for Genomic Applications. In Proceedings of the 2021 IEEE International Conference on Bioinformatics and Biomedicine (BIBM), Houston, TX, USA, 9–12 December 2021. [CrossRef]
15. Afgan, E.; Baker, D.; Batut, B.; van den Beek, M.; Bouvier, D.; Čech, M.; Chilton, J.; Clements, D.; Coraor, N.; Grüning, B.A.; et al. The Galaxy platform for accessible, reproducible and collaborative biomedical analyses: 2018 update. *Nucleic Acids Res.* **2018**, *46*, W537–W544. [CrossRef] [PubMed]
16. Meyer, F.; Paarmann, D.; D'Souza, M.; Olson, R.; Glass, E.M.; Kubal, M.; Paczian, T.; Rodriguez, A.; Stevens, R.; Wilke, A.; et al. The metagenomics RAST server—A public resource for the automatic phylogenetic and functional analysis of metagenomes. *BMC Bioinform.* **2008**, *9*, 1–8. [CrossRef] [PubMed]
17. Mitchell, A.L.; Almeida, A.; Beracochea, M.; Boland, M.; Burgin, J.; Cochrane, G.; Crusoe, M.R.; Kale, V.; Potter, S.C.; Richardson, L.J.; et al. MGnify: The microbiome analysis resource in 2020. *Nucleic Acids Res.* **2020**, *48*, D570–D578. [CrossRef] [PubMed]
18. Bolyen, E.; Rideout, J.R.; Dillon, M.R.; Bokulich, N.A.; Abnet, C.C.; Al-Ghalith, G.A.; Alexander, H.; Alm, E.J.; Arumugam, M.; Asnicar, F.; et al. Reproducible, interactive, scalable and extensible microbiome data science using QIIME 2. *Nat. Biotechnol.* **2019**, *37*, 852–857.
19. What Makes qbase+ Unique? Available online: https://www.qbaseplus.com/features (accessed on 7 June 2021).
20. Hellemans, J.; Mortier, G.; de Paepe, A.; Speleman, F.; Vandesompele, J. qBase relative quantification framework and software for management and automated analysis of real-time quantitative PCR data. *Genome Biol.* **2007**, *8*, R19,
21. Reis, T.; Bornschlegl, M.X.; Hemmje, M.L. Toward a Reference Model for Artificial Intelligence Supporting Big Data Analysis. In *Advances in Data Science and Information Engineering*; Stahlbock, R., Weiss, G.M., Abou-Nasr, M., Yang, C.Y., Arabnia, H.R., Deligiannidis, L., Eds.; Transactions on Computational Science and Computational Intelligence; Springer: Cham, Switzerland, 2021._38. [CrossRef]
22. Krause, T.; Jolkver, E.; Bruchhaus, S.; Kramer, M.; Hemmje, M.L. An RT-qPCR Data Analysis Platform. In Proceedings of the Collaborative European Research Conference (CERC 2021), Cork, Ireland, 9–10 September 2021; Afli, H., Bleimann, U., Burkhardt, D., Hasanuzzaman, M., Loew, R., Reichel, D., Wang, H., Zheng, H., Eds.; CEUR Workshop Proceedings; CERC: New Delhi, India, 2021.

23. Berwind, K.; Bornschlegl, M.X.; Kaufmann, M.A.; Hemmje, M.L. Towards a Cross Industry Standard Process to support Big Data Applications in Virtual Research Environments. In Proceedings of the Collaborative European Research Conference (CERC 2016), Cork, Ireland, 23–24 September 2016; Bleimann, U., Humm, B., Loew, R., Stengel, I., Walsh, P., Eds.; CERC: New Delhi, India, 2016.
24. Barrat, F.J.; Crow, M.K.; Ivashkiv, L.B. Interferon target-gene expression and epigenomic signatures in health and disease. *Nat. Immunol.* **2019**, *20*, 1574–1583.
25. Nunamaker, J.F.; Chen, M.; Purdin, T.D. Systems Development in Information Systems Research. *J. Manag. Inf. Syst.* **1990**, *7*, 89–106. [CrossRef]
26. Krause, T.; Jolkver, E.; Mc Kevitt, P.; Kramer, M.; Hemmje, M. A Systematic Approach to Diagnostic Laboratory Software Requirements Analysis. *Bioengineering* **2022**, *9*, 144.
27. Pabinger, S.; Rödiger, S.; Kriegner, A.; Vierlinger, K.; Weinhäusel, A. A survey of tools for the analysis of quantitative PCR (qPCR) data. *Biomol. Detect. Quantif.* **2014**, *1*, 23–33.

BioMedInformatics

Article

Automated Detection of Ear Tragus and C7 Spinous Process in a Single RGB Image—A Novel Effective Approach

Ivanna Kramer [1,2,*,†], Sabine Bauer [2,†] and Anne Matejcek [1]

1 Institute for Computational Visualistics, University Koblenz-Landau, 56070 Koblenz, Germany; amatejcek@uni-koblenz.de
2 Institute of Medical Technology and Information Processing, University Koblenz-Landau, 56070 Koblenz, Germany; bauer@uni-koblenz.de
* Correspondence: ivannamyckhal@uni-koblenz.de
† These authors contributed equally to this work.

Abstract: Biophotogrammetric methods for postural analysis have shown effectiveness in the clinical practice because they do not expose individuals to radiation. Furthermore, valid statements can be made about postural weaknesses. Usually, such measurements are collected via markers attached to the subject's body, which can provide conclusions about the current posture. The craniovertebral angle (CVA) is one of the recognized measurements used for the analysis of human head–neck postures. This study presents a novel method to automate the detection of the landmarks that are required to determine the CVA in RGBs. Different image processing methods are applied together with a neuronal network Openpose to find significant landmarks in a photograph. A prominent key body point is the spinous process of the cervical vertebra C7, which is often visible on the skin. Another visual landmark needed for the calculation of the CVA is the ear tragus. The methods proposed for the automated detection of the C7 spinous process and ear tragus are described and evaluated using a custom dataset. The results indicate the reliability of the proposed detection approach, particularly head postures.

Keywords: automated detection; craniovertebral angle; neuronal network; Openpose; RGB; C7; tragus

Citation: Kramer, I.; Bauer, S.; Matejcek, A. Automated Detection of Ear Tragus and C7 Spinous Process in a Single RGB Image—A Novel Effective Approach. *Biomedinformatics* **2022**, 2, 318–331. https://doi.org/10.3390/biomedinformatics2020020

Academic Editor: Pentti Nieminen

Received: 22 April 2022
Accepted: 2 June 2022
Published: 8 June 2022

1. Introduction

The number of smart device users is increasing every year. The year 2013 recorded a total of more than 4.01 billion smartphone users, which increased to 5.07 billion users in 2019 [1]. It is forecast that the subscriptions associated with smartphones will continue to rise and will reach 7.7 billion in 2027 [2,3]. Moreover, tablet computer usage has increased dramatically in recent years, in terms of both the number of users and the type of applications [4].

With such increased use of smart devices, the number of people who report neck pain has also risen. Scientific studies show that more and more physiological and musculoskeletal complaints are being reported that can be traced to the use of smart devices [5–8]. The bent body position that is often taken when using a smart device can lead to an abnormal head posture and also affects the postural apparatus and thus the spinal structures. To investigate these effects on the human body, researchers evaluate the biomechanics of the head–neck system and the associated impairments such as dizziness or headaches associated with a variety of conditions.

In order to quantify these postural alterations, the neck flexion and forward head position (FHP) can be determined with the help of, e.g., the craniovertebral angle (CVA), head tilt angle (HTA), and shoulder angle (SHA).

The research in [9–11] showed that prolonged smartphone use has a direct effect on the HTA, SHA, and FHP as determined by the CVA.

In order to gain insights into the tendency towards scoliosis, the naked dorsal surface of 98 volunteers was scanned with Microsoft Kinect to determine the shoulder angle [12]. The position of the C7 spinous process was estimated using the method of pixel-shade difference. The method used to determine the C7 spinous process was not presented in detail, and it was not checked for validity. The aim of the study presented in [13] was the assessment of the relative angles between vertebral adjacent segments during gait using IMUs. The proposed method proved the usability of inertial sensors for the assessment of spinal posture. Statistically significant differences were shown with regard to the influence of gender, speed, and imposed cadence. In addition to the analysis of the head position, Ormos et al. [14,15] measured the range of motion of the cervical spine using a goniometer and determined the isometric strength of the neck muscles with a dynamometer for flexion, extension, and head tilt on both sides. People with FHP showed a lower pressure pain threshold (PPT) in all locations except for the upper trapezius and scalenus medius muscles. They also showed less extension and right-rotation range of motion. The objectives of the study in [16,17] were to quantify the neck posture using CVA and fatigue in neck muscles. Both studies used markers attached to the participant's tragus and C7 to measure the CVA.

Furthermore, different studies investigated the relation between a bent posture and neck pain, headache, and spinal deformations. For example, Ref. [18] investigated the effects of smartphone use for less than and more than four hours per day between two groups. They found a significant difference in forward head angle and the intensity of neck pain after prolonged use of smartphones. To explore the working mechanism of manual therapy, Ref. [19] investigated whether aspects of cervical spine function, such as cervical ROM, neck flexor endurance, and FHP, were mediators of the effect of manual therapy on headache frequency. The effect whereby FHP causes spinal deformation, which increases scapula deformation, lordosis of the cervical vertebra, and kyphosis of the upper thoracic vertebra, was confirmed by [20,21]. The craniocervical angle was manually measured on the basis of markers using a lateral digital photograph with a digital camera. In addition, the authors of [22] quantified neck postures using electrogoniometers. It was observed that the ergonomic loads were increased when compact and slate computers were used, especially when used in non-traditional work environments.

The study by [23] is a prospective, cross-sectional, observational investigation, evaluating 3D quantitative standing posture proprioceptive perception through an instinctive self-correction maneuver in nonspecific chronic and sub-acute patients with lower back pain. To measure the subjects' 3D whole-skeleton pose, a non-ionizing 3D optoelectronic stereophotogrammetric approach with 27 passive retro-reflective markers was used.

The methods reported in the previous publications are based on marker-based approaches or semi-automatic recording, or they need additional recording devices to determine the body position. To the best of our knowledge, no markerless, fully-automatic detection method for head and neck angles in a single RGB image exists. Therefore, the focus of our study was to propose a fully automated approach to analyze cervical spine posture using RGB images, without using additional markers as landmarks, to detect defined key points such as the tragus of the ear or the spinous process of C7. By means of this automatic landmark detection method, the craniovertebral angle (CVA) is an established indicator of the severity of forward head position [10,15,16,24–26], is determined.

2. Materials and Methods

The CVA [27,28] is determined using lateral view images of the head–neck postures as the angle formed between the horizontal and a line drawn from the midpoint of the ear tragus to the point on the skin overlying the tip of the spinous process of the seventh cervical vertebra, C7 (see Figure 1). In order to automatically calculate the CVA, two anatomical landmarks, i.e., the ear tragus and the spinous process of C7, must be detected first.

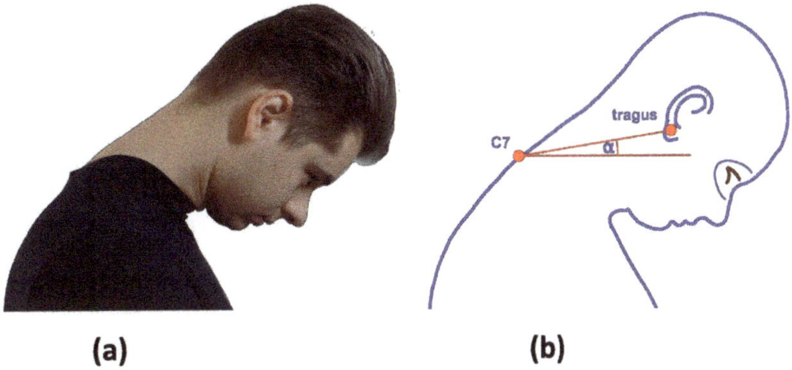

Figure 1. Image of a subject with flexed head position: (**a**) craniovertebral angle α was defined as the angle formed between the line drawn from the tragus of the ear to the skin tip location of the spinous process C7 and the horizontal line (**b**).

2.1. Determination of Spinous Process

The spinous process of the seventh human vertebra is an important landmark in the analysis of head–neck postures. When lowering or stretching the head forward, the spinous process of C7 forms a clear bulge in the skin on the back of the neck. In order to find a 2D pixel position of the skin tip of the spinous process in a single RGB image, a method based on the approximation of the line to the neck contour is proposed.

Openpose is a neural network that can recognize the 2D positions of landmarks on the human body and facial structures in an RGB image. In the context of this study, Openpose was used to determine a region of interest (RoI) surrounding the landmarks in the neck region. The proposed method, depicted in Figure 2, is to take a photograph of the subject and extract 18 key body points using the real-time skeleton detection model of Openpose [29] on it. The determination of the RoI is an essential part of the proposed approach. If the neck curvature is outside of the RoI, the C7 spinous process cannot be detected. Otherwise, if the RoI was too large, the image filters applied in the further steps could extract too many features in the background, which could lead to errors in the landmark detection.

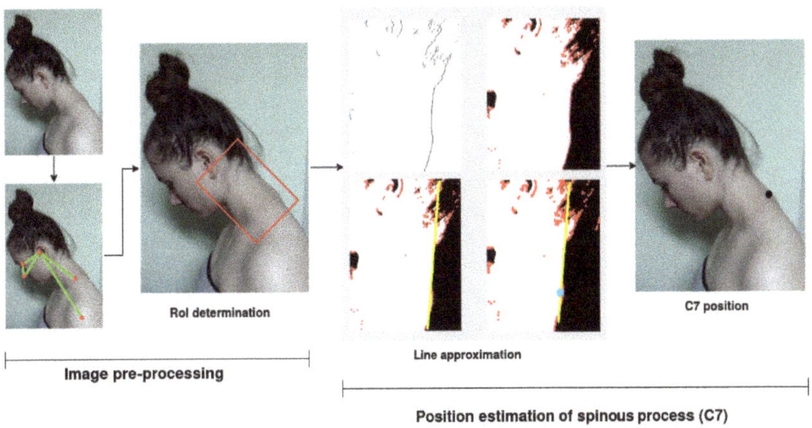

Figure 2. Determination of the position of the skin bulging through the C7 spinous process in an RGB image: based on 2D body key points (marked red) detected in the image, the RoI was determined. Using computer vision methods, corner detection was performed. The 2D position of the spinous process of C7 was estimated through the line (marked yellow) approximated to the neck curvature.

The RoI was calculated based on the 2D coordinates of the selected body parts in the Openpose output such as the x and y pixel positions of the nose and the ear (see Figure 3):

$$upper_{left} = nose_x + \frac{ear_x - nose_x}{2}, \quad nose_y + \frac{ear_y - nose_y}{2}, \tag{1}$$

$$upper_{right} = ear_x + (ear_x - nose_x), \quad ear_y + (ear_y - nose_y), \tag{2}$$

$$lower_{left} = upper_{left_x} - ((ear_y - nose_y) \cdot 2), upper_{left_y} + ((ear_x - nose_x) \cdot 2), \tag{3}$$

$$lower_{right} = upper_{right_x} - ((ear_y - nose_y) \cdot 2), upper_{right_y} + ((ear_x - nose_x) \cdot 2). \tag{4}$$

The input image was cropped to only the relevant area where the neck curvature and C7 spinous process bulge were visible, and at the same time, the area of the background was kept as small as possible.

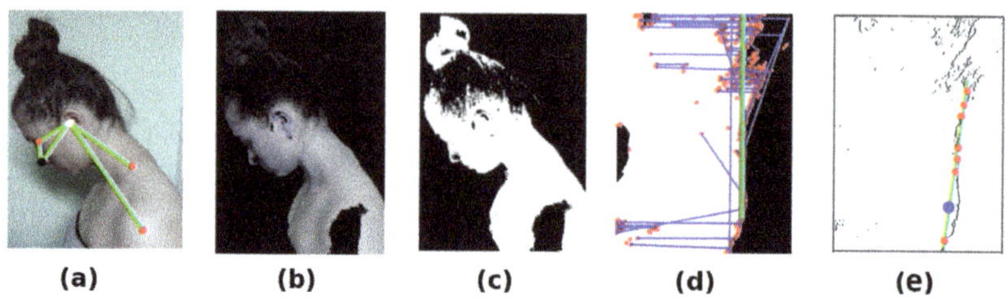

Figure 3. Body positions of the nose (marked black) and ear (marked white), which are used for the determination of RoI, are extracted using a pre-trained Openpose model (**a**). For the separation of the body from the background, color segmentation (**b**) is applied to the image. Then the body is marked white and the background black (**c**). In the binary image, the 2D corner-point coordinates are detected. For each of the corner points (marked red) and its neighbor, a straight line (marked blue) is generated. Subsequently, the number of corner points lying on each line is determined and compared. The line with the most corner points located on it is selected as the approximation line of the neck contour (green line). (Note: for clarity, not all lines are visualized in the image) (**d**). In order to calculate the position of the intersection, points (marked red) between the approximation line (marked green) and the neck contour (black) are used (**e**). The C7 spinous process is located in the middle of the adjacent intersection points with the maximum distance from each other.

Before computer vision methods for the edge extraction could be applied to the image, a color segmentation was used in order to separate the human body from the background. A color interval was first determined in the HSV color space. The output of this step is shown in Figure 3b. In the next step, the binary image was created (see Figure 3c). All pixels whose color value was inside the color interval of the skin were set as white, and every other pixel was set as black. This binary image was then passed to the Sobel operator [30] to select prominent contours in the RoI. The Sobel filter is a classical edge detector, which is commonly used in image processing. It extracts edges by performing the gradient on the image and emphasizes edges in the vertical or horizontal direction. A binary image favors the use of the Sobel filter. When using an RGB image instead, results can vary widely due to different lighting and color values. Using a binarized image, the Sobel operator can easily find the edges between the person and the background, since factors such as light and shadow are no longer taken into account. For a better interpretation of the edge detector results, corner points were calculated on each found contour using the Harris operator [31]. The 2D coordinates of the calculated corners points were then used to determine a straight line that approximated the neck contour. In order to determine this approximation line, the corner points found were first sorted according to their y-coordinate. For each corner point and its successor, a straight line was calculated. We then checked how many other corner points lay on each of the lines. Finally, the line with the most corner points was chosen to be the approximation line for the neck contour. The reason that the number of corner points on the line was also taken as a criterion was that the number of corner points on the neck contour was always significantly higher than the number of vertices on, for example, hair contours.

Once the approximation line was determined, its intersection points with the neck contour were calculated utilizing the edges extracted by the Sobel operator in the neck region. In Figure 3e, it is shown that the estimated position of the C7 spinous process is located between two adjacent intersection points with a distance greater than a predefined threshold.

2.2. Estimation of the Ear Tragus

The ear tragus was the second most important reference point for the CVA determination. The pipeline for the calculation of the ear tragus position was similar to the method proposed in Section 2.1 for the detection of C7. The RoI with the ear tragus was determined using the same pre-trained Openpose model as the RoI used for the C7 spinous process. However, in this case, rather than the neck contour, the ear should be mainly visible. For the RoI extraction, the Euclidean distance $dist_{NE}$ between the nose's key point and the ear was calculated. The vertices of the RoI were determined in such a way that the ear was located in the center:

$$upper_{left} = ear_x - \frac{dist_{NE}}{2}, \quad ear_y - \frac{dist_{NE}}{2} \tag{5}$$

$$upper_{right} = ear_x + \frac{dist_{NE}}{2}, \quad ear_y - \frac{dist_{NE}}{2} \tag{6}$$

$$lower_{left} = ear_x - \frac{dist_{NE}}{2}, \quad ear_y + \frac{dist_{NE}}{2} \tag{7}$$

$$lower_{right} = ear_x + \frac{dist_{NE}}{2}, \quad ear_y + \frac{dist_{NE}}{2}. \tag{8}$$

For the localization of the ear tragus, the ear contour was first detected by approximating an ellipse model on the outer shape of the ear, and then the pixel intensities inside the selected ellipse were analyzed. For this purpose, the Canny algorithm [32] was applied to the ear's RoI in order to detect edges. The Canny edge detector was chosen since the ear had many complex structures that could be missed by the Sobel operator. Afterward, the edges that were close to each other were connected to the contours, which were used to fit an ellipse to the ear's outer boundaries. The ellipses were generated in such a way that they maximally surrounded the found contours in the image (see Figure 4). In the last step, the ellipse whose center was the closest to the ear landmark point found by Openpose was selected to build a bounding ellipse of the outer ear contours.

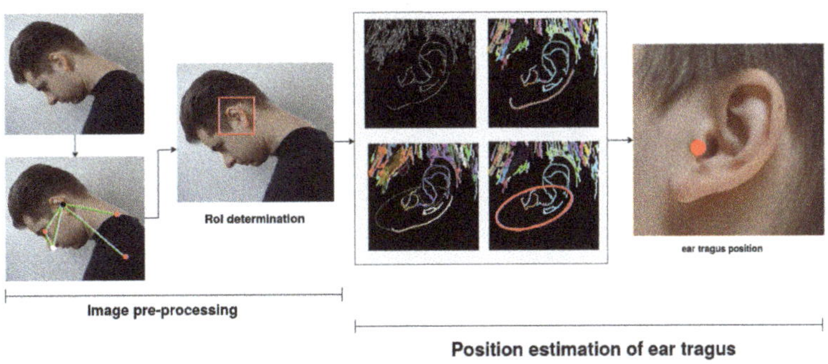

Figure 4. Estimation of the ear tragus in the lateral-view image of the subject: in the first step, image pre-processing was performed, which includes the extraction of the RoI (marked by red frame) based on the Openpose output. In the further processing steps, image features such as edges and contours were detected in the RoI. An ellipse was associated with each contour. The ellipse positioned closest to the Openpose ear point was then selected. Intensities were analyzed inside of the chosen ellipse. The ear tragus was estimated to be located in the direction of the smallest distance from the ear channel to the ear border represented through an ellipse.

In the next step, the area inside the ear ellipse was analyzed. The goal was to find the region with the darkest pixels, since this is where the auditory canal is most likely to be found. To do so, the minimum intensity value of all points within the ellipse was determined. The position of the ear tragus can be derived by applying an edge detector in the direction of the closest distance to the bounding ellipse that surrounds the ear.

2.3. Data Acquisition

In order to validate the proposed method for the automated calculation of the CVA in RGB images, a custom dataset was generated with a total of 79 subjects, of whom 45 were male and 34 were female.

For each test participant, the following additional data, required for the CVA analysis, were collected: demographic data such as age and gender, spinal disorders, and average daily duration of smartphone usage. Their mean age was 26.6 years, with the youngest person being 21 years old and the oldest being 61 years old. The height of the test subjects ranged from 163 cm to 196 cm. Of the 79 participants, 6 had been diagnosed with cervical spine disorders. The estimated daily duration of smartphones usage among the test subjects was 3.16 h on average, in a range from 0.3 h to 7 h.

The images in the dataset showed each subject performing four head–neck postures: straight neck, maximal head flexion, forward head posture, and head-down position (see Figure 5). The dataset resulted in a total of 316 images. The aim of the recorded dataset was twofold: on the one hand, the validation of the proposed methods for the detection of the anatomical points needed for calculation of the CVA and, on the other hand, the analysis of the CVA in four different head–neck positions.

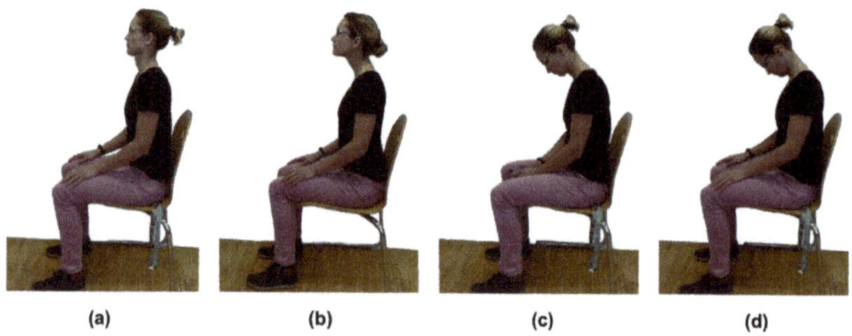

Figure 5. Sample images of different head–neck postures: straight-neck (**a**), forward-head (**b**), and head-down position during smartphone use (**c**) and maximal head flexion (**d**).

The images were recorded with a widely available Microsoft Kinect v2 3D camera, which captured 2D RGB images, as well as the depth data with a separate depth sensor [33]. The resolution of the RGB camera was 1920 × 1080 pixels, and the depth sensor had a resolution of 512 × 424 pixels. The camera and the data recorded in the dataset are depicted in Figure 6a. Although the dataset was intended for the evaluation of the automated calculation of the craniocervical angle in a single RGB image, depth maps were captured for each RGB frame and can be used for future research projects.

The photographs were taken in sitting positions in a left lateral view with the same background. For each recording, the camera was located at a distance of 1.3 m away from the subject on a tripod at a height of 1.2 m from the floor. In particular, to be able to determine the position of C7's skin bulge, the area of the neck bulge through C7 should not be covered by clothing or hair. The participants were asked to wear suitable clothing to keep the region of the head and neck uncovered and tie their hair back. In addition, all participants looked in the same direction and followed the instructions given to the participants before recording. Some of the subjects were asked to cover their neck, and 48 images were obtained, which could be used to validate whether the method could correctly predict the negative classes or not.

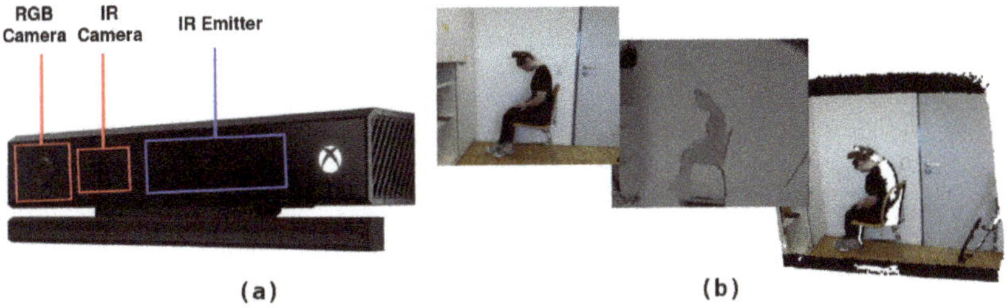

Figure 6. Microsoft Kinect v2 camera with included sensors (**a**) and illustration of three modalities captured in the the dataset (**b**): RGB image, depth map, and 3D point cloud.

The labeling of the captured photographs was performed by three experts on the 2D data. The experts were asked to mark the posterior position of the C7 spinous process, the ear tragus, and the ear lobula (see Figure 7). In this study, two points, the C7 spinous process and the ear tragus, were used for analysis and validation. In order to evaluate the quality of the annotation performed by the experts, inter-rater reliability (IRR) [34,35] was chosen as a validation metric. To calculate the IRR for three ratings, Krippendorff's α_K coefficient [35] was applied, which measures the extent of the agreement between multiple raters. A α_K value that approaches 1.0 indicates high confidence in the labeling accuracy and results in the high-quality dataset. The calculated reliability coefficient for the given data showed a high inter-rater agreement with an α_K of 0.991186.

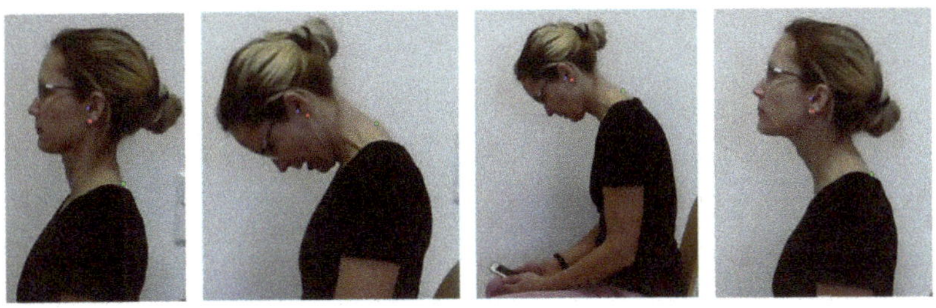

Figure 7. Labeled sample images of recorded head–neck postures: straight posture (**a**), maximal flexed head (**b**), using smartphone (**c**), and forward head position (**d**). The C7 spinous process is marked green, the ear tragus is blue, and the ear lobula is shown in red.

3. Results

In order to validate the performance of the proposed methods, the general detection accuracy was determined by calculating the ratio of the correct outcomes to all possible method responses:

$$acc = \frac{TP + TN}{TP + FP + FN + TN}, \tag{9}$$

where TP denotes true positive, TN denotes true negative, FP denotes false positive, and FN denotes false negative predictions. The detection accuracy for two detected anatomical points is shown in Table 1.

Table 1. Detection accuracy determined for C7 spinous process and ear tragus.

	C7 Spinous Process	Ear Tragus
Detection accuracy (acc)	80%	83%

The performance of the proposed detection methods was analyzed by considering the detected and observed values of the x and y coordinates for the chosen landmarks. The relationships of the observed and detected x and y coordinates for the C7 spinous process and ear tragus are visualized in Figure 8. From the presented diagrams, it can be seen that the proposed detection approaches performed well for the most of the images in the dataset. In general, the detected points are aligned to the line of the optimal fit in all of the sub-plots.

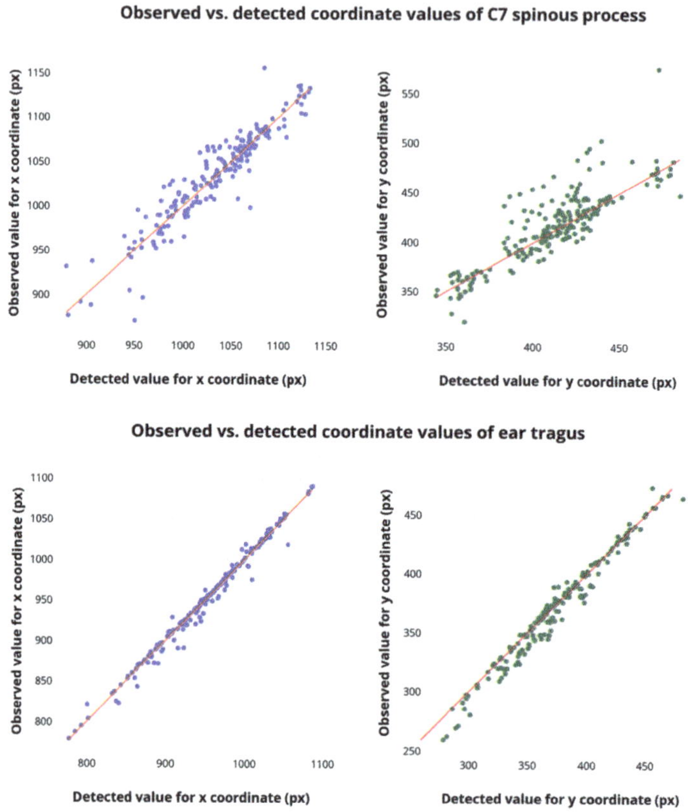

Figure 8. Comparison of the observed and detected values of the 2D coordinate of C7 spinous process and ear tragus. Values of x and y coordinates for the corresponding anatomical landmarks are visualized in the separate sub-plots. The line for the optimal fit is marked in red in each diagram.

By comparing the determined points for the C7 spinous process to the detected points of the ear tragus, it can be seen that the detection of the ear tragus provided more accurate results. In some datapoints, the detector for the C7 spinous process computed a slightly higher y coordinate value compared to its ground truth. However, the proposed method for ear tragus detection showed a relatively small number of incorrect outcomes.

In order to quantify the performance of the proposed detectors, PRESS statistics were calculated for each coordinate of the corresponding landmark points by using the following equation:

$$PRESS_{coordinate} = \sum_{i=1}^{N} (v_{coordinate,i} - \hat{v}_{coordinate,i})^2, \tag{10}$$

where v_i is the observed value of the corresponding coordinate, $\hat{v}_i$ is its predicted value, and N is the number of images in the dataset. Additionally, the coefficient of determination R^2 was calculated:

$$R^2_{coordinate} = \frac{PRESS}{\sum_{i=1}^{N}(v_{coordinate,i} - \overline{v}_{coordinate,i})^2}, \quad (11)$$

The results of the PRESS statistics are presented in Table 2. High values of R_x^2 and R_y^2 for the C7 spinous process and ear tragus indicate strong correlation between predicted datapoints and the corresponding ground truth. While comparing proposed detection approaches for the C7 spinous process and for the ear tragus much lower PRESS statistics are shown for the ear tragus demonstrating high predictive ability of this method.

Table 2. PRESS statistics and coefficient of determination R^2 calculated for x and y coordinates of C7 spinous process and ear tragus.

Measure	C7 Spinous Process	Ear Tragus
$PRESS_x$	68,760.81	11,094.77
$PRESS_y$	80,683.63	13,316.21
R_x^2	0.99	0.99
R_y^2	0.99	0.99

To assess the success of the methods graphically, the residuals for the x and y coordinates of the determined landmarks are depicted in the scatter-plots in Figure 9. The upper sub-plots representing residual values for the determined point of the C7 spinous process show that most residuals for the x and y coordinates are distributed symmetrically between 20 px and -20 px, and the only exceptions are a few outliers, which demonstrate a difference of up to 80 px from the ground truth value in the x coordinate and up to -60 px in the y coordinate. The residual datapoints for ear tragus detection are located mostly between 0 px and 5 px for both coordinates of the calculated landmark. However, in the validation dataset used, some incorrect detections were performed by the ear tragus detector, which are shown as outliers in the corresponding diagram. The minimum residual of the x coordinate was -36 px, while the minimum residual for the y coordinate was -22 px.

Considering the detection error of the proposed methods, the mean distance error $\bar{e}$ between the predicted point p_i and the corresponding ground truth $\hat{p}_i$ point for each posture class was determined. The mean distance error was calculated by applying the Euclidean distance in each of the images i:

$$\bar{e}_{class} = \frac{1}{N}\sqrt{\sum_{i=1}^{N}(p_{class,i} - \hat{p}_{class,i})^2}, \quad (12)$$

where N is the total number of images in the dataset. The results of the mean detection errors and of the standard deviation of the detection for the C7 spinous process and ear tragus are depicted in Figure 10. It can be seen that the smallest detection error was indicated for the posture class smartphone use, where $\bar{e}_{C7}$ for the C7 spinous process was 15.75 $\pm$ 12.06 px, and $\bar{e}_{ear}$ was 6.7 $\pm$ 7.4 px for the ear tragus and maximal flexed where we observed the values of 14.18 $\pm$ 8.03 px for the C7 spinous process and 7.02 $\pm$ 7.07 px for the ear tragus. For the C7 spinous process, the maximum mean distance error of 22.01 $\pm$ 18.06 px was calculated for the straight posture. The highest mean distance error for the ear tragus detection of 9.27 $\pm$ 7.34 px was indicated in the posture class of head forward.

The overall mean distance error for the detection of the C7 spinous process $\bar{e}_{c7}$ was calculated to be 18.07 $\pm$ 13.67 px, and the overall mean distance error for the ear tragus $\bar{e}_{ear}$ was 7.96 $\pm$ 7.45 px.

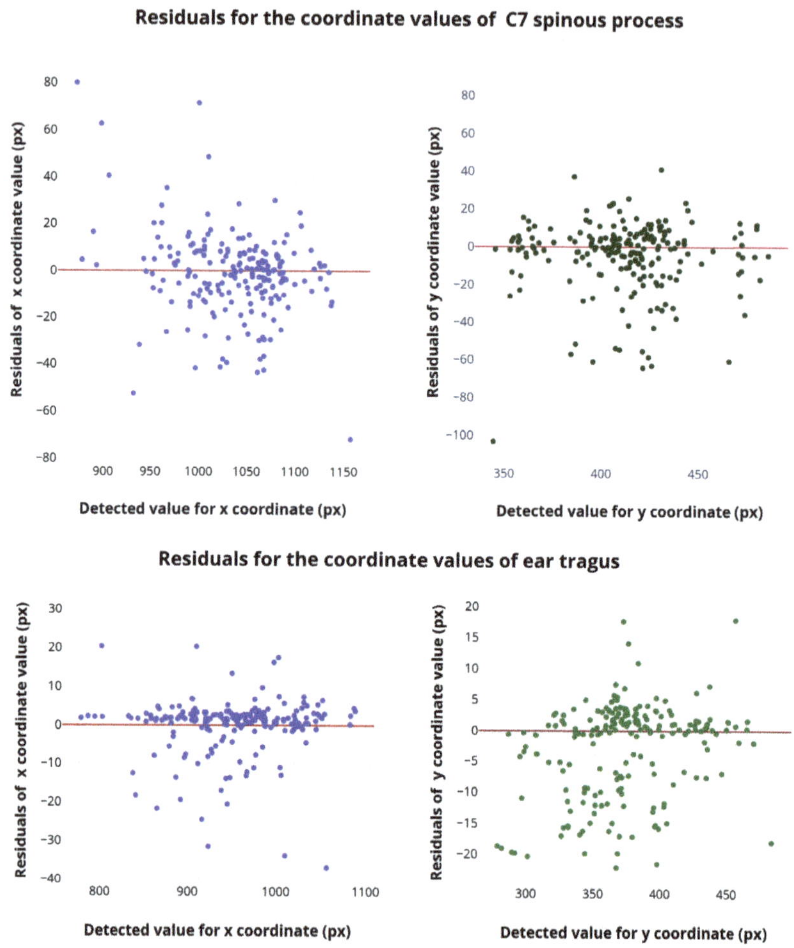

Figure 9. Residuals calculated for x and y coordinates of the detected landmarks: the zero-line is marked in red, the points for the x coordinates are marked in blue, and the green points represent residuals for the y coordinate.

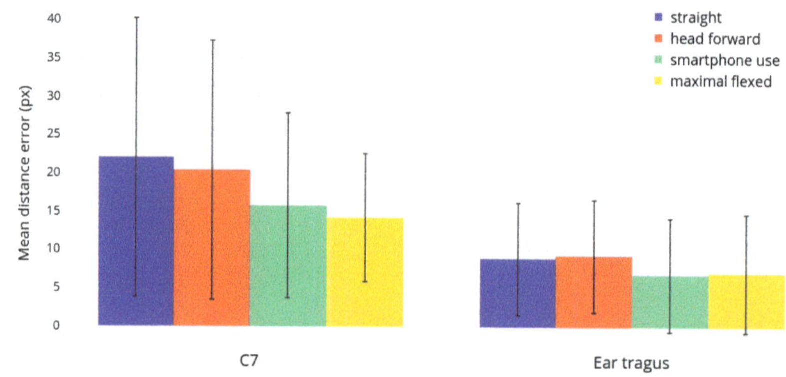

Figure 10. Mean distance error calculated for the detected landmarks. The distance error together with standard deviation is visualized separately for each posture class.

Figure 11 shows sample images from the recorded validation dataset and detected landmark points for the C7 spinous process as well as for the ear tragus. For the subject depicted in Figure 11a, the determined point of the C7 spinous process is slightly offset from the observed point in the horizontal direction.

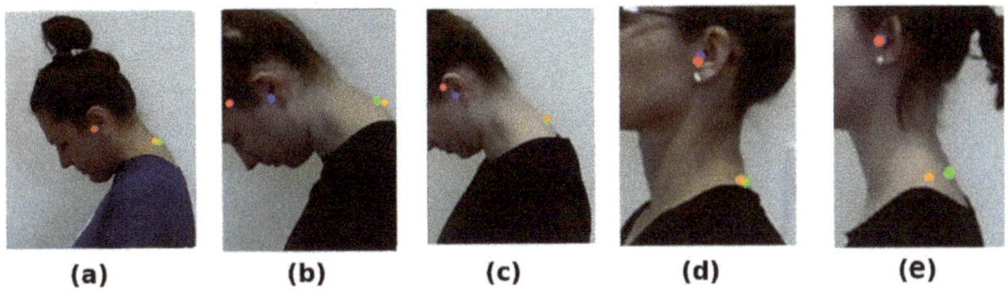

Figure 11. Sample predictions for different postures: minor deviation between the predicted and labeled points for the C7 spinous process and the ear tragus (**a**), the wrongly detected ear tragus (**b**), the found point for the ear tragus is located on the outer ear border (**c**), good prediction sample (**d**), the found position of the C7 spinous process with the slight deviation from the corresponding ground truth point (**e**). Green marks the positions of the C7 spinous process and blue indicates the ear tragus annotated by experts; predicted positions are marked using red for the ear tragus and orange for the C7 spinous process.

A higher displacement can be seen for the tragus point in Figure 11b. It is falsely positioned outside of the ear border, in contrast to the detection in Figure 11c, where it is still localized in the ear region, but in the wrong position. Moreover, as shown in Figure 11b, the detector estimated the position of the C7 spinous process over the skin tip. An example of a small shift for both the tragus point and the C7 spinous process point is shown in Figure 11d. There is also the possibility that one of the two key points is found well, but there are deviations for the other. While the key point of the ear tragus is well estimated, the key point for the C7 spinous process is localized in the middle of the neck (Figure 11e).

There is also a possibility that one of the two key points may be found successfully while the other landmark is miscalculated, such as the case shown in Figure 11e, where the point of the C7 spinous process is detected in the middle of the neck and the ear tragus is located correctly.

4. Discussion

The CVA is an important characteristic in head–neck postural assessment. However, the automatic detection of the head–neck landmarks, such as the C7 spinous process and ear tragus, which are required for the calculation of the CVA, is a challenging task.

The methods proposed in this study utilize image filters in order to detect landmarks required for CVA calculation in a single RGB image. In the first step of the proposed approach, the RoI was extracted based on the output from a body pose prediction model. For the localization of the C7 spinous process, line approximation was applied to the neck curvature. The intersection points between the neck contour and the approximation line were extracted in the subsequent step, and the distance for each pair of adjacent intersection points was calculated. Finally, the position of the C7 spinous process was determined as the midpoint of the vector built from the intersection points with the maximum distance.

For the ear tragus detection, the ear RoI was first extracted similarly to that of the C7 spinous process. Using a classical edge detector, the contours were extracted inside the RoI. From the extracted contours, an ellipse was fitted to contour of the ear. The ear tragus was then determined by analyzing the intensities inside the associated ellipse.

In general, the presented results demonstrated the capability of the developed method to detect the desired landmarks in an RGB image. The detector for the C7 spinous process as well as for the ear tragus showed the best performance for the subjects performing the smartphone use and maximal flexed postures. In these postures the bulge of the C7 spinous process was prominently expressed on the skin for most of the subjects, so the values of the detected C7 spinous process points remained within the error-tolerance range. The ear tragus detection showed good prediction results in the images of these postures as well. In some rare cases, the ear detector falsely located the position of the ear tragus shifted to the left side of the determined RoI, as shown in Figure 11b. The reason for this miscalculation was the incorrect estimation of the ear contour. In this case, multiple edges in the hair region given by the Sobel filter were taken into account during the determination of the ear contours. Subsequently, the wrong ellipse was associated with the ear, and the ear tragus was found in the wrong position. In future work, we can overcome this issue by filtering the hair region out from the edge detection.

From the high values of the PRESS statistics as well as from the graphical representation of the residuals, relatively large deviations between the detected and labeled points of the C7 spinous process could be observed for some datapoints. Furthermore, based on the mean detection error, it can be stated that the most mismatched points were found for the subjects performing the straight head and forward head postures. In general, the morphological conditions of humans are subject to high natural variance. While in one person the spinous process of the C7 vertebra might be clearly visible, it may hardly be seen in another subject. In addition, when the head is held upright or positioned forward, the spinous process generally does not stand out as prominently as when the head is bent.

5. Conclusions

This study aimed to present and evaluate a novel approach for the automated detection of the body landmarks, namely the C7 spinous process and the ear tragus, required for the determination of the CVA. The proposed methods take a single RGB image and localize the 2D position in pixel coordinates for the desired key points using simple but effective computer vision methods. Both detection methods utilize the Sobel edge detector for their core calculations.

The proposed detectors demonstrated robust detection results for the smartphone use and maximal flexed posture groups; however, they showed some discrepancy in the detection of the straight and forward head posture classes. In order to improve the detection of the C7 spinous process in these particular poses, machine learning approaches can be used. In these approaches, the models learn to localize the pre-defined landmarks in the image from the data provided.

A limitation of the method is that the background where the person is recorded needs to be homogeneous. Otherwise, the color segmentation can detect some false-positive regions. Another limitation of this approach is that landmark occlusion is not considered in the method; i.e., landmarks covered by hair or clothing cannot be determined. To overcome this problem in the future, a machine learning model will be trained using the recorded dataset in order to detect the C7 spinous process.

Another future task is to extend the current method's implementation to the automatic determination and analysis of CVAs for different postures and compare them with the data recorded in the dataset.

A particularly attractive feature of this method is that the current posture can be automatically deduced without attaching additional physical markers. This rules out the possibility that a changed posture, which is caused by potentially interfering markers, will unknowingly influence the actual posture and thus falsify the measurement results. Especially when using physical markers during movement, there is the possibility that these markers will move away from their initial positions and shift with the skin. This implies that the unintentionally changed local position of the markers can lead to incorrect positions of joints.

Furthermore, markerless analysis of the head–neck postures can be beneficial in different experimental scenarios, especially if a study with specific vulnerable participants needs to be carried out. The proposed methods are a promising approach that can be extended to include the detection of other prominent landmarks on the human body. Therefore, this approach could also be of interdisciplinary interest—for example, to dentists, physical therapists, speech therapists, and other professionals, since it may assist them in their clinical practice and in the context of scientific research.

All of the presented results so far relate to detection in 2D pixel space. However, using depth maps recorded in the dataset, a projection of the detected points in the 3D world is possible. This will be addressed in future works.

Author Contributions: Conceptualization, I.K. and S.B.; methodology, S.B.; software, A.M.; validation, I.K.; formal analysis, A.M.; investigation, S.B.; data curation, I.K.; writing—original draft preparation, S.B. and I.K.; writing—review and editing; visualization, I.K.; supervision, S.B.; project administration, S.B. and I.K. All authors have read and agreed to the published version of the manuscript.

Funding: This research received no external funding.

Institutional Review Board Statement: Not applicable.

Informed Consent Statement: Informed consent was obtained from all subjects involved in the study. Written informed consent has been obtained from the patient(s) to publish this paper.

Data Availability Statement: Not applicable.

Conflicts of Interest: The authors declare no conflict of interest.

Abbreviations

The following abbreviations are used in this manuscript:

CVA	craniovertebral angle
FHP	forward head position
HTA	head tilt angle
RoI	region of interest
IRR	inter-rater reliability
PRESS	predicted residual error sum of squares

References

1. Abdulla, M.; Smaeel, A. Providing Information through Smart Platforms: An Applied Study on Academic Libraries in Saudi Universities. *J. Educ. Soc. Behav. Sci.* **2019**, *30*, 1–24. [CrossRef]
2. Saksena, R.; Lu, D.; Celik, I. Ericsson Mobility Report. Report, Ericsson. 2021. Available online: https://www.ericsson.com/en/reports-and-papers/mobility-report/reports/november-2021 (accessed on 15 December 2021).
3. Number of Smartphone Users from 2016 to 2021. Website. 2021. Available online: https://www.statista.com/statistics/330695/number-of-smartphone-users-worldwide/ (accessed on 15 December 2021).
4. Vasavada, A.N.; Nevins, D.D.; Monda, S.M.; Hughes, E.; Lin, D.C. Gravitational demand on the neck musculature during tablet computer use. *Ergonomics* **2015**, *58*, 990–1004. [CrossRef] [PubMed]
5. Jacobs, K.; Hudak, S.; McGiffert, J. Computer-Related posture and musculoskeletal discomfort in middle school students. *Work* **2009**, *32*, 275–283. [CrossRef] [PubMed]
6. Siu, D.C.H.; Tse, L.A.; Yu, I.T.S.; Griffiths, S.M. Computer products usage and prevalence of computer related musculoskeletal discomfort among adolescents. *Work* **2009**, *34*, 449–454. [CrossRef]
7. Palmer, K.; Ciccarelli, M.; Falkmer, T.; Parsons, R. Associations between exposure to Information and Communication Technology (ICT) and reported discomfort among adolescents. *Work* **2014**, *48*, 165–173. [CrossRef]
8. Park, J.; Kim, J.; Kim, J.; Kim, K.; Kim, N.; Choi, I.; Lee, S.; Yim, J. The effects of heavy smartphone use on the cervical angle, pain threshold of neck muscles and depression. *Adv. Sci. Technol. Lett.* **2015**, *91*, 12–17. [CrossRef]
9. Shousha, T.; Hamada, H.; Abo-zaid, N.; Abdelsamee, M.; Behiry, M. The effect of smartphone use on neck flexion angle and hand grip power among adolescents: Cross-sectional study. *J. Hum. Sport Exerc.* **2021**, *16*, 883–891. [CrossRef]
10. Shaghayeghfard, B.; Ahmadi, A.; Maroufi, N.; Sarrafzadeh, J. Evaluation of forward head posture in sitting and standing positions. *Eur. Spine J.* **2016**, *25*, 3577–3582. [CrossRef]
11. Kang, J.H.; Park, R.Y.; Lee, S.J.; Kim, J.Y.; Yoon, S.R.; Jung, K.I. The effect of the forward head posture on postural balance in long time computer based worker. *Ann. Rehabil. Med.* **2012**, *36*, 98–104. [CrossRef]
12. Castro, A.; Pacheco, J.; Lourenço, C.; Queirós, S.; Moreira, A.; Rodrigues, N.; Vilaça, J. Evaluation of spinal posture using Microsoft Kinect™: A preliminary case-study with 98 volunteers. *Porto Biomed. J.* **2017**, *2*, 18–22. [CrossRef]

13. Digo, E.; Pierro, G.; Pastorelli, S.; Gastaldi, L. Evaluation of spinal posture during gait with inertial measurement units. *Proc. Inst. Mech. Eng. Part H J. Eng. Med.* **2020**, *234*, 1094–1105. [CrossRef] [PubMed]
14. Ormos, G. Survey of neck posture, mobility and muscle strength among schoolchildren. *Man. Med.* **2016**, *54*, 156–162. [CrossRef]
15. Martinez-Merinero, P.; Nuñez-Nagy, S.; Achalandabaso-Ochoa, A.; Fernandez-Matias, R.; Pecos-Martin, D.; Gallego-Izquierdo, T. Relationship between Forward Head Posture and Tissue Mechanosensitivity: A Cross-Sectional Study. *Ann. Rehabil. Med.* **2012**, *36*, 98–104. [CrossRef]
16. Choi, K.H.; Cho, M.U.; Park, C.W.; Kim, S.Y.; Kim, M.J.; Hong, B.; Kong, Y.K. A Comparison Study of Posture and Fatigue of Neck According to Monitor Types (Moving and Fixed Monitor) by Using Flexion Relaxation Phenomenon (FRP) and Craniovertebral Angle (CVA). *Int. J. Environ. Res. Public Health* **2020**, *17*, 6345. [CrossRef]
17. Lee, S.; Choi, Y.H.; Kim, J. Effects of the cervical flexion angle during smartphone use on muscle fatigue and pain in the cervical erector spinae and upper trapezius in normal adults in their 20s. *J. Phys. Ther. Sci.* **2017**, *29*, 921–923. [CrossRef] [PubMed]
18. Marina Samaan, E.E.; Elnahhas, A.; Hendawy, A. Effect of prolonged smartphone use on cervical spine and hand grip strength in adolescence. *Int. J. Multidiscip. Res. Dev.* **2018**, *5*, 49–53.
19. Castien, R.; Blankenstein, N.; van der Windt, D.; Heymans, M.; Dekker, J. The Working Mechanism of Manual Therapy in Participants With Chronic Tension-Type Headache. *J. Orthop. Sport. Phys. Ther.* **2013**, *43*, 693–699. [CrossRef]
20. Shin, Y.; Kim, W.; Kim, S. Correlations among visual analogue scale, neck disability index, shoulder joint range of motion, and muscle strength in young women with forward head posture. *J. Exerc. Rehabil.* **2017**, *13*, 413–417. [CrossRef]
21. Singla, D.; Veqar, Z. Association Between Forward Head, Rounded Shoulders, and Increased Thoracic Kyphosis: A Review of the Literature. *J. Chiropr. Med.* **2017**, *16*, 220–229. [CrossRef]
22. Werth, A.J.; Babski-Reeves, K. Effects of portable computing devices on posture, muscle activation levels and efficiency. *Appl. Ergon.* **2014**, *45*, 1603–1609. [CrossRef]
23. Kinel, E.; Roncoletta, P.; Pietrangelo, T.; D'Amico, M. 3D Stereophotogrammetric Quantitative Evaluation of Posture and Spine Proprioception in Subacute and Chronic Nonspecific Low Back Pain. *J. Clin. Med.* **2022**, *11*, 546. [CrossRef] [PubMed]
24. Brunton, J.; Brunton, E.; Mhuiri, A.N. Reliability of measuring natural head posture using the craniovertebral angle. In *Proceedings of the Irish Ergonomics Society Annual Conference*; Irish Ergonomics Society: Limerick, Ireland, 2003; pp. 37–40.
25. van Niekerk, S.M.; Louw, Q.; Vaughan, C.; Grimmer-Somers, K.; Schreve, K. Photographic measurement of upper-body sitting posture of high school students: A reliability and validity study. *BMC Musculoskelet. Disord.* **2008**, *9*, 113. [CrossRef] [PubMed]
26. Salahzadeh, Z.; Maroufi, N.; Ahmadi, A.; Behtash, H.; Razmjoo, A.; Gohari, M.; Parnianpour, M. Assessment of forward head posture in females: Observational and photogrammetry methods. *J. Back Musculoskelet. Rehabil.* **2013**, *27*, 131. [CrossRef] [PubMed]
27. Weber, P.; Corrêa, E.C.R.; Milanesi, J.M.; Soares, J.C.; Trevisan, M.E. Craniocervical posture: Cephalometric and biophotogrammetric analysis. *Braz. J. Oral Sci.* **2012**, *11*, 416–421.
28. Iunes, D.; Bevilaqua-Grossi, D.; Oliveira, A.; Castro, F.; Salgado, H. Comparative analysis between visual and computerized photogrammetry postural assessment. *Braz. J. Phys. Ther.* **2009**, *13*, 308–315. [CrossRef]
29. Osokin, D. Real-time 2d multi-person pose estimation on cpu: Lightweight openpose. *arXiv* **2018**, arXiv:1811.12004.
30. Vincent, O.R.; Folorunso, O. A descriptive algorithm for sobel image edge detection. *Proc. Informing Sci. Educ. Conf. (InSITE)* **2009**, *40*, 97–107.
31. Derpanis, K.G. *The Harris Corner Detector*; York University: Toronto, ON, Canada, 2004; Volume 2.
32. Canny, J. A computational approach to edge detection. *IEEE Trans. Pattern Anal. Mach. Intell.* **1986**, *PAMI-8*, 679–698. [CrossRef]
33. Brancati, R.; Cosenza, C.; Niola, V.; Savino, S. Experimental Measurement of Underactuated Robotic Finger Configurations via RGB-D Sensor. Advances in Service and Industrial Robotics. RAAD 2018. *Mech. Mach. Sci.* **2019**, *67*, 533. [CrossRef]
34. Viera, A.J.; Garrett, J.M. Understanding interobserver agreement: The kappa statistic. *Fam. Med.* **2005**, *37*, 360–363.
35. Krippendorff, K. *Content Analysis: An Introduction to Its Methodology*, 4th ed.; Sage Publications, International Educational and Professional Publisher: Thousand Oaks, CA, USA; London, UK; New Delhi, India, 2018; pp. 221–285.

BioMedInformatics

Article

Meal and Physical Activity Detection from Free-Living Data for Discovering Disturbance Patterns of Glucose Levels in People with Diabetes

Mohammad Reza Askari [1], Mudassir Rashid [1], Xiaoyu Sun [2], Mert Sevil [2], Andrew Shahidehpour [1], Keigo Kawaji [2] and Ali Cinar [1,2,*]

[1] Department of Chemical and Biological Engineering, Illinois Institute of Technology, 10 W 33rd Street, Perlstein Hall, Suite 127, Chicago, IL 60616, USA; maskari@hawk.iit.edu (M.R.A.); mrashid3@iit.edu (M.R.); ashahide@hawk.iit.edu (A.S.)

[2] Department of Biomedical Engineering, Illinois Institute of Technology, Chicago, IL 60616, USA; xsun49@hawk.iit.edu (X.S.); msevil@hawk.iit.edu (M.S.); kkawaji@iit.edu (K.K.)

* Correspondence: cinar@iit.edu; Tel.: +1-312-567-3042

Abstract: Objective: The interpretation of time series data collected in free-living has gained importance in chronic disease management. Some data are collected objectively from sensors and some are estimated and entered by the individual. In type 1 diabetes (T1D), blood glucose concentration (BGC) data measured by continuous glucose monitoring (CGM) systems and insulin doses administered can be used to detect the occurrences of meals and physical activities and generate the personal daily living patterns for use in automated insulin delivery (AID). Methods: Two challenges in time-series data collected in daily living are addressed: data quality improvement and the detection of unannounced disturbances of BGC. CGM data have missing values for varying periods of time and outliers. People may neglect reporting their meal and physical activity information. In this work, novel methods for preprocessing real-world data collected from people with T1D and the detection of meal and exercise events are presented. Four recurrent neural network (RNN) models are investigated to detect the occurrences of meals and physical activities disjointly or concurrently. Results: RNNs with long short-term memory (LSTM) with 1D convolution layers and bidirectional LSTM with 1D convolution layers have average accuracy scores of 92.32% and 92.29%, and outperform other RNN models. The F1 scores for each individual range from 96.06% to 91.41% for these two RNNs. Conclusions: RNNs with LSTM and 1D convolution layers and bidirectional LSTM with 1D convolution layers provide accurate personalized information about the daily routines of individuals. Significance: Capturing daily behavior patterns enables more accurate future BGC predictions in AID systems and improves BGC regulation.

Keywords: recurrent neural networks; event detection; data preprocessing; outlier removal; type 1 diabetes

Citation: Askari, M.R.; Rashid, M.; Sun, X.; Sevil, M.; Shahidehpour, A.; Kawaji, K.; Cinar, A. Meal and Physical Activity Detection from Free-Living Data for Discovering Disturbance Patterns to Glucose Levels in People with Diabetes. *Biomedinformatics* **2022**, *2*, 297–317. https://doi.org/10.3390/biomedinformatics2020019

Academic Editor: Pentti Nieminen

Received: 23 April 2022
Accepted: 27 May 2022
Published: 1 June 2022

1. Introduction

Time series data are widely used in many fields, and various data-driven modeling techniques are developed to represent the dynamic characteristics of systems and forecast the future behavior. The growing research in artificial intelligence has provided powerful machine learning (ML) techniques to contribute to data-driven model development. Real-world data provide several challenges to modeling and forecasting, such as missing values and outliers. Such imperfections in data can reduce the accuracy of ML and the models developed. This necessitates data preprocessing for the imputation of missing values, down- and up-sampling, and data reconciliation. Data preprocessing is a laborious and time-consuming effort since big data are usually stacked on a large scale [1]. When models are used for forecasting, the accuracy of forecasts improve if the effects of future possible disturbances based on behavior patterns extracted from historical data are incorporated in the forecasts. This paper focuses on these two problems and investigates the benefits of preprocessing the real-world data and the performance of different recurrent neural network (RNN) models for detecting various events that affect blood glucose concentration (BGC) in people with type 1 diabetes (T1D). The behavior patterns detected are used for more accurate predictions of future BGC variations, which can be used for warnings and for increasing the effectiveness of automated insulin delivery (AID) systems.

Time series data captured in daily living of people with chronic conditions have many of these challenges to modeling, detection, and forecasting. Focusing on people with T1D, the medical objective is to forecast the BGC of a person with T1D and prevent the excursion of BGC outside a "desired range" (70–180 mg/dL) to reduce the probability of hypo- and hyperglycemia events. In recent years, the number of people with diabetes has grown rapidly around the world, reaching pandemic levels [2,3]. Advances in continuous glucose monitoring (CGM) systems, insulin pump and insulin pen technologies, and in novel insulin formulations has enabled many powerful treatment options [4–9]. The current treatment options available to people with T1D range from manual insulin injections to AID. Manual injection (insulin bolus) doses are computed based on the person's characteristics and the properties of the meal consumed. Current AID systems necessitate the manual entry of meal information to give insulin boluses for mitigating the effects of meal on the BGC. A manual adjustment of the basal insulin dose and increasing the BGC target level and/or consumption of snacks are the options to mitigate the effects of physical activity. Some people may forget to make these manual entries and a system that can nudge them to provide appropriate information can reduce the extreme excursions in BGC. Commercially available AID systems are hybrid closed-loop systems, and they require these manual entries by the user. AID systems, also called artificial pancreas (AP), consist of a CGM, an insulin pump, and a closed-loop control algorithm that manipulates the insulin infusion rate delivered by the pump based on the recent CGM values reported [10–23]. More advanced AID systems that use a multivariable approach [10,24–26] use additional inputs from wearable devices (such as wristbands) to automatically detect the occurrence of physical activity and incorporate this information to the automated control algorithms for a fully automated AID system [27]. Most AID systems use model predictive control techniques that predict future BGC values in making their insulin dosing decisions. Knowing the habits of the individual AID user improves the control decisions since the prediction accuracy of the future BGC trajectories can explicitly incorporate the future potential disturbances to the BGC, such as meals and physical activities, that will occur with high likelihood during the future BGC prediction window [24,26]. Consequently, the detection of meal and physical activity events from historical free-living data of a person with T1D will provide useful information for decision making by both the individual and by the AID system.

CGM systems report subcutaneous glucose concentration to infer BGC with a sampling rate of 5 min. Self-reported meal and physical activity data are often based on diary entries. Physical activity data can also be captured by wearable devices. The variables reported by wearable devices may have artifacts, noise, missing values, and outliers. The data used in this work include only CGM values, insulin dosing information, and diary entries of meals and physical activities.

Analyzing long-term data of people with T1D indicates that individuals tend to repeat daily habitual behaviors. Figure 1 illustrates the probability of physical activity and meal (indicated as carbohydrate intake) events, either simultaneously or disjointly, for 15 months of self-reported CGM, meal, insulin pump, and physical activity data of individuals with T1D. Major factors affecting BGC variations usually occur at specific time windows and conditions, and some combinations of events are mutually exclusive. For example, insulin-bolusing and physical activity are less likely to occur simultaneously or during hypoglycemia episodes, since people do not exercise when their BGC is low. People may have different patterns of behavior during the work week versus weekends or holidays. Predicting the probabilities of exercise, meal consumption, and their concurrent occurrence based on historical data using ML can provide important information on the behavior patterns for making medical therapy decisions in diabetes.

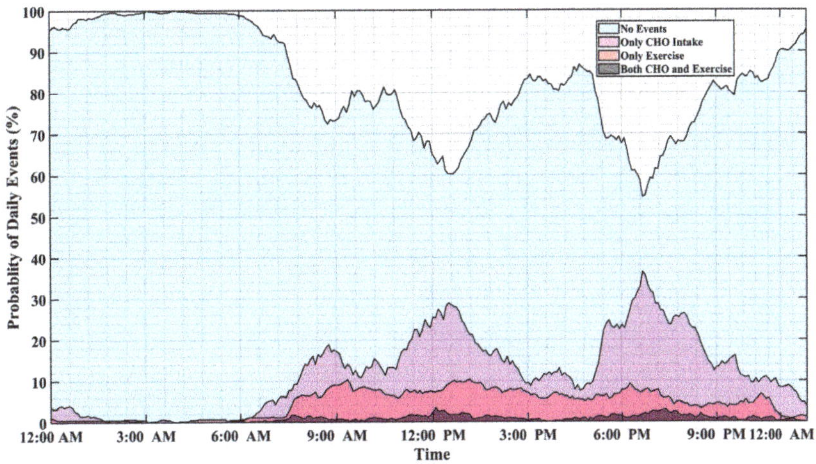

Figure 1. The probabilities of meal and physical activity events during one day obtained by analyzing 15 months of the pump–CGM sensor, meal, and physical activity data collected from a randomly selected person with T1D.

Motivated by the above considerations, this work develops a framework for predicting the probabilities of meal and physical activity events, including their independent and simultaneous occurrences. A framework is built to handle the inconsistencies and complexities of real-world data, including missing data, outlier removal, feature extraction, and data augmentation. Four different recurrent neural network (RNN) models are developed and evaluated for estimating the probability of events causing large variations in BGC. The advent of deep neural networks (NNs) and their advances have paved the way for processing and analyzing various types of information, namely: time-series, spatial, and time-series–spatial data. Long short-term memory (LSTM) NN models are specific sub-categories of recurrent NNs introduced to reduce the computational burden of storing information over extended time intervals [28,29]. LSTMs take advantage of nonlinear dynamic modeling without knowing time-dependency information in the data. Moreover, their multi-step-ahead prediction capability makes them an appropriate choice for detecting upcoming events and disturbances that can deteriorate the accuracy of model predictions.

The main contributions of this work are the development of NN models capable of estimating the occurrences of meals and physical activities without requiring additional bio-signals from wearable devices, and the integration of convolution layers with LSTM that enable the NN to accurately estimate the output from glucose–insulin input data. The proposed RNN models can be integrated with the control algorithm of an AID system to enhance its performance by readjusting the conservativeness and aggressiveness of the AID system.

The remainder of this paper is organized as follows: the next section provides a short description of the data collected from people with T1D. The preprocessing step, including outlier removal, data imputation, and feature extraction is presented in Section 3. Section 4 presents various RNN configurations used in this study. A case study with real-world data and a discussion of the results are presented in Section 5 and Section 6, respectively. Finally, Section 6 provides the conclusions.

2. Free-Living, Self-Reported Dataset of People with T1D

A total of 300 self-collected T1D datasets were made available for research, and each dataset represents a unique individual. Among all of the datasets, 50 T1D datasets include CGM-sensor–insulin-pump recordings and exercise information such as the time, type, and duration of physical activity recorded from either open or closed-loop insulin-pump–sensor data. Meal information is reported as the amount of carbohydrates (CHO) consumed in the meal as estimated by the subject. An over or underestimation of CHO in meals is common.

The subjects with T1D selected for this study used insulin-pump–CGM-sensor therapy for up to two years, and some of them have lived with diabetes for more than fifty years. Tables 1 and 2 summarize the demographic information of the selected subjects and the definition of the variables collected, respectively. Separate RNN models were developed for each person in order to capture personalized patterns of meal consumption and physical activity.

Table 1. The general demographic information of 11 subjects with T1D and the durations of recorded samples.

Subject	Gender	Age	Duration of Data [1]	Missing Samples (%)	Max Gap Size [2]
1	M	36	283 days	12.36%	273
2	M	33	368 days	7.11%	71
3	F	72	280 days	1.10%	28
4	M	43	468 days	10.03%	435
5	F	52	655 days	4.91%	233
6	F	26	206 days	14.45%	107
7	M	51	278 days	6.12%	34
8	-	41	390 days	8.87%	177
9	-	42	279 days	19.70%	311
10	M	27	695 days	14.32%	571
11	F	35	413 days	8.97%	147

[1] The duration of data is calculated after imputation of missing data and counting gaps between samples.
[2] Number of samples, sampling time 5 min.

Table 2. The name and the definition of measured variables.

Variable/Symbol	Definition	Units
CGM	Continuous glucose monitoring values sampled every five minutes	mmol/L
Smbg	Self-monitored BGC for sensor calibration	mmol/L
Rate (Ins_{Basal})	The basal insulin rate	unit/h
Bolus (Ins_{Bolus})	The actual delivered amount of normal bolus insulin	unit
Time	UTC time stamp	Format: yyyy-mm-yy hh:mm:ss
Duration	The actual duration of a suspend, basal, or dual/square bolus	milliseconds
Activity.name	The type of physical activity	-
Activity.duration (AD)	The duration of a physical activity	milliseconds
Distance.value (DV)	The value of the distance traveled	miles
Energy.value (EV)	The amount of energy spent during activity	kilocalories
Nutrition.carbohydrate (CHO)	The carbohydrates entered in a health kit food entry	grams

3. Data Preprocessing

This is a computational study for the development of detection and classification of infrequent events (eating, exercising) that affect the main variable of interest in people with diabetes: their blood glucose concentrations. It is based on data collected from patients in free living; hence, it contains many windows of data with missing values and outliers. Using real-world data for developing models usually has numerous challenges: (i) the datasets can be noisy and incomplete; (ii) there may be duplicate CGM samples in some of the datasets; (iii) inconsistencies exist in the sampling rate of CGM and insulin values; (iv) gaps in the time and date can be found due to insulin pump or CGM sensor disconnection. Therefore, the datasets need to be preprocessed before using them for model development.

3.1. Sample Imputation

Estimating missing data is an important step before analyzing the data [30]. Missing data are substituted with reasonable estimates (imputation) [31]. In dealing with time-series data such as CGM, observations are sorted according to their chronological order. Therefore, the variable "Time", described in Table 2, is converted to "Unix time-stamp", samples are sorted in ascending order of "Unix time-stamp", and gaps without observations are filled with pump–sensor samples labeled as "missing values".

Administered basal insulin is a piecewise constant variable and its amount is calculated by the AID system or by predefined insulin injection scenarios. Applying a simple forward or backward imputation for basal insulin with gaps in duration lasting a maximum of two hours gives reasonable reconstructed values for the missing observations. Gaps lasting more than two hours in missing recordings are imputed with basal insulin values recorded in the previous day at the same time, knowing that insulin injection scenarios usually follow a daily pattern [32].

The variable "Bolus" is a sparse variable (usually nonzero only at times of meals) and its missing samples were imputed with the median imputation approach, considering that the bolus injection policy is infrequently altered. Similarly, missing recordings of variables "Nutrition.carbohydrate", "Smbg", "Duration", "Activity.duration", and "Distance.value" were imputed with the median strategy. A multivariate strategy that uses CGM, total injected insulin, "Nutrition.carbohydrate", the "Energy.value", and "Activity.duration" was employed to impute missing CGM values.

This choice of variables has to do with the dynamic relationship between CGM and the amount of carbohydrate intake, the duration and the intensity of physical activity, and the total injected insulin. Estimates of missing CGM samples were obtained by performing probabilistic principal component analysis (PPCA) on the lagged matrices of the CGM data. PPCA is an extension of principal component analysis, where the Gaussian conditional distribution of the latent variables is assumed [33]. This formulation of the PPCA facilitates tackling the problem of missing values in the data through the maximum likelihood estimation of the mean and variance of the original data. Before performing PPCA on the feature variables, the lagged array of each feature variable, $\mathcal{X}_{k,j}, k \in \{CGM, Ins, CHO, EV, AD\}$, at the jth sampling index was constructed from the past two hours of observations as:

$$\begin{aligned} \mathcal{X}_{k,j} &= \left[X_{k,j}, X_{k,j-1} \dots \quad X_{k,j-24}\right]_{1\times 25}, \quad k \in \{CGM, Ins, CHO, EV, AD\} \\ X_j &= [\mathcal{X}_{1,j}, \dots, \mathcal{X}_{k,j} \dots, \mathcal{X}_{M,j}]^T, \quad X = \left[X_1, \dots, X_N\right]_{M\times N} \end{aligned} \tag{1}$$

For an observed set of feature variables X_j, let $\mathcal{T}_j = [\mathcal{T}_{1,j}, \dots, \mathcal{T}_{q,j}]^T$ be its q-dimensional ($q \leq M$) Gaussian latent transform [34] such that

$$X_{i,j} = W_i \mathcal{T}_j + \mu_i + \epsilon_{i,j} \tag{2}$$

where $W_i = [W_{i,1}, \dots, W_{i,q}] \in \mathbb{R}^q$ and $\underline{\mu} = [\mu_1, \dots, \mu_M]^T \in \mathbb{R}^M$ represent the ith row of the loading matrix $W \in \mathbb{R}^{M\times q}$ and mean value of the data. $\epsilon_{i,j} \in \mathbb{R}$ is also the measurement noise with the probability distribution

$$p(\epsilon_{i,j}|\sigma^2) = \mathcal{N}(\epsilon_{i,j}|0, \sigma^2)\,. \tag{3}$$

Based on the Gaussian distribution assumption of $\mathcal{T}_j$ and the Gaussian probability distribution of $\epsilon_{i,j}$, one can deduce that

$$\begin{cases} p(\mathcal{T}_j) = \mathcal{N}(\mathcal{T}_j|0, I_q) \\ p(X_{i,j}|\mu_i, W_i, \sigma^2) = \mathcal{N}(X_{i,j}|\mu_i, W_i W_i^T + \sigma^2) \\ p(X_{i,j}|\mathcal{T}_j, \mu_i, W_i, \sigma^2) = \mathcal{N}(X_{i,j}|W_i\mathcal{T}_j + \mu_i, \sigma^2) \end{cases} . \tag{4}$$

The joint probability distribution $p(X_{i,j}, \mathcal{T}_j, \mu_i, W_i, \sigma^2)$ can be derived from (4) and Bayes' joint probability rule as

$$p(X_{i,j}, \mathcal{T}_j, \mu_i, W_i, \sigma^2) = \frac{1}{(2\pi\sigma^2)^{\frac{M}{2}}} exp\frac{(X_{i,j} - W_i\mathcal{T}_j - \mu_i)^2}{-2\sigma^2} \frac{1}{(2\pi)^{\frac{q}{2}}} exp\frac{-\mathcal{T}_j^T\mathcal{T}_j}{2} \tag{5}$$

Define the set $\eta = \{(i,j)|1 \le i \le M, 1 \le j \le N, X_{i,j} \neq NaN\}$. The log-likelihood of the joint multivariate Gaussian probability distribution of (5) is calculated over all available observations as

$$\begin{aligned} ln(p(X_{i,j}, \mathcal{T}_j|\mu_i, W_i, \sigma^2)) &= \sum_{i,j\in\eta}\sum [ln(p(X_{i,j}|\mathcal{T}_j, \mu_i, W_i, \sigma^2)) + lnp(\mathcal{T}_j)] \\ &= \sum_{i,j\in\eta}\sum \frac{-M}{2} ln(2\pi\sigma^2) - \frac{q}{2} ln(2\pi) - \frac{(X_{i,j} - W_i\mathcal{T}_j - \mu_i)^2}{2\sigma^2} - \frac{\mathcal{T}_j^T\mathcal{T}_j}{2} \end{aligned} \tag{6}$$

where the log-likelihood (6) is defined for all available observations $X_{i,j}, i,j \in \eta$. By applying the expectation operation with respect to the posterior probability distribution over all latent variables $\mathcal{T}_j, j \in \eta_i$, where $\eta_i = \{j|1 \le j \le N, X_{i,j} \neq NaN\}$, (6) becomes

$$\begin{aligned} \mathbb{E}\{\mathcal{L}\} = -\sum_{i,j\in\eta}\sum & \frac{M}{2} ln(\sigma^2) + \frac{1}{2}\mathbb{E}\{\mathcal{T}_j^T\mathcal{T}_j\} + \frac{1}{2\sigma^2}(X_{i,j} - \mu_i)^2 \\ & - \frac{1}{\sigma^2}\mathbb{E}\{\mathcal{T}_j^T\}W_i^T(X_{i,j} - \mu_i) + \frac{1}{2\sigma^2}\mathbb{E}\{\mathcal{T}_j^T\mathcal{T}_j\}W_iW_i^T \end{aligned} \tag{7}$$

Maximizing (7) is feasible by setting all partial derivatives $\frac{\partial\mathbb{E}\{\mathcal{L}\}}{\partial\sigma^2}$, $\frac{\partial\mathbb{E}\{\mathcal{L}\}}{\partial\mu_i^2}$, and $\frac{\partial\mathbb{E}\{\mathcal{L}\}}{\partial W_i^2}, i = 1, \ldots, M, j = 1, \ldots, N$ to zero [34].

$$\begin{aligned} Cvar_{\mathcal{T}_j} &= \frac{\sigma^2}{(\sigma^2 I_q + \sum_{i\in\eta_j} W_iW_i^T)} \\ \mu_{\mathcal{T}_j} &= \frac{Cvar_{\mathcal{T}_j}}{\sigma^2} \sum_{i\in\eta_j} W_i^T(X_{i,j} - \mu_i) \\ \mu_i &= \frac{1}{|\eta_i|} \sum_{j\in\eta_i} [X_{i,j} - W_i\mu_{\mathcal{T}_j}] \\ W_i &= \frac{1}{\sum_{j\in\eta_i}[\mu_{\mathcal{T}_j}\mu_{\mathcal{T}_j}^T + Cvar_{\mathcal{T}_j}]} \sum_{j\in\eta_i} \mu_{\mathcal{T}_j}(X_{i,j} - \mu_i) \\ \sigma^2 &= \frac{1}{|\eta|} \sum_{i,j\in\eta} [(X_{i,j} - W_i\mu_{\mathcal{T}_j} - \mu_i)^2 + W_iCvar_{\mathcal{T}_j}W_i^T] \end{aligned} \tag{8}$$

Parameters μ_i, σ^2, and W_i in (8) are updated recursively until they converge to their final values. The final estimation of missing CGM samples is obtained by performing a diagonal averaging of the reconstructed lagged matrix $\widehat{X} \in \mathbb{R}^{M\times N}$ over rows/columns filled with CGM values. Long gaps in CGM recordings might exist in the data, and imputing their values causes problems in accuracy and reliability. Therefore, CGM gaps of no more than twenty-five consecutive missing samples (approximately two hours) are imputed by PPCA.

3.2. Outlier Removal

Signal reconciliation and outlier removal are necessary to avoid misleading interpretation of data and biased results, and to improve the quality of CGM observations. As a simple outlier removal approach for a variable with Gaussian distribution, observations outside ± 2.72 standard deviations from the mean, known as inner Tukey fences, can be labeled as outliers and extreme values [35]. The probability distribution of the CGM data shows a skewed distribution compared to the Gaussian probability distribution. Thus, labeling samples as outliers only based on their probability of occurrence is not the proper way of removing extreme values from the CGM data since it can cause a loss of useful CGM information, specifically during hypoglycemia ($CGM < 70$ mg/dL) and hyperglycemia ($CGM > 180$ mg/dL) events. As another alternative, extreme values and spikes in the CGM data can be labeled from the prior knowledge and by utilizing other feature variables, namely: "Smbg", "Nutrition.carbohydrate", "Bolus", and "Activity.duration". Algorithm 1 is proposed to remove outliers from CGM values. Usually, BGC is slightly different from the recordings of the CGM signal because of the delay between BGC and the subcutaneous glucose concentration measured by the CGM device and sensor noise. The noisy signal can deteriorate the performance of data-driven models. Therefore, Algorithm 2, which is based on eigendecomposition of the Hankel matrix of CGM values, is used to reduce the noise in the CGM recordings.

Algorithm 1 Outlier rejection from CGM readings

procedure OUTLIERREJECTION($CGM, Smbg, CHO, AD, Ins_{Bolus}$)
  for $i = 1 : N$ **do** ▷ Removing samples outside of the calibration range
    if $CGM_k > 400$ mg/dL or $CGM_k < 0$ mg/dL **then**
      $CGM_k \leftarrow NaN$
    end if
  end for
  for $i = 2 : N$ **do**
    $\Delta CGM_k \leftarrow CGM_k - CGM_{k-1}$
    if $\Delta CGM_k > 30$ mg/dL & all $(\{CHO_k, \ldots, CHO_{k-9}\} == 0)$ **then**
      $CGM_k \leftarrow$ NaN
    end if
    if $\Delta CGM_k < 30$ mg/dL & all $(\{Ins_{Bolus,k}, \ldots, Ins_{Bolus,k-6}\} == 0)$ **then**
      $CGM_k \leftarrow$ NaN
    end if
    if $\Delta CGM_k < 30$ mg/dL & all $(\{AD_k, \ldots, AD_{k-6}\} == 0)$ **then**
      $CGM_k \leftarrow$ NaN
    end if
    if $Smbg_k \neq$ NaN & $CGM_k \neq$ NaN & abs$(Smbg_k - CGM_k) > 18$ mg/dL **then**
      $CGM_k \leftarrow$ NaN
    end if
  end for
  return CGM
end procedure

Algorithm 2 Smoothing CGM recordings

procedure CGMDENOISING(CGM) ▷ Smoothing CGM recordings
  $Q_i = [CGM_d, \ldots, CGM_{d+q_i-1}]$ ▷ $Q_i \in \mathbb{R}^{q_i}$ is ith consecutive CGM recordings
  $q_i \leftarrow |Q_i|,\ p_i \leftarrow floor(\frac{q_i}{2}),\ w_i \leftarrow q_i - p_i + 1$
  $[U_i, S_i, V_i] = SVD(A_i)$ ▷ $A_i \in \mathbb{R}^{w_i \times p_i}$ is the Hankel matrix made of Q_i
  $\widehat{S}_i \leftarrow zeros(p_i, p_i)$
  $\eta \leftarrow \frac{cumsum([s_1, \ldots, s_{p_i}])}{sum([s_1, \ldots, s_{p_i}])}$ ▷ $s_j > 0$ are eigenvalues of S_i in descending order
  for j=1 : p_i **do**
    if $\eta_j > 0.95$ **then**
      $\widehat{S}_i(j,j) \leftarrow 0$
    else
      $\widehat{S}_i(j,j) \leftarrow S_i(j,j)$
    end if
  end for
  $\widehat{A}_i = U_i \widehat{S}_i V_i^T$
  $\widehat{Q}_i \leftarrow \text{Diagonalaveraging}\left(\widehat{A}_i\right)$ ▷ $\widehat{Q}_i = \left[C\widehat{G}M_d, \ldots, C\widehat{G}M_{d+q_i-1}\right]$
  return $C\widehat{G}M$
end procedure

3.3. Feature Extraction

Converting raw data into informative feature variables or extracting new features is an essential step of data preprocessing. In this study, four groups of feature variables, including frequency domain, statistical domain, nonlinear domain, and model-based features, were calculated and added to each dataset to enhance the prediction power of models. The summarized description of each group of features and the number of past samples required for their calculation are listed in Table 3.

A qualitative trend analysis of variables can extract different patterns caused by external factors within a specified time [36,37]. A pairwise multiplication of the sign and magnitude of the first and second derivatives of CGM values indicates the carbohydrate intake [38,39], exogenous insulin injection, and physical activity. Therefore, the first and second derivatives of CGM values, calculated by the fourth-order backward difference method, were added as feature variables. The sign and magnitude product of the first and second derivatives of CGM, their covariance, Pearson correlation coefficient, and Gaussian kernel similarity were extracted. Statistical feature variables, e.g., mean, standard deviation, variance, skewness, etc., were obtained from the specified time window of CGM values. Similar to the first and second derivatives of CGM values, a set of feature variables, including covariance and correlation coefficients, from pairs of CGM values and derivatives was extracted and augmented to the data.

As a result of the daily repetition in the trends of CGM and glycemic events and the longer time window of CGM values, samples collected during the last twenty-four hours were used for frequency-domain feature extraction. Therefore, magnitudes and frequencies of the top three dominant peaks in the power spectrum of CGM values, conveying past long-term variation of the BGC, were included in the set of feature maps.

Table 3. The type and definition of the extracted feature variables and the length of time window required for their calculations.

Domain	Feature Description	No. of Required Samples
Time	First derivative calculated by 4th backward differences	5
	Second derivative calculated by 4th backward differences	6
Nonlinear	Sign-product of the 1st and the 2nd derivatives	6
	Magnitude-product of the 1st and the 2nd derivatives	6
Statistical	Statistical measures, namely mean, variance, median, etc., of windowed CGM values	24
	Pair-wise covariance and correlation coefficient between CGM and its 1st and 2nd derivatives	24
Frequency	The magnitudes and frequencies of three dominant peaks in the power spectrum of CGM	288
Model-based	Plasma insulin concentration (PIC) and gut absorption rate (U_g) [40,41].	1

The plasma insulin concentration (PIC) is another feature variable that informs about the carbohydrate intake information and exogenous insulin administration. PIC accounts for the accumulation of subcutaneously injected insulin within the bloodstream, which is gradually consumed by the body to enable the absorption of carbohydrates released from the gastrointestinal track to various cells and tissues. Usually, dynamic physiological models are used to describe and model the glucose and insulin concentration dynamics in diabetes. The main idea of estimating PIC from physiological models stems from predicting the intermediate state variables of physiological models by designing a state observer and utilizing the total infused insulin and carbohydrate intake as model inputs, and CGM values as the output of the model [40–42]. In this work, the estimation of the PIC and glucose appearance rate were obtained from a physiological model known as Hovorka's model [43]. Equation (9) presents this nonlinear physiological (compartment) model:

$$
\begin{aligned}
\frac{dS_1(t)}{dt} &= Ins(t) - \frac{S_1(t)}{t_{max,I}} \\
\frac{dS_2(t)}{dt} &= \frac{S_1(t)}{t_{max,I}} - \frac{S_2(t)}{t_{max,I}} \\
\frac{dI(t)}{dt} &= \frac{S_2(t)}{t_{max,I}V_I} - K_e I(t) \\
\frac{dx_1(t)}{dt} &= k_{b,1}I(t) - k_{a,1}x_1(t) \\
\frac{dx_2(t)}{dt} &= k_{b,2}I(t) - k_{a,2}x_2(t) \\
\frac{dx_3(t)}{dt} &= k_{b,3}I(t) - k_{a,3}x_3(t) \\
\frac{dQ_1(t)}{dt} &= U_g(t) - F_{0,1}^c(t) - F_R(t) - x_1(t)Q_1(t) + k_{12}Q_2(t) + EGP_0(1 - x_3(t)) \\
\frac{dQ_2(t)}{dt} &= x_1(t)Q_1(t) - (k_{12} + x_2(t))Q_2(t) \\
\frac{dG_{sub}(t)}{dt} &= \frac{1}{\tau}\left(\frac{Q_1(t)}{V_g} - G_{sub}(t)\right)
\end{aligned}
\tag{9}
$$

Model (9) comprises four sub-models, describing the action of insulin on glucose dynamics, the insulin absorption dynamics, plasma–interstitial-tissue glucose concentration dynamics, and the blood glucose dynamics.The state variables of (9), the nominal values of the parameters, and their units are listed in Table 4 [43].

Table 4. The description of variables and parameters and the nominal values of parameters in Hovorka's model [43].

Variable/Parameter	Description	Value/Unit
$S_1(t), S_2(t)$	Two-compartment chain representing absorption of subcutaneously administered short-acting insulin	mU
$Ins(t)$	Subcutaneously infused insulin	mU min^{-1}
$I(t)$	Plasma insulin concentration (PIC)	mU L^{-1}
$x_1(t)$	The remote effect of insulin on glucose distribution	min^{-1}
$x_2(t)$	The remote effect of insulin on glucose disposal	min^{-1}
$x_3(t)$	The remote effect of insulin on endogenous glucose production (EGP)	min^{-1}
$Q_1(t)$	The mass of glucose in accessible compartments	mmol
$Q_2(t)$	The mass of glucose in non-accessible compartments	mmol
$G_{sub}(t)$	Measurable subcutaneous glucose concentration	mmol L^{-1}
$U_G(t)$	Gut absorption rate	mmol min^{-1}
K_e	The fractional elimination rate of PIC	0.138 min^{-1}
$k_{a,1}$		0.006 min^{-1}
$k_{a,2}$	The deactivation rate constants	0.06 min^{-1}
$k_{a,3}$		0.03 min^{-1}
S^f_{ID}	The sensitivity of insulin disposal	0.00082 L min^{-1} mU^{-1}
S^f_{IT}	The sensitivity of insulin distribution	0.00512 L min^{-1} mU^{-1}
S^f_{IE}	The sensitivity of EGP	0.052 L mU^{-1}
$k_{b,1}$		$k_{a,1} \times S^f_{IT}$
$k_{b,2}$	The activation rate constants	$k_{a,2} \times S^f_{ID}$
$k_{b,3}$		$k_{a,3} \times S^f_{IE}$
EGP_0	EGP extrapolated to zero insulin concentration	0.0161 mmol kg^{-1} min^{-1}
k_{12}	The transfer rate constant from the non-accessible to the accessible compartment	0.066 min^{-1}
τ	The time constant of subcutaneous glucose concentration dynamic	min
V_g	The glucose distribution volume in the accessible compartment	$0.16 \times BW(L)$
V_I	The insulin distribution volume in the accessible compartment	$0.12 \times BW(L)$
$F_R(t)$	The renal glucose clearance above the glucose threshold of 9 mmol L^{-1}	$\begin{cases} 0.003(G_{sub}-9), G_{sub} \geq 9 \\ 0, G_{sub} < 9 \end{cases}$
F_{01}	Non-insulin-dependent glucose flux	0.0097 mmol kg^{-1} min^{-1}
$F^c_{0,1}(t)$	The total non-insulin-dependent glucose flux (mmol min^{-1})	$\begin{cases} F_{01}, G_{sub} \geq 4.5 \\ F_{01}(G_{sub}/4.5), G_{sub} < 4.5 \end{cases}$

Body weight has a significant effect on the variations in the PIC and other state variables as it is used for determining the amount of exogenous insulin to be infused. Although estimating body weight as an augmented state variable of the insulin-CGM model is an effective strategy to cope with the problem of unavailable demographic information, estimating body weight from the total amount of daily administered insulin is a more reliable approach. As reported in various studies, the total daily injected insulin can have a range of 0.4–1.0 units kg^{-1} day^{-1} [44–46]. A fair estimation of body weight can be obtained by calculating the most common amount of injected basal/bolus insulin for each subject and using a conversion factor of 0.5 units kg^{-1} day^{-1} as a rule of thumb to estimate the body weight.

The insulin–glucose dynamics (9) in discrete-time format are given by

$$\begin{aligned} X'_{k+1} &= f'(X'_k, U_k) + G_k\omega_k, & \omega_k &\approx N(0,Q) \\ Y'_k &= h'(X'_k) + \nu_k, & \nu_k &\approx N(0,R) \end{aligned} \tag{10}$$

where $X'_k = [S_{1,k}, S_{2,k}, I_k, x_{1,k}, x_{2,k}x_{3,k}, Q_{1,k}, Q_{2,k}, G_{sub,k}, t_{max,I,k}, k_{e,k}, U_{G,k}] \in \mathcal{R}^{n_x}$ denotes the extended state variables and U_k is the total injected exogenous insulin. Symbols ω_k and ν_k denote zero-mean Gaussian random process and measurement noises (respectively), representing any other uncertainty and model mismatch that are not taken into account. Further, $Q \in \mathcal{R}^{n_x \times n_x}$ and $R \in \mathcal{R}$ represent the positive definite system uncertainty and measurement noise covariance matrices, respectively.

Tracking the dynamics of the internal state variables of the model (10) is feasible by using a class of sequential Monte Carlo algorithms known as particle filters. A generic form of the particle filter algorithm proposed by [47] with an efficient adaptive Metropolis–Hastings resampling strategy developed in [48] was employed to predict the trajectory of the PIC and other state variables. In order to avoid any misleading state estimations, each state variable was subjected to a constraint to maintain all estimations within meaningful intervals [41].

3.4. Feature Selection and Dimensionality Reduction

Reducing the number of redundant feature variables lowers the computational burden of their extraction and hinders over-parameterized modeling. In this work, a two-step feature selection procedure was used to obtain the optimal subset of feature variables that boost the efficiency of the classifier the most. In the first step, the deviance statistic test was performed to filter out features with low significance (p-value > 0.05). In the second step, the training split of all datasets was used in the wrapper feature selection strategy to maximize the accuracy of the classifier in estimating the glycemic events. A sequential floating forward selection (SFFS) approach [49] was applied on a random forest estimator with thirty decision tree classifiers with a maximum depth of six layers to sort out features with the most predictive power in descending order. Consequently, the top twenty feature variables with the highest contribution to the classification accuracy enhancement were used for model development.

4. Detection and Classification Methods

Detecting the occurrence of events causing large glycemic variations requires solving a supervised classification problem. Hence, all samples required labeling using the information provided in the datasets, specifically using variables "Activity.duration" and "Nutrition.carbohydrate". In order to determine the index sets of each class, let N be the total number of samples and $T(k) = ceil\big(AD(k)/(3 \times 10^5)\big)$ be the sample duration of physical activity at each sampling time k. Define sets of sample indexes as:

$$\begin{cases} Label.Index_{\{1,1\}} := & \{i|k \le i \le k+T(k)-1, \quad k=1,\dots,N, \quad T(k) \neq 0, \\ & Nutrition.carbohydrate(j) \neq 0, \quad j=k+1,\dots,k+T(k)\} \\ Label.Index_{\{0,1\}} := & \{i|k \le i \le k+T(k)-1, \quad k=1,\dots,N, \quad T(k) \neq 0, \\ & Nutrition.carbohydrate(j) = 0, \quad j=k+1,\dots,k+T(k)\} \\ Label.Index_{\{1,0\}} := & \{k|1 \le k \le N, \quad T(k)=0, \quad Nutrition.carbohydrate(k) \neq 0\} \\ Label.Index_{\{0,0\}} := & \{k|1 \le k \le N, \quad T(k)=0, \quad Nutrition.carbohydrate(k) = 0\} \end{cases} \tag{11}$$

The label indexes defined by (11) corresponds to classes "Meal and Exercise", "no Meal but Exercise", "no Exercise but Meal", "neither Meal nor Exercise", respectively.

Four different configurations of the RNN models were studied to assess the accuracy and performance of each in estimating the joint probability of the carbohydrate intake and physical activity. All four models used 24 past samples of the selected feature variables, and event estimations were performed one sample backward. Estimating the co-occurrences of the external disturbances should be performed at least one step backward as the effect of disturbance variables needs to be seen first, before parameter adjustment and event prediction can be made.

Since the imputation of gaps with a high number of consecutive missing values adversely affects the prediction of meal–exercise classes, all remaining samples with missing values after the data imputation step were excluded from parameter optimization. Excluding missing values inside the input tensor can be carried out either by using a placeholder for missing samples and filtering samples through masking layer or by manually removing incomplete samples.

Each recurrent NN models used in this study encompasses a type of LSTM units [50] (see Figure 2) to capture the time-dependent patterns in the data. The first NN model consists of a masking layer to filter out unimputed samples, followed by a LSTM layer, two dense layers, and a softmax layer to estimate the probability of each class. The LSTM and dense layers undergo training with dropout and parameter regularization strategies to avoid the drastic growth of hyperparameters. Additionally, the recurrent information stream in the LSTM layer was randomly ignored in the calculation at each run. At each layer of the network, the magnitude of both weights and intercept coefficients was penalized by adding a L_1 regularizer term to the loss function. The rectified linear unit (ReLu) activation function was chosen as a nonlinear component in all layers. The input variables of the regular LSTM network will have the shape of $N \times m \times L$, which denotes the size of samples, the size of lagged samples, and the number of feature variables, respectively.

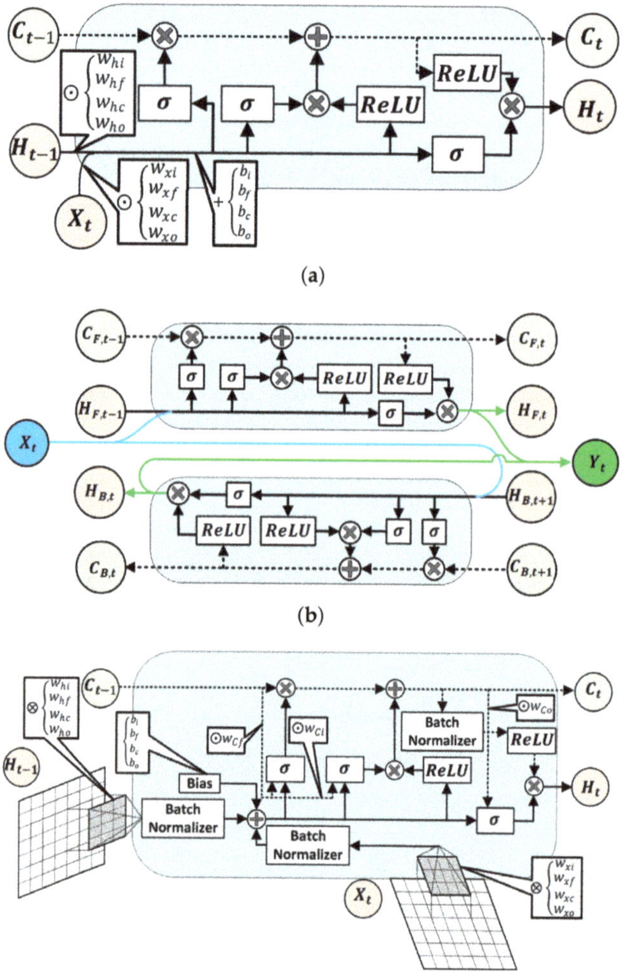

(c)

Figure 2. Structures of a regular LSTM unit (**a**), a Bi-LSTM unit (**b**), and schematic demonstration of a 2D ConvLSTM cell (**c**) [50].

The second model encompasses a series of two 1D convolution layers, each one followed by a max pool layer for downsampling feature maps. The output of the second max pool layer was flattened to achieve a time-series extracted feature to feed to to the LSTM layer. A dense layer after LSTM was added to the model and the joint probability of events was estimated by calculating the output of the softmax layer. Like the first RNN model, the ReLU activation function was employed in all layers to capture the nonlinearity in the data. A L_1 regularization method was applied to all hyperparameters of the model. Adding convolution layers with repeated operations to an RNN model paves the way for extracting features for the sequence regression or classification problem. This approach has shown a breakthrough in visual time-series prediction from the sequence of images or videos for various problems, such as activity recognition, textual description, and audio and word sequence prediction [51,52]. Time-distributed convolution layers scan and elicit features from each block of the sequence of the data [53]. Therefore, each sample was reshaped into $m \times n \times L$, with $n = 1$ blocks at each sample.

The third classifier has a 2D convolutional LSTM (ConvLSTM) layer, one dropout layer, two dense layers, and a softmax layer for the probability estimation of each class from the sequences of data. A two-dimensional ConvLSTM structure was designed to capture both temporal and spatial correlation in the data, moving pictures in particular, by employing a convolution operation in both input-to-state and state-to-state transitions [50]. In comparison to a regular LSTM cell, ConvLSTMs perform the convolution operation by an internal multiplication of inputs and hidden states into kernel filter matrices (Figure 2c). Similar to previously discussed models, the L_1 regularization constraint and ReLU activation function were considered in constructing the ConvLSTM model. A two-dimensional ConvLSTM import sample of spatiotemporal data in the format of $m \times s \times n \times L$, where $s = 1$ and $n = 1$, stands for the size of the rows and columns of each tensor, and $L = 20$ is the number of channels/features on the data [54].

Finally, the last model comprises two 1D convolution layers, two max pooling layers, a flatten layer, a bidirectional LSTM (Bi-LSTM) layer, a dense layer, and a soft max layer to predict classes. Bi-LSTM units capture the dependency in the sequence of the data in two directions. Hence, as a comparison to a regular LSTM memory unit, Bi-LSTM requires reversely duplicating the same LSTM unit and employing a merging strategy to calculate the output of the cell [55]. The use of this approach was primarily observed in speech recognition tasks, where, instead of real-time interpretation, the whole sequence of the data was analyzed and its superior performance over the regular LSTM was justified [56]. The joint estimation of glycemic events was made one step backward. Therefore, the whole sequence of features were recorded first, and the use of an RNN model with Bi-LSTM units for the detection of unannounced disturbances was quite justifiable. The tensor of input data is similar to LSTM with 1D convolutional layers. Figure 2 is the schematic diagram of a regular LSTM, a Bi-LSTM, and a ConvLSTM unit.

Figure 3 depicts the structure of the four RNN models to estimate the probability of meal consumption, physical activity, and their concurrent occurrence. The main difference between models (a) and (b) in Figure 3 is the convolution and max-pooling layers added before the LSTM layer to extract features map from time series data. Although adding convolutional blocks to an RNN model increases the number of learnable parameters, including weights, biases, and kernel filters, calculating temporal feature maps from input data better discriminates the target classes.

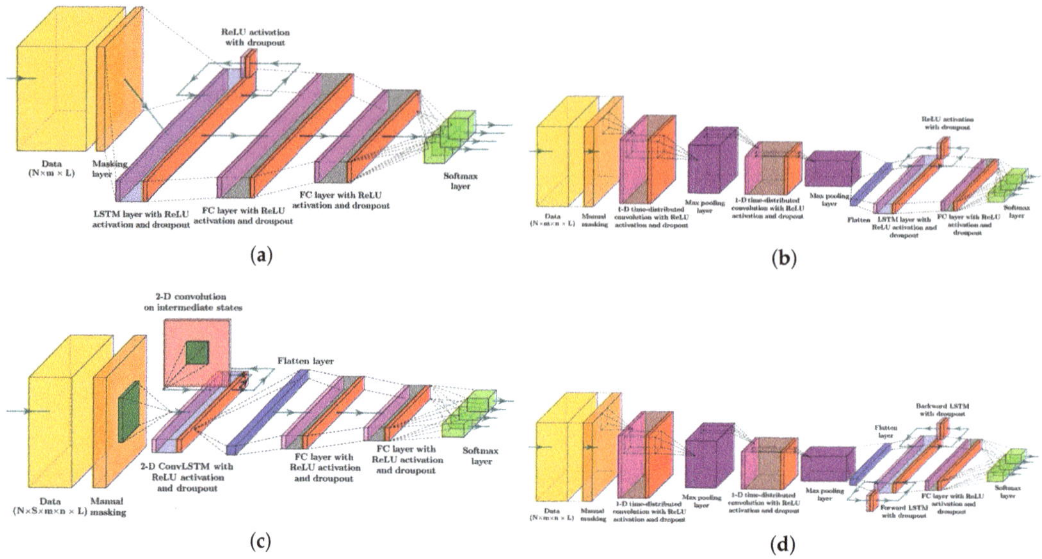

Figure 3. Systematic structures of the different RNN models included in the study: (**a**) LSTM NN model, (**b**) LSTM with 1D convolutional layers, (**c**) 2D ConvLSTM NN model, and (**d**) Bi-LSTM with 1D convolutional layers. Color dictionary: Yellow: tensor of data, Orange: Masking to exclude missing samples, Magenta: Relu activation, Light blue: LSTM layer, Red: dropout, Grey: dense layer, Green: softmax activation, Blue: flatten layer, Purple: max pool layer, Dark green: kernel filter, Light red: the matrix of intermediate states.

5. Case Study

Eleven datasets containing CGM-sensor–insulin-pump, physical activity, and carbohydrate intake information were selected randomly from subject records for a case study. Data imputation and reconciliation, RNN training, and an evaluation of the results were conducted individually for each subject. Hence, the RNN models were personalized, using only that person's data. All datasets were preprocessed by the procedure elaborated on in the data preprocessing section and feature variables were rescaled to have zero-mean and unit variance. Stratified six-fold cross-validation was applied to 87.5% of samples of each dataset to reduce the variance of predictions. Weight values proportional to the inversion of class sizes were assigned to the corresponding samples to avoid biased predictions caused by imbalanced samples in each class. In order to better assess the performance of each model and to avoid the effects of randomization in the initialization step of the back propagation algorithm, each model was trained five times with different random seeds. Hyperparameters of all models were obtained through an adaptive moment estimation (Adam) optimization algorithm, and 2% of the training sample size was chosen as the size of the training batches. In model training with different random seeds, the number of adjustable parameters, including weights, biases, the size and number of filter kernels, and the learning rate remained constant.

One difficulty associated with convolution layers in models (b) and (d) is the optimization of the hyperparameters of the convolutional layers. Usually, RNN models with convolution layers require a relatively high computation time. As a solution, learning rates with small values are preferred for networks with convolutional layers since they lead to a more optimal solution compared to large learning weights, which may result in non-optimality and instability.

The data preprocessing part of the work was conducted in a Matlab 2019a environment, and Keras/Keras-gpu 2.3.1 were used to construct and train all RNN models. Keras is a high-class API library with Tensorflow as the backend; all are available in the Python environment. We used two computational resources for data preparations and model training. Table 5 provides the details of hardware resources.

Table 5. Hardware specifications.

	Data Preprocessing Task	Model Training Task
CPU Model	Intel i9 9900 k	Intel i7 8700 k
CPU Frequency	3.6–5.0 GHz	3.7–4.7 GHz
Threads	16	12
RAM Capacity	64 GB (DDR IV)	32 GB (DDR IV)
Graphics Processor	RTX 2080 Ti × 2	GTX 1050 Ti (GDDR5)
Graphics Memory	11 GB	4 GB
Clock Frequency	1545–1750 MHz	1290–1392 MHz
Cuda Kernels	4352	768

6. Discussion of Results

Each classifier was evaluated by testing a 12.5% split of all sensor and insulin pump recordings for each subject, corresponding to 3–12 weeks of data for a subject. The average and the standard deviation of performance indexes are reported in Table 6. The lowest performance indexes were achieved by 2D ConvLSTM models. Bi-LSTM with 1D convolution layer RNN models achieve the highest accuracy for six subjects out of eleven, and LSTM with 1D convolution RNN for three subjects. Bi-LSTM with 1D convolution layer RNN models outperformed other models for four subjects, with weighted F1 scores ranging from 91.41–96.26%. Similarly, LSTM models with 1D convolution layers achieved the highest weighted F1 score for another four subjects, with score values within 93.65–96.06%. Glycemic events for the rest of the three subjects showed to be better predicted by regular LSTM models, with a weighted F1 score between 93.31–95.18%. This indicates that 1D convolution improves both the accuracy and F1 scores for most of the subjects. Based on the number of adjustable parameters for the four different RNN models used for a specific subject, LSTMs are the most computational demanding blocks in the model. To assess the computational load of developing the various RNN models, we compared the number of learnable parameters (details provided in Supplementary Materials). These values can be highly informative, as the number of dropouts in each model and the number of learnable parameters at each epoch (iteration) are invariant.

A comparison between 1D conv-LSTM and 1D-Bi-LSTM for one randomly selected subject shows that the number of learnable parameters increases by at least 54%, mainly stemming from an extra embedded LSTM in the bidirectional layer (Table S1). While comparing adjustable parameters may not be the most accurate way of determining the computational loads for training the models, they provide a good reference to compare the computational burden of different RNN models.

Figure 4 displays a random day selected from the test data to compare the effectiveness of each RNN model in detecting meal and exercise disturbances. Among four possible realizations for the occurrence of events, detecting joint events, $Class_{1,1}$, is more challenging as it usually shows overlaps with $Class_{0,1}$ and $Class_{1,0}$. Another reason for the lower detection is the lack of enough information on $Class_{1,1}$, knowing that people would usually rather have a small snack before and after exercise sessions over having a rescue carbohydrate during physical activity. Furthermore, the AID systems used by subjects automatically record only CGM and insulin infusion values, and meal and physical activity sessions need to be manually entered to the device, which is, at times, an action that may be forgotten by the subject. Meal consumption and physical activity are two prominent disturbances that disrupt BGC regulation, but their opposite effect on BGC makes the prediction of $Class_{1,1}$ less critical than each of meal intake or only physical activity classes.

Table 6. The average performance indexes of LSTM, LSTM with 1D convolution layers, 2D ConvLSTM, and Bi-LSTM with 1D convolution layers RNN models for the event detection problem. Standard deviations are given in parentheses and values with bold notation denote the highest performance indexes.

Subject No.	Model	Total Accuracy (%)	Weighted Recall (%)	Weighted Precision (%)	Weighted F1 Score (%)
1	$LSTM$	92.03 (0.37)	92.03 (0.37)	94.59 (0.29)	93.06 (0.30)
	$LSTM(1D\ Convolution)$	94.61 (0.15)	94.61 (0.15)	**97.67 (0.20)**	**96.06 (0.13)**
	$2D\ ConvLSTM$	89.89 (0.27)	89.89 (0.27)	94.36 (0.16)	91.73 (0.13)
	$Bi-LSTM(1D\ Convolution)$	**94.72 (0.31)**	**94.72 (0.31)**	96.85 (0.34)	95.68 (0.29)
2	$LSTM$	93.17 (0.21)	93.17 (0.21)	96.17 (0.09)	94.37 (0.10)
	$LSTM(1D\ Convolution)$	**94.69 (0.33)**	**94.69 (0.33)**	96.58 (0.20)	**95.31 (0.16)**
	$2D\ ConvLSTM$	91.29 (0.38)	91.29 (0.38)	95.90 (0.20)	93.20 (0.17)
	$Bi-LSTM(1D\ Convolution)$	93.56 (0.21)	93.56 (0.21)	**96.99 (0.25)**	95.17 (0.11)
3	$LSTM$	89.93 (0.22)	89.93 (0.22)	**93.98 (0.24)**	91.38 (0.22)
	$LSTM(1D\ Convolution)$	88.98 (0.28)	88.98 (0.28)	93.53 (0.09)	90.61 (0.22)
	$2D\ ConvLSTM$	88.40 (0.25)	88.40 (0.25)	93.13 (0.12)	90.21 (0.11)
	$Bi-LSTM(1D\ Convolution)$	**89.98 (0.17)**	**89.98 (0.17)**	93.87 (0.05)	**91.41 (0.10)**
4	$LSTM$	92.55 (0.27)	92.55 (0.27)	95.49 (0.09)	93.48 (0.17)
	$LSTM(1D\ Convolution)$	**94.67 (0.31)**	**94.67 (0.31)**	**96.62 (0.17)**	**95.34 (0.22)**
	$2D\ ConvLSTM$	88.87 (0.33)	88.87 (0.33)	94.61 (0.16)	90.93 (0.16)
	$Bi-LSTM(1D\ Convolution)$	94.49 (0.28)	94.49 (0.28)	96.47 (0.25)	95.13 (0.15)
5	$LSTM$	**94.41 (0.21)**	**94.41 (0.21)**	96.46 (0.10)	**95.18 (0.13)**
	$LSTM(1D\ Convolution)$	91.65 (0.26)	91.65 (0.26)	96.16 (0.12)	93.38 (0.22)
	$2D\ ConvLSTM$	89.81 (0.18)	89.81 (0.18)	95.62 (0.10)	92.02 (0.17)
	$Bi-LSTM(1D\ Convolution)$	92.66 (0.21)	92.66 (0.21)	**96.93 (0.28)**	94.73 (0.20)
6	$LSTM$	94.50 (0.27)	94.50 (0.27)	95.15 (0.22)	94.78 (0.15)
	$LSTM(1D\ Convolution)$	95.67 (0.26)	95.67 (0.26)	96.69 (0.09)	95.04 (0.14)
	$2D\ ConvLSTM$	91.10 (0.25)	91.10 (0.25)	94.37 (0.10)	92.60 (0.16)
	$Bi-LSTM(1D\ Convolution)$	**95.86 (0.17)**	**95.86 (0.17)**	**96.72 (0.21)**	**96.26 (0.11)**
7	$LSTM$	**91.81 (0.22)**	**91.81 (0.22)**	95.43 (0.22)	**93.31 (0.16)**
	$LSTM(1D\ Convolution)$	89.85 (0.22)	89.85 (0.22)	94.19 (0.17)	91.68 (0.14)
	$2D\ ConvLSTM$	87.47 (0.27)	87.47 (0.27)	**99.83 (0.22)**	93.15 (0.18)
	$Bi-LSTM(1D\ Convolution)$	90.03 (0.24)	90.03 (0.24)	95.01 (0.16)	92.32 (0.17)
8	$LSTM$	89.19 (0.22)	89.19 (0.22)	**99.68(0.27)**	**94.13 (0.16)**
	$LSTM(1D\ Convolution)$	90.99 (0.18)	90.99 (0.18)	97.68 (0.19)	94.11 (0.20)
	$2D\ ConvLSTM$	83.92 (0.28)	83.92 (0.28)	94.60 (0.33)	88.73 (0.12)
	$Bi-LSTM(1D\ Convolution)$	**91.42 (0.30)**	**91.42 (0.30)**	95.17 (0.37)	93.12 (0.12)
9	$LSTM$	92.70 (0.18)	92.70 (0.18)	96.53 (0.28)	94.10 (0.12)
	$LSTM(1D\ Convolution)$	93.10 (0.32)	93.10 (0.32)	95.70 (0.31)	94.10 (0.30)
	$2D\ ConvLSTM$	91.56 (0.34)	91.56 (0.34)	94.81 (0.30)	93.10 (0.31)
	$Bi-LSTM(1D\ Convolution)$	**93.33 (0.27)**	**93.33 (0.27)**	**97.24 (0.21)**	**95.21 (0.22)**
10	$LSTM$	89.30 (0.34)	89.30 (0.34)	95.57 (0.08)	91.73 (0.22)
	$LSTM(1D\ Convolution)$	**91.89 (0.25)**	**91.89 (0.25)**	**96.14 (0.08)**	**93.65 (0.12)**
	$2D\ ConvLSTM$	85.87 (0.27)	85.87 (0.27)	95.69 (0.08)	89.73 (0.22)
	$Bi-LSTM(1D\ Convolution)$	89.51 (0.25)	89.51 (0.25)	96.11 (0.03)	92.30 (0.17)
11	$LSTM$	87.17 (0.44)	87.17 (0.44)	92.26 (0.12)	89.10 (0.23)
	$LSTM(1D\ Convolution)$	89.41 (0.35)	89.41 (0.35)	94.39 (0.06)	91.19 (0.23)
	$2D\ ConvLSTM$	86.90 (0.29)	86.90 (0.29)	94.84 (0.21)	90.05 (0.25)
	$Bi-LSTM(1D\ Convolution)$	**89.62 (0.15)**	**89.62 (0.15)**	**96.51 (0.13)**	**92.64 (0.14)**

The confusion matrices of the classification results for one of the subjects (No. 2) are summarized in Table 7. As can be observed from Figure 4 and Table 7, detecting $Class_{0,1}$ (physical activity) is more challenging in comparison to the carbohydrate intake ($Class_{1,0}$) and $Class_{0,0}$ (no meal or exercise). One reason for this difficulty is the lack of biosignal information, such as 3D accelerometer, blood volume pulse, and heart rate data. Some erroneous detections, such as confusing meals and exercise, are dangerous, since meals necessitate an insulin bolus while exercise lowers BGC, and the elimination of insulin infusion and/or increase in target BGC are needed. RNNs with LSTM and 1D convolution layers provide the best overall performance in minimizing such confusions: two meals events are classified as exercise (0.003%) and eight exercise events are classified as meals (0.125%).

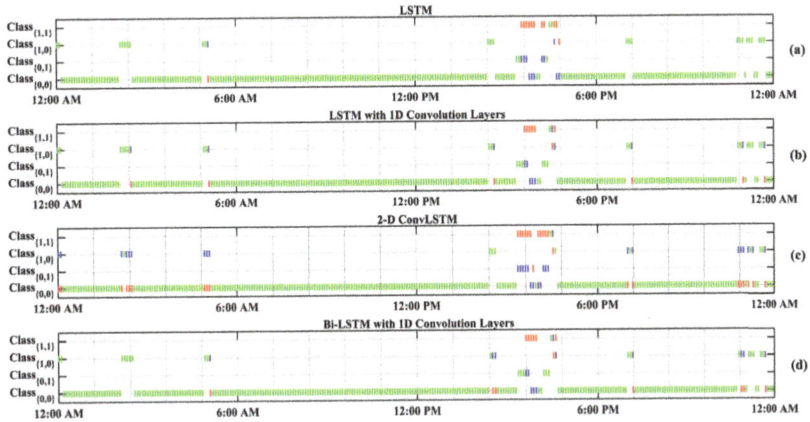

Figure 4. One-step-backward predicted Meal and Exercise events for one randomly selected dataset (Subject 2).Vertical green bars represent correctly predicted classes. Vertical red bars denote incorrectly predicted classes, and their actual labels are shown by blue bars. Class Dictionary: $Class_{0,0}$: "neither Meal nor Exercise", $Class_{0,1}$: "only Exercise", $Class_{1,0}$: "only Meal", $Class_{1,1}$: "Meal and Exercise".

Two limitations of the study are the quality and accuracy of data collected in free living and the variables that are measured. As stated in the Introduction and Data Preprocessing sections, the missing data in the time series of CGM readings is one limitation that we addressed by developing data preprocessing techniques. The second limitation is the number of variables that are measured. In this data set, there are only CGM and insulin pump data and the voluntary information provided by the patients about meal consumption and exercising. This information is usually incomplete (sometimes people may forget or have no time to enter this information). These events can be captured objectively by other measurements from wearable devices. Such data were not available in this data set and limited the accuracy of the results, especially when the meal and exercise occurred concurrently.

The proportion of correctly detected exercise and meal events to all actual exercise and meal events for all subjects reveals that a series of convolution–max-pooling layers could elicit informative feature maps for classification efficiently. Although augmented features, such as the first and second derivatives of CGM and PIC, enhance the prediction power of the NN models, the secondary feature maps, extracted from all primary features, show to be a better fit for this classification problem. In addition, repeated 1D kernel filters in convolution layers better suit the time-series nature of the data, as opposed to extracting feature maps by utilizing 2D convolution filters on the data.

Table 7. Confusion matrices calculated from the predicted and actual classes of testing samples collected from Subject 2.

(a) LSTM

		Actual			
		Class$_{\{0,0\}}$	**Class$_{\{0,1\}}$**	**Class$_{\{1,0\}}$**	**Class$_{\{1,1\}}$**
Predicted	**Class$_{\{0,0\}}$**	11,154	12	46	2
	Class$_{\{0,1\}}$	310	598	2	0
	Class$_{\{1,0\}}$	263	21	593	1
	Class$_{\{1,1\}}$	217	5	27	6

(b) LSTM (1D Convolution)

		Actual			
		Class$_{\{0,0\}}$	**Class$_{\{0,1\}}$**	**Class$_{\{1,0\}}$**	**Class$_{\{1,1\}}$**
Predicted	**Class$_{\{0,0\}}$**	11,297	14	8	1
	Class$_{\{0,1\}}$	274	596	2	2
	Class$_{\{1,0\}}$	311	8	655	1
	Class$_{\{1,1\}}$	62	18	3	5

(c) 2D ConvLSTM

		Actual			
		Class$_{\{0,0\}}$	**Class$_{\{0,1\}}$**	**Class$_{\{1,0\}}$**	**Class$_{\{1,1\}}$**
Predicted	**Class$_{\{0,0\}}$**	10,984	14	29	1
	Class$_{\{0,1\}}$	560	574	16	2
	Class$_{\{1,0\}}$	157	6	541	2
	Class$_{\{1,1\}}$	243	42	82	4

(d) Bi-LSTM (1D Convolution)

		Actual			
		Class$_{\{0,0\}}$	**Class$_{\{0,1\}}$**	**Class$_{\{1,0\}}$**	**Class$_{\{1,1\}}$**
Predicted	**Class$_{\{0,0\}}$**	11,324	14	29	1
	Class$_{\{0,1\}}$	110	537	16	2
	Class$_{\{1,0\}}$	257	6	538	2
	Class$_{\{1,1\}}$	253	79	85	4

7. Conclusions

This work focuses on developing RNN models for detection and classification tasks using time series data containing missing and erroneous values. The first modeling issue arose from the quality of the recorded data in free living. An outlier rejection algorithm was developed based on multivariable statistical analysis and signal denoising by decomposition of the Hankel matrix of CGM recordings. A multivariate approach based on PPCA for CGM sample imputation was used to keep the harmony and relationship among the variables. The second issue addressed is the detection of events that affect the behavior of dynamic systems and the classification of these events. Four different RNN models were developed to detect meal and exercise events in the daily lives of individuals with T1D. The results indicate that models with 1D convolution layers can classify events better than regular LSTM RNN and 2D ConvLSTM RNN models, with very low confusion between the events that may cause dangerous situations by prompting erroneous interventions, such as giving insulin boluses during exercise.

Supplementary Materials: The following supporting information can be downloaded at: https://www.mdpi.com/article/10.3390/biomedinformatics2020019/s1, File S1: Assessing the computational load of training the RNN models.

Author Contributions: M.R.A., M.R., X.S., M.S., A.S., K.K. and A.C. conceived the research. M.R.A. and M.R. developed the theory, and M.R.A. performed the computations. M.R.A., M.R. and A.C. wrote the manuscript. All authors discussed the results and contributed to the final manuscript. A.C. supervised the project. All authors have read and agreed to the published version of the manuscript.

Funding: Financial support from JDRF under Grant No. 1-SRA-2019-S-B, NIH under Grant No. K25 HL141634 and the Hyosung S. R. Cho Endowed Chair to Ali Cinar at Illinois Institute of Technology are gratefully acknowledged.

Institutional Review Board Statement: Not applicable.

Informed Consent Statement: Not applicable.

Data Availability Statement: Not applicable.

Conflicts of Interest: The authors declare no conflict of interest.

References

1. Cai, L.; Zhu, Y. The challenges of data quality and data quality assessment in the big data era. *Data Sci. J.* **2015**, *14*, 2. [CrossRef]
2. Centers for Disease Control and Prevention. *National Diabetes Statistics Report, 2020*; Centers for Disease Control and Prevention, US Department of Health and Human Services: Atlanta, GA, USA, 2020.
3. Roglic, G. WHO Global report on diabetes: A summary. *Int. J. Noncommun. Dis.* **2016**, *1*, 3. [CrossRef]
4. Horowitz, M.E.; Kaye, W.A.; Pepper, G.M.; Reynolds, K.E.; Patel, S.R.; Knudson, K.C.; Kale, G.K.; Gutierrez, M.E.; Cotto, L.A.; Horowitz, B.S. An analysis of Medtronic MiniMed 670G insulin pump use in clinical practice and the impact on glycemic control, quality of life, and compliance. *Diabetes Res. Clin. Pract.* **2021**, *177*, 108876. [CrossRef] [PubMed]
5. Berget, C.; Lange, S.; Messer, L.; Forlenza, G.P. A clinical review of the t:slim X2 insulin pump. *Expert Opin. Drug Deliv.* **2020**, *17*, 1675–1687. [CrossRef]
6. Cobry, E.C.; Berget, C.; Messer, L.H.; Forlenza, G.P. Review of the Omnipod® 5 Automated Glucose Control System Powered by Horizon™ for the treatment of Type 1 diabetes. *Ther. Deliv.* **2020**, *11*, 507–519. [CrossRef]
7. Sangave, N.A.; Aungst, T.D.; Patel, D.K. Smart Connected Insulin Pens, Caps, and Attachments: A Review of the Future of Diabetes Technology. *Diabetes Spectr.* **2019**, *32*, 378–384. [CrossRef]
8. Hoskins, M. New Diabetes Technology Expected in 2022. Available online: https://www.healthline.com/diabetesmine/new-diabetes-technology-in-2022 (accessed on 20 May 2022).
9. Tanzi, M.G. FDA approves first interchangeable biosimilar insulin product for treatment of diabetes. *Pharmacy Today* **2021**, *27*, 21.
10. Sevil, M.; Rashid, M.; Hajizadeh, I.; Askari, M.R.; Hobbs, N.; Brandt, R.; Park, M.; Quinn, L.; Cinar, A. Automated insulin delivery systems for people with type 1 diabetes. In *Drug Delivery Devices and Therapeutic Systems*; Chappel, E., Ed.; Developments in Biomedical Engineering and Bioelectronics, Academic Press: Cambridge, MA, USA, 2021; Chapter 9; pp. 181–198.
11. Boughton, C.K.; Hovorka, R. New closed-loop insulin systems. *Diabetologia* **2021**, *64*, 1007–1015. [CrossRef]
12. Brown, S.A.; Kovatchev, B.P.; Raghinaru, D.; Lum, J.W.; Buckingham, B.A.; Kudva, Y.C.; Laffel, L.M.; Levy, C.J.; Pinsker, J.E.; Wadwa, R.P.; et al. Six-Month Randomized, Multicenter Trial of Closed-Loop Control in Type 1 Diabetes. *N. Engl. J. Med.* **2019**, *381*, 1707–1717. [CrossRef]
13. Forlenza, G.P.; Buckingham, B.A.; Brown, S.A.; Bode, B.W.; Levy, C.J.; Criego, A.B.; Wadwa, R.P.; Cobry, E.C.; Slover, R.J.; Messer, L.H.; et al. First Outpatient Evaluation of a Tubeless Automated Insulin Delivery System with Customizable Glucose Targets in Children and Adults with Type 1 Diabetes. *Diabetes Technol. Ther.* **2021**, *23*, 410–424. [CrossRef]
14. Ware, J.; Hovorka, R. Recent advances in closed-loop insulin delivery. *Metab.-Clin. Exp.* **2022**, *127*, 154953. [CrossRef] [PubMed]
15. Garcia-Tirado, J.; Lv, D.; Corbett, J.P.; Colmegna, P.; Breton, M.D. Advanced hybrid artificial pancreas system improves on unannounced meal response—In silico comparison to currently available system. *Comput. Methods Programs Biomed.* **2021**, *211*, 106401. [CrossRef] [PubMed]
16. Haidar, A.; Legault, L.; Raffray, M.; Gouchie-Provencher, N.; Jacobs, P.G.; El-Fathi, A.; Rutkowski, J.; Messier, V.; Rabasa-Lhoret, R. Comparison Between Closed-Loop Insulin Delivery System (the Artificial Pancreas) and Sensor-Augmented Pump Therapy: A Randomized-Controlled Crossover Trial. *Diabetes Technol. Ther.* **2021**, *23*, 168–174. [CrossRef]
17. Paldus, B.; Lee, M.H.; Morrison, D.; Zaharieva, D.P.; Jones, H.; Obeyesekere, V.; Lu, J.; Vogrin, S.; LaGerche, A.; McAuley, S.A.; et al. First Randomized Controlled Trial of Hybrid Closed Loop Versus Multiple Daily Injections or Insulin Pump Using Self-Monitoring of Blood Glucose in Free-Living Adults with Type 1 Diabetes Undertaking Exercise. *J. Diabetes Sci. Technol.* **2021**, *15*, 1399–1401. [CrossRef]
18. Ekhlaspour, L.; Forlenza, G.P.; Chernavvsky, D.; Maahs, D.M.; Wadwa, R.P.; Deboer, M.D.; Messer, L.H.; Town, M.; Pinnata, J.; Kruse, G.; et al. Closed loop control in adolescents and children during winter sports: Use of the Tandem Control-IQ AP system. *Pediatr. Diabetes* **2019**, *20*, 759–768. [CrossRef]
19. Deshpande, S.; Pinsker, J.E.; Church, M.M.; Piper, M.; Andre, C.; Massa, J.; Doyle, F.J., III; Eisenberg, D.M.; Dassau, E. Randomized Crossover Comparison of Automated Insulin Delivery Versus Conventional Therapy Using an Unlocked Smartphone with Scheduled Pasta and Rice Meal Challenges in the Outpatient Setting. *Diabetes Technol. Ther.* **2020**, *22*, 865–874. [CrossRef] [PubMed]
20. Wilson, L.M.; Jacobs, P.G.; Riddell, M.C.; Zaharieva, D.P.; Castle, J.R. Opportunities and challenges in closed-loop systems in type 1 diabetes. *Lancet Diabetes Endocrinol.* **2022**, *10*, 6–8. [CrossRef]
21. Franc, S.; Benhamou, P.Y.; Borot, S.; Chaillous, L.; Delemer, B.; Doron, M.; Guerci, B.; Hanaire, H.; Huneker, E.; Jeandidier, N.; et al. No more hypoglycaemia on days with physical activity and unrestricted diet when using a closed-loop system for 12 weeks: A post hoc secondary analysis of the multicentre, randomized controlled Diabeloop WP7 trial. *Diabetes Obes. Metab.* **2021**, *23*, 2170–2176. [CrossRef]
22. Jeyaventhan, R.; Gallen, G.; Choudhary, P.; Hussain, S. A real-world study of user characteristics, safety and efficacy of open-source closed-loop systems and Medtronic 670G. *Diabetes Obes. Metab.* **2021**, *23*, 1989–1994. [CrossRef]
23. Jennings, P.; Hussain, S. Do-it-yourself artificial pancreas systems: A review of the emerging evidence and insights for healthcare professionals. *J. Diabetes Sci. Technol.* **2020**, *14*, 868–877. [CrossRef]
24. Hajizadeh, I.; Askari, M.R.; Kumar, R.; Zavala, V.M.; Cinar, A. Integrating MPC with Learning-Based and Adaptive Methods to Enhance Safety, Performance and Reliability in Automated Insulin Delivery. *IFAC-PapersOnLine* **2020**, *53*, 16149–16154. [CrossRef]

25. Hajizadeh, I.; Askari, M.R.; Sevil, M.; Hobbs, N.; Brandt, R.; Rashid, M.; Cinar, A. Adaptive control of artificial pancreas systems for treatment of type 1 diabetes. In *Control Theory in Biomedical Engineering*; Boubaker, O., Ed.; Academic Press: Cambridge, MA, USA, 2020; Chapter 3; pp. 63–81.
26. Askari, M.R.; Hajizadeh, I.; Rashid, M.; Hobbs, N.; Zavala, V.M.; Cinar, A. Adaptive-learning model predictive control for complex physiological systems: Automated insulin delivery in diabetes. *Annu. Rev. Control.* **2020**, *50*, 1–12. [CrossRef]
27. Garcia-Tirado, J.; Brown, S.A.; Laichuthai, N.; Colmegna, P.; Koravi, C.L.; Ozaslan, B.; Corbett, J.P.; Barnett, C.L.; Pajewski, M.; Oliveri, M.C.; et al. Anticipation of Historical Exercise Patterns by a Novel Artificial Pancreas System Reduces Hypoglycemia During and After Moderate-Intensity Physical Activity in People with Type 1 Diabetes. *Diabetes Technol. Ther.* **2021**, *23*, 277–285. [CrossRef] [PubMed]
28. Hochreiter, S.; Schmidhuber, J. Long short-term memory. *Neural Comput.* **1997**, *9*, 1735–1780. [CrossRef]
29. Yu, Y.; Si, X.; Hu, C.; Zhang, J. A Review of Recurrent Neural Networks: LSTM Cells and Network Architectures. *Neural Comput.* **2019**, *31*, 1235–1270. [CrossRef]
30. Efron, B. Missing data, imputation, and the bootstrap. *J. Am. Stat. Assoc.* **1994**, *89*, 463–475. [CrossRef]
31. Moritz, S.; Bartz-Beielstein, T. imputeTS: Time series missing value imputation in R. *R J.* **2017**, *9*, 207. [CrossRef]
32. Ahola, A.J.; Mutter, S.; Forsblom, C.; Harjutsalo, V.; Groop, P.H. Meal timing, meal frequency, and breakfast skipping in adult individuals with type 1 diabetes–associations with glycaemic control. *Sci. Rep.* **2019**, *9*, 1–10. [CrossRef]
33. Tipping, M.E.; Bishop, C.M. Probabilistic principal component analysis. *J. R. Stat. Soc. Ser. Stat. Methodol.* **1999**, *61*, 611–622. [CrossRef]
34. Ilin, A.; Raiko, T. Practical approaches to principal component analysis in the presence of missing values. *J. Mach. Learn. Res.* **2010**, *11*, 1957–2000.
35. Hoaglin, D.C.; John, W. Tukey and Data Analysis. *Stat. Sci.* **2003**, *18*, 311–318. [CrossRef]
36. Bakshi, B.; Stephanopoulos, G. Representation of process trends-III. Multiscale extraction of trends from process data. *Comput. Chem. Eng.* **1994**, *18*, 267–302. [CrossRef]
37. Cheung, J.Y.; Stephanopoulos, G. Representation of process trends-Part I. A formal representation framework. *Comput. Chem. Eng.* **1990**, *14*, 495–510. [CrossRef]
38. Samadi, S.; Turksoy, K.; Hajizadeh, I.; Feng, J.; Sevil, M.; Cinar, A. Meal Detection and Carbohydrate Estimation Using Continuous Glucose Sensor Data. *IEEE J. Biomed. Health Inf.* **2017**, *21*, 619–627. [CrossRef] [PubMed]
39. Samadi, S.; Rashid, M.; Turksoy, K.; Feng, J.; Hajizadeh, I.; Hobbs, N.; Lazaro, C.; Sevil, M.; Littlejohn, E.; Cinar, A. Automatic Detection and Estimation of Unannounced Meals for Multivariable Artificial Pancreas System. *Diabetes Technol. Ther.* **2018**, *20*, 235–246. [CrossRef] [PubMed]
40. Eberle, C.; Ament, C. The Unscented Kalman Filter estimates the plasma insulin from glucose measurement. *Biosystems* **2011**, *103*, 67–72. [CrossRef] [PubMed]
41. Hajizadeh, I.; Rashid, M.; Turksoy, K.; Samadi, S.; Feng, J.; Frantz, N.; Sevil, M.; Cengiz, E.; Cinar, A. Plasma insulin estimation in people with type 1 diabetes mellitus. *Ind. Eng. Chem. Res.* **2017**, *56*, 9846–9857. [CrossRef]
42. Hajizadeh, I.; Rashid, M.; Samadi, S.; Feng, J.; Sevil, M.; Hobbs, N.; Lazaro, C.; Maloney, Z.; Brandt, R.; Yu, X.; et al. Adaptive and Personalized Plasma Insulin Concentration Estimation for Artificial Pancreas Systems. *J. Diabetes Sci. Technol.* **2018**, *12*, 639–649. [CrossRef]
43. Hovorka, R.; Canonico, V.; Chassin, L.J.; Haueter, U.; Massi-Benedetti, M.; Federici, M.O.; Pieber, T.R.; Schaller, H.C.; Schaupp, L.; Vering, T.; et al. Nonlinear model predictive control of glucose concentration in subjects with type 1 diabetes. *Physiol. Meas.* **2004**, *25*, 905–920. [CrossRef]
44. Ivers, N.M.; Jiang, M.; Alloo, J.; Singer, A.; Ngui, D.; Casey, C.G.; Catherine, H.Y. Diabetes Canada 2018 clinical practice guidelines: Key messages for family physicians caring for patients living with type 2 diabetes. *Can. Fam. Physician* **2019**, *65*, 14–24.
45. Care, F. Standards of Medical Care in Diabetes 2019. *Diabetes Care* **2019**, *42*, S124–S138.
46. NICE. *Type 1 Diabetes in Adults: Diagnosis and Management*; National Institute for Health and Care Excellence (NICE): London, UK, 2015; pp. 1–87.
47. Arulampalam, M.; Maskell, S.; Gordon, N.; Clapp, T. A tutorial on particle filters for online nonlinear/non-Gaussian Bayesian tracking. *IEEE Trans. Signal Process.* **2002**, *50*, 174–188. [CrossRef]
48. Pitt, M.; Silva, R.; Giordani, P.; Kohn, R. Auxiliary particle filtering within adaptive Metropolis-Hastings sampling. *arXiv* **2010**, arXiv:1006.1914.
49. Pudil, P.; Novovičová, J.; Kittler, J. Floating search methods in feature selection. *Pattern Recognit. Lett.* **1994**, *15*, 1119–1125. [CrossRef]
50. Shi, X.; Chen, Z.; Wang, H.; Yeung, D.Y.; Wong, W.K.; Woo, W.c. Convolutional LSTM network: A machine learning approach for precipitation nowcasting. *Adv. Neural Inf. Process. Syst.* **2015**, *28*, 802–810.
51. Vinyals, O.; Toshev, A.; Bengio, S.; Erhan, D. Show and tell: A neural image caption generator. In Proceedings of the IEEE Conference on Computer Vision and Pattern Recognition, Boston, MA, USA, 7–12 June 2015; pp. 3156–3164.
52. Donahue, J.; Anne Hendricks, L.; Guadarrama, S.; Rohrbach, M.; Venugopalan, S.; Saenko, K.; Darrell, T. Long-term recurrent convolutional networks for visual recognition and description. In Proceedings of the IEEE Conference on Computer Vision and Pattern Recognition, Boston, MA, USA, 7–12 June 2015; pp. 2625–2634.

53. Géron, A. *Hands-on Machine Learning with Scikit-Learn, Keras, and TensorFlow: Concepts, Tools, and Techniques to Build Intelligent Systems*; O'Reilly Media: Newton, MA, USA, 2019.
54. Brownlee, J. *Deep Learning for Time Series Forecasting: Predict the Future with MLPs, CNNs and LSTMs in Python*; Machine Learning Mastery. 2018. Available online: https://machinelearningmastery.com/deep-learning-for-time-series-forecasting/ (accessed on 20 May 2022).
55. Schuster, M.; Paliwal, K. Bidirectional recurrent neural networks. *IEEE Trans. Signal Process.* **1997**, *45*, 2673–2681. [CrossRef]
56. Graves, A.; Schmidhuber, J. Framewise phoneme classification with bidirectional LSTM and other neural network architectures. *Neural Netw.* **2005**, *18*, 602–610. [CrossRef]

BioMedInformatics

MDPI

Review

Towards Automated Meta-Analysis of Clinical Trials: An Overview

Stella C. Christopoulou

Department of Business and Organization Administration, University of Peloponnese, Antikalamos, 24100 Kalamata, Greece; stellachristop@gmail.com

Abstract: Background: Nowadays, much research deals with the application of the automated meta-analysis of clinical trials through appropriate machine learning tools to extract the results that can then be applied in daily clinical practice. Methods: The author performed a systematic search of the literature from 27 September 2022–22 November 2022 in PUBMED, in the first 6 pages of Google Scholar and in the online catalog, the Systematic Review Toolbox. Moreover, a second search of the literature was performed from 7 January 2023–20 January 2023 in the first 10 pages of Google Scholar and in the Semantic Google Scholar. Results: 38 approaches in 39 articles met the criteria and were included in this overview. These articles describe in detail machine learning approaches, methods, and tools that have been or can potentially be applied to the meta-analysis of clinical trials. Nevertheless, while the other tasks of a systematic review have significantly developed, the automation of meta-analyses is still far from being able to significantly support and facilitate the work of researchers, freeing them from manual, difficult and time-consuming work. Conclusions: The evaluation of automated meta-analysis results is presented in some studies. Their approaches show positive and promising results.

Keywords: machine learning; clinical trials; RCT; automated meta-analysis; deep learning; automation

Citation: Christopoulou, S.C. Towards Automated Meta-Analysis of Clinical Trials: An Overview. *Biomedinformatics* **2023**, *3*, 115–140. https://doi.org/10.3390/biomedinformatics3010009

Academic Editor: Pentti Nieminen

Received: 31 December 2022
Revised: 24 January 2023
Accepted: 29 January 2023
Published: 1 February 2023

1. Introduction

Today clinical trials are considered as an established experimental clinical tool suitable not only for evaluating the effectiveness of interventions, but also for supporting the conduct of an adequately designed systematic review [1]. In addition, meta-analysis is a systematic review of a focused topic in the literature that provides a quantitative estimate of the effect of a therapeutic intervention or exposure [2]. This effect is inferred from outputs usually from more than one previously published clinical trial. A meta-analysis is necessary for making correct medical decisions (such as prognosis, diagnosis, treatment, recording side effects in taking drugs, etc.). It is the prevailing method applied in clinical trials for generating qualitative and quantitative evidence and conclusions. Meta-analysis and synthesis of the results of clinical trials are gaining rapid momentum in the research to generate quantitative information [3]. Thus, clinical trials are at the forefront of clinical decision support.

In parallel, since in the present time the volume of clinical studies is increasing exponentially, automating their processing by applying machine learning (ML) is a great challenge and a dominant research topic.

The automation in the management of clinical studies refers to dealing with the individual processes related to the search, collection, selection, and extraction of results. In detail these tasks are the following: Design Systematic Search, Run Systematic Search, Deduplicate, Obtain full texts, Snowballing, Screen abstracts, Data extraction and Text Mining Tool, Automated bias assessments, Automated Meta-Analysis, Summarize/Synthesis of data (analysis), Write up, and Data Miner/Analysis of Data for General-Purpose [4].

More specifically, the meta-analysis is a systematic approach for understanding a phenomenon by analyzing the results of many previously published experimental studies.

Unfortunately, the conventional meta-analysis requires a great deal of human effort, is labor-intensive, and vulnerable to human bias [2,5].

The task of the automated meta-analysis and synthesis of data is the part of their management in which the least research has been done in terms of their mechanical processing and automation [4].

The authors of many studies [6–11] demonstrated the feasibility and acceptance of semi-automated and automated meta-analyses yielding promising results. The outcomes of these studies suggest that automated meta-analysis through machine learning approaches reduces the time required for a meta-analysis without altering the expert confidence in methodological and scientific rigor. Moreover, these results suggest acceptance for risk assessment and improve the quality of reporting.

In this direction, the author of this article deals with the application of automated meta-analysis of clinical trials through appropriate machine learning tools to extract the results that can then be applied in daily clinical practice.

In addition, deep learning methods and tools as a subcategory of ML, are also included in this study. Deep learning based on learning data representations are part of the larger family of machine learning algorithms that use multiple layers to progressively extract higher-level features from the raw input [12].

The novelty of this overview is that until yet very few review articles have been published which describe all these mentioned frameworks, techniques, and tools alongside their applications in a complete and effective way in order to contribute to their further development and improvement.

Thus, initially, the author searched for relevant work and described it in detail below in Section 3.1.

More specifically, the author in this article performed an overview exploring the applied state-of-the-art ML methods, approaches, frameworks, and tools in automating the meta-analysis and synthesis of data extracted from clinical trials.

The main research questions were as follows:

- RQ1. What are the trends and key characteristics of studies showing automation in the meta-analysis and synthesis of clinical trial data.
- RQ2. What are the most common technologies, methods, tools, and software used in the meta-analysis and synthesis of data extracted from clinical trials.
- RQ3. What are the impacts that derive from the usage of the automation in the meta-analysis in clinical trials.
- RQ4. What are the challenges, guidelines, and obstacles to be addressed and what studies and research are proposed to achieve automation and maximum and reliable application of clinical trial results in daily medical practices.

The rest of this study is organized as follows: Section 2 discusses other relevant studies. Section 3 presents the materials and methods of this study. Section 4 summarizes the results. Section 5 discusses the key issues arising from this study. Section 6 concludes the study and presents future directions.

2. Related Work

There are many studies in the field of the management of studies and clinical trials and the extraction of their knowledge [4,13–16] but only a limited number deal with the automation of the meta-analysis task.

Wang et al. [12] conducted a review and assessment of 18 common deep learning frameworks and libraries (Caffe, Caffe2, Tensorflow, Theano including Keras Lasagnes and Blocks, MXNet, CNTK, Torch, PyTorch, Pylearn2, Scikit-learn, Matlab including MatconvNet Matlab deep learning and Deep learning toolbox, Chainer, Deeplearning4j) and introduced a large number of benchmarking data.

In order to provide a basis for comparing and selecting between software tools that support Systematic reviews, the authors of [17] performed a feature-by-feature comparison of Systematic reviews tools.

Finally, the Systematic Review Toolbox [9] is an online catalog of tools that support various tasks within the systematic review and wider evidence synthesis process. The updated version of the Systematic Review Toolbox was launched on 13 May 2022, with 235 software tools and 112 guidance documents included.

3. Materials and Methods

3.1. Study Design

In this study design the author used the overview approach [18]. An overview is a generic term used for "any summary of the literature" [19] that attempts to survey the literature and describe its characteristics. As such, it can be used for many different types of literature review, with differing degrees of systematicity. Overviews can provide a broad and often comprehensive summation of a topic area and, as such, have value for those coming to a subject for the first time [20]. They are also important in cases where either a subject is not yet mature and well-known enough to be treated with a thorough systematic review or there is not the necessary time to perform it.

Additionally, the forward and backward snowball method is used [21]. It has been proposed that in reviews of complex or heterogeneous evidence in the field of health services research, "snowball" methods of forward (citation) and backwards (reference) searching are powerful. This method allows researchers using the references and citations of an article to find specific literature on an issue quickly and easily.

3.2. Literature Search and Study Selection

The author performed a systematic search of the literature from 27 September 2022–22 November 2022 in PUBMED (http://www.pubmed.org, accessed on 27 December 2022), in the first 6 pages of Google Scholar and in the online catalog: Systematic Review Toolbox (http://www.systematicreviewtools.com/, accessed on 28 December 2022) using combinations of search strings ("automated meta-analysis" AND "trials"). Moreover, a second search of the literature was performed from 7 January 2023–20 January 2023 in the first 10 pages of Google Scholar and in the Semantic Google Scholar using combinations of search strings ("automated meta-analysis" OR "automatic meta-analysis").

The author did not find records in clinical trials.gov, or in the COCHRANE library.

In addition, forward and reverse citation searches (snowball method) were performed for specific studies to ensure inclusion of the most relevant studies. Snowballing was undertaken, starting from the included citations and from the references of each article.

Restrictions are related to the language (only English articles are included).

In addition, studies involving tools and techniques for image management (e.g., [22–27]) were out of the scope of this study and excluded.

3.3. Data Screening

The data were screened in a two-stage review process (Figure 1) that the author performed, (a) initially excluding assignments based on the titles and their abstracts, and (b) then the remaining assignments were screened based on the reading of the full text of the article.

One researcher reviewed the articles.

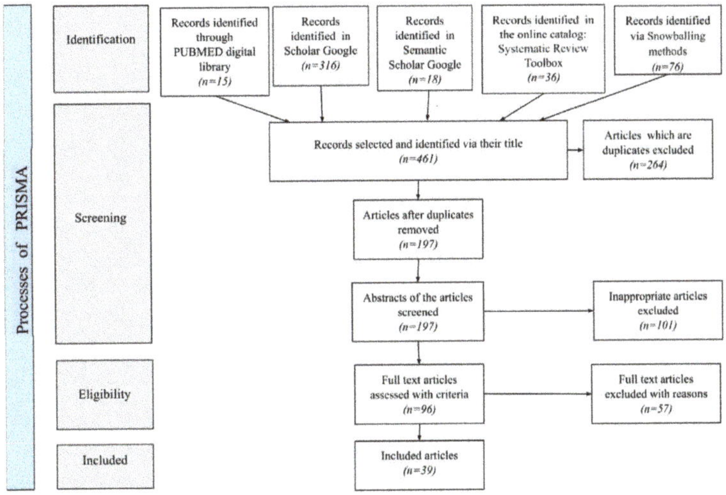

Figure 1. The flow diagram of the literature search.

3.4. Data Extraction and Analyses

The following data were extracted from the included studies:

- Bibliographic elements of the included articles:
    - Name of the studies' object
    - Reference
    - Title
    - Year
    - Author(s)
    - Journal
- Characteristics of the studies' object:
    - Name studies' object
    - Domain
    - Type
    - (Not)Free/(Not)Open
    - Source Code
    - Method/Language

4. Results

There were 38 approaches in 39 articles that met the criteria and were included in this overview (Table 1).

These articles describe in detail ML approaches, methods, and tools that have been or can potentially be applied to the meta-analysis of clinical trials.

All articles in the review range from the years 2010–2023, most of which were identified during the years 2016–2022. (There were 3 articles in 2016, 4 in 2017, 6 in 2018, 4 in 2019, 2 in 2020, 5 in 2021, and 7 in 2022) (Table 1).

The dominant technologies used for the development and application of the automated meta-analysis are Python and R programming languages. Some studies also used Java, Excel, and either C++ or another version of it (i.e., C, ANSI C++, C++11). More rarely were found CUDA, Docker environment, Lua, and LuaJIT. In addition, some studies combined the use of several different technologies to achieve their goals (Table 2).

Table 1. The bibliographic elements of the included studies.

Name	Reference	Title	Year	Author(s)	Journal
A Logic of Meta-Analysis approach	[28]	Towards a Logic of Meta-Analysis	2020	Peñaloza, R	Proceedings of the International Conference on
Amamida R Package	[29]	Amanida: An R package for meta-analysis of metabolomics non-integral data	2022	Llambrich, Maria; Correig, Eudald; Gumà, Josep; Brezmes, Jesús; Cumeras, Raquel	Bioinformatics
Amazon SageMaker	[30,31]	Getting Started with Amazon SageMaker Studio: Learn to build end-to-end machine learning projects in the SageMaker machine learning IDE	2022	Hsieh, M	Packt Publishing Ltd.
Automated Meta-analysis of Biomedical Texts	[10]	Towards Automated Meta-analysis of Biomedical Texts in the Field of Cell-based Immunotherapy	2019	Devyatkin DA, Molodchenkov AI, Lukin AV et al.	Research and Methods
Caffe2	[32]	Applied Machine Learning at Facebook: A Datacenter Infrastructure Perspective	2018	Hazelwood, K; et al.	IEEE International Symposium on High Performance Computer Architecture
Causal Learning Perspective	[5]	Automated Meta-Analysis: A Causal Learning Perspective	2021	Cheng, L; Katz-Rogozhnikov, D A; Varshney, K R; others	arXiv preprint
CINeMA	[33]	CINeMA: An approach for assessing confidence in the results of a network	2020	Nikolakopoulou, Adriani; Higgins, Julian P T; Papakonstantinou, Theodoros; Chaimani, Anna; Del Giovane, Cinzia; Egger, Matthias; Salanti, Georgia	PLOS Medicine
DIAeT	[11]	Synthesizing evidence from clinical trials with dynamic interactive	2022	Sanchez-Graillet; Witte, Olivia; Grimm, Christian; Grautoff, Frank; Ell, Steffen; Cimiano, Basil; Philipp	J. Biomed. Semantics
dmetar	[34]	Doing Meta-Analysis with R: A Hands-On Guide	2021	Harrer, Mathias; Cuijpers, Pim; Furukawa, Toshi A; Ebert, David D	CRC Press

Table 1. *Cont.*

Name	Reference	Title	Year	Author(s)	Journal
DTA MA (Diagnostic Test Accuracy Meta-Analysis) (MetaDTA)	[35]	Graphical enhancements to summary receiver operating characteristic plots to facilitate the analysis and reporting of meta-analysis of diagnostic test accuracy data	2021	Patel, Amit; Cooper, Nicola; Freeman, Suzanne; Sutton, Alex	Res Synth Methods
Keras	[36]	Introduction to keras. In Deep learning with Python	2017	Ketkar, Nikhil	Apress, Berkeley, CA
Meta-Essentials	[37]	Introduction, comparison, and validation of Meta-Essentials: A free and simple tool for meta-analysis	2017	Suurmond, Robert; van Rhee, Henk; Hak, Tony	Res Synth Methods
metafor	[38]	Conducting Meta-Analyses in R with the metafor Package	2010	Viechtbauer, Wolfgang	Journal of Statistical Software
MetaInsight	[39]	MetaInsight: An interactive web-based tool for analyzing, interrogating, and visualizing network meta-analyses using R-shiny and netmeta	2019	Owen, Rhiannon K; Bradbury, Naomi; Xin, Yiqiao; Cooper, Nicola; Sutton, Alex	Res Synth Methods
metamisc	[40]	A framework for meta-analysis of prediction model studies with binary and time-to-event outcomes	2019	Debray, Thomas Pa; Damen, Johanna Aag; Riley, Richard D; Snell, Kym; Reitsma, Johannes B; Hooft, Lotty; Collins, Gary S; Moons, Karel Gm	Stat. Methods Med. Res.
MetaXL	[41]	Advances in the meta-analysis of heterogeneous clinical trials I: The	2015	Doi, Suhail A R; Barendregt, Jan J; Khan, Shahjahan; Thalib, Lukman; Williams, Gail M	Contemp. Clin. Trials
Nested-Knowledge	[17]	Web-Based Software Tools for Systematic Literature Review in Medicine: A Review and Feature Analysis	2021	Cowie; Rahmatullah, Kathryn; Hardy, Asad; Holub, Nicole; Kallmes, Karl; Kevin	Nested Knowledge, Inc.
netmeta	[42]	Network Meta-Analysis using Frequentist Methods [R package netmeta version 0.9-8	2022	Rücker, Gerta; Krahn, Ulrike; König, Jochem; Efthimiou, Orestis; Davies, Annabel; Papakonstantinou, Theodoros; Schwarzer, Guido	CRAN package repository

Table 1. *Cont.*

Name	Reference	Title	Year	Author(s)	Journal
OpenNN	[43]	Open NN: An Open Source Neural Networks C++ Library	2022	Lopez, Roberto	International Center for Numerical Methods in Engineering (CIMNE)
Pymeta	[44]	PyMeta	2018	Hongyong, Deng	PythonMeta Website
PythonMeta	[45]	PythonMeta 1.26	2018	Hongyong, Deng	PythonMeta Website
PyTorch	[46]	PyTorch	Not found	PyTorch–Linux Foundation	
scikit-learn	[47]	scikit-learn	2016	Python Software Foundation	Python Software Foundation
ShinyMDE	[48]	ShinyMDE: Shiny tool for microarray meta-analysis for differentially expressed gene detection	2016	Shashirekha, H. L.; Wani, Agaz Hussain	HLS and team
Spark ML	[49]	Scaling Machine Learning with Spark: Distributed ML with MLlib, TensorFlow, and Pytorch	2023	Polak, A.	O'Reilly Media
TensorFlow	[50]	Learning TensorFlow: A Guide to Building Deep Learning Systems	2017	Hope, Tom; Resheff, Yehezkel S.; Lieder, Itay	O'Reilly Media
Torch	[51]	Torch7: A Matlab-like Environment for Machine Learning	2019	Collobert, Ronan; Kavukcuoglu, Koray; Farabet, Clement	Neural Information Processing Systems
Whyis	[52]	Developing Scientific Knowledge Graphs Using Whyis	2018	McCusker, J.P., Rashid, S.M., Agu, N., Bennett, K.P. and McGuinness, D.L.	SemSci
Comprehensive gene expression meta-analysis	[53]	A comprehensive gene expression meta-analysis identifies novel immune signatures in rheumatoid arthritis patients	2017	Afroz, S.; Giddaluru, J.; Vishwakarma, S.; Naz, S.; Khan, A.A.; Khan, N.	Frontiers in
NeuroSynth	[54]	Large-scale automated synthesis of human functional neuroimaging data	2011	Yarkoni T, Poldrack RA, Nichols TE, Van Essen DC, Wager TD	Nat. Methods
Text-mining the neurosynth corpus (NeuroSynth #2)	[55]	Text-mining the neurosynth corpus using deep boltzmann machines	2016	Monti R, Lorenz R, Leech R, Anagnostopoulos C, Montana G	2016 International Workshop on Pattern Recognition in Neuroimaging

Table 1. *Cont.*

Name	Reference	Title	Year	Author(s)	Journal
Social brain (NeuroSynth #3)	[56]	The "social brain" is highly sensitive to the mere presence of social information: An automated meta-analysis and an independent study	2018	Tso, Ivy F; Rutherford, Saige; Fang, Yu; Angstadt, Mike; Taylor, Stephan F	PLoS One
MetaCyto	[57]	MetaCyto: A Tool for Automated Meta-analysis of Mass and Flow Cytometry Data	2018	Hu Z, Jujjavarapu C, Hughey JJ, Andorf S, Lee HC, Gherardini PF et al.	Cell Rep.
Automated meta-analysis of the ERP literature	[58]	Automated meta-analysis of the event-related potential (ERP) literature	2022	Donoghue T, Voytek B	Sci. Rep.
CancerMA	[59]	CancerMA: a web-based tool for automatic meta-analysis of public cancer microarray data	2012	Feichtinger J, McFarlane RJ, Larcombe LD	Database
CancerEST	[60]	CancerEST: a web-based tool for automatic meta-analysis of public EST data	2014	Feichtinger J, McFarlane RJ, Larcombe LD	Database
Research Method Classification	[61]	Research Method Classification with Deep Transfer Learning for Semi-Automatic Meta-Analysis of Information Systems Papers	2021	Anisienia A, Mueller RM, Kupfer A, Staake T	Proceedings of the Annual Hawaii International Conference on System Sciences
AUTOMETA	[62]	AUTOMETA: Automatic Meta-Analysis System Employing Natural Language Processing	2022	Mutinda FW, Yada S, Wakamiya S, Aramaki E	Stud. Health Technol. Inform.

Table 2. The characteristics of the studies' objects.

Name	Domain	Type	(Not)Free (Not)Open	Source Code	Method/Language
A Logic of Meta-Analysis approach	General purpose	Approach	No need	Not supported	Not supported
Amamida R Package	Metabolomic studies	Package	Open source	(https://github.com/mariallr/amanida, accessed on 23 December 2022)	R package

Table 2. *Cont.*

Name	Domain	Type	(Not)Free (Not)Open	Source Code	Method/Language
Amazon SageMaker	General purpose	Tool	Not free	(https://aws.amazon.com/sagemaker/resources/, accessed on 23 December 2022)	Python
Automated Meta-analysis of Biomedical Texts	Biomedical	All	Not described	No need	MetaMap; Fasttext model; Eclat algorithm/Python package
Caffe2	General purpose	Framework	Open Source	(https://github.com/pytorch/pytorch, accessed on 22 December 2022)	Graph representation is shared among all backend implementation; C++ & Python API
Causal Learning Perspective	General purpose	Approach	No need	No need	Multiple Causal inference for automated Meta-Analysis (MCMA)
CINeMA	General purpose	Tool	Open source	(https://github.com/esm-ispm-unibe-ch/cinema, accessed on 25 December 2022)	Salanti approach; JavaScript, Docker, and R package
DIAeT	Evidence-based medicine (EBM)	Model/Method	Open source	(https://doi.org/10.5281/zenodo.5604516, accessed on 24 December 2022)	model Toulmin; Java
dmetar	General purpose	Package	Open source	(https://github.com/MathiasHarrer/Doing-Meta-Analysis-in-R, accessed on 25 December 2022; https://dmetar.protectlab.org/, accessed on 25 December 2022)	R package
DTA MA (Diagnostic Test Accuracy Meta-Analysis) (MetaDTA)	General purpose	Software	Open source	(https://github.com/CRSU-Apps/MetaDTA; https://crsu.shinyapps.io/dta_ma/, accessed on 25 December 2022)	R package
Keras	General purpose	Software	Open source	(https://keras.io/; https://github.com/keras-team/keras, accessed on 25 December 2022)	Python
Meta-Essentials	General purpose	Software	Open source	(https://www.erim.eur.nl/research-support/meta-essentials/download/, accessed on 26 December 2022; https://www.meta-essentials.com, accessed on 26 December 2022)	Excel files

Table 2. *Cont.*

Name	Domain	Type	(Not)Free (Not)Open	Source Code	Method/Language
metafor	General purpose	Software	Open source	(https://www.jstatsoft.org/article/view/v036i03, accessed on 27 December 2022)	R package
MetaInsight	General purpose	Web application	Not Open; Freely available	(https://crsu.shinyapps.io/metainsight, accessed on 22 December 2022)	Not described
metamisc	General purpose	Model/Method	Open source	(https://cran.r-project.org/web/packages/metamisc/index.html, accessed on 25 December 2022; https://github.com/smartdata-analysis-and-statistics/metamisc, accessed on 28 December 2022)	R package
MetaXL	Evidence-based medicine (EBM)	Software	Freely available	(http://www.epigear.com/index_files/metaxl.html, accessed on 27 December 2022)	Excel files
Nested-Knowledge	Evidence-based medicine (EBM)	Web application	Not free	(https://nested-knowledge.com/nest/qualitative/371, accessed on 26 December 2022)	Not described
netmeta	General purpose	Web application	Open source	(https://cran.r-project.org/web/packages/netmeta/index.html, accessed on 23 December 2022; https://github.com/guido-s/netmeta, accessed on 28 December 2022; https://link.springer.com/book/10.1007/978-3-319-21416-0, accessed on 26 December 2022; https://rdrr.io/cran/netmeta/src/R/netmeta.R, accessed on 26 December 2022)	R package
OpenNN	General purpose	Tool	Open source	(https://github.com/Artelnics/OpenNN, accessed on 27 December 2022; http://opennn.cimne.com/download.asp, accessed on 28 December 2022)	ANSI C++
Pymeta	Evidence-based medicine (EBM)	Tool	Not Open	(https://www.pymeta.com/, accessed on 28 December 2022	Python

Table 2. *Cont.*

Name	Domain	Type	(Not)Free (Not)Open	Source Code	Method/Language
PythonMeta	Evidence-based medicine (EBM)	Tool	Open source	https: //pypi.org/project/PythonMeta/, accessed on 28 December 2022)	Python
PyTorch	Evidence-based medicine (EBM)	Tool	Open source	(https://github.com/pytorch/pytorch, accessed on 28 December 2022)	Python
scikit-learn	General purpose	Tool	Open source	(scikit-learn/scikit-learn: scikit-learn: machine learning in Python (github.com), accessed on 21 December 2022)	Python
ShinyMDE	genomics, molecular genetics	Tool	Not Open; Freely available	(https://hussain.shinyapps.io/App-1, accessed on 21 December 2022)	R package
Spark ML	General purpose	Tool	Open source	(https://github.com/apache/spark, accessed on 22 December 2022)	Java; Python; R
TensorFlow	General purpose	Tool	Open source	(https: //github.com/tensorflow/tensorflow, accessed on 22 December 2022)	C++; Python
Torch	General purpose	Framework	Open source	(https://github.com/torch/torch7, accessed on 22 December 2022)	C++11; Lua; LuaJIT, C; CUDA and C++
Whyis	General purpose	All	Open	(https://whyis.readthedocs.io/en/latest/index.html, accessed on 22 December 2022; https: //github.com/tetherless-world/whyis, accessed on 22 December 2022)	probabilistic knowledge graphs by using Stouffer's Z-Method/ Python; Flask framework; Fuseki; SPARQL; Graph Store HTTP Protocol; FileDepot Python library
Comprehensive gene expression meta-analysis	Biomedical	Method	Open	No need	Weighted Z-method/ survcomp R package
NeuroSynth	Medical	Framework	Open	(https://github.com/neurosynth, accessed on 26 December 2022)	naïve Bayes classification
Text-mining the neurosynth corpus (NeuroSynth #2)	Medical	Method	No need	No need	unsupervised study/ Deep Boltzmann machines for text-mining

Table 2. *Cont.*

Name	Domain	Type	(Not)Free (Not)Open	Source Code	Method/Language
Social brain (NeuroSynth #3)	Medical	Method	No need	(http://neurosynth.org/analyses/terms/social/, accessed on 28 December 2022)	Regions Of Interest (ROIs) analysis
MetaCyto	Biomedical	Method	No need	(http://bioconductor.org/packages/release/bioc/html/MetaCyto.html, accessed on 28 December 2022)	clustering methods with a scanning method/R package
Automated meta-analysis of the ERP literature	Medical	Tool	Open	(https://erpscanr.github.io/, accessed on 28 December 2022; https://github.com/ERPscanr/ERPscanr, accessed on 28 December 2022)	text-mining and word co-occurrence analyses
CancerMA	Biomedical	Tool	Open	(http://www.cancerma.org.uk, accessed on 28 December 2022) (not found)	HTML/CSS; Twitter Bootstrapp; Javascript/jQuery; Perl; R package; Bioconductor package
CancerEST	Biomedical	Tool	Open	(http://www.cancerest.org.uk/help.html http://www.cancerest.org.uk, accessed on 28 December 2022) (not found)	HTML/CSS; Twitter Bootstrapp; Javascript/jQuery; Perl; R package; Bioconductor package
Research Method Classification	General purpose	Method	No need	No need	Support Vector Models
AUTOMETA	Medical	Approach	No need	No need	BERT-based model

The research for automation of meta-analyses in some studies is specialized to handle strictly specialized issues such as the biomedical domain (5 articles), evidence-based medicine (6 articles), genomics and molecular genetics (1 article), and medical (5 articles) and metabolomic domain (1 article) (Table 2).

According to the findings of this overview, the types of research most frequently encountered to achieve automated meta-analysis are: the development and implementation of appropriate tools (13 studies), the development and implementation of software (5 studies), and the development of appropriate models and methods (7 studies). More analytically this overview basically identified four types of applications related to supporting or developing an automated meta-analysis. These are the following:

A Framework or Tool: this category includes the development of an integrated framework or the development of a specific tool to support automated meta-analysis. Most of the studies included in this review fall into this category.

A Package or Software: this category includes the development of package software to support automated meta-analysis.

A Model, Method, or Approach: this category includes the development of models and/or methods in the field of automated meta-analysis.

A Web application: This category includes web-based applications that implement automated meta-analyses and are either already implemented or may potentially be implemented in the future in clinical studies as well.

Some of the applications may be included in more than one category. Moreover, some of them can be a complete implementation and include all of the above. More analytically, it is worth noting that 2 studies ([10,52]) fully and comprehensively deal with the topic under discussion here by presenting an integrated modeling and application framework (Table 2).

Below are briefly described the applications found in this overview as classified based on the above four categories.

4.1. Framework/Tool (Includes 16 Studies)

- Amazon SageMaker [30,31]

Description: Amazon SageMaker Studio is the first integrated development environment in the cloud for machine learning and is designed to integrate the following machine learning workflows: data preparation, feature engineering, statistical bias detection, automated machine learning, training, hosting, ML explainability, monitoring, and machine learning operations in one environment.

Features: The features available in Amazon SageMaker Studio include the following issues: build, train, and deploy machine learning models quickly using Amazon SageMaker; analyze, detect, and receive alerts relating to various business problems using machine learning algorithms and techniques; improve productivity by training and fine-tuning machine learning models in production.

Inputs: datasets; csv files; models.

Outputs: models; Python script; data flow; data.

- Caffe2 [32]

Caffe2 is Facebook's in-house production framework for training and deploying large-scale machine learning models. Caffe2 is a deep learning framework that provides an easy and straightforward way for you to experiment with deep learning and leverage community contributions of new models and algorithms.

Features: Caffe2 focuses on several key features required by products: performance, cross-platform support, and coverage for fundamental machine learning algorithms and multi-layer perceptions. The design involves a modular approach, where a unified graph representation is shared among all backend implementations.

Inputs: Python and C++ files; models.

Outputs: everything.

- CINeMA [33]

  Description: the Confidence in Network Meta-Analysis (CINeMA) approach is broadly based on the GRADE (Grading of Recommendations Assessment, Development and Evaluation) framework, with several conceptual and semantic differences [5]. It covers the following domains: (i) within-study bias, (ii) reporting bias, (iii) indirectness, (iv) imprecision, (v) heterogeneity, and (vi) incoherence. The reviewer's input is required at the study level. Then, CINeMA assigns judgments at three levels (no concerns, some concerns, or major concerns) to each domain. Judgments across domains can be summarized to obtain four levels of confidence (very low, low, moderate, or high) for each relative treatment effect.

  Features: the CINeMA framework has been implemented in a freely available, user-friendly web application aiming to facilitate the evaluation of confidence in the results from network meta-analysis. The web application applies the Salanti approach and is programmed in JavaScript, uses Docker, and is linked with R; in particular, packages meta and netmeta are used, and an R package to calculate the contribution of studies in network meta-analysis treatment effects.

  Inputs: csv files.

  Outputs: outputs a downloadable report with a summary of the evaluations.

- OpenNN [43]

  Description: OpenNN is a software library that implements neural networks, a major area of deep learning research.

  Features: OpenNN includes: a multilayer perceptron software implementation; many examples; unit testing.

  Inputs: C++ code.

  Outputs: data; plots.

- Pymeta [44]

  Description: Pymeta is an online meta-analysis tool, as a web-based application it is created and supported with PythonMeta, a Python package of meta-analysis.

  Features: performs: combining effect measures (OR, RR, RD for count data and MD, SMD for continuous data); heterogeneity testing (the Q/Chi-square test); subgroup analysis; cumulative meta-analysis; and sensitivity analysis (one or two factors).

  Inputs: Python code.

  Outputs: data; plots; bar-lines.

- PythonMeta [45]

  Description: PythonMeta package performs the meta-analysis on an open-access dataset from COCHRANE..

  Features: meta-analysis package by and for the Python language. This module was designed to perform some evidence-based medicine (EBM) tasks, such as: combining effect measures (OR, RR, RD, MD, SMD), heterogeneity testing (the Q/Chi-squared test), subgroup analysis, and plots (forest, funnel, etc.).

  Inputs: dataset from COCHRANE.

  Outputs: data; plots.

- PyTorch [46]

  Description: PyTorch is a deep learning research platform that provides maximum flexibility and speed.

  Features: PyTorch is a library that consists of the following components: torch which is a Tensor library with strong GPU support; torch.autograd which is a tape-based automatic differentiation library; torch.jit which is a compilation stack; torch.nn which is a neural networks library deeply integrated with autograd designed for maximum flexibility; torch.multiprocessing which is Python multiprocessing useful for data loading and Hogwild training; torch.utils which is a DataLoader; and other utility functions.

  Inputs: Python code.

  Outputs: data; plots.

- scikit-learn [47]

Description: Scikit-learn is a Python library.

Features: it includes functions that are integral to the machine learning pipeline such as data preprocessing steps, data resampling techniques, evaluation parameters, and search interfaces for tuning/optimizing an algorithm's performance.

Inputs: datasets.

Outputs: data; plots.

- ShinyMDE [48]

Description: ShinyMDE supports an automated meta-analysis of gene expression data facilitating screening and downloading the results.

The tool handles processed and raw data generated from the most widely used data platforms. In addition, the tool provides users with an option of choosing the method of their choice from the list for meta-analysis.

Features: ShinyMDE consists of a web interface, a standalone version to work remotely, and a database holding GPL files. The general workflow of the ShinyMDE system visualizes the steps of the meta-analysis, which is carried out automatically once a user submits the data and selects the necessary parameters.

Inputs: CSV and txt files.

Outputs: data; web.

- Spark ML [49]

Description: Spark is a unified analytics engine for large-scale data processing. The package spark.ml aims to provide a uniform set of high-level APIs that help users create and tune practical machine learning pipelines.

Features: Spark provides high-level APIs in Scala, Java, Python, and R, and an optimized engine that supports general computation graphs for data analysis. It also supports a rich set of higher-level tools including Spark SQL for SQL and DataFrames, pandas API on Spark for pandas workloads, MLlib for machine learning, GraphX for graph processing, and Structured Streaming for stream processing.

Inputs: Java and Python code.

Outputs: data results; plots.

- TensorFlow [50]

Description: TensorFlow 2 is an end-to-end, open-source machine learning platform which operates as an infrastructure layer for differentiable programming.

Features: It combines the following key abilities: efficiently executing low-level tensor operations on the CPU, GPU, or TPU; computing the gradient of arbitrary differentiable expressions; scaling computation to many devices; and exporting programs ("graphs") to external runtimes such as servers, browsers, and mobile and embedded devices.

Inputs: Python and C++ code.

Outputs: data; graphs; and plots.

- Torch [51]

Description: Torch is not in active development. The functionality provided by the C backend of Torch, which are the TH, THNN, THC, and THCUNN libraries, is actively extended and re-written in the ATen C++11 (which is a new version of C++) library (https://github.com/pytorch/pytorch/tree/master/aten, accessed on 30 December 2022). ATen exposes all operators you would expect from torch7, nn, cutorch, and cunn directly in C++11 and includes additional support for sparse tensors and distributed operations. Thus, Torch is the main package in Torch7 where data structures for multi-dimensional tensors and mathematical operations over these are defined. Moreover, it provides many utilities for accessing files, serializing objects of arbitrary types, and other useful utilities.

Features: Torch includes the following libraries: Tensor Library, File I/O Interface Library, and Useful Utilities. Moreover, Torch7 is a versatile numeric computing framework and machine learning library that extends Lua. Its goal is to provide a flexible environment to design and train learning machines. Flexibility is obtained via Lua, an extremely lightweight scripting language. Torch7 can easily be interfaced to third-party software thanks to Lua's light interface.

Inputs: code; scripts.

Outputs: data results; plots.

- NeuroSynth [54]

Description: In this article the authors describe and validate an automated brain mapping framework that uses text mining, meta-analysis, and machine learning techniques to generate a large database of mappings between neural and cognitive states.

Features: in this article the authors describe and validate a framework for the brain mapping, NeuroSynth, that takes an instrumental step towards automated large-scale synthesis of the neuroimaging literature. NeuroSynth combines text mining, meta-analysis, and machine learning techniques (naïve Bayes classification) to generate probabilistic mappings between cognitive and neural states.

Inputs: data.

Outputs: data; plots.

- Automated meta-analysis of the ERP literature [58]

Description: event-related potentials (ERP) are a common signal of analysis in medicine experiments, with a large existing literature of ERP-related work. This work uses automated literature collection and the text-mining of research articles to summarize the ERP literature, examining patterns and associations within and between components.

Features: all code for this project is written in the Python programming language and uses the LISC [63] Python tool to collect and analyze scientific literature. The data is collected from Pubmed, a database of biomedical literature. From there, the authors use text-mining and word co-occurrence analyses to derive data-driven summaries for each ERP, as well as to compare across these profiles to summarize patterns across the literature.

Inputs: Python code.

Outputs: data; plots.

- CancerMA [59]

Description: CancerMA is an online, integrated bioinformatic pipeline for automated identification of novel candidate cancer markers/targets. CancerMA operates by means of meta-analyzing expression profiles of user-defined sets of biologically significant and related genes across a manually curated database of 80 publicly available cancer microarray datasets covering 13 cancer types. A simple-to-use web interface allows experts to initiate new analyses as well as to view and retrieve the meta-analysis results.

Features: CancerMA consists of a web interface, a set of pipelined analyses, and two relational databases, one holding the analysis data for each user and another one holding the gene annotation data.

Inputs: R code and data.

Outputs: data; plots.

- CancerEST [60]

Description: CancerEST was developed as a user-friendly and intuitive tool to compute cancer marker/target potential as well as to obtain comprehensive expression profiles and information about the tissue specificity for genes of interest to biologists/clinicians. The CancerEST web interface for viewing the analysis results consists of three sections: the overview, the information, and the results section. The overview section provides basic information about the submitted job and a brief explanation on how to interpret the results.

Features: CancerEST consists of a web interface, pipelined analyses, and three relational databases; one holding the analysis data, one holding the Unigene data, and another one holding the gene annotation data.

Inputs: R code and data.

Outputs: data; plots.

4.2. Package/Software (Includes 7 Studies)

- Amamida R Package [29]

Description: the Amanida R package allows a meta-analysis of metabolomics data, combining the results of different studies addressing the same question. The Amanida package contains a collection of functions for computing a meta-analysis in R only using significance and effect size. It covers the lack of data provided on metabolomic studies. Amanida also computes qualitative meta-analysis.

Features: Amanida is a meta-analysis approach using only the most reported statistical parameters in this field: P-value and fold-change. The P-values are combined via Fisher's method and fold-changes by averaging, both weighted by the study size.

Inputs: supported files are csv, xls/xlsx, and txt.

Outputs: the Amanida package includes several visualization options: a volcano plot for quantitative results, a vote plot for total regulation behaviors for each compound, and an explore plot of the vote-counting results.

- dmetar [34]

Description: the dmetar package using the meta, metafor, netmeta, and meta-SEM packages as a base is provided as a companion to the R package to support more functions that improve the workflow of a meta-analysis.

Features: dmetar provides tools for various stages of the systematic review process, e.g., visualizing the risk of bias, standard inverse variance meta-analysis, network meta-analysis, three-level meta-analysis, and exploration of the between-study heterogeneity.

Inputs: R code.

Outputs: data results.

- DTA MA (Diagnostic Test Accuracy Meta-Analysis) (MetaDTA) [35]

Description: MetaDTA is an online interactive application for conducting the meta-analysis of diagnostic test accuracy studies (DTA), requiring no specialist software for the user to install, but leveraging established analysis routines (specifically the lme4 package in R).

Features: the application allows users to upload their own data, customize SROC plots, obtain statistics such as sensitivity and specificity, and conduct sensitivity analyses. All plots and tables are downloadable.

The tool is interactive and uses an intuitive "point and click" interface and presents results in visually intuitive and appealing ways. It is hoped that this tool will assist those in conducting a DTA meta-analysis who are not statistical experts, and, in turn, increase the relevance of published meta-analyses, and in the long term contribute to improved healthcare decision making as a result.

Inputs: csv files.

Outputs: data results; plots.

- Keras [36]

Description: Keras is a library that provides highly powerful and abstract building blocks to build deep learning networks. It is a deep learning API written in Python, running on top of the machine learning platform TensorFlow. It was developed with a focus on enabling fast experimentation.

Features: Keras supports both CPU and GPU computation and is a great tool for quickly prototyping ideas. It reduces the developer's cognitive load to free him up to focus on the parts of the problem that really matter. It also adopts the principle of the progressive disclosure of complexity. Finally, it provides industry-strength performance and scalability.

Inputs: Python code.

Outputs: data results.

- Meta-Essentials [37]

Description: this is a free excel tool for meta-analysis that facilitates the integration and synthesis of effect sizes from different studies.

Features: Meta-Essentials automatically calculates effect sizes from a wide range of statistics and can be used for a wide range of meta-analysis applications, including subgroup analysis, moderator analysis, and publication bias analysis.

Inputs: xls files.

Outputs: xls files.

- metafor [38]

Description: The metafor package is a free and open-source add-on for conducting meta-analyses with the statistical software environment R.

Features: the package consists of a collection of functions that allow the user to calculate various effect sizes or outcome measures, fit equal-, fixed-, random-, and mixed-effects models to such data, carry out moderator and meta-regression analyses, and create various types of meta-analytical plots.

Inputs: R code.

Outputs: data results; plots.

- MetaXL [41]

Description: MetaXL is an add-in for meta-analysis in Microsoft Excel for Windows. It supports all major meta-analysis methods, plus, uniquely, the inverse variance heterogeneity and quality effects models. Starting with v4.0, it also implements a powerful, yet easy-to-use way to perform network meta-analyses. Output is in table and graphical formats.

Features: MetaXL employs almost the same meta-analysis methods that can be accessed in general statistical packages and in dedicated meta-analysis software.

Inputs: Excel files.

Outputs: Excel files.

4.3. *Model/Method/Approach (Includes 10 Studies)*

- A Logic of the Meta-Analysis approach [28]

Description: in this position paper, the authors propose, the first as far as is known, an approach for automated reasoning in meta-analyses.

Features: thus, they considered the first steps towards a logic for performing automated meta-analysis based on a finite class of confidence intervals and subset relationships as background knowledge.

Inputs: A machine learning problem.

Outputs: The solution of the problem.

- Causal Learning Perspective [5]

Description: this work demonstrates the efficacy of using causal models to process the outputs of natural language processing (NLP)-based data extraction and achieve the goal of meta-analysis. In this article the authors initially extract information from scientific publications written in natural language. Sequently, from a novel causal learning perspective, they then propose to frame automated meta-analysis—based on the input of the first step—as a multiple causal inference problem where the summary effect is obtained through intervention.

Features: the authors of this article worked toward automating meta-analysis with a focus on controlling for risks of bias. Thus, they proposed the Multiple Causal inference for automated Meta-Analysis (MCMA). MCMA employs existing NLP systems for the extraction of risks of bias and therapeutic association, which are then used to estimate the summary therapeutic association across several Randomized Clinical Trials (RCTs). More analytically, from this perspective, the authors suggest to frame automated meta-analysis—based on the input of the first step—as a multiple causal inference problem where the summary effect is obtained through intervention. Built upon existent efforts for automating the primary steps of the meta-analysis, the proposed approach achieves the goal of automated meta-analysis and largely reduces the human effort involved.

Inputs: free text and data.

Outputs: data; plots.

- DIAeT [11]

Description: DIAeT (Dynamic Interactive Argumentation Trees) is a method of synthesizing the evidence available in clinical trials in an ad-hoc and on-demand manner that automatically organizes such evidence into a hierarchical argument that recommends a treatment as superior to another based on a series of key dimensions corresponding to the clinical points of interest.

Features: the DIAeT method is an argumentation-based method that contributes to supporting the synthesis of clinical trial evidence. A limitation of the method is that it relies on a manually populated knowledge base. This problem can be addressed by applying natural language processing methods to extract relevant information from publications. The method has been implemented as a web tool.

Inputs: SPARQL queries.

Outputs: results on the web.

- metamisc [40]

Description: the metamisc package includes the meta-analysis of diagnostic and prognostic modeling studies. In addition, it summarizes estimations of prognostic factors, diagnostic test accuracy, and prediction model performance. Finally, it validates, updates, and combines published prediction models. It also develops new prediction models with data from multiple studies.

Features: This R package deals with the incomplete availability of study-specific results (performance estimates and their precision), and produces summary estimates of the c-statistic and the observed: the expected ratio and the calibration slope. Furthermore, it tackles the implementation of frequentist and Bayesian meta-analysis methods and proposes novel empirically based prior distributions to improve the estimation of between-study heterogeneity in small samples.

Inputs: R code.

Outputs: data results.

- Comprehensive gene expression meta-analysis [53]

Description: this approach plans a comprehensive gene expression meta-analysis that labels novel immune signatures in patients with rheumatoid arthritis. This pattern suggests meta-analysis to recognize novel gene signatures that take care of providing mechanistic visions into disease initiation, progression, and the development of better therapeutic attacks.

Features: the aim of the meta-analysis method was firstly to extract the intersected genes, then to exclude genes with inconsistent expression, and finally to test them for significance. The weighted Z-method was used to combine the individual q-values of each gene [64] and was implemented using an R package (https://github.com/bhklab/survcomp, accessed on 28 December 2022), [65].

The meta-analysis algorithm was implemented using R.

Inputs: R code.

Outputs: data.

- Text-mining the neurosynth corpus (NeuroSynth #2) [55]

Description: in this work the authors demonstrate that an unsupervised study of the NeuroSynth text corpus using Deep Boltzmann Machines (DBMs) can be effectively employed to learn the distribution of the text corpus. The results of this study show some of the clusters obtained when k-means clustering is applied to word embeddings obtained from the DBM model. The clusters display clear semantic context.

Features: a two-layer DBM was employed consisting of a visible layer of multinomial visible units followed by two binary hidden layers. During pre-training and model selection, DBMs were trained. Briefly, annealed importance sampling was employed to estimate the partition function for each DBM. Thus, the proposed DBM model can be used to obtain both word as well as document embeddings in a high-dimensional vector space.

Inputs: data.

Outputs: data; plots.

- Social brain (NeuroSynth #3) [56]

Description: how the human brain processes social information is an increasingly researched topic in psychology and neuroscience, advancing our understanding of basic human cognition and psychopathologies. In this study, the authors investigated whether these brain regions are evoked by the mere presence of social information using an automated meta-analysis and confirmatory data from an independent study. Results of 1000 published fMRI studies containing the keyword of "social" were subject to an automated meta-analysis. The social/non-social contrast in the independent study showed a strong resemblance to the NeuroSynth map. The Region Of Interest (ROI) analyses revealed that a social effect was credible in most of the NeuroSynth regions in the independent dataset.

Features: the first part of the analyses of this study aimed to identify the brain regions that have shown significant activation in published fMRI studies with a prominent social element in the literature. Using the keyword "social" yielded 1000 published fMRI studies to include in an automated meta-analysis on neurosynth.org. The authors used the reverse inference map of the results of the automated meta-analysis, which represent z-scores corresponding to the likelihood that the term "social" is used in a study given the presence of the reported activation. The significant brain regions showing up in the reverse inference map represent those that are more likely to be reported in "social" studies than in "non-social" studies.

Inputs: data.

Outputs: data; plots.

- MetaCyto [57]

Description: the authors of this article developed MetaCyto for the automated meta-analysis of flow cytometry and mass spectrometry (CyTOF) data.

Features: by combining clustering methods with a scanning method, MetaCyto can identify commonly labeled subsets of cells, thereby enabling meta-analysis. Thus, the application of MetaCyto to a set of cytometric studies allowed for the identification of cell populations that show differences in abundance between demographic groups.

Inputs: R package.

Outputs: data; plots.

- Research Method Classification [61]

Description: this research work presents a prototype that applies deep transfer learning to predict the research methods in scientific publications, which facilitates an automatic discovery of crucial research information from large numbers of publications. The current state-of-the-art for classification of research methods uses Support Vector Models (SVMs).

This article provides the following research contributions: (a) developing an artifact that uses deep transfer learning and outperforms the state-of-the-art of research method classification, (b) using full papers and classifying them into predefined research methods, and (c) demonstrating the performance based on an extensive Information Systems corpus.

Features: the proposed approach outperforms state-of-the-art research method classification that deploys the Support Vector Model (SVM). The proposed deep transfer learning models can lead to a better recognition of research methods than shallower word embedding approaches such as word2vec or GloVe. The results illustrate the potential of establishing semi-automated methods for meta-analysis.

Inputs: free text and data.

Outputs: data.

- AUTOMETA [62]

Description: the proposed system for automating meta-analysis employs existing natural language processing methods for identifying Participants, Intervention, Control, and Outcome (PICO) elements. This system can perform advanced meta-analyses by parsing numeric outcomes to identify the number of patients having certain outcomes. In this study, the authors used the BERT-based approach which is a general-purpose language model trained on a large dataset and uses an attention mechanism that learns contextual relations between words in a text.

Features: the proposed system consists of four major components: crawling PubMed articles, NLP module, creating structured data, and aggregation and visualization. First, a user queries the PubMed database and related articles are returned. Abstracts are then extracted from the articles and passed to the NLP module for preprocessing and extraction of PICO elements. The extracted data are then converted into a structured form. It also parses numeric texts to identify the number of patients having certain outcomes. Identification of the number of patients having certain outcomes is important for statistical analysis to determine the effectiveness of an intervention.

Inputs: free text and data.

Outputs: data.

4.4. Web Application and Integrated Systems (Includes 5 Studies)

- Automated meta-analysis of biomedical texts [10]

Description: in this research article the authors present the results of the automated analysis of the data extracted from abstracts of scientific articles available in PubMed. These results demonstrate the associations between types of tumors and the most used methods for their cell-based immunotherapy.

Features: the proposed method automates the meta-analysis by standardizing the process in a series of steps. In summary, the following are mentioned: (a) crawling abstracts from Pubmed via the Scrapy based web-crawler, (b) rich linguistic features extraction by using the ISANLP framework which is a Python library to obtain the morphology, syntax parsing, and semantic role labeling features [66], (c) combining tumor and cell dictionaries and morphology-based rules to extract entity candidates from the abstracts, d) using syntactic relations and constructing all their possible combinations and applying models (e.g., UMLS Metathesaurus, MetaMap [67] Fasttext model [68]) to map the terms, (e) using syntactic relations and semantic roles to reveal the links between entities and their roles in the sentence, (f) applying a pre-trained sequence-labeling machine learning model to filter uninformative entity candidates, and g) computing co-occurrence statistics and mining associative rules for the extracted entities [69,70] to obtain stable combinations of tumors, therapy, and cell types. We used the Eclat algorithm [71] because of its scalability.

Inputs: biomedical texts; abstracts of scientific articles available in PubMed; Python code.

Outputs: data; plots.

- MetaInsight [39]

Description: MetaInsight is a new tool that is freely available and that conducts network meta-analysis (NMA) via the web.

Features: MetaInsight is a web-based tool allowing users with only standard internet browser software to be able to conduct NMAs using an intuitive "point and click" interface and present the results using visual plots.

Inputs: .csv files.

Outputs: data results; plots.

- Nested-Knowledge [72]

Description: Nested Knowledge offers a comprehensive software platform for systematic literature review and meta-analysis.

Features: the software is composed of two parts which work in tandem. Search, screen, tag, and extract data with AutoLit, and visualize, analyze, publish, and share insights with Synthesis.

Inputs: RIS files.

Outputs: data results; plots; RIS or nBIB files.

- netmeta [42]

Description: an R package for frequentist meta-analysis, this has a comprehensive set of functions providing a lot of methods for network meta-analysis.

Features: this package supports a comprehensive set of functions providing frequentist methods for network meta-analysis such as: the frequentist network meta-analysis; the net heat plot and design-based decomposition of Cochran's Q; the measurements of characterizing the flow of evidence between two treatments; the ranking of treatments based on the frequentist analogue of SUCRA; the partial order of treatment rankings and the Hasse diagram; and the contribution matrix, etc.

Inputs: R code.

Outputs: data results.

- Whyis [52]

Description: Whyis is the first framework for creating custom provenance-driven knowledge graphs. Whyis knowledge graphs are based on nanopublications, which simplify and standardize the production of structured, provenance-supported knowledge in knowledge graphs.

To create probabilistic knowledge graphs, Whyis [52] implements a method of automated meta-analysis. The authors refined the methods used in [73] by using Stouffer's Z-Method [64].

Features: Whyis is written in Python using the Flask framework. The RDF database used by default is Fuseki. Whyis uses the SPARQL Query, Update, and Graph Store HTTP Protocol. Storage is provided using the FileDepot Python library to provide the file-based persistence of nanopublications and uploaded files. Whyis also relies on Celery which is a task queuing system that can be scaled by adding more task workers on remote machines. Thus, knowledge graph developers create their knowledge graphs by generating a Python module that contains the configuration, templates, and code adapted to their purposes.

Inputs: Python code and script modules.

Outputs: Views; data; plots.

5. Discussion

5.1. Purpose of This Study

The aim of this article is to discover the most modern and complete tools used to automate the conduct of meta-analyses of clinical trials. In this way, it will contribute, on the one hand, to the identification and promotion of the most suitable candidates, and on the other hand, to the development of research in this field.

5.2. Benefits Arising from Automated Meta-Analysis

The evaluation of automated meta-analysis results is presented in some studies [5,9–11,29,37]. Their approaches show positive and promising results in the feasibility, acceptance, reliability, and time consumption. More analytically, the most important benefits are the ability to process large data sets in shorter times without altering expert confidence in the methodological and scientific rigor [6].

5.3. Comparison of Systems and Tools Currently Available

Built upon existent efforts for automating the basic steps of meta-analysis, the proposed approaches achieve the goal of automated meta-analysis and largely reduce the human effort involved [5].

However, although important steps have been taken to date, currently there is no application that can fully replace the human effort in conducting a systematic review to draw conclusions from clinical trials. Thus, while the other tasks of a systematic review have significantly developed, the automation of meta-analyses is still far from being able to significantly support and facilitate the work of researchers, freeing them from manual, difficult, and time-consuming work.

At the same time, it is worth noting that most of the tools are either open source or some are freely available (Table 2). Therefore, the strengthening of research in this field should be important in the immediate future.

The benefits of automating meta-analysis are expected to be particularly important in all areas of evidence-based medicine and especially in cutting edge areas of medical research such as gene therapy and cancer treatment.

5.4. Limitations of This Study

In addition, this overview has some methodological limitations. Initially the author had difficulty in identifying suitable articles. This limitation was partially addressed using snowballing methods. Secondly, the author included articles written only in English.

6. Conclusions and Future Directions

ML is the fastest growing field in computer science, and Health Informatics is amongst the greatest application challenges, providing significant benefits in improved medical prognosis, diagnosis, and pharmaceutical development [74].

Meta-analysis is a systematic approach for understanding a wonder by resolving the results of many previously published exploratory studies. It is used mainly to extract knowledge and decisions about the summary effect of situations, interventions, and treatments in medicine. Unfortunately, meta-analysis involves excellent human exertion, rendering a process that is extremely inefficient and vulnerable to human bias. To overcome these issues, many researchers are studying and proposing architectures, methods, and tools to automate meta-analysis [5]. The researchers' main goal is to provide a system for automating the meta-analysis process as much as possible to reduce the time taken in conducting a meta-analysis [62].

Moreover, the development and application of ML in the meta-analysis of clinical trials is a promising approach to implement more effective daily clinical practices.

However, extensive future studies are needed to validate the performance of ML tools in their application domain.

Funding: This research received no external funding.

Institutional Review Board Statement: Not applicable.

Informed Consent Statement: Not applicable.

Data Availability Statement: Data from this research are not available elsewhere. Please contact the author for more information, if required.

Conflicts of Interest: The author declares no conflict of interest.

References

1. Sargeant, J.M.; Kelton, D.F.; O'Connor, A. Study Designs and Systematic Reviews of Interventions: Building Evidence Across Study Designs. *Zoonoses Public Health* **2014**, *61*, 10–17. [CrossRef]
2. Russo, M.W. How to Review a Meta-analysis. *Gastroenterol. Hepatol.* **2007**, *3*, 637–642.
3. Masoumi, S.; Shahraz, S. Meta-analysis using Python: A hands-on tutorial. *BMC Med. Res. Methodol.* **2022**, *22*, 193. [CrossRef] [PubMed]
4. Christopoulou, S.C. Machine Learning Tools and Platforms in Clinical Trial Outputs to Support Evidence-Based Health Informatics: A Rapid Review of the Literature. *Biomedinformatics* **2022**, *2*, 511–527. [CrossRef]
5. Cheng, L.; Katz-Rogozhnikov, D.A.; Varshney, K.R.; Baldini, I.; Cheng, L.; Katz-Rogozhnikov, D.A.; Varshney, K.R.; Baldini, I. Automated Meta-Analysis: A Causal Learning Perspective. *arXiv* **2021**, arXiv:2104.04633.

6. Ajiji, P.; Cottin, J.; Picot, C.; Uzunali, A.; Ripoche, E.; Cucherat, M.; Maison, P. Feasibility study and evaluation of expert opinion on the semi-automated meta-analysis and the conventional meta-analysis. *Eur. J. Clin. Pharmacol.* **2022**, *78*, 1177–1184. [CrossRef]
7. O'Connor, A.M.; Glasziou, P.; Taylor, M.; Thomas, J.; Spijker, R.; Wolfe, M.S. A focus on cross-purpose tools, automated recognition of study design in multiple disciplines, and evaluation of automation tools: A summary of significant discussions at the fourth meeting of the International Collaboration for Automation of Systematic Reviews (ICASR). *Syst. Rev.* **2020**, *9*, 100. [CrossRef]
8. Zintzaras, E.; Lau, J. Trends in meta-analysis of genetic association studies. *J. Hum. Genet.* **2008**, *53*, 1–9. [CrossRef]
9. Johnson, E.E.; O'Keefe, H.; Sutton, A.; Marshall, C. The Systematic Review Toolbox: Keeping up to date with tools to support evidence synthesis. *Syst. Rev.* **2022**, *11*, 258. [CrossRef]
10. Devyatkin, D.; Molodchenkov, A.; Lukin, A.; Kim, Y.; Boyko, A.; Karalkin, P.; Chiang, J.-H.; Volkova, G.; Lupatov, A. Towards Automated Meta-analysis of Biomedical Texts in the Field of Cell-based Immunotherapy. *Biomed. Chem. Res. Methods* **2019**, *2*, e00109. [CrossRef]
11. Sanchez-Graillet, O.; Witte, C.; Grimm, F.; Grautoff, S.; Ell, B.; Cimiano, P. Synthesizing evidence from clinical trials with dynamic interactive argument trees. *J. Biomed. Semant.* **2022**, *13*, 16. [CrossRef] [PubMed]
12. Wang, Z.; Liu, K.; Li, J.; Zhu, Y.; Zhang, Y. Various Frameworks and Libraries of Machine Learning and Deep Learning: A Survey. *Arch. Comput. Methods Eng.* **2019**, 1–24. [CrossRef]
13. Scott, A.M.; Forbes, C.; Clark, J.; Carter, M.; Glasziou, P.; Munn, Z. Systematic review automation tools improve efficiency but lack of knowledge impedes their adoption: A survey. *J. Clin. Epidemiol.* **2021**, *138*, 80–94. [CrossRef]
14. Jaspers, S.; De Troyer, E.; Aerts, M. Machine learning techniques for the automation of literature reviews and systematic reviews in EFSA. *EFSA Support. Publ.* **2018**, *15*, 1427E. [CrossRef]
15. Khalil, H.; Ameen, D.; Zarnegar, A. Tools to support the automation of systematic reviews: A scoping review. *J. Clin. Epidemiol.* **2021**, *144*, 22–42. [CrossRef]
16. Beller, E.; On behalf of the founding members of the ICASR group; Clark, J.; Tsafnat, G.; Adams, C.; Diehl, H.; Lund, H.; Ouzzani, M.; Thayer, K.; Thomas, J.; et al. Making progress with the automation of systematic reviews: Principles of the International Collaboration for the Automation of Systematic Reviews (ICASR). *Syst. Rev.* **2018**, *7*, 77. [CrossRef]
17. Cowie, K.; Rahmatullah, A.; Hardy, N.; Holub, K.; Kallmes, K. Web-Based Software Tools for Systematic Literature Review in Medicine: Systematic Search and Feature Analysis. *JMIR Med. Inform.* **2021**, *10*, e33219. [CrossRef]
18. Khangura, S.; Konnyu, K.; Cushman, R.; Grimshaw, J.; Moher, D. Evidence summaries: The evolution of a rapid review approach. *Syst. Rev.* **2012**, *1*, 10. [CrossRef]
19. Oxman, A.D. Users' guides to the medical literature. VI. How to use an overview. Evidence-Based Medicine Working Group. *JAMA* **1994**, *272*, 1367–1371. [CrossRef]
20. Grant, M.J.; Booth, A. A typology of reviews: An analysis of 14 review types and associated methodologies. *Health Inf. Libr. J.* **2009**, *26*, 91–108. [CrossRef]
21. Greenhalgh, T.; Peacock, R. Effectiveness and efficiency of search methods in systematic reviews of complex evidence: Audit of primary sources. *BMJ* **2005**, *331*, 1064–1065. [CrossRef] [PubMed]
22. Shehzad, Z.; Kelly, C.; Reiss, P.T.; Craddock, R.C.; Emerson, J.W.; McMahon, K.; Copland, D.A.; Castellanos, F.X.; Milham, M.P. A multivariate distance-based analytic framework for connectome-wide association studies. *Neuroimage* **2014**, *93*, 74–94. [CrossRef] [PubMed]
23. Ewendelken, C. Meta-analysis: How does posterior parietal cortex contribute to reasoning? *Front. Hum. Neurosci.* **2015**, *8*, 1042. [CrossRef] [PubMed]
24. Chavez, R.S.; Heatherton, T.F. Representational Similarity of Social and Valence Information in the Medial pFC. *J. Cogn. Neurosci.* **2015**, *27*, 73–82. [CrossRef]
25. Chawla, M.; Miyapuram, K.P. Comparison of meta-analysis approaches for neuroimaging studies of reward processing: A case study. In Proceedings of the 2015 International Joint Conference, Killarney, Ireland, 12–17 July 2015; pp. 1–5. [CrossRef]
26. Dockès, J.; A Poldrack, R.; Primet, R.; Gözükan, H.; Yarkoni, T.; Suchanek, F.; Thirion, B.; Varoquaux, G. NeuroQuery, comprehensive meta-analysis of human brain mapping. *Elife* **2020**, *9*, e53385. [CrossRef]
27. Muller, A.M.; Meyer, M. Language in the brain at rest: New insights from resting state data and graph theoretical analysis. *Front. Hum. Neurosci.* **2014**, *8*, 228. [CrossRef]
28. Peñaloza, R. Towards a Logic of Meta-Analysis. In Proceedings of the 17th International Conference on Principles of Knowledge Representation and Reasoning, Rhodes, Greece, 12–18 September 2020.
29. Llambrich, M.; Correig, E.; Gumà, J.; Brezmes, J.; Cumeras, R. Amanida: An R package for meta-analysis of metabolomics non-integral data. *Bioinformatics* **2021**, *38*, 583–585. [CrossRef]
30. Hsieh, M. *Getting Started with Amazon SageMaker Studio: Learn to Build End-to-End Machine Learning Projects in the SageMaker Machine Learning IDE.*; Packt Publishing Ltd.: Birmingham, UK, 2022.
31. Simon, J. *Learn Amazon SageMaker: A Guide to Building, Training, and Deploying Machine Learning Models for Developers and Data Scientists*; Packt Publishing Ltd.: Birmingham, UK, 2020.
32. Hazelwood, K.; Bird, S.; Brooks, D.; Chintala, S.; Diril, U.; Dzhulgakov, D.; Fawzy, M.; Jia, B.; Jia, Y.; Kalro, A. Applied machine learning at Facebook: A datacenter infrastructure perspective. In Proceedings of the 2018 IEEE International Symposium on High-Performance Computer Architecture (HPCA), Vienna, Austria, 24–28 February 2018; pp. 620–629.

33. Nikolakopoulou, A.; Higgins, J.P.T.; Papakonstantinou, T.; Chaimani, A.; Del Giovane, C.; Egger, M.; Salanti, G. CINeMA: An approach for assessing confidence in the results of a network meta-analysis. *PLoS Med.* **2020**, *17*, e1003082. [CrossRef]
34. Harrer, M.; Cuijpers, P.; Furukawa, T.A.; Ebert, D.D. *Doing Meta-Analysis with R: A Hands-On Guide*; CRC Press: Boca Raton, FL, USA, 2021.
35. Patel, A.; Cooper, N.; Freeman, S.; Sutton, A. Graphical enhancements to summary receiver operating characteristic plots to facilitate the analysis and reporting of meta-analysis of diagnostic test accuracy data. *Res. Synth. Methods* **2020**, *12*, 34–44. [CrossRef]
36. Ketkar, N. Introduction to Keras. In *Deep Learning with Python*; Apress: Berkeley, CA, USA, 2017; pp. 97–111.
37. Suurmond, R.; van Rhee, H.; Hak, T. Introduction, comparison, and validation of *Meta-Essentials*: A free and simple tool for meta-analysis. *Res. Synth. Methods* **2017**, *8*, 537–553. [CrossRef]
38. Viechtbauer, W. Conducting Meta-Analyses in R with the metafor Package. *J. Stat. Softw.* **2010**, *36*, 1–48. [CrossRef]
39. Owen, R.K.; Bradbury, N.; Xin, Y.; Cooper, N.; Sutton, A. MetaInsight: An interactive web-based tool for analyzing, interrogating, and visualizing network meta-analyses using R-shiny and netmeta. *Res. Synth. Methods* **2019**, *10*, 569–581. [CrossRef] [PubMed]
40. Debray, T.P.; Damen, J.A.; Riley, R.D.; Snell, K.; Reitsma, J.B.; Hooft, L.; Collins, G.S.; Moons, K.G. A framework for meta-analysis of prediction model studies with binary and time-to-event outcomes. *Stat. Methods Med. Res.* **2018**, *28*, 2768–2786. [CrossRef] [PubMed]
41. Doi, S.A.; Barendregt, J.J.; Khan, S.; Thalib, L.; Williams, G.M. Advances in the meta-analysis of heterogeneous clinical trials I: The inverse variance heterogeneity model. *Contemp. Clin. Trials* **2015**, *45*, 130–138. [CrossRef]
42. Network Meta-Analysis Using Frequentist Methods [R Package Netmeta Version 0.9-8]. Available online: https://CRAN.R-project.org/package=netmeta (accessed on 29 December 2022).
43. Open NN: An Open Source Neural Networks C++ Library. Available online: http://opennn.cimne.com (accessed on 30 December 2022).
44. Hongyong, D. PyMeta. 2018. Available online: www.pymeta.com (accessed on 27 November 2022).
45. Hongyong, D. PythonMeta 1.26. 2018. Available online: https://pypi.org/project/PythonMeta/ (accessed on 28 December 2022).
46. The Linux Foundation. PyTorch. Available online: https://pytorch.org/ (accessed on 31 December 2022).
47. Kramer, O. *Machine Learning for Evolution Strategies*; Springer: Cham, Switzerland, 2016; p. 20. [CrossRef]
48. Shashirekha, H.L.; Wani, A.H. ShinyMDE: Shiny tool for microarray meta-analysis for differentially expressed gene detection. In Proceedings of the 2016 International Conference on Bioinformatics and Systems Biology (BSB), Allahabad, India, 4–6 March 2016; pp. 1–5. [CrossRef]
49. Polak, A. *Scaling Machine Learning with Spark: Distributed ML with MLlib, TensorFlow, and Pytorch*; O'Reilly Media: Sebastopol, CA, USA, 2023.
50. Hope, T.; Resheff, Y.; Lieder, I. *Learning TensorFlow: A Guide to Building Deep Learning Systems*; O'Reilly Media, Inc.: Sebastopol, CA, USA, 2017.
51. Collobert, R.; Kavukcuoglu, K.; Farabet, C. Torch7: A Matlab-like Environment for Machine Learning. Available online: https://ronan.collobert.com/pub/matos/2011_torch7_nipsw.pdf (accessed on 31 December 2022).
52. McCusker, J.P.; Rashid, S.M.; Agu, N.; Bennett, K.P.; McGuinness, D.L. Developing Scientific Knowledge Graphs Using Whyis. In *SemSci@ ISWC*; Rensselaer Polytechnic Ins.: Troy, NY, USA, 2018; pp. 52–58.
53. Afroz, S.; Giddaluru, J.; Vishwakarma, S.; Naz, S.; Khan, A.A.; Khan, N. A Comprehensive Gene Expression Meta-analysis Identifies Novel Immune Signatures in Rheumatoid Arthritis Patients. *Front. Immunol.* **2017**, *8*, 74. [CrossRef]
54. Yarkoni, T.; Poldrack, R.; Nichols, T.; Van Essen, D.C.; Wager, T.D. Large-scale automated synthesis of human functional neuroimaging data. *Nat. Methods* **2011**, *8*, 665–670. [CrossRef]
55. Monti, R.; Lorenz, R.; Leech, R.; Anagnostopoulos, C.; Montana, G. Text-mining the neurosynth corpus using deep boltzmann machines. In Proceedings of the 2016 International Workshop on Pattern Recognition in Neuroimaging (PRNI), Trento, Italy, 22–24 June 2016; pp. 1–4. [CrossRef]
56. Tso, I.F.; Rutherford, S.; Fang, Y.; Angstadt, M.; Taylor, S.F. The "social brain" is highly sensitive to the mere presence of social information: An automated meta-analysis and an independent study. *PLoS ONE* **2018**, *13*, e0196503. [CrossRef]
57. Hu, Z.; Jujjavarapu, C.; Hughey, J.J.; Andorf, S.; Lee, H.-C.; Gherardini, P.F.; Spitzer, M.H.; Thomas, C.G.; Campbell, J.; Dunn, P.; et al. MetaCyto: A Tool for Automated Meta-analysis of Mass and Flow Cytometry Data. *Cell Rep.* **2018**, *24*, 1377–1388. [CrossRef]
58. Donoghue, T.; Voytek, B. Automated meta-analysis of the event-related potential (ERP) literature. *Sci. Rep.* **2022**, *12*, 1867. [CrossRef]
59. Feichtinger, J.; McFarlane, R.J.; Larcombe, L.D. CancerMA: A web-based tool for automatic meta-analysis of public cancer microarray data. *Database* **2012**, *2012*, bas055. [CrossRef]
60. Feichtinger, J.; McFarlane, R.J.; Larcombe, L.D. CancerEST: A web-based tool for automatic meta-analysis of public EST data. *Database* **2014**, *2014*, bau024. [CrossRef] [PubMed]
61. Anisienia, A.; Mueller, R.M.; Kupfer, A.; Staake, T. Research Method Classification with Deep Transfer Learning for Semi-Automatic Meta-Analysis of Information Systems Papers. In Proceedings of the 54th Hawaii International Conference on System Sciences, online, 4–9 January 2021; pp. 6099–6108. [CrossRef]
62. Mutinda, F.W.; Yada, S.; Wakamiya, S.; Aramaki, E. AUTOMETA: Automatic Meta-Analysis System Employing Natural Language Processing. *Stud. Health Technol. Inform.* **2022**, *290*, 612–616. [CrossRef]

63. LISC-Literature Scanner-Lisc 0.2.0 Documentation. Available online: https://lisc-tools.github.io/lisc/ (accessed on 23 January 2023).
64. Whitlock, M.C. Combining probability from independent tests: The weighted Z-method is superior to Fisher's approach. *J. Evol. Biol.* **2005**, *18*, 1368–1373. [CrossRef] [PubMed]
65. Schröder, M.S.; Culhane, A.C.; Quackenbush, J.; Haibe-Kains, B. survcomp: An R/Bioconductor package for performance assessment and comparison of survival models. *Bioinformatics* **2011**, *27*, 3206–3208. [CrossRef] [PubMed]
66. Larionov, D.; Moscow, R.F.C.R.; Shelmanov, A.; Chistova, E.; Smirnov, I. Semantic Role Labeling with Pretrained Language Models for Known and Unknown Predicates. In *Proceedings of the International Conference on Recent Advances in Natural Language Processing (RANLP 2019)*; INCOMA Ltd.: Varna, Bulgaria, 2019; pp. 619–628. [CrossRef]
67. Aronson, A.R.; Lang, F.-M. An overview of MetaMap: Historical perspective and recent advances. *J. Am. Med. Inform. Assoc.* **2010**, *17*, 229–236. [CrossRef]
68. Joulin, A.; Grave, E.; Bojanowski, P.; Mikolov, T. Bag of tricks for efficient text classification. In Proceedings of the 15th Conference of the European Chapter of the Association for Computational Linguistics: Volume 2, Short Paper, Valencia, Spain, 3–7 April 2017.
69. Srikant, R. *Fast Algorithms for Mining Association Rules and Sequential Patterns*; The University of Wisconsin-Madison: Madison, WI, USA, 1996.
70. Srikant, R.; Agrawal, R. Mining quantitative association rules in large relational tables. In Proceedings of the 1996 ACM SIGMOD International Conference on Management of Data—SIGMOD '96, Montreal, QC, Canada, 4–6 June 1996. [CrossRef]
71. Zaki, M. Scalable algorithms for association mining. *IEEE Trans. Knowl. Data Eng.* **2000**, *12*, 372–390. [CrossRef]
72. Nested Knowledge Features. Available online: https://about.nested-knowledge.com/ (accessed on 31 December 2022).
73. McCusker, J.P.; Dumontier, M.; Yan, R.; He, S.; Dordick, J.S.; McGuinness, D.L. Finding melanoma drugs through a probabilistic knowledge graph. *Peer J. Comput. Sci.* **2017**, *3*, e106. [CrossRef]
74. Holzinger, A. *Machine Learning for Health Informatics: State-of-the-Art and Future Challenges*; Springer International Publishing: Cham, Switzerland, 2016. [CrossRef]

BioMedInformatics MDPI

Review

In Silico Protein Structure Analysis for SARS-CoV-2 Vaccines Using Deep Learning

Yasunari Matsuzaka [1,2,*] and Ryu Yashiro [2,3]

[1] Division of Molecular and Medical Genetics, Center for Gene and Cell Therapy, The Institute of Medical Science, University of Tokyo, Minato-ku, Tokyo 108-8639, Japan
[2] Administrative Section of Radiation Protection, National Institute of Neuroscience, National Center of Neurology and Psychiatry, Kodaira, Tokyo 187-8551, Japan
[3] Department of Infectious Diseases, Kyorin University School of Medicine, 6-20-2 Shinkawa, Mitaka-shi, Tokyo 181-8611, Japan
* Correspondence: yasunari80808@ims.u-tokyo.ac.jp; Tel.: +81-3-5449-5372

Abstract: Protein three-dimensional structural analysis using artificial intelligence is attracting attention in various fields, such as the estimation of vaccine structure and stability. In particular, when using the spike protein in vaccines, the major issues in the construction of SARS-CoV-2 vaccines are their weak abilities to attack the virus and elicit immunity for a short period. Structural information about new viruses is essential for understanding their properties and creating effective vaccines. However, determining the structure of a protein through experiments is a lengthy and laborious process. Therefore, a new computational approach accelerated the elucidation process and made predictions more accurate. Using advanced machine learning technology called deep neural networks, it has become possible to predict protein structures directly from protein and gene sequences. We summarize the advances in antiviral therapy with the SARS-CoV-2 vaccine and extracellular vesicles via computational analysis.

Keywords: SARS-CoV-2 vaccines; deep learning; spike protein; ACE2; CpG DNA

Citation: Matsuzaka, Y.; Yashiro, R. In Silico Protein Structure Analysis for SARS-CoV-2 Vaccines Using Deep Learning. *Biomedinformatics* **2023**, *3*, 54–72. https://doi.org/10.3390/biomedinformatics3010004

Academic Editor: Pentti Nieminen

Received: 20 December 2022
Revised: 6 January 2023
Accepted: 10 January 2023
Published: 11 January 2023

1. Introduction

Vaccines for the new coronavirus disease (COVID-19) are on track around the world, but it is still difficult to predict when this pandemic will end. Furthermore, the possibility of achieving "herd immunity" that if a sufficient proportion of people develop immunity to severe acute respiratory syndrome coronavirus 2 (SARS-CoV-2), is beginning to be considered unlikely. This thinking reflects the complexity and difficulty of responding to a pandemic and does not deny the fact that vaccination is beneficial. As more people in the population acquire immunity, another problem arises. A higher percentage of people who acquire immunity creates selective pressure, favoring mutant strains that can infect those who acquire immunity. Furthermore, new SARS-CoV-2 variants emerge that are highly contagious and are resistant to vaccine, and once acquired immunity is attenuated. Thus, antibodies induced by current vaccines are 'strain-specific' and cannot respond to antigenic mutation of virus strains, and it is necessary to activate antibodies that match the latest epidemic strains. By vaccinating as many as possible as soon as possible, it is possible to prevent new variants from gaining footholds. However, it is almost inevitable that vaccines will create new selective pressure and lead to the emergence of mutant strains, so it is necessary to develop infrastructure and processes to monitor this. In this way, vaccines are a double-edged sword that can immunize many people and create many new patients. Furthermore, the persistence of induced antibodies is not as good as that of live vaccines, such as the measles vaccine [1,2]. It will also be important to clarify how long immunity from vaccines lasts and whether booster vaccinations are necessary after vaccination.

Additionally, considerable attention has been focused on antibodies that acquire 'cross-reactivity' by targeting epitopes that are difficult to mutate to improve the strain specificity of vaccines [3–7]. Because this cross-reactive antibody is a rare antibody that is difficult to induce with current vaccines, structural analysis has clarified the binding sites and B cell epitopes of monoclonal cross-reactive antibodies, and it has become possible to produce vaccines with artificially increased antigenicity to facilitate the induction of these antibodies through structural biology approaches, such as epitope-focused vaccines [8,9]. Although vaccine formulations based on this strategy have shown steady efficacy in animal models, clinical studies have suggested that the persistence of induced cross-reactive antibodies may be even lower than that of normal antibodies. Therefore, in the future, it will be necessary to devise ways to increase the amount and persistence of antibodies induced. To develop vaccines that are both safe and effective, it is important to understand the in vivo infection mechanisms of the virus. The amount and persistence of antibodies induced by influenza vaccines are largely dependent on the amount and quality of helper signals supplied by activated T cells to B cells [10,11]. Therefore, vaccine antigens must bind to T cell antigen receptors in addition to binding to antibodies, which are B cell antigen receptors that elicit helper signals from T cells [12–20]. Because T-cell epitopes consist of peptides of 20 amino acids or less, antigenicity is mainly determined by the primary amino acid sequence [21,22]. On the other hand, by mutating the part that binds to the antibody made by the vaccine, the virus can escape from the antibody while maintaining the ability to invade cells. At the time, a new vaccine containing the mutated part will be needed. In such a case, although there is a protein property prediction that predicts a change in stability for a single amino acid mutation from the amino acid sequence of the protein, not only the static structure but also the dynamic structure greatly contributes to the expression of protein function. Therefore, the molecular dynamics (MD) method has come to be used frequently as a means of analyzing the dynamic structure of proteins by simulation, but the amount of trajectory, molecular motion, obtained as a result of MD simulation is enormous. Moreover, since it is time-series data, in silico technology, including machine learning or deep learning is actively applied. Then, using the learning results, pseudo-MD is performed for single amino acid mutants of the protein without performing MD simulation calculation, which takes a long time, similar results, such as trajectory etc. can be obtained. Therefore, it is relatively easy to predict antigenicity using the bioinformatics tools. In this review, we summarize the applications of in silico analysis including deep learning for SARS-CoV-2 vaccine.

2. Anti-Virus Therapy via Vaccine

Two strategies are available for the development of antiviral drugs: (1) suppress the life cycle of the virus in the host cell and (2) control the runaway of the host immune system [23–44]. Three-dimensional (3D) protein structure information is extremely useful in searching for drug candidates that inhibit the functions of viral proteins based on strategy (1) [45,46]. Therefore, it is necessary to develop therapeutic drugs and vaccines as soon as possible; therapeutic drugs and vaccines against COVID-19 are underway. SARS-CoV-2 is classified as a single-stranded positive-strand RNA virus, and its genome size is approximately 30,000 bases, encoding 11 open reading frames and genes (Figure 1A) [47–57]. Each gene contains one non-structural protein (orf1ab) and four structural proteins (spike (S) protein, envelope (E), membrane (M), and nucleocapsid (N) protein) and encodes six accessory proteins (ORF3a, ORF6, ORF7a, ORF7b, ORF8, and ORF10) (Figure 1B) [58–64]. After translation, orf1ab is cleaved by the papain-like protease (nsp3, PL-pro) and the main protease (M-pro) that it encodes and is divided into 16 proteins (Nsp1 to Nsp16) [65–67]. SARS-CoV-2 is similar to SARS coronavirus (SARS-CoV), the pathogen of the severe acute respiratory syndrome (SARS), with approximately 80% genome sequence identity, and many encoded proteins are highly conserved [68,69]. Homology of the amino acid sequence of the SARS-CoV-2 protein revealed that 17 of the 26 proteins had structurally known proteins with significant sequence similarity, of which 16, excluding nsp4, had

SARS-CoV protein conformations. Many SARS-CoV-2 proteins have postulated conformational models in the form of homo- or hetero- multimers [70,71]. For example, M-pro is a homodimer, nsp10 is a heterodimer with exonuclease (ExoN), respectively, and 2-O′-ribose methyltransferase (2oMT), and a model of inhibitor complex is assumed [72–75]. In addition, the S protein forms a homotrimer, and a complex model of the receptor-binding domain (RBD) and human angiotensin-converting enzyme 2 (ACE2) is assumed [76–95]. Virtual screening is an in silico analysis method for identifying drug candidates, which are compounds that bind to specific sites on viral proteins, based on 3D structural models. Typically, this method defines the site at which the drug molecule is bound to the 3D structure of the target protein. Compound library molecules are comprehensively docked on a computer, and candidate compounds are extracted by evaluating bond stability using evaluation functions, such as the energy function [96,97]. Although significant seed-up has been achieved using parallel computing and machine learning, it is not easy to apply in situations where the target protein or compound library has not been narrowed down. A ligand bound to a target protein homologue in a known complex structure is highly likely to contain a pharmacophore, where a structural feature is specifically recognized by the site where the compound is bound, such as the ligand-binding site. If there is an approved drug with a structure similar to that of the ligand that can be reasonably docked to the structural model, the molecule is expected to become a therapeutic drug candidate. Three of the SARS-CoV-2 protein models, the M-pro homodimer, S protein-ACE2 complex, and 2oMT-nsp10 heterodimer, have ligand molecules bound to the template structure [98–101]. M-pro is an essential enzyme for viral protein production and is considered a promising drug target for SARS-CoV-2. Therefore, complex structures with many peptidomimetic inhibitors have been analyzed; however, no existing drug molecules showing high similarity to these known ligands have been found. This suggests that the M-pro of SARS-CoV-2 is a cysteine protease, whereas many of the targets of existing antiviral protease inhibitors, such as the HIV protease, are aspartate or zinc proteases [23,102–104]. Moreover, carfilzomib, which showed the highest similarity among known ligands, is an irreversible inhibitor of proteasome and approved for the clinical treatment of multiple myeloma or Walden Strom's macroglobulinemia [105–107]. The target of carfilzomib is a threonine protease with a nucleophilic attacking group: Thr; however, it also reacts with the nucleophilic attacking group Cys of M-pro. Because the S protein on the virus surface uses human angiotensin-converting enzyme 2 (ACE2) as a receptor when infecting host cells, the S protein-ACE2 binding site is an important target. ACE2 is a homologue, with 44% amino acid sequence identity, of ACE, which is a major target of anti-hypertensive ACE-inhibitor complex structures [108]. Approved drugs analogous to these inhibitors were found to be lisinopril, enalaprilat, and captopril, all of which are antihypertensive drugs.

However, these molecules were bound at a position different from the S protein-ACE2 interaction site; therefore, they could not directly inhibit the interaction with the S protein. Clinical trials of antibody drugs targeting the receptor-binding domain (RGD) as antigens are currently being conducted for drugs that target the S protein [109,110]. As a low-molecular-weight drug targeting the site, catharanthine, a component derived from Tamasaki Tsutsurugi, which has been approved as a treatment for alopecia areata and leukopenia, inhibits S protein-ACE2 interaction and suppresses SARS-CoV-2 infection [111,112]. This finding suggests the possibility of developing a drug to prevent COVID-19 infection by expanding catharanthine. The 2oMT-nsp10 complex is an enzyme that modifies the methyl group on the 5′-terminal cap structure of viral RNA. The cap structure protects viral RNA from degradation by the host and is essential for synthesizing its proteins using the host's translational machinery [113]. Several existing drugs were discovered from the 2oMT ligand complex structure of SARS-CoV, which was used as the template for the model, and antiviral activity was reported in in vitro experiments. Additionally, the adenosine A1 receptor agonists tecadenoson, serodenosone, and travodenosone are expected to target 2oMT, of which tecadenoson and travodenosone have passed phase I clinical trials, and their safety has been confirmed [114]. In addition, there should be a guanylyl transferase that adds a cap structure to the 5′ end of the viral RNA molecule, but the protein that plays that role is currently unknown; if it is identified in the future, it can become a drug discovery target [115].

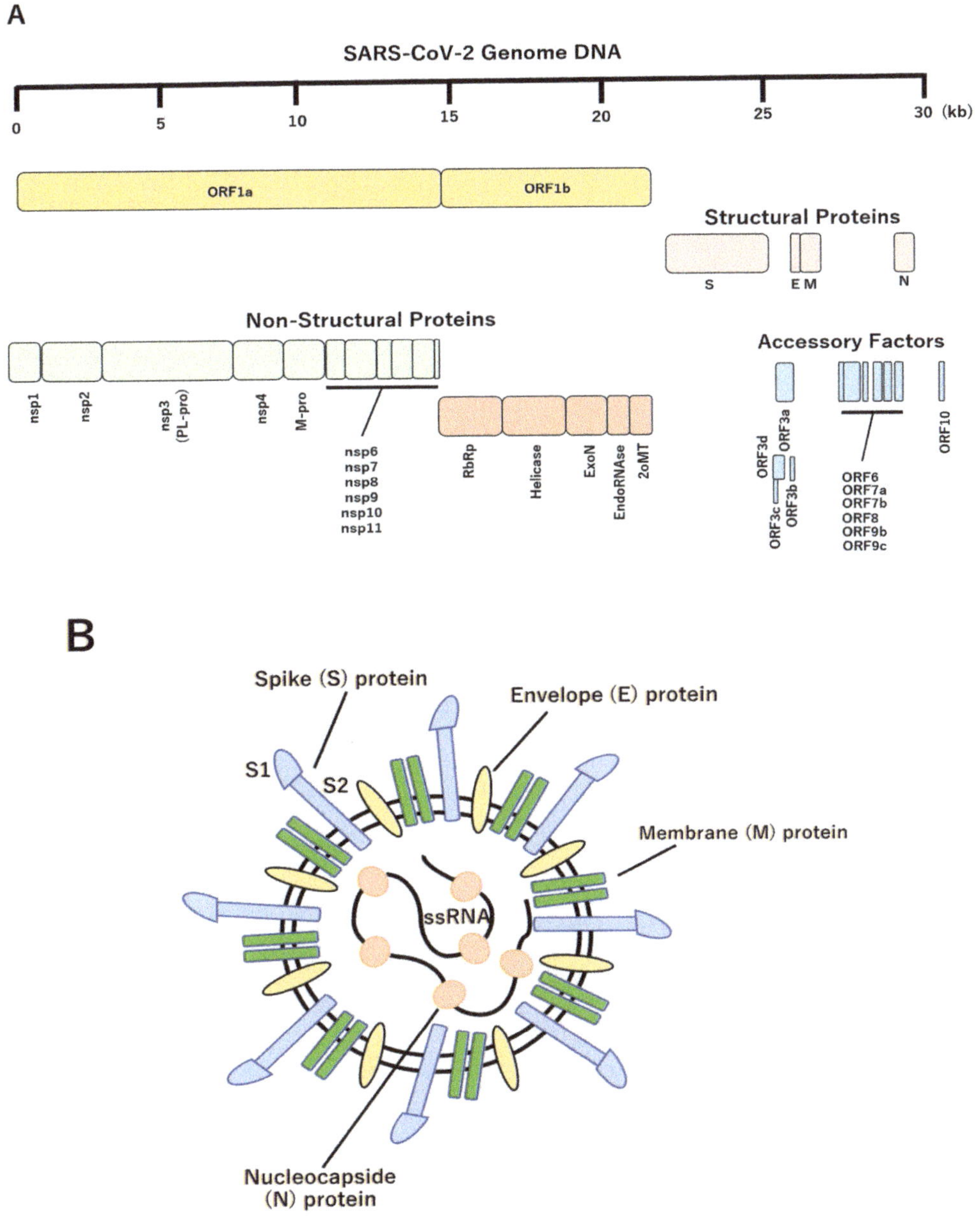

Figure 1. Schematic structure of SARS-CoV-2. (**A**) The genomic organization of SARS-CoV-2. Upper line indicates genomic scale. Sixteen non-structural proteins, four structural proteins, and eleven accessory factors were represented. (**B**) Schematic diagram of the SARS-CoV-2 virus. The four structural proteins, including S, M, N and E proteins are shown.

Since protein interactions between humans and viruses play a crucial role in viral infections, their identification will lead to elucidation of viral infection mechanisms and discovery of targets for antiviral drugs. However, since biological experiments for this identification require a huge amount of time and cost, the prediction of the interaction by in silico analysis is expected. Conventional computer prediction method of the protein interaction is docking simulation using molecular dynamics method based on protein 3D-structure information, which examines the shape of the key and the keyhole of the protein and uses computer simulation to find the conditions that the key fits into the keyhole. However, it is difficult to elucidate the 3D-structure information, and the application of the molecular dynamics method for mutant viruses is limited. On the other hand, high-throughput experimental methods make it easy to obtain amino acid sequence information of viral proteins. By applying a deep learning model that predicts the future from time series data and taking the amino acid sequence of a protein as a flow of context, it is possible to extract 3D features of keys and keyholes from the order patterns of long-chain amino acid sequences. Thus, COVID-19 runaway of the host immune system is investigated by AI-based analytical approaches [116,117].

3. SARS-CoV-2 Vaccine with Extracellular Vesicles

Furthermore, modified extracellular vesicles (EV), i.e., vesicles with a heterogeneous lipid bilayer structure that are secreted from almost all living cells, are roughly divided into three types: exosomes, macrovesicles, and apoptotic bodies, based on differences in intracellular production mechanisms, loaded with an antibody consisting only of a heavy chain, which is a type of low-molecular-weight antibody against the spike protein of SARS-CoV-2, and IFN-b, a cytokine with antiviral effect, which inhibits the SARS-CoV-2 pseudo-virus derived from infecting cells and can induce the cells into an antiviral state [118]. In particular, exosomes are expected as new preventive and therapeutic strategies that exhibit antiviral activity. As the new coronavirus establishes infection by binding the SARS-CoV-2 spike protein to ACE2 on cells, blocking the spike protein with antibodies to render it incapable of binding to ACE2 is an important strategy for preventing SARS-CoV-2 infection and aggravation. Anti-spike neutralizing antibodies are expected to be therapeutic agents for COVID-19. Although the SARS-CoV-2 vaccine also promotes antibody production against the spike protein, among mutant strains, such as the Omicron strain, some strains that reduce the infection prevention effect of the SARS-CoV-2 vaccine have appeared [119–124]. Therefore, it is difficult to completely prevent SARS-CoV-2 infection and aggravation using the anti-spike neutralizing antibody alone. A large number of modified EV-mounted fusion proteins consisting of IFN-b, which induces an antiviral state in cells, an antibody comprising only heavy chains, which is a type of low-molecular-weight anti-spike antibody, and MFG-E8 protein, which can bind to EVs, showed significant anti-inhibitory effects on SARS-CoV-2 pseudo virus infectivity [118].

In addition, two mRNA vaccines have been developed against SARS-CoV-2, designed to induce systemic immunity via intramuscular injection [125–146]. However, it is necessary to develop a cold chain for real-world inoculation. Therefore, it has been reported that the vaccine is administered directly to the lungs, not via intramuscular injection, and EVs secreted from lung spheroid cells (LSC) are used as carriers [147,148]. The receptor binding domain (RBD) is more tightly retained in both muscle-lined respiratory airways and lung parenchyma than in liposome-based vaccines by inhaling LSC-EV virus-like particles (VLPs) modified with the RBD of the recombinant SARS-CoV-2 spike protein. In mice, this vaccine induces lung CD4+/CD8+ T cells with RBD-specific IgG antibodies, mucosal IgA responses, and a Th1-like cytokine expression profile, leading to the removal of the challenged SARS-CoV-2 pseudo virus [149]. In hamsters, two doses of this vaccine attenuated severe pneumonia and reduced inflammatory infiltrates after the SARS-CoV-2 challenge. RBD-modified LSC-EV vaccines (RBD-EVs) induce mucosal and systemic immunity in the lungs.

4. Vaccination Process and Nuclei Acids

Plasmid DNA (pDNA) is a safe and highly productive vector for DNA vaccines and gene therapies [150,151]. Antigen-presenting cells, such as macrophages and dendritic cells, which play an important role in the immune response and defense against foreign substances, recognize pDNA administered to the body as a 'foreign substance', and have a significant effect on its pharmacokinetics and gene expression. Therefore, it is important to optimize the gene expression profile obtained by pDNA administration for each target disease. DNA derived from bacteria, including pDNA, has a high frequency of unmethylated CpG sequences, known as CpG motifs. When mammalian macrophages and dendritic cells take them up, they are recognized as danger signals via intracellular toll-like receptor 9 (TLR9), and immune activation reactions, such as the production of various inflammatory cytokines, are induced [152–155]. Inflammatory cytokines are responsible for reducing gene expression in target cells owing to their cytotoxic effects. However, in the case of cancer treatment, in addition to the effects of transgenes, immune activation by inflammatory cytokine production can be expected, and the immune response to pDNA is thought to have complex effects on therapeutic efficacy. However, the mechanism of cellular uptake and activity of pDNA in macrophages and dendritic cells has not been fully elucidated. In particular, in the case of complexes with cationic carriers, which are commonly used to increase gene expression, immune activation by a mechanism different from cell activation by CpG motifs has been suggested, but the details are unknown. Non-parenchymal cells in the liver are significantly involved in the pharmacokinetics of pDNA, and this cellular uptake involves a mechanism similar to that of scavenger receptors, which specifically recognize the conformation of polyanions. In addition, a similar uptake mechanism exists in dendritic cells [156]. In contrast, by complexing DNA with cationic liposomes, cytokines are produced from macrophages

Regardless of the presence or absence of CpG motifs [157]. TLR9 is not involved in this CpG motif-independent phenomenon in mouse-derived macrophages, and a similar CpG motif-independent activation occurs in mouse dendritic cells as well as in human-derived cells. Furthermore, cell activation is highly dependent on the type of liposomes used for complex formation. In contrast, mouse peritoneal macrophages and RAW264.7, a cultured macrophage cell line, differ significantly in DNA uptake and cytokine production between the two cell groups. Because peritoneal macrophages efficiently take up naked pDNA but produce few cytokines, inhibition of TLR9 recognition by DNA binding factors is envisioned. Th1-type cytokine production induced by CpG DNA administration exhibits effective therapeutic effects against cancer and allergic diseases [158]. Y-shaped DNA is constructed by combining three short DNA strands with partially complementary sequences, and this unique structure induces cytokine production more efficiently than identical double-stranded DNA.

Chemokines are secretory proteins that promote cell migration and contribute to inflammatory reactions by attracting leukocytes. In addition, CXCL14, a chemokine, binds to CpG DNA and significantly enhances the induction of innate immunity and inflammatory responses through its uptake by dendritic cells (Figure 2) [159]. Furthermore, CXCL4, the CXC-type chemokine CXCL14, has functions similar to those of CXCL14 and enhances CpG DNA-induced dendritic cell activation [160]. CXCL14 has both CpG DNA and cell surface receptor-binding domains, and uptake of the CXCL14/CpG DNA complex into dendritic cells via the clathrin-dependent endocytosis pathway is required for the enhancement of CpG DNA activity [161]. In addition, by simulating the binding of CXCL14/CpG DNA, multiple amino acids on the N-terminal and C-terminal sides of CXCL14 act cooperatively to stabilize binding. Thus, the activation of dendritic cells by CXCL14 and CpG DNA is expected to function as a vaccine adjuvant to enhance vaccine efficacy [162]. Further elucidation of the cooperative action of CXCL14 and CpG DNA may lead to the development of more efficient cancer immunopotentiators and vaccine adjuvants. However, the immunological mechanisms of action of DNA vaccines, which are next-generation vaccines under development against infectious diseases, such as influenza, cancer, and allergies, are still not well understood. In contrast, the right-handed double-helical structure of DNA acts as an endogenous adjuvant for vaccines by activating the innate immune system via tank-binding kinase 1 (TBK1) in cells, and signals for activating the innate immune system are essential for the efficacy in DNA vaccines [163]. Among the effects of DNA vaccines, activation of TBK1-dependent innate immunity in immune cells, such as dendritic cells, is important for antibody production. Activation of TBK1 in non-immune cells, such as muscle cells, that take up DNA is important for the activation of cell-mediated immunity by T cells. In other words, the effects of DNA vaccines involve a pathway that induces type I interferon without being mediated by TLRs. Although the innate immunostimulatory action of nucleic acids is due to a special base sequence, CpG motif, often found in pathogens, such as bacteria and viruses, mediated by TLR9, it was shown that the right-handed structure of double-stranded DNA found in both viruses and host cells has a strong TLR-independent ability to produce interferon. Furthermore, innate immune activations in both immune and nonimmune cells interact with each other.

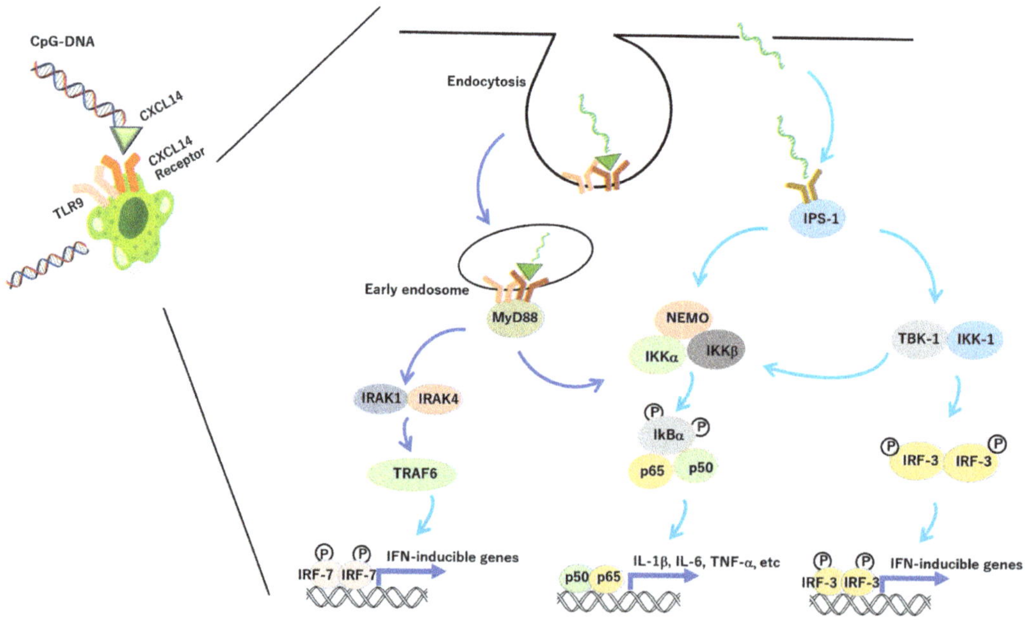

Figure 2. Molecular pathways of inflammation induced by CXCL14 and CpG-DNA. CXCL14: chemokine (C-X-C motif) ligand 14, TLR9: toll-like receptor 9, TRAF6:TNF receptor-associated factor 6, MyD88: myeloid differentiation primary response gene 88, NEMO: NF-κB essential modulator, IκB: inhibitor kappa B, IKK: IκB kinase, p50: NF-κB p50, p65: NF-κB p65, IPS-1: IFN-inducing β promoter stimulator-1, TBK1: TANK-binding kinase 1, IRF: interferon regulatory factor, IFN: interferon, IRAK: IL-1 receptor associated kinase, IL-6: interleukin-6, IL-1b: interleukin-1b, TNF-α: tumor necrosis factor α.

5. Construction of Vaccine and Protein Structure in Silico Analysis

The methodology of analyzing the results of experiments using the information science method is the same as that of bioinformatics and computational biology and is a pioneering study that utilizes bioinformatics in virology (Figure 3) [164–170]. There are ethical issues with artificial intelligence (AI), but it has the potential to revolutionize science and solve some of the most complex problems facing modern biology. In particular, it is expected to predict the structure of unknown proteins, solve the mysteries of cells, and quickly elucidate diseases that affect cells. However, determining the structure of a protein through experiments is a lengthy and laborious process. Structural information about new viruses is essential for understanding their properties and for creating effective vaccines. Thus, researchers have accelerated the unravelling process and made predictions more accurate with a new computational approach. With the remarkable development of AI, it is now possible to predict the 3D structure of complex proteins with a high degree of accuracy. The AI system AlphaFold2 has accomplished a feat of identified several protein structures that make up the previously little-known novel SARS-CoV-2 within a fairly short time [171]. Thus, the tireless efforts of scientists and international collaboration, combined with cutting-edge AI technologies, such as AlphaFold2, have enabled a rapid response to the pandemic. AlphaFold2 uses advanced machine learning techniques, called deep learning neural networks, to predict protein structures directly from protein gene sequences [172–177]. In addition, AI must first learn the sequences and structures of approximately 100,000 known proteins from the experimental data published in the scientific community. This has made it possible to predict the 3D models of any protein with high accuracy. Because protein structure is related to protein function, it is important to clarify protein function and is essential and even more important information. There are several methods for experimentally determining protein structures, such as NMR and X-ray crystallography, but they are both time-consuming and expensive [178]. Therefore, researchers have been actively researching to predict 3D structures for some time, and many modelling methods have been devised [173,179–182]. There are various modelling techniques, and with regard to comparative modelling, different proteins used as templates yield different results; thus, a variety of predicted 3D structures can be obtained. However, it is necessary to choose the most natural structure among the predicted 3D structures. Herein, 'natural structure-like' implies that the structure is highly similar to the natural structure, and this is called the model quality assessment program (MQAP) [183]. Many MQAPs comprise single or multiple statistical potential functions that express natural structure-likeness, and prediction models with machine learning based on explicitly created feature values have also been proposed [184]. This statistical potential function is a statistically constructed potential function based on the distribution of structural features from the natural structures known in the Protein Data Bank and has been devised many times. Many of these statistical potential functions mainly capture the interactions between two bodies, such as the original pairs and residue pairs. However, because proteins have a 3D structure, it is difficult to capture their features. Therefore, although many-body potential functions have been devised, they are not as accurate as existing two-body functions. This is because the problem becomes more complicated, and the number of parameters increases in the case of many bodies. Therefore, to capture the interactions between many bodies, a new method that differs from the conventional method of creating a statistical potential function is required.

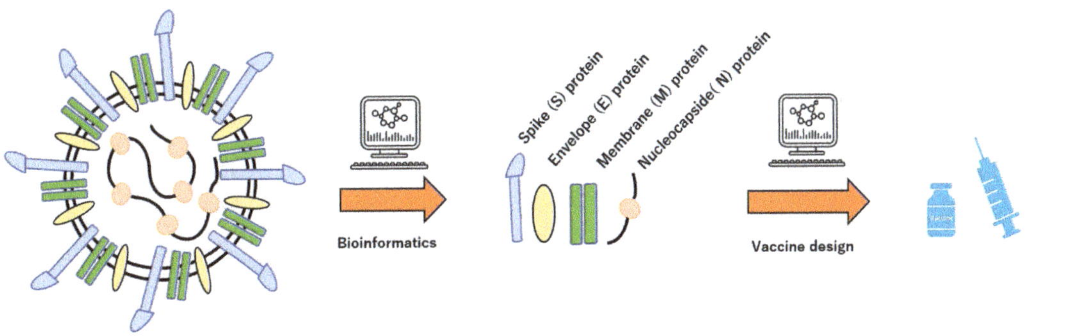

Figure 3. Schematic procedure of vaccine design by bioinformatics of virus characterizations. Structural information and biological activity of viruses can automatically extract the molecular futures by AI.

Convolutional neural networks (CNN), which are neural networks with convolutional layers, have been successfully applied in many fields [185]. A 3D CNN, which is an extension of this to 3D, has been used for motion recognition and object recognition in the past, but it is also beginning to be used for the analysis of the 3D structures of proteins. Among them, 3D-CNN achieved better accuracy than existing methods that used machine learning with explicit feature values, suggesting the effectiveness of 3D-CNN in analyzing 3D structures of proteins. Based on this, it was expected that 3D-CNN would be effective in the MQAP field. Therefore, to develop a method for evaluating the predicted 3D structure that captures the interaction between many bodies, a method for evaluating the predicted conformation that analyses the local environment of a protein using 3D-CNN and outputs the overall score of the protein as the average of the evaluations of the local environment was developed. Consequently, the validity of evaluating the local structure of proteins using a 3D-CNN was suggested [184–189].

In addition, many studies have been conducted to predict the local and secondary structures of proteins from amino acid sequence information using machine learning [190–194]. The secondary structure can be classified into two types: α-helix and β-sheet (Table 1). The alpha-helix is a right-handed helical structure with an average of 3.6 residues per cycle. In this helical structure, all the amino acids form hydrogen bounds with amino acids residues to maintain an energetically stable structure. In contrast, the beta-strand contains a series of amino acids in a straight line. This secondary structure prediction is defined as a classification problem called sequence labelling, which predicts secondary structures from information, such as amino acid sequences. Furthermore, a secondary structure prediction model using a deep neural network (DNN) has been proposed, and it has been reported that highly accurate predictions can be made [195–197]. Conversely, a DNN is a nonlinear function involving a large number of parameters ranging from thousands to millions [198,199]. As the inside is a black box, it is unclear whether the prediction is based on biologically plausible features, and the prediction results for unknown proteins cannot be guaranteed. DNN can be input from both ends of the amino acid sequence using bidirectional LSTM with a convolution layer and bidirectional LSTM layer [200–202]. The output layer of the DNN had the same number of neurons as the number of classes to be discriminated. Given an input vector $x0 \in R^{c}$, we find the largest output value Sl of each neuron l = {L, B, E, G, I, H, S, T, NoSeq} in the output layer. Then, the label argmaxlSl corresponding to that neuron was selected as the prediction result. At this time, saliency, which is a characteristic of the spatial arrangement of visual stimuli that induces bottom-up attention, is defined as the value of the partial differential with respect to the input x, as shown in Equation (1):

$$(\text{Saliency}) = \text{maxc} \mid \partial Sl / \partial x \mid x0 \mid \quad (1)$$

Table 1. Secondary structure of amino acids.

No.	Name
1	irregular
2	beta-bridge
3	beta-strand
4	3qo-helix
5	pai-helix
6	alpha-helix
7	bend
8	beta-turn

Saliency represents the result of a type of sensitivity analysis [203–206]. For example, consider the case of obtaining saliency for neurons in the output layer corresponding to an α-helix, where saliency indicates the part of the input that should be changed locally to fire the neuron in the output layer corresponding to the α-helix. For example, a large value at a certain position in the amino acid sequence on saliency indicates that changing the input at that position has a large effect on the output. By using saliency, when predicting the secondary structure label Lx of a certain position x, it is possible to determine which amino acid, feature value, at the surrounding position contributes greatly. For example, it is expected that the effect tends to approach zero at positions that are not related to the prediction, such as positions far enough away. If these results are consistent with what is known biologically, a trained DNN can be considered to capture biologically plausible features. In particular, for the α-helix and β-strand, which have high prediction accuracy, visualization with saliency is important to determine what type of amino acid exists at a position three or four residues away when predicting whether the secondary structure at a certain position in an amino acid sequence is an α-helix, because the α-helix has a right-handed helical structure with an average of 3.6 residues. Conversely, the β-strand has a structure in which amino acids are linked in a straight chain, and when making predictions, the relationship with amino acids that are close to each other is important. When the DNN acquires the correct prediction model, the saliency values at positions three or four residues away are higher when predicting the α-helix than when predicting the β-strand. This saliency is a method to obtain the value corresponding to each feature quantity of each input for each output neuron. In β-strand prediction, the saliency value gradually decreases as the distance between the sequences increases. Conversely, regarding α-helix prediction, the saliency value did not decrease from the first residue, that is, from the next amino acid to the third residue, which is consistent with the α-helix cycle length of 3.6 residues. However, when a DNN that predicts the secondary structure is visualized using saliency, a large amount of saliency is created. For human interpretation, it is necessary to obtain statistics from that saliency, and design the types of statistics to obtain. Therefore, activation maximization has been proposed in addition to saliency as a visualization method for DNN. By using these alternative visualization methods, we may extract insights without explicitly designing the statistics. Moreover, it is reported some AI-based prediction systems of protein structure with high-performance [207–220]. However, there are issues about time-consumption, high-throughput, or versatility, etc.

Research on the structures of such proteins and their associated functions has been applied to vaccine development. In particular, simulating the 'spike protein' present on the surface of SARS-CoV-2 and clarifying the molecular mechanism that causes the structural change of the spike protein necessary for viral infection will lead to the establishment of infection prevention and treatment methods.

6. Conclusions

By more accurately predicting the distance between the beta carbon of each amino acid residue and the beta carbon of another amino acid residue, it is possible to more accurately predict the formation of 3D structures from the amino acid sequences of proteins. Running computer simulations related to SARS-CoV-2 vaccine development can dramatically accelerate the design process and may further aid drug discovery to improve diagnostic and therapeutic outcomes.

Author Contributions: Writing, review, and editing, Y.M.; supervision, R.Y.; funding acquisition, Y.M. All authors have read and agreed to the published version of the manuscript.

Funding: This review was funded by the Fukuda Foundation for Medical Technology, and APC was funded by the Fukuda Foundation for Medical Technology.

Informed Consent Statement: Not applicable.

Data Availability Statement: Not applicable.

Conflicts of Interest: The authors declare no conflict of interest.

References

1. Winkler, N.E.; Dey, A.; Quinn, H.E.; Pourmarzi, D.; Lambert, S.; McIntyre, P.; Beard, F. Australian vaccine preventable disease epidemiological review series: Measles, 2012–2019. *Commun. Dis. Intell.* **2022**, *46. in press*. [CrossRef] [PubMed]
2. Paret, M.; Trillo, R.; Lighter, J.; Youngster, I.; Ratner, A.J.; Pellett Madan, R. Poor Uptake of MMR Vaccine 1-year Post-Measles Outbreak: New York City and Israel. *J. Pediatric Infect. Dis. Soc.* **2022**, *11*, 322–328. [CrossRef] [PubMed]
3. Takahashi, Y.; Kelsoe, G. Role of germinal centers for the induction of broadly-reactive memory B cells. *Curr. Opin. Immunol.* **2017**, *45*, 119–125. [CrossRef] [PubMed]
4. Ura, T.; Takeuchi, M.; Kawagoe, T.; Mizuki, N.; Okuda, K.; Shimada, M. Current Vaccine Platforms in Enhancing T-Cell Response. *Vaccines* **2022**, *10*, 1367. [CrossRef] [PubMed]
5. Antoñanzas, J.; Rodríguez-Garijo, N.; Estenaga, Á.; Morelló-Vicente, A.; España, A.; Aguado, L. Generalized morphea following the COVID vaccine: A series of two patients and a bibliographic review. *Dermatol. Ther.* **2022**, *35*, e15709. [CrossRef]
6. Bostan, H.; Ucan, B.; Kizilgul, M.; Calapkulu, M.; Hepsen, S.; Gul, U.; Ozturk Unsal, I.; Cakal, E. Relapsed and newly diagnosed Graves' disease due to immunization against COVID-19: A case series and review of the literature. *J. Autoimmun.* **2022**, *128*, 102809. [CrossRef]
7. Pereira, D.F.S.; Ribeiro, H.S.; Gonçalves, A.A.M.; da Silva, A.V.; Lair, D.F.; de Oliveira, D.S.; Boas, D.F.V.; Conrado, I.D.S.S.; Leite, J.C.; Barata, L.M.; et al. Rhipicephalus microplus: An overview of vaccine antigens against the cattle tick. *Ticks. Tick. Borne Dis.* **2022**, *13*, 101828. [CrossRef]
8. Gan, S.K.; Phua, S.X.; Yeo, J.Y. Sagacious epitope selection for vaccines, and both antibody-based therapeutics and diagnostics: Tips from virology and oncology. *Antib. Ther.* **2022**, *5*, 63–72. [CrossRef]
9. Stepanova, E.; Matyushenko, V.; Rudenko, L.; Isakova-Sivak, I. Prospects of and Barriers to the Development of Epitope-Based Vaccines against Human Metapneumovirus. *Pathogens* **2020**, *9*, 481. [CrossRef]
10. Moritzky, S.A.; Richards, K.A.; Glover, M.A.; Krammer, F.; Chaves, F.A.; Topham, D.J.; Branche, A.; Nayak, J.L.; Sant, A.J. The negative effect of pre-existing immunity on influenza vaccine responses transcends the impact of vaccine formulation type and vaccination history. *J. Infect. Dis.* **2022**, *in press*. [CrossRef]
11. Devarajan, P.; Vong, A.M.; Castonguay, C.H.; Kugler-Umana, O.; Bautista, B.L.; Jones, M.C.; Kelly, K.A.; Xia, J.; Swain, S.L. Strong influenza-induced T_{FH} generation requires CD4 effectors to recognize antigen locally and receive signals from continuing infection. *Proc. Natl. Acad. Sci. USA* **2022**, *119*, e2111064119. [CrossRef]
12. Wylie, B.; Ong, F.; Belhoul-Fakir, H.; Priebatsch, K.; Bogdawa, H.; Stirnweiss, A.; Watt, P.; Cunningham, P.; Stone, S.R.; Waithman, J. Targeting Cross-Presentation as a Route to Improve the Efficiency of Peptide-Based Cancer Vaccines. *Cancers* **2021**, *13*, 6189. [CrossRef]
13. Tagliamonte, M.; Mauriello, A.; Cavalluzzo, B.; Ragone, C.; Manolio, C.; Luciano, A.; Barbieri, A.; Palma, G.; Scognamiglio, G.; Di Mauro, A.; et al. MHC-Optimized Peptide Scaffold for Improved Antigen Presentation and Anti-Tumor Response. *Front. Immunol.* **2021**, *12*, 769799. [CrossRef]
14. Li, W.H.; Su, J.Y.; Li, Y.M. Rational Design of T-Cell- and B-Cell-Based Therapeutic Cancer Vaccines. *Acc. Chem. Res.* **2022**, *55*, 2660–2671. [CrossRef]
15. He, B.; Liu, S.; Xu, M.; Hu, Y.; Lv, K.; Wang, Y.; Ma, Y.; Zhai, Y.; Yue, X.; Liu, L.; et al. Comparative global B cell receptor repertoire difference induced by SARS-CoV-2 infection or vaccination via single-cell V(D)J sequencing. *Emerg. Microbes Infect.* **2022**, *11*, 2007–2020. [CrossRef]
16. Kumar, P.; Shiraz, M.; Akif, M. Multiepitope-based vaccine design by exploring antigenic potential among leptospiral lipoproteins using comprehensive immunoinformatics and structure-based approaches. *Biotechnol. Appl. Biochem.* **2022**, *in press*. [CrossRef]
17. Gupta, S.L.; Khan, N.; Basu, S.; Soni, V. B-Cell-Based Immunotherapy: A Promising New Alternative. *Vaccines* **2022**, *10*, 879. [CrossRef]
18. Lee, A.; Wimmers, F.; Pulendran, B. Epigenetic adjuvants: Durable reprogramming of the innate immune system with adjuvants. *Curr. Opin. Immunol.* **2022**, *77*, 102189. [CrossRef]
19. Jarisch, A.; Wiercinska, E.; Huenecke, S.; Bremm, M.; Cappel, C.; Hauler, J.; Rettinger, E.; Soerensen, J.; Hellstern, H.; Klusmann, J.H.; et al. Immune Responses to SARS-CoV-2 Vaccination in Young Patients with Anti-CD19 Chimeric Antigen Receptor T Cell-Induced B Cell Aplasia. *Transplant Cell Ther.* **2022**, *28*, 366.e1–366.e7. [CrossRef]
20. Srinivasan, S.; Selvaraj, G.F.; Gopalan, V.; Padmanabhan, P.; Ramesh, K.; Govindan, K.; Chandran, A.; Dhandapani, P.; Krishnasamy, K.; Kitambi, S.S. Epitope Identification and Designing a Potent Multi-epitope Vaccine Construct against SARS-CoV-2 Including the Emerging Variants. *J. Glob. Infect. Dis.* **2022**, *14*, 24–30. [CrossRef]
21. Khanum, S.; Carbone, V.; Gupta, S.K.; Yeung, J.; Shu, D.; Wilson, T.; Parlane, N.A.; Altermann, E.; Estein, S.M.; Janssen, P.H.; et al. Mapping immunogenic epitopes of an adhesin-like protein from Methanobrevibacter ruminantium M1 and comparison of empirical data with in silico prediction methods. *Sci. Rep.* **2022**, *12*, 10394. [CrossRef] [PubMed]
22. Dhiman, G.; Lohia, N.; Jain, S.; Baranwal, M. Metadherin peptides containing CD4(+) and CD8(+) T cell epitopes as a therapeutic vaccine candidate against cancer. *Microbiol. Immunol.* **2016**, *60*, 646–652. [CrossRef] [PubMed]
23. La Monica, G.; Bono, A.; Lauria, A.; Martorana, A. Targeting SARS-CoV-2 Main Protease for Treatment of COVID-19: Covalent Inhibitors Structure-Activity Relationship Insights and Evolution Perspectives. *J. Med. Chem.* **2022**, *65*, 12500–12534. [CrossRef] [PubMed]

24. Hu, X.; Jia, C.; Wu, J.; Zhang, J.; Jiang, Z.; Ma, K. Towards the Antiviral Agents and Nanotechnology-Enabled Approaches Against Parvovirus B19. *Front. Cell Infect. Microbiol.* **2022**, *12*, 916012. [CrossRef] [PubMed]
25. Lee, M.; Park, J.; Cho, I.H. Target-Specific Drug Discovery of Natural Products against SARS-CoV-2 Life Cycle and Cytokine Storm in COVID-19. *Am. J. Chin. Med.* **2022**, *50*, 927–959. [CrossRef]
26. Leowattana, W.; Leowattana, T. Chronic hepatitis B: New potential therapeutic drugs target. *World J. Virol.* **2022**, *11*, 57–72. [CrossRef]
27. Gorai, S.; Junghare, V.; Kundu, K.; Gharui, S.; Kumar, M.; Patro, B.S.; Nayak, S.K.; Hazra, S.; Mula, S. Synthesis of Dihydrobenzofuro[3,2-b]chromenes as Potential 3CLpro Inhibitors of SARS-CoV-2: A Molecular Docking and Molecular Dynamics Study. *Chem. Med. Chem.* **2022**, *17*, e202100782. [CrossRef]
28. Zhai, J.; He, X.; Man, V.H.; Sun, Y.; Ji, B.; Cai, L.; Wang, J. A multiple-step *in silico* screening protocol to identify allosteric inhibitors of Spike-hACE2 binding. *Phys. Chem. Chem. Phys.* **2022**, *24*, 4305–4316. [CrossRef]
29. Rashid, F.; Xie, Z.; Suleman, M.; Shah, A.; Khan, S.; Luo, S. Roles and functions of SARS-CoV-2 proteins in host immune evasion. *Front. Immunol.* **2022**, *13*, 940756. [CrossRef]
30. Jiang, J.; Li, J.; Zhang, Y.; Zhou, C.; Guo, C.; Zhou, Z.; Ming, Y. The Protective Effect of the Soluble Egg Antigen of *Schistosoma japonicum* in A Mouse Skin Transplantation Model. *Front. Immunol.* **2022**, *13*, 884006. [CrossRef]
31. Wang, M.; Tan, W.; Li, J.; Fang, L.; Yue, M. The Endless Wars: Severe Fever with Thrombocytopenia Syndrome Virus, Host Immune and Genetic Factors. *Front. Cell Infect. Microbiol.* **2022**, *12*, 808098. [CrossRef]
32. Gori Savellini, G.; Anichini, G.; Gandolfo, C.; Cusi, M.G. Nucleopore Traffic Is Hindered by SARS-CoV-2 ORF6 Protein to Efficiently Suppress IFN-β and IL-6 Secretion. *Viruses* **2022**, *14*, 1273. [CrossRef]
33. Naman, Z.T.; Kadhim, S.; Al-Isawi, Z.J.K.; Butch, C.J.; Muhseen, Z.T. Computational Investigations of Traditional Chinese Medicinal Compounds against the Omicron Variant of SARS-CoV-2 to Rescue the Host Immune System. *Pharmaceuticals* **2022**, *15*, 741. [CrossRef]
34. Dong, S.; Kong, N.; Wang, C.; Li, Y.; Sun, D.; Qin, W.; Zhai, H.; Zhai, X.; Yang, X.; Ye, C.; et al. FUBP3 Degrades the Porcine Epidemic Diarrhea Virus Nucleocapsid Protein and Induces the Production of Type I Interferon. *J. Virol.* **2022**, *96*, e0061822. [CrossRef]
35. Zhang, H.; Sha, H.; Qin, L.; Wang, N.; Kong, W.; Huang, L.; Zhao, M. Research Progress in Porcine Reproductive and Respiratory Syndrome Virus-Host Protein Interactions. *Animals* **2022**, *12*, 1381. [CrossRef]
36. Wu, S.; Yi, W.; Gao, Y.; Deng, W.; Bi, X.; Lin, Y.; Yang, L.; Lu, Y.; Liu, R.; Chang, M.; et al. Immune Mechanisms Underlying Hepatitis B Surface Antigen Seroclearance in Chronic Hepatitis B Patients with Viral Coinfection. *Front. Immunol.* **2022**, *13*, 893512. [CrossRef]
37. Chakraborty, A.; Diwan, A.; Arora, V.; Thakur, Y.; Chiniga, V.; Tatake, J.; Pandey, R.; Holkar, P.; Holkar, N.; Pond, B. Mechanism of Antiviral Activities of Nanoviricide's Platform Technology based Biopolymer (NV-CoV-2). *AIMS Public Health* **2022**, *9*, 415–422. [CrossRef]
38. Poirson, J.; Suarez, I.P.; Straub, M.L.; Cousido-Siah, A.; Peixoto, P.; Hervouet, E.; Foster, A.; Mitschler, A.; Mukobo, N.; Chebaro, Y.; et al. High-Risk Mucosal Human Papillomavirus 16 (HPV16) E6 Protein and Cutaneous HPV5 and HPV8 E6 Proteins Employ Distinct Strategies To Interfere with Interferon Regulatory Factor 3-Mediated Beta Interferon Expression. *J. Virol.* **2022**, *96*, e0187521. [CrossRef]
39. Farzana, M.; Shahriar, S.; Jeba, F.R.; Tabassum, T.; Araf, Y.; Ullah, M.A.; Tasnim, J.; Chakraborty, A.; Naima, T.A.; Marma, K.K.S.; et al. Functional food: Complementary to fight against COVID-19. *Beni. Suef. Univ. J. Basic Appl. Sci.* **2022**, *11*, 33. [CrossRef]
40. Ramdhan, P.; Li, C. Targeting Viral Methyltransferases: An Approach to Antiviral Treatment for ssRNA Viruses. *Viruses* **2022**, *14*, 379. [CrossRef]
41. Gong, L.; Ou, X.; Hu, L.; Zhong, J.; Li, J.; Deng, S.; Li, B.; Pan, L.; Wang, L.; Hong, X.; et al. The Molecular Mechanism of Herpes Simplex Virus 1 UL31 in Antagonizing the Activity of IFN-β. *Microbiol. Spectr.* **2022**, *10*, e0188321. [CrossRef] [PubMed]
42. Hong, Y.; Truong, A.D.; Vu, T.H.; Lee, S.; Heo, J.; Kang, S.; Lillehoj, H.S.; Hong, Y.H. Exosomes from H5N1 avian influenza virus-infected chickens regulate antiviral immune responses of chicken immune cells. *Dev. Comp. Immunol.* **2022**, *130*, 104368. [CrossRef] [PubMed]
43. Sencanski, M.; Perovic, V.; Milicevic, J.; Todorovic, T.; Prodanovic, R.; Veljkovic, V.; Paessler, S.; Glisic, S. Identification of SARS-CoV-2 Papain-like Protease (PLpro) Inhibitors Using Combined Computational Approach. *Chem. Open* **2022**, *11*, e202100248. [CrossRef] [PubMed]
44. Qian, Z.; Yang, C.; Xu, L.; Mickael, H.K.; Chen, S.; Zhang, Y.; Xia, Y.; Li, T.; Yu, W.; Huang, F. Hepatitis E virus-encoded microRNA promotes viral replication by inhibiting type I interferon. *FASEB J.* **2022**, *36*, e22104. [CrossRef] [PubMed]
45. Chatterjee, R.I.; Ghosh, M.; Sahoo, S.; Padhi, S.; Misra, N.; Raina, V.; Suar, M.; Son, Y.O. Next-Generation Bioinformatics Approaches and Resources for Coronavirus Vaccine Discovery and Development-A Perspective Review. *Vaccines* **2021**, *9*, 812. [CrossRef]
46. Chen, J.; Gao, K.; Wang, R.; Nguyen, D.D.; Wei, G.W. Review of COVID-19 Antibody Therapies. *Annu. Rev. Biophys.* **2021**, *50*, 1–30. [CrossRef]
47. Park, C.; Kim, K.W.; Park, D.; Hassan, Z.U.; Park, E.C.; Lee, C.S.; Rahman, M.T.; Yi, H.; Kim, S. Rapid and sensitive amplicon-based genome sequencing of SARS-CoV-2. *Front. Microbiol.* **2022**, *13*, 876085. [CrossRef]

48. Asif, M.; Amir, M.; Hussain, A.; Achakzai, N.M.; Natesan Pushparaj, P.; Rasool, M. Role of tyrosine kinase inhibitor in chronic myeloid leukemia patients with SARS-CoV-2 infection: A narrative Review. *Medicine* **2022**, *101*, e29660. [CrossRef]
49. Srivastava, K.; Singh, M.K. Drug repurposing in COVID-19: A review with past, present and future. *Metabol. Open* **2021**, *12*, 100121. [CrossRef]
50. Zhu, M.; Shen, J.; Zeng, Q.; Tan, J.W.; Kleepbua, J.; Chew, I.; Law, J.X.; Chew, S.P.; Tangathajinda, A.; Latthitha, N.; et al. Molecular Phylogenesis and Spatiotemporal Spread of SARS-CoV-2 in Southeast Asia. *Front. Public Health* **2021**, *9*, 685315. [CrossRef]
51. Amarilla, A.A.; Sng, J.D.J.; Parry, R.; Deerain, J.M.; Potter, J.R.; Setoh, Y.X.; Rawle, D.J.; Le, T.T.; Modhiran, N.; Wang, X.; et al. A versatile reverse genetics platform for SARS-CoV-2 and other positive-strand RNA viruses. *Nat. Commun.* **2021**, *12*, 3431. [CrossRef]
52. Islam, M.A.; Rahman, M.A.; Jakariya, M.; Bahadur, N.M.; Hossen, F.; Mukharjee, S.K.; Hossain, M.S.; Tasneem, A.; Haque, M.A.; Sera, F.; et al. A 30-day follow-up study on the prevalence of SARS-COV-2 genetic markers in wastewater from the residence of COVID-19 patient and comparison with clinical positivity. *Sci. Total Environ.* **2023**, *858*, 159350. [CrossRef]
53. Azzarà, A.; Cassano, I.; Paccagnella, E.; Tirindelli, M.C.; Nobile, C.; Schittone, V.; Lintas, C.; Sacco, R.; Gurrieri, F. Genetic variants determine intrafamilial variability of SARS-CoV-2 clinical outcomes in 19 Italian families. *PLoS ONE* **2022**, *17*, e0275988. [CrossRef]
54. Reno, U.; Regaldo, L.; Ojeda, G.; Schmuck, J.; Romero, N.; Polla, W.; Kergaravat, S.V.; Gagneten, A.M. Wastewater-Based Epidemiology: Detection of SARS-CoV-2 RNA in Different Stages of Domestic Wastewater Treatment in Santa Fe, Argentina. *Water Air Soil. Pollut.* **2022**, *233*, 372. [CrossRef]
55. Iqbal, N.; Rafiq, M.; Tareen, S.; Ahmad, M.; Nawaz, F.; Khan, S.; Riaz, R.; Yang, T.; Fatima, A.; Jamal, M.; et al. The SARS-CoV-2 differential genomic adaptation in response to varying UVindex reveals potential genomic resources for better COVID-19 diagnosis and prevention. *Front. Microbiol.* **2022**, *13*, 922393. [CrossRef]
56. Kim, H.S.; Lee, H.; Park, J.; Abbas, N.; Kang, S.; Hyun, H.; Seong, H.; Yoon, J.G.; Noh, J.Y.; Kim, W.J.; et al. Collection and detection of SARS-CoV-2 in exhaled breath using face mask. *PLoS ONE* **2022**, *17*, e0270765. [CrossRef]
57. Huang, J.; Zhang, Z.; Hao, C.; Qiu, Y.; Tan, R.; Liu, J.; Wang, X.; Yang, W.; Qu, H. Identifying Drug-Induced Liver Injury Associated With Inflammation-Drug and Drug-Drug Interactions in Pharmacologic Treatments for COVID-19 by Bioinformatics and System Biology Analyses: The Role of Pregnane X Receptor. *Front. Pharmacol.* **2022**, *13*, 804189. [CrossRef]
58. Chen, Z.; Ng, R.W.Y.; Lui, G.; Ling, L.; Chow, C.; Yeung, A.C.M.; Boon, S.S.; Wang, M.H.; Chan, K.C.C.; Chan, R.W.Y.; et al. Profiling of SARS-CoV-2 Subgenomic RNAs in Clinical Specimens. *Microbiol. Spectr.* **2022**, *10*, e0018222. [CrossRef]
59. Hassan, S.S.; Choudhury, P.P.; Dayhoff, G.W., II; Aljabali, A.A.A.; Uhal, B.D.; Lundstrom, K.; Rezaei, N.; Pizzol, D.; Adadi, P.; Lal, A.; et al. The importance of accessory protein variants in the pathogenicity of SARS-CoV-2. *Arch. Biochem. Biophys.* **2022**, *717*, 109124. [CrossRef]
60. Mohammed, M.E.A. SARS-CoV-2 Proteins: Are They Useful as Targets for COVID-19 Drugs and Vaccines? *Curr. Mol. Med.* **2022**, *22*, 50–66. [CrossRef]
61. Dolan, K.A.; Dutta, M.; Kern, D.M.; Kotecha, A.; Voth, G.A.; Brohawn, S.G. Structure of SARS-CoV-2 M protein in lipid nanodiscs. *Elife* **2022**, *11*, e81702. [CrossRef] [PubMed]
62. Araújo, L.P.; Dias, M.E.C.; Scodeler, G.C.; Santos, A.S.; Soares, L.M.; Corsetti, P.P.; Padovan, A.C.B.; Silveira, N.J.F.; de Almeida, L.A. Epitope identification of SARS-CoV-2 structural proteins using in silico approaches to obtain a conserved rational immunogenic peptide. *Immunoinformatics* **2022**, *7*, 100015. [CrossRef] [PubMed]
63. Rodríguez-Enríquez, A.; Herrera-Camacho, I.; Millán-Pérez-Peña, L.; Reyes-Leyva, J.; Santos-López, G.; Rivera-Benítez, J.F.; Rosas-Murrieta, N.H. Predicted 3D model of the M protein of Porcine Epidemic Diarrhea Virus and analysis of its immunogenic potential. *PLoS ONE* **2022**, *17*, e0263582. [CrossRef] [PubMed]
64. Thomas, S. Towards Determining the Epitopes of the Structural Proteins of SARS-CoV-2. *Methods Mol. Biol.* **2022**, *2410*, 265–272. [CrossRef] [PubMed]
65. Emam, M.; Oweda, M.; Antunes, A.; El-Hadidi, M. Positive selection as a key player for SARS-CoV-2 pathogenicity: Insights into ORF1ab, S and E genes. *Virus Res.* **2021**, *302*, 198472. [CrossRef]
66. Boccia, A.; Tufano, R.; Ferrucci, V.; Sepe, L.; Bianchi, M.; Pascarella, S.; Zollo, M.; Paolella, G. SARS-CoV-2 Pandemic Tracing in Italy Highlights Lineages with Mutational Burden in Growing Subsets. *Int. J. Mol. Sci.* **2022**, *23*, 4155. [CrossRef]
67. Urrutia-Cabrera, D.; Liou, R.H.; Wang, J.H.; Chan, J.; Hung, S.S.; Hewitt, A.W.; Martin, K.R.; Edwards, T.L.; Kwan, P.; Wong, R.C. Comparative analysis of loop-mediated isothermal amplification (LAMP)-based assays for rapid detection of SARS-CoV-2 genes. *Sci. Rep.* **2021**, *11*, 22493. [CrossRef]
68. Li, L.; Zhang, L.; Zhou, J.; He, X.; Yu, Y.; Liu, P.; Huang, W.; Xiang, Z.; Chen, J. Epidemiology and Genomic Characterization of Two Novel SARS-Related Coronaviruses in Horseshoe Bats from Guangdong, China. *mBio* **2022**, *13*, e0046322. [CrossRef]
69. Portakal, S.H.; Kanat, B.; Sayan, M.; Berber, B.; Doluca, O. A novel method for conserved sequence extraction with prospective mutation prediction for SARS-CoV-2 PCR primer design. *J. Virol. Methods* **2021**, *293*, 114146. [CrossRef]
70. Yan, W.; Zheng, Y.; Zeng, X.; He, B.; Cheng, W. Structural biology of SARS-CoV-2: Open the door for novel therapies. *Signal Transduct. Target Ther.* **2022**, *7*, 26. [CrossRef]
71. Selvaraj, C.; Dinesh, D.C.; Krafcikova, P.; Boura, E.; Aarthy, M.; Pravin, M.A.; Singh, S.K. Structural Understanding of SARS-CoV-2 Drug Targets, Active Site Contour Map Analysis and COVID-19 Therapeutics. *Curr. Mol. Pharmacol.* **2022**, *15*, 418–433. [CrossRef]

72. Ebrahim, A.; Riley, B.T.; Kumaran, D.; Andi, B.; Fuchs, M.R.; McSweeney, S.; Keedy, D.A. The tem-per-ature-dependent conformational ensemble of SARS-CoV-2 main protease (M^{pro}). *IUCrJ.* **2022**, *9*, 682–694. [CrossRef]
73. Siddiqa, M.A.; Rao, D.S.; Suvarna, G.; Chennamachetty, V.K.; Verma, M.K.; Rao, M.V.R. In-Silico Drug Designing of Spike Receptor with Its ACE2 Receptor and Nsp10/Nsp16 MTase Complex Against SARS-CoV-2. *Int. J. Pept. Res. Ther.* **2021**, *27*, 1633–1640. [CrossRef]
74. Sharma, K.; Morla, S.; Goyal, A.; Kumar, S. Computational guided drug repurposing for targeting 2′-O-ribose methyltransferase of SARS-CoV-2. *Life Sci.* **2020**, *259*, 118169. [CrossRef]
75. El Khoury, L.; Jing, Z.; Cuzzolin, A.; Deplano, A.; Loco, D.; Sattarov, B.; Hédin, F.; Wendeborn, S.; Ho, C.; El Ahdab, D.; et al. Computationally driven discovery of SARS-CoV-2 M^{pro} inhibitors: From design to experimental validation. *Chem. Sci.* **2022**, *13*, 3674–3687. [CrossRef]
76. Kim, Y.S.; Kim, B.; Kwon, E.B.; Chung, H.S.; Choi, J.G. Mulberrofuran G, a Mulberry Component, Prevents SARS-CoV-2 Infection by Blocking the Interaction between SARS-CoV-2 Spike Protein S1 Receptor-Binding Domain and Human Angiotensin-Converting Enzyme 2 Receptor. *Nutrients* **2022**, *14*, 4170. [CrossRef]
77. Verkhivker, G.; Agajanian, S.; Kassab, R.; Krishnan, K. Probing Mechanisms of Binding and Allostery in the SARS-CoV-2 Spike Omicron Variant Complexes with the Host Receptor: Revealing Functional Roles of the Binding Hotspots in Mediating Epistatic Effects and Communication with Allosteric Pockets. *Int. J. Mol. Sci.* **2022**, *23*, 11542. [CrossRef]
78. Sarma, S.; Herrera, S.M.; Xiao, X.; Hudalla, G.A.; Hall, C.K. Computational Design and Experimental Validation of ACE2-Derived Peptides as SARS-CoV-2 Receptor Binding Domain Inhibitors. *J. Phys. Chem. B.* **2022**, *126*, 8129–8139. [CrossRef]
79. Eka Saputri, M.; Aisyah Rahmalia Effendi, S.; Nadila, R.; Azzam Fajar, S.; Damajanti Soejoedono, R.; Handharyani, E.; Nadia Poetri, O. Immunoglobulin yolk targeting spike 1, receptor binding domain of spike glycoprotein and nucleocapsid of SARS-CoV-2 blocking RBD-ACE2 binding interaction. *Int. Immunopharmacol.* **2022**, *112*, 109280. [CrossRef]
80. Lv, N.; Cao, Z. RBD spatial orientation of the spike protein and its binding to ACE2: Insight into the high infectivity of the SARS-CoV-2 Delta variant from MD simulations. *Phys. Chem. Chem. Phys.* **2022**, *24*, 24155–24165. [CrossRef]
81. Singh, J.; Vashishtha, S.; Rahman, S.A.; Ehtesham, N.Z.; Alam, A.; Kundu, B.; Dobrindt, U. Energetics of Spike Protein Opening of SARS-CoV-1 and SARS-CoV-2 and Its Variants of Concern: Implications in Host Receptor Scanning and Transmission. *Biochemistry* **2022**, *61*, 2188–2197. [CrossRef] [PubMed]
82. Taft, J.M.; Weber, C.R.; Gao, B.; Ehling, R.A.; Han, J.; Frei, L.; Metcalfe, S.W.; Overath, M.D.; Yermanos, A.; Kelton, W.; et al. Deep mutational learning predicts ACE2 binding and antibody escape to combinatorial mutations in the SARS-CoV-2 receptor-binding domain. *Cell* **2022**, *185*, 4008–4022.e14. [CrossRef] [PubMed]
83. Seifert, S.N.; Bai, S.; Fawcett, S.; Norton, E.B.; Zwezdaryk, K.J.; Robinson, J.; Gunn, B.; Letko, M. An ACE2-dependent Sarbecovirus in Russian bats is resistant to SARS-CoV-2 vaccines. *PLoS Pathog.* **2022**, *18*, e1010828. [CrossRef] [PubMed]
84. Huhn, G.; Poorbaugh, J.; Zhang, L.; Beasley, S.; Nirula, A.; Brothers, J.; Welbel, S.; Wilson, J.; Gillani, S.; Weber, K.M.; et al. COVID-19 symptom relationship to antibody response and ACE2 neutralization in recovered health systems employees before and after mRNA BNT162b2 COVID-19 vaccine. *PLoS ONE* **2022**, *17*, e0273323. [CrossRef] [PubMed]
85. Ching, W.Y.; Adhikari, P.; Jawad, B.; Podgornik, R. Effect of Delta and Omicron Mutations on the RBD-SD1 Domain of the Spike Protein in SARS-CoV-2 and the Omicron Mutations on RBD-ACE2 Interface Complex. *Int. J. Mol. Sci.* **2022**, *23*, 10091. [CrossRef] [PubMed]
86. Lai, H.T.T.; Nguyen, L.H.; Phan, A.D.; Kranjc, A.; Nguyen, T.T.; Nguyen-Manh, D. A comparative study of receptor interactions between SARS-CoV and SARS-CoV-2 from molecular modeling. *J. Mol. Model.* **2022**, *28*, 305. [CrossRef]
87. Thébault, S.; Lejal, N.; Dogliani, A.; Donchet, A.; Urvoas, A.; Valerio-Lepiniec, M.; Lavie, M.; Baronti, C.; Touret, F.; Da Costa, B.; et al. Biosynthetic proteins targeting the SARS-CoV-2 spike as anti-virals. *PLoS Pathog.* **2022**, *18*, e1010799. [CrossRef]
88. Barroso da Silva, F.L.; Giron, C.C.; Laaksonen, A. Electrostatic Features for the Receptor Binding Domain of SARS-COV-2 Wildtype and Its Variants. Compass to the Severity of the Future Variants with the Charge-Rule. *J. Phys. Chem. B.* **2022**, *126*, 6835–6852. [CrossRef]
89. Pitsillou, E.; Liang, J.J.; Beh, R.C.; Hung, A.; Karagiannis, T.C. Molecular dynamics simulations highlight the altered binding landscape at the spike-ACE2 interface between the Delta and Omicron variants compared to the SARS-CoV-2 original strain. *Comput. Biol. Med.* **2022**, *149*, 106035. [CrossRef]
90. Erausquin, E.; Glaser, F.; Fernández-Recio, J.; López-Sagaseta, J. Structural bases for the higher adherence to ACE2 conferred by the SARS-CoV-2 spike Q498Y substitution. *Acta. Crystallogr. D Struct. Biol.* **2022**, *78*, 1156–1170. [CrossRef]
91. Verma, S.; Patil, V.M.; Gupta, M.K. Mutation informatics: SARS-CoV-2 receptor-binding domain of the spike protein. *Drug Discov. Today* **2022**, *27*, 103312. [CrossRef]
92. Singh, D.D.; Sharma, A.; Lee, H.J.; Yadav, D.K. SARS-CoV-2: Recent Variants and Clinical Efficacy of Antibody-Based Therapy. *Front. Cell Infect. Microbiol.* **2022**, *12*, 839170. [CrossRef]
93. Liu, H.; Wei, P.; Kappler, J.W.; Marrack, P.; Zhang, G. SARS-CoV-2 Variants of Concern and Variants of Interest Receptor Binding Domain Mutations and Virus Infectivity. *Front. Immunol.* **2022**, *13*, 825256. [CrossRef]
94. Ghosh, N.; Nandi, S.; Saha, I. A review on evolution of emerging SARS-CoV-2 variants based on spike glycoprotein. *Int. Immunopharmacol.* **2022**, *105*, 108565. [CrossRef]

95. Kumar, A.; Parashar, R.; Kumar, S.; Faiq, M.A.; Kumari, C.; Kulandhasamy, M.; Narayan, R.K.; Jha, R.K.; Singh, H.N.; Prasoon, P.; et al. Emerging SARS-CoV-2 variants can potentially break set epidemiological barriers in COVID-19. *J. Med. Virol.* **2022**, *94*, 1300–1314. [CrossRef]
96. Afolabi, R.; Chinedu, S.; Ajamma, Y.; Adam, Y.; Koenig, R.; Adebiyi, E. Computational identification of Plasmodium falciparum RNA pseudouridylate synthase as a viable drug target, its physicochemical properties, 3D structure prediction and prediction of potential inhibitors. *Infect. Genet. Evol.* **2022**, *97*, 105194. [CrossRef]
97. Shimizu, Y.; Yonezawa, T.; Sakamoto, J.; Furuya, T.; Osawa, M.; Ikeda, K. Identification of novel inhibitors of Keap1/Nrf2 by a promising method combining protein-protein interaction-oriented library and machine learning. *Sci. Rep.* **2021**, *11*, 7420. [CrossRef]
98. Santiago-Silva, K.M.; Camargo, P.; Felix da Silva Gomes, G.; Sotero, A.P.; Orsato, A.; Perez, C.C.; Nakazato, G.; da Silva Lima, C.H.; Bispo, M. In silico approach identified benzoylguanidines as SARS-CoV-2 main protease (M^{pro}) potential inhibitors. *J. Biomol. Struct. Dyn.* **2022**, *in press*. [CrossRef]
99. Macip, G.; Garcia-Segura, P.; Mestres-Truyol, J.; Saldivar-Espinoza, B.; Ojeda-Montes, M.J.; Gimeno, A.; Cereto-Massagué, A.; Garcia-Vallvé, S.; Pujadas, G. Haste makes waste: A critical review of docking-based virtual screening in drug repurposing for SARS-CoV-2 main protease (M-pro) inhibition. *Med. Res. Rev.* **2022**, *42*, 744–769. [CrossRef]
100. de Azevedo Junior, W.F.; Bitencourt-Ferreira, G.; Godoy, J.R.; Adriano, H.M.A.; Dos Santos Bezerra, W.A.; Dos Santos Soares, A.M. Protein-Ligand Docking Simulations with AutoDock4 Focused on the Main Protease of SARS-CoV-2. *Curr. Med. Chem.* **2021**, *28*, 7614–7673. [CrossRef]
101. Zhang, Y.; Yan, R.; Zhou, Q. ACE2, B^0AT1, and SARS-CoV-2 spike protein: Structural and functional implications. *Curr. Opin. Struct. Biol.* **2022**, *74*, 102388. [CrossRef] [PubMed]
102. Hu, Q.; Xiong, Y.; Zhu, G.H.; Zhang, Y.N.; Zhang, Y.W.; Huang, P.; Ge, G.B. The SARS-CoV-2 main protease (M^{pro}): Structure, function, and emerging therapies for COVID-19. *MedComm* **2022**, *3*, e151. [CrossRef] [PubMed]
103. Nocentini, A.; Capasso, C.; Supuran, C.T. Perspectives on the design and discovery of α-ketoamide inhibitors for the treatment of novel coronavirus: Where do we stand and where do we go? *Expert. Opin. Drug Discov.* **2022**, *17*, 547–557. [CrossRef] [PubMed]
104. Mahato, S. Recent Development in Small Molecules for SARS-CoV-2 and the Opportunity for Fragment-Based Drug Discovery. *Med. Chem.* **2022**, *18*, 847–858. [CrossRef] [PubMed]
105. Georgoulis, V.; Haidich, A.B.; Bougioukas, K.I.; Hatzimichael, E. Efficacy and safety of carfilzomib for the treatment of multiple myeloma: An overview of systematic reviews. *Crit. Rev. Oncol. Hematol.* **2022**, *180*, 103842. [CrossRef]
106. Terao, T.; Tsushima, T.; Miura, D.; Ikeda, D.; Fukumoto, A.; Kuzume, A.; Tabata, R.; Narita, K.; Takeuchi, M.; Matsue, K. Carfilzomib-induced thrombotic microangiopathy is underestimated in clinical practice: A report of five patients and literature review. *Leuk. Lymphoma* **2022**, *63*, 1102–1110. [CrossRef]
107. Chaudhry, M.; Steiner, R.; Claussen, C.; Patel, K.; Lee, H.; Weber, D.; Thomas, S.; Feng, C.; Amini, B.; Orlowski, R.; et al. Carfilzomib-based combination regimens are highly effective frontline therapies for multiple myeloma and Waldenström's macroglobulinemia. *Leuk. Lymphoma* **2019**, *60*, 964–970. [CrossRef]
108. Carlos-Escalante, J.A.; de Jesús-Sánchez, M.; Rivas-Castro, A.; Pichardo-Rojas, P.S.; Arce, C.; Wegman-Ostrosky, T. The Use of Antihypertensive Drugs as Coadjuvant Therapy in Cancer. *Front. Oncol.* **2021**, *11*, 660943. [CrossRef]
109. Zhan, Y.; Zhu, Y.; Wang, S.; Jia, S.; Gao, Y.; Lu, Y.; Zhou, C.; Liang, R.; Sun, D.; Wang, X.; et al. SARS-CoV-2 immunity and functional recovery of COVID-19 patients 1-year after infection. *Signal Transduct. Target Ther.* **2021**, *6*, 368. [CrossRef]
110. Zhang, P.; Li, B.; Wang, Y.; Min, W.; Wang, X.; Zhou, Y.; Li, Z.; Zhao, Y.; Zhang, H.; Jiang, M.; et al. Development and multi-center clinical trials of an up-converting phosphor technology-based point-of-care (UPT-POCT) assay for rapid COVID-19 diagnosis and prediction of protective effects. *BMC Microbiol.* **2022**, *22*, 42. [CrossRef]
111. Grau-Expósito, J.; Perea, D.; Suppi, M.; Massana, N.; Vergara, A.; Soler, M.J.; Trinite, B.; Blanco, J.; García-Pérez, J.; Alcamí, J.; et al. Evaluation of SARS-CoV-2 entry, inflammation and new therapeutics in human lung tissue cells. *PLoS Pathog.* **2022**, *18*, e1010171. [CrossRef]
112. Ohashi, H.; Watashi, K.; Saso, W.; Shionoya, K.; Iwanami, S.; Hirokawa, T.; Shirai, T.; Kanaya, S.; Ito, Y.; Kim, K.S.; et al. Potential anti-COVID-19 agents, cepharanthine and nelfinavir, and their usage for combination treatment. *iScience* **2021**, *24*, 102367. [CrossRef]
113. Kasprzyk, R.; Jemielity, J. Enzymatic Assays to Explore Viral mRNA Capping Machinery. *Chembiochem* **2021**, *22*, 3236–3253. [CrossRef]
114. Jiang, Y.; Liu, L.; Manning, M.; Bonahoom, M.; Lotvola, A.; Yang, Z.-Q. Repurposing Therapeutics to Identify Novel Inhibitors Targeting 2′-O-Ribose Methyltransferase Nsp16 of SARS-CoV-2. *ChemRxiv* **2020**, *25*, 2965. [CrossRef]
115. Walker, A.P.; Fan, H.; Keown, J.R.; Knight, M.L.; Grimes, J.M.; Fodor, E. The SARS-CoV-2 RNA polymerase is a viral RNA capping enzyme. *Nucleic Acids Res.* **2021**, *49*, 13019–13030. [CrossRef]
116. Zhang, H.; Saravanan, K.M.; Yang, Y.; Hossain, M.T.; Li, J.; Ren, X.; Pan, Y.; Wei, Y. Deep Learning Based Drug Screening for Novel Coronavirus 2019-nCov. *Interdiscip. Sci.* **2020**, *12*, 368–376. [CrossRef]
117. Gao, K.; Wang, R.; Chen, J.; Cheng, L.; Frishcosy, J.; Huzumi, Y.; Qiu, Y.; Schluckbier, T.; Wei, X.; Wei, G.W. Methodology-Centered Review of Molecular Modeling, Simulation, and Prediction of SARS-CoV-2. *Chem. Rev.* **2022**, *122*, 11287–11368. [CrossRef]
118. Lyu, X.; Imai, S.; Yamano, T.; Hanayama, R. Preventing SARS-CoV-2 Infection Using Anti-spike Nanobody-IFN-β Conjugated Exosomes. *Pharm. Res.* **2022**, *in press*. [CrossRef]

119. Hielscher, F.; Schmidt, T.; Klemis, V.; Wilhelm, A.; Marx, S.; Abu-Omar, A.; Ziegler, L.; Guckelmus, C.; Urschel, R.; Sester, U.; et al. NVX-CoV2373-induced cellular and humoral immunity towards parental SARS-CoV-2 and VOCs compared to BNT162b2 and mRNA-1273-regimens. *J. Clin. Virol.* **2022**, *157*, 105321. [CrossRef]
120. Wiedemann, A.; Pellaton, C.; Dekeyser, M.; Guillaumat, L.; Déchenaud, M.; Krief, C.; Lacabaratz, C.; Grimbert, P.; Pantaleo, G.; Lévy, Y.; et al. Longitudinal evaluation of the impact of immunosuppressive regimen on immune responses to COVID-19 vaccination in kidney transplant recipients. *Front. Med.* **2022**, *9*, 978764. [CrossRef]
121. Grikscheit, K.; Rabenau, H.F.; Ghodratian, Z.; Widera, M.; Wilhelm, A.; Toptan Grabmair, T.; Hoehl, S.; Layer, E.; Helfritz, F.; Ciesek, S. Characterization of the Antibody and Interferon-Gamma Release Response after a Second COVID-19 Booster Vaccination. *Vaccines* **2022**, *10*, 1163. [CrossRef] [PubMed]
122. Seki, Y.; Yoshihara, Y.; Nojima, K.; Momose, H.; Fukushi, S.; Moriyama, S.; Wagatsuma, A.; Numata, N.; Sasaki, K.; Kuzuoka, T.; et al. Safety and immunogenicity of the Pfizer/BioNTech SARS-CoV-2 mRNA third booster vaccine dose against the BA.1 and BA.2 Omicron variants. *Med* **2022**, *3*, 406–421.e4. [CrossRef] [PubMed]
123. Lee, H.K.; Go, J.; Sung, H.; Kim, S.W.; Walter, M.; Knabl, L.; Furth, P.A.; Hennighausen, L.; Huh, J.W. Heterologous ChAdOx1-BNT162b2 vaccination in Korean cohort induces robust immune and antibody responses that includes Omicron. *iScience* **2022**, *25*, 104473. [CrossRef] [PubMed]
124. Karaba, A.H.; Johnston, T.S.; Aytenfisu, T.Y.; Akinde, O.; Eby, Y.; Ruff, J.E.; Abedon, A.T.; Alejo, J.L.; Blankson, J.N.; Cox, A.L.; et al. A Fourth Dose of COVID-19 Vaccine Does Not Induce Neutralization of the Omicron Variant Among Solid Organ Transplant Recipients with Suboptimal Vaccine Response. *Transplantation* **2022**, *106*, 1440–1444. [CrossRef] [PubMed]
125. Benfield, T.L.; Iversen, K.K.; Mustafa, A.B.; Juhl, M.R.; Petersen, K.T.; Ostrowski, S.R.; Lindvig, S.O.; Rasmussen, L.D.; Schleimann, M.H.; Andersen, S.D.; et al. Comparison of vaccine-induced antibody neutralization against SARS-CoV-2 variants of concern following primary and booster doses of COVID-19 vaccines. *Front. Med.* **2022**, *9*, 994160. [CrossRef]
126. Zafar, U.; Zafar, H.; Ahmed, M.S.; Khattak, M. Link between COVID-19 vaccines and myocardial infarction. *World J. Clin. Cases* **2022**, *10*, 10109–10119. [CrossRef]
127. Morgan, M.C.; Atri, L.; Harrell, S.; Al-Jaroudi, W.; Berman, A. COVID-19 vaccine-associated myocarditis. *World J. Cardiol.* **2022**, *14*, 382–391. [CrossRef]
128. Ho, J.Y.K.; Siu, I.C.H.; Ng, K.H.L.; Tam, M.; Chow, S.C.Y.; Lim, K.; Kwok, M.W.T.; Wan, S.; Fujikawa, T.; Wong, R.H.L. Retrospective record review on timing of COVID-19 vaccination and cardiac surgery. *J. Card. Surg.* **2022**, *37*, 3634–3638. [CrossRef]
129. Risk, M.; Hayek, S.S.; Schiopu, E.; Yuan, L.; Shen, C.; Shi, X.; Freed, G.; Zhao, L. COVID-19 vaccine effectiveness against omicron (B.1.1.529) variant infection and hospitalisation in patients taking immunosuppressive medications: A retrospective cohort study. *Lancet Rheumatol.* **2022**, *4*, E775–E784. [CrossRef]
130. Tan, E.; Salman, S. Unusual Case of Painful Glossitis and Xerostomia Following Vaccination with Pfizer-BioNTech SARS-CoV-2 (BNT162b2). *Am. J. Case Rep.* **2022**, *23*, e937212. [CrossRef]
131. Numakura, T.; Murakami, K.; Tamada, T.; Yamaguchi, C.; Inoue, C.; Ohkouchi, S.; Tode, N.; Sano, H.; Aizawa, H.; Sato, K.; et al. A Novel Development of Sarcoidosis Following COVID-19 Vaccination and a Literature Review. *Intern. Med.* **2022**, *61*, 3101–3106. [CrossRef]
132. Patel, S.; Wu, E.; Mundae, M.; Lim, K. Myocarditis and pericarditis following mRNA vaccination in autoimmune inflammatory rheumatic disease patients: A single-center experience. *Rheumatol. Autoimmun.* **2022**, *2*, 92–97. [CrossRef]
133. Chandra, P.; Roldao, M.; Drachenberg, C.; Santos, P.; Washida, N.; Clark, A.; Bista, B.; Mitsuna, R.; Yango, A. Minimal change disease and COVID-19 vaccination: Four cases and review of literature. *Clin. Nephrol. Case Stud.* **2022**, *10*, 54–63. [CrossRef]
134. Yong, S.J.; Halim, A.; Halim, M.; Al Mutair, A.; Alhumaid, S.; Al-Sihati, J.; Albayat, H.; Alsaeed, M.; Garout, M.; Al Azmi, R.; et al. Rare Adverse Events Associated with BNT162b2 mRNA Vaccine (Pfizer-BioNTech): A Review of Large-Scale, Controlled Surveillance Studies. *Vaccines* **2022**, *10*, 1067. [CrossRef]
135. Ritskes-Hoitinga, M.; Barella, Y.; Kleinhout-Vliek, T. The Promises of Speeding Up: Changes in Requirements for Animal Studies and Alternatives during COVID-19 Vaccine Approval-A Case Study. *Animals* **2022**, *12*, 1735. [CrossRef]
136. Zou, Y.; Huang, D.; Jiang, Q.; Guo, Y.; Chen, C. The Vaccine Efficacy Against the SARS-CoV-2 Omicron: A Systemic Review and Meta-Analysis. *Front. Public Health* **2022**, *10*, 940956. [CrossRef]
137. Jawalagatti, V.; Kirthika, P.; Lee, J.H. Oral mRNA Vaccines Against Infectious Diseases- A Bacterial Perspective. *Front. Immunol.* **2022**, *13*, 884862. [CrossRef]
138. Shi, J.; Huang, M.W.; Lu, Z.D.; Du, X.J.; Shen, S.; Xu, C.F.; Wang, J. Delivery of mRNA for regulating functions of immune cells. *J. Control. Release* **2022**, *345*, 494–511. [CrossRef]
139. Banerjee, S.; Banerjee, D.; Singh, A.; Saharan, V.A. A Comprehensive Investigation Regarding the Differentiation of the Procurable COVID-19 Vaccines. *AAPS PharmSciTech* **2022**, *23*, 95. [CrossRef]
140. Gasmi, A.; Srinath, S.; Dadar, M.; Pivina, L.; Menzel, A.; Benahmed, A.G.; Chirumbolo, S.; Bjørklund, G. A global survey in the developmental landscape of possible vaccination strategies for COVID-19. *Clin. Immunol.* **2022**, *237*, 108958. [CrossRef]
141. Feikin, D.R.; Higdon, M.M.; Abu-Raddad, L.J.; Andrews, N.; Araos, R.; Goldberg, Y.; Groome, M.J.; Huppert, A.; O'Brien, K.L.; Smith, P.G.; et al. Duration of effectiveness of vaccines against SARS-CoV-2 infection and COVID-19 disease: Results of a systematic review and meta-regression. *Lancet* **2022**, *399*, 924–944. [CrossRef] [PubMed]
142. Buckley, J.E.; Landis, L.N.; Rapini, R.P. Pityriasis rosea-like rash after messenger RNA COVID-19 vaccination: A case report and review of the literature. *JAAD Int.* **2022**, *7*, 164–168. [CrossRef] [PubMed]

143. Patel, R.; Kaki, M.; Potluri, V.S.; Kahar, P.; Khanna, D. A comprehensive review of SARS-CoV-2 vaccines: Pfizer, Moderna & Johnson & Johnson. *Hum. Vaccin. Immunother.* **2022**, *18*, 2002083. [CrossRef] [PubMed]
144. Pratama, N.R.; Wafa, I.A.; Budi, D.S.; Putra, M.; Wardhana, M.P.; Wungu, C.D.K. mRNA Covid-19 vaccines in pregnancy: A systematic review. *PLoS ONE* **2022**, *17*, e0261350. [CrossRef] [PubMed]
145. Simnani, F.Z.; Singh, D.; Kaur, R. COVID-19 phase 4 vaccine candidates, effectiveness on SARS-CoV-2 variants, neutralizing antibody, rare side effects, traditional and nano-based vaccine platforms: A review. *3 Biotech.* **2022**, *12*, 15. [CrossRef]
146. Sapkota, B.; Saud, B.; Shrestha, R.; Al-Fahad, D.; Sah, R.; Shrestha, S.; Rodriguez-Morales, A.J. Heterologous prime-boost strategies for COVID-19 vaccines. *J. Travel. Med.* **2022**, *29*, taab191. [CrossRef]
147. Wang, Z.; Popowski, K.D.; Zhu, D.; de Juan Abad, B.L.; Wang, X.; Liu, M.; Lutz, H.; De Naeyer, N.; DeMarco, C.T.; Denny, T.N.; et al. Exosomes decorated with a recombinant SARS-CoV-2 receptor-binding domain as an inhalable COVID-19 vaccine. *Nat. Biomed. Eng.* **2022**, *6*, 791–805. [CrossRef]
148. Mustajab, T.; Kwamboka, M.S.; Choi, D.A.; Kang, D.W.; Kim, J.; Han, K.R.; Han, Y.; Lee, S.; Song, D.; Chwae, Y.J. Update on Extracellular Vesicle-Based Vaccines and Therapeutics to Combat COVID-19. *Int. J. Mol. Sci.* **2022**, *23*, 11247. [CrossRef]
149. Stewart, E.L.; Counoupas, C.; Johansen, M.D.; Nguyen, D.H.; Miemczyk, S.; Hansbro, N.G.; Ferrell, K.C.; Ashhurst, A.; Alca, S.; Ashley, C.; et al. Mucosal immunization with a delta-inulin adjuvanted recombinant spike vaccine elicits lung-resident immune memory and protects mice against SARS-CoV-2. *Mucosal. Immunol.* **2022**, *15*, 1405–1415. [CrossRef]
150. Martínez-Puente, D.H.; Pérez-Trujillo, J.J.; Zavala-Flores, L.M.; García-García, A.; Villanueva-Olivo, A.; Rodríguez-Rocha, H.; Valdés, J.; Saucedo-Cárdenas, O.; Montes de Oca-Luna, R.; Loera-Arias, M.J. Plasmid DNA for Therapeutic Applications in Cancer. *Pharmaceutics* **2022**, *14*, 1861. [CrossRef]
151. Fomsgaard, A.; Liu, M.A. The Key Role of Nucleic Acid Vaccines for One Health. *Viruses* **2021**, *13*, 258. [CrossRef]
152. Kayraklioglu, N.; Horuluoglu, B.; Klinman, D.M. CpG Oligonucleotides as Vaccine Adjuvants. *Methods Mol. Biol.* **2021**, *2197*, 51–85. [CrossRef]
153. Zhang, Z.; Kuo, J.C.; Yao, S.; Zhang, C.; Khan, H.; Lee, R.J. CpG Oligodeoxynucleotides for Anticancer Monotherapy from Preclinical Stages to Clinical Trials. *Pharmaceutics* **2021**, *14*, 73. [CrossRef]
154. Chen, W.; Jiang, M.; Yu, W.; Xu, Z.; Liu, X.; Jia, Q.; Guan, X.; Zhang, W. CpG-Based Nanovaccines for Cancer Immunotherapy. *Int. J. Nanomedicine.* **2021**, *16*, 5281–5299. [CrossRef]
155. Jin, Y.; Zhuang, Y.; Dong, X.; Liu, M. Development of CpG oligodeoxynucleotide TLR9 agonists in anti-cancer therapy. *Expert Rev. Anticancer Ther.* **2021**, *21*, 841–851. [CrossRef]
156. Putzke, S.; Feldhues, E.; Heep, I.; Ilg, T.; Lamprecht, A. Cationic lipid/pDNA complex formation as potential generic method to generate specific IRF pathway stimulators. *Eur. J. Pharm. Biopharm.* **2020**, *155*, 112–121. [CrossRef]
157. Yasuda, S.; Yoshida, H.; Nishikawa, M.; Takakura, Y. Comparison of the type of liposome involving cytokine production induced by non-CpG Lipoplex in macrophages. *Mol. Pharm.* **2010**, *7*, 533–542. [CrossRef]
158. Gupta, G.K.; Agrawal, D.K. CpG oligodeoxynucleotides as TLR9 agonists: Therapeutic application in allergy and asthma. *BioDrugs* **2010**, *24*, 225–235. [CrossRef]
159. Tsujihana, K.; Tanegashima, K.; Santo, Y.; Yamada, H.; Akazawa, S.; Nakao, R.; Tominaga, K.; Saito, R.; Nishito, Y.; Hata, R.I.; et al. Circadian protection against bacterial skin infection by epidermal CXCL14-mediated innate immunity. *Proc. Natl. Acad. Sci. USA* **2022**, *119*, e2116027119. [CrossRef]
160. Bi, X.; Liu, W.; Ding, X.; Liang, S.; Zheng, Y.; Zhu, X.; Quan, S.; Yi, X.; Xiang, N.; Du, J.; et al. Proteomic and metabolomic profiling of urine uncovers immune responses in patients with COVID-19. *Cell Rep.* **2022**, *38*, 110271. [CrossRef]
161. Iwase, R.; Naruse, N.; Nakagawa, M.; Saito, R.; Shigenaga, A.; Otaka, A.; Hara, T.; Tanegashima, K. Identification of Functional Domains of CXCL14 Involved in High-Affinity Binding and Intracellular Transport of CpG DNA. *J. Immunol.* **2021**, *207*, 459–469. [CrossRef] [PubMed]
162. Tanegashima, K.; Takahashi, R.; Nuriya, H.; Iwase, R.; Naruse, N.; Tsuji, K.; Shigenaga, A.; Otaka, A.; Hara, T. CXCL14 Acts as a Specific Carrier of CpG DNA into Dendritic Cells and Activates Toll-like Receptor 9-mediated Adaptive Immunity. *EBioMedicine* **2017**, *24*, 247–256. [CrossRef] [PubMed]
163. Larsen, K.C.; Spencer, A.J.; Goodman, A.L.; Gilchrist, A.; Furze, J.; Rollier, C.S.; Kiss-Toth, E.; Gilbert, S.C.; Bregu, M.; Soilleux, E.J.; et al. Expression of tak1 and tram induces synergistic pro-inflammatory signalling and adjuvants DNA vaccines. *Vaccine* **2009**, *27*, 5589–5598. [CrossRef] [PubMed]
164. Hoque, M.N.; Sarkar, M.M.H.; Khan, M.A.; Hossain, M.A.; Hasan, M.I.; Rahman, M.H.; Habib, M.A.; Akter, S.; Banu, T.A.; Goswami, B.; et al. Differential gene expression profiling reveals potential biomarkers and pharmacological compounds against SARS-CoV-2: Insights from machine learning and bioinformatics approaches. *Front. Immunol.* **2022**, *13*, 918692. [CrossRef] [PubMed]
165. Maghsoudi, S.; Taghavi Shahraki, B.; Rameh, F.; Nazarabi, M.; Fatahi, Y.; Akhavan, O.; Rabiee, M.; Mostafavi, E.; Lima, E.C.; Saeb, M.R.; et al. A review on computer-aided chemogenomics and drug repositioning for rational COVID-19 drug discovery. *Chem. Biol. Drug Des.* **2022**, *100*, 699–721. [CrossRef] [PubMed]
166. Kumar, S.; Kumar, G.S.; Maitra, S.S.; Malý, P.; Bharadwaj, S.; Sharma, P.; Dwivedi, V.D. Viral informatics: Bioinformatics-based solution for managing viral infections. *Brief Bioinform.* **2022**, *23*, bbac326. [CrossRef]
167. Marques-Pereira, C.; Pires, M.; Moreira, I.S. Discovery of Virus-Host interactions using bioinformatic tools. *Methods Cell Biol.* **2022**, *169*, 169–198. [CrossRef]

168. Swain, S.S.; Singh, S.R.; Sahoo, A.; Panda, P.K.; Hussain, T.; Pati, S. Integrated bioinformatics-cheminformatics approach toward locating pseudo-potential antiviral marine alkaloids against SARS-CoV-2-Mpro. *Proteins* **2022**, *90*, 1617–1633. [CrossRef]
169. Ghaznavi, H.; Shirvaliloo, M.; Sargazi, S.; Mohammadghasemipour, Z.; Shams, Z.; Hesari, Z.; Shahraki, O.; Nazarlou, Z.; Sheervalilou, R.; Shirvalilou, S. SARS-CoV-2 and influenza viruses: Strategies to cope with coinfection and bioinformatics perspective. *Cell Biol. Int.* **2022**, *46*, 1009–1020. [CrossRef]
170. Gorbalenya, A.E.; Anisimova, M. Editorial overview: Virus bioinformatics—Empowering genomics of pathogens, viromes, and the virosphere across divergence scales. *Curr. Opin. Virol.* **2022**, *52*, 161–165. [CrossRef]
171. Robertson, A.J.; Courtney, J.M.; Shen, Y.; Ying, J.; Bax, A. Concordance of X-ray and AlphaFold2 Models of SARS-CoV-2 Main Protease with Residual Dipolar Couplings Measured in Solution. *J. Am. Chem. Soc.* **2021**, *143*, 19306–19310. [CrossRef]
172. Beuming, T.; Martín, H.; Díaz-Rovira, A.M.; Díaz, L.; Guallar, V.; Ray, S.S. Are Deep Learning Structural Models Sufficiently Accurate for Free-Energy Calculations? Application of FEP+ to AlphaFold2-Predicted Structures. *J. Chem. Inf. Model.* **2022**, *62*, 4351–4360. [CrossRef]
173. Lee, D.; Xiong, D.; Wierbowski, S.; Li, L.; Liang, S.; Yu, H. Deep learning methods for 3D structural proteome and interactome modeling. *Curr. Opin. Struct. Biol.* **2022**, *73*, 102329. [CrossRef]
174. Tsaban, T.; Varga, J.K.; Avraham, O.; Ben-Aharon, Z.; Khramushin, A.; Schueler-Furman, O. Harnessing protein folding neural networks for peptide-protein docking. *Nat. Commun.* **2022**, *13*, 176. [CrossRef]
175. McCoy, A.J.; Sammito, M.D.; Read, R.J. Implications of AlphaFold2 for crystallographic phasing by molecular replacement. *Acta. Crystallogr. D Struct. Biol.* **2022**, *78*, 1–13. [CrossRef]
176. Jumper, J.; Evans, R.; Pritzel, A.; Green, T.; Figurnov, M.; Ronneberger, O.; Tunyasuvunakool, K.; Bates, R.; Žídek, A.; Potapenko, A.; et al. Applying and improving AlphaFold at CASP14. *Proteins* **2021**, *89*, 1711–1721. [CrossRef]
177. Cramer, P. AlphaFold2 and the future of structural biology. *Nat. Struct. Mol. Biol.* **2021**, *28*, 704–705. [CrossRef]
178. Marzolf, D.R.; Seffernick, J.T.; Lindert, S. Protein Structure Prediction from NMR Hydrogen-Deuterium Exchange Data. *J. Chem. Theory Comput.* **2021**, *17*, 2619–2629. [CrossRef]
179. Andreini, C.; Rosato, A. Structural Bioinformatics and Deep Learning of Metalloproteins: Recent Advances and Applications. *Int. J. Mol. Sci.* **2022**, *23*, 7684. [CrossRef]
180. Park, S.; Seok, C. GalaxyWater-CNN: Prediction of Water Positions on the Protein Structure by a 3D-Convolutional Neural Network. *J. Chem. Inf. Model.* **2022**, *62*, 3157–3168. [CrossRef]
181. Perez, M.A.S.; Cuendet, M.A.; Röhrig, U.F.; Michielin, O.; Zoete, V. Structural Prediction of Peptide-MHC Binding Modes. *Methods Mol. Biol.* **2022**, *2405*, 245–282. [CrossRef] [PubMed]
182. Yalcin-Ozkat, G. Molecular Modeling Strategies of Cancer Multidrug Resistance. *Drug Resist. Updat.* **2021**, *59*, 100789. [CrossRef] [PubMed]
183. Jing, X.; Dong, Q. MQAPRank: Improved global protein model quality assessment by learning-to-rank. *BMC Bioinform.* **2017**, *18*, 275. [CrossRef] [PubMed]
184. Sato, R.; Ishida, T. Protein model accuracy estimation based on local structure quality assessment using 3D convolutional neural network. *PLoS ONE* **2019**, *14*, e0221347. [CrossRef] [PubMed]
185. Dankelman, L.H.M.; Schilstra, S.; IJpma, F.F.A.; Doornberg, J.N.; Colaris, J.W.; Verhofstad, M.H.J.; Wijffels, M.M.E.; Prijs, J. Artificial intelligence fracture recognition on computed tomography: Review of literature and recommendations. *Eur. J. Trauma Emerg. Surg.* **2022**, *in press*. [CrossRef]
186. Islam, M.M.; Nooruddin, S.; Karray, F.; Muhammad, G. Human activity recognition using tools of convolutional neural networks: A state of the art review, data sets, challenges, and future prospects. *Comput. Biol. Med.* **2022**, *149*, 106060. [CrossRef]
187. Baur, D.; Kroboth, K.; Heyde, C.E.; Voelker, A. Convolutional Neural Networks in Spinal Magnetic Resonance Imaging: A Systematic Review. *World Neurosurg.* **2022**, *166*, 60–70. [CrossRef]
188. Lin, Y.; Xu, J.; Zhang, Y. Identification Method of Citrus Aurantium Diseases and Pests Based on Deep Convolutional Neural Network. *Comput. Intell. Neurosci.* **2022**, *2022*, 7012399. [CrossRef]
189. Loddo, A.; Fadda, C.; Di Ruberto, C. An Empirical Evaluation of Convolutional Networks for Malaria Diagnosis. *J. Imaging.* **2022**, *8*, 66. [CrossRef]
190. Ren, H.; Zhang, Q.; Wang, Z.; Zhang, G.; Liu, H.; Guo, W.; Mukamel, S.; Jiang, J. Machine learning recognition of protein secondary structures based on two-dimensional spectroscopic descriptors. *Proc. Natl. Acad. Sci. USA* **2022**, *119*, e2202713119. [CrossRef]
191. Yu, C.H.; Chen, W.; Chiang, Y.H.; Guo, K.; Martin Moldes, Z.; Kaplan, D.L.; Buehler, M.J. End-to-End Deep Learning Model to Predict and Design Secondary Structure Content of Structural Proteins. *ACS Biomater. Sci. Eng.* **2022**, *8*, 1156–1165. [CrossRef]
192. Robson, B. Testing machine learning techniques for general application by using protein secondary structure prediction. A brief survey with studies of pitfalls and benefits using a simple progressive learning approach. *Comput. Biol. Med.* **2021**, *138*, 104883. [CrossRef]
193. Goodswen, S.J.; Kennedy, P.J.; Ellis, J.T. Predicting Protein Therapeutic Candidates for Bovine Babesiosis Using Secondary Structure Properties and Machine Learning. *Front. Genet.* **2021**, *12*, 716132. [CrossRef]
194. Bouvier, B. Protein-Protein Interface Topology as a Predictor of Secondary Structure and Molecular Function Using Convolutional Deep Learning. *J. Chem. Inf. Model.* **2021**, *61*, 3292–3303. [CrossRef]

195. Chelur, V.R.; Priyakumar, U.D. BiRDS—Binding Residue Detection from Protein Sequences Using Deep ResNets. *J. Chem. Inf. Model.* **2022**, *62*, 1809–1818. [CrossRef]
196. Du, Z.; Su, H.; Wang, W.; Ye, L.; Wei, H.; Peng, Z.; Anishchenko, I.; Baker, D.; Yang, J. The trRosetta server for fast and accurate protein structure prediction. *Nat. Protoc.* **2021**, *16*, 5634–5651. [CrossRef]
197. Liu, Z.; Gong, Y.; Bao, Y.; Guo, Y.; Wang, H.; Lin, G.N. TMPSS: A Deep Learning-Based Predictor for Secondary Structure and Topology Structure Prediction of Alpha-Helical Transmembrane Proteins. *Front. Bioeng. Biotechnol.* **2021**, *8*, 629937. [CrossRef]
198. Wu, B.; Zheng, C. Pattern Recognition of Holographic Image Library Based on Deep Learning. *J. Healthc. Eng.* **2022**, *2022*, 2129168. [CrossRef]
199. Yu, B.; Zhou, L.; Wang, L.; Yang, W.; Yang, M.; Bourgeat, P.; Fripp, J. SA-LuT-Nets: Learning Sample-Adaptive Intensity Lookup Tables for Brain Tumor Segmentation. *IEEE Trans. Med. Imaging* **2021**, *40*, 1417–1427. [CrossRef]
200. Jeong, S.; Cheon, W.; Cho, S.; Han, Y. Clinical applicability of deep learning-based respiratory signal prediction models for four-dimensional radiation therapy. *PLoS ONE* **2022**, *17*, e0275719. [CrossRef]
201. Wang, C.; Garlick, S.; Zloh, M. Deep Learning for Novel Antimicrobial Peptide Design. *Biomolecules* **2021**, *11*, 471. [CrossRef] [PubMed]
202. Sharma, R.; Shrivastava, S.; Kumar Singh, S.; Kumar, A.; Saxena, S.; Kumar Singh, R. Deep-ABPpred: Identifying antibacterial peptides in protein sequences using bidirectional LSTM with word2vec. *Brief Bioinform.* **2021**, *22*, bbab065. [CrossRef] [PubMed]
203. Ayhan, M.S.; Kümmerle, L.B.; Kühlewein, L.; Inhoffen, W.; Aliyeva, G.; Ziemssen, F.; Berens, P. Clinical validation of saliency maps for understanding deep neural networks in ophthalmology. *Med. Image Anal.* **2022**, *77*, 102364. [CrossRef] [PubMed]
204. Zhou, F.; Yao, R.; Liao, G.; Liu, B.; Qiu, G. Visual Saliency via Embedding Hierarchical Knowledge in a Deep Neural Network. *IEEE Trans. Image Process.* **2020**, *29*, 8490–8505. [CrossRef] [PubMed]
205. Yan, K.; Wang, X.; Kim, J.; Feng, D. A New Aggregation of DNN Sparse and Dense Labeling for Saliency Detection. *IEEE Trans. Cybern.* **2021**, *51*, 5907–5920. [CrossRef]
206. Lu, Y.; Liu, A.A.; Chen, M.; Nie, W.Z.; Su, Y.T. Sequential Saliency Guided Deep Neural Network for Joint Mitosis Identification and Localization in Time-Lapse Phase Contrast Microscopy Images. *IEEE J. Biomed. Health Inform.* **2020**, *24*, 1367–1378. [CrossRef]
207. Jumper, J.; Hassabis, D. Protein structure predictions to atomic accuracy with AlphaFold. *Nat. Methods* **2022**, *19*, 11–12. [CrossRef]
208. Jumper, J.; Evans, R.; Pritzel, A.; Green, T.; Figurnov, M.; Ronneberger, O.; Tunyasuvunakool, K.; Bates, R.; Žídek, A.; Potapenko, A.; et al. Highly accurate protein structure prediction with AlphaFold. *Nature* **2021**, *596*, 583–589. [CrossRef]
209. Peng, Z.; Wang, W.; Han, R.; Zhang, F.; Yang, J. Protein structure prediction in the deep learning era. *Curr. Opin. Struct. Biol.* **2022**, *77*, 102495. [CrossRef]
210. Nikam, R.; Yugandhar, K.; Gromiha, M.M. DeepBSRPred: Deep learning-based binding site residue prediction for proteins. *Amino Acids* **2022**, *in press*. [CrossRef]
211. Ferruz, N.; Heinzinger, M.; Akdel, M.; Goncearenco, A.; Naef, L.; Dallago, C. From sequence to function through structure: Deep learning for protein design. *Comput. Struct. Biotechnol. J.* **2022**, *21*, 238–250. [CrossRef]
212. Lee, S.; Kim, S.; Lee, G.R.; Kwon, S.; Woo, H.; Seok, C.; Park, H. Evaluating GPCR modeling and docking strategies in the era of deep learning-based protein structure prediction. *Comput. Struct. Biotechnol. J.* **2022**, *21*, 158–167. [CrossRef]
213. Wang, P.H.; Zhu, Y.H.; Yang, X.; Yu, D.J. GCmapCrys: Integrating graph attention network with predicted contact map for multi-stage protein crystallization propensity prediction. *Anal. Biochem.* **2022**, *663*, 115020. [CrossRef]
214. Derry, A.; Altman, R.B. COLLAPSE: A representation learning framework for identification and characterization of protein structural sites. *Protein Sci.* **2022**, *15*, e4541. [CrossRef]
215. Yuan, L.; Hu, X.; Ma, Y.; Liu, Y. DLBLS_SS: Protein secondary structure prediction using deep learning and broad learning system. *RSC Adv.* **2022**, *12*, 33479–33487. [CrossRef]
216. Lin, P.; Yan, Y.; Huang, S.Y. DeepHomo2.0: Improved protein-protein contact prediction of homodimers by transformer-enhanced deep learning. *Brief Bioinform.* **2022**, *in press*. [CrossRef]
217. Kang, Y.; Xu, Y.; Wang, X.; Pu, B.; Yang, X.; Rao, Y.; Chen, J. HN-PPISP: A hybrid network based on MLP-Mixer for protein-protein interaction site prediction. *Brief Bioinform.* **2022**, *19*, bbac480. [CrossRef]
218. Aybey, E.; Gümüş, Ö. SENSDeep: An Ensemble Deep Learning Method for Protein-Protein Interaction Sites Prediction. *Interdiscip. Sci.* **2022**, *in press*. [CrossRef]
219. Soleymani, F.; Paquet, E.; Viktor, H.; Michalowski, W.; Spinello, D. Protein-protein interaction prediction with deep learning: A comprehensive review. *Comput. Struct. Biotechnol. J.* **2022**, *20*, 5316–5341. [CrossRef]
220. Li, Y.; Zhang, C.; Yu, D.J.; Zhang, Y. Deep learning geometrical potential for high-accuracy ab initio protein structure prediction. *iScience* **2022**, *25*, 104425. [CrossRef]

BioMedInformatics

MDPI

Review

Application of Standardized Regression Coefficient in Meta-Analysis

Pentti Nieminen

Medical Informatics and Data Analysis Research Group, University of Oulu, 90014 Oulu, Finland; pentti.nieminen@oulu.fi

Abstract: The lack of consistent presentation of results in published studies on the association between a quantitative explanatory variable and a quantitative dependent variable has been a long-term issue in evaluating the reported findings. Studies are analyzed and reported in a variety of ways. The main purpose of this review is to illustrate the procedures in summarizing and synthesizing research results from multivariate models with a quantitative outcome variable. The review summarizes the application of the standardized regression coefficient as an effect size index in the context of meta-analysis and describe how it can be estimated and converted from data presented in original research articles. An example of synthesis is provided using research articles on the association between childhood body mass index and carotid intima-media thickness in adult life. Finally, the paper shares practical recommendations for meta-analysts wanting to use the standardized regression coefficient in pooling findings.

Keywords: standardized regression coefficient; statistics; meta-analysis; research synthesis; data presentation; carotid intima-media thickness; overweight; childhood

Citation: Nieminen, P. Application of Standardized Regression Coefficient in Meta-Analysis. *Biomedinformatics* **2022**, *2*, 434–458. https://doi.org/10.3390/biomedinformatics2030028

Academic Editor: Jörn Lötsch

Received: 15 August 2022
Accepted: 29 August 2022
Published: 31 August 2022

1. Introduction

Systematic reviews and meta-analyses are used to synthesize the available evidence for a given question in several scientific disciplines [1,2]. A review of the original articles and research synthesis extends our knowledge through the combination and comparison of the original studies. A major problem in analyzing, evaluating and summarizing the reported findings of studies on the association between a quantitative explanatory variable and a quantitative dependent variable is that the results are analyzed and reported in many ways [3–5]. When using a systematic literature review with a meta-analytical approach to learn from combined studies, we are dependent on the research methodology and reporting of the underlying studies. When the reviewed research articles contain inadequate statistical reporting of applied research methods and poor data presentation, the pooling of the findings will be even more difficult for the meta-analyst.

Among studies measuring the relationship between an explanatory factor and a response variable, some use correlation coefficients, some apply multivariable regression methods, and some studies compare mean values [5,6]. In addition, different measurement methods are used to assess the explanatory factors in the original studies. The quality of data presentation also varies. Detailed descriptive statistics of the variables under study are not given in all articles, and necessary measures of variation (standard errors) for coefficients of associations are not directly provided. Multivariable relationships present additional special challenges to meta-analysis because the statistics of interest depend on the other variables that are included in the multivariable analysis. Pooling these studies often requires data transformations and additional computations and estimations of effect sizes [1,7]. Thus, a coherent synthesis of studies analyzing the relation of an explanatory variable with a continuous outcome variable is challenging.

The measure used to represent the study findings in a meta-analysis is called an effect-size statistic. Several effect sizes have been proposed to synthesize results from multivariable regression models [8]. These include the unstandardized regression coefficient (*b*) and correlation coefficient (*r*). One effect-size approach is based on standardized regression coefficients. By definition, a standardized regression coefficient β (also called a beta weight) represents the estimated number of standard deviations of change in the outcome variable for one standard deviation unit change in the explanatory or predictor variable, while controlling for other predictors. The synthesis of standardized regression coefficients has received attention over the last few decades because standardized regression coefficients are effect sizes commonly used in various domains [4,9–11]. Examples of applied disciplines include public-health and environmental research [12–14], psychology [15,16], and educational sciences [17,18].

As an example of using the standardized regression coefficient, I perform a meta-analysis to evaluate the association of childhood obesity and carotid intima-media thickness (cIMT) in adult life. Obesity induces multiple metabolic abnormalities that contribute to the pathogenesis of atherosclerosis and cardiovascular disease [19,20]. The carotid artery intima-media thickness is a marker of cardiovascular disease risk [21]. Thus, it is important to quantify the impact of childhood and adolescent body mass index (BMI) on common cIMT measurement in adulthood.

In this review, I first provide a description of the standardized regression coefficient (β) as an effect-size index. This is followed by a brief literature review of studies using these coefficients in different domains during the last ten years. An example is presented to illustrate the use of the meta-analysis technique for combining regression coefficients to synthesize findings from multivariable studies. The next chapter provides formulas to convert different statistics and effect sizes to standardized regression coefficients. After this, I discuss issues regarding the use of the standardized regression coefficient for combining effects. The main purposes of this paper are to point out the complexities and potential problems in a critical review of the association between a quantitative response variable and one primary quantitative explanatory variable, and to present a practical effect-size approach based on standardized regression coefficients.

2. Standardized Regression Coefficient as an Effect-Size Index in Meta-Analysis

Multivariable linear-regression models are used to analyze the associations between one quantitative dependent variable and several explanatory variables. The unstandardized regression coefficient (*b*) estimated from the linear-regression model is an easy-to-interpret statistic to describe how the explanatory variable affects the values of the outcome variable. These coefficients are usually provided with their standard errors (SEs) or confidence intervals (CIs) in articles reporting findings from regression models [22,23]. The unstandardized regression coefficient *b* describes the effect of changing the explanatory variable by one unit, and hence its size depends on the scale used to measure the explanatory variable. However, the main explanatory characteristic is often measured using different methods and metrics in the reviewed studies. Thus, the direct pooling of unstandardized regression coefficients is not meaningful across studies. To pool the effects of explanatory variables measured with different scales, we must express them in a comparable manner. In such a case, the standardized regression coefficient β may offer an option to synthetize the findings [5,17]. The β coefficient is the estimate resulting from an analysis carried out on variables that have been standardized so that their standard deviations (and variances) are equal to one [22,23]. Therefore, the standardized coefficient refers to how many standard deviations the response or outcome variable will change per a standard deviation increase in the explanatory or predictor variable. Thus, the standardized coefficient β can be regarded as an attempt to make regression coefficients more comparable, and can be used as an effect-size estimate when the exposure levels in original studies are measured in different units of measurement.

The statistical significance of the standardized regression coefficient can be tested using the t-test of the null hypothesis H_0: $\beta = 0$, or in substantive terms, no systematic relationship between the predictor and outcome. A p-value higher than 0.05 supports the null hypothesis that there is no association. A confidence interval for the coefficient β provides information about the range of the β. A positive (negative) β-value supports the hypothesis that a high exposure level increases (decreases) the response. When the confidence interval does not include 0, then the association between the explanatory variable and outcome variable is considered statistically significant, in accordance with the p-value of the t-test <0.05.

When considering effect sizes, a natural question to ask is what constitutes a large, medium, and small effect size. Cohen's [24] guidelines for the classification of effect sizes are widely cited in scientific reports. For a coefficient β, effect sizes between 0.10–0.29 are said to be only small, effect sizes between 0.30–0.49 are medium, and effect sizes of 0.50 or greater are large [24,25].

An essential feature of the quantitative meta-analysis is its ability to compare the magnitude of effects across studies, which requires the use of a single effect-size metric for measuring these effects. Using the standardized regression coefficient β as the common effect-size measure involves extracting the findings of reviewed studies expressed as unstandardized regression coefficients, correlation coefficients or mean differences. These statistics are then re-expressed as standardized regression coefficients and their standard errors. This process includes several conversions, calculations, and approximations. The different approaches are summarized in Section 5.

In a meta-analysis, the findings (and effect sizes) are pooled from reviewed studies. However, every observed effect size is not equal with regard to the reliability of the information it carries [1]. Therefore, each effect-size value must be weighted by a term that represents its precision. An optimal approach is to use the inverse of the squared standard error of the effect-size value as a weight. Thus, larger studies, which have smaller standard errors, are given more weight than smaller studies, which have larger standard errors. The formula for computing the associated standard error must also be identified. To obtain the summary effect of all the reviewed studies, the weighted average effect size can be computed using the following formula:

$$M = \frac{\sum_{i=1}^{k} w_i \beta_i}{\sum_{i=1}^{k} w_i},$$

where k = number studies, β_i is the standard regression coefficient from study I, SE(β_i) is the standard error of βi, and w_i is the inverse of $(\mathrm{SE}(\beta_i))^2$. The variance $(\mathrm{SE}(\beta_i))^2$ can be calculated using the fixed-effects or random-effects model [1,26]. This version of the meta-analysis procedure is commonly referred to as the generic inverse-approach [27]. The approach is implemented in all standard software packages for meta-analysis.

Meta-analyses typically report the summary effect size M with a measure of precision (SE or CI) and a p-value in a figure. This figure, the forest plot, displays the effect estimates and confidence intervals for individual studies as well as the summary effect. Figure 1 provides two examples of forest plots. Following Cohen's guidelines [24] and substantive empirical reviews [25,28], for the absolute (non-negative) value of the pooled effect size $|M|$, a value of 0.10–0.19 is a small effect size, a pooled value of 0.20–0.29 is classified as a medium effect size, and a pooled value of 0.30 or greater is a large effect size.

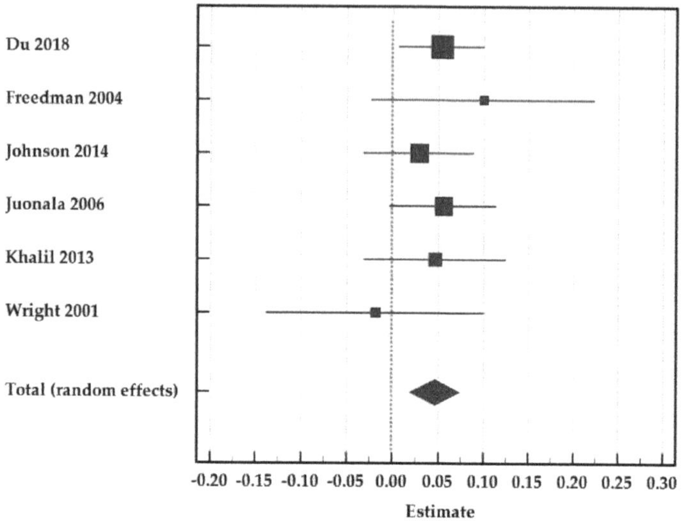

(**A**)

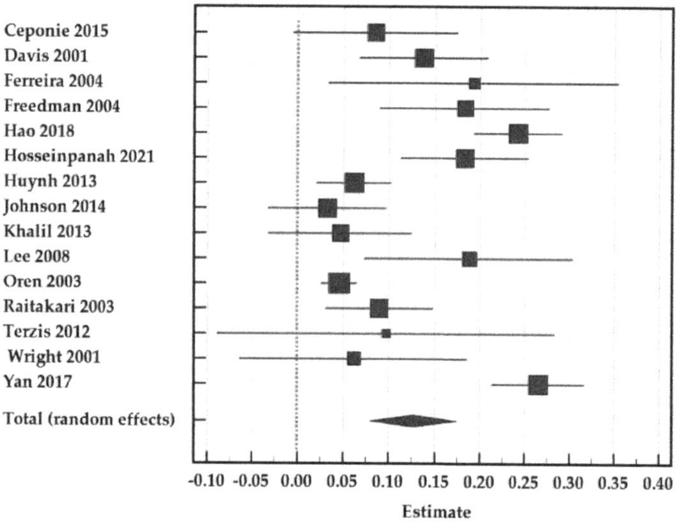

(**B**)

Figure 1. Forest plots for the association between childhood (**A**) and adolescent (**B**) and adult cIMT. Total number of individuals was 5796 in childhood and 11,859 in adolescent in the meta-analysis. (**A**) Childhood. (**B**) Adolescent.

3. Literature Review of Applications

In the following sub-chapters, I provide examples of meta-analytical studies where the use of the standardized regression coefficient served as a useful tool for synthesizing the results of numerous studies on a particular topic. Unfortunately, I also found meta-analyses where the coefficients r, b and β were confused [29–31].

3.1. Public Health

In environmental and public-health research, several outcomes and explanatory factors are often measured by different methods and units of measurement. Dzhambov and co-workers [13] studied whether green spaces and general greenery in the living environment of pregnant women were associated with the birth weight of their infants and what the direction of that effect was. They performed meta-analyses on eight published studies exploring the association of residential greenness and birth weight. The majority of the studies used multivariable linear regression to determine the effect of residential greenery on birthweight adjustments for personal covariates. In the original studies, different indicators were chosen as a proxy for residential greenness. Thus, the standardized regression coefficient offers one solution to pool the findings. The reported pooled β was 0.001 (95% CI = −0.001 to 0.003), showing a non-significant association between greenness and birth weight. The authors noted that the findings were similar when the correlation coefficient was used as an effect-size index.

Keenan A. Ramsay and her co-authors [32] presented in their meta-analysis that higher physical activity (PA) and lower sedentary behavior (SB) are associated with greater skeletal muscle strength and muscle power in older adults. Articles were included in the meta-analyses if the associations between PA or SB measures and hand grip strength or the chair stand test were expressed as adjusted standardized regression coefficients (β) and their 95% CI or SE, or when these could be calculated. They identified considerable heterogeneity in the study design, the definitions of measures of outcome and explanatory variables, and the statistical analyses used to present the associations. This posed methodological challenges to comparing and synthesizing the results.

In healthy individuals and people with chronic pain, an inverse association between physical-activity level and pain has been reported (e.g., more activity and less pain). Jones et al. [33] examined the relation between aerobic capacity and pain in healthy individuals and people with fibromyalgia. They collated their new data with data from previous original studies in healthy individuals. To pool the findings identified by the literature search, standardized regression coefficients and their standard errors were calculated. This involved converting the results of analyses using the correlation, linear regression, or effect sizes of differences between groups and converting these to standardized β coefficients with their standard errors. Then, 95% confidence intervals of the βs were calculated for presentation of the data on forest plots. Interestingly, the authors noted that a pooled effect size for these studies was not calculated, because they presented several effect sizes between various measures of pain and explanatory variables estimated from the same studies. Thus, the findings do not provide independent estimates of an effect. The presented forest plots (standardized β coefficients with their 95% confidence intervals) of findings from studies illustrate clearly that the associations between physical fitness and pain are generally small and are highly variable within and across studies [33].

In 2020, Wang et al. [14] published a well-constructed quantitative summary of prenatal lead (Pb) exposure on birth weight. Because the quantitative variables from each reviewed article were reported using different metrics and different measures of association, they used standardized regression coefficients to allow a combination of findings from the reviewed studies. The pooling of findings was conducted separately for maternal blood and cord blood as measures of exposure variables. In addition, the analyses were restricted to unadjusted findings and to studies that adjusted for potential confounders. There was a significant negative association between prenatal Pb exposure and birth weight. In the unadjusted studies, birth-weight reduction was weakly associated with elevated lead levels in maternal blood (pooled $\beta = -0.094$, 95% CI = −0.157 to −0.030) and cord blood (pooled $\beta = -0.120$, 95% CI = −0.239 to −0.001). When restricted to the adjusted studies, these associations were weaker.

The study by Nicholas Burrows and his co-authors [34] reported meta-analyses of studies that examined correlations between pain from knee osteoarthritis and physical activity or fitness. The effect sizes from the evaluated original studies were converted to standardized regression coefficients in order to be included on the forest plots and to estimate the pooled standardized coefficient. Data from their own new study were also included in the meta-analysis. From the 33 included studies, 13 provided data for the analysis of the associations between pain and physical activity, and 21 provided data for the associations between pain and fitness. The extracted physical-activity variables were either questionnaire-based measures of activity or objectively measured activity using pedometers or accelerometers. Separate meta-analyses were performed for muscle strength, muscle power, and aerobic capacity. Statistically significant pooled βs were found between objectively measured physical activity and pain severity. The more physically active individuals reported less pain at a baseline measurement, and across the seven-day period of physical-activity measurement.

McLaughlin et al. [35] reviewed studies related to the association between engagement with a physical-activity digital health intervention and physical-activity outcomes. A variety of different methods of association were used across the included studies. For the clearly reported meta-analysis, authors were required to transform several estimates into one consistent effect index. A standardized regression coefficient was chosen as the effect index. Many included studies reported more than one association. For meta-analyses, they used hierarchical selection criteria to select a single association from each study for inclusion in the pooled synthesis. When a study did not provide sufficient data required for meta-analysis (i.e., information to calculate an effect estimate and measure of variability of the effect estimate), the authors excluded this study from the meta-analysis. A meta-analysis of 11 included studies indicated a very small but statistically significant positive association between digital health engagement and physical activity (pooled $\beta = 0.08$, 95% CI = 0.01 to 0.14).

3.2. Psychology

Charlie Rioux and co-authors [16] published an interesting study where βs were used to represent the effect size of the interaction between temperament and family variables on substance use or externalizing behaviors while controlling for the other variables included in the tested model of the various studies. The authors searched for studies examining the interactions between temperament and the family environment on the outcome variables. Analyses of the interactions between two explanatory variables can be conducted using ANOVA techniques or with multiple regression models. The interpretation of the interactions is difficult because different patterns of interaction among temperament and family variables may have different implications. Due to issues with interaction terms and differences in measurements, the researchers were cautious and did not report pooled effect sizes. However, the reported individual effect sizes and their interpretation in the text still provide useful information about the possible interaction between the analyzed explanatory variables.

Kaitlin Woolley and Ayelet Fishbach [36] examined the relationship between immediate versus delayed rewards and persistence in long-term goals (e.g., healthy eating, exercising). The authors conducted five different intervention studies to examine the associations. In each study, they conducted a regression analysis to estimate the associations and reported βs. Finally, they pooled the βs using a meta-analytic approach to estimate an overall pattern across the five studies. In summary, whereas delayed rewards may motivate goal setting and the intentions to pursue long-term goals, a meta-analysis of their studies found that immediate rewards are more strongly associated with actual persistence in a long-term goal. The effect of immediate rewards on persistence, controlling for delayed rewards, was considered to be of medium size and statistically significant, (pooled $\beta = 0.35$, 95% CI = 0.28 to 0.42, $p < 0.001$).

Choi et al. [37] used a similar approach to Wooley and Fishbach [36] and combined the findings from five different studies using β as the effect size. In each sub-study, they examined predictors of success in different achievement domains using regression models. By conducting meta-analyses, they explored the overall pattern across the studies. Their findings indicate that self-control is predictive of success in achievement-related domains (β = 0.27, 95% CI = 0.21 to 0.32), while emotional well-being is predictive of success in relationship-related domains (β = 0.36, 95% CI = 0.29 to 0.43).

Two meta-analyses have examined the pain-related factors in individuals with chronic musculoskeletal pain [38,39]. In both studies, standardized regression coefficients and their 95% confidence intervals were calculated for the pooled results. Reviewed studies were excluded from these analyses if they did not provide sufficient information for computing the SE of the regression coefficient. Greater levels of fear of pain, pain-related anxiety, and fear-avoidance beliefs were significantly associated with greater pain intensity and disability [38]. In addition, higher levels of overly negative thoughts in response to pain or pain-related cues were associated with more pain intensity and disability levels [39]. The authors comment that an important observation in their reviews was that despite the very large number of studies that have been performed to evaluate the associations between pain-related factors and both pain and disability, the quality of the studies tended to be very low. These included issues in statistical analyses and reporting. These shortcomings made it difficult to carry out meta-analyses.

3.3. Other Sub-Fields

The paper by Yong Jei Lee and collaborators [40] is an example from criminology. The aim of their work was to show how many standard deviations in the number of crimes will change per a standard-deviation increase (or decrease) in the police-force size variable in the USA. They pooled standardized regression coefficients from 62 studies to estimate the overall effect size. The estimated pooled effect size was −0.030 (95% CI = −0.078 to 0.019). The nonsignificant and tiny mean effect size between police-force size and crime suggests that simply increasing police-force size may not help reduce crime, and if it does, then it does not reduce crime by much.

Meta-regression can be used in a meta-analysis to assess the relationship between study-level covariates and effect size [1]. Sanghee Park [41] applied meta-regression to study the effect of various study characteristics on the observed association between gender representation in the workforce and public-organization performance using the pooled β as an effect-size index in 72 studies published between 1999 and 2017. Several covariates explained the variations in the reported βs. Unfortunately, the message of Park's article is hampered by an inadequate linkage between meta-regression theory and the reporting of the applied field of meta-analysis.

Yahui Tian and Jijun Yao [18] applied meta-analysis to analyze a total of 20 effect sizes from 11 articles on the impact of Chinese school resource investment on student performance. They found that the overall impact of school resources on student performance is significant (pooled β = 0.093, 95% CI = 0.039 to 0.147). Since the standard regression coefficient was used as the effect size in this study, an increase of one standard deviation in school resource investment will increase student performance by 0.093 standard points. It should be noted that combining the effects of human, material and financial resources to an overall amount of resource investment in each study required multiple computational steps.

Standardized regression coefficients have also been applied in economics research. A paper published by Araujo et al. in 2020 provides a comprehensive synthesis of the evidence on macroprudential policies [42]. Drawing from 58 empirical studies, authors summarized the effects of macroprudential policy on several outcomes (e.g., credit, household credit, and house prices). The economic literature does not have a standard definition of the variables used to measure the effects of macroprudential policy. Enhancing the comparability of the effects across studies required the standardization approach to the regression coefficient between the macroprudential-policy variable and the corresponding outcome variable. The paper then used a meta-analysis framework to quantitatively synthesize estimated βs. In addition, meta-regression was used to examine how the βs varied with the study characteristics. Relying on β as an effect size in meta-analysis techniques, this paper demonstrated that on average, macroprudential-policy tools have statistically significant effects on credit.

4. Meta-Analysis Example

4.1. Research Question

With the rise in childhood obesity to epidemic portions across the world in the past few decades, many studies have sought to find out the long-term effects of childhood obesity on adulthood diseases [20]. The carotid artery intima-media thickness measured by ultrasound imaging represents a marker of preclinical atherosclerosis [43]. It correlates with vascular risk factors, associates with the severity of coronary artery disease, and predicts the likelihood of cardiovascular events in population groups. Several longitudinal cohort studies have tried to assess the relationship between childhood BMI or obesity and adulthood cIMT. The studies have shown conflicting results with some showing a positive association [43–47] while the other showing no significant association [48,49]. A systematic review [50], a pooled data analysis [51], and a meta-analysis [30] have also been conducted to assess these associations and have found qualitative positive associations between the two. Two of these studies [50,51] did not quantify the relationship, and the study of Ajala et al. [30] includes errors in pooling different effect-size metrics. With my example, I aim to clarify and quantify the association between childhood obesity and adulthood cIMT by combining evidence from the available studies.

4.2. Material and Methods

4.2.1. Search Strategy

A literature search was carried out using Medline and Scopus from the year of inception to April 2022 with no language restrictions. The search strategy used a combination of medical subject headings and keywords to identify publications. The following search terms were used for the childhood-exposure variable: body mass index; BMI; child*; adolescen*; pediatric*; paediatric*. I combined these search terms with the search terms for the outcome variable: carotid intima-media thickness; intima-media thickness; carotid atherosclero*; carotid intima media; intimal-medial thickness; subclinical atherosclero*. Additional search terms were added to the aforementioned terms: prospective; retrospective; longitudinal; cohort; lifetime; long term; follow-up.

4.2.2. Screening of Studies

The following criteria were used for the inclusion or exclusion of studies:

(a) Type of study: prospective/retrospective longitudinal
(b) Exposure: body mass index (BMI)
(c) Age at measurement of body mass index: 2–19 years (childhood: 2–9 years; adolescence: 10–19 years)
(d) Outcome: carotid intima-media thickness measured in adult ($\geq$20 years)
(e) Length of follow-up: at least 5 years
(f) Mode of ascertainment of exposure and outcome: all measurements taken by health professionals or trained investigators or from medical records.

Interventional studies, review articles and studies with selective groups, e.g., preterm babies, low- or high-birth-weight infants, obese children, etc. were excluded. In addition, studies using the categorized outcome variable cIMT and reporting odds ratios (ORs) or relative risks (RRs) were not included in this meta-analysis.

4.2.3. Data Synthesis and Analysis

The effect sizes extracted from the original studies included correlation coefficients, mean differences, and unstandardized and standardized regression coefficients measuring the relationship between childhood and adolescent BMI and adult cIMT. Results from both unadjusted and adjusted analyses were included if they were included in the original studies. Since BMI was measured in childhood or adolescence, most studies used a BMI variable standardized by age and sex.

I performed a meta-analysis to estimate the pooled effect of childhood and adolescent BMI on adult cIMT. In this analysis, standardized regression coefficients were used as effect-size estimates because different measurement methods and metrics were used across the original studies. Some studies provided the association between childhood BMI and adolescent BMI with maximum cIMT, whereas the other studies reported the association with mean cIMT measurements. Furthermore, childhood and adolescent BMI measurements were age- and sex-standardized using different growth charts. In these articles, the standard deviation of BMI (SD(BMI)) was equal to 1. If original studies presented correlation coefficients or unstandardized regression coefficients, then these were transformed to standardized regression coefficients using the formulas presented in Section 5.

4.3. Results

A total of 17 articles analyzing individuals from 16 different longitudinal cohort studies met the inclusion criteria and were included in the systematic review.

Table 1 reports the main characteristics of the 17 longitudinal studies included in this systematic review and meta-analysis. Sample sizes varied between 112 and 2628. Outcome (cIMT) was most frequently measured in individuals who were aged between 20–50 years.

Table 1. Characteristics of studies included in the meta-analysis.

Study and Year of Publication	Country of Study	BMI Measured		Sample Size	Baseline Age (Years)	Final Age (Years)
		Childhood	Adolescent			
Ceponiene 2015 [52]	Lithuania		✓	380	12–13	48–49
Davis 2001 [44]	United States		✓	725	8–18	33–42
Du 2018 [53]	United States	✓		1052	9.8 (3.2) [a]	23–43
Ferreira 2004 [54]	Netherlands		✓	159	13–16	36.5 (0.6) [a]
Freedman 2004 [55]	United States	✓	✓	513	4–17	23–40
Hao 2018 [56]	United States		✓	626	10–18	24 [b]
Hosseinpanah 2021 [57]	Iran		✓	1295	10.9 (4.0)	29.8 (4.0) [a]
Huynh 2013 [58]	Australia		✓	2328	7–15	26–36
Johnson 2014 [59]	United Kingdom		✓	1273	15	60–64
Juonala 2006 [60]	Finland	✓		1081	3–9	24–30
Khalil 2013 [46]	India	✓	✓	600	2, 11	33–38
Lee 2008 [61]	South Korea		✓	256	16	25
Oren 2003 [47]	Netherlands		✓	750	12–16	27–30
Raitakari 2003 [43]	Finland		✓	1170	12–18	33–39
Terzis 2012 [49]	Greece		✓	106	12–17	40.5 (1.1) [a]
Wright 2001 [62]	United Kingdom	✓	✓	412	9, 13	50
Yan 2017 [63]	China		✓	1252	6–18	27–42

[a] Mean (SD), [b] median.

Table 2 shows the effect sizes and computations applied to obtain the standardized regression coefficient β with standard error SE(β) for each evaluated study. Only 3 articles from the 17 included studies directly reported β-value estimated by linear-regression modeling [45,50,58]. These were used as the effect sizes in the meta-analysis. The standard error of β or b was not reported in several of the reviewed articles. In two studies, the authors were contacted to obtain SE(β) for their study [54,62]. In other studies, SE(β) was obtained from a confidence interval, or from a reported p-value or t-value of Wald's test statistic.

Table 2. Reported effect sizes and computations applied to obtain the standardized regression coefficient β with standard error SE(β) for each evaluated study. The numbers in columns refer to sub-sections of Chapter 5 where detailed formulas are provided.

	Reported Effect Size	Obtaining β and SE(β)	Combining within a Study	Estimating SD	Other Computations
Ceponiene [52]	b	5.3.3	5.4	5.6.4	
Davis [44]	r	5.2.2	5.4		
Du [53]	b	5.2.3		5.6.4	5.7.1
Ferreira [54]	β	5.7.2			5.7.2
Freedman [55]	r	5.2.2	5.5		
Hao [56]	b	5.2.5			5.7.3
Hosseinpanah [57]	b	5.2.5		5.6.4	
Huynh [58]	b	5.3.3		5.6.4	
Johnson [59]	b	5.3.3	5.4 and 5.5	5.6.2	5.7.1
Juonala [60]	r	5.2.2	5.4		
Khalil [46]	b	5.3.3		5.6.4	
Lee [61]	b	5.3.2	5.4	5.6.4	5.7.3
Oren [47]	b	5.3.3		5.6.4	
Raitakari [43]	b	5.2.3			
Terzis [49]	β	5.3.2			
Wright [62]	β	5.7.2	5.4		5.7.2
Yan [63]	r	5.2.2	5.4		

β = standardized regression coefficient, r = correlation coefficient, b = unstandardized regression coefficient, SD = standard deviation of cIMT or BMI.

A total of six studies reported effect sizes separately for males and females and one for age groups. Two studies analyzed data with repeated measurements where BMI was measured more than once at different age phases on the same children. For these studies I calculated composite effect sizes.

Standard deviations of BMI and cIMT were needed for the calculations of β and SE(β). In most of the studies SD(BMI) was 1. SD(cIMT) was not available in several of the evaluated articles. I applied the available data in eight articles to obtain the required standard deviation.

Tables 3 and 4 show the estimated β effect sizes from the cohorts included in the meta-analysis. The first analysis included the studies in which the age at the assessment of BMI of the individuals was in childhood (Table 3, Figure 1, Childhood BMI). A 1 SD increase in childhood BMI leads to an increase of 0.047 SD (95% CI = 0.019 to 0.074; $p = 0.001$) in adult cIMT. Although statistically significant, this effect can be considered very small or negligible. The pooled standard deviation of cIMT among all the individuals included in this meta-analysis was 0.103. Using the Formula (8) of relationship between coefficients b and β from Section 5.7.1, a 1 SD increase in childhood BMI leads to an increase in adult cIMT by $0.047 \times 0.103 = 0.005$ mm (95% CI = 0.002 to 0.008 mm).

The second meta-analysis included studies where the individuals were in their adolescence at the time of the assessment of BMI (Table 4, Figure 1, Adolescent BMI). A 1 SD increase in adolescent BMI leads to a 0.127 SD (95% CI = 0.080 to 0.175; $p < 0.001$) or $0.127 \times 0.103 = 0.013$ mm (95% CI = 0.008 to 0.018 mm) increase in adult cIMT. According to this effect size, the relationship between the adolescent BMI and adult cIMT was small.

Table 3. Observed standardized regression coefficient β with standard error SE(β) and 95% confidence interval, sample size and weight in pooled analysis from seven studies estimating the relationship between childhood BMI and adult cIMT.

	β	SE(β)	Lower Limit of 95% CI	Upper Limit of 95% CI	Sample Size	Weight (%)
Du 2018	0.054	0.024	0.007	0.101	1052	34.5
Freedman 2004	0.100	0.063	−0.023	0.223	246	5.0
Johnson 2014	0.029	0.031	−0.032	0.090	1273	20.7
Juonala 2006	0.056	0.030	−0.003	0.115	1078	22.1
Khalil 2013	0.047	0.040	−0.031	0.125	600	12.4
Wright 2001	−0.018	0.061	−0.138	0.102	274	5.3
Combined effect	0.047	0.014	0.019	0.074	4523	

Table 4. Observed standardized regression coefficient β with standard error $SE(\beta)$ and 95% confidence interval, sample size and weight in pooled analysis from 15 studies estimating the relationship between adolescent BMI and adult cIMT.

	β	$SE(\beta)$	Lower Limit of 95% CI	Upper Limit of 95% CI	Sample Size	Weight (%)
Ceponie 2015	0.085	0.046	−0.005	0.175	380	6.5
Davis 2001	0.138	0.036	0.067	0.209	725	7.2
Ferreira 2004	0.194	0.082	0.033	0.355	161	4.3
Freedman 2004	0.184	0.048	0.090	0.278	825	6.4
Hao 2018	0.243	0.025	0.194	0.292	496	7.8
Hosseinpanah 2021	0.184	0.036	0.113	0.255	1295	7.2
Huynh 2013	0.052	0.022	0.021	0.103	2328	8.0
Johnson 2014	0.033	0.033	−0.032	0.098	1273	7.3
Khalil 2013	0.047	0.040	−0.031	0.125	600	6.9
Lee 2006	0.189	0.059	0.073	.0305	256	5.7
Oren 2003	0.046	0.010	0.026	0.066	750	8.4
Raitakari 2003	0.090	0.030	0.031	0.149	1170	7.5
Terzis 2012	0.098	0.095	−0.088	0.284	106	3.7
Wright 2001	0.062	0.064	−0.063	0.187	242	5.4
Yan 2017	0.266	0.026	0.215	0.317	1252	7.7
Combined effect	0.127	0.024	0.080	0.175	11859	

5. Detailed Description of Computations and Conversions

5.1. General

Often, evaluators confront the problem of different statistical methods and strategies being used to analyze the relationship between the response and explanatory variables [1,5,7]. The studies address the same broad question, and the reviewers want to include them in a meta-analysis. They need to convert the reported findings to a common index before they can proceed. The results expressed as linear-regression coefficients, correlation coefficients or mean differences can be re-expressed as standardized regression coefficients. This chapter provides formulas and procedures for computing standardized regression coefficients with standard errors from a variety of reported statistical data.

Studies vary in the usage of statistics to summarize the basic characteristics, sometimes using medians rather than means and sometimes using standard errors, confidence intervals, interquartile ranges and ranges to report variation. They also vary in the reporting of linear-regression models, sometimes reporting unstandardized or standardized regression coefficients, standard errors, or confidence intervals for coefficients, sometimes only p-values or models estimated in sub-groups. Inadequate data presentation and reporting problems are common in scientific articles in the evaluated articles [5,64].

In the literature review of the published meta-analysis using β as the effect size (Section 3) and in my meta-analysis example (Section 4), I noticed that authors often confuse the unstandardized b and the standardized β coefficients in the description of their methods and in reported regression analysis tables. In addition, different symbols are used for these statistics in textbooks and statistical software. In healthcare and medicine, you can recognize a reporting error only if you are familiar both with the statistical methods used and the field under study. Interpreting the clinical meaning of the finding should reveal possible errors. For example, something is wrong if the article reports a standardized regression coefficient of 4.187.

To perform a meta-analysis of continuous data using β as an effect-size index, researchers seek values of β and SE(β) from these numbers. Software procedures for performing meta-analyses using generic inverse-variance weighted averages take input data in the form of these estimates from each study [1,27].

When β and SE(β) are not directly available from the included article, procedures to estimate them from other reported data can be used. These calculations and conversions often require the standard deviation (SD) for response and explanatory variables. In several evaluated articles these are not given. In those articles they can be approximated using various methods depending on the data available in the article. In the following sections I describe how to calculate the standardized regression coefficient effect-size measure β and its standard error SE(β) in different research approaches and reporting styles of the original studies.

5.2. *Obtaining Standardized Regression Coefficients*

5.2.1. Coefficient β Reported from a Linear-Regression Model

In an included article, when the standardized regression coefficient β for the explanatory variable is reported from the estimated linear-regression model, it can be used directly as an effect size. An unadjusted or adjusted β can be selected depending on the purpose of the meta-analysis. If the standard error of the β is not reported, then it should be calculated from the other available information; see Section 5.3. Often models are estimated in subgroups, e.g., males and females separately. In these cases, effect sizes should be combined; see Section 5.4.

5.2.2. Correlation Coefficient r Reported

A study may only report a regression coefficient between the outcome and explanatory variables. In such a situation, the standardized regression coefficient is equal to the Pearson correlation coefficient r between the variables. If the Spearman correlation coefficient is reported, then it can used as an approximation of r and β. Basically, a Spearman coefficient is a Pearson correlation coefficient calculated with the ranks of the values of each of the two variables instead of their actual values. SE(β) can be obtained using the formula

$$\mathrm{SE}(\beta) = \frac{1 - r^2}{\sqrt{n-1}} \tag{1}$$

where r is the reported correlation coefficient and n is the sample size [1,7].

5.2.3. Unstandardized Regression Coefficient b Reported

If a study has estimated a simple linear regression $Y = a + b\,X$ or multivariable linear-regression model to report the regression coefficient b between response Y and explanatory variable X, then the β-value can be obtained by applying the formula

$$\beta = \frac{\mathrm{SD}(X)}{\mathrm{SD}(Y)} b \tag{2}$$

where SD(Y) is the standard deviation of response variable and SD(X) is the standard deviation of the exposure measure used in the study [5,23]. When SD(X) or SD(Y) are not provided, the methods described in Section 5.6 can be used to calculate these statistics from other available data.

The standard error for β is obtained as follows:

$$\mathrm{SE}(\beta) = \frac{\mathrm{SD}(X)}{\mathrm{SD}(Y)}\mathrm{SE}(b). \tag{3}$$

5.2.4. Mean Values of Outcome Variable Reported between Two Exposure Groups

When mean values of the response variable are compared between two groups (low- and high-exposure groups), the following statistics are usually given:

n_1 = sample size in group 1 and n_2 = sample size in group 2,
M_1 = mean value of response Y in group 1 and M_2 = mean value in group 2
SD_1= standard deviation of Y in group 1 and SD_2 standard deviation in group 2
SD(Y) = full sample standard deviation oy outcome variable Y.

Now

$$b = M_1 - M_2$$

and the standard deviation of the dichotomous variable X is

$$\mathrm{SD}(X) = \sqrt{\frac{n_1\, n_2}{(n_1+n_2)^2}}$$

Using Equation (2) the standardized regression coefficient β can be obtained by applying the formula

$$\beta = \sqrt{\frac{n_1\, n_2}{(n_1+n_2)^2}}\,\frac{b}{\mathrm{SD}(Y)} = \sqrt{\frac{n_1\, n_2}{(n_1+n_2)^2}}\,\frac{(M_1-M_2)}{\mathrm{SD}(Y)}.$$

When SD(Y) is not reported in the article, it can be calculated using the formula

$$\mathrm{SD}(Y) = \sqrt{\frac{(n_1-1)\mathrm{SD}_1^2 + (n_2-1)\mathrm{SD}_2^2 + \frac{n_1\, n_2}{n_1+n_2}\,(M_1-M_2\,)^2}{n_1+n_2-1}}.$$

From Formula (3) the standard error of β is given by

$$\mathrm{SE}(\beta) = \frac{\mathrm{SD}(X)}{\mathrm{SD}(Y)}\mathrm{SE}(b) = \sqrt{\frac{n_1\, n_2}{(n_1+n_2)^2}}\,\frac{\mathrm{SE}(b)}{\mathrm{SD}(Y)}.$$

SE(b) can be obtained from the confidence interval of b (=$M_1 - M_2$), or from the t-value or p-value of the t-test statistic to test the hypothesis $M_1 - M_2 = 0$. If these are not given, then the SE(b) can be estimated by

$$\mathrm{SE}(b) = \mathrm{SE}(M_1 - M_2) = \mathrm{SD}_{pooled}(Y)\sqrt{\frac{1}{n_1}+\frac{1}{n_2}},$$

where the statistic

$$\mathrm{SD}_{pooled}(Y) = \sqrt{\frac{(n_1-1)\mathrm{SD}_1^2 + (n_2-1)\mathrm{SD}_2^2}{n_1+n_2-2}} \tag{4}$$

is usually known as the pooled standard deviation of the outcome variable Y.

An alternative method is to covert the mean difference effect-size statistic

$$d = (M_1 - M_2)/\mathrm{SD}_{pooled}(Y)$$

to the regression coefficient r [1,5,7]. This approach is not derived from the general relationship between b and β as described by Formula (2).

5.2.5. Mean Values of Outcome Variable Reported between More Than Two Exposure Groups

In some articles, authors have categorized using cut-off values of the explanatory variable X to more than two groups with different ordered exposure levels, e.g., low, medium, high levels. Researchers have reported the mean response values by these groups and used an analysis of variance to compare the statistical significance of the mean values between these groups. A similar approach is to use dummy variables (indicator variables) in multivariable linear-regression modeling to indicate the groups of categorized explanatory levels and report the mean differences between these groups.

In the case of a categorized explanatory variable, a simple linear-regression line can be used to estimate the β coefficient. In this approach, the group means of the outcome variable Y are set as the dependent variable, and the selected values (contrasts) denoting the levels of the explanatory variable X are the explanatory variable in the regression line [65]. Usually, values of 0, 1, 2, 3, ... k are selected as contrast values when the explanatory variable is categorized to k ordered groups. The β coefficient with SE(β) can be obtained as follows:

$$\beta = \frac{\mathrm{SD}(contrast)}{\mathrm{SD}(Y)}\, b_c$$

and

$$\mathrm{SE}(\beta) = \frac{\mathrm{SD}(contrast)}{\mathrm{SD}(Y)}\, \mathrm{SE}(b_c),$$

where SD(*contrast*) is the standard deviation of the selected contrast values, SD(Y) is standard deviation of the outcome variable Y, and b_c is the regression slope (regression coefficient of contrast values). This approach is also known as the linear trend test, and b_c can be interpreted as the effect size for the trend between the exposure categories.

5.3. *Obtaining Standard Error of Regression Coefficient from t-Value, p-Value or Confidence Interval*

The standard error of the unstandardized (b) or standardized (β) regression coefficient can be obtained from a model output (if reported), from a reported confidence interval, from a t-statistic or a p-value to test the statistical significance of the coefficient or contacting authors of the original article. In addition, in an unadjusted analysis, SE(β) can be obtained by applying Formula (1) from Section 5.2.2 for the standard error of the Pearson correlation coefficient r. I describe first how a t-statistic can be obtained from a p-value, then how SE can be obtained from a t-statistic, and finally how a confidence interval can be used to calculate SE. Meta-analysists may select the appropriate steps in this process according to what results are available to them.

5.3.1. Standard Error from t-Value

The t-statistic tests the hypotheses that a regression coefficient (b or β) equals to 0. The t-value is the ratio of the estimated regression coefficient to the standard error of the coefficient, i.e., $t = b/\mathrm{SE}(b)$ or $t = \beta/\mathrm{SE}(\beta)$. Thus, the standard error of the regression coefficient b and β can be obtained by applying the formulas

$$\mathrm{SE}(b) = \left|\frac{b}{t}\right|$$

and

$$\mathrm{SE}(\beta) = \left|\frac{\beta}{t}\right|$$

where t is the observed value of the t-test to test the null hypothesis H_0: $b = 0$ (or $\beta = 0$).

5.3.2. Standard Error from p-Value

When only actual p-values obtained from t-tests are quoted, the corresponding t-value may be obtained from the t-distribution with $n - k - 1$ degrees of freedom, where n is the sample size and k is the number of explanatory variables in the regression model [65]. Standard statistical programs include a function to calculate the corresponding t-value. Difficulties are encountered when levels of significance are reported (such as $p < 0.05$ or even NS ('not significant', which usually implies $p > 0.05$) rather than actual p-values. A conservative approach would be to take the p-value at the upper limit (e.g., for $p < 0.05$ take $p = 0.05$, for $p < 0.01$ take $p = 0.01$, and for $p < 0.001$ take $p = 0.001$). However, this is not a solution for results that are reported as p = NS, or $p > 0.05$.

5.3.3. Standard Error from Confidence Interval

If a 95% confidence interval is available for b or β, then the standard error SE can be calculated as:

$$\text{SE} = (upper\ limit - lower\ limit)/3.92\,.$$

where *upper limit* and *lower limit* refer to the 95% confidence interval of the regression coefficient. For 90% confidence intervals 3.92 should be replaced by 3.29, and for 99% confidence intervals it should be replaced by 5.15.

5.4. Pooling Betas from Two or More Independent Sub-Groups

In this section I consider cases where studies report data for two sub-groups of participants. For example, a study might report effect sizes separately for males and females. The defining feature here is that the sub-groups are independent of each other, so that each provides unique information. For this reason, it is possible to treat each sub-group as though it were a separate study [1]. This is one option to include the reported data into the meta-analysis. A second option is to compute a composite effect size for each study and use this in the meta-analysis. I consider this option in the following.

Let:

β_1 = standardized regression coefficient among females,
β_2 = standardized regression coefficient among males,
$\text{SE}(\beta_1)$ = SE of β_1,
$\text{SE}(\beta_2)$ = SE of β_2,
$W_1 = 1/(\text{SE}(\beta_1))^2$ weight for females,
$W_2 = 1/(\text{SE}(\beta_2))^2$ weight for males.

The combined effect of β_p and $\text{SE}(\beta_p)$ can be obtained as follows:

$$\beta_p = (W_1\,\beta_1 + W_2\,\beta_2)/(W_1 + W_2)$$

$$\text{SE}(\beta_p) = \sqrt{\frac{1}{W_1 + W_2}}\,.$$

If the number of sub-groups is more than two, then the above formulas can be extended to the situation of several independent groups [1].

5.5. Pooling Effect Sizes Measured in More Than One Time Point

Some studies may report findings where the outcome variable or the explanatory variable was measured more than once at different time points on the same participants. For example, in assessing the effect of BMI on cIMT, in one article BMI was measured at ages 3 and 9 years for the same children, and the effect on cIMT was reported separately for BMI at age 3 years and BMI at age 9 years. In another article, BMI was measured only at age 9 years, but cIMT was measured during adulthood twice, at ages 30 and 50 years. The effect size β was reported separately for each adult age, but both measures were based on the same members of the cohort. This study design is also known as repeated measurements.

The effect sizes are not measured at independent groups but come from the same group of children or adolescents. Measurements at different time points are positively correlated. If the non-independent information is ignored in the combining of βs and their standard errors, then this will underestimate the standard error of the summary effect [66]. The procedure proposed by Bornstein et al. [1] can be used to combine the estimated βs across age phases (time points). This approach allows one to address the problem of repeated measurements, since the formula for the SE of combined effect sizes will take into account the correlation among the repeated measurements.

Let β_j refer to the standardized regression coefficient estimated at the j time point (age phase), $j = 1, 2, \ldots, m$. Thus, m represents the number of different time points. Let the variance of coefficient β_j be $V_j = (\mathrm{SE}(\beta_j))^2$. The composite effect size β_{ct} and the variance $V(\beta_{ct}) = (\mathrm{SE}(\beta_{ct}))^2$ can be computed as

$$\beta_{ct} = \frac{1}{m}\left(\sum_{j=1}^{m}\beta_j\right)$$

and

$$\mathrm{V}(\beta_{ct}) = \left(\frac{1}{m}\right)^2\left(\sum_{j=1}^{m}V_j + \sum_{j\neq k}\left(r_{jk}\sqrt{V_j}\,\sqrt{V_k}\right)\right), \quad (5)$$

where r_{jk} is the correlation between effect sizes β_j and β_k. Thus, the standard error of b_{ct} is

$$\mathrm{SE}(\beta_{ct}) = \sqrt{V(\beta_{ct})}\,.$$

If the variances V_j are all equal to V and the correlations are all equal to r, then Formula (5) of $V(\beta_{ct})$ simplifies to

$$V(\beta_{ct}) = \frac{1}{m}V(1 + (m-1)r).$$

The composite effect size of two correlated effect sizes ($m = 2$) is

$$\beta_{c2} = \frac{1}{2}(\beta_1 + \beta_2)$$

and variance

$$V(\beta_{c2}) = \frac{1}{4}\left(V_1 + V_2 + 2r\sqrt{V_1}\sqrt{V_2}\right).$$

5.6. *Estimating SD of Reponse and Explonatory Variables*

To calculate β and SE(β) from b and SE(b) using Formulas (2) and (3), the full-sample SD for Y and X are needed. Sometimes they are not available from the evaluated article. However, for the standard deviations there is an approximate or direct algebraic relationship with other measures of variation, so that it is possible to obtain the required statistic even if it is not published in the article.

5.6.1. SD from Ranges

If *minimum* and *maximum* values of response variable are given, then they can be used to estimate standard deviation. Ranges (*maximum–minimum*) are very unstable and, unlike other measures of variation, increase when the sample size increases. They describe the extremes of observed outcomes rather than the average variation. One common approach has been to make use of the fact that, with normally distributed data, 95% of values will lie within 2 SD of either side of the mean. The standard deviation SD may therefore be estimated to be approximately one-quarter of the typical range of data values, i.e., (*maximum- minimum*)/4. This method may not work well in practice when the sample size is large ($n > 70$) [67,68]. To overcome this problem, the following improved range rule of thumb is often used

$$\mathrm{SD}(Y) = \frac{(maximum - minimum)}{6}.$$

Alternative methods have been proposed to estimate SDs from ranges [67–69].

5.6.2. SD from Interquartile Range

An interquartile range is defined as the difference between the *upper quartile* and *lower quartile* (75th and 25th percentiles) of the analyzed variable. It describes where the central 50% of participants' outcomes lie. When sample sizes are large and the distribution of the outcome is similar to the normal distribution, the width of the interquartile range will be approximately 1.35 SD. Thus

$$\mathrm{SD}(Y) = \frac{(upper\ quartile - lower\ quartile)}{1.349}.$$

Wan and colleagues [68] provided a sample-size-dependent extension to the formula for approximating the SD using the interquartile range.

5.6.3. SD from SE

If the standard error SE(Y) of the response variable Y is reported, then SD(Y) is given by

$$\mathrm{SD}(Y) = \sqrt{n}\mathrm{SE}(Y), \tag{6}$$

where n is the sample size.

If SE(Y) is not given, then it can be estimated from the confidence interval for the mean value of response Y. Then by (6)

$$\mathrm{SE}(Y) = \frac{\sqrt{n}\,(upper\ limit - lower\ limit)}{3.92}$$

where *upper limit* and *lower limit* refer to the 95% confidence interval for the mean value of Y.

5.6.4. Pooling Groups to Obtain SD

Sometimes it is necessary to combine two reported sub-groups into a single group to obtain the full-sample SD of Y or X. For example, a study may report results separately for men and women. The following formula can be used to combine standard deviations into a full sample SD:

$$\mathrm{SD}_{full\ sample} = \sqrt{\frac{(n_1-1)\mathrm{SD}_1^2 + (n_2-1)\mathrm{SD}_2^2 + \frac{n_1 n_2}{n_1+n_2}(M_1 - M_2)^2}{n_1+n_2-1}} \tag{7}$$

where n_1 and n_2 are sample sizes, SD_1 and SD_2 are standard deviations, and M_1 and M_2 are mean values of groups 1 and 2.

Note that the rather complex-looking Formula (7) for the SD produces the SD of outcome measurements as if the combined group had never been divided into two. This SD is different from the usual pooled SD in (4) that is used to compute a confidence interval for a mean difference or as the denominator in computing the standardized mean difference. The pooled SD provides a within-sub-group SD rather than an SD for the combined group, and thus provides an underestimate of the desired SD.

When there are more than two groups to combine, the simplest strategy is to apply the above Formula (7) sequentially (i.e., combine Group 1 and Group 2 to create Group '1 + 2', then combine Group '1 + 2' and Group 3 to create Group '1 + 2 + 3', and so on).

There are also other methods to estimate the full-sample standard deviation of a variable when findings are reported only in sub-groups [70]. However, these more complex calculation formulas need additional information that is not necessarily available.

5.7. Other Topics

5.7.1. Interpretation with the Unit of Measurement of the Outcome Variable

The results represented by the standardized coefficient β can also be expressed in terms of the original measurement unit of the outcome variable. By Equation (2) the standardized regression coefficient β represents how many standard deviation units the outcome variable Y will change per a standard deviation increase in the explanatory variable X. If SD(X) equals to one, then Equation (2) gives

$$b = \frac{\mathrm{SD}(Y)}{\mathrm{SD}(X)}\beta = \mathrm{SD}(Y)\beta \quad (8)$$

If we know the standard deviation of the outcome variable Y, then we can estimate how much variable Y will change per one standard deviation change in the explanatory variable. For example, in the previous chapter, the outcome variable was cIMT and the predictor factor was childhood or adolescent BMI. A positive β-value equal to 0.08 demonstrates that a one-standard-deviation increase in childhood BMI leads to a cIMT increase (in mm) equal to the standard deviation SD(cIMT) of cIMT multiplied by 0.08. Further, if the pooled SD of cIMT from all the included studies is 0.10 mm, then we obtain a cIMT increase (in mm) of β SD(cIMT) = 0.08 $\times$ 0.10 mm = 0.008 mm per one-standard-deviation increase in childhood BMI.

5.7.2. Log-Transformed Data

The standardized regression coefficient can be used as an effect-size index to pool both raw and log-transformed outcomes (or explanatory variables). The standardized regression coefficient does not estimate effects on the original scales of variables but refers to the standard deviations of the variables.

When an original study involves an outcome variable with a skewed distribution, the reported data can sometimes be a mixture of results presented on the raw scale and results presented on the logarithmic scale [71]. A common approach to dealing with skewed outcome data is to take a logarithmic transformation of each observation and to conduct the regression modeling using log-transformed values. However, for ease of interpretation, basic characteristics are often reported using the initial unit of measurement (raw scale). When the estimated regression coefficient b and SE(b) are estimated for the log-transformed variable (lnY), then we need SD(lnY) to calculate the standardized regression coefficient (and SE) for the (lnY).

To obtain the approximate standard deviation of the outcome variable Y on the log-transformed scale, the following formula can be used:

$$\mathrm{SD}(lnY) = \sqrt{\ln(1 + \frac{\mathrm{SD}_Y^2}{M_Y^2})},$$

where SD_Y is the reported standard deviation and M_Y is the mean value of variable Y [71].

5.7.3. Contacting Authors

Missing data and clarification about the statistics required for the meta-analysis could be sought from the authors of the original studies. Although challenging, obtaining additional data through author contacts can enable reviewers to synthesize data more readily and completely. Authors of more recent studies are more likely to be located and provide data compared to authors of older studies [72]. Contacting authors may be time-consuming, not only for meta-analysists but also for the study authors. They need to locate the data before being able to provide the statistics. However, when needed, authors of studies with missing or discrepant data should be contacted.

5.7.4. Imputing Missing Statistics

Missing SEs of the effect size or standard deviations of the main variables are a common feature of meta-analyses of continuous outcome data. When none of the methods described in the previous sections allow the calculation of the SEs or SDs from the study report (and the information is not available from the authors), then a meta-analysist may be forced to impute ('fill in') the missing data if they are not to exclude the study from the meta-analysis [73,74].

There are several obvious advantages to imputing the missing data compared to a meta-analysis using only the studies with reported statistics. Imputing allows the inclusion of more studies, thus reducing the overall standard error of the estimate of the effect size, compared to using only studies reporting information [74]. The simplest imputation is to borrow the missing value of a statistic from one or more other studies. If several candidate SDs are available, reviewing researchers should decide whether to use their average, the highest, a 'reasonably high' value, or some other strategy. Choosing a higher SD down-weights a study and yields a wider confidence interval. Thus, choosing a higher SD will bias the result towards a lack of effect.

6. Discussion

Many original studies addressing the same research question are relatively small and differ in their statistical content for various reasons. It is important to have practicable research methods to pool findings from different studies to quantify the relationships between predictor variables and outcomes. This article summarizes the procedures of applying the standardized regression coefficient β for the synthesis of an association between a quantitative dependent variable and one focal explanatory factor when the measurement methods and controlling of other potential covariates varies between the reviewed studies. I described how it is possible to use β as a workable effect-size statistic that can be applied to the research findings of interest. I applied this method in a systematic review of studies to provide evidence for the relationship between childhood and adulthood BMI and cIMT in adult life using effect sizes that were continuous variables.

6.1. Issues Regarding the Conduction of Standardized Regression Coefficient

There are issues in combining and analyzing the standardized regression coefficients. These potential problems are related to the variation of the variables to be controlled, multiple conversions of effect sizes and data presentation in the original studies. Riley et al. [75] gives the following detailed list of challenges for the meta-analysis of multivariable findings:

(a) Different types of effect measures (e.g., correlation coefficients, regression coefficients, risk ratios, odd ratios and mean differences), which are not necessarily comparable.
(b) Estimates without standard errors, which is a problem because meta-analysis methods typically weight each study by their standard error.
(c) Estimates relating to various time points of the outcome occurrence or measurement.
(d) Different methods of measurement for explanatory variables and outcomes.
(e) Various sets of adjustment factors.
(f) Different approaches to handling continuous explanatory variables (e.g., categorization, linear, non-linear trends, log-transforms), including the choice of cut point value when dichotomizing continuous values into "high" and "normal" groups.

In addition, shortcomings in the reporting of the included publications makes meta-analysis challenging.

6.1.1. Different Adjusted Covariates

Several researchers have discussed the problem that the covariates in multiple regression models can vary across studies [9,10,76,77]. In the original studies, multivariable regression models have been used to estimate the independent effect of the main explanatory variable on a response variable when confounding factors are controlled. It is ideal, but highly unlikely, that the estimated effect sizes from different studies are adjusted for the same confounding factors (covariates) [75]. In the synthesis of standardized regression coefficients, pooling the independent effects of the focal explanatory variable is still important to obtain an estimate of the association between the explanatory and outcome variables. If adjustment factors are omitted, then the observed effects could be too optimistic. Estimates adjusted for a different set of covariates creates difficulty in interpreting meta-analysis results. To overcome this issue, Riley et al. [75] recommended considering meta-analysis only on those estimates that are adjusted for at least a predefined minimum core set of established covariates. This core set of covariates for the outcome can be defined in consultation with experts. In addition, separate meta-analyses could be performed for unadjusted and adjusted prognostic effect estimates. Even when control variables and other predictors differ between studies, the pooling of βs still provide useful information about the size of the effect. Generally, meta-analysis results will be most interpretable, and therefore useful, when a separate meta-analysis is undertaken for groups of "similar" prognostic variables. However, it is evident that enhancements to the associated synthesis methodologies are urgently needed. Becker and Wu described existing methods of analysis and presented a multivariate generalized least-squares approach to the synthesis of regression coefficients [9]. Yoneoka and Henmi [78] extended this approach and proposed a synthesis methodology for regression results under different covariate sets by using a generalized least-squares method that includes bias-correction terms. However, the combination will be exponentially complex as the number of covariates increases.

6.1.2. Several Transformations and Conversions

Converting reported effect sizes from estimated regression models to β coefficients requires several transformations, and on some occasions, data imputation or manipulation of the statistical information available in a report. Converting from a reported effect size to a β coefficient may not go smoothly. The data conversion begins with the extraction of the information from an original article. This can be frustrating if the article fails to report the statistics required in the formulas for computing the β-values. In addition, understanding the analysis approach and methods used in the original article may sometimes be difficult.

However, effect-size transformation provides an opportunity to make a study available for meta-analysis. Data transformation facilitates the compatibility between studies with same research question. The question of whether or not it is appropriate to combine effect sizes from studies that used different statistical methods or metrics must be considered on a case-by-case basis. It only makes sense to compute a summary effect from studies that we assess to be comparable in a meaningful way. If it would be comfortable to combine these studies if they had used the same method, then the fact that they used different methods or metrics should not be an obstacle [1]. Although not without concerns, this approach produces reasonably similar results from other methods [9]. The decision to use these conversions is often better than the alternative, which is to simply omit studies that happened to use an alternative measure effect size. This would involve the loss of information, and possibly result in a biased sample of studies.

6.1.3. Insufficient Reported Data

One obstacle in conducting a meta-analysis is insufficiently reported data in evaluated articles to compute effect-size estimates. Detailed descriptive statistics of the variables under study are not given in all articles, and standard errors for regression coefficients are not always available [5]. In some cases, the incomplete reporting of statistics in the studies limits or prevents the use of these studies in the systematic review [4].

The validity and practical utility of observational research critically depends on good study design, appropriate analysis methods and high-quality reporting and data presentation [79,80]. In reviewed studies, the reporting of observational findings often exhibits serious shortcomings [80]. An efficient way to help readers to extract the necessary data is to develop guidance documents of data presentation that are disseminated to the research community at large. We need a much more structured framework in scientific reporting, which emphasizes that today's scientific evidence is based on the synthesis of studies reporting findings with similar effect-size indices [64]. Especially, the reporting of estimated multivariable regression models needs attachments such as tables and figures reporting descriptive statistics about the distributions of the response variables and explanatory variables. This would help other researchers to utilize the results in their approaches to summarize and meta-analyze the magnitude of the effects.

In the future, this issue could be even more pronounced with the application of machine-learning methods. Machine-learning methods do not provide effect sizes (indices) that can be combined or that are interpretable for clinicians.

6.2. Meta-Analysis of Association between BMI and cIMT

In the illustrative meta-analysis study, I aimed to provide evidence for the relationship between childhood and adulthood BMI and cIMT in adult life using the β coefficient as the effect-size index. This approach helped us to quantify the relationship. Findings from my meta-analysis indicate that elevated childhood and adult BMI is associated with only a modest increase in carotid intima-media thickness in adult life. Adolescent BMI had a marginally stronger relation with adult cIMT than childhood BMI. In general, the results are consistent with those of previous systematic reviews [30,50,51]. However, these previous reviews used different approaches and different effect sizes that were not entirely suitable for the research problem.

The quantification of the associations made in my study showed that these significant effect sizes reflect only a modest increase in cIMT. These small increases in cIMT might be difficult to equate to true clinical significance. One explanation for these small increases in cIMT might be the younger age of most of the participants at the time of the evaluation of cIMT. Longer follow-ups might be necessary to demonstrate the utility of these findings.

There were some limitations in this study. First, BMI is not an ideal measure of obesity and caution must be used while interpreting these results. However, BMI remains to be the most basic and the most commonly used tool for the assessment of obesity due to the ease of measurement, the ease of interpretation of the results, and its low expense. While tests like dual-energy X-ray absorptiometry, computed tomography and magnetic resonance imaging are the gold standards for assessing regional obesity, their use is limited by their high cost, lack of availability, and non-portable, required equipment for use in routine clinical practice. In the presence of these constraints, BMI has remained a valuable tool for the assessment of obesity in clinics, hospitals, and in large epidemiological studies. Second, multiple transformations of effect sizes for some studies were needed to translate them into one common effect size. A comparison of the effect sizes produced by different statistical techniques is a challenge for readers and especially those wanting to carry out a meta-analysis [Nieminen 2013]. However, it is often informative to translate the effect-size results from the original studies to one effect-size index to reveal the pooled effects.

7. Conclusions

Statistical methods used in studies should not be the basis for the inclusion of the studies in a meta-analysis. The same research question can be analyzed with different statistical methods. Measurements methods, data transformations, descriptive statistics, and statistical inference methods may vary between studies. In addition, authors may focus on reporting in different ways. This reflects the reality when reviewing published research articles and trying to summarize the findings from observational studies. The proposed approach based on standardized regression coefficients provides a workable effect-size index that can be applied to the systematic review of diverse multivariable studies with quantitative outcomes. I applied this method in a meta-analysis providing evidence that BMI in childhood and adult have a minimal effect on adult cIMT. As the observed effect sizes are very low, they are unlikely to correlate with clinically significant differences. In addition, from the public-health point of view, the small effect sizes suggest that the introduction of interventions to reduce obesity in childhood might not have a high impact on the subsequent cIMT measurements in young-adult life.

Funding: This research received no external funding.

Institutional Review Board Statement: Not applicable.

Informed Consent Statement: Not applicable.

Data Availability Statement: Data for the meta-analyses are presented in Tables 3 and 4.

Acknowledgments: I am grateful to Jasleen Kaur for her valuable and constructive suggestions during the development of this research work, especially in the literature search and screening of studies.

Conflicts of Interest: I declare no conflict of interest.

References

1. Borenstein, M.; Hedges, L.V.; Higgins, J.P.T.; Rothstein, H.R. *Introduction to Meta-Analysis*, 2nd ed.; John Wiley & Sons, Ltd.: Oxford, UK, 2021; ISBN 978-1-119-55835-4.
2. Lasserson, T.; Thomas, J.; Higgins, J.P.T. Chapter 1: Starting a review. In *Cochrane Handbook for Systematic Reviews of Interventions*; Higgins, J.P.T., Thomas, J., Chandler, J., Cumpston, M., Li, T., Page, M.J., Welch, V.A., Eds.; Cochrane: London, UK, 2022.
3. Cooper, H.; Hedges, L.V. Research synthesis as a scientific process. In *The Handbook of Research Synthesis and Meta-Analysis*; Cooper, H., Hedges, L.V., Valentine, J.C., Eds.; Russell Sage Foundation: New York, NY, USA, 2009; pp. 3–16, ISBN 978-0-87154-163-5.
4. Aloe, A.M.; Becker, B.J. An Effect Size for Regression Predictors in Meta-Analysis. *J. Educ. Behav. Stat.* **2012**, *37*, 278–297. [CrossRef]
5. Nieminen, P.; Lehtiniemi, H.; Vähäkangas, K.; Huusko, A.; Rautio, A. Standardised regression coefficient as an effect size index in summarising findings in epidemiological studies. *Epidemiol. Biostat. Public Health* **2013**, *10*, e8854-2. [CrossRef]
6. Epure, A.M.; Rios-Leyvraz, M.; Anker, D.; Di Bernardo, S.; da Costa, B.R.; Chiolero, A.; Sekarski, N. Risk factors during first 1000 days of life for carotid intima-media thickness in infants, children, and adolescents: A systematic review with meta-analyses. *PLoS Med.* **2020**, *17*, e1003414. [CrossRef]
7. Lipsey, M.W.; Wilson, D.B. *Practical Meta-Analysis*; SAGE Publications: London, UK, 2000; ISBN 0-7619-2168-1.
8. Aloe, A.M. Inaccuracy of regression results in replacing bivariate correlations. *Res. Synth. Methods* **2015**, *6*, 21–27. [CrossRef] [PubMed]
9. Becker, B.J.; Wu, M.J. The synthesis of regression slopes in meta-analysis. *Stat. Sci.* **2007**, *22*, 414–429. [CrossRef]
10. Kim, R.S. Standardized Regression Coefficients as Indices of Effect Sizes in Meta-Analysis. Ph.D. Thesis, The Florida State University, Tallahassee, FL, USA, 2011.
11. Peterson, R.A.; Brown, S.P. On the use of beta coefficients in meta-analysis. *J. Appl. Psychol.* **2005**, *90*, 175–181. [CrossRef]
12. Paul, P.A.; Lipps, P.E.; Madden, L.V. Meta-analysis of regression coefficients for the relationship between fusarium head blight and deoxynivalenol content of wheat. *Phytopathology* **2006**, *96*, 951–961. [CrossRef] [PubMed]
13. Dzhambov, A.M.; Dimitrova, D.D.; Dimitrakova, E.D. Association between residential greenness and birth weight: Systematic review and meta-analysis. *Urban For. Urban Green.* **2014**, *13*, 621–629. [CrossRef]
14. Wang, D.; Fu, X.; Zhang, J.; Xu, C.; Hu, Q.; Lin, W. Association between blood lead level during pregnancy and birth weight: A meta-analysis. *Am. J. Ind. Med.* **2020**, *63*, 1085–1094. [CrossRef]
15. Pratt, T.C.; Cullen, F.T.; Sellers, C.S.; Winfree, L.T.; Madensen, T.D.; Daigle, L.E.; Fearn, N.E.; Gau, J.M. The Empirical Status of Social Learning Theory: A Meta-Analysis. *Justice Q.* **2010**, *27*, 765–802. [CrossRef]
16. Rioux, C.; Castellanos-Ryan, N.; Parent, S.; Séguin, J.R. The interaction between temperament and the family environment in adolescent substance use and externalizing behaviors: Support for diathesis-stress or differential susceptibility? *Dev. Rev.* **2016**, *40*, 117–150. [CrossRef]
17. Bowman, N.A. Effect Sizes and Statistical Methods for Meta-Analysis in Higher Education. *Res. High. Educ.* **2012**, *53*, 375–382. [CrossRef]
18. Tian, Y.; Yao, J. The Impact of School Resource Investment on Student Performance: A Meta-analysis Based on Chinese Literature. *SSRN Electron. J.* **2020**, *4*, 389–410. [CrossRef]
19. Abate, N. Obesity and cardiovascular disease: Pathogenetic role of the metabolic syndrome and therapeutic implications. *J. Diabetes Complicat.* **2000**, *14*, 154–174. [CrossRef]

20. Sahoo, K.; Sahoo, B.; Choudhury, A.; Sofi, N.; Kumar, R.; Bhadoria, A. Childhood obesity: Causes and consequences. *J. Fam. Med. Prim. Care* **2015**, *4*, 187. [CrossRef]
21. Lorenz, M.W.; Markus, H.S.; Bots, M.L.; Rosvall, M.; Sitzer, M. Prediction of clinical cardiovascular events with carotid intima-media thickness: A systematic review and meta-analysis. *Circulation* **2007**, *115*, 459–467. [CrossRef]
22. Vach, W. *Regression Models as a Tool in Medical Research*; CRC Press: Boca Raton, FL, USA, 2013; ISBN 978-1-4665-17486.
23. Vittinghoff, E.; Shiboski, S.C.; Glidden, D.V.; McCullogh, C.E. *Regression Methods in Biostatistics: Linear, Logistic, Survival and Repeated Measures Models*; Springer: Berlin/Heidelberg, Germany, 2005; ISBN 0-387-20275-7.
24. Cohen, J. *Statistical Power Analysis for the Behavioral Sciences*, 2nd ed.; Erlbaum: Hillsdale, MI, USA, 1988; ISBN 0-8058-0283-5.
25. Fey, C.F.; Hu, T.; Delios, A. The Measurement and Communication of Effect Sizes in Management Research. *Manag. Organ. Rev.* **2022**, 1–22. [CrossRef]
26. Shadish, W.R.; Haddock, C.K. Combining estimates of effect size. In *The Handbook of Research Synthesis and Meta-Analysis*, 2nd ed.; Russell Sage Foundation: New York, NY, USA, 2009; pp. 257–277, ISBN 978-0-87154-163-5.
27. Deeks, J.J.; Higgins, J.P.; Altman, D.G. Chapter 10: Analysing data and undertaking meta-analyses. In *Cochrane Handbook for Systematic Reviews of Interventions*; Higgins, J.P.T., Thomas, J., Chandler, J., Cumpston, M., Li, T., Page, M.J., Welch, V.A., Eds.; Cochrane: London, UK, 2022.
28. Gignac, G.E.; Szodorai, E.T. Effect size guidelines for individual differences researchers. *Personal. Individ. Differ.* **2016**, *102*, 74–78. [CrossRef]
29. García-Hermoso, A.; Saavedra, J.M.; Ramírez-Vélez, R.; Ekelund, U.; del Pozo-Cruz, B. Reallocating sedentary time to moderate-to-vigorous physical activity but not to light-intensity physical activity is effective to reduce adiposity among youths: A systematic review and meta-analysis. *Obes. Rev.* **2017**, *18*, 1088–1095. [CrossRef]
30. Ajala, O.; Mold, F.; Boughton, C.; Cooke, D.; Whyte, M. Childhood predictors of cardiovascular disease in adulthood. A systematic review and meta-analysis. *Obes. Rev.* **2017**, *18*, 1061–1070. [CrossRef]
31. Ribeiro, C.; Mendes, V.; Peleteiro, B.; Delgado, I.; Araújo, J.; Aggerbeck, M.; Annesi-Maesano, I.; Sarigiannis, D.; Ramos, E. Association between the exposure to phthalates and adiposity: A meta-analysis in children and adults. *Environ. Res.* **2019**, *179*, 108780. [CrossRef]
32. Ramsey, K.A.; Rojer, A.G.M.; D'Andrea, L.; Otten, R.H.J.; Heymans, M.W.; Trappenburg, M.C.; Verlaan, S.; Meskers, C.G.M.; Maier, A.B. The association of objectively measured physical activity and sedentary behavior with skeletal muscle strength and muscle power in older adults: A systematic review and meta-analysis. *Ageing Res. Rev.* **2021**, *67*, 101266. [CrossRef]
33. Jones, M.D.; Booth, J.; Taylor, J.L.; Barry, B.K. Limited association between aerobic fitness and pain in healthy individuals: A cross-sectional study. *Pain Med.* **2016**, *17*, 1799–1808. [CrossRef]
34. Burrows, N.J.; Barry, B.K.; Sturnieks, D.L.; Booth, J.; Jones, M.D. The Relationship between Daily Physical Activity and Pain in Individuals with Knee Osteoarthritis. *Pain Med.* **2020**, *21*, 2481–2495. [CrossRef]
35. Mclaughlin, M.; Delaney, T.; Hall, A.; Byaruhanga, J.; Mackie, P.; Grady, A.; Reilly, K.; Campbell, E.; Sutherland, R.; Wiggers, J.; et al. Associations Between Digital Health Intervention Engagement, Physical Activity, and Sedentary Behavior: Systematic Review and Meta-analysis. *J. Med. Internet Res.* **2021**, *23*, e23180. [CrossRef]
36. Woolley, K.; Fishbach, A. Immediate Rewards Predict Adherence to Long-Term Goals. *Personal. Soc. Psychol. Bull.* **2017**, *43*, 151–162. [CrossRef]
37. Choi, I.; Lim, S.; Catapano, R.; Choi, J. Comparing two roads to success: Self-control predicts achievement and positive affect predicts relationships. *J. Res. Pers.* **2018**, *76*, 50–63. [CrossRef]
38. Martinez-Calderon, J.; Flores-Cortes, M.; Morales-Asencio, J.M.; Luque-Suarez, A. Pain-Related Fear, Pain Intensity and Function in Individuals With Chronic Musculoskeletal Pain: A Systematic Review and Meta-Analysis. *J. Pain* **2019**, *20*, 1394–1415. [CrossRef]
39. Martinez-Calderon, J.; Jensen, M.P.; Morales-Asencio, J.M.; Luque-Suarez, A. Pain Catastrophizing and Function in Individuals with Chronic Musculoskeletal Pain. *Clin. J. Pain* **2019**, *35*, 279–293. [CrossRef]
40. Lee, Y.J.; Eck, J.E.; Corsaro, N. Conclusions from the history of research into the effects of police force size on crime—1968 through 2013: A historical systematic review. *J. Exp. Criminol.* **2016**, *12*, 431–451. [CrossRef]
41. Park, S. Gender and performance in public organizations: A research synthesis and research agenda. *Public Manag. Rev.* **2021**, *23*, 929–948. [CrossRef]
42. Araujo, J.; Patnam, M.; Popescu, A.; Valencia, F.; Yao, W. *Effects of Macroprudential Policy: Evidence from Over 6000 Estimates*; IMF Working Paper; International Monetary Fund: Washington, DC, USA, 2020.
43. Raitakari, O.T.; Juonala, M.; Kähönen, M.; Taittonen, L.; Laitinen, T.; Mäki-Torkko, N.; Järvisalo, M.J.; Uhari, M.; Jokinen, E.; Rönnemaa, T.; et al. Cardiovascular Risk Factors in Childhood and Carotid Artery Intima-Media Thickness in Adulthood: The Cardiovascular Risk in Young Finns Study. *J. Am. Med. Assoc.* **2003**, *290*, 2277–2283. [CrossRef] [PubMed]
44. Davis, P.H.; Dawson, J.D.; Riley, W.A.; Lauer, R.M. Carotid intimal-medial thickness is related to cardiovascular risk factors measured from childhood through middle age the muscatine Study. *Circulation* **2001**, *104*, 2815–2819. [CrossRef]
45. Freedman, D.S.; Patel, D.A.; Srinivasan, S.R.; Chen, W.; Tang, R.; Bond, M.G.; Berenson, G.S. The contribution of childhood obesity to adult carotid intima-media thickness: The Bogalusa Heart Study. *Int. J. Obes.* **2008**, *32*, 749–756. [CrossRef] [PubMed]

46. Khalil, A.; Huffman, M.D.; Prabhakaran, D.; Osmond, C.; Fall, C.H.D.; Tandon, N.; Lakshmy, R.; Prabhakaran, P.; Biswas, S.K.D.; Ramji, S.; et al. Predictors of carotid intima-media thickness and carotid plaque in young Indian adults: The New Delhi Birth Cohort. *Int. J. Cardiol.* **2013**, *167*, 1322–1328. [CrossRef]
47. Oren, A.; Vos, L.E.; Uiterwaal, C.S.P.M.; Gorissen, W.H.M.; Grobbee, D.E.; Bots, M.L. Change in body mass index from adolescence to young adulthood and increased carotid intima-media thickness at 28 years of age: The Atherosclerosis Risk in Young Adults study. *Int. J. Obes.* **2003**, *27*, 1383–1390. [CrossRef]
48. Charakida, M.; Khan, T.; Johnson, W.; Finer, N.; Woodside, J.; Whincup, P.H.; Sattar, N.; Kuh, D.; Hardy, R.; Deanfield, J. Lifelong patterns of BMI and cardiovascular phenotype in individuals aged 60-64 years in the 1946 British birth cohort study: An epidemiological study. *Lancet Diabetes Endocrinol.* **2014**, *2*, 648–654. [CrossRef]
49. Terzis, I.D.; Papamichail, C.; Psaltopoulou, T.; Georgiopoulos, G.A.; Lipsou, N.; Chatzidou, S.; Kontoyiannis, D.; Kollias, G.; Iacovidou, N.; Zakopoulos, N.; et al. Long-term BMI changes since adolescence and markers of early and advanced subclinical atherosclerosis. *Obesity* **2012**, *20*, 414–420. [CrossRef]
50. Lloyd, L.J.; Langley-Evans, S.C.; McMullen, S. Childhood obesity and adult cardiovascular disease risk: A systematic review. *Int. J. Obes.* **2010**, *34*, 18–28. [CrossRef]
51. Juonala, M.; Magnussen, C.G.; Berenson, G.S.; Venn, A.; Burns, T.L.; Sabin, M.A.; Srinivasan, S.R.; Daniels, S.R.; Davis, P.H.; Chen, W.; et al. Childhood Adiposity, Adult Adiposity, and Cardiovascular Risk Factors. *N. Engl. J. Med.* **2011**, *365*, 1876–1885. [CrossRef]
52. Ceponiene, I.; Klumbiene, J.; Tamuleviciute-Prasciene, E.; Motiejunaite, J.; Sakyte, E.; Ceponis, J.; Slapikas, R.; Petkeviciene, J. Associations between risk factors in childhood (12–13 years) and adulthood (48–49 years) and subclinical atherosclerosis: The Kaunas Cardiovascular Risk Cohort Study. *BMC Cardiovasc. Disord.* **2015**, *15*, 89. [CrossRef] [PubMed]
53. Du, Y.; Zhang, T.; Sun, D.; Li, C.; Bazzano, L.; Qi, L.; Krousel-Wood, M.; He, J.; Whelton, P.K.; Chen, W.; et al. Effect of Serum Adiponectin Levels on the Association Between Childhood Body Mass Index and Adulthood Carotid Intima-Media Thickness. *Am. J. Cardiol.* **2018**, *121*, 579–583. [CrossRef] [PubMed]
54. Ferreira, I.; Twisk, J.W.R.; Van Mechelen, W.; Kemper, H.C.G.; Seidell, J.C.; Stehouwer, C.D.A. Current and adolescent body fatness and fat distribution: Relationships with carotid intima-media thickness and large artery stiffness at the age of 36 years. *J. Hypertens.* **2004**, *22*, 145–155. [CrossRef]
55. Freedman, D.S.; Dietz, W.H.; Tang, R.; Mensah, G.A.; Bond, M.G.; Urbina, E.M.; Srinivasan, S.; Berenson, G.S. The relation of obesity throughout life to carotid intima-media thickness in adulthood: The Bogalusa Heart Study. *Int. J. Obes.* **2004**, *28*, 159–166. [CrossRef] [PubMed]
56. Hao, G.; Wang, X.; Treiber, F.A.; Harshfield, G.; Kapuku, G.; Su, S. Body mass index trajectories in childhood is predictive of cardiovascular risk: Results from the 23-year longitudinal Georgia Stress and Heart study. *Int. J. Obes.* **2018**, *42*, 923–925. [CrossRef] [PubMed]
57. Hosseinpanah, F.; Seyedhoseinpour, A.; Barzin, M.; Mahdavi, M.; Tasdighi, E.; Dehghan, P.; Momeni Moghaddam, A.; Azizi, F.; Valizadeh, M. Comparison analysis of childhood body mass index cut-offs in predicting adulthood carotid intima media thickness: Tehran lipid and glucose study. *BMC Pediatr.* **2021**, *21*, 494. [CrossRef]
58. Huynh, Q.; Blizzard, L.; Sharman, J.; Magnussen, C.; Schmidt, M.; Dwyer, T.; Venn, A. Relative contributions of adiposity in childhood and adulthood to vascular health of young adults. *Atherosclerosis* **2013**, *228*, 259–264. [CrossRef]
59. Johnson, W.; Kuh, D.; Tikhonoff, V.; Charakida, M.; Woodside, J.; Whincup, P.; Hughes, A.D.; Deanfield, J.E.; Hardy, R. Body mass index and height from infancy to adulthood and carotid intima-media thickness at 60 to 64 years in the 1946 British Birth cohort study. *Arterioscler. Thromb. Vasc. Biol.* **2014**, *34*, 654–660. [CrossRef]
60. Juonala, M.; Raitakari, M.; Viikari, J.S.A.; Raitakari, O.T. Obesity in youth is not an independent predictor of carotid IMT in adulthood: The Cardiovascular Risk in Young Finns Study. *Atherosclerosis* **2006**, *185*, 388–393. [CrossRef]
61. Lee, Y.J.; Nam, C.M.; Kim, H.C.; Hur, N.W.; Suh, I. The association between obesity indices in adolescence and carotid intima-media thickness in young adults: Kangwha study. *J. Prev. Med. Public Health* **2008**, *41*, 107–114. [CrossRef]
62. Wright, C.M.; Parker, L.; Lamont, D.; Craft, A.W. Implications of childhood obesity for adult health: Findings from thousand families cohort study. *BMJ* **2001**, *323*, 1280–1284. [CrossRef] [PubMed]
63. Yan, Y.; Hou, D.; Liu, J.; Zhao, X.; Cheng, H.; Xi, B.; Mi, J. Childhood body mass index and blood pressure in prediction of subclinical vascular damage in adulthood: Beijing blood pressure cohort. *J. Hypertens.* **2017**, *35*, 47–54. [CrossRef] [PubMed]
64. Sauerbrei, W.; Collins, G.S.; Huebner, M.; Walter, S.D.; Cadarette, S.M.; Abrahamowicz, M. Guidance for designing and analysing observational studies. *Med. Writ.* **2017**, *26*, 17–21.
65. Altman, D.G. *Practical Statistics for Medical Research*; Chapman and Hall: London, UK, 1991; ISBN 0-412-27630-5.
66. Fitzmaurice, G.M.; Laird, N.M.; Ware, J.H. *Applied Longitudinal Analysis*, 2nd ed.; John Wiley & Sons: Hoboken, NJ, USA, 2011; ISBN 978-0-470-38027-7.
67. Hozo, S.P.; Djulbegovic, B.; Hozo, I. Estimating the mean and variance from the median, range, and the size of a sample. *BMC Med. Res. Methodol.* **2005**, *5*, 13. [CrossRef]
68. Wan, X.; Wang, W.; Liu, J.; Tong, T. Estimating the sample mean and standard deviation from the sample size, median, range and/or interquartile range. *BMC Med. Res. Methodol.* **2014**, *14*, 135. [CrossRef]
69. Bland, M. Estimating Mean and Standard Deviation from the Sample Size, Three Quartiles, Minimum, and Maximum. *Int. J. Stat. Med. Res.* **2015**, *4*, 57–64. [CrossRef]

70. Armitage, P.; Berry, G.; Matthews, J.N.S. *Statistical Methods in Medical Research*, 4th ed.; Blackwell Science: Oxford, UK, 2002; ISBN 9780632052578.
71. Higgins, J.P.; White, I.R.; Anzures-Cabrera, J. Meta-analysis of skewed data: Combining results reported on log-transformed or raw scales. *Stat. Med.* **2008**, *27*, 6072–6092. [CrossRef]
72. Selph, S.S.; Ginsburg, A.D.; Chou, R. Impact of contacting study authors to obtain additional data for systematic reviews: Diagnostic accuracy studies for hepatic fibrosis. *Syst. Rev.* **2014**, *3*, 107. [CrossRef]
73. Higgins, J.P.; Li, T.; Deeks, J.J. Chapter 6: Choosing effect measures and computing estimates of effect. In *Cochrane Handbook for Systematic Reviews of Interventions*; Higgins, J., Thomas, J., Chandler, J., Cumpston, M., Li, T., Page, M., Welch, V., Eds.; Cochrane: London, UK, 2022.
74. Idris, N.R.N.; Robertson, C. The effects of imputing the missing standard deviations on the standard error of meta analysis estimates. *Commun. Stat. Simul. Comput.* **2009**, *38*, 513–526. [CrossRef]
75. Riley, R.D.; Moons, K.G.M.; Snell, K.I.E.; Ensor, J.; Hooft, L.; Altman, D.G.; Hayden, J.; Collins, G.S.; Debray, T.P.A. A guide to systematic review and meta-analysis of prognostic factor studies. *BMJ* **2019**, *364*, k4597. [CrossRef]
76. Greenland, S.; Schesselman, J.J.; Criqui, M.H. The Fallacy of Employing Standardized Regression. *J. Epidemiol.* **1986**, *123*, 203–208. [CrossRef]
77. Fernández-Castilla, B.; Aloe, A.M.; Declercq, L.; Jamshidi, L.; Onghena, P.; Natasha Beretvas, S.; Van den Noortgate, W. Concealed correlations meta-analysis: A new method for synthesizing standardized regression coefficients. *Behav. Res. Methods* **2019**, *51*, 316–331. [CrossRef] [PubMed]
78. Yoneoka, D.; Henmi, M. Synthesis of linear regression coefficients by recovering the within-study covariance matrix from summary statistics. *Res. Synth. Methods* **2017**, *8*, 212–219. [CrossRef] [PubMed]
79. Baillie, M.; le Cessie, S.; Schmidt, C.O.; Lusa, L.; Huebner, M. Ten simple rules for initial data analysis. *PLoS Comput. Biol.* **2022**, *18*, e1009819. [CrossRef] [PubMed]
80. Nieminen, P. Ten Points for High-Quality Statistical Reporting and Data Presentation. *Appl. Sci.* **2020**, *10*, 3885. [CrossRef]

BioMedInformatics

MDPI

Opinion

Big Data in Chronic Kidney Disease: Evolution or Revolution?

Abbie Kitcher [1], UZhe Ding [1], Henry H. L. Wu [2,*] and Rajkumar Chinnadurai [1,3]

1 Department of Renal Medicine, Northern Care Alliance NHS Foundation Trust, Salford M6 8HD, UK
2 Renal Research Laboratory, Kolling Institute of Medical Research, Royal North Shore Hospital & The University of Sydney, Sydney, NSW 2065, Australia
3 Faculty of Biology, Medicine and Health, University of Manchester, Manchester M13 9PL, UK
* Correspondence: honlinhenry.wu@health.nsw.gov.au; Tel.: +61-9926-4751

Abstract: Digital information storage capacity and biomedical technology advancements in recent decades have stimulated the maturity and popularization of "big data" in medicine. The value of utilizing big data as a diagnostic and prognostic tool has continued to rise given its potential to provide accurate and insightful predictions of future health events and probable outcomes for individuals and populations, which may aid early identification of disease and timely treatment interventions. Whilst the implementation of big data methods for this purpose is more well-established in specialties such as oncology, cardiology, ophthalmology, and dermatology, big data use in nephrology and specifically chronic kidney disease (CKD) remains relatively novel at present. Nevertheless, increased efforts in the application of big data in CKD have been observed over recent years, with aims to achieve a more personalized approach to treatment for individuals and improved CKD screening strategies for the general population. Considering recent developments, we provide a focused perspective on the current state of big data and its application in CKD and nephrology, with hope that its ongoing evolution and revolution will gradually identify more solutions to improve strategies for CKD prevention and optimize the care of patients with CKD.

Keywords: big data; machine learning; nephrology; chronic kidney disease; prediction models; outcomes; personalized medicine; primary prevention; treatment

Citation: Kitcher, A.; Ding, U.; Wu, H.H.L.; Chinnadurai, R. Big Data in Chronic Kidney Disease: Evolution or Revolution? *BioMedInformatics* **2023**, *3*, 260–266. https://doi.org/10.3390/biomedinformatics3010017

Academic Editor: Pentti Nieminen

Received: 14 February 2023
Revised: 28 February 2023
Accepted: 6 March 2023
Published: 14 March 2023

In 1965, Gordon Moore described Moore's law, which rightfully predicted the exponential growth of computational capacity. Subsequently, the cost of 1 MB of storage has dropped from USD 1331 to less than USD 0.01 in the past 5 decades [1]. The drastic improvement in digital information storage capacity over the past few decades has led to a propagation in the size and number of available datasets. The result of these advancements is "big data"—colossal and complex data sets that are impossible to process with traditional methods. Big data can be defined by the three Vs—volume, velocity, and variety—initially described in 2001 by Doug Laney. Veracity and value were later added on to form the 'five Vs' in describing big data. The value of big data does not simply reside in its sheer volume, but rather from the analytical processes which can uncover and explore hidden patterns and correlations, and provide better insight and accuracy in the prediction of future events. Predicting potential trajectories in healthcare is imperative as it will aid governing bodies to decide upon longstanding investments and implement effective health policies.

Chronic Kidney Disease (CKD) is a progressive non-communicable disease that affects >10% of the general population worldwide, with 843.6 million individuals being in CKD stages 1–5 [2]. The Global Burden of Disease Studies show that CKD has surfaced as one of the leading causes of worldwide mortality since 1990 [3], and that all-age mortality rate related to CKD rose by 41.5% between 1990 and 2017. In that period, CKD also climbed in rank among the leading causes of death, from 17th in 1990 to 12th in 2017 [4]. Based on a study forecasting life expectancy, Kyle et al.'s model predicted that by 2040, deaths related to CKD diagnosis will rise to 2.2 million per year in a best-case scenario and even further to 4 million in the worst-case scenario [5]. The cost involved in the care for CKD patients is getting higher—many patients have other comorbidities that necessitate multidisciplinary team care, risk of medical complications that require hospitalisation, and the potential need for dialysis when they reach end-stage kidney disease, which drives up the cost significantly. In the United States alone, the spending for Medicare beneficiaries with kidney disease by 2015 was close to USD 100 billion [6]. Given the immense cost of looking after CKD patients, it is therefore not surprising that there is a huge variation between disability-adjusted life years (DALYs) caused by CKD, more so in countries which are in the lower socio-demographic index quintiles [7].

In comparison to kidney disease, the use of big data in medicine has been more well-established for conditions such as skin cancer and diabetic retinopathy, where over hundreds of thousands of clinical images are fed into data-driven models which are then used for the classification and detection of the aforementioned conditions based on deep convolutional neural networks [8,9]. Another example of big data analysis being successfully utilized is in cardiology, with Loghmanpour et al. [10] demonstrating the superiority of the Bayesian network—a graphical model that is ideal for predicting probable relationships between two events—against the pre-existing traditional risk prediction model in predicting right ventricular failure following left ventricular assist device therapy. In oncology, Jang et al. [11] have also built an extensive clinical and genomic information system from several public databases that aim to aid clinicians in improving diagnostic decision-making, risk assessment, and providing targeted and precise treatment. However, a review of PubMed citations over the previous 2 decades still demonstrates that nephrology is lagging behind other specialties in terms of big data research [12]. In an analysis by Joshi et al. [13], radiology and cardiology were shown to be two of the specialties which showed a drastic increase in the numbers of United States Food and Drug Administration (FDA)-approved machine learning medical devices in the past decade, with the former taking up to 75% of the total amount. Interestingly, there were no nephrology-related machine learning medical devices listed on the FDA website at the time this review was written [14].

There have been increased efforts in the application of big data in CKD (Table 1). Having the ability to predict patient outcomes is essential to achieve targeted preventive medicine. Using traditional regression models based on large cohort studies, Tangri et al. [15] were able to formulate an equation to predict the progression of CKD patients towards end-stage kidney disease. A machine learning algorithm was developed by Ravizza et al. [16] to predict and quantify the risk of CKD progression using real-world data, demonstrating similar or even better predictive accuracy compared to using clinical trial data. Sandokii et al. [17] and Inaguma et al. [18] also replicated successful studies in using machine learning algorithms to identify risk factors and variables in AKI and CKD progression, respectively. A prediction model for end-stage renal disease in primary IgA nephropathy with a 91% success rate was developed by Schena et al. [19]. By applying deep learning techniques to a large data set of 703,872 patients, Tomasev et al. [20] were able to generate a model which had 90.2% accuracy in predicting AKIs requiring dialysis within 90 days.

Inaguma et al. [18] also replicated a similar machine learning algorithm to predict the risk factors for CKD progression. The examples above would not have been possible without pre-existing epidemiological big data. Epidemiological big datasets can come from national registries, surveillance programmes, and electronic health records. For example, the United States Renal Data System (USRDS) is a national surveillance system that compiles and evaluates demographic and clinical information for patients diagnosed with CKD [21]. Similar surveillance projects have also been replicated in Ireland and Canada, which are useful for identifying and describing the prevalence of CKD and improving the care for CKD patients [22,23]. The China Kidney Disease Network (CK-NET) is set up to integrate and analyse data from China's national database, covering 39 million inpatient electronic records [24].

Developments in biomedical technology over recent years have led to a decrease in the costs of performing high throughput sequencing—also known as next-generation sequencing (NGS)—as well as other biomedical technologies in parallel. This has stimulated an abundance of research efforts focusing on genome-wide association studies (GWAS) and other omics data, such as proteomics (quantification of protein), metabolomics (quantification of metabolites), and transcriptomics (measurement of RNA transcripts), just to name a few. In nephrology, these multi-omics studies paved the way to building "biobanks", such as that of NEPTUNE (Nephrotic Syndrome STudy Network), ERCB (European Renal cDNA Bank), EURenOmics, C-PROBE (Clinical Phenotyping and Resource Biobank), PKU-IgAN, TRIDENT (for diabetic nephropathy), CureGN (for glomerulopathies), the National Institute of Diabetes and Digestive and Kidney Diseases (NIDDK), and the Kidney Precision Medicine Project (KPMP) [12,25,26]. When combined with machine learning methods, they can provide clinicians with a deeper understanding of the complexity of molecular events and the pathogenesis of kidney diseases and thus lead to the development of a more precise treatment strategy [12,25,26].

The use of electronic notes and images coupled with artificial intelligence technology has been considered in nephrology research. This has resulted in the design of algorithms that could detect risk factors and identify different stages of CKD from electronic health records [27]. By feeding a convolutional neural network (CNN) with virtual slides of biopsy samples obtained from the Academia and Industry Collaboration for Digital Pathology (AIDPATH) kidney database, Pedraza et al. [28] were also able to demonstrate the encouraging application of artificial intelligence technology at a histopathological level, in which the algorithm they developed was able to achieve a level of accuracy up to 99.5% in differentiating between glomerular and non-glomerular samples. A deep learning framework that could analyse and grade digitized kidney biopsies for fibrosis was generated by using deidentified whole slide images obtained from the Kidney Precision Medicine Project (KPMP) [29].

Table 1. Completed and ongoing research studies relating to the application of big data in chronic kidney disease.

Research Study (Author(s), Journal, Country of Publication, Year of Publication if Specific Details Available)	Summary of Findings and Conclusions
Tangri et al. [15], JAMA, Canada, 2011	• Development and validation of prediction models included 3449 patients and 4942 patients, respectively, from 2 independent Canadian cohorts • A model using routine lab tests can accurately predict the risk of kidney failure in chronic kidney disease patients
Ravizza et al. [16], Nature Medicine, Switzerland, 2019	• Data from 417,912 individual electronic health records were used for the study • Predictive analytic algorithms taught using real world data were shown to be equivalent, if not more accurate, than those taught using clinical trial data
Inaguma et al. [18], PLoS One, Japan, 2020	• Machine-learning-based model included 118,584 patients obtained from an electronic medical records system • Increased urine tendency was found to be a risk factor for rapid decline in kidney function

Table 1. *Cont.*

Research Study (Author(s), Journal, Country of Publication, Year of Publication if Specific Details Available)	Summary of Findings and Conclusions
Pedraza et al. [28], Medical Image Understanding and Analysis, 2017	• Digital/virtual slides were obtained from the AIDPATH (Academia and Industry Collaboration for Digital Pathology) kidney database—a compilation of kidney tissue cohorts from institutions and labs around Europe • Accuracy of convolutional neural networks was observed at 99.95% in differentiating glomerular and non-glomerular samples
Shang et al. [27], NPJ Digital Medicine, United States, 2021	• An algorithm with a 95% positive predictive value in identifying CKD cases in Electronic Health Records (EHR) • The algorithm was validated in EHR from more than 5 institutions and over 1.3 million patients from the Columbia Clinical Data Warehouse
NEPTUNE (Nephrotic Syndrome STudy Network) United States, study due for completion in 2024	• Established to collect long-term observational data with corresponding biological specimens from 1200 patients with nephrotic syndrome across 44 separate institutions in North America
ERCB (European Renal cDNA Bank) database study Germany, ongoing	• A consortium of more than 2600 anonymized kidney biopsies with matching genomic analysis developed from the collaboration of multiple kidney research centres across Europe
EURenOmics database Germany, 2012–2017 Multiple Publications Refer to https://eurenomics.eu/publications/index.html, accessed on 1 February 2023.	• A consortium built with data from more than 15,000 patients to study the pathogenesis of rare nephropathies and to explore new treatment therapies
C-PROBE (Clinical Phenotyping and Resource Biobank) United States, study due for completion in 2025	• Prospective observational study aiming to collect clinical phenotyping of up to 1600 kidney disease patients, laboratory, and histopathology samples
TRIDENT (Transformative Research in diabetic nephropathy) United States, study due for completion in 2023	• Prospective observational study aiming to collect laboratory and histopathology samples combined with high-throughput genomic analysis for patients with diabetic nephropathy
CureGN database study United States and Europe, ongoing	• A multi-centre international consortium of both children and adults with glomerular disease aiming to identify and understand epidemiology, genetics, biomarkers, and patient-related outcomes

Ultimately, potential applications of big data and big data analysis in nephrology are promising, but various limitations and challenges remain. It would make sense that with more information, we would be able to identify previously unrecognized patterns, though this may also provide misleading concepts between causality and correlation. A lot of primary kidney diseases are rare diseases, and the lack of data can sometimes limit the development of accurate prediction models. A relatively smaller funding budget for nephrology research in general compared to other medical specialties has been observed historically, with less clinical trials being conducted in nephrology compared to specialties such as cardiology [30,31]. This may be a hindering factor for the application of big data and big data analysis in nephrology, given a considerable number of clinical trials exclude patients with CKD as well [32]. It is encouraging that greater efforts have been made by international nephrology societies (e.g., the International Society of Nephrology Advancing Clinical Trials Group) to address these issues over recent years, with initiatives to garner increased industry funding, government support, and patient participation. Another key issue with big data, not only limited to nephrology, is that of 'veracity'—which is the reliability of the collected data—as large retrospective cohort data can suffer from biases, and the data from clinical trials is sometimes not representative of what occurs within the real world [33]. In the current climate where patient privacy is considered invaluable for patients, families, and the clinical team, restrictions and regulations surrounding the collection of health data from wearables, implantable devices, and smartphones remains an issue that needs to be overcome. Protecting patient confidentiality is of the utmost importance and not to be disregarded.

In summary, it appears that the utility of big data in CKD and nephrology research, and integration in clinical practice, is undergoing an evolutionary phase, albeit at a slower pace when compared to other conditions and specialties. The revolutionary aspect of this should take place at an operator level where the users of big data—data scientists, statisticians, health informatics experts, and clinicians—need to gain the skills and direction to effectively translate the findings from big data analysis into clinical practice. At a global health level, we will also need to continuously brainstorm strategies on how best to combine information from big data acquired across various demographics, and search for optimal pathways in utilizing information from big data analysis to prevent CKD and improve CKD outcomes for individuals and populations.

Author Contributions: Conceptualization, H.H.L.W. and R.C.; resources, U.D. and A.K.; writing—original draft preparation, U.D. and A.K.; writing—review and editing, H.H.L.W. and R.C.; visualization, H.H.L.W.; supervision, H.H.L.W. and R.C. All authors have read and agreed to the published version of the manuscript.

Funding: This research received no external funding.

Institutional Review Board Statement: Not applicable.

Informed Consent Statement: Not applicable.

Data Availability Statement: Not applicable; no new data were created.

Conflicts of Interest: The authors declare no conflict of interest.

References

1. McCallum, J.; Blok, H. *Historical Cost of Computer Memory and Storage. Our World in Data*; Oxford Martin School, The University of Oxford: Oxford, UK, 2022; Available online: https://ourworldindata.org/grapher/historical-cost-of-computer-memory-and-storage?country=~OWID_WRL (accessed on 1 February 2023).
2. Kovesdy, C.P. Epidemiology of chronic kidney disease: An update 2022. *Kidney Int. Suppl.* **2022**, *12*, 7–11. [CrossRef]
3. Abubakar, I.I.; Tillmann, T.; Banerjee, A. Global, regional, and national age-sex specific all-cause and cause-specific mortality for 240 causes of death, 1990–2013: A systematic analysis for the Global Burden of Disease Study 2013. *Lancet* **2015**, *385*, 117–171.
4. Bikbov, B.; Purcell, C.A.; Levey, A.S.; Smith, M.; Abdoli, A.; Abebe, M.; Adebayo, O.M.; Afarideh, M.; Agarwal, S.K.; Agudelo-Botero, M.; et al. Global, regional, and national burden of chronic kidney disease, 1990–2017: A systematic analysis for the Global Burden of Disease Study 2017. *Lancet* **2020**, *395*, 709–733. [CrossRef]
5. Foreman, K.J.; Marquez, N.; Dolgert, A.; Fukutaki, K.; Fullman, N.; McGaughey, M.; Pletcher, M.A.; Smith, A.E.; Tang, K.; Yuan, C.W.; et al. Forecasting life expectancy, years of life lost, and all-cause and cause-specific mortality for 250 causes of death: Reference and alternative scenarios for 2016–40 for 195 countries and territories. *Lancet* **2018**, *392*, 2052–2090. [CrossRef] [PubMed]
6. Saran, R.; Robinson, B.; Abbott, K.C.; Agodoa, L.Y.; Bhave, N.; Bragg-Gresham, J.; Balkrishnan, R.; Dietrich, X.; Eckard, A.; Eggers, P.W.; et al. US Renal Data System 2017 Annual Data Report: Epidemiology of Kidney Disease in the United States. *Am. J. Kidney Dis.* **2018**, *71*, A7. [CrossRef]
7. Cockwell, P.; Fisher, L.-A. The global burden of chronic kidney disease. *Lancet* **2020**, *395*, 662–664. [CrossRef]
8. Esteva, A.; Kuprel, B.; Novoa, R.A.; Ko, J.; Swetter, S.M.; Blau, H.M.; Thrun, S. Dermatologist-level classification of skin cancer with deep neural networks. *Nature* **2017**, *542*, 115–118. [CrossRef]

9. Gulshan, V.; Peng, L.; Coram, M.; Stumpe, M.C.; Wu, D.; Narayanaswamy, A.; Venugopalan, S.; Widner, K.; Madams, T.; Cuadros, J.; et al. Development and validation of a deep learning algorithm for detection of diabetic retinopathy in retinal fundus photo-graphs. *JAMA* **2016**, *316*, 2402–2410. [CrossRef]
10. Loghmanpour, N.A.; Kormos, R.L.; Kanwar, M.K.; Teuteberg, J.J.; Murali, S.; Antaki, J.F. A Bayesian Model to Predict Right Ventricular Failure Following Left Ventricular Assist Device Therapy. *JACC: Hear. Fail.* **2016**, *4*, 711–721. [CrossRef] [PubMed]
11. Jang, Y.; Choi, T.; Kim, J.; Park, J.; Seo, J.; Kim, S.; Kwon, Y.; Lee, S.; Lee, S. An integrated clinical and genomic information system for cancer precision medicine. *BMC Med. Genom.* **2018**, *11*, 34. [CrossRef]
12. Saez-Rodriguez, J.; Rinschen, M.M.; Floege, J.; Kramann, R. Big science and big data in nephrology. *Kidney Int.* **2019**, *95*, 1326–1337. [CrossRef]
13. Joshi, G.; Jain, A.; Adhikari, S.; Garg, H.; Bhandari, M. FDA approved Artificial Intelligence and Machine Learning (AI/ML)-Enabled Medical Devices: An updated 2022 landscape. *medRxiv* **2022**. [CrossRef]
14. Food and Drug Administration, US. Artificial Intelligence and Machine Learning (AI/ML)-Enabled Medical Devices. 2022. Available online: https://www.fda.gov/media/145022 (accessed on 1 February 2023).
15. Tangri, N.; Stevens, L.A.; Griffith, J.; Tighiouart, H.; Djurdjev, O.; Naimark, D.; Levin, A.; Levey, A.S. A Predictive Model for Progression of Chronic Kidney Disease to Kidney Failure. *JAMA* **2011**, *305*, 1553–1559. [CrossRef]
16. Ravizza, S.; Huschto, T.; Adamov, A.; Böhm, L.; Büsser, A.; Flöther, F.F.; Hinzmann, R.; König, H.; McAhren, S.M.; Robertson, D.H.; et al. Predicting the early risk of chronic kidney disease in patients with diabetes using real-world data. *Nat. Med.* **2019**, *25*, 57–59. [CrossRef] [PubMed]
17. Sandokji, I.; Yamamoto, Y.; Biswas, A.; Arora, T.; Ugwuowo, U.; Simonov, M.; Saran, I.; Martin, M.; Testani, J.M.; Mansour, S.; et al. A Time-Updated, Parsimonious Model to Predict AKI in Hospitalized Children. *J. Am. Soc. Nephrol.* **2020**, *31*, 1348–1357. [CrossRef]
18. Inaguma, D.; Kitagawa, A.; Yanagiya, R.; Koseki, A.; Iwamori, T.; Kudo, M.; Yuzawa, Y. Increasing tendency of urine protein is a risk factor for rapid eGFR decline in patients with CKD: A machine learning-based prediction model by using a big database. *PLoS ONE* **2020**, *15*, e0239262. [CrossRef]
19. Schena, F.P.; Anelli, V.W.; Trotta, J.; Di Noia, T.; Manno, C.; Tripepi, G.; D'Arrigo, G.; Chesnaye, N.C.; Russo, M.L.; Stangou, M.; et al. Development and testing of an artificial intelligence tool for predicting end-stage kidney disease in patients with im-munoglobulin A nephropathy. *Kidney Int.* **2021**, *99*, 1179–1188. [CrossRef] [PubMed]
20. Tomašev, N.; Harris, N.; Baur, S.; Mottram, A.; Glorot, X.; Rae, J.W.; Zielinski, M.; Askham, H.; Saraiva, A.; Magliulo, V.; et al. Use of deep learning to develop continuous-risk models for adverse event prediction from electronic health records. *Nat. Protoc.* **2021**, *16*, 2765–2787. [CrossRef]
21. Port, F.K.; Held, P.J. The US Renal Data System at 30 Years: A Historical Perspective. *Am. J. Kidney Dis.* **2019**, *73*, 459–461. [CrossRef] [PubMed]
22. Stack, A.G.; Casserly, L.F.; Cronin, C.J.; Chernenko, T.; Cullen, W.; Hannigan, A.; Saran, R.; Johnson, H.; Browne, G.; Ferguson, J.P. Prevalence and variation of Chronic Kidney Disease in the Irish health system: Initial findings from the National Kidney Disease Surveillance Programme. *BMC Nephrol.* **2014**, *15*, 185. [CrossRef] [PubMed]
23. Bello, A.K.; E Ronksley, P.; Tangri, N.; Singer, A.; Grill, A.; Nitsch, D.; A Queenan, J.; Lindeman, C.; Soos, B.; Freiheit, E.; et al. A national surveillance project on chronic kidney disease management in Canadian primary care: A study protocol. *BMJ Open* **2017**, *7*, e016267. [CrossRef]
24. Saran, R.; Steffick, D.; Bragg-Gresham, J. The China kidney disease network (CK-NET): "big data-big dreams". *Am. J. Kidney Dis.* **2017**, *69*, 713–716. [CrossRef] [PubMed]
25. Cisek, K.; Krochmal, M.; Klein, J.; Mischak, H. The application of multi-omics and systems biology to identify therapeutic targets in chronic kidney disease. *Nephrol. Dial. Transplant.* **2015**, *31*, 2003–2011. [CrossRef]
26. Wuttke, M.; Köttgen, A. Insights into kidney diseases from genome-wide association studies. *Nat. Rev. Nephrol.* **2016**, *12*, 549–562. [CrossRef] [PubMed]
27. Shang, N.; Khan, A.; Polubriaginof, F.; Zanoni, F.; Mehl, K.; Fasel, D.; Drawz, P.E.; Carrol, R.J.; Denny, J.C.; Hathcock, M.A.; et al. Medical records-based chronic kidney disease phenotype for clinical care and "big data" observational and genetic studies. *NPJ Digit. Med.* **2021**, *4*, 1–13. [CrossRef]
28. Pedraza, A.; Gallego, J.; Lopez, S.; Gonzalez, L.; Laurinavicius, A.; Bueno, G. Glomerulus classification with convolutional neural networks. In Proceedings of the Medical Image Understanding and Analysis: 21st Annual Conference, MIUA 2017, Edinburgh, UK, 11–13 July 2017; Springer International Publishing: Berlin/Heidelberg, Germany; pp. 839–849.
29. Zheng, Y.; Cassol, C.A.; Jung, S.; Veerapaneni, D.; Chitalia, V.C.; Ren, K.Y.; Bellur, S.S.; Boor, P.; Barisoni, L.M.; Waikar, S.S.; et al. Deep-Learning–Driven Quantification of Interstitial Fibrosis in Digitized Kidney Biopsies. *Am. J. Pathol.* **2021**, *191*, 1442–1453. [CrossRef]
30. Erickson, K.F.; Hostetter, T.H.; Winkelmayer, W.C.; Olan, G.; Meyer, R.N.; Hakim, R.; Sedor, J.R. Federal Funding for Kidney Disease Research: A Missed Opportunity. *Am. J. Public Heal.* **2016**, *106*, 406–407. [CrossRef]
31. Strippoli, G.F.M.; Craig, J.; Schena, F.P. The Number, Quality, and Coverage of Randomized Controlled Trials in Nephrology. *J. Am. Soc. Nephrol.* **2004**, *15*, 411–419. [CrossRef]

32. Banerjee, D.; Lowe-Jones, R.; Damster, S.; Thomas, N.; Scholes-Robertson, N.; Tong, A.; Levin, A. International perspectives on patient involvement in clinical trials in nephrology. *Kidney Int.* **2020**, *98*, 566–571. [CrossRef]
33. Glicksberg, B.; Johnson, K.; Dudley, J.T. The next generation of precision medicine: Observational studies, electronic health records, biobanks and continuous monitoring. *Hum. Mol. Genet.* **2018**, *27*, R56–R62. [CrossRef]

MDPI
St. Alban-Anlage 66
4052 Basel
Switzerland
www.mdpi.com

BioMedInformatics Editorial Office
E-mail: biomedinformatics@mdpi.com
www.mdpi.com/journal/biomedinformatics

www.ingramcontent.com/pod-product-compliance
Lightning Source LLC
Chambersburg PA
CBHW061815210926
51850CB00006B/709
9783725810437